South University Library
Richmond Campus
2151 Old Brick Road
Glen Allen, Va 23060

MAR 0 6 2018

Organizing Academic Work in Higher Education

Organizing Academic Work in Higher Education explores how managers influence teaching, learning and academic identities and how new initiatives in teaching and learning change the organizational structure of universities. By building on organizational studies and higher education studies literatures, *Organizing Academic Work in Higher Education* offers a unique perspective, presenting empirical evidence from different parts of the world. This edited collection provides a conceptual frame of organizational change in universities in the context of New Public Management reforms and links it to the core activities of teaching and learning.

Split into four main sections:

- University from the organizational perspective,
- Organizing teaching,
- Organizing learning and
- Organizing identities,

this book uses a strong international perspective to provide insights from three continents regarding the major differences in the relationships between the university as an organization and academics.

It contains highly pertinent, scientifically driven case studies on the role and boundaries of managerial behaviour in universities. It supplies evidence-based knowledge on the effectiveness of management behaviour and tools to university managers and higher education policy-makers worldwide. Academics who aspire to institutionalize their successful academic practices in certain university structures will find this book of particular value.

Organizing Academic Work in Higher Education will be a vital companion for academic interest in higher education management, transformation of universities, teaching, learning, academic work and identities. Bringing together the study of the organizational transformation in higher education with the study of teaching, learning and academic identity, *Organizing Academic Work in Higher Education* presents a unique cross-national and cross-regional comparative perspective.

Liudvika Leišytė is Professor of Higher Education at the Centre for Higher Education (zhb), TU Dortmund.

Uwe Wilkesmann is Professor of Organizational Studies and Director of the Centre for Higher Education (zhb), TU Dortmund.

International Studies in Higher Education

Series Editors:
David Palfreyman, OxCHEPS
Ted Tapper, OxCHEPS
Scott Thomas, Claremont Graduate University

The central purpose of this series is to see how different national and regional systems of higher education are responding to widely shared pressures for change. The most significant of these are: rapid expansion; reducing public funding; the increasing influence of market and global forces; and the widespread political desire to integrate higher education more closely into the wider needs of society and, more especially, the demands of the economic structure. The series will commence with an international overview of structural change in systems of higher education. It will then proceed to examine on a global front the change process in terms of topics that are both traditional (for example, institutional management and system governance) and emerging (for example, the growing influence of international organizations and the blending of academic and professional roles). At its conclusion the series will have presented, through an international perspective, both a composite overview of contemporary systems of higher education, along with the competing interpretations of the process of change.

Published titles:

Structuring Mass Higher Education
The Role of Elite Institutions
Edited by David Palfreyman and Ted Tapper

International Perspectives on the Governance of Higher Education
Alternative Frameworks for Coordination
Edited by Jeroen Huisman

International Organizations and Higher Education Policy
Thinking Globally, Acting Locally?
Edited by Roberta Malee Bassett and Alma Maldonado-Maldonado

Academic and Professional Identities in Higher Education
The Challenges of a Diversifying Workforce
Edited by Celia Whitchurch and George Gordon

International Research Collaborations
Much to Be Gained, Many Ways to Get in Trouble
Melissa S. Anderson and Nicholas H. Steneck

Cross-border Partnerships in Higher Education
Strategies and Issues
Robin Sakamoto and David Chapman

Accountability in Higher Education
Global Perspectives on Trust and Power
Bjorn Stensaker and Lee Harvey

The Engaged University
International Perspectives on Civic Engagement
David Watson, Robert M. Hollister, Susan E. Stroud, and Elizabeth Babcock

Universities and the Public Sphere
Knowledge Creation and State Building in the Era of Globalization
Edited by Brian Pusser, Ken Kempner, Simon Marginson, and Imanol Ordorika

The Future University
Ideas and Possibilities
Edited by Ronald Barnett

Universities in the Knowledge Economy
Higher Education Organisation and Global Change
Edited by Paul Temple

Tribes and Territories in the 21st Century
Rethinking the Significance of Disciplines in Higher Education
Edited by Paul Trowler, Murray Saunders, and Veronica Bamber

Universities and Regional Development
A Critical Assessment of Tensions and Contradictions
Edited by Rómulo Pinheiro, Paul Benneworth, and Glen A. Jones

The Global Student Experience
An International and Comparative Analysis
Edited by Camille B. Kandiko and Mark Weyers

Enhancing Quality in Higher Education
International Perspectives
Edited by Ray Land and George Gordon

Student Financing of Higher Education
A Comparative Perspective
Edited by Donald Heller and Claire Callender

The Physical University
Contours of Space and Place in Higher Education
Edited by Paul Temple

Affirmative Action Matters
Creating Opportunities for Students Around the World
Edited by Laura Dudley Jenkins and Michele S. Moses

Diversity and Inclusion in Higher Education
Emerging perspectives on institutional transformation
Edited by Daryl Smith

International Trends in University Governance
Autonomy, Self-Government and the Distribution of Authority
Edited by Michael Shattock

Access and Expansion Post-Massification
Opportunities and Barriers to Further Growth in Higher Education Participation
Edited by Ben Jongbloed and Hans Vossensteyn

Organizing Academic Work in Higher Education

Teaching, learning and identities

Edited by Liudvika Leišytė
and Uwe Wilkesmann

LONDON AND NEW YORK

First published 2016
by Routledge
2 Park Square, Milton Park, Abingdon, Oxon OX14 4RN

and by Routledge
711 Third Avenue, New York, NY 10017

Routledge is an imprint of the Taylor & Francis Group, an informa business

© 2016 selection and editorial matter, Liudvika Leišytė and Uwe Wilkesmann; individual chapters, the contributors

The right of the editor to be identified as the author of the editorial material, and of the authors for their individual chapters, has been asserted in accordance with sections 77 and 78 of the Copyright, Designs and Patents Act 1988.

All rights reserved. No part of this book may be reprinted or reproduced or utilised in any form or by any electronic, mechanical, or other means, now known or hereafter invented, including photocopying and recording, or in any information storage or retrieval system, without permission in writing from the publishers.

Trademark notice: Product or corporate names may be trademarks or registered trademarks, and are used only for identification and explanation without intent to infringe.

British Library Cataloguing in Publication Data
A catalogue record for this book is available from the British Library

Library of Congress Cataloging-in-Publication Data
Names: Leisyte, Liudvika, editor. | Wilkesmann, Uwe, editor.
Title: Organizing academic work / edited by Liudvika Leisyte and Uwe Wilkesmann.
Description: New York, NY : Routledge, 2016. | Includes bibliographical references.
Identifiers: LCCN 2015040930 | ISBN 9781138909908 (hbk) | ISBN 9781315693729 (ebk)
Subjects: LCSH: Universities and colleges–Administration. | Universities and colleges–United States–Business management. |Education, Higher–Aims and objectives. | Organizational change.
Classification: LCC LB2341 .O835 2016 | DDC 378.1/01–dc23
LC record available at http://lccn.loc.gov/2015040930

ISBN: 978-1-138-90990-8 (hbk)
ISBN: 978-1-315-69372-9 (ebk)

Typeset in Minion
by Cenveo Publisher Services

Printed and bound in Great Britain by
TJ International Ltd, Padstow, Cornwall

Contents

	List of illustrations	ix
	Acknowledgements	xi
	Contributors	xii
	Series editors' introduction DAVID PALFREYMAN, TED TAPPER, AND SCOTT L. THOMAS	xvii
	Organizing academic work in higher education: teaching, learning, and identities – an introduction LIUDVIKA LEIŠYTĖ AND UWE WILKESMANN	1
I	**University from the organizational perspective**	**11**
1	Universities, teaching, and learning JAY R. DEE	13
2	Teaching matters, too: different ways of governing a disregarded institution UWE WILKESMANN	33
3	Bridging the duality between universities and the academic profession: a tale of protected spaces, strategic gaming, and institutional entrepreneurs LIUDVIKA LEIŠYTĖ	55
4	Organizing and managing university education HAMISH COATES AND EMMALINE BEXLEY	68
II	**Organizing teaching**	**87**
5	Towards a conceptualization of faculty decision-making about curricular and instructional change LISA R. LATTUCA AND JENNIFER R. POLLARD	89
6	Institutional (teaching) entrepreneurs wanted! – Considerations on the professoriate's agentic potency to enhance academic teaching in Germany CHRISTIAN J. SCHMID AND SABINE LAUER	109

7	Organizing teaching in Chinese universities SHUANGYE CHEN	132
III	**Organizing learning**	**149**
8	Learners and organizations: competing patterns of risk, trust, and responsibility RAY LAND	151
9	Organizing teaching in project teacher teams across established disciplines using wearable technology: digital didactical designing, a new form of practice ISA JAHNKE, EVA MÅRELL-OLSSON, AND THOMAS MEJTOFT	169
10	Changing organizational structure and culture to enhance teaching and learning: cases in a university in Hong Kong SAMUEL K. W. CHU AND SANNY S. W. MOK	186
IV	**Organizing identities**	**203**
11	Multiversities and academic identities: change, continuities, and complexities MARY HENKEL	205
12	Boundary crossing and maintenance among UK and Dutch bioscientists: towards hybrid identities of academic entrepreneurs LIUDVIKA LEIŠYTĖ AND BENGÜ HOSCH-DAYICAN	223
13	University academic promotion system and academic identity: an institutional logics perspective YUZHUO CAI AND GAOMING ZHENG	243
	Conclusion ROSEMARY DEEM	262
	Index	268

Illustrations

Figures

1.1	How the organizational context shapes teaching and learning	15
2.1	Governance types at three levels: HES, universities, and academic staff	37
5.1	Initial model of faculty decision-making about curricular change	92
5.2	Proposed model of faculty decision-making about curricular change	103
7.1	Loop of specialization-centred, tightly coupled organizing of teaching	139
7.2	Context for reactive de-specialization during the post-1985 stage	141
9.1	Digital didactics from a broad view: organizational prerequisites	173
9.2a	Technical application: seeing the real world, 'the wall in a tunnel' with the Swedish text added through Google Glass	177
9.2b	Pedagogical design example	177
9.3	Pupils' learning situation	178
9.4	Phases of finding ideas and synergizing (Group 1)	182
10.1	TWiki templates for 'group progress' and 'group discussion'	189
10.2	An integrated KM cycle	192
10.3	A two-dimensional BSTL model with examples of different matrix points	195
10.4	The process of organization change	198
13.1	Analytical framework for understanding influences of policies on identities	248
13.2	Process of academic promotion at B University	250
13.3	Changes of academic identities in China from an institutional logics perspective	258

Tables

1.1	How the external environment can affect teaching and learning	17
1.2	The roles of managers and academics in reform	26
2.1	Sample structure of interviews per country	40

3.1	Governance mechanisms and two institutional logics	58
3.2	Types of academic responses to threats to professional autonomy	63
7.1	Selected educational statistics describing the context of organizing teaching in Chinese universities	136
7.2	Comparison of course structures and workloads	144
8.1	Emergent learning technologies	155
8.2	The learner's pedagogic rights	161
8.3	Contexts of enhancement	163
10.1	Student responses on the use of TWiki	190
10.2	Distribution of coded blogs and Facebook entries in the theme of KM processes	193
10.3	Distribution of coded blogs and Facebook in the theme of socio-emotional expressions	193
10.4	Students' perceived support received on blogs and Facebook	194
13.1	Institutional logics aligned with changes of university academic promotion system	252

Acknowledgements

We would like to thank the series editors David Palfreyman, Ted Tapper and Scott L. Thomas for their encouragement to write this book and support in finalizing the manuscript. We would also like to acknowledge the help from Olga Wagner, without whose keen eye on detail and continuous support with finalizing the manuscript this book would not be what it is now. Many thanks also go to Anna-Lena Rose for her assistance.

Contributors

Emmaline Bexley is a Senior Lecturer in Higher Education at the Centre for the Study of Higher Education (CSHE), University of Melbourne. Her research interests include equity and participation in higher education, national and international higher education policy and funding practices, and the nature of academic work.

Yuzhuo Cai is a Senior Lecturer and Adjunct Professor at the Higher Education Group (HEG), School of Management, University of Tampere, Finland, and was the acting professor of the unit from August 2013 to July 2014. He is currently a guest professor at the Institute of International and Comparative Education, Beijing Normal University, China, and the co-convener of the Thematic Research Group on 'Entrepreneurial Universities' in the Triple Helix Association. His main teaching and research areas are organization theory, higher education policy and management, internationalization of higher education, and innovation studies; he has published six books and over 50 articles.

Shuangye Chen is currently Assistant Professor in the Department of Educational Administration and Policy at the Chinese University of Hong Kong. Her research interests span higher education, educational leadership, and education policy, with special regional knowledge in China and the wider Chinese societies. Her journal publications appear in *Higher Education Policy*, *Higher Education Research and Development*, *London Review of Education*, *Journal of Educational Administration*, *Education Management Administration and Leadership*, *Journal of Research on Leadership Education*, *Frontiers of Education in China*, *Peking University Review of Education*, and *Global Education*.

Samuel Kai Wah Chu is Associate Professor and the Head of Division of Information and Technology Studies and an Associate Professor at the Faculty of Education. He is also the Deputy Director (Centre for Information Technology in Education) in the Faculty of Education, University of Hong Kong. He has published over 200 articles and books, including key journals in the area of IT in education, information and library science, school librarianship, academic librarianship, and knowledge management. Dr Chu is the Managing Editor for *Journal of Information and Knowledge Management* and the Associate Editor (Asia) for *Online Information Review*. Dr Chu has been involved in over 50 research/project grants totalling over $3 million. He is also the recipient of his faculty's Outstanding Researcher Award in 2013.

Hamish Coates is a Professor of Higher Education at the Centre for the Study of Higher Education (CSHE), University of Melbourne. He was Founding Director of Higher Education Research at the Australian Council for Educational Research (ACER) from 2006–13, and between 2010 and 2013 also Program Director at the LH Martin Institute for Tertiary Leadership and Management. Hamish completed his PhD in 2005 at the University of Melbourne, and subsequent executive training at INSEAD and MBS. Through research and development, Hamish focuses on improving the quality and productivity of higher education. Interests include large-scale evaluation, tertiary education policy, institutional strategy, assessment methodology, learner engagement, and academic work and leadership. He has initiated and led many successful projects, including numerous national and international student surveys. He was Founding International Director of the OECD's Assessment of Higher Education Learning Outcomes (AHELO).

Jay R. Dee is Associate Professor and Director of the Higher Education graduate programme at the University of Massachusetts Boston. His research interests include organizational change, the academic workplace, and higher education administration and governance. His publications have focused on organizational learning, conflict, and decision-making in colleges and universities. He has also studied innovative professional development models that help academics improve their teaching.

Rosemary Deem is currently Vice-principal (Education), Dean of the Doctoral School and Professor of Higher Education Management at Royal Holloway, University of London. She has also worked at Bristol, Lancaster and the Open University, has twice chaired the British Sociological Association, directed the UK Learning and Teaching Support Network Education Subject Centre 2001–4 and was Vice-chair of the Society for Research into Higher Education from 2007–9. She is currently Chair of the UK Council for Graduate Education and a co-editor of the international journal *Higher Education*.

Mary Henkel, now retired, was until recently Professor and then Professor Associate of the Department of Politics and History, Brunel University, London. She has researched and published extensively on higher education, science, and evaluation policies. Her primary focus during the last 20 years has been on the implications of such policies for academic work and identities. Her main publication in this field is *Academic Identities and Policy Change in Higher Education* (Jessica Kingsley, 2000).

Bengü Hosch-Dayican holds a PhD in Political Science from the University of Twente. She is a post-doctoral researcher for Professor of Higher Education at the Centre for Higher Education (zhb) at TU Dortmund University. Her research interests include the processes and influences of higher education governance and policies, particularly on the nature of academic work as well as on the gender differences in academic career advancement. Her work has been published in *Acta Politica*, *Journal of Workplace Rights* and *Social Science Computer Review*.

Isa Jahnke is Director of Research for the Information Experience Lab and Associate Professor at the University of Missouri, School of Information Science and Learning Technologies. She studied online learning communities and creativity in higher education and was subproject-manager of a European initiative about remote-controlled labs in engineering education, as well as principal investigator of iPad-didactics in schools in Denmark, Sweden, and Finland. Her research interest is the innovative use of technologies for learning and teaching. Her new book, *Digital Didactical Designs* (Routledge, 2015), draws an alternative view of teaching and learning in the digital world and future classrooms.

Ray Land is Professor of Higher Education at Durham University and Director of Durham's Centre for Academic Practice. He has been a higher education consultant for the OECD and the European Commission and has recently been involved in two European Commission higher education projects in Europe and Latin America. He is currently advisor to the Norwegian TRANSark project on architectural education. He has published widely in the field of educational research, particularly in the area of threshold concepts and troublesome knowledge. He is a Fellow of the Royal Society of Arts and a Principal Fellow of the Higher Education Academy.

Lisa R. Lattuca is Professor of Higher Education at the University of Michigan. She studies curriculum, teaching, and learning using a systems perspective to understand the different and interacting influences, internal and external to institutions, that shape learning environments, experiences, and outcomes. Her studies of US engineering and science programmes have been funded by the US National Science Foundation, the Accreditation Board for Engineering and Technology, and the Helmsley Foundation. She is the author of *Creating Interdisciplinarity: Interdisciplinary Research among College and University Faculty* (Vanderbilt University Press, 2001), and co-author of *Shaping the College Curriculum: Academic Plans in Context* (Jossey Bass, 2009).

Sabine Lauer holds a major in Sociology and Statistics. She is currently a research assistant and PhD candidate at the chair of Organizational Studies, Continuing Education and Social Management at the Centre for Higher Education (zhb) at TU Dortmund University. Her current research interests focus on higher education research and advanced statistical modelling.

Liudvika Leišytė is Professor of Higher Education at the Centre for Higher Education (zhb) at TU Dortmund University. She has worked or was a visiting fellow at the Center for Higher Education Policy Studies (CHEPS) at the University of Twente, Harvard University, Oslo University, Bristol University, Pennsylvania State University, University of Michigan, and Boston College. Her major research interests lie in the nexus between organizational change and academic work, including impact of governance shifts and evaluation practices on the teaching–research nexus, professional autonomy, academic entrepreneurship and academic identities. In her work she builds on the sociology of organizations, sociology of knowledge, and sociology of valuation and evaluation. Professor Leišytė has published two monographs and numerous chapters and articles in higher education and science policy, as well as public management journals. She is the co-convener of *Higher Education Section* (22) at the European Association of Educational Research.

Eva Mårell-Olsson is Senior Lecturer at the Department of Educational Sciences at Umeå University and has many years of experience in process development in the education sector supported by technology. Her research interest is the innovative use of mobile and wearable technology and how these technologies can enhance teaching and learning. Her research focuses on digital documentation and assessment for learning, and how technology can support these processes. Her most recent study is about digital didactical designs and how innovative teachers design their teaching and the use of media tablets in 1:1 classrooms in Sweden. Another part of her research concerns wearable technology and, more specifically, how smart glasses can be used in various fields.

Thomas Mejtoft is Associate Professor of Media Technology at Umeå University and Program Director for the Master of Science Study Program in Interaction Technology and Design. He holds a PhD from the Royal Institute of Technology (KTH) and has worked as a Senior Research Associate at the STFI-Packforsk research institute. His research and teaching interests include media and interaction technology in persuasive and learning systems, along with business development and strategies for implementation of new technology.

Sanny S. W. Mok is a Research Assistant at the Centre for Information Technology in Education, University of Hong Kong. Projects she has participated in include using a game-based learning approach to enhance secondary students' reading ability and interest, as well as on sex education. She has also participated in writing a book on twenty-first-century skills. She has recently completed a master's degree in Applied Linguistics at the University of Edinburgh.

Jennifer R. Pollard is a doctoral student in the Center for the Study of Higher and Postsecondary Education at the University of Michigan. Her research interests lie in professional development for teaching and learning in higher education institutions, and the success and retention of undergraduate students who have been historically underrepresented in science, engineering, and mathematics fields in the USA. As a graduate research assistant, she is contributing to several research projects, including a multi-year evaluation of a comprehensive academic and social support programme for students pursuing sciences, engineering, and mathematics degrees at the University of Michigan.

Christian J. Schmid holds a major in sociology. He is a PhD candidate and holds a position as a Research Assistant at the chair of Organizational Studies, Continuing Education and Social Management at the Centre for Higher Education (zhb) at TU Dortmund University. His current research interests focus on the managerial governance of higher education institutions and the social organization of deviants in outlaw biker clubs.

Uwe Wilkesmann is Director of the Centre for Higher Education (zhb), TU Dortmund University. He holds a chair for Organization Studies, Continuing Education and Social Management. He was Adjunct Professor at the Hong Kong Polytechnic University between 2008 and 2014 and has chaired the German Organization Sociology. He has published a lot of articles and books about higher education research and knowledge management – for example, in *Organization Studies*, *Higher Education*, and *Tertiary Education and Management*. His current research interests focus on higher education research and knowledge transfer.

Gaoming Zheng is a doctoral candidate at Higher Education Group (HEG), University of Tampere, Finland. Her main research interests are quality assurance, the academic profession, doctoral education, internationalization of higher education, and organizational studies.

Series editors' introduction

International Studies in Higher Education

This series is constructed around the premise that higher education systems are experiencing common pressures for fundamental change, reinforced by differing national and regional circumstances that also impact upon established institutional structures and procedures. There are four major dynamics for change that are of international significance.

1. Mass higher education is a universal phenomenon.
2. National systems find themselves located in an increasingly global marketplace that has particular significance for their more prestigious institutions.
3. Higher education institutions have acquired (or been obliged to acquire) a wider range of obligations, often under pressure from governments prepared to use state power to secure their policy goals.
4. The balance between the public and private financing of higher education has shifted – markedly in some cases – in favour of the latter.

In response to such pressures many higher education systems have demonstrated their ability to be highly innovative. There are three significant developments. First, the idea of higher education as a private as well as a public good is expressed concretely in the search for market funding, incorporating the rise of for-profit universities. Second, there has been a marked increase in trans-institutional cooperation, which includes the emergence of international ties; coupled with this has been the move by some universities to establish overseas campuses. Third, we see the rise of the MOOCs (Massive Open Online Courses), which represent the severest challenge to traditional pedagogies, including our very understanding of what it means to acquire the experience of higher education. The world of the universities is in a state of flux. Change rather than stability is the order of the day.

Each volume in the series will examine how systems of higher education are responding to this new and demanding political and socio-economic environment. Although it is easy to overstate the uniqueness of the present situation, it is not an exaggeration to say that higher education is undergoing a fundamental shift in its character, and one that is truly international in scope. We are witnessing a major transition in the relationship of higher education to state and society. What makes the present circumstances particularly interesting is to see how different systems – a product of social, cultural, economic and political contexts that have interacted and evolved over time – respond in their own peculiar ways to the changing environment. There is no assumption that the pressures for change have set in motion the trend towards a converging model of higher education, but we do believe that in the present circumstances no understanding of 'the idea of the university' remains sacrosanct.

Although this is a series with an international focus, it is not expected that each individual volume should cover every national system of higher education. This would be an impossible task. While aiming for a broad range of case studies, with each volume addressing a particular theme, the focus will be upon the most important and interesting examples of responses to the pressures for change. Most of the individual volumes will bring together a range of comparative quantitative and qualitative information, but the primary aim of each volume will be to present differing interpretations of critical developments in key aspects of the experience of higher education. The dominant overarching objective is to explore the conflict of ideas and the political struggles that inevitably surround any significant policy development in higher education.

It can be expected that volume editors and their authors will adopt their own interpretations to explain the emerging patterns of development. There will be conflicting theoretical positions drawn from the increasingly multi-disciplinary field of higher education research. Thus we can expect in most volumes to find an inter-marriage of approaches drawn from sociology, economics, history, political science, cultural studies, and the administrative sciences. However, while there will be different approaches to understanding the process of change in higher education, each volume editor(s) will impose a framework upon the volume inasmuch as chapter authors will be required to address common issues and concerns.

This volume in the series, edited by two distinguished continental European scholars, examines the changing relationship between the organizational structure of the university and the process of teaching and learning, along with the formation of academic identities. How do organizational structures impact upon teaching and learning, and academic identity formation? Conversely, how does the process of teaching, learning, and academic identity formation shape the organizational structure of the university? Underwriting the volume are two central beliefs: the importance of understanding the interdependence between teaching, learning, and academic identity formation within the university and the university as an organizational structure; and the contention that we are currently in an age in which organizational structure is being purposefully changed in an endeavour to create new modes of teaching and learning, and also to encourage academics to interpret their roles differently. In this respect, note the rise of the ideology of New Public Management, and the marketization of higher education. These are matters which are increasingly less likely to be shaped at the chalkface of the university and driven by its academic labour force, but are now more under the central direction of an internal managerial class influenced by state-driven public policy initiatives. The editors argue that this is a change that occurred initially within the Anglo-American universities, but now has a wider impact, penetrating university culture in continental Europe as well as Asia. It is necessary to think of the university as less likely to pursue a tradition of scholarship as it is embraced by the values of academic capitalism and that its academics may be on the way to becoming entrepreneurs rather than scholars.

The volume recognizes that these developments are more pronounced in some university systems than others, that there is no universal one-dimensional process of change, and that some of these pressures also have led to what are widely agreed to be positive developments (like the enhanced possibilities for distance learning) – but it also points to the significant challenges that face contemporary universities, and the need to recognize the central role that organizational structure will play in mitigating those challenges in a way that enables the university to retain what is best about its past while responding constructively to present challenges.

David Palfreyman
Director of OxCHEPS, New College, University of Oxford
Ted Tapper
OxCHEPS, New College, University of Oxford
Scott L. Thomas
Professor of Educational Studies,
Claremont Graduate University, California

Organizing academic work in higher education
Teaching, learning, and identities – an introduction

LIUDVIKA LEIŠYTĖ AND UWE WILKESMANN

Traditionally, universities are often characterized as loosely coupled institutions with underdeveloped technologies that are not conducive for promoting learning (Bess and Dee, 2008; Musselin, 2007). They are also known for being change averse (Orton and Weick, 1990; Paradeise *et al.*, 2009). Specifically, high levels of specialization and structural differentiation, cultural values, and reward systems that promote autonomy and individual achievement, combined with weak feedback loops regarding performance and outcomes, often make it difficult for universities to promote change (Kezar and Elrod, 2012). Most universities consist of various faculties that represent different disciplines that are culturally different regarding their own epistemologies, organizational patterns, divisions between teaching and research tasks, and attitudes towards academic and administrative duties.

As professional organizations, universities have been subject to many ongoing reforms in Europe following the trend of the 'marketization' of public sectors, ranging from the partial retreat of state financing to the allocation of strategic authority directed to university management, with an increasing focus on economic utility, the monitoring of teaching, and research performance. In the USA, state provision to higher education has dramatically decreased during the recent recession years; thus, universities have also faced harsh demands to 'earn' money from alternative sources, which usually means students and their parents (Leišytė and Dee, 2012). The emphasis on quality teaching and student satisfaction in this context has been reinforced by university managers.

The Anglo-American universities have served as a role model for the European and Asian transformation of universities for all ongoing university transformation processes. With recent changes in university governance arrangements and with financial stringencies, it is possible to observe a tighter organization, where decision-making is more centralized and the boundaries between different units are increasingly blurred. Numerous studies show significant university transformation (de Boer *et al.*, 2007; Leišytė and Dee, 2012;

Kezar, 2014; Musselin, 2007; Krücken et al., 2013; Paradeise et al., 2009; Wilkesmann and Schmid, 2012, 2014) and reveal the complexity of the governance reforms, which cover many different areas such as formal structures, management, financing, quality control and evaluation, human resources, course planning, access, and internationalization. The introduction of managerial tools in universities strengthens the role of the top management and deans as they shift into more professional managerial roles. A lot of empirical evidence indicates that universities have become more corporate and competitive organizations.

During these reforms, universities have remained professional organizations. We observe some 'imaginary contradictions of university governance' (Wilkesmann, 2015): profession versus organization, monitoring versus autonomy, intrinsic versus extrinsic motivation, and transactional versus transformational governance. The first imaginary contradiction describes the conflict between the establishment of principal agent relations in universities and self-governance by professionals. The second one emphasizes the monitoring and sanction capacity of accounting tools versus the professional autonomy that research and teaching need for innovation. The third contradiction labels the crowding-out effect of intrinsic motivation by selective incentives such as the new steering instruments. The last contradiction addresses different governance styles. Monitoring and sanction are examples of transactional governance, in which each behaviour of a member is related to an organizational exchange. Transformational governance creates leeway for intellectual innovation and common visions. However, both transactional and transformational governance are necessary for a university (Wilkesmann, 2013). The modern university must balance these four imaginary contradictions.

One of the main reasons for the restructuring of universities is the 'massification' of higher education. In all OECD countries, more than 50 per cent of a birth cohort are enrolled in some type of higher education. As a result, universities have recently become one of the main education institutions in our societies as they prepare graduates for the labour market and contribute to economic development. However, this development has consequences for teaching, learning, and academic identities, and these consequences are not typically considered in policy-making and scholarly debates. Based on the number of students, academic teaching may turn into scholastic instruction. In the case of 'schoolification', more surface learning can be observed (Trigwell et al., 1999). To manage the mass of students, the organizational decision-making processes of the universities are more top down; as a consequence, the academic identity changes from a vocation to a 'normal' job identity, whereby a splintering of academic roles may be observed in some cases (Leišytė, 2015). Additionally, intrinsic motivation can shift to extrinsic job and teaching motivation (Wilkesmann and Schmid, 2014). All of these changes are not 'natural' or compulsory consequences of 'massification'. They can be organized and, to a certain extent, managed in different ways. Additionally, 'massification' implies the advantage that many more people acquire the opportunity for an academic career and societal mobility.

Another reason for the change in higher education systems (HESs) is technological development. In earlier times, books and articles were written on typewriters. The author had to pre-formulate the whole article up to the last word. A subsequent correction was nearly impossible or associated with high costs. The PC dramatically restructured academic writing. Currently, an article revision is easily accomplished without any additional cost from a technological perspective. To drag and drop a paragraph, to insert new sentences and to delete words are now common practices of writing that were a nightmare for every previous author. The same is true for academic teaching. New IT systems, such as wikis, MOOCs, apps, and logs, have altered the teaching situation at universities (see Jahnke, Mårell-Olsson and Mejtoft, and Chu and Mok in this book). Some professors and almost all students use mobile phones and tablets, which play a new and decisive part in the teaching–learning situation. In the future, new IT systems will likely obviate the need for traditional forms of academic classroom teaching. Thus, new technologies matter in the academic world and higher education institutions.

After the New Public Management (NPM) hype, and given the above-mentioned major changes, a new consensus about an appropriate organization structure for universities emerges (see Henkel in this book). Bottom-up initiatives must be accompanied by top-down initiatives. The university must act as a cooperative actor with common goals that give leeway, autonomy for teaching and research for the academic staff. The four above-mentioned imaginary contradictions need to be balanced in the organizational structure of the universities. All of these criteria and factors are well known from the discussion about knowledge-intensive organizations. In particular, the German universities represent an organizational structure that lies between companies and German clubs (Wilkesmann, 2013). They have participative, democratic, self-governance elements mixed-up with accountable, hierarchical, and monitoring components. From this perspective, the organization structure of a (German) university is or could be a role model for all knowledge-intensive companies.

The above-described paradoxes and problems in university transformation show the complexity of the linkages between the university structures and individual behaviour. Therefore, we want to align this book to an organizational perspective and shed light on the interdependency between university transformation and behaviour in teaching and learning and describe the implications of this transformation for academic identities.

The recursive relationship between organizational structure and individual behaviour is a main topic of sociology theory (Giddens, 1984) and institutional approaches (Lawrence et al., 2009). Lawrence et al. (2009) call the mutual dependency 'institutional work' (see Leišytė and Wilkesmann in this book). Similarly, the relationship between organization structure and the behaviour of its members is a central topic in organizational theory. On the one hand, the organizational structure is a constraint for the individual behaviour of its members. On the other hand, (collective) action of the members can change the organizational structure. We want to highlight these recursive relationships in this book. Although action can change structure, we must define the prime mover. Who takes the initiative and why? Why do some professors act as 'institutional entrepreneurs' but not others (see Schmid and Lauer in this book)?

The literature on university governance, the academic profession and working conditions, research and research governance, and teaching and learning all contribute to a better understanding of the changes that are taking place at universities, including changes within academic work. Only a few accounts, however, use multi-level analysis to reveal the complexities between changing institutional environment and teaching, learning and academic identities, and the relationship between structure and agency. Further, the communities of higher education studies seem to avoid the connection between organization and the core processes of teaching and learning. The rich literature on teaching and learning is quite often, to a large extent, decoupled from higher education studies that explore organizational transformation and changes in governance of higher education. By focusing on the gap between these studies, we offer a unique perspective on the linkages between the organizational transformation of the university and its teaching, learning, and academic identities.

Therefore, our aim is to answer the following main research question:

How can managers from the organizational side of universities influence teaching, learning, and academic identities? Alternatively, to turn the question around: how can new initiatives in teaching and learning change the organizational structure?

To answer this question, we take a closer look at the following three sub-questions:

- What are interdependences between organizational structures and teaching?
- What are interdependences between organizational structures and learning?
- What are interdependences between organizational structures and academic identities?

Regarding the first sub-question, we will discuss how organizational structures influence teaching approaches. Have different organizational designs led to a more student- or teacher-focused approach to teaching? Under what circumstances are new initiatives for improving teaching methods successful? What motivates academics to engage in curriculum changes? In comparison to research, teaching is always collective action. You need faculty to deliver a study programme. As a consequence, managing teaching is much more of a main task for the organization than conducting and managing research. The interdependence between the organizational structure and teaching is highly important but is neglected in the literature.

The second sub-question focuses on the interdependence between the organizational structure and learning. The teaching–learning nexus can only be analysed under structural conditions. Does the organizational environment put pressure on academics? If so, will they pass the pressure along to the students? How will students then react? What are the organizational prerequisites for establishing a long-term learning process? Under what organizational conditions can new digital teaching methods change students' learning outcomes?

The third question addresses the relation between organizational conditions and academic identities. Academic identities have traditionally been linked with disciplines and related to the main academic roles of teaching and research. University managers across the globe have increasingly started to use performance indicators, which may multiply or marginalize academic roles. Furthermore, with increasingly blurring organizational boundaries, the duality between disciplinary academic and organizational identities can shrink. However, we know little of what the organizational demands for productivity and multiplication of roles in different disciplines mean for the self-concepts from the international perspective. How do changing working conditions and blurring organizational boundaries affect academic identity?

We explore these questions from an international perspective by providing empirically grounded insights from the Anglo-American, Asian, and European university contexts. We systematically cover the three sub-questions across the three continents, thus providing a grounded and global view on the key developments of linking the core processes of teaching, learning, academic identities, and university transformation.

The book is divided into four sections. The first section provides theoretical insights into the questions of linkages between organizational transformation, teaching, learning, and academic identities and problematizes the linear relationship between organizational change, teaching, and learning. Here, we are interested in how the university organizes teaching and learning: what are the key drivers for these changes and where are the locus and agency of change to be found?

The first section starts with Jay R. Dee's contribution, which highlights the organizational principles that are requisite knowledge for academics and managers who seek to design and implement new initiatives to improve teaching and learning. At the outset, the chapter identifies how organizational structure, culture, and power configurations affect teaching and learning in universities. It further describes the exogenous and endogenous factors that affect the types of organizational configurations that have been adopted by universities. Finally, Dee identifies the organizational components that affect and shape the change process in universities, particularly in terms of reforms that aim to improve teaching and learning. Most importantly, the chapter identifies organizational obstacles to change and structures and practices that can foster innovative practices.

Uwe Wilkesmann theorises how the institution of teaching importance is supported and leveraged at universities. The chapter argues that specific types of governance lead to different outcomes of importance for teaching in the universities. Based on two models – transactional and transformative governance – and considering the multi-level causal relationships, Wilkesmann elegantly provides an answer to universities that aim to fulfil the goal of academic teaching. This answer is supported with empirical evidence from a comparative case study that covers universities in Germany, the UK, and Hong Kong.

Liudvika Leišytė concentrates on the institutional logics perspective in understanding the creation and maintenance of protected spaces in academia in the context of governance reforms and the responses of academics when negotiating these spaces within the organizations where they teach. This chapter discusses the implications of the presence of the protected spaces and specific responses of academics for their academic identities under the quasi-market logic.

Hamish Coates and Emmaline Bexley clarify and advance our understanding of new scenarios for organizing and managing university education. They look at contemporary change forces which are homogenizing and diversifying facets of higher education, and emerging organizational forms. The authors provide a taxonomy of emerging organizational architectures, which is exemplified via institutional case studies from the Australian context, and discuss the linkages between the management of higher education and academic work.

The second part of the book concentrates on the questions of organizing teaching and emphasizes the linkages between organizational change and teaching at universities from an international perspective.

Lisa R. Lattuca and Jennifer R. Pollard explore factors that direct faculty members' behaviour in curricular and instructional changes at American universities. Based on solid empirical evidence, they discuss the engagement of academics in curricular reforms in their universities and salient individual and organizational influences. They use Stark and Lattuca's model, the academic plan-in-context, as a heuristic approach to distinguish between socio-cultural factors, external influences, internal factors, and individual-level influences as contextual impacts for academic staff.

Christian J. Schmid and Sabine Lauer discuss empirical case studies from German public universities that have received the national 'teaching excellence' award. Interviews with various actors in these organizations have revealed the importance of agency, specifically, the role of teachers as 'institutional entrepreneurs' in making changes in teaching innovations at the studied universities. For a variety of socio-biographical or institutional reasons, a few professors take full individual responsibility to improve academic teaching, regardless of or in actual opposition to their institutional environments. Different types of 'institutional entrepreneurs' are characterized.

Shuangye Chen analyses the development of the Chinese HES and the way teaching was organized under the perspective of Weick's concept of organizing and social grammar. She distinguishes five different time periods during which teaching was organized differently: 1949–78, 1979–85, 1986–93, 1994–99, and 2000–13. Each period describes very different political impact factors on the HES that lead to varying constraints that influence the principles of teaching in these organizations.

The third section centres around the question of organizing learning. Ray Land's contribution focuses on the notion of troublesome knowledge and discursive shifts in the current debates of teaching and learning in the context of organizational transformation of universities towards market-oriented models. He observes the discursive shift that has occurred over the last three decades from a language of education to a language of learning and the student experience. He argues that as a result of the organizational shifts and accountability practices in universities, learning becomes depicted within the organization as an undertaking that is easy, without any significant risk. Thus, the chapter problematizes this view, positing that tensions and contradictions arise for the organization when it is required to produce graduates for society who can act in complex, uncertain, risk-laden and unpredictable environments. In his view, this requirement entails radically different forms of curriculum, student–staff relationships and student encounters. He argues that viewing learning as an educational transaction implies an altered relation of trust with the student teachers and fellow learners. As organizational actors, students become co-enquirers, co-creators, and co-producers. In turn, teachers must assume a different form of responsibility, operating within risk and uncertainty, which cannot be predicated on the assumed certainties of a conventional accountability protocol of the organization.

Isa Jahnke, Eva Mårell-Olsson and Thomas Mejtoft explore how teachers meet the new challenges of technological change in their teaching. Adopting a European digital didactical design (DDD) approach, the authors study how academics organize their teaching in a different way due to these changes at a Swedish university that uses media tablets and Google Glass when teaching. They observed a change in organizing teaching and, more concretely, their findings provide evidence that the traditional course-based teaching has moved away from a common routine activity towards a design project. Additionally, organizational prerequisites for the use of DDD are discussed, such as freedom and support for teachers, an institutionalized moving towards 'design for learning', a community of reflecting peers, and a scrutiny of existing structures of study programmes.

With the help of three case studies at a Hong Kong university, Samuel Kai Wah Chu and Sanny S. W. Mok analyse the prerequisites of organizational structure and organizational culture for realizing new teaching and learning initiatives. They provide empirical evidence for prerequisites and the impacts of new IT tools, such as TWikis, blogs, and Facebook, in teaching. For them, the most powerful condition is the funding of new teaching and learning initiatives.

In the fourth section of the book, we discuss organizing academic identities. This section begins with Mary Henkel's chapter, which highlights the complexity and new meanings of multiversities and their implications for academic work and academic identities. She questions whether it is possible for the organization 'university' to be the source of an academic identity. Until now, the disciplines are the sources of professional identity. On the one hand, more power is shifted from the academic profession (and thus the disciplines) to the organization. On the other hand, universities are not homogeneous organizations and can be better characterized as 'multiversities'. In her contribution, Henkel shows the consequences of these developments for changes in professional academic identity.

Liudvika Leišytė and Bengü Hosch-Dayican report on boundary maintenance and the boundary crossing behaviour of life scientists in UK and Dutch universities. Building on the literature on symbolic boundaries and the notions of academic identities, this chapter explores the entrepreneurship behaviour of bioscientists, their teaching and research roles and the implications of boundary crossing and maintenance for their academic identities. This chapter has shown that bioscientists are crossing the boundaries of academia and industry when they commercialize their research results via patenting and spin-off company creation. They also do so by performing contract research with industry. Overall, Leišytė and Hosch-Dayican see differences between the responses in UK and the Dutch universities, which imply that differences in the governance regimes and managerial context matter for boundary crossing in academia. This chapter reveals that bioscientists find it challenging to combine entrepreneurship roles with teaching and research roles. Sometimes, it leads to conflicts in terms of producing timely research output or determining the focus of teaching programmes. At the same time, this chapter shows that financial incentives are strong drivers for combining these roles and acquiring a hybrid identity of an academic entrepreneur.

Finally, Yuzhuo Cai and Gaoming Zheng concentrate on the changing academic profession and academic identities at a Chinese university. Based on the institutional logics perspective, this chapter offers an insightful account of how Chinese universities have adopted a variety of managerial approaches to promote education quality, research performance, social engagement, and internationalization with a focus on academic promotion policies. The core of the contribution explores how the introduction of current academic promotion policy affects academic identities. They argue that academics are embedded in social institutions and that their identity change is a matter of changes in institutional environment.

We hope that these contributions will shed light on the previously neglected interdependence between organizational structure on the one side and teaching, learning, and academic identities on the other side by answering our three research sub-questions. The Asian HESs are developing particularly fast and will generate many interesting changes for teaching and learning and require a rapid organizational transformation of their higher education institutions in the near future. This transformation will serve as a fantastic lab for many empirical research settings and provide wonderful conditions for further research on organizational change and academic work.

References

Bess, J. L. and Dee, J. R. (2008) *Understanding College and University Organization: The State of the System, vol. I.* Sterling, VA: Stylus

de Boer, H., Endres, J. and Schimank, U. (2007) 'On the way towards new public management? The governance of university systems in England, the Netherlands, Austria, and Germany' in Jansen, D. (Ed.) *New Forms of Governance in Research Organizations.* Springer: Dordrecht, pp. 137–54

Giddens, A. (1984) *The Constitution of Society, Outline of the Theory of Structuration.* Cambridge: Polity Press

Kezar, A. (2014) *How Colleges Change: Understanding, Leading, and Enacting Change.* New York: Routledge

Kezar, A. and Elrod, S. L. (2012) 'Facilitating interdisciplinary learning: lessons from project Kaleidoscope'. *Change: The Magazine of Higher Education,* 44 (1), pp. 16–25

Krücken, G., Blümel, A. and Kloke, K. (2013) 'The managerial turn in higher education? On the interplay of organizational and occupational change in German academia'. *Minerva,* 51 (4), 417–42

Lawrence, T. B., Suddaby, R. and Leca, B. (Eds) (2009) *Institutional Work: Actors and Agency in Institutional Studies of Organization.* Cambridge, NY: Cambridge University Press

Leišytė, L. (2015) 'Changing academic identities in the context of a managerial university: bridging the duality between professions and organizations' in Cummings, W. and Teichler, U. (Eds) *The Relevance of Academic Work in Comparative Perspective.* Dordrecht: Springer, pp. 59–73

Leišytė, L. and Dee, J. R. (2012) 'Changing academic practices and identities in Europe and the US. Critical perspectives' in Smart, J. C. and Paulsen, M. B. (Eds) *Higher Education: Handbook of Theory and Research.* Dordrecht: Springer, pp. 123–206

Musselin, C. (2007) 'Are universities specific organisations?' in Krücken, G., Kosmützky, A. and Torka, M. (Eds) *Towards a Multiversity? Universities between Global Trends and National Traditions.* Bielefeld: Transcript, pp. 63–84

Orton, J. D. and Weick, K. E. (1990) 'Loosely coupled systems: a reconceptualization'. *Academy of Management Review,* 15, pp. 203–23

Paradeise, C., Reale, E., Bleiklie, I. and Ferlie, E. (Eds) (2009) *University Governance. Western European Comparative Perspectives.* Dordrecht: Springer

Trigwell, K., Prosser, M. and Waterhouse, F. (1999) 'Relations between teachers' approaches to teaching and students' approaches to learning'. *Higher Education,* 37, pp. 57–70

Wilkesmann, U. (2013) 'Effects of transactional and transformational governance on academic teaching: empirical evidence from two types of higher education institutions'. *Tertiary Education and Management,* 19 (4), 281–300

Wilkesmann, U. (2015) 'Imaginary contradictions of university governance' in Welpe, M., Wollersheim, J., Ringelhan, S. and Osterloh, M. (Eds) *Incentives and Performance: Governance of Research Organizations*. Berlin: Springer, pp. 189–205

Wilkesmann, U. and Schmid, C. J. (2012) 'The impacts of new governance on teaching at German universities: findings from a national survey in Germany'. *Higher Education*, 63, pp. 33–52

Wilkesmann, U. and Schmid, C. J. (2014) 'Intrinsic and internalized modes of teaching motivation'. *Evidence-based HRM*, 2 (1), pp. 6–27

I
University from the organizational perspective

1
Universities, teaching, and learning

JAY R. DEE

Introduction

Higher education managers and academics have at their disposal a range of pedagogical practices that research has shown to be effective for improving teaching and learning. Specifically, researchers in the cognitive sciences have developed a growing body of knowledge that explains how people learn (Blakemore and Frith, 2005; Zull, 2011). This research suggests that students can learn more effectively through experiential, collaborative, and problem-based activities that integrate and synthesize multiple domains of content. Additionally, the research indicates that teaching practices can be more effective when they build upon students' prior knowledge, and when they take into account students' emotions and motivations (Immordino-Yang and Damasio, 2007; Pintrich, 2003). This research lends empirical support to a range of potential reforms, including service learning, problem-based learning, learning communities, internships, interdisciplinary studies, and capstone projects. While there is no one best way to improve teaching and learning, academics and managers now have a repertoire of practices that can be customized to fit the goals of specific academic programmes and particular institutional missions.

The path towards change, however, is exceptionally difficult. The challenge is not a shortage of reforms, but rather limited organizational capacity for implementing them. While individual academics can readily and relatively easily make changes in their own courses, instituting changes at the level of the academic department or the institution as a whole is much more problematic. The difficulties associated with large-scale change are attributable, in part, to the unique organizational characteristics of higher education institutions (Bess and Dee, 2008; Birnbaum, 1988; Kezar, 2014). These institutions lack clear goals around which reform efforts can be organized. Seldom is there a consensus regarding institutional priorities; instead, conflict over competing claims is more likely to characterize planning and decision-making. In the absence of clear goals, political conflict, bargaining, and negotiation are more likely to shape decisions than objective data or rational analysis. Higher education institutions also have high levels of structural differentiation, which can impede collaboration and limit interaction across departmental boundaries (Holley, 2009). In this context, academic departments tend to function independently from each other and, thus, academics seldom learn from effective practices implemented elsewhere in the institution. Furthermore, the cultural values of a higher education institution are more likely fragmented than unified. Managers and academics may espouse different sets of beliefs regarding appropriate courses of action for their institution, and academics themselves are seldom in agreement regarding their beliefs about what constitutes effective teaching and learning (Becher and Trowler, 2001).

Given the challenges associated with implementing large-scale change, higher education reform efforts often remain isolated and disconnected (Kezar, 2012; Kezar and Lester, 2009). The bottom-up reforms initiated by individual academics are seldom scaled up for wider implementation, and the top-down reforms instituted by managers may not be widely embraced by academics and therefore may not influence teaching practices. These disconnected, piecemeal changes are unlikely to address the need to improve learning outcomes, foster higher levels of degree completion, and comply with governmental and stakeholder expectations for accountability and efficiency.

Building consensus around a clear set of institutional goals and priorities is frequently prescribed as a remedy for addressing the obstacles to change (Keller, 1983; Lutz, 1982; Schuster et al., 1994). But this remedy could generate more harm than good. Clarity is often the enemy of innovation. When organizations have clear goals and priorities, incentives and rewards are directed towards behaviours that support those goals. Incentives for venturing beyond the established goals are largely absent; hence, the status quo is reinforced. Clearly prescribed goals would likely restrict the range of bottom-up innovation that has historically characterized the functioning of higher education institutions and that has allowed these institutions to become driving forces in the production and dissemination of knowledge (Rhoades, 2000; Tierney, 1992). Moreover, if institutional leaders seek to clarify goals and priorities, then some groups within the institution may feel excluded from these newly clarified priorities. Goals and priorities, by definition, cannot be all inclusive. When precise goals are set, some activities are deemed more valuable to the institution than others. As a result, some organizational members may believe that their goals and preferred activities are no longer a priority for the institution. This inclusion–exclusion dynamic may alienate some departments whose members believe that their goals and values are not reflected in the institution's priorities (Bess and Dee, 2014). The overall result, in this scenario, would be less innovation across the organization, and lower morale for some departments and units.

Rather than aim for consensus around a clear set of goals, managers and academics can seek to capitalize on the diversity of ideas and perspectives found within their institution. Higher education institutions are comprised of groups with divergent goals and conflicting interests. Efforts to improve teaching and learning may be more successful if related reforms are designed in flexible ways that can accommodate the goals and values of different groups. This type of flexibility can be achieved in three ways. First, institutional leaders can create incentives and offer resources to support grassroots innovation in academic programmes. Second, institutional leaders can establish horizontal structures that link and connect grassroots innovators from different departments and units in the organization. Through these horizontal structures, groups of innovators can collaborate, share ideas and resources, and learn from each other. Third, institutional leaders can work with groups of innovators to design new initiatives that address the diverse goals and priorities of multiple academic units. This approach recognizes that the same reform can achieve multiple goals simultaneously (Bergquist and Pawlak, 2008).

This chapter provides a framework that can serve as a useful guide for managers and academics who aspire to improve teaching and learning. The framework (see Figure 1.1) indicates how dimensions of the external environment, institutional missions and strategies, and features of the organizational context can shape teaching practices and learning outcomes. First, the framework shows that the external environment can have a direct effect on teaching and learning. The external environment can also have an indirect effect that is mediated through the organizational context. In other words, the external environment can affect the organizational context, which, in turn, influences teaching and learning. Second, the framework highlights how institutional

External environment

Government policies
Market-based competition
Academic disciplines
Accreditation associations
Employers
Community stakeholders

Endogenous forces

Institutional strategy
Institutional mission

Organizational context

Structural arrangements
Power dynamics
Cultural values and beliefs

Teaching and learning

Pedagogy
Curriculum
Academic programmes of study
Quality of learning environment
Learning outcomes

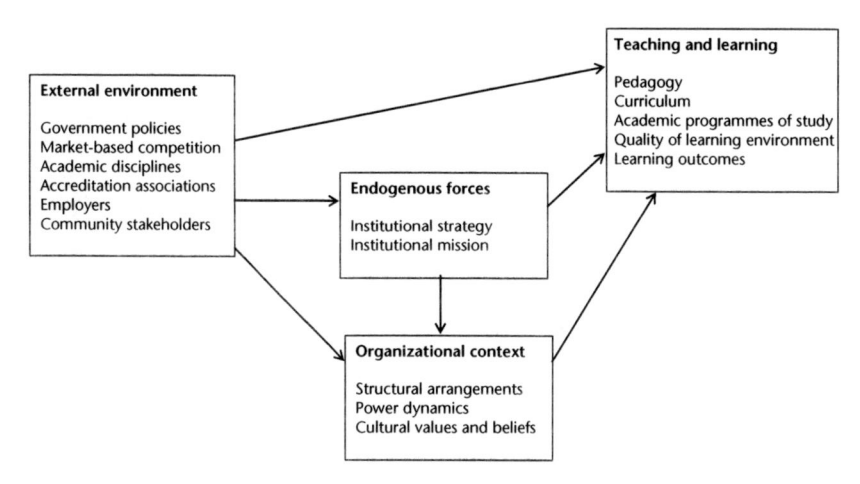

Figure 1.1 How the organizational context shapes teaching and learning

missions and strategies shape the organizational context and influence teaching and learning. Finally, the framework indicates that three features of the organizational context – structure, power dynamics, and culture – can shape teaching practices and learning outcomes. This framework is more of a heuristic device, rather than an empirically derived model. Nevertheless, the framework does reflect insights from the large body of literature in higher education studies that focuses on how the external environment and the organizational characteristics of colleges and universities can affect teaching and learning.

The chapter begins with a discussion of the external environments, missions, and strategies of higher education institutions in relation to teaching and learning. Then, the chapter explains how the structural, political, and cultural context of a higher education institution can foster or impede efforts to improve teaching and learning. After the chapter discusses these elements of the framework, the focus returns to the three proposed mechanisms for fostering change and improvement in teaching and learning: grassroots innovation, horizontal structures, and flexibly designed initiatives that connect divergent goals and interests. The chapter concludes with a case study that illustrates the recommended approach to reform.

External environment

The external environment has a significant impact on higher education policies and practices, including those that pertain to teaching and learning. Burton Clark (1983) identified three external forces that impact the governance and internal operations of colleges and universities: government policies, the marketplace for students and other resources, and the disciplines and fields of study that shape the preferences and behaviours of academics. In addition to those three forces, teaching and learning practices can also be influenced by accreditation associations, employers, and community stakeholders. Table 1.1 illustrates how these components of the external environment can affect teaching and learning in higher education institutions.

Forces in the external environment can serve as a catalyst for efforts to improve teaching and learning, or they can severely complicate academic reform initiatives. As Bess and Dee (2014) note, pressures from policy-makers, government agencies, accreditation associations, and other external constituencies have generated many positive changes in the operations of higher education institutions. Greater attention towards diversity, a stronger focus on student learning, and increasing levels of engagement with community stakeholders can each be attributed, in part, to external influences. In fact, research suggests that external pressures are among the most powerful driving forces for collaboration and change in colleges and universities (Kezar and Lester, 2009). External influences, however, can also generate conflict and tension within higher education

Table 1.1 How the external environment can affect teaching and learning

Components of the external environment	Potential effects on teaching and learning
Government policies	Emphasis on workforce development and career skills Desire to increase post-secondary degree attainment rates Concerns regarding institutional costs, efficiency, and affordability for students Attention to quality assurance through implementation of performance measurement systems Policies that seek the standardization of degrees and curriculum so that students can move more easily between institutions (e.g. Bologna Agreement)
Market-based competition	Development of institutional strategies and marketing campaigns that seek to increase enrolment and generate revenue Some institutions may embrace cost-cutting measures to keep tuition low, in order to attract more students; such measures may include hiring larger numbers of part-time academics Some institutions may strive for higher rankings of their academic programmes; higher-ranked programmes may be better able to compete for resources because they accrue the benefits of perceived quality and are therefore more attractive to potential funding sources and prospective students May contribute to the commodification of higher education and student consumerism, in which students value education as a means to obtain a high-paying job, rather than develop an appreciation of knowledge for its own sake Competition occurs in a global marketplace; some institutions may seek to internationalize their academic programmes
Academic disciplines	The disciplines shape how academics think about teaching and learning; given ontological and epistemological differences among the disciplines, academics from different departments are likely to have different views regarding what constitutes effective teaching and learning Disciplinary differences complicate any effort to create standardized teaching practices for an entire institution Disciplinary differences complicate any effort to create standardized practices to assess student learning outcomes

(Continued)

Table 1.1 (Continued)

Components of the external environment	Potential effects on teaching and learning
Academic disciplines	Academics may affiliate extensively with colleagues in their own discipline at other institutions, but seldom communicate with academics in other disciplines at their own institution; academics who have a strong external orientation may have little desire to participate in academic reform initiatives at their own institution Despite substantial differences among the disciplines, academics often share a common set of professional values for autonomy, academic freedom, shared governance, and the pursuit of knowledge; these academic values represent a powerful force that can motivate and unite academics to work across disciplinary boundaries to improve teaching and learning
Accreditation associations	Institutional and programmatic accreditation associations have shifted their emphasis from an examination of inputs (e.g. library resources, student qualifications) to an assessment of outcomes, including student learning outcomes Assessment does not focus on the grades that students receive in specific courses; instead, it seeks to determine what students are learning from their study programme as a whole Assessment data are sometimes generated through the use of a standardized exam (e.g. a test that measures content knowledge in biology) or through capstone projects in which students integrate knowledge across a range of courses Academics and managers can use assessment data to identify areas for improvement in teaching practices and curriculum
Employers and community stakeholders	Employers may encourage government agencies to develop programmes that foster workforce development Corporate and industrial leaders may serve on the institution's governing board, and the board may have authority to approve new academic programmes at the institution Employers can provide direct input to academic programmes through advisory boards; academic programmes can establish advisory boards that seek to ensure that the curriculum is relevant for the types of jobs that students are likely to obtain after graduation Employers and community organizations can provide venues for internships and service-learning activities

institutions. Different groups of managers and academics will interpret the external environment in different ways. Competing interpretations of the external environment are likely to emerge and, as a result, organizational members may disagree significantly about how the institution should engage with its external environment (Esterberg and Wooding, 2012). They might disagree, for example, about how the institution should respond to a new government policy, or how the institution should address the expectations of business and industry.

Organizational context

In addition to the influence of the external environment, research has demonstrated that the organizational context of a higher education institution plays an important role in shaping how academics teach and how students learn (Berger, 2000; Kezar and Lester, 2009). This organizational context can be analysed in terms of structural, political, and cultural dimensions. Efforts to improve teaching and learning are more likely to be successful when managers and academics take into consideration the structures, power dynamics, and cultures of their institution (Bess and Dee, 2008; Kezar and Eckel, 2002). This section of the chapter begins with a discussion of how two endogenous factors – institutional strategy and mission statement – shape the organizational context of higher education institutions. Then, this section considers each of the three components of the organizational context – structure, power, and culture – in relation to teaching and learning.

Institutional strategy

Organizational strategies provide a plan for achieving desired outcomes (Hatch, 1997). Strategy signals what the organization views as important, and it can guide organizational members as they encounter novel challenges and opportunities in their work. Strategies are often the outgrowth of a planning process that is directed by top-level managers, who may solicit advice and recommendations from academics, students, and staff (Keller, 1983; Schuster et al., 1994). Occasionally, strategies offer a creative vision for the future. More often, strategies are reactive to external pressures or simply mimic what other institutions are doing (O'Meara, 2007).

Higher education institutions have pursued a range of entrepreneurial strategies in response to market-based competition (Clark, 1998; Morphew and Eckel, 2009). To generate revenues and prestige, institutions have added new academic programmes, created new research centres and institutes, and developed new domains of operation that include interdisciplinary initiatives, online education, and the internationalization of teaching and research. While entrepreneurial strategies can enhance the reputation and profile of an institution, these approaches may also crowd out other priorities that are not revenue generating, such as working with community organizations to combat poverty or improve access to health care. While revenue generation is important to the financial health of institutions, institutional strategies can be designed to accommodate a wide range of goals that reflect the diverse interests of students and academics (Rhoads and Szelényi, 2011).

Managers and academics can leverage institutional strategies to support efforts to improve teaching and learning. They can build a compelling case for reform by linking their ideas for change to themes expressed in institutional strategic plans. This linkage to the strategic plan is important because, at many institutions, leaders allocate resources based on the extent to which a proposed initiative can contribute to the institution's strategic priorities. Top-level leaders, however, can ensure that those strategic priorities are not so tightly prescribed that they discourage new and innovative proposals from coming forward.

Institutional mission

In contrast to strategy, which varies based on the preferences of the organization's current leadership group, institutional mission is relatively enduring, held in place by tradition and values or prescribed by government policy. Missions convey a belief system regarding teaching and learning. They suggest which forms of learning are valued in the curriculum, and they indicate, although usually indirectly, desired roles for academics and students in terms of teaching, learning, and research (Morphew and Hartley, 2006). Missions can also convey a sense of place by referring to the region or area in which the institution is located.

Missions are closely related to institutional type and control. Institutional type refers to the mix of degrees and academic programmes provided by an institution. Research universities, for example, offer both undergraduate and graduate degrees in a large number of disciplines. In contrast, comprehensive regional universities and universities of applied sciences offer a broad range of undergraduate programmes, and a smaller set of graduate programmes that tend to be concentrated in professional fields, such as business and education. Institutional control refers to the governance and financing of the institution, namely whether it is public, private, or for-profit.

Just as managers and academics can link their ideas for reform to institutional strategies, they can also seek to explain how proposed changes can advance the values espoused in institutional missions. Institutional missions are often criticized for being vague and ambiguous (Delucchi, 1997). But this ambiguity allows diverse constituencies within the institution to construct their own interpretations and assign their own meanings to the mission. Organizational members can, in spite of their differences, find ways to connect to and shape their work around a flexible and somewhat ambiguous mission (Bess and Dee, 2014). More precise missions, in contrast, would likely exclude certain ideas and activities from further consideration, thus diminishing the potential for innovation and creativity.

Organizational structure

The structural designs of higher education institutions can have a significant effect on efforts to improve teaching and learning. The typical higher education institution is structurally differentiated into a large number of academic departments. These departments typically set their own curriculum, identify appropriate learning outcomes for students, and pursue research agendas that are relevant to their respective disciplines. Thus, most decisions regarding teaching and learning are made at the level of the department, while centralized coordination at the level of the institution as a whole is fairly limited (Alpert, 1985; Bess, 1988). This arrangement reflects the influence of academic disciplines on the structures of most colleges and universities. Teaching and learning are organized largely on the basis of disciplinary communities, and the structural arrangements of most higher education institutions reflect that logic.

The highly differentiated and decentralized structures that characterize most higher education institutions can foster high levels of innovation and experimentation at the local departmental level, but those same structural characteristics can complicate larger organization-wide reforms. Specifically, decentralized departments can become disconnected from each other, and begin to function as separate silos (Benjamin and Carroll, 1998). Under these conditions, academics tend to focus on the goals and priorities of their own department, and neglect institution-wide efforts to improve teaching and learning. Furthermore, departmental groupings based on discipline may not always support the integration of learning across disciplines. Many institutions require students to complete a general curriculum that educates them broadly in a range of disciplines, including the humanities, arts, and sciences (Kanter et al., 1997). While research has shown that students learn more effectively when learning is integrated across the courses they are taking, little integration may occur if academics focus only on their own discipline and neglect the general curriculum (Keeling et al., 2007). Required courses in the social sciences, for instance, may seem disconnected from the required courses in the humanities and, thus, students experience a fragmented curriculum.

Given the potential for decentralized departments to drift away from each other, the structural challenge for managers and academics is to establish sufficient cross-departmental linkages to support institution-wide reforms and to promote the sharing of knowledge and expertise across the organization. Cross-departmental linkages can be established through formal structures that span departmental boundaries. These structures include centralized offices that support the work of academics (such as professional development centres and instructional technology offices), interdisciplinary centres and programmes, and institution-wide initiatives that seek to improve some dimension of organizational performance (such as assessment or benchmarking). In addition to these formal structures, informal networks can also facilitate cross-departmental linkages. For example, through informal conversations, academics in biology and academics in economics could identify a common interest in policies regarding environmental sustainability and, in turn, they could collaborate to design new interdisciplinary courses in that area.

In higher education institutions, cross-departmental linkages are more likely established and sustained through informal networks, rather than through formal structures (Kezar, 2014). These informal networks produce a form of structural coordination known as loose coupling (Orton and Weick, 1990; Weick, 1976). Loose coupling refers to coordination that occurs informally through existing social networks. Loosely coupled departments are responsive to each other because the members of those units have established informal relationships with each other. Under these conditions, coordination is largely organic; it emerges informally from the bottom up. Loose coupling is consistent with the norms of a highly professionalized organization in which workers are granted extensive autonomy to shape their own work tasks.

In contrast, tight coupling establishes coordination through prescribed rules and standard operating procedures that indicate how each unit is expected to interact with and respond to other units. Under these conditions, coordination is primarily mechanistic; it emerges formally through centralized control. Top-level managers, for example, could establish environmental sustainability as a priority for the institution, and then create formal committees for academics in biology and economics to develop the curriculum. Tight coupling, however, would likely be resisted by academics because it interferes with their professional autonomy. Academics in biology and economics, for instance, might not view environmental sustainability as an area in which they desire to collaborate and, therefore, they may be dismissive of plans to develop curriculum in that area.

Loose coupling can foster coordination without compromising the professional autonomy of academics and their respective departments (Bess and Dee, 2008; Tierney, 2001). This form of coordination, however, cannot be centrally planned. Loose coupling cannot be created by managerial directives. Instead, it emerges informally, through interpersonal interactions that build relationships and shared interests. To foster loose coupling, institutional leaders can establish venues for informal communication across departmental boundaries. Such interactions may subsequently build internal networks that foster collaboration and support the development of innovative approaches to teaching and learning.

Power and politics

A group of managers and academics may have a promising idea for improving teaching and learning. They might gather extensive data and evidence of its effectiveness, and attempt to persuade others that this reform should be adopted. Rather than receive praise or support for their efforts, they might encounter vociferous resistance. Perhaps the group members did not realize that their idea might conflict with an initiative preferred by a different group of managers and academics. Perhaps the group did not understand that their idea would require the cooperation of a powerful department that has no interest in reform. Perhaps the group did not cultivate a sufficient number of allies and supporters for their idea before it was introduced. Organizational power dynamics can derail even the most promising academic initiative. Thus, managers and academics need to take into account the balance of power within their institution before initiating any reform.

The power dynamics of higher education institutions are somewhat unique because they revolve largely around conflicting goals (Cohen and March, 1974). Many organizations have clear, measurable goals, such as profit for a corporation. In those organizations, people may disagree about the best way to achieve the goal, but they all understand the goal in similar ways. In contrast, the goals of colleges and universities are multiple and vague, such as enhancing learning, creating new knowledge, and serving society. Organizational members will interpret and prioritize those goals in different ways; hence, the organization will lack consensus around goals and how to pursue them. Furthermore, vague goals do not provide an objective basis for institutional decision-making. In this case, data, evidence, and rational arguments may not persuade organizational members who interpret the institution's goals differently. Thus, as Temple (2008) argues, the test of many decisions is not whether they meet some rational objective standard, but whether they will work in political terms; that is, whether they will attract sufficient support from key constituency groups in the organization.

Conflict over goals tends to emerge during the institution's budget-setting process. The budget process often pits academic units against each other in a competition for resources. Some institutions allocate resources on the basis of enrolments; departments that enrol more students receive a larger share of institutional funds. Enrolment-based budgeting, however, serves as a disincentive for interdisciplinary collaboration and works against the pursuit of institution-wide reforms. Under a system of enrolment-based budgeting, each unit will attempt to maximize its own enrolment, rather than look for ways to improve the institution as a whole (Bealing and Riordan, 1996). In a study of research universities, for example, Rhoades (2000) found that during the budget process deans and department chairs attempted to politically position their units to gain more resources, rather than work to advance the institution's strategic plan.

In addition to goals-based conflict, higher education power dynamics are also shaped by unclear patterns of authority. In most higher education institutions, some degree of power sharing occurs between managers and academics. This system of shared authority – sometimes described as shared governance – delegates some decisions to academics, particularly those that deal with curricular issues (AAUP, 2001; Birnbaum, 1988). For other decisions, such as setting the institution's budget or developing the institution's strategy, academics are customarily provided opportunities to offer advice and feedback to the managers who ultimately make those decisions. This system of shared authority seems rational because it allows decisions to be made at the level where expertise resides – academics for curricular matters and managers for budgets and strategy. But the boundary between these domains is not entirely clear. A curricular decision is likely to have budgetary implications. And managers may make strategic decisions about academic programme development that are not aligned with the curricular expertise of academics. Thus, systems of shared governance are likely to produce some degree of conflict between managers and academics. As Kezar (2014) notes, the intersection of academic and managerial decision-making frequently produces a tension between managerial desires to centralize and standardize practices and procedures (to promote efficiency and coordination) and the desires of academics to maintain decentralized and customized approaches (to promote freedom of thought and action).

Organizational culture

The organizational culture of a higher education institution will influence not only the types of academic reforms adopted, but also the processes through which these reforms occur. In terms of the types of reforms adopted, organizational members are more likely to select and support reforms that are consistent with their values. An institution that values social change and engagement in the community, for example, might adopt service learning, while an institution that values the practical application of knowledge might embrace problem-based learning. Organizational change processes are also sensitive to the institution's cultural values (Kezar and Eckel, 2002; Kezar, 2014). If the organizational culture is entrepreneurial, then the reform process might be more effective if it includes external stakeholders from industry, government, and the surrounding community. If the organizational culture is more bureaucratic, then the change process would likely be more successful if it unfolds through formal committees and follows a clear chain of command. According to this line of research, efforts to improve teaching and learning are more likely to be successful if the type of reform and the process of change are both aligned with the cultural values of the institution.

Aligning an academic reform with the culture of an institution, however, is challenging because the organizational culture of a college or university seldom presents a unified set of values and beliefs. In fact, higher education institutions are often comprised of multiple, and sometimes conflicting, subcultures. Each academic department is likely to have a distinct subculture based on disciplinary traditions (Becher and Trowler, 2001). Furthermore, the cultural values of academic units (for freedom and flexibility) are likely to clash with the values of administrative units (for consistency and efficiency). The overarching culture that links these disparate subcultures might be weak or in dispute (Bess and Dee, 2014). Thus, higher education institutions may lack a common set of values with which to identify promising reforms or to guide the change process. In such circumstances, managers and academics may need to design flexible reforms that can accommodate different subcultural values. For example, efforts to internationalize the curriculum might address the social justice values of some academics, but also connect to the values of managers who seek to enhance the prestige and visibility of the institution.

Organizational culture can also shape academic reform initiatives through its impact on institutional rewards and incentives. The cultural values of an institution will likely be reflected in the activities and achievements that are rewarded, for example, in tenure and promotion decisions for academics. If teaching is not highly valued in an institution, then few rewards will be provided for instructional accomplishments. In that context, academics are likely to direct their efforts towards other activities that are more likely to gain recognition and support. In many institutions, reward systems for academics tend to emphasize individual accomplishments within a discipline, rather than collective achievements that span disciplines (O'Meara, 2005). In such cases, existing reward systems may serve as a disincentive for participating in institution-wide change initiatives, where the accomplishments are collective and not discipline specific. Thus, managers and academics may need to expand institutional reward systems so that they recognize contributions to organizational change and academic reform, in addition to accomplishments within a discipline.

Fostering change

Academic reform occurs within a complex organizational context in which institutional missions are ambiguous, goals and values are in conflict, and different people have quite different visions and preferences for the future. A potential response to these conditions might be to clarify the mission, align goals and values, and achieve a consensus regarding the future direction of the institution. While such a response might seem rational, the likely outcome would be high levels of resistance, diminished levels of innovation, and a sense of exclusion and alienation among those who believe that more powerful interests have marginalized their priorities and values. Rather than aim for clarity and consensus, managers and academics might be more successful if they attempt to establish some degree of integration among divergent goals and interests (Bess and Dee, 2014; Temple, 2008). Institutional leaders can view divergent perspectives as a resource to foster critical reflection, promote organizational learning, and create innovative approaches to improve teaching and learning.

This chapter proposes three approaches for treating divergent perspectives as a resource for improving teaching and learning. Specifically, managers and academics can support grassroots innovations, connect those innovations through horizontal structures, and encourage the development of new initiatives that can link or accommodate disparate goals. Table 1.2 shows that managers and academics have somewhat different roles in terms of carrying out these three approaches.

To support grassroots innovation, managers may need to abandon the notion that they must steer the institution towards a specific set of goals and outcomes.

Table 1.2 The roles of managers and academics in reform

Approach to reform	Role of managers	Role of academics
Grassroots innovation	Provide incentives for grassroots innovation; identify patterns of connection among grassroots initiatives	Engage the external environment to identify promising innovations to reshape practice
Horizontal structures	Based on patterns of connection, develop new horizontal structures that link innovators, and modify existing horizontal structures to support the identified patterns of activity	Invest effort in the horizontal structures because it will build capacity for related innovations to be successful – mutual learning across related projects
Flexible reforms	Rather than try to prioritize or select among competing options, instead, weave together strands from various interests; build initiatives that can achieve disparate goals or that can bridge the divide between different groups	Be willing to engage in new initiatives in which the goals seem ambiguous; that ambiguity actually provides the opportunity for groups with different goals to attribute their own meaning to the initiative and thus establish their own sense of connection to it

Centralized, top-down initiatives may not be needed to generate change. In a study of research universities, Rhoades (2000) found that innovation in academic departments was not primarily a function of centralized initiatives; instead, innovations emerged through grassroots experimentation and through the department's own interpretation of external trends and opportunities. As Rhoades notes, the primary role of managers is to 'recognize the initiatives already being undertaken by many units, to support them, and to seed strategic efforts elsewhere through selective and gentle persuasion' (p. 60). Specifically, managers can create an 'energizing context' that links innovators across departments (Spender and Grinyer, 1995, p. 921). Managers can establish venues for informal communication among academics, and between academics and managers. These interactions can forge the internal networks needed to support academic reform.

Academics can also take an active role in generating grassroots innovations. They can engage more extensively in the external environment to identify promising innovations that can improve practice. This would involve a willingness to move beyond disciplinary communities and explore practices that have emerged in other venues, such as professional associations and conferences that focus on service learning, first-year seminars, or learning communities.

As grassroots innovations become more numerous, the foci of these innovations are likely to cluster together in certain ways. Managers can identify patterns that connect the innovations that emerge in different parts of the organization. For instance, academics in sociology and academics in business management might be independently developing new courses in problem-based learning. A manager could introduce these academics to each other and, if those initial interactions generate ideas for collaboration, then the manager could provide some funding for a pilot project. In addition to connecting innovators, managers may also need to modify existing structures so that they can better support the identified patterns of activity. If several departments begin to explore problem-based learning, for example, then managers could direct the institution's professional development centre to offer workshops and training sessions on this teaching approach.

If the institution is to successfully link innovations horizontally across the organization, then academics will need to invest the time and energy necessary to build relationships with colleagues in other departments. These relationships can yield mutual learning that will be beneficial to all parties. Academics can bring new ideas back to their departments, and they might also develop new collaborative activities that span departmental boundaries.

Finally, managers and academics can work together to design flexible reforms that accommodate different goals and values. Academic reforms can accommodate diverse goals and interests if the description and focus of the initiative are left somewhat open to interpretation. This approach to reform relates to Eisenberg's (1984) concept of strategic ambiguity. According to Eisenberg, when people receive an ambiguous message, they will often 'fill in what they believe to be the appropriate context and meaning' (p. 233). When people fill in the meaning of an ambiguous message, they tend to do so in ways that are consistent with their own beliefs and values. When the message is somewhat vague, different groups with different goals can attach their own meanings to the idea, and thus find a way to connect to it. For instance, the description of an internationalization initiative could be left somewhat ambiguous. Academics in a sociology department might become interested in the initiative because they believe that it will allow their students to apply their knowledge to address practical social concerns in other nations. Academics in a business management department might become interested in the same initiative because they believe that it will allow their students to build entrepreneurial skills. If the reform effort is designed flexibly enough, then both groups of academics could pursue their separate goals within the same initiative.

Bergquist and Pawlak (2008) offer additional examples of higher education reforms that can accommodate different goals and values. Service learning, for example, can address managerial values for improving relationships with the community, as well as accommodate the values of academics who want to engage in pedagogical innovation and advance the public good. Similarly, the development of learning communities can improve student retention and degree completion rates, thus addressing managerial values for institutional effectiveness, as well as provide opportunities for academics to promote collaborative, team-based approaches to learning, thus fulfilling academic values.

A reform case study

This section provides a case study that illustrates how an academic reform can accommodate both managerial and academic values. The case is based on research conducted by the author, who studied managers and academics in a large public university system in the USA. Based on interviews with 40 managers, 40 full-time academics, and 20 part-time academics, the study examined how managers and academics work together to promote academic reform and improve teaching and learning.

Top-level leaders at Academic Reform University (ARU, pseudonym) initiated a strategic planning process that sought to improve organizational performance, particularly in the areas of student retention and degree completion. The planning process was carried out by a strategic planning group, which was appointed by the president of ARU. The group included the chief academic officer and several deans of colleges, as well as middle managers such as academic department chairs. The planning group recommended the adoption of several reforms that they had identified as having potential to improve institutional performance. These new practices were identified through an environmental scan that was conducted by members of the planning group. Environmental scanning activities included a review of websites of similar universities, participation by some group members in a national conference on university reform, and informal enquiries made to colleagues at other universities.

One of the recommended reforms was the development of a first-year experience (FYE) programme. FYE programmes seek to address the drop-out problem by providing higher levels of academic and social support to students during their first year of college – the year in which drop-out rates are highest (Braxton, 2000). Typically, FYE courses are taught by academics with expertise in building the academic and social skills of first-year college students.

The president of ARU approved the strategic planning document, which included the reforms recommended by the planning group. Implementation teams were then created for each reform that university managers planned to adopt. When the implementation plan for FYE was shared with academics, many expressed opposition. Specifically, academics were concerned that the FYE courses would lack significant content from the disciplines. In response, university managers convened two organization-wide meetings to convey information about the FYE programme, but academics continued to view the proposed programme as lacking academic rigour.

After two organization-wide meetings failed to reduce resistance to FYE, university managers discarded the original FYE proposal. A university-wide committee, comprised of managers and academics, was then established to design a new FYE model. As a result of the work of this committee, the previous conflict regarding course content was alleviated through the development of an FYE model that accommodated the interests of both managers (to reduce drop-out rates) and academics (to teach courses consistent with the principles of their discipline). One academic summarized the overall process:

> They [university managers] went to us with a plan that we didn't like. The FYE was a little too touchy-feely. I mean, it focused on study skills and how to get along with others. Faculty wanted more of an academic focus. So they went back and reworked the plan more to our liking. Now, lots of faculty want to teach FYE seminars. If they had gone forward with that other proposal, there is no way they would have got that many of us on board.
>
> (Interview with author)

In the new model, academics were given greater authority to determine the content of the FYE courses, while, at the same time, the courses continued to emphasize academic skill development so that first-year students could receive assistance before they become at-risk for dropping out. A top-level manager contrasted the current level of support for the FYE programme to the previous effort to establish first-year seminars.

> The previous attempt to implement a first-year seminar generated some faculty resistance to what they perceived as non-academic content [e.g. helping

students adjust to college life]... Now, the seminar is very academic. A faculty committee designed it. The theme is the value of liberal education and it can be taught through the lens of any discipline. The FYE has helped to build a community of colleagues who are committed to our first-year students.

(Interview with author)

Managers and academics noted that the FYE programme contributed to significant improvements in undergraduate student retention rates. A top-level manager noted that ARU has seen a 12 per cent increase in first-year to second-year retention since implementing the programme. The FYE programme was also a catalyst for creating new professional development opportunities, including a summer institute for academics who teach FYE seminars.

Academics held to their view that FYE seminars should adhere to the norms of their disciplines, while managers retained their perspective on FYE as a mechanism for improving undergraduate student retention. Neither group surrendered its interests. Instead, both groups established a shared commitment to FYE, but for different reasons. Academics became committed to FYE because they believed that the programme would provide them with an opportunity to engage in innovative teaching practices within their respective disciplines. Managers were committed to FYE because they saw the value of the programme for improving retention of students.

Conclusion

To improve teaching and learning, managers and academics may need to become familiar with two bodies of literature: the research on how students learn, and studies of how higher education institutions function. Not only must managers and academics select appropriate reforms, but they must also navigate those reforms through a complex organizational context that includes structural, political, and cultural dimensions. This chapter has highlighted the features of the organizational context that are unique to higher education institutions. While common organizational features are found at nearly every college and university, the organizational context is also specific to each institution, shaped by distinctive missions and strategies. Managers and academics can also benefit from understanding how the organizational context for teaching and learning is shaped by external forces, such as government policies, market-based competition, and academic disciplines.

Efforts to improve teaching and learning can be viewed as organizational change processes that unfold in complex, ambiguous, and non-linear ways. Fostering change in higher education institutions is exceptionally difficult, and the organizational features that would make change easier – clear goals, precise missions, tightly coupled structures, and unified cultures – are also the things that would stifle innovation and extinguish the spark of creativity that drives teaching and learning. A more feasible path towards change can be achieved through supporting grassroots innovations, building internal networks that link innovators who share common interests, and designing flexible reforms that can accommodate diverse goals and values. This path towards change acknowledges the unique organizational context of colleges and universities, and has the potential to build an enduring institutional capacity for developing and implementing successful academic reforms.

References

AAUP (American Association of University Professors) (2001) 'Statement on governance of colleges and universities (1967)' in *Policy Documents and Reports* (9th edn). Washington, DC: AAUP, pp. 217–23

Alpert, D. (1985) 'Performance and paralysis: the organizational context of the American research university'. *Journal of Higher Education*, 56 (3), pp. 241–81

Bealing, W. and Riordan, D. (1996) 'Institutional theory: what does it mean for college administrative behavior?' *Spectrum*, 69, pp. 32–7

Becher, T. and Trowler, P. R. (2001) *Academic Tribes and Territories: Intellectual Inquiry and the Culture of Disciplines* (2nd edn). Buckingham: Open University Press/Society for Research into Higher Education

Benjamin, R. and Carroll, S. (1998) 'The implications of the changed environment for governance in higher education' in Tierney, W. (Ed.), *The Responsive University: Restructuring for High Performance*. Baltimore: Johns Hopkins University Press, pp. 92–119

Berger, J. (2000) 'Organizational behavior at colleges and student outcomes: a new perspective on college impact'. *Review of Higher Education*, 23 (2), pp. 177–98

Bergquist, W. and Pawlak, K. (2008) *Engaging the Six Cultures of the Academy*. San Francisco: Jossey-Bass

Bess, J. (1988) *Collegiality and Bureaucracy in the Modern University: The Influence of Information and Power on Decision-making Structures*. New York: Teachers College Press

Bess, J. and Dee, J. R. (2008) *Understanding College and University Organization: Theories for Effective Policy and Practice, vol. I* and *II*. Sterling, VA: Stylus

Bess, J. and Dee, J. R. (2014) *Bridging the Divide between Faculty and Administration: A Guide to Understanding Conflict in the Academy*. New York: Routledge

Birnbaum, R. (1988) *How Colleges Work: The Cybernetics of Academic Organization and Leadership*. San Francisco: Jossey-Bass

Blakemore, S. and Frith, U. (2005) *The Learning Brain: Lessons for Education*. Malden, MA: Blackwell

Braxton, J. (Ed.) (2000) *Reworking the Student Departure Puzzle*. Nashville: Vanderbilt University Press

Clark, B. (1983) *The Higher Education System: Academic Organization in Cross-national perspective*. Berkeley: University of California Press

Clark, B. (1998) *Creating Entrepreneurial Universities: Organizational Pathways of Transformation*. New York: Pergamon

Cohen, M. and March, J. (1974) *Leadership and Ambiguity: The American College President*. Boston: Harvard Business School Press

Delucchi, M. (1997) '"Liberal arts" colleges and the myth of uniqueness'. *Journal of Higher Education*, 68 (4), pp. 414–26

Eisenberg, E. (1984) 'Ambiguity as a strategy in organizational communication'. *Communication Monographs*, 51, pp. 227–42

Esterberg, K. and Wooding, J. (2012) *Divided Conversations: Identities, Leadership, and Change in Public Higher Education*. Nashville: Vanderbilt University Press

Hatch, M. (1997) *Organization Theory: Modern, Symbolic, and Postmodern Perspectives*. New York: Oxford University Press

Holley, K. (2009) *Understanding Interdisciplinary Challenges and Opportunities in Higher Education*. San Francisco: Jossey-Bass

Immordino-Yang, M. and Damasio, A. (2007) 'We feel, therefore we learn: the relevance of affective and social neuroscience to education'. *Mind, Brain, and Education*, 1 (1), pp. 3–10

Kanter, S., Gamson, Z. and London, H. (1997) *Revitalizing General Education in a Time of Scarcity: A Navigational Chart for Administrators and Faculty*. Boston: Allyn and Bacon

Keeling, R., Underhile, R. and Wall, A. (2007) 'Horizontal and vertical structures: the dynamics of organization in higher education'. *Liberal Education*, 93 (4), pp. 22–31

Keller, G. (1983) *Academic Strategy: The Management Revolution in Higher Education*. Baltimore: Johns Hopkins University Press

Kezar, A. (2012) 'Bottom-up, top-down leadership: contradiction or hidden phenomenon'. *Journal of Higher Education*, 83 (5), pp. 725–60

Kezar, A. (2014) *How Colleges Change: Understanding, Leading, and Enacting Change*. New York: Routledge

Kezar, A. and Eckel, P. (2002) 'The effects of institutional culture on change strategies in higher education: universal principles or culturally responsive concepts'. *Journal of Higher Education*, 73 (4), pp. 443–60

Kezar, A. and Lester, J. (2009) *Organizing Higher Education for Collaboration: A Guide for Campus Leaders*. San Francisco: Jossey-Bass

Lutz, F. (1982) 'Tightening up loose coupling in organizations of higher education'. *Administrative Science Quarterly*, 27, pp. 653–69

Morphew, C. and Eckel, P. (Eds) (2009) *Privatizing the Public University: Perspectives from Across the Academy*. Baltimore: Johns Hopkins University Press

Morphew, C. and Hartley, M. (2006) 'Mission statements: a thematic analysis of rhetoric across institutional type'. *Journal of Higher Education*, 77 (3), pp. 456–71

O'Meara, K. (2005) 'Encouraging multiple forms of scholarship in faculty reward systems: does it make a difference?' *Research in Higher Education*, 46 (5), pp. 479–510

O'Meara, K. (2007) 'Striving for what? Exploring the pursuit of prestige' in Smart, J. (Ed.), *Higher Education: Handbook of Theory and Research, vol. 22*. New York: Springer, pp. 121–79

Orton, J. and Weick, K. (1990) 'Loosely coupled systems: a reconceptualization'. *Academy of Management Review*, 15, pp. 203–23

Pintrich, P. (2003) 'A motivational science perspective on the role of student motivation in learning and teaching contexts'. *Journal of Educational Psychology*, 95 (4), pp. 667–86

Rhoades, G. (2000) 'Who's doing it right? Strategic activity in public research universities'. *Review of Higher Education*, 24 (1), pp. 41–66

Rhoads, R. and Szelényi, K. (2011) *Global Citizenship and the University: Advancing Social Life and Relations in an Interdependent World*. Stanford, CA: Stanford University Press

Schuster, J., Smith, D., Corak, K. and Yamada, M. (1994) *Strategic Academic Governance: How to Make Big Decisions Better*. Phoenix: Oryx Press

Spender, J.-C. and Grinyer, P. (1995) 'Organizational renewal: top management's role in a loosely coupled system'. *Human Relations*, 48 (8), pp. 909–26

Temple, P. (2008) 'The integrative university'. *Perspectives: Policy and Practice in Higher Education*, 12 (4), pp. 99–102

Tierney, W. (1992) 'Cultural leadership and the search for community'. *Liberal Education*, 78 (5), pp. 16–21

Tierney, W. (2001) 'Why committees don't work: creating a structure for change'. *Academe*, 87 (3), pp. 25–9

Weick, K. (1976) 'Educational organizations as loosely coupled systems'. *Administrative Science Quarterly*, 21, pp. 1–19

Zull, J. (2011) *From Brain to Mind: Using Neuroscience to Guide Change in Education*. Sterling, VA: Stylus

2
Teaching matters, too
Different ways of governing a disregarded institution

UWE WILKESMANN

Introduction[1]

Universities throughout the world have at least two organizational goals: research and education. Both goals require complex and knowledge-intensive processes that need a special kind of organizational structure, culture, and institution. The main problem regarding teaching is that the teaching–research nexus is unbalanced – that is, research is much more highly valued than teaching. All professors working at a research university prefer research because their academic career, job promotion, and reputation belong primarily to their research performance. Individual researchers cannot use an hour of their work for both research and teaching. Preferring research while neglecting teaching mostly solves this conflict of interest and is why the institution of 'only research matters' is the most dominant logic in the field of higher education (Leišytė and Dee, 2012).

In this sense, the organizational goal of conducting research is closely linked to the individual goal of all academics. In the words of Coleman (1990, p. 74), a conjoint authority relation is given here. He defines a conjoint authority as one in which 'the subordinate's directives implement the subordinate's interest' (ibid.). In contrast, in research universities, the organizational goal of teaching is often not the primarily individual goal. Because teaching is part of a collective action, it must therefore be managed by the organization. In this case, a disjoint authority relation is likely preferred, in which 'the subordinate's interests must be satisfied by extrinsic means' (ibid.) because the organization must sometimes prioritize the academic education against the individual goals of the organization's members. Here, the interesting question arises whether teaching is only related to disjoint authority relations. This question additionally could be related to research versus teaching institutions, in which research universities are more linked to conjoint and

33

teaching universities are more linked to disjoint authority relations (Wilkesmann, 2013).

If a higher education system or a university as an organization wants to fulfil the goal of academic teaching, the institution of 'only research matters' must be disrupted and replaced by the institution 'teaching matters, too'. The main research question of this chapter will address the development and implementation of this new institution: how can the institution 'teaching matters, too' be supported and leveraged? A related question is: which type of governance leads to which kind of outcome?

The analysis of how this institution is governed must distinguish among three levels: the macro-level, which describes the governance in a nationwide higher education system (HES); the meso-level, which analyses the governance structure in the organization university; and the micro-level, which includes the behaviour of the academic staff.

The chapter starts with the theoretical underpinning of institutions and transformational and transactional governance. After giving empirical evidence from three case studies where a nexus between the macro-level, the meso-level, and the micro-level can be shown, the chapter will conclude with a discussion of the results and some concluding remarks.

Theoretical framework

Institutions

For theoretical underpinning, the difference between transformational and transactional governance (Wilkesmann, 2013) will be combined with the neo-institutional approach of institutional work (Lawrence et al., 2009). Institutions can be defined as 'rules, norms, and beliefs that describe reality for the organization, explaining what is and is not, what can be acted upon and what cannot' (Hoffman, 1999, p. 351). We find institutions at the macro-level, such as the above-mentioned institution of 'only research matters', and at the meso-level, such as the unequal interaction during examinations where the professors define what an appropriate question is that the student has to answer. Another example of an institution of teaching in Germany is the 'academic quarter' – that is, all lectures or classes start 15 minutes later than advertised.

In the following section, the aspect of governance will broaden the perspective of institutions. Governance can be seen as an institution itself when it defines standard operating procedures or constraints for teaching behaviour. Moreover, the type of governance enables and socializes specific forms and opportunities of action; similarly, action maintains, develops, or destroys forms of governance. To explain the change or the maintenance of governance and institutions in an organization, we will elucidate the recursive process among the three above-mentioned levels (see Figure 2.1). Lawrence et al. (2009) describe this recursive process as institutional work:

> If one thinks of institutions and action as existing in a recursive relationship …, in which institutions provide templates for action, as well as a regulative mechanism that enforce those templates, and action affects those templates and regulative mechanism …, then we are centrally concerned in the study of institutional work.
>
> (pp. 6–7)

Transformational and transactional governance

To answer both research questions ((1) how can the institution's message 'teaching matters, too' be supported and leveraged and (2) which type of governance leads to which kind of outcome) two different forms of organizational governance of teaching must be described: transformational and transactional. These terms originate in the 'Full Range Leadership Model' of Bass and Avolio (1993). Each type of governance enables or enforces a special kind of decision-making at the macro- and meso-level. Transformational governance is an opportunity structure for a bottom-up decision capacity, whereas transactional governance implicates a top-down reproduction of routines. Additionally, both types of governance enable, support, or enforce different types of agency at the micro-level. In the following section, the chapter will analyse this nexus in depth.

Transformational governance

Bass and Riggio (2006) characterize the transformational aspect of organizing as follows:

> there is a sense of purpose and feeling of family. Commitments are long term. Mutual interests are shared, along with a sense of shared fates and interdependence of leaders and followers. Leaders serve as role models, mentors, and coaches …. Leaders and followers go beyond their self-interests or expected rewards for the good of the team and the good of the organization.
>
> (pp. 103–4)

In the 'Full Range Leadership Model', transformational leadership is divided into the following four components (ibid., pp. 6–7):

1. Idealized influence: leaders behave as role models for their followers.
2. Inspirational motivation: transformational leaders inspire and motivate their team with enthusiasm and optimism.

3. Intellectual stimulation: followers are encouraged to introduce new ideas, and they are not criticized because their ideas differ from others' ideas.
4. Individualized consideration: leaders act as coaches and mentors. New learning opportunities are supported and created, along with an encouraging climate.

Transformational governance describes social norms (vision), expected social behaviour (supportive action), and the interactive negotiated belief system (trust the teachers) and prescribes the organizational structure that covers the leeway and autonomy of the organization's members (Wilkesmann, 2013). This type of governance could manage conjoint authority relations. In the empirical analysis, this approach will be adapted to the case of academic teaching governance.

Transactional governance

Avolio *et al.* (2009) define transactional as 'largely based on the exchange of rewards contingent on performance' (p. 427). Bass and Riggio (2006) characterize the transactional mode of organizing as follows:

> [It]… concentrates on explicit and implicit contractual relationships. Job assignments are in writing, accompanied by statements about conditions of employment, rules, regulations, benefits, and disciplinary codes…. Motivation to work is a matter of trade-offs of worker effort in exchange for rewards and the avoidance of disciplinary actions. Commitments remain short term, and self-interests are underscored …. The partly transactional organization is an internal, competitive marketplace of individuals whose rewards are contingent on their performance …. Cooperation depends on the organization's ability to satisfy the self-interests of the employees.
> (p. 103)

Agreements, codes, controls, directions, and standard operating procedures characterize transactional governance. Many managerial instruments in the style of transactional governance have been introduced in the public sector since the 1990s. At that time, various reforms and regulatory measures under the heading of New Public Management (NPM) were initiated to control public services (de Boer *et al.*, 2007). In addition to these measures, new rules, norms, and routines needed to be institutionalized by monitoring, controlling, and rewarding or punishing deviant members of the organization. In this sense, new teaching methods need transactional governance to be distributed throughout the organization. Transactional governance describes a superior–subordinate relationship in which both have different interests and the superior could only lead the subordinate with reward and punishment. Therefore, this style is more related to disjoint authority relations. The most well-known transactional management tool is merit pay.

The two types of governance can be differentiated at the macro-level: an HES with a government-produced quasi-market or a top-down state regulation or an HES with a soft governmental regime at the macro-level (e.g. little state regulation and low competition). In the first case, institutions with clear rules for decision-making will be leveraged because standard operating routines will be enforced. Either the market competition or the state defines these routines. The second case gives leeway for a bottom-up recursive feedback loop. The theoretical approach can be summarized with the following assumptions (see Figure 2.1): a quasi-market or a top-down regime at the macro-level typically supports transactional governance, and a soft governmental regime enables transformational governance. Moreover, transactional governance at the meso-level will leverage existing institutions and socialize mainstream actors, whereas transformational governance at the meso-level will enable a recursive loop and will support opportunity structures for institutional entrepreneurs (see Schmid and Lauer in this volume).

Methodology: a multiple case study of three HESs

A multiple case study design (Yin, 2014) compared three different countries with different NPM regimes at the macro-level: Germany, Hong Kong, and the UK.

The HES in Germany can be characterized as a soft governmental regime at the macro-level. Admittedly, the governance in the German system has changed in the direction of NPM since the 1990s (Schmid and Wilkesmann, 2015;

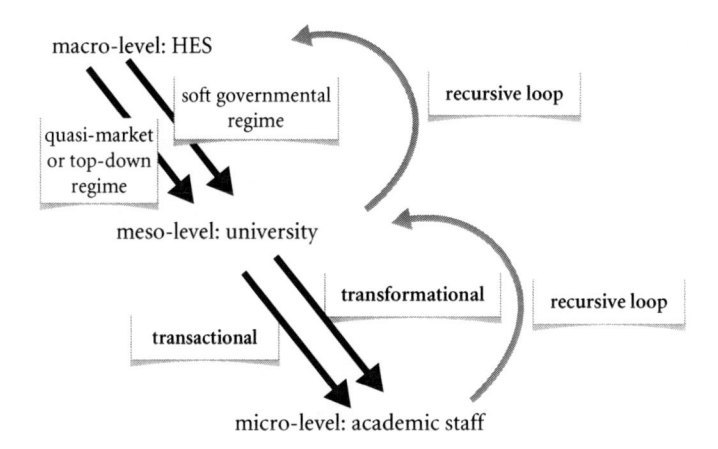

Figure 2.1 Governance types at three levels: HES, universities, and academic staff

Wilkesmann and Schmid 2012; Jansen, 2010; de Boer *et al.*, 2007; Enders *et al.*, 2002). The New Steering Instruments (NSIs), such as merit pay with a bonus, performance-related budgets, and management by objectives, have strengthened the hierarchical decision-making processes at the meso-level, which prevails in universities. Unfortunately, empirical evidence indicates that the monetary incentives of pay-for-performance and management by objectives have not had the expected influence on teaching activities (Wilkesmann and Schmid, 2012; Wilkesmann, 2013); rather, they reinforce the power of the senior management. The NSI and, additionally, the newly created university boards (Hochschulräte) have strengthened the organizational autonomy of universities and increased the managerial governance capacity. With very few exceptions, all universities are governmentally financed, and the public money is assigned as global budgets. The senior management has a wide scope in spending the budget. In sum, NPM strengthens mostly (managerial) self-governance at the meso-level but not the dependency from the state. Additionally, studying is free in Germany; no tuition fees exist at all. Therefore, a competition or quasi-market does not exist for students.

The UK describes the opposite HES. The quasi-market regime at the macro-level is highly developed with the Research Excellence Framework (REF) and the National Student Survey (NSS). High tuition fees constitute a market for higher education in the UK, with strong nationwide competition (REF, 2014; Reidpath and Allotey, 2010; Leišytė *et al.*, 2009; de Boer *et al.*, 2007; Elton, 2000). The Hong Kong case is in-between. A moderate top-down regime and moderate tuition fees characterize the HES of Hong Kong. The hierarchy at the Hong Kong university is stricter than in Germany. Last, but not least, Hong Kong was selected because pressure from the government and public opinion introduced a shift towards new teaching methods for generating innovative students and generally focusing more on academic education (Currie, 2008; UGC, 2010, recommendation 22).

The interesting question is whether these three cases disrupt the institution of 'only research matters' at the macro-level in different ways. Does high or low state regulation and strong or minor competition support different types of governance, and do they lead to different ways in building up a new institution in which 'teaching matters, too'?

Sample

In Germany, the data consist of 21 interviews at two research universities and two universities of applied sciences. The German higher education institutions (HEIs) are divided into these two categories, which exhibit the following major differences. First, to become a professor at a research university, a candidate must have, in addition to a PhD, the 'habilitation' (professorship examination) or a successfully assessed assistant professorship. For a professorship at a university of applied sciences (UAS), a candidate must have, in addition to a PhD, five years' job experience, including three years outside the university. Second, the teaching load at research universities is normally eight to nine hours per week; at the UASs, it is twice as high as at research universities. Third, the organizational goal at the UASs is much more directed towards teaching and professional development than at research universities.

The data collection in Germany followed a purposive sampling by choosing cases of best practices for teaching. The aim of the data collection was to discover explorative organizational possibilities to enhance the status of academic teaching. The German association Stifterverband für die Deutsche Wissenschaft (Foundation of the German Industry for Higher Education) rewarded ten universities in their programme 'Excellence in Teaching', a highly competitive funding project that recognizes best practices in academic education. The study includes experts from four of the rewarded universities.

In the UK, six in-depth interviews were conducted at a research university. The UK case – and especially the selected middle-ranked university – highlights the high impact of student evaluation on internal decisions.[2]

In Hong Kong, 13 in-depth interviews were conducted on-site at three research universities and one teaching university in Hong Kong. Due to scheduling difficulties, two additional interviews were conducted via Skype afterwards.

All interviews were conducted in 2014. The sample consisted of academic staff at all universities from different hierarchical levels: vice-rectors for teaching and learning (the term 'vice-rector' also includes the vice-president and pro-vice-chancellor), professors, lecturers, and the department heads of the centres for excellence in teaching and learning (CETL).

The length of the interviews varied between one and one and a half hours. All interviews were recorded, transcribed, coded, and analysed by using the 'content-analysing method' (Mayring, 2007; Berg, 2004). In the following section, all quoted interviews are referred to at the hierarchical level (professors are counted per country), including teaching award winners and heads of the CETL, with the related country in brackets. When the interviewee is a member of a UAS or teaching university, it is mentioned; otherwise, the interviewee is not a member.

Empirical results

In the field of higher education, the previously mentioned idea of 'only research matters' is the most powerful in research universities. Nevertheless, in all countries, official initiatives were introduced to disrupt this idea. The deductive content analysis initially focused on this aspect at the macro-level. Then, the different governance types of teaching were analysed at the meso-level, with all the implications for agency at the micro-level.

Table 2.1 Sample structure of interviews per country

	Germany (four universities) number	Hong Kong (four universities) number	UK (one university) number
Vice-rectors	4	3	2
Heads of CETL	4 (+ 2 evaluation managers)	4	1
Teaching award winners	2	2	1
Professors	9	6 (includes an associate head of school)	2 (includes a vice-dean)
Total number	21	15	6

The macro-level of HES

Germany

In Germany, the Federal Ministry of Education and Research (BMBF) spent more than €2 billion on the Quality Initiative for Teaching (Qualitätspakt Lehre) and more money in other teaching supporting activities. This money was distributed as funded projects for which universities had to apply with proposals. This special type of money distribution meant that many bottom-up initiatives started at each university. Especially for the UASs, which are typically much smaller and have less third-party money than research universities, this chance to obtain extra money for teaching had an impact because it noticeably increased the whole budget (vice-rector UAS, Germany). Moreover, every year the German Stifterverband awards Germany's best professor in teaching with €50,000. Such a nationwide teaching award matters as a German professor described:

> Even the president will acknowledge when the Stifterverband decides to give a fellowship and rewards a professor with €50,000. He will then get a letter: 'Congratulations to the appointment of honourable Prof. (X) as Fellow. Prize money amounting to €50,000.' Then, you will be noticed for the first time.
> (Teaching award winner, Germany)

The rectorate at this research university confirms this perception:

> employees then regularly rise to the competition at the Stifterverband. Our results are very successful, which is a kind of evaluation in my opinion

because ultimately it is an external expert's assessment. And it can't be so wrong if the Stifterverband, which I regard highly because they have a good overview, certifies 'Your employees have a good concept, or are innovative in some cases', which does not automatically imply good teaching but is a start.
(Vice-rector, Germany)

Traditionally, in Germany, the 'freedom of teaching' ensures a high degree of autonomy, especially for the tenured professors. The governmental money is 'only' a selective incentive to disrupt the institution of 'only research matters' and pushes the whole system into the designated direction. The main purpose is not to implement a new top-down incentive but to give leeway for developing many bottom-up initiatives.

The UK

In the UK, the situation is very different. The governance of the HES pressures the universities by implementing top-down measures and thereby creating a quasi-market. In former times, the Research Assessment Exercise (RAE) (now the Research Excellence Framework (REF)) and the National Student Survey (NSS) are the implemented ranking systems in the HES. With these rankings and the high tuition fees, the government produces a quasi-market for higher education. A high ranking in the first framework is essential for the universities because only then are they allowed to submit proposals to the national research councils. Otherwise, they could be downgraded to a teaching university (Shattock, 2007). The only organizational goal is then more or less teaching without enough resources for research.

Additionally, the nationwide teaching evaluation by the NSS is a powerful tool to enforce teaching interests. Each bachelor student is asked during their last year to complete the NSS questionnaire. The results will be published on the university ranking and compared at the programme level. Last, but not least, these results are also used at the professor level as an individual performance criterion. The investigated university was very successful in the university ranking based on NSS in the previous few years and therefore attracted many students. 'Yes, and as it happens [university name] has managed to become the number one for two years running. Does [university name] have any trouble in recruiting the best students? Absolutely not, there are ten applicants for every place, so that's really helpful' (former vice-rector, UK). The NSS rankings are published as national league tables in the newspapers, 'and universities are very sensitive to that because our funding depends on the number of students and, for most of our academic departments, even in the research-intensive, you're looking at about three-quarters to 80 per cent of the funding coming in from students' (head CETL, UK). Thus, all departmental budgets are affected if the university is at the bottom of the table. 'However, if we are 25th in the *Daily*

Telegraph then we are 25th. That's going to affect your recruitment. That's ultimately going to affect the departments' (vice-rector, UK). In conclusion, tuition fees and rankings matter.

All students have to pay a tuition fee of up to £9,000 per year. From the rectorate's perspective, this fee changes a lot. In our case, it is the largest budget item and is over 60 per cent of the whole university budget. Additionally, other income related to the number of students, such as dormitory or other loans, is also relevant. Thus, strong competition is present between the universities in terms of attracting students. The senior management perceives a very high and recently increasing importance of tuition fees; therefore, increasing attention is given to teaching. Marketing activities such as open days are becoming more significant, as a vice-rector mentioned:

> Now, when we have an open day we get approximately 10,000 people here. Every one of the students who is coming here is with at least one parent and often two. They are the ones asking me questions; the kids don't. It's the parents. It is different.
>
> (Vice-rector, UK)

And the parents are prepared.

> This is expensive business in this country. Therefore, the parents and the students would do much homework on the websites and do their research, and they come armed with good questions. I've even been asked questions about selection criteria for new academics; how important is teaching when you recruit new academics? Fortunately, I sit on selection panels, you know what it's like, and I can speak with honesty as to what we look at, but that gives you an idea. Parents are interested; parents and applicants, but parents especially are interested in teaching excellence. They want to know how good you are, what steps you take ... because [of] the whole fee issue in this country.
>
> (Vice-dean, UK)

Hong Kong

In Hong Kong, the University Grants Committee (UGC), which is the government body in Hong Kong that distributes money to the universities, awards an annual Hong Kong-wide teaching price of HK$500,000. Persons who are rewarded at the faculty level could be nominated for the university award, and those award winners are automatically candidates for the UGC award (head CETL, HK). The UGC grant receives significant public attention because all newspapers and TV stations report about it. Afterward, the award winner is very often asked to serve as an interview partner in the media. Therefore, his or her face is publicly well known (vice-rector, HK).

Between 2012 and 2015, HK$112.7 million was spent by the UGC for 'teaching development grants' (UGC, 2015). All undergraduate and PhD programmes are generally financed by the UGC, but all master's programmes must be self-financed by tuition fees without contributing to basic structures, such as buildings or IT. Therefore, the tuition fees for master's programmes are 2.5 higher than those for bachelor's or PhD programmes (vice-rector, HK). As a consequence, tuition fees matter for master's programmes.

In Hong Kong, some more external factors partially disrupt the institution of 'only research matters'. The government developed the political goal to educate innovative students at universities. From the government's perspective, a knowledge-intensive society does not need employees who copy only western goods but innovative academics who develop new products. Therefore, the teaching style at universities changes from a teacher-focused to a student-focused approach (for the German case, see Wilkesmann and Lauer, 2015). Students are encouraged to be more creative, deal with uncertainty, and be thirsty for knowledge (associate head of school, HK). This challenge is a strong political argument to change to a more student-focused teaching approach. Problem-based learning (PBL), small classes, and open discussions are moving in this direction. Globalization and competition are the main forces to emphasize teaching and learning activities throughout Hong Kong society.

Based on this political issue, teachers perceive their students in two different categories: the Hong Kong (student-focused) and the Mainland Chinese (teacher-focused) students. Hong Kong people perceive the Mainland students as over-ambitious who are learning '48 hours a day' (professor teaching university, HK). All interviewed professors described Mainland students as persons who gather knowledge and only memorize but without transforming the knowledge into new contexts. Caused by their socialization at school, they demand a teacher-focused, lecturing teaching approach so they know what to learn for the examination (professors 1, 4, 12, HK). They passively listen in the classroom, are not used to discussing things, are less interactive than the Hong Kong students, and they do not speak up for themselves. From the professor's perspective, it is challenging to engage them (teaching award winner, HK). Therefore, some professors use IT tools to allow the Mainland students to post their questions, and the professors will answer them anonymously in class; thus, the students do not have to fear losing face (professor 6; teaching award winner, HK). In comparison, the Hong Kong students are described as demanding a student-focused teaching approach in classes (head CETL, HK).

Last, but not least, a struggle in the teaching–learning nexus is based on Chinese culture. On the one side, teaching is highly valued in Chinese culture because education is one of the most outstanding social values. The teacher is seen as a lifelong advisor, and the students must honour her or him. Teachers and professors have a high social status. On the other side, the HES in Hong

Kong has recently forced professors to put more emphasis on research. The universities in Hong Kong are ranked in the QS World University Ranking (2014) between place 28 (26) and place 162 (161). The research output of professors is measured and rewarded with many incentives, such as merit pay bonuses (vice-head CETL, HK), renewed contracts, and promotions up the academic career ladder (head CETL, HK). As a consequence, this strong motivation leads the professors to pass the pressure on to the students. A common strategy, for example, is to coerce the PhD candidates, and even the master's candidates, to publish papers with the professors in highly ranked journals. At some faculties, the informal rule is that PhD students must publish four papers in collaboration with the supervisor before they can submit their thesis (professor 6, 14, HK).

Additionally, a history of the drive that 'teaching matters, too' exists in Germany and the UK. The UAS and polytechnics are or were teaching universities, but both are now universities (UK) or are trying to achieve the status of research universities (Germany).

In Hong Kong, an example of the recursive loop at the macro-level was also given. One of the vice-rectors was a proponent for the UGC teaching award and the teaching development grants. An important reason why the recursive loop between the meso- and the macro-level is easy to implement is the size of the country. Hong Kong is a city where all relevant persons know each other.

The meso-level of universities

Transformational governance in Germany and Hong Kong

The data show clear evidence for transformational governance at some German and Hong Kong universities. Intellectual stimulation and inspirational motivation are particularly relevant in the best practice examples for developing new teaching methods and new institutions in organizations that support the status of teaching.

From a government perspective, intellectual stimulation fosters the perception of leeway and autonomy that is essential for innovative teaching activities. One interviewee who pushed PBL at her faculty emphasizes how important intellectual stimulation is: 'They allow you to have the space and time to think' (associate head of school, HK). Intellectual stimulation must also be visible in the senior management's behaviour, that is, a vision must be communicated by the rectorate, as one interviewee noted (associate head of school, HK). In this case, the professor perceives the vision by the open-mindedness of the senior management and the idea that all university members can speak freely about new, innovative ideas without repercussion. Furthermore, the vision must be lived in the organization. The senior management must act as a role model.

One vice-rector summarized this process as follows: 'The teachers have to feel that you have the passion' (vice-rector, HK).

In addition, intellectual stimulation is necessary because no top-down defaults are caused by the 'freedom of teaching' (head CETL; vice-rector; professor 3, 12, HK). Bottom-up agency is needed to improve academic teaching. As one vice-rector describes it from the senior management perspective: 'You have to have confidence in your own teachers – you have to believe in them!' (vice-rector, HK). A corresponding style of leadership is also required:

> Leadership is not about telling people what they should do or not do. Leadership is about looking at the situation and identifying what are the elements that can come together which will change things. And the elements have got to be there. These elements come from the teachers.
> (Vice-rector, HK)

From her point of view, her job is to identify, recognize, and gather all innovative initiatives; learn from her findings and support these initiatives. Therefore, she has many informal face-to-face interactions with professors, for example, during lunch or coffee breaks. Furthermore, she builds up communities of practice, so innovative colleagues do not feel isolated and can learn from each other. Thus, she identified excellent courses and invited the instructors to speak about their experiences.

In the best practice examples, inspirational motivation also plays an important role. During a talk that a German teaching award winner gave regarding teaching problems, he reported:

> and at a point in the talk our rector said 'So Mr (XY), we are familiar with this but what can we tangibly do?' And I had already read about the Professional Teaching–Learning Communities and had looked for solutions and was serendipitously able to suggest them and he said willingly, 'Okay, we can try that here, what is necessary to do so?' and I mentioned 'Those who participate should be discharged of teaching load' and he agreed, 'Okay, let's give it a try next summer term.'
> (Teaching award winner, UAS, Germany)

Another practice that is not taken for granted at universities is the following recognition:

> The rectorate endeavours, I mean, it was positive regarding the teaching project: when I do something, the rector approaches me, hugs me, not in a physical way but figuratively speaking, and says 'Mr (XY), fantastic, I really think it's great that you are so involved.'
> (Teaching award winner, UAS, Germany)

Transformational governance not only includes leaders who behave as role models; all of the best practice cases in teaching are visible and will be transferred to all members in the university. For example, at a university in Germany, a professor developed computer games for his students, so they would be able to repeat and deepen their knowledge when playing the game. Because this game was successful, the rectorate appointed him as the official university's expert for educational games and forwarded all requests regarding this topic to him.

Within universities with the transformational leading vice-rectors, an open culture exists in several departments. Teachers commonly share their teaching material (teaching award winner, HK). In another department, the teaching material from all academic staff is made available on a protected online database, so all colleagues can mutually share it. No one has hesitated to publish material such as his or her slides, PBL cases, games, group work instructions, and questions (professor 3, HK).

Transformational governance enables autonomy and leeway for the organizational members and provides wide leeway for self-motivated behaviour for both teaching and learning. This organizational freedom is necessary for the recursive loop because only then can the professors reflect on their teaching and learning experience and take appropriate action from this critical distance. In one case, a professor told us that being a student was a hard-luck story for him. After graduating, the student recognized during his first practical experience that he had learned unimportant concepts:

> I think it might be my personal tale of woe ... with every second move in my daily work life I realize that wherever I turn to, that I have never heard of it, nobody has ever told me about it at the university, and the information I got was mostly rubbish and out of date.
> (Teaching award winner, Germany)

Additionally, the transformational governance enables the academic staff to be highly intrinsically motivated (Ryan and Deci, 2000). The staff emphasize that one has to speak about learning and not teaching. 'The learning of the students has to occupy the centre stage' (teaching award winner, HK). That is why the professors want to change the focus to the students. Therefore, the professors want to be very close to the students, in terms of what they think and believe, how they act, and what they desire (associate head of school, HK). 'I see them [students] to be individuals, people who I enjoy being with, people who I enjoy seeing develop' (teaching award winner, HK). Her motivation is based on 'seeing students after a certain period of time, after they have graduated, being special people in life [...] becoming really famous, popular; developing in different ways'. From her perspective, 'Teaching is part of my life. It is not extra work.' Her basic motivation is 'seeing myself as a role model'.

In alignment with Maguire *et al.* (2004) and Garud *et al.* (2007), this innovative academic staff can be described as institutional entrepreneurs because they build up the institution 'teaching matters, too' within their universities. Institutional entrepreneurship refers to the 'activities of actors who have an interest in particular institutional arrangements and who leverage resources to create new institutions or to transform existing ones' (Maguire *et al.*, 2004, p. 657; for more details, see Schmid and Lauer in this volume). Institutional entrepreneurs are the basis of new initiatives. Additionally, an organizational opportunity structure is needed, so the initiative can grow. The organization comes back into mind when you have to institutionalize, formalize, and evaluate the new innovation (vice-rector, HK). These activities describe the recursive loop between the transformational governance as an opportunity structure for institutional entrepreneurs. This is what Lawrence and Suddaby (2006) call institutional work. They broaden the concept of institutional entrepreneurs because:

> such work tends to overemphasize the rational and 'heroic' dimension of institutional entrepreneurship while ignoring the fact that all actors, even entrepreneurs, are embedded in an institutionally defined context. Institutional entrepreneurship has thus been criticized as a *deus ex machina* within institutional theory, used to explain institutional change as the outcome of attempts by a few rational and powerful actors.
>
> (Lawrence *et al.*, 2009, p. 5)

Transactional governance in the UK, Hong Kong, and part of Germany

The data show five transactional modes of teaching governance in our cases. Mostly, the data belong to the UK and Hong Kong cases, but also partially to the German case.

1. Teaching evaluation: in the UK and Hong Kong, the teaching evaluation is an important management tool at the individual and programme level. As mentioned before, the NSS generates data on the university, programme, and individual level in the UK. Within the university at the personal level, each professor has to receive 3.5 or above on average (on a five-point Likert scale) to be on the safe side. If a professor is below that threshold, he or she has a serious discussion with the dean. Additionally, individual performance on the teaching evaluation is used for promotion decisions on the career track.

    > There are a variety of explanations, so everybody below 3.5 has to come up with an action plan for their course and that has to be approved by our quality group with the school, and then we follow it

up and see what's happened to their scores the next year. We've got quite a tight system, so it's completely circular. There are no gaps in it.

(Vice-dean, UK)

Furthermore, evaluations such as the NSS rearrange the power balance within the organization and change the micro-politics:

The NSS has been one of the catalysts because it provides people like me with a mandate to affect change, and this is hard currency, if you get my flavour, this is hard currency, and therefore the Dean knows our scores.

(Vice-dean, UK)

Additionally, the senior management could sanction poor performers in teaching: 'Well, you can make life uncomfortable for somebody' (former vice-rector, UK). The professors perceive this sanction capacity. A professor explained that the NSS quality management 'hasn't distinguished well enough between monitoring and control', and as a consequence,

it really transforms the relationship between the students and the teacher. That's seriously problematic for me. It makes it a transaction. I think it takes away the joy of being a good teacher and it erodes that teacher–student relationship.

(Professor 2, UK)

In Hong Kong, the Student Evaluation of Teaching and Learning exists, although the usage of the evaluation in each university is slightly different. In one university, the vice-rector emphasizes that the results are not for accountability but only for feedback and enhancement (vice-rector, HK). She also revised the questionnaire from a teacher-focused to a student-focused perspective. Now, the learning outcomes have priority as opposed to the personal assessment of the teachers. The survey shifted to a more competence-oriented perspective.

On the programme level at some Hong Kong universities and the university in the UK, the vice-rector analyses the data. If a programme has a poor evaluation, the programme director must write a report concerning how the whole programme can be improved. If the evaluation is still substandard in the following year, the vice-rector will act. In some cases in Hong Kong, the senior management will sanction the whole programme. If a programme is poorly evaluated twice, they will cut the budget by approximately 30 per cent (vice-rector, HK). With visible improvement, the programme director will get the budget refunded.

2. Arranged competition: a university can fund its own teaching development grants (TDGs) in addition to the nationwide ones. For example, in

Hong Kong, the TDGs amount to HK$10 million each year per university. Some of the interviewees successfully applied for TDGs (e.g. professor 3, HK). All of the TDGs combine enhancement in teaching with research about teaching. Such research projects are only attractive for professors in the field of education research, didactics, and psychology who cover that topic. Most interviewees – even if they have no TDGs – classify them as a success story for developing and testing new teaching tools and methods because other colleagues can also participate in the results.

3. Career track based on teaching: universities in the UK can provide extra career tracks for teaching. An assistant professor can be promoted to an associate or full professor based on teaching criteria. If someone is very engaged in developing new teaching programmes or is managing bachelor's or master's programmes, he or she can be promoted without having the required number of A- or B-journal papers. Interestingly, this career option does not lead to a teaching professorship. The teaching load is as high as in the research-based track. The former vice-rector, who created the new career track, provided the following reasons:

> Now, why did I do it? It's partly to do with a belief that students should get a better deal out of teaching by making teaching slightly more important in the institution. It also had to do with the fact of the way in which the market was starting to operate in UK, so that the government certainly was trying to say, teaching is very important, we will reward those institutions that take teaching seriously, and that with the National Student Survey being an important contributor to league table position, I was able to persuade the Vice-chancellor that it was in our interest to do something like this.
>
> (Former vice-rector, UK)

Teaching performance is also sometimes linked to the 'normal' research-based career track. In Hong Kong, all professors are evaluated based on their tasks as follows: 60 per cent research performance, 30 per cent to 20 per cent teaching quality, and 20 per cent to 10 per cent engagement for service and administration (vice-rector; professor 2, HK). For lecturers, the breakdown changes to 60 per cent teaching, 20 per cent research, and 20 per cent service and administration (teaching award winner, HK). This order implies that research is more important than teaching for professors but that lecturers are linked to their teaching performance. This organizational segregation between a research track and a teaching track creates an organizational and an individual responsibility. Not all members of the organization must simultaneously fulfil both organizational goals – as in the German case, where the ratio for all academic staff is 50:50. When an organization has different goals, segregation is a typical organizational solution. Different departments produce one solution for each goal.

4. Peer coaching and sabbatical for teaching: at some universities in Germany and in Hong Kong, peer coaching was implemented. Professors build voluntary peer groups where they sit in on the classes of colleagues and give checklist-based feedback to them. One German university awarded a sabbatical for teaching. If a professor wants to develop an innovative, new method for teaching, the person can apply for the sabbatical and will get a teaching load of zero during the next semester. However, the main problem with this sabbatical is that only very few professors apply for it.

5. Centres for excellence in teaching and learning (CETL): from the organizational perspective, a classical solution is to build a new department that is responsible for finding a solution. The organization is then relieved and can address further problems within the department. In our case, all universities established CETLs. In the UK, these centres are responsible for looking at 'academic standards … we look at systems and approaches around to make sure that staff and students engage on making teaching the best it can be' (head CETL, UK). Moreover, their mission is to support, coach, and improve those academic staff who score less than 3.5 on the NSS.

In Hong Kong, for example, all four CETL have a staff of from 30 to 70 employees. In comparison to the centres in Europe, they are very well equipped. Sometimes, the vice-rectors use the centre as their executive arm. They are obliged to implement the vice-rector's strategic decisions (vice-rector, HK). In this case, the director of the centre tries to guard against them having the 'police function – only the coach function' (head CETL, HK).

Support from senior management is very important for these centres:

> The pro-vice-chancellor for Learning and Teaching we have now and pro-vice chancellor for Learning and Teaching we've had before were very much looking at the recognition of learning and teaching …. It's funny because I looked at some email that I got from the pro-vice-chancellor in 2006. It was a draft email that he was about to send out to all of the heads of departments and says, if you don't care enough about how well you do on learning and teaching, you should not be academics. I mean, that's quite something.
>
> (Head of CETL, UK)

New routines in teaching are implemented via transactional governance. The corresponding agency for this type of governance is an actor who must be socialized in the new routines, norms, and methods. This agency type can be defined as a mainstream actor because the actor meets the requirements of the new teaching institution. The mainstream actor is a member who is following the required institutional behaviour and therefore 'only' reproducing the organizational structure. In contrast with the institutional entrepreneur, the mainstream actor will not disrupt, develop, or rebuild (new) institutions but maintain the existing ones. From the organizational perspective, mainstream actors who reproduce the institutions are very important for the 'daily teaching work' because such institutionalized behaviour is the main coordination and management instrument in universities, which are hybrid forms of conjoint and disjoint organizations.

Discussion

The data analysis shows two central findings for the main research question, which was how the goal of 'teaching matters, too' could be supported and leveraged. First, in an HES with a quasi-market regime at the macro-level (the UK case), transactional governance at the meso-level is common. The competition from the environment is handed down via the corresponding competitive rules within the organization. Transformational governance is more probable in a soft governmental regime at the macro-level (Germany and, partially, Hong Kong) because universities have more freedom and autonomy to choose their own governance type. Second, transformational governance enables new, innovative action from the bottom-up, which can create new rules, norms, and ideas about academic teaching. Only this type of governance enables a recursive loop to the meso-level. In this case, transactional governance is then needed to leverage these new ideas as institutions within the whole organization. If the monitoring and sanction system is too strict, teaching motivation can decrease and be crowded-out.

Inspirational motivation and intellectual stimulation, which is supported by a wide leeway of action, are prerequisites for developing innovative actions. Additionally, a vision that highlights the route of development in the organization is important, and the new behaviour must be supported by the hierarchy. Power, specifically power distance, 'the blessing from the senior management' (professor 2, HK), is necessary to support innovation and to leverage new routines and new rules within the organization. Furthermore, when professors engage in the recursive loop in terms of transformational governance, they also need financial resources and the competency to use micro-political strategies. Resources, especially monetary, are necessary to implement new teaching projects, such as flipped classrooms, where the lectures are filmed in advance.

To answer the initial question, whether teaching is only related to a disjointed authority, the data show that a conjoint authority with transformational governance is necessary for developing new ideas, rules, or norms. For developing and leveraging the institution that decides 'teaching matters, too', both kinds of governance and both types of authority are important.

The transformational governance at universities is sometimes in accordance with the newly described fluidly organized communities (Marquis et al., 2011;

Adler and Heckscher, 2006). 'Communities are collections of actors whose membership in the collective provides social and cultural resources that shape their action. Membership can result from a number of factors including propinquity, interest in a common goal, or common identity' (Marquis *et al.*, 2011, p. xvi). These communities are grounded in an affective shared identity, but membership in such a community is an active decision, not a question of genealogy, and based on value-based actions. The correlation between communities and transformational governance is that both support innovation. Both emphasize that action is governed by value, social norms, and shared visions. However, the community approach focuses on the prerequisites of collective action and forms of self-organizing, which can be enabled under transformational governance. In contrast, the transformational governance's perspective focuses more on structural aspects. In addition, transactional governance is necessary to leverage innovation. This aspect is neglected in the collaborative community approach. The latter stresses only the self-organizing, self-determination process of collective action. In communities, it is rather difficult to establish decisions because every member has veto power.

In summary, a mixed transformational–transactional governance approach could be a good pattern for analysing and describing teaching governance and solving the problem of how to enhance the social status and recognition of teaching within the university as an organization. This combined approach could be a blueprint for disrupting routines and organizing innovations in universities and companies.

Nevertheless, further quantitative research is needed to generalize these findings from the selected best practice examples in this study.

Notes

1 The data collection has been financed by the German Federal Ministry of Education and Research (Project: Transformational governance of academic teaching, TeachGov). In addition to the author, Sabine Lauer and Christian Schmid were involved in the data collection.
2 The sample does not cover the traditional old polytechnics.

References

Adler, P. S. and Heckscher, C. (2006) 'Towards collaborative community' in Heckscher, C. and Adler, P. S. (Eds), *The Firm as Collaborative Community: Reconstructing Trust in the Knowledge Economy*. Oxford: Oxford University Press, pp. 11–105

Avolio, B., Walumba, F. and Weber, T. J. (2009) 'Leadership: current theories, research, and future directions'. *Annual Review of Psychology*, 60, pp. 421–49

Bass, B. M. and Avolio, B. J. (1993) 'Transformational leadership and organizational culture'. *PAQ Spring 1993*, pp. 112–21

Bass, B. M. and Riggio, R. E. (2006) *Transformational Leadership* (2nd edn). New York: Psychology Press

Berg, B. L. (2004) *Qualitative Research Methods for the Social Sciences*. Boston: Allyn and Bacon Press

Coleman, J. S. (1990) *Foundations of Social Theory*. Cambridge, MA: Belknap Press
Currie, J. (2008) 'The Research Assessment Exercise in Hong Kong: positive and negative consequences'. *International Education Journal: Comparative Perspectives*, 9 (1), pp. 47–58
de Boer, H., Endres, J. and Schimank, U. (2007) 'On the way towards new public management? The governance of university systems in England, the Netherlands, Austria, and Germany' in Jansen, D. (Ed.), *New Forms of Governance in Research Organizations*. Dordrecht: Springer, pp. 137–54
Elton, L. (2000) 'The UK Research Assessment Exercise: unintended consequences'. *Higher Education Quarterly*, 54 (3), pp. 274–83
Enders, J., Kehm, B. and Schimank, U. (2002) 'Structures and problems of research in German higher education' in McAdams, R. (Ed.), *Trends in American and German Higher Education*. Cambridge, MA.: American Academy of Arts and Sciences, pp. 85–119
Garud, R., Hardy, C. and Maguire, S. (2007) 'Institutional entrepreneurship as embedded agency: an introduction to the special issue'. *Organization Studies*, 28, pp. 957–69
Hoffman, A. J. (1999) 'Institutional evolution and change: environmentalism and the US chemical industry'. *Academy of Management Journal*, 42 (4), pp. 351–71
Jansen, D. (Ed.) (2010) *Governance and Performance in the German Public Research Sector*. Dordrecht: Springer
Lawrence, T. B. and Suddaby, R. (2006) 'Institutions and institutional work' in Clegg, S. R., Hardy, C., Lawrence, T. and Nord, W. R. (Eds), *The Sage Handbook of Organization Studies* (2nd edn). London and Thousand Oaks: Sage, pp. 215–54
Lawrence, T. B., Suddaby, R. and Leca, B. (2009) 'Introduction: theorizing and studying institutional work' in Lawrence, T. B., Suddaby, R. and Leca, B. (Eds), *Institutional Work: Actors and Agency in Institutional Studies of Organization*. Cambridge, NY: Cambridge University Press
Leišytė, L. and Dee, J. R. (2012) 'Understanding academic work in a changing institutional environment' in Smart, J. C. and Paulsen, M. B. (Eds), *Higher Education: Handbook of Theory and Research*. New York: Springer, pp. 123–206
Leišytė, L., Enders, J. and de Boer, H. (2009) 'The balance between teaching and research in Dutch and English universities in the context of university governance reforms'. *Higher Education*, 58, pp. 619–35
Maguire, S., Hardy, C. and Lawrence, T. B. (2004) 'Institutional entrepreneurship in emerging fields: HIV/AIDS treatment advocacy in Canada'. *Academy of Management Journal*, 47, pp. 657–79
Marquis, C., Lounsbury, M, and Greenwood, R. (Eds) (2011) *Communities and Organizations*. Bingley: Emerald
Mayring, P. (2007) 'On generalization in qualitative oriented research'. *Forum: Qualitative Social Research*, 8 (3), Art. 26. Retrieved from http://www.qualitative-research.net/index.php/fqs/article/viewArticle/291/641.%208
QS World University Ranking (2014) QS World University Ranking. http://www.topuniversities.com
REF (Research Excellence Framework) (2014) *Overview Report by Main Panel A and Sub-panels 1 to 6*. Retrieved from http://www.ref.ac.uk/media/ref/content/expanel/member/Main%20Panel%20A%20-%20Final%20List%20%28Jan%202015%29.pdf
Reidpath, D. D. and Allotey, P. (2010) 'Can national research assessment exercises be used locally to inform research strategy development? The description of a methodological approach to the UK RAE 2008 results with focus on one institution'. *Higher Education*, 59, pp. 785–97
Ryan, R. M. and Deci, E. L. (2000) 'Self-determination theory and the facilitation of intrinsic motivation, social development and well-being'. *American Psychologist*, 55, pp. 68–78
Schmid, C. J. and Wilkesmann, U. (2015) 'Ansichtssache Managerialismus an deutschen Hochschulen – Ein empirisches Stimmungsbild und Erklärungen'. *Beiträge zur Hochschulforschung*, 37 (2), pp. 56–87. Dordrecht: Springer

Shattock, M. (2007) 'United Kingdom' in Forest, J. F. and Altbach, P. G. (Eds), *International Handbook of Higher Education*. Netherlands: Springer, pp. 1019–33

UGC (Universities Grants Committee) (2010) *Aspirations for Higher Education Systems in Hong Kong. Report of the University Grants Committee*. Hong Kong. Retrieved from http://www.voced.edu.au/content/ngv58227

UGC (Universities Grants Committee) (2015) *About the UGC*. Hong Kong. Retrieved from http://www.ugc.edu.hk/eng/ugc/about/about.htm

Wilkesmann, U. (2013) 'Effects of transactional and transformational governance on academic teaching: empirical evidence from two types of higher education institutions'. *Tertiary Education and Management*, 19 (4), pp. 281–300

Wilkesmann, U. and Lauer, S. (2015) 'What affects the teaching style of German professors? Evidence from two nationwide surveys'. *Zeitschrift für Erziehungswissenschaft*. Online First; doi: 10.1007/s11618-015-0628-4

Wilkesmann, U. and Schmid, C. J. (2012) 'The impacts of new governance on teaching at German universities: findings from a national survey in Germany'. *Higher Education*, 63, pp. 33–52

Yin, R. K. (2014) *Case Study Research. Design and Methods* (5th edn). Thousand Oaks, CA: Sage

3
Bridging the duality between universities and the academic profession
A tale of protected spaces, strategic gaming, and institutional entrepreneurs

LIUDVIKA LEIŠYTĖ

Introduction

In past decades, scholars have observed that the transnational and local competition in higher education, as well as the expansion of higher education, have led to unprecedented transformation of universities and have affected its core processes and core staff – academics – in manifold ways (Bleiklie *et al.*, 2011). Since the 1980s, new public management-inspired reforms in the European systems (both Western and Central Eastern Europe) have fostered a more business-like management at universities (de Boer, Enders, and Schimank, 2007). Performance measurement in teaching and research, increased competition for resources, and increased accountability to the funding agencies have become important characteristics of higher education systems.

These changed conditions at universities have had serious repercussions about what constitutes academic work and where, how, and under what conditions academics can pursue knowledge creation and dissemination activities. In many cases, teaching and learning, which were the core activities in European universities, have become 'secondary' activities because they do not really 'count' for research performance evaluations and overall individualistic performance reviews under a managerialist regime. At the same time, the accountability following the quasi-market logics has increased the oversight over all academic activities, including teaching and learning. The tensions abound for academic work in this context. This chapter aims to unravel some of these tensions, with specific emphasis on the tensions between the profession and the organization, and tensions between the logics of the quasi-market and collegiality. Specifically, we aim to answer two questions. How are protected academic spaces created under different logics in different governance regimes? How do academics respond to threats to these protected academic spaces?

To address these questions, we first conceptualize the shifts in the governance arrangements of higher education and the implications of these shifts for the protected academic work spaces. Further, we reflect on the relationship between the level of the protected spaces and the level of discretion academics have and, finally, discuss the implications of this relationship for academic identities.

Understanding governance change from the institutional logics perspective

Governance studies of higher education show significant university transformation in European countries (Paradeise *et al.*, 2009; Jansen, 2010). They reveal the complexity of the governance reforms, which cover many different areas including formal structures, management, financing, quality control and evaluation, human resources, course planning, access, and internationalization. Given their different backgrounds and political realities, countries have developed their own versions of managerialism in higher education. There is convergence across Europe at the level of rhetoric, but at the operational level one can observe a wide variety of systems. Governance of higher education has become a complex, multi-layered and multi-actor activity in every country (Braun and Merrien, 1999; de Boer, Enders, and Leišytė, 2007). In this context, universities have been targeted to become more 'complete and corporate' organizations, and this targeting has resulted in more managed universities (Krücken and Meier, 2006; Parker, 2013). Today, one can see a patchwork of state control and quasi-markets coupled with professional and managerial self-governance among the European higher education systems (Leišytė and Dee, 2012).

The institutional norms of governing academic work at universities are thus changing, and the academic logic that has guided academic self-regulation, which encompasses professional and institutional autonomy, is being challenged by a different type of quasi-market logic that may lead to a very different environment for academic work, thus encompassing mixed logics (Greenwood *et al.*, 2010; Thornton and Ocasio, 2008; Thornton *et al.*, 2012). In this context, institutional logic is 'the socially constructed, historical pattern of material practices, assumptions, values, beliefs, and rules by which individuals produce and re-produce their material substance, organize time and space, and provide meaning to their social reality' (Thornton and Ocasio, 1999, p. 804). Institutional logics guide the modes of governance in higher education. The traditional logic guiding the governance of higher education has been the academic logic (see Fini and Lacetera, 2010; Murray, 2010) and is based on the Mertonian (1973) values of science in which peer review is central as the key justification of value and prestige, and science and higher education are for the public good. The principle of collegiality is at the centre in this logic.

In contrast, the opposing quasi-market logic, which may be increasingly guiding higher education governance, is based on proprietary values and is manifested in the private appropriation of financial returns (Dill *et al.*, 2004). Following this logic, higher education is governed by centralized bureaucratic control, restrictions on disclosure in science, and rationalized performance measurement (Sauermann and Stephan, 2013, p. 891). The role of management is crucial in this paradigm. The control of value and prestige is in the hands of the bureaucratic procedures and in vested stakeholders, such as industry. Following the quasi-market logic, the performance criteria of universities are defined outside the academic community. Moreover, following this logic, monetary rewards are sought after.

To understand the shift of logics in governing higher education in a comparative systematic way across different systems, five governance mechanisms in higher education can be used (see de Boer, Enders, and Schimank, 2007). The five dimensions of governance that are specifically identified in this article are: academic self-governance, competition for resources, managerial self-governance, (state) regulation, and stakeholder guidance.

- Academic self-governance is based on the functioning of disciplinary communities and the collegial decision-making practices at universities and in the national agencies in which academic communities participate in deciding on resources. The participation of academics in decision-making processes (committees) that decide the strategic direction of the university, decentralization of power within the university to lower units (e.g. departments), peer review-based research funding mechanisms, and academic participation in the quality assurance procedures are examples of academic self-governance in higher education systems. Historically, academic self-governance goes hand-in-hand with the institutional autonomy of universities, where collegiate decision-making prevails.
- Competition is another governance mechanism, which in higher education is usually state-induced quasi-market competition for resources, such as research funds, personnel, students, and prestige. Differentiated pay systems for academic staff, performance-based funding of universities, performance agreements between university and the government are examples of competition as a governance mechanism in higher education.
- Managerial self-governance concerns the role of the university leadership, organizational decision-making structures, and the centralization of decision-making processes, professional management, and professional administration at universities. Centralization of decision-making powers, professional managers instead of elected professors running the institutions, few collegial committees, strategic and budgetary powers at the strategic apex of the institution, global budgeting, performance contracts, and standardized performance criteria are some of the key features of managerial self-governance. Strong institutional autonomy, especially in regard to financial procedural autonomy, ownership of buildings, freedom to charge fees, and hiring/firing of academic staff are the strong indicators of this dimension of governance.
- State regulation is the traditional mechanism of governance, with the top-down authority vested in the state. Regulation by directives prescribes the

behaviour of higher education institutions in detail. Typical examples of state regulation are line-item budgeting; state ownership of university property; and ultimate control over planning, hiring, and overseeing staff.
- Stakeholder guidance is the mechanism based on goal setting and advice provided by various societal stakeholders (including the government). The plurality of advice; delegation of certain state powers to other actors, such as representatives of business and industry or intermediary bodies; and employers in governance of higher education are examples of this governance mechanism. At the institutional level, the role of external stakeholders in governing universities and setting the priorities at universities is an indicator of stakeholder guidance.

To understand the linkages between different types of logics and the five governance mechanisms, the use of a low–medium–high scale model is useful, with 'low' denoting limited presence of a particular logic and 'high' signifying the dominating role of a particular logic guiding a particular governance mechanism (Leišytė, 2014). These governance mechanisms are not mutually exclusive because each of them can change irrespective of stability or change in the other mechanism. In this context, the configuration of governance within a country is assumed to comprise a specific mixture of these five dimensions (de Boer, Enders, and Schimank, 2007).

A certain dominant logic is posited to shape the creation of a particular configuration of governance of higher education in a given system at a particular time. The academic logic provides the grounds for strong academic self-governance, as observed in the Humboldtian model of the university. Following this logic, competition for resources is low, while managerial self-governance and state regulation can be low to medium (Leišytė, 2014). Stakeholder guidance can be medium, especially in relation to state guidance (see Table 3.1). In contrast, one can see strong competition for resources, strong managerial self-governance and strong stakeholder guidance according to the quasi-market logic in higher education. This logic would also facilitate low state regulation and low academic self-governance (see Table 3.1).

Table 3.1 Governance mechanisms and two institutional logics

	Logic of quasi-markets	Academic logic
Academic self-governance	Low	High
Competition for resources	High	Low
Managerial self-governance	High	Low/medium
State regulation	Low	Low/medium
Stakeholder guidance	High	Medium

Source: Leišytė, 2014

Protected spaces and their nestedness under different institutional logics

The academic profession is seen as threatened by the quasi-market logic and the related governance regime. It has been portrayed as a 'victim' of organizational standards and performance monitoring, while managers are portrayed as the 'carriers of neo-liberal reforms and organizational control' (Noordegraaf, 2011, p. 1350; Ackroyd et al., 2007; Scott, 2008). The reaction to these threats results in academics creating protected spaces within their organizations by a 'return to professionalism' (Freidson, 2001; Noordegraaf, 2011; Rip, 2011).

At the core of the need to 'protect' the profession is its professional autonomy. We understand professional autonomy as the freedom of academics to decide on the lines and priorities of research, curriculum design, course content, and modes of instruction. This understanding is very much in agreement with the notion of substantive autonomy – one of the most cherished and protected values in academia (Berdahl, 1990) – and the autonomy of academic affairs (Braun and Merrien, 1999). Many accounts show that the independence of pursuing one's own priorities in research depends on the availability of 'protected spaces' (Rip, 2011; Whitley, 2012; Laudel, 2012).

Academics typically respond to the pressures of quasi-market logics by resisting change and creating 'protected spaces' (Leišytė, 2014). However, such spaces can be created also in the managerial type of universities, which are more strongly guided by quasi-market logic, although then they are the co-creation of academics and managers with mixes of old processes and structures that preserve collegiality and new structures that, while based on quasi-market logic, still preserve academic freedom. What is actually happening at universities with the protected spaces remains a question for empirical research.

The key feature of these spaces is their multi-level nestedness (Rip, 2011), which point to the interlinkages among the macro- (state), meso- (funding agencies, disciplines) and micro- (organizational and sub-organizational) levels. The key insight here is that the protection of professional autonomy is not only an issue at one level, as usually described in the literature (usually the laboratory or university level), but it is a multi-level issue. Another important point in understanding protected spaces is the agency of academics in the creation and maintenance of these protected spaces. Given the multi-level nature of these spaces, the academic lobby must be involved at all levels to maintain these spaces over time. Thus, conceptualizing protected spaces needs to be understood at different levels with the view of academics as institutional entrepreneurs who create and maintain them. Finally, when discussing protected spaces, it is important to underscore that they may be continuously changing, depending on the level of agency academics exhibit, their power positions at a particular time, and the contextual conditions and situations in which they find themselves at that particular time. Thus, the temporal dimension is important.

Following the governance shifts described above, we imagine two types of protected spaces and their nestedness based on the dominant logic. We envisage the ideal type scenarios, which may vary strongly depending on the discipline because some disciplines require more time to produce research outputs, or teaching takes place in different formats and modes, and because the dependence on external resources provided by the state or other sponsors differs per discipline (Whitley and Gläser, 2014).

Under the dominance of academic logic, one could imagine the protection of spaces at all levels – state, discipline, intermediary organizations, organization, and sub-organization. One scenario here would be the state giving full funding to science without much accountability, and with rather 'weak' monitoring and university management, they would also not interfere in any way in academic affairs or setting research priorities. An example of this strategy is the famous Vannevar Bush's *Science the Endless Frontier* in 1945 in the USA. In the ample funding environment, competition for resources is rather low, which also partially provides protected space in this regard (Rip, 2012). When the academic oligarchy is strong, the norms and rules designed by academic elites penetrate the intermediary organizations, which provide funding to institutions and individual academics, while professors are in their 'kingdoms', where they ensure the protected space for the work of the sub-organizational unit, such as a laboratory or department. In such a scenario, the academic identities are strongly connected to the values and norms of the scientific communities they inhabit, and their role as institutional entrepreneurs centres on maintaining power positions at the multiple levels of governance.

Under the dominance of the quasi-market logic, however, the nestedness of protected spaces becomes more complex, and the power positions of academics may be less pronounced. Following this logic, the state gives more autonomy to higher education institutions, and external research funding is no longer an entitlement (Rip, 2012) but a competitive game. At the same time, the funding bodies are concerned not only with providing the funding for top scientists, but they are concerned about efficient funding and spending, and so monitoring scientific performance. Similarly, the state is also concerned with measuring the performance of academic systems, which adds time pressures and certain performance requirements to universities and individual academics. These performance requirements may include certain numbers and types of publications or production of a certain number of graduates in certain fields. The accountability, performance drive, competition, and limited time horizons due to short-term project funding may reduce protected spaces for academics at the micro-level.

Although academics as institutional entrepreneurs are still engaged in the funding of the science agenda, state official and professional managers from funding agencies and industry/business representatives are also getting involved in defining those spaces at the macro-level. The stakeholder guidance increases; thus, identifying the protected space at the macro- and meso-levels depends on the concrete mixture and power of different stakeholders in a given situation. These spaces may be reduced when this competitive type of state instrumentation is nested with strong managerialism at universities and powerful influences from other stakeholders at the meso-level regarding priorities and types of funding for research and performance measurement policies and practices at the universities. Then, the effects on sub-unit and individual levels for protected spaces may be harsh, especially if these effects are also exacerbated by scarce funding possibilities, which increases competition from the intermediary agencies. This scenario would lead to shrinking protected spaces in academia. However, what happens with the academics who are institutional entrepreneurs in creating and maintaining protected spaces under the scenario of quasi-markets in higher education governance? In the following section, we aim to understand the responses of academics to the threat to the protected spaces under the quasi-market logic, which will help answer this question.

Understanding the responses of academics to managerial organizational settings

Traditionally, being an academic means belonging to an academic profession and a specific disciplinary community and adhering to a set of scientific norms and values. We define professional identities as an individual's self-definition as a member of a profession and this self-definition is associated with the enactment of a professional role (Pratt and Dutton, 2000; Chreim et al., 2007). Disciplinary communities have the features of the classic Tönnies' Gemeinschaft, such as commonality, limited interaction with people outside the community (boundary maintenance), closeness via shared beliefs, and norms and traditions that presuppose a clear pattern of behaviour (Leišytė, 2015). As an academic, the core interest is the maintenance of discretion over the content and methods of one's work, either in teaching or in research (i.e. professional autonomy), for which protected spaces are needed.

In this understanding, the identity of the academics stems from their socialization into and belonging to the disciplinary community. Academics belong to tribes with 'gatekeepers' and 'hostile natives', which allude to the adherence to disciplinary norms and ways of performing our scientific enquiry and teaching (Becher, 1989). In line with the demands of the new institutional context, academics are expected to adjust their work roles and identities to the mission and profile of the organizations in which they work (Leišytė, 2015). They may choose from a more diversified pallet of roles, from teaching to academic entrepreneurship, and are offered the chance to build credibility in multiple arenas (Enders and de Weert, 2009). Academic identities can become heterogeneous (Whitchurch, 2012) and be redefined (Chreim et al., 2007). However, this type and extent of redefinition will depend on the conflict between the level of discretion that academics have and organizational and institutional pressures (ibid.).

To understand these changes in academic identities as related to protected spaces in the context of shifting governance arrangements, one may imagine academics adopting a range of responses to managerial demands impinging on their protected spaces, depending on their own predisposition, their disciplinary standing, their social and academic capital (i.e. their discretion). Elite academics would engage at multiple levels to ensure the reconstruction of protected spaces and extensive institutional work at the funding agencies and government, and they may maintain and renegotiate the order of worth of their discipline and protected spaces. They will act as institutional entrepreneurs, propagating redefinition of their academic identities while maintaining their protected spaces and power.

The other scenario, especially in the case of peripheral disciplines or with respect to academics less endowed in their academic and social capital, may face difficulties in rearranging and preserving protected spaces at different levels and would have difficulties in acting as institutional entrepreneurs. At the same time, as institutional entrepreneurs, academics would find ways to engage in bricolage (Louvel, 2013), and they can find ways to extend beyond their disciplinary communities and engage with broader audiences and stakeholders or with academics from other disciplines. In this way, they can expand the boundaries of protected spaces. For example, as argued by Leišytė (2014), the growing policy emphasis on profiling, specific societal problem solving, and bringing 'society' and communities of practice into the process of knowledge creation suggests that the academic discipline may be only one of many sources from which academics can derive their sense of identity.

At the organizational and sub-organization levels, such boundary expansion could be observed in the strongly managerial organizational environment. For example, one can imagine three types of sub-organizational units, each differing in terms of the level of autonomy from the central control at university; the degree of available protected academic space within each unit varies from high to low. High levels of protected space within the unit means it is an autonomous unit that determines its own academic agenda, both in teaching and research and has its own discretionary resources. A low degree of protected academic space means that the unit is integrated into the organizational structures and agendas and has a low degree of autonomy from the university's central control. Professional development units that report directly to the top management would exemplify these units.

We argue that academics respond to institutional reform processes that threaten their professional autonomy in various ways, depending on how much room for discretion they have and in which organizational unit they are embedded. Here, discretion is understood as the power academics possess to assert authority over the content and methods of their work and the prestige they hold within the academic community (Chreim *et al.*, 2007; Leišytė, 2007). Discretion may also be influenced by the prestige of their discipline within the discipline pecking order, in which physics would claim first place (Rip, 2012). Thus, even though a professor may have high prestige in her/his community, this person may not have high discretion organizationally because the power of other disciplines may be higher when negotiating the autonomy and resources within the organization in which the academics from different disciplines meet (see Table 3.2).

As shown in Table 3.2, in the highly autonomous unit, which is a strongly protected space at a higher education institution, one could find two types of responses. The academics with high discretion would exhibit an open resistor response to the top down-initiated change process. Resisting changes in academic roles would be observed, which would include maintaining their own self-concepts of teacher and researcher. At the same time, the proactive manipulation

Table 3.2 Types of academic responses to threats to professional autonomy

Level of discretion/ degree of available protected space	High discretion	Low discretion
Autonomous units	*Open resistor:* resists change in academic roles and maintains self-concept of teacher and researcher, proactive manipulation of the environment and redefinition of academic identity based on own initiative	*Deviant resistor:* symbolically compliant with new initiatives, avoiding new roles (e.g. administration), maintains academic identity
Semi-autonomous units	*Strategic gamer:* compliant with the new roles, which only builds credibility for new audiences (management included) and maintains the old roles, which strengthens academic credibility (mainly research)	*New professional:* embraces change to incorporate organizational roles and redefine some academic roles
Units integrated in institutional structures and agendas	*Elite manager:* gives up most academic roles to run the institution/faculty and design its policies	*Professional manager:* gives up academic roles and switches fully to administrative work

of the environment and redefinition of academic identity based on their own initiatives may occur in such a protected space, given this high level of discretion.

In the case of a low level of discretion (e.g. junior academics), one could imagine a deviant resistor type emerging. These academics would be symbolically compliant with new initiatives for change, and they would avoid these new initiatives (e.g. increase in administrative tasks). In such cases, the academic identity will be maintained following similar framing as open resistors with high discretion, but it will less likely include being institutional entrepreneurs in terms of their initiatives for redefining roles.

In cases when academics are located in semi-autonomous units, have medium levels of protected spaces, and high discretion and power, we would find strategic game-playing. They would renegotiate but also partially comply with the new roles to build credibility for new audiences (including organizational management) in addition to maintaining the 'traditional' roles, which would strengthen academic credibility and discretion (e.g. research activities and standing in the disciplinary community). For those academics with lower amounts of discretion, one could find 'new professionals'. These academics would embrace change to incorporate organizational roles and redefine some of their academic roles (Leišytė, 2015).

Finally, when protected spaces are very limited and we look at the academics within units that are integrated into institutional structures and agendas within higher education institutions, we would find elite managers and professional managers. Elite managers would be academics with high levels of discretion who give up most of their academic roles to run the institution/faculty and design its policies. Professional managers would be the academics who have lower discretion; thus, they would give up their academic roles and switch fully to administrative work.

Given the temporal dimension of protected spaces and the variability in agency among academics, one could imagine switching occurring over time in terms of changing the amount of protected spaces at the sub-organizational level and the level of discretion. The units may shift from being semi-autonomous to autonomous, for example. Additionally, switching or blurring between different roles and identities may occur. One can hypothesize that the direction of switching in terms of protected spaces under the quasi-market logic-dominated governance regime would be downward – from autonomous to integrated units, rather than the other way around.

Conclusion

This chapter has focused on the tensions between professions and organizations and tensions between the logics of the quasi-market and collegiality. We posed two questions. How are academic spaces protected under different logics in different governance regimes? How do academics respond to threats to protected academic spaces?

We have shown that, under the quasi-market logic, academic governance shifts towards changing protected spaces for academics in higher education institutions. Academics maintain and create protected space at different levels, which may result in their nestedness. Our enquiry into governance shifts in higher education has showed that the quasi-market logic results in a specific set of governance mechanisms that may invade academic protected spaces through managerial interventions. Additionally, depending on their level of discretion, academics may act as institutional entrepreneurs and respond to various reform initiatives as open and deviant resistors, strategic gamers, new professionals, elite managers or professional managers. Blurring boundaries of protected spaces over time seems to elicit different responses, depending on the level of discretion academics have and the type of organizational settings they inhabit.

However, the proposed theoretical account needs to be further substantiated by empirical evidence to ascertain the types of responses in attempts to create, maintain, and expand protected spaces across different institutional and disciplinary settings.

References

Ackroyd, S., Kirkpatrick, I. and Walker, R. (2007) 'Public management reform and its consequences for professional organisation: a comparative analysis'. *Public Administration*, 8 (1), pp. 9–26

Becher, T. (1989) *Academic Tribes and Territories: Intellectual Enquiry and the Cultures of Disciplines*. Buckingham: Open University Press/SRHE

Berdahl, R. (1990) 'Academic freedom, autonomy and accountability in British universities'. *Studies in Higher Education*, 15 (2), pp. 169–80

Bleiklie, I., Enders, J., Lepori, B. and Musselin, C. (2011) 'New public management, network governance and the university as a changing professional organization'. *The Ashgate Research Companion to New Public Management*, pp. 161–76

Braun, D. and Merrien, F.-X. (1999) *Governance of Universities and Modernisation of the State: Analytical Aspects. Towards a New Model of Governance for Universities? A Comparative View*. London, Philadelphia: Jessica Kingsley

Chreim S, Williams, B. E. and Hinings, C. R. (2007) 'Interlevel influences on the reconstruction of professional role identity'. *Academy of Management Journal*, 50 (6), pp. 1515–39

de Boer, H., Enders, J. and Leišytė, L. (2007) 'On striking the right notes: shifts in governance and the organizational transformation of universities'. *Public Administration*, 85 (1), pp. 27–46

de Boer, H., Enders, J. and Schimank, U. (2007) 'On the way towards New Public Management? The governance of university systems in England, the Netherlands, Austria, and Germany' in Jansen, D. (Ed.), *New Forms of Governance in Research Organizations: Disciplinary Approaches, Interfaces, and Integration*. Dordrecht: Springer, pp. 137–52

Dill, D., Texeira, P., Jongbloed, B. and Amaral, A. (2004) *Markets in Higher Education: Rhetoric or Reality*. Dordrecht: Kluwer, pp. 327–52

Enders, J. and de Weert, E. (2009) *The Changing Face of Academic Life: Analytical and Comparative Perspectives*. Basinstoke: Palgrave Macmillan

Fini, R. and Lacetera, N. (2010) 'Different yokes for different folks: individual preferences, institutional logics, and the commercialization of academic research' in Libecap, G. (Ed.),

Spanning Boundaries and Disciplines: University Technology Commercialization in the Idea Age. Bingley: Emerald Group, pp. 1–25

Freidson, E. (2001) *Professionalism: The Third Logic*. Cambridge: Polity

Greenwood, R., Díaz, A. M., Li, S. X. and Lorente, J. C. (2010) 'The multiplicity of institutional logics and the heterogeneity of organizational responses'. *Organization Science*, 21 (2), pp. 521–39

Jansen, D. (2010) *Governance and Performance in the German Public Research Sector*. Dordrecht: Springer

Krücken, G. and Meier, F. (2006) 'Turning the university into an organizational actor' in Drori, G., Meyer, J. and Hwang, H. (Eds), *Globalization and Organization: World Society and Organizational Change*. Oxford: Oxford University Press, pp. 241–57

Laudel, G. (2012). 'Doing something new in the Netherlands: the impact of research organisations and funding agencies on the start of new research lines'. Paper presented at the 28th EGOS colloquium, July. Helsinki, Finland

Leišytė, L. (2007) 'University governance and academic research: case studies of research units in Dutch and English universities. PhD thesis. University of Twente, CHEPS, Enschede, Netherlands

Leišytė, L. (2014) 'The transformation of university governance in Central and Eastern Europe: its antecendents and consequences'. *Leadership and Governance in Higher Education*, 1 (E-1-4). Retrived from www.lg-handbook.info

Leišytė, L. (2015) 'Changing academic identities in the context of a managerial university: bridging the duality between professions and organizations' in Cummings, W. K. and Teichler, U. (Eds), *The Relevance of Academic Work in Comparative Perspective*. Dordrecht: Springer International, pp. 59–73

Leišytė, L. and Dee, J. (2012) 'Changing academic practices and identities in Europe and the US: critical perspectives' in Smart, J. C. and Paulsen, M. B. (Eds), *Higher Education: Handbook of Theory and Research*. Dordrecht: Springer, pp. 123–206

Louvel, S. (2013) 'Understanding change in higher education as bricolage: how academics engage in curriculum change'. *Higher Education*, 66 (6), pp. 669–91

Merton, R. K. (1973) *The Sociology of Science: Theoretical and Empirical Investigations*. Chicago: University of Chicago Press

Murray, F. (2010) 'The Onco Mouse that roared: hybrid exchange strategies as a source of distinction at the boundary of overlapping institutions'. *American Journal of Sociology*, 116 (2), pp. 341–88

Noordegraaf, M. (2011) 'Risky business: how professionals and professional fields (must) deal with organizational issues'. *Organization Studies*, 32 (10), pp. 1349–71

Noordegraaf, M. and Schinkel, W. (2010) 'Professional capital contested: a Bourdieusian analysis of conflicts between professionals and managers'. *Comparative Sociology*, 10 (1), pp. 1–29

Paradeise, C., Reale, E., Bleiklie, I. and Ferlie, E. (Eds) (2009) *University Governance*. Dordrecht: Springer

Parker, L. D. (2013) 'Contemporary university strategizing: the financial imperative'. *Financial Accountability and Management*, 29 (1), pp. 1–25

Pratt, M. and Dutton, J. (2000) 'Owning up or opting out: the role of identities and emotions in issue ownership' in Ashkanasy, N., Hartel, C. and Zerbe, W. (Eds), *Emotions in the Workplace: Research, Theory, and Practice*. London: Quorum, pp. 103–29

Rip, A. (2011) 'Protected spaces of science: their emergence and future evolution in a changing world' in Carrier, M. and Nordmann, A. (Eds), *Science in the Context of Application*. Dordrecht: Springer, Boston Studies in Philosophy of Science, pp. 197–220

Rip, A. (2012) 'The context of innovation journeys'. *Creativity and Innovation Management*, 21 (2), pp. 158–70

Sauermann, H. and Stephan, P. (2013) 'A multidimensional view of industrial and academic science'. *Organization Science*, 24 (3), pp. 889–909

Scott, W. R. (2008) 'Lords of the dance: professionals as institutional agents'. *Organization Studies*, 29 (2), pp. 219–38

Thornton, P. H. and Ocasio, W. (1999) 'Institutional logics and the historical contingency of power in organizations: executive succession in the higher education publishing industry, 1958–1990'. *American Journal of Sociology*, 105 (3), pp. 801–43

Thornton, P. H. and Ocasio, W. (2008) 'Institutional logics' in Greenwood, R., Oliver, C., Sahlin, K. and Suddaby, R. (Eds), *The Sage Handbook of Organizational Institutionalism*. Thousand Oaks and London: Sage, pp. 99–129

Thornton, P. H., Ocasio, W. and Lounsbury, M. (2012) *The Institutional Logics Perspective*. Oxford: Oxford University Press

Whitchurch, C. (2012) *Reconstructing Identities in Higher Education: The Rise of 'Third Space' Professionals*. New York: Routledge

Whitley, R. (2012) 'Transforming universities: national conditions of their varied organisational actorhood'. *Minerva*, 50 (4), pp. 493–510

Whitley, R. and Gläser, J. (Eds) (2014) *Organizational Transformation and Scientific Change: The Impact of Institutional Restructuring on Universities and Intellectual Innovation*. Research in the Sociology of Organisations, vol. 42. Bingley, W. Yorkshire: Emerald, doi: 10.1108/S0733-558X201442

4
Organizing and managing university education

HAMISH COATES AND EMMALINE BEXLEY

Introduction

In most countries university education is in demand like never before. Governments and the public are seeking more higher education, and students are diversifying including via unprecedented transnational flows. Yet many traditional approaches to university education do not scale well from quality or productivity perspectives. Ensuring the efficient supply of quality educational services has increasingly required new and different ways of doing core education business. This provides obvious stimulus for investigation of the design and practice of academic work, workforce, and management.

This chapter clarifies and advances our understanding of new scenarios for organizing and managing university education. It looks at contemporary change forces which are homogenizing and diversifying facets of higher education, and emerging organizational forms. A taxonomy of emerging organizational architectures is presented, which is exemplified via institutional case studies. This leads to the penultimate section, which explores consequences for academic management and work.

As this focus conveys, the chapter responds to the key questions framing the book, namely the interdependences between organizational structures and individuals' work. Our analysis is pitched at the level of management or leadership, so is inclusive of the essentially broad range of phenomena that constitute this core facet of higher education. As such, it touches on the ideas and arguments of other contributors to this volume, and provides foundations for subsequent analyses of education concepts and practices.

While pitched to be broadly international in nature, the chapter draws in spirit and substance from analysis of the Australian context. This offers insight into the Australian system. It also contributes broader international perspectives, given what might be characterized as the 'hyper-internationalization' of higher education in Australia. We emphasize this cultural dimension because of the contemporary and growing significance of such 'borderlessness' for higher education. Such a stance aligns with the more balanced global perspective advanced in this book, revealing differences and similarities across national systems and cultures.

In framing our analysis we draw on several precursor studies that we have conducted into academic work, workforce, leadership, and policy. In this chapter we concentrate not so much on the detailed findings of this prior work – please see the in-text citations for further information – but on higher-level syntheses. Such synthesis is important, for the complex ideas we address go beyond any attempt at reductive or compartmentalized research and necessarily require such broader strategic analysis.

The balance of this chapter unfolds in four main parts. First, we analyse key forces provoking change in traditional ways of doing business and education. In essence, we distill the strategic parameters pertinent to planning contemporary higher education. Second, we review organizational forms arising in response to such challenges, and also being positioned to capture new opportunities. Third, drawing from analysis of international institutional practice, and with an eye on ongoing development, we advance a taxonomy of emergent organizational scenarios relevant to teaching in higher education. Case studies are given from the Australian context. Fourth, the balance of the chapter investigates implications of current changes for institutional management and the organization of teaching at universities. Paying particular attention to workforce and technology, we conclude by forecasting management capabilities required for future higher education.

Shaping contexts

Higher education is a very contextualized activity, even in its most elite or conceptual instantiations. Working from Coates and Mahat (2013, 2014), this section reviews a handful of intersecting and intensifying contexts shaping systems, institutions, and people. It addresses how each context drives greater interest in the organization and management of tertiary education.

Cost is perhaps the key pressure reshaping higher education and various facets of tertiary education. Even among other service industries, higher education stands out as being particularly afflicted by what Baumol (1967) described as the 'cost disease'. Universities have large infrastructure costs, large labour costs – traditionally at least – and reliance on expensive face-to-face provision. This underpins high fixed and variable costs, and limited economies of scale. The 'traditional' university model is not highly expandable without seeing diseconomies of scale, particularly in such a highly person-centric services sector that manifests several growth-inhibiting factors. This puts increasing pressure on institutions to explore revised cost structures and, indeed, in many instances simply to develop better systems for measuring, hence managing, cost. The urgent need to boost university productivity has been noted by many (see Massy, 2013; Sullivan et al., 2012; Auguste et al., 2010). Of course, such high costs intensify requests for increased financial disclosure.

Revenue as well as expenditure is squeezed. Coupled with cost pressures, universities in most countries have only limited capacity to set tuition prices. In domestic markets regulation and subsidization tend to nourish elite oligopolistic clubs which would enable universities to function as 'price-makers' were it not for the typical imposition of tuition price ceilings. Internationally, and regional relativities aside, universities tend to be 'price-takers' like any others, competing on the open market for student enrolment. Compounding these pricing pressures is the emergence of new institutional players that can offer higher education services at substantially lower cost and often without the kinds of price regulation that touch public providers. Coates and Mahat (2014) provide examples of education service firms and providers – for instance: SEEK (www.seeklearning.com.au), Laureate Education (www.laureate.net), and the Apollo Education Group (www.apollo.edu). Understandably, pressures on higher education mount with tilts towards decreased regulation or price control.

As explored below, the proliferation of institution and programme rankings pointedly highlights the evolving thirst for greater transparency regarding education. But, more broadly, governments are demanding that institutions detail activity, and prove performance and standards (European Commission, 2013; TEQSA, 2013). Potential students and their families are seeking information on learning to guide investments in education. Business is seeking reliable data to guide graduate recruitment and research partnerships. Many of these transparency developments are international, working off 'found data' and restricting the capacity of institutions or governments to establish or control reporting. Institutions can attempt to manage and assure the data that feeds into such processes (various institutions have hired 'rankings coordinators', and an increasing number are hiring consultants to assist with positioning), but much can already be sourced passively by third parties.

At the same time, universities are confronting new commercial constraints. Though various facets of university research activity have long had a commercial flavour, new economic pressures are enveloping core education business. In many countries, new streams of often private finance are flowing into higher education, seemingly in loose counterpoint to the diminution of government subsidy as a proportion of overall revenue. This kind of money can create problems for universities, imposing new obligations – for instance, around intellectual property and disclosure – which mix uneasily with basic tenets of scholarly work and conventional collegial demands. While various intellectual property models attempt to span the divide, 'commercial transparency' and 'scholarly openness' differ in theory and practice. This situation puts pressure on universities to rethink collegial conventions regarding knowledge creation and dissemination, many of which are tacit. Who owns knowledge and how freely can it be accessed and shared? Deliberation about these matters multiplies in certain areas which also must embrace complexities around confidentiality and security.

Among all this flux, institutions appear to be facing enormous stratification pressures in new global ecosystems. National systems are not knowledge islands – academics, students, and ideas travel widely among systems. In many advanced economies it seems increasingly fruitless to seek 'national sense' out of either research or education, for so much of higher education is international in essence. The national barriers that protected most universities are being eroded by new transnational hierarchies. Institutions are situating, though mostly being situated, in emerging borderless orders partly driven by student markets and preferences. Kennie and Price (2012), for instance, detail a taxonomy of an emerging international ecosystem which structures the landscape by selectivity (open/elite) and funding (public/private). Van Vught (2012) writes of a hierarchy consisting of the top echelon, international research universities, a range of niche/specialized institutions, a plethora of local teaching institutions, and a set of virtual global players. In another version, Barber et al. (2013) propose another taxonomy – the elite university, the mass university, the niche university, the local university, and the lifelong learning mechanism. Within Australia, while all universities espouse that they are comprehensive research institutions, detailed empirical analysis reveals a more complex arrangement which the rise of non-university niche providers affirms (Coates et al., 2013). Of course, taxonomies to date are driven by available metrics and perceived correlates of reputation and prestige, and profoundly different orders may emerge given different status markers.

Against these stratification pressures sit a host of policy and strategic desires for a diverse higher education system. Systems desire policies that maximize the value and reach of ever scarcer public dollars. Institutions seek 'blue oceans' (Kim and Mauborgne, 2005) that deliver 'alpha' performance beyond expectation in increasingly contested terrain. Both eschew isomorphism that leads to structural inertia. Finding and establishing difference gets harder just as it becomes more important. Beyond initial decision-making, detecting, driving, and substantiating strategic difference hinges ultimately on evidence of quality and performance. Institutions that seek differentiation in terms of education, for instance, will need evidence of their efforts and success.

The rudiments of education are changing. Like many other goods, knowledge is being reconfigured and repackaged. As flagged, universities are facing business pressures arising from the promulgation of online open-access proprietary curriculum products. Protecting access to knowledge resources once gave higher education a strategic edge. Until very recently, universities could distinguish themselves through the substance and quality of curriculum materials. Institutions with access to leading professors/experts, with ownership of distinctive technologies, and with expensive facilities held the keys to relatively exclusive access to knowledge. In many areas of higher education this exclusivity has gone, with the internet and global flow of talent servicing what major research institutions referred to nearly a decade ago as the 'open courseware initiative' (MIT, 2015). The new knowledge architectures lead to reconceptualization and reform of how higher education is conducted. Providers can recode and recompile information, repackaging this in myriad ways to suit different individuals and groups. Easier access to curriculum, however, doesn't imply competence, redistributing energy from inputs (like access and admission) to outcomes (such as learning and professional outcomes).

A decade ago, aspirations shaping books on 'virtual universities' (see Robins and Webster, 2002; van der Molen, 1999) seemed to trump sales, but such literature is being reprinted now that more sophisticated software is meeting expectations (Christensen and Eyring, 2011; Siemens *et al.*, 2015). What once higher education eschewed as 'programmed learning' today may constitute 'authentic pedagogy'. The physical university has not died, but e-learning has proliferated and been incorporated within existing institutions. Despite persistent shortcomings (Coates *et al.*, 2005), learning management systems can now automate many core teaching functions. Far from being a backwards slide, however, this refiguring of teaching creates space for innovation, positioning, and diversification. The same 'Psychology 101' may be 'implemented' by a robotic algorithm, a fully tenured professor, or a sessional lecturer, all with different financial structures, market potentials, and intellectual textures. Institutions capture more degrees of freedom to locate themselves in the market. The disruptive consequences for higher education are well documented even though sustainable and fully assured business models for these new forms of provision are yet to be established. Finding quality and cost effective ways of automating assessment is a prevailing edge of e-learning innovation. As picked up in the next section, these new hybrid forms of provision have substantial implications for tertiary education.

Looking afresh at core facets of higher education, and changes to fundamental academic and corporate business, stimulates and magnifies questions about higher education quality. The more standardized production of curriculum and provision via learning management systems, for instance, may work to compress quality while at the same time ensuring above minimal levels of provision. Revised assumptions and approaches to core business require new quality assurance perspectives and practices. Invariably, broad-ranging work on education raises fresh questions and pressures about quality assurance perspectives and methods.

Anyone working in or around higher education recognizes that these pressures play out in varying ways at different moments, that each pressure analysed is only part of a very much larger story, and that the above analysis is inevitably broad and incomplete. Yet, taken together, these pressures are provoking more than a little of the current reconfiguration in the organization and management of university education.

Emerging organizational forms

These contextual remarks set the scene for the chapter. They also help frame analysis of emerging institutional architectures being developed to support business models that deliver new education services that distribute emerging knowledge products. Organizations are hard to pin down, like any complex, dynamic, and highly contextualized phenomenon. They can take infinite forms and functions, even when restricted to the field of higher education, and it is helpful to view them with respect to broad underpinning parameters. Doing this helps chart the flow of emerging institutional forms in higher education from the contextual forces sketched above. The following analysis is structured in terms of ownership, leadership, management, and activities.

The ownership of organizations is a complex matter, but is fundamental to teasing out basic changes to higher education institutions. Ownership can be characterized broadly as either public (i.e. governmental) or private (i.e. by one or more equity-holders), though particular arrangements play out in very specific ways. Two notable trends can be detected with respect to the changing ownership of higher education institutions.

First, there are an increasing number of private institutions. There are various reasons for this, not least growing political and social beliefs in many parts of the world in the private value of higher education, increasing emphasis on knowledge in advanced economies, and the desire by governments to expand higher education in times of fiscal constraint. In Australia, for instance, the institutional landscape has changed from having none to around 130 private institutions in the last 25 years, with these providing around a tenth of all higher education (Commonwealth of Australia, 1993; TEQSA, 2015). These private institutions themselves exhibit many ownership structures distinguished, for instance, by whether they are for profit or not, the nature and extent of the shareholders, and whether they are discrete organizations or owned by larger and often multinational firms.

Second, many public institutions are becoming increasingly privatized. Such privatization can be distinguished from the growth of fully private institutions as there is no enduring transfer of public ownership. Such privatization takes myriad forms, and while these can be opaque and difficult to unpack, the literature on 'public–private partnerships' (Grimsey and Lewis, 2013) offers a useful conceptual lens. In essence, arrangements can be described in terms of which entity is responsible for construction, management, different facets of ownership, and financial flows. Examples in higher education could range from the construction and operation by private firms of student residences, student management, curriculum development, and teaching, with all of such developments governed by an existing public university (Norton et al., 2013).

Institutions vary in terms of how authority is structured and enacted. Authority plays out in governance and executive architectures, and in terms of strategy. Institutional changes are observable in each of these areas. The governance of higher education takes myriad forms, and can be asserted through direct or indirect mechanisms. Changes in both are spurring new institutional forms. Direct forms of governance are exerted through governing boards or councils. While the composition of the councils that govern public universities may be relatively invariant, sub-structures with a more commercial flavour may be established to govern specific institutional entities and interests. The councils or boards of private institutions tend to be more commercially oriented to start with. Governance happens via indirect channels, too, via the influence of external forces on institutional planning and operations. Here, the big shift is from government to market forms of regulation. As well, as institutions open out to play a greater role in public life many broader forms of community stakeholder fora are emerging, either playing a formal review role, or as broader consultative mechanisms.

Similar shifts carry implications for the leadership, which is now more important and challenging than ever. Leaders are under constant pressure to be more responsive to the mounting expectations of governments, the fluctuating requirements of industries, and the diverse needs of communities and individuals. Commercial pressures have been with tertiary leaders for some time, but they now face renewed pressures arising from the recognition of higher education as a key vehicle for workforce development and productivity. Research on tertiary leaders has revealed the additional capabilities such contexts demand (Coates et al., 2012). Along with enduring educational and institutional management capabilities, leaders must be adept at managing commercial pressures of an external nature as well as the institutional implications these convey. Responding to increased demands relating to industry, business and research translation, for instance, requires more agile and productive organizations. This has implications for leadership development. New formal and on-the-job training is required, as are new forms of recruitment (Coates and Goedegebuure, 2010; Scott et al., 2008). Rather than simply work up through academic and managerial ranks, for instance, leaders benefit from the kind of commercial acumen gained through industry experience. Rather than spend a sabbatical at a like university, for instance, there may be more return from a secondment at an industry partner or government agency.

Changes in institutional governance and leadership are linked with changes in strategy. Of course, the very term 'strategy' carries commercial connotations, signalling a shift from a centrally planned supply-driven system to a more commercially oriented demand-driven market (Gallagher, 2014). Institutions shift from providing education as a public good, to positioning themselves in lucrative market niches (Mahat and Coates, 2015). This commercial tilt is nuanced in varying ways across countries, but even so there are notable shifts towards the specification of 'missions', 'visions', 'goals', and 'values', which signal more externally inflected institutional dispositions and intentions. Almost necessarily, this rouses forms of competitive and commercial behaviour which, as detailed above, place added and often conflicting demands on existing collegial arrangements.

Institutional management is another vector of change. The most evident change is to the distribution of the managerial workforce. In Australia, the percentage of non-academic to total staff has remained stable in recent decades at just over 50 per cent of total non-casual university staff (Australian Government, 2015). Yet beneath this apparent stability lie fundamental changes in the distribution of work roles. For instance, Dobson (2012) calculates that the proportion of non-academic staff in the higher levels of non-academic employment increased from 22.7 per cent of the non-academic workforce in 1997 to 38.2 per cent in 2010. Academic management structures have changed too, with changes in size and purpose seeding development of new administrative and matrix arrangements (Leišytė and Dee, 2012). This is evidenced in particular through growth in portfolio positions such as that of pro-vice-chancellor and associate or deputy heads and deans, and by the elaboration of increasingly complex organograms and functional structures. The nature of management is changing too. Emerging capability requirements mirror those regarding leadership. New roles are being designed, such as hybrid roles which blend academic and professional functions, examples being learning designers, academic advisors, and teaching fellows (Coates and Goedegebuure, 2010; Leišytė, 2015). Combined, these developments provoke substantial changes in the managerial workforce, sparking new patterns of hiring and development.

The changes in ownership, leadership, and management mirror changes in academic work. In essence, it manifests a shift from boutique forms of knowledge production and dissemination, to increasingly distributed, virtualized, recombined, packaged, and 'just-in-time', 'just-enough', and 'just-for-me' forms of higher education provision. New models for business and education emerge, as flagged above, with these designed to better match supply with new forms of demand. The identity of a student plays an ever-more contingent role in people's lives as they dip in and out of accessing subjects from a range of online providers, paying to build individualized credentials to fit particular professional futures. The applied literature produced by governments and stakeholder agencies is charting thinking in this area (see ACE, 2014a, 2014b; Kennie and Price, 2012; Barber *et al.*, 2013).

Taxonomy of emergent organizational scenarios

This analysis reveals the emerging institutional architectures in higher education. These new forms of higher education are transfiguring core business. Institutions have long outsourced various corporate and research functions, but now they are outsourcing core academic business – and not just to contingent/sessional staff. Accredited institutions are forming hybrid alliances with non-accredited service organizations, seeding derivative joint ventures, bolstering academic governance arrangements, and reviewing the costs of provision (see Coates and Mahat, 2014). Generally, these service firms (for want of better term) are now well established in many fields and, as the case given below suggests, can do curriculum and teaching cheaper than institutions like universities operating on a legacy business model. The academic ventures vary in structure and substance, and manifest a range of business models and implications for work and outcomes. Essentially, institutions are increasingly commercial, private, virtual, and managed. Despite such trends, it has to be noted that many such arrangements are new and untested (Daniel, 2012), resembling the assertions made more than a decade ago about universities and faculty being unbundled into a credentialing skeleton (see Coaldrake, 2000).

One of the indicators of such transformation is the expanded presence in higher education of consulting firms reaching beyond straight audit functions into the world of strategy and academic design. One of the largest – Ernst and Young – advanced a portrait of institutional futures for higher education. Somewhat mirroring the stratification analysed above, Ernst and Young (2012, p. 5) predict that the institutional landscape will include three core entities:

- 'Streamlined Status Quo' – some established universities [that] will continue to operate as broad-based teaching and research institutions, but will progressively transform the way they deliver their services and administer their organizations – with major implications for the way they engage with students, government, industry stakeholders, TAFEs, secondary schools, and the community;
- 'Niche Dominators' – some established universities and new entrants [that] will fundamentally reshape and refine the range of services and markets they operate in, targeting particular 'customer' segments with tailored education, research and related services – with a concurrent shift in the business model, organization and operations; and
- 'Transformers' – private providers and new entrants [that] will carve out new positions in the 'traditional' sector and also create new market spaces that merge parts of the higher education sector with other sectors, such as media, technology, innovation, venture capital and the like. This will create new markets, new segments and new sources of economic value. Incumbent universities that partner with the right new entrants will create new lines of business that deliver much needed incremental revenue to invest in the core business – internationally competitive teaching and research.

Leaders steering these organizations, the authors assert, will need to adeptly embrace contestable markets and funding, global mobility of students and staff, integration with industry, digital technologies, and the democratization of knowledge and access. Institutions will change to sustain new value propositions and functions, with shifts in customers, product offerings, sales, delivery, student services, and the back office. As always, market power will shape the nature and extent of change.

It is helpful to unpack these architectures with reference to a few case studies. Hence we explore institutions which appear to resemble the 'streamlined status quo', 'niche dominators' and 'transformers'. These are drawn from the Australian context as flagged.

The University of Melbourne is a traditional comprehensive research university that is one of Australia's largest in terms of budget and research outcomes. Melbourne has the lowest attrition rates of any Australian university and concentrates educational provision to over 40,000 students on a single inner-city campus (University of Melbourne, 2015a, 2015b). While building its core value has worked well for Melbourne, the institution has also engaged in substantial reform. Educationally, curriculum reform around a decade ago saw Melbourne implement a hybrid model which coupled a refined suite of foundation bachelor's degrees each with a liberal arts nuance, with a more vocationally oriented suite of master's degrees. Subsequent education development has sought to increase the extent of online provision, and to establish a virtual borderless campus with a major Chinese partner university. Two rounds of institutional reform have helped to, first, devolve management responsibility to faculties, then, second, to separate academic from service functions and the institution's executive. Such reform has been conducted to place the institution in a stronger position, given the more uncertain context sketched above.

'Niche dominators' are characterized by their focus on strategic targeting of a focused market or service. This might play out via existing institutions taking steps to target particular segments of the student and disciplinary market. Deakin University in Victoria, Australia, is an example of this kind of institutional change. Deakin's strategy is encapsulated in its 'Deakin offer', which it presents as 'a personalized experience with premium digital engagement, creating the power and opportunities to live in a connected and evolving world' (Deakin University, 2015, p. 16). The delivery aligns closely with the institution's target market, offering 'an educational experience which will widen participation and support students from diverse backgrounds'. Deakin targets 'first-in-family' students, and has maintained a strong focus on providing a 'second chance' to mature-age students (Deakin University, 2014, p. 9), one quarter of whom study entirely online (Deakin University, 2015).

The Australian Catholic University (ACU) can also be characterized as a 'niche dominator'. A multi-state university, it is one of the only universities in Australia with a Christian mission, positioning itself as providing 'innovative and distinctive learning and teaching experience within the Catholic intellectual tradition' (ACU, 2015). ACU also maintains strong provision of higher education to non-traditional students. This is evident in its disciplinary focus on health, education, theology and philosophy, and social justice (ibid.).

Indeed, it is by emphasizing these niche professional fields that ACU has differentiated itself. Between 2013 and 2014 the institution saw double-digit growth in full-time student loads in its core fields of health, education, law, and business.

The 'transformers' group includes providers who create new market spaces and business/education models. This includes straight private institutions and also privatized arrangements involving partnerships between public and private institutions.

As might be expected given the deliberately invisible nature of this trade, case studies are hard to find. The company Online Education Services was founded in 2011 as a joint venture between Swinburne University and SEEK, an online employment recruitment company listed on the Australian Stock Exchange. Online Education Services trades as Swinburne Online (see www.seeklearning.com.au/swinburne-online). Commercially, this partnership diversified SEEK's education profile giving access to government-subsidized students at an institution with a proven track record in online education, and gave Swinburne access to an equity partner and rapid exposure through an employment agency reportedly touching around 20 per cent of the world's GDP. Academically, Swinburne University staff design, accredit, and develop programmes, while e-learning advisors employed through Swinburne Online support students and assess student learning outcomes. This division of labour, which separates production from delivery, casts new dynamics for academic and teaching responsibilities. These interlinked workforces are framed by different industrial arrangements and provoke new governance questions.

Implications for managing teaching and learning

A great strength of universities is their organizational capacity to morph, but there are limits and, as the above discussion brings out, key boundaries have already been well stretched. Much more could be said, but these remarks are sufficient to fuel uncertainties about 'traditional' academic systems and to frame the following section, which focuses on how new system and institution contexts carry implications for work, workforce, management, and leadership.

Growth in the scope and complexity of higher education carries implications for academic work. In mass and universal systems of higher education, the reasonably formalized assumption of 'traditional' academic work being comprised of relatively equal proportions of teaching-related duties, self-directed research, and service responsibilities is becoming increasingly untenable. As Trow (2007) has rightly observed, the per capita cost levels that suit an elite system educating only 5 per cent of the relevant age group are unsustainable for systems educating 40 per cent of that group. The most obvious example of this kind of economic tension is the increased reliance on casual labour for teaching, prevalent across the OECD (Anibas *et al.*, 2009; Brown *et al.*, 2008; Dawson, 2007; Bexley and Baik, 2011). Similarly, as research inevitably becomes a proportionately smaller component of total person-hours due to the increase in teaching brought about by massification, research-related work tends to be tied to income streams (grants, consultancies, and the like). For universities, this approach makes sense.

In turn, changes in academic work functions carry implications for roles. New role configurations can be described in terms of activity-based typologies. Coates and Goedegebuure (2010), for instance, propose a new set of descriptors, from the 'entrepreneurial researcher', whose activities barely touch on teaching or leadership tasks, to the likely later-career 'senior academic', focused heavily on leadership. Function-based descriptors fit more readily into a human resources framework, and may include roles that are well outside traditional academic – for example, learning designers, partnership facilitators, and those developing e-learning curricula. Further disaggregation is evident in the development of specialized non-academic roles focused on tasks peripheral to core academic duties around teaching and research, but which have historically been undertaken by academics themselves. Examples include reporting activities for audits and performance measurements (of publications, grant histories, etc.), preparation of grant applications, and subject coordination tasks (such as data entry for grading and other administration). Such tasks often require expertise in academic management, but need not be undertaken by academics (Bexley *et al.*, 2011).

The atomization of institutional activities does not just necessitate new forms of work and role, but extends to reconsideration of aspects of the central mission of universities. An example here is the so-called 'teaching/research nexus'. The teaching/research nexus can only be analysed under structural conditions, for, in the contemporary university, it is unrealistic for all teaching staff to be actively engaged in disciplinary research. That said, the primacy of the teaching/research nexus in the work of universities must be maintained, albeit in new forms, for it is integral to maintaining the quality and meaning of higher education. In practical terms, the present settings often throw teaching and research into direct competition for academics' time, given that productivity and effectiveness in one area is achieved at the expense of the other. A less simplistic consideration of the nexus, which focuses on the interplay between teaching and research at the department level, rather than in the work of the individual academic, is a practical approach in the present, mass higher education setting.

These shifts in the way higher education institutions organize their various functions, and the resultant changes to academic work roles, require new forms of management (Leišytė and Dee, 2012). In many ways, the post-mass participation higher education landscape is still in its infancy, and struggling to find ways to badge 'quality' outside of the old assumptions around excellence inherent in the previous, elite system of higher education. These challenges, and the radically increased complexity and instability of the operating environment over recent decades, has necessitated the introduction of specialized, professional management in higher education institutions, challenging old forms of collegial self-governance.

In part, such management of tertiary institutions has been characterized by the displacement of what might be termed 'traditional academic values' – such as collegial governance, autonomy of time management, implicit and discipline-based systems of professional recognition – by more business-oriented styles of management such as line-management structures, vertical accountability, and performance management. The importation from the public sector of New Public Management (NPM) practices has become common in universities, with the preference for disaggregation that is central to NPM at least superficially well suited to the atomization of academic work roles. But in other public organizations there is an increasing realization that NPM-style disaggregation of work roles can lead to negative consequences – that efficiency can come at the cost of institutional development and strategic capability (van de Walle and Hammerschmid, 2011). The challenge for tertiary managers is how to maintain a workforce that is sufficiently flexible to allow for changes in income streams and role requirements while not losing sight of the main game – high-quality teaching and research.

The changes sketched above do not come easily or without cost. The effects on academic identity of the changed relationship between academic and institution have been keenly observed internationally (see Chandler *et al.*, 2002; Churchman, 2006; Deem and Brehony, 2005; Leišytė, 2015; Winter, 2009), and are discussed in some detail elsewhere in this volume. Most problematically, perceived differences in the values of academics and managers are often treated as a binary divide – whether as a 'schism' (Winter, 2009) or worse, as a kind of ground war (Head, 2011). Winter observes, for example, that 'lost in this fractured work environment are values that broaden, transcend or unify disparate conceptions of what is central, distinctive and enduring about higher education' (Winter, 2009, p. 121). Ideally, the relationship between teaching and learning, and the organization itself, must be not just reflexive, but reciprocal. O'Byrne and Bond (2014) argue that a new consensus needs to be formed between the values and expectations of academics, students and managers. Such a consensus,

> must require a reinstatement of some of the traditional academic values. [But] this need not imply a return to the crusty old idealist model of the university as some kind of sacred space operating outside the acceptable laws and processes of accountability to which others are answerable, because such a model was surely elitist.
>
> (Ibid., p. 581)

They conclude that there is 'an inherent value in knowledge itself which cannot be reduced to the mathematics of the marketplace' (ibid.).

The traditional 'chalk and talk' lecture with supplementary tutorials is no longer the norm, and universities are increasingly turning to concepts like the 'flipped classroom' and the introduction of online elements to otherwise face-to-face learning environments. The rise of the Massive Open Online Course (MOOC), while initially seen as a potential threat to bricks and mortar institutions, is providing a valuable evidence base for understanding how people learn, and how technology can facilitate better learning. The massive banks of user data collected in MOOCs is providing the basis for a transformation of pedagogy (Coffrin *et al.*, 2014). But not all is good news. Increased use of ICT in teaching and learning can enable a lack of connection between students and their teachers and institution. A rise in student disengagement has been observed in Australia, with a troubling connection between disengagement and attrition (Baik *et al.*, 2015). The challenge is to find new ways to engage learners, even when they are studying remotely from the host institution (Bower *et al.*, 2014).

Similarly, the variety of institutional architectures offers a high degree of choice to students, at least on the surface. Steep status hierarchies remain in practice. Private higher education is yet to overtake traditional public universities in the status game. Yet these traditional values around tertiary education are unlikely to go long unchallenged. Small private institutions are able to offer higher education in niche markets, with small classes and deep industry engagement (Wheelahan *et al.*, 2012). For universities, the pressure to demonstrate that participation will result in direct, or at least strong, pathways to employment are becoming very strong. 'Graduate employability' is the new mantra, spawning practices like work-integrated learning, 'capstone' subjects offering industry experience, and a growth in vocational and professional disciplines. Problematically for managers and coordinators of teaching and learning, this drive to more closely align educational activities with employability requires close links with industry, in an economic context where industry and business does not necessarily have the time or resources to form such partnerships. Innovative approaches are emerging, such as 'work-simulated' learning, and an increasing use of portfolio-style assessments that can provide an evidence base for skills when graduates move into the workforce (an overview of related activities taking place in Australian universities are surveyed by Arkoudis *et al.*, 2014).

Concluding observations

What general implications flow from revised operating, institutional, and educational contexts? A great deal, obviously, and a few observations are made by way of conclusion.

Obviously, teaching hence learning will be different in future forms of higher education. This refers to the service provided, and also how students will expect to interact and achieve. Academics will value-add rather than serve content. The experience people receive will be priced. The way people study will be managed via technology in much more explicit, albeit often indirect, ways. Changes in this core pillar of higher education will reverberate through research, the complex and uncertain interplays between teaching and research, hence through institutions are proposed. Higher education institutions of today and the future will be better equipped to deal with the demands from graduate employers and research clients, though in ways which reflect a shock to contemporary ways of doing business.

New forms of leadership will be required. Conventionally, higher education leaders have worked 'up from the ranks', which means that people have led as they have experienced leadership, and that their skills and expectations have been shaped through a complex apprenticeship. The fruitful serendipity which has carried higher education to date is unlikely to prevail in the future. Tertiary systems and institutions – and not least the borderless operating context – carry big budgets and stakes. Leadership training via formal and informal methods plays a role in creating the leadership capability required for the future. Such training needs to ensure people have both the managerial skills, interpersonal and personal capacities, and also intellectual capability to succeed. As in many other sectors, experience is a necessary though not sufficient condition for leadership effectiveness.

Evidently, it is not just leaders but also the broader workforce that requires training and regeneration. The prompt here comes not just from transformations to and around the higher education industry, but also from exogenous factors like retirement of the baby boomers, productivity pressures, and evolution of new technologies. Benefits would flow from upskilling incumbent academics by helping them improve the quality and productivity of their teaching. As well, the PhD – now the effective gateway to an academic post – would benefit from incorporation of training in pedagogy.

This chapter has reviewed changes in the management of teaching and learning in higher education. Such change flows from broader transitions, as well as carrying implications for these. The word 'change' is used, noting that with any major shift in higher education this often plays out at what might be considered glacial speed over a period of five-to-ten years. Incumbent powerful institutions with less incentive to innovate may take longer to evolve, affirming the stable foundations of much of higher education. Even in such contexts, however, the dynamics explored in this chapter still apply, not least as people grasp the improvement potential implied by effective teaching and learning innovation.

References

ACE (American Council on Education) (2014a) *Beyond the Inflection Point: Reimagining Business Models for Higher Education*. Washington, DC: ACE

ACE (American Council on Education) (2014b) *The Students of the Future*. Washington, DC: ACE

ACU (Australian Catholic University) (2015) *ACU Strategic Plan 2015–2020*. Retrieved from http://www.acu.edu.au/about_acu/our_university/mission_and_profile/strategic_plan_2015-2020

Anibas, M., Hanson-Brenner, G. and Zorn, C. (2009) 'Experiences described by novice teaching academic staff in baccalaureate nursing education: a focus on mentoring'. *Journal of Professional Nursing*, 25 (4), 211–27

Arkoudis, S., Baik, C., Bexley, E. and Doughney, L. (2014) *English Language Proficiency and Employability Framework*. Melbourne: CSHE

Auguste, B. G., Cota, A. Jayaram, K. and Laboissière, M. C. A. (2010) *Winning by Degrees: The Strategies of Highly Productive Higher-education Institutions*. Retrieved from http://mckinseyonsociety.com/winning-by-degrees

Australian Government (2015) *Staff Data*. Canberra: Department of Education and Training

Baik, C., Naylor, R. and Arkoudis, S. (2015) *The First Year Experience in Australian Universities: Findings from Two Decades 1994–2014*. Parkville: Centre for the Study of Higher Education

Barber, M., Donnelly, K. and Rizvi, S. (2013) *An Avalanche is Coming: Higher Education and the Revolution Ahead*. London: Institute for Public Policy Research

Baumol, W. J. (1967) 'Macroeconomics of unbalanced growth: the anatomy of urban crisis'. *The American Economic Review*, 57 (3), pp. 415–42

Bexley, E. and Baik, C. (2011) *Casual Academics: Australia's Hidden Workforce*. Hiroshima: Research Institute of Higher Education

Bexley, E., James, R. and Arkoudis, S. (2011) *The Australian Academic Profession in Transition: Addressing the Challenge of Reconceptualising Academic Work and Regenerating the Academic Workforce*. Canberra: Department of Education, Employment and Workplace Relations, Commonwealth of Australia

Bower, M., Kenney, J., Dalgarno, B., Lee, M. J. and Kennedy, G. E. (2014) 'Patterns and principles for blended synchronous learning: engaging remote and face-to-face learners in rich-media real-time collaborative activities'. *Australasian Journal of Educational Technology*, 30 (3), pp. 261–72

Brown, T., Goodman, J. and Yasukwa, K. (2008) 'Casualisation of academic work: industrial justice and quality education'. *Dialogue*, 27 (1), pp. 17–29

Chandler, J., Barry, J. and Clark, H. (2002) 'Stressing academe: the wear and tear of the new public management'. *Human Relations*, 55 (9), pp. 1051–69

Christensen, C. and Eyring, H. J. (2011) *The Innovative University: Changing the DNA of Higher Education from the Inside Out*. New York: John Wiley and Sons

Churchman, D. (2006) 'Institutional commitments, individual compromises: identity-related responses to compromise in an Australian university'. *Journal of Higher Education Policy and Management*, 28 (1), pp. 3–15

Coaldrake, P. (2000) 'Rethinking academic and university work'. *Higher Education Management*, 12 (3), pp. 7–20

Coates, H. and Goedegebuure, L. (2012) 'Recasting the academic workforce: why the attractiveness of the academic profession needs to be increased and eight possible strategies for how to go about this from an Australian perspective'. *Higher Education*, 64, pp. 875–89

Coates, H. and Mahat, M. (2013) 'Assessing student engagement and outcomes: modelling insights from Australia and around the world'. *International Journal of Chinese Education*, 2 (2), pp. 241–26

Coates, H. and Mahat, M. (2014) 'Threshold quality parameters in hybrid higher education'. *Higher Education*, 68(4), pp. 577–90

Coates, H., James, R. and Baldwin, G. (2005) 'A critical examination of the effects of learning management systems on university teaching and learning'. *Tertiary Education and Management*, 11, pp. 19–36

Coates, H., Edwards, D., Goedegebuure, L., Mahat, M., van der Brugge, E. and van Vught, F. (2013) *Profiling Diversity of Australian Universities. LH Martin Institute for Tertiary Education Leadership and Management and ACER Research Briefing*. Camberwell: ACER

Coates, H., Meek, L., Brown, J., Friedman, T., Noonan, P. and Mitchell, J. (2012) 'VET leadership for the future: characteristics, contexts and capabilities'. *Further and Higher Education*, 37 (6), pp. 819–43

Coffrin, C., Corrin, L., de Barba, P. and Kennedy, G. (2014) 'Visualizing patterns of student engagement and performance in MOOCs'. LAK '14, Proceedings of the Fourth International Conference on Learning Analytics and Knowledge, March. Indianapolis

Commonwealth of Australia (1993) *National Report on Australia's Higher Education Sector.* Canberra: Australian Government

Daniel, J. (2012) *Making Sense of Musings in a Maze of Myth, Paradox and Possibility.* Retrieved from www.academicpartnerships.com

Dawson, N. (2007) 'Post postdoc: are new scientists prepared for the real world?' *Bioscience*, 57 (1), 16. doi: 10.1641/B570104

Deakin University (2014) *Deakin at a Glance.* Geelong: Deakin University

Deakin University (2015) *Live the Future: Agenda 2020.* Retrieved from http://www.deakin.edu.au/__data/assets/pdf_file/0009/363357/2015_live_plan_on_a_page.pdf

Deem, R. and Brehony, K. J. (2005) 'Management as ideology: the case of "new managerialism" in higher education'. *Oxford Review of Education*, 31 (2), pp. 217–35

Dobson, I. R. (2012) 'How the other half lives: university general staff today and tomorrow'. Paper presented at the NTEU conference, February. Sydney, Australia. Retrieved from http://www.nteu.org.au/library/view/id/2288

Ernst and Young (2012) *University of the Future: A Thousand Year Old Industry on the Cusp of Profound Change.* Sydney: Ernst and Young

European Commission (2013) *Horizon 2020 Programme.* Retrieved from http://ec.europa.eu/research/horizon2020

Gallagher, M. (2014) *Micro-economic Reform of Australia's Higher Education Industry.* Canberra: Group of Eight

Grimsey, D. and Lewis, M. K. (2013) *Public Private Partnerships.* London: Edward Elgar

Head, S. (2011) 'The grim threat to British universities'. *The New York Review of Books*, 13 January. Retrieved from http://www.nybooks.com/articles/archives/2011/jan/13/grim-threat-british-universities/

Kennie, T. and Price, I. (2012) *Disruptive Innovation and the Higher Education Ecosystem Post-2012.* London: Leadership Foundation for Higher Education

Kim, W. C. and Mauborgne, R. (2005) *Blue Ocean Strategy: How to Create Uncontested Market Space and Make Competition Irrelevant.* Cambridge: Harvard Business Press

Leišytė, L. (2015) 'Changing academic identities in the context of a managerial university: bridging the duality between professions and organisations' in Cummings, W. and Teichler, U. (Eds), *The Relevance of Academic Work in Comparative Perspective. The Changing Academy: The Changing Academic Profession in International Comparative Perspective,* 13. Dordrecht: Springer

Leišytė, L. and Dee, J. R. (2012) 'Understanding academic work in a changing institutional environment: faculty autonomy, productivity, and identity in Europe and the United States' in Smart, J. C. and Paulsen, M. B. (Eds), *Higher Education: Handbook of Theory and Research.* Dordrecht: Springer

Mahat, M. and Coates, H. (2015) 'Strategic planning and institutional research: the case of Australia' in Webber, K. L. and Calderon, A. J. (Eds), *Institutional Research and Planning in Higher Education: Global Contexts and Themes.* London: Routledge

MIT (Massachusetts Institute of Technology) (2015) *MIT OpenCourseWare (OCW).* Retrieved from http://ocw.mit.edu/index.htm

Massy, B. (2013) *Initiatives for Containing the Cost of Higher Education.* Washington, DC: American Enterprise Institute

Norton, A., Sonnemann, J. and McGannon, C. (2013) *The Online Evolution: When Technology Meets Tradition in Higher Education.* Parkville: Grattan Institute

O'Byrne, D. and Bond, C. (2014) 'Back to the future: the idea of a university revisited'. *Journal of Higher Education Policy and Management,* 36 (6), pp. 571–84

Robins, K. and Webster, F. (Eds) (2002) *The Virtual University? Knowledge, Markets and Management*. Oxford: Oxford University Press

Scott, G., Coates, H. and Anderson, M. (2008) *Learning Leaders in Times of Change: Academic Leadership Capabilities for Australian Higher Education*. Sydney: Australian Learning and Teaching Council

Siemens, G., Gašević, D. and Dawson, S. (2015) *Preparing for the Digital University: A Review of the History and Current State of Distance, Blended, and Online Learning*. Retrieved from http://linkresearchlab.org/PreparingDigitalUniversity.pdf

Sullivan, T. A., Mackie, C., Massy, W. F. and Sinha, E. (2012) *Improving Measurement of Productivity in Higher Education*. Washington, DC: National Academies Press

TEQSA (Tertiary Education Quality and Standards Agency) (2013) *Draft Standards for Course Design and Learning Outcomes*. Retrieved from http://www.HEstandards.gov.au

TEQSA (Tertiary Education Quality and Standards Agency) (2015) *National Register of Higher Education Providers*. Melbourne: TEQSA

Trow, M. (2007) 'Reflections on the transition from elite to mass to universal access: forms and phases of higher education in modern societies since WWII' in Forest, J. J. F. and Altbach, P. G. (Eds), *International Handbook of Higher Education*. Dordrecht: Springer, pp. 243–80

University of Melbourne (2015a) *The University of Melbourne Strategic Plan 2015–2020: Growing Esteem*. Parkville: University of Melbourne

University of Melbourne (2015b) *The University of Melbourne Annual Report 2014*. Parkville: University of Melbourne

van de Walle, S. and Hammerschmid, G. (2011) 'The impact of the new public management: challenges for coordination and cohesion in European public sectors'. *Halduskultuur – Administrative Culture*, 12 (2), pp. 190–209

van der Molen, H. J. (Ed.) (1999) *Virtual University? Educational Environments of the Future*. London: Portland Press

van Vught, F. (2012) 'Diversity, transparency and institutional profiling in higher education'. Paper presented at the LH Martin Institute Symposium on Strategic Differentiation and Sameness in Australian Higher Education: Institutional Profiling and Transparency. Australia, Melbourne

Wheelahan, L., Arkoudis, S., Moodie, G., Fredman, N. and Bexley, E. (2012) *Shaken Not Stirred? The Development of One Tertiary Education Sector in Australia*. Adelaide: NCVER

Winter, R. (2009) 'Academic manager or managed academic? Academic identity schisms in higher education'. *Journal of Higher Education Policy and Management*, 31 (2), pp. 121–31

II
Organizing teaching

5
Towards a conceptualization of faculty decision-making about curricular and instructional change

LISA R. LATTUCA AND JENNIFER R. POLLARD

Introduction

The question of why academics do or do not engage in curricular and instructional change is increasingly important as changes in the socio-political context of higher education pressures institutions to respond to accountability initiatives, student demand, workforce needs, and quality assurance efforts to quantify educational value and return on investment (Shavelson, 2010). The cultural traditions of academic institutions, which have historically placed great value on professional autonomy and individual decision-making inside and outside the classroom, are assumed to counter these external influences and complicate the process of curricular and instructional change (e.g. Fairweather, 1996; Trowler *et al.*, 2003); however, limited research exists to support such assumptions, particularly in a dynamic higher education context. As national and global higher education contexts change, it is important to study how external, organizational, and individual factors interact to shape decisions about teaching and curricula (Lattuca and Stark, 2009).

The goal of this this chapter is to bring together the research literature that explores factors that shape US college and university faculty members' engagement in curricular change to produce a conceptualization of faculty decision-making about curricular change. There is a longstanding literature on organizational change in higher education institutions that generally implicates faculty members as influences on the failure, success, or sustainability of organizational change. Often, however, the change rather than the faculty and instructors who make or implement change, is the primary concern. Here we place faculty attitudes and behaviours in the forefront, identifying potential influences on their decisions to engage (or not) in curricular change. To make our case, we synthesize findings from the literatures on faculty work, curriculum planning, curricular change, organizational change, and learning. Since space limitations prohibit an exhaustive review of all the literature that might be brought to bear on this topic, our work should be considered a step towards the development of a comprehensive framework for further study and refinement.

This work responds to calls for more nuanced views of instructor thinking. Seeking more holistic understandings of faculty members' decision-making about instruction, Hora (2012) called for researchers 'to focus on the constituent parts and processes that comprise decision-making in specific contexts', suggesting that researchers seek to understand how faculty members' mental representations of practice interact with organizational factors to affect instructional decisions (p. 229). This chapter also seeks to extend Lattuca and Stark's work on curriculum planning in US colleges and universities, viewing the decision to engage (or not) in a curricular change effort as a logical antecedent to the actual work of curriculum planning.

Our focus on instructors as individuals may initially appear narrow. In her review of the literature on change in higher education, Graham (2012, p. 8) challenged 'the assumption that influencing the beliefs, priorities, and behaviours of the individual faculty member holds the key to successful and sustainable educational reform'. Graham's concern, rightfully taken, reflects the reality that most educational change efforts are small-scale, isolated efforts that have little impact beyond the innovator's classroom or unit (Kezar, 2012). Successful curricular change, Graham argues, requires department-level buy-in and effort. This does not obviate the need to influence faculty beliefs and behaviours to achieve curricular change. Indeed, Graham identifies the following in her list of 'critical features of success and failure': faculty engagement; faculty development; resources and time; faculty networks; and faculty perceptions of institutional culture (Graham, 2012, pp. 10–11). Since the goal of curricular change cannot be realized without the participation of faculty members, the task of building a conceptualization of faculty decision-making regarding curricular change, grounded in the empirical and theoretical literature, remains relevant. Moreover, research suggests that limited attention to, and understanding of, the beliefs, knowledge, motivations, and experiences of faculty and instructors is at least in part to blame for failed attempts to generate collective buy-in to curricular innovation, to provide needed support to faculty during the change process, and to sustain faculty commitment to specific curricular innovations as well as to build a culture of concern for ongoing curriculum improvement.

In the sections that follow, we identify the components of a comprehensive framework for studying – and understanding – how faculty in higher education institutions make decisions about curricular change efforts – whether these change efforts would require making significant changes in their own course(s) or that faculty engage in larger curricular change efforts with colleagues in their own or other academic programmes.

Defining curricular change

In the academic-plan-in-context model, Lattuca and Stark (2009) define an academic plan as consisting of eight elements, or decision points, that are addressed in every academic plan – whether intentionally or not – by instructors as they develop courses and programmes. These include purposes (the views of education that inform decisions about the goals of programmes and of courses); content; sequence (for example, of topics in a course, courses in a programme, and other kinds of learning experiences); instructional processes;[1] instructional resources; assessment strategies; and approaches to evaluation of courses or programmes. An eighth element is the feedback loop of changes that instructors make to courses or programmes after they are delivered and assessed, either formally or informally. Following this model, we define 'curricular change' as change in one or more elements of an academic plan.

Defining curriculum in this way raises the question of when a decision to modify one or more of the elements of an academic plan rises to the level of a 'curricular change'. Instructors regularly adjust aspects of their courses, often while they are in progress (Jaschik, 2010), and often as they prepare to teach a course that they have previously taught (Lattuca and Stark, 2009). Without diminishing the importance of these ongoing efforts at improvement, we have in mind curricular changes that are larger in scope.

The distinctions made by Eckel *et al.* (1998) regarding the broader topic of organizational change are useful in considering curricular change. They suggest two measures – depth and pervasiveness – that describe the impact of a change. Depth is a measure of the extent to which a change affects behaviours or alters institutional structures. Taking an existing course and modifying it for an online environment is an example of a deep curricular change that alters the actions of faculty and students. The move to the online course management system alters the learning environment significantly as the technology presents new and different ways of engaging with course materials, the instructor, and students. Expectations regarding 'participation' in the course change in the absence of face-to-face contact, even in blended courses that combine face-to-face and technologically mediated interaction. While modifying a course for an online environment is a deep change, it may not be a pervasive one if it affects only the instructor making the change and the students who take her course. A change is pervasive if it affects many students and faculty or many units across the institution. Taking an existing course and creating a Massive Open Online Course (MOOC) may be an example of a pervasive change if it affects the learning of thousands of students internationally. A better example might be the adoption of a new course management system that will be used by many faculty members across programmes in a single university, thus affecting the learning experience of the majority of its students.

By combining the dimensions of depth and pervasiveness, we can broadly define the kinds of curricular changes that concern us in this chapter. Eckel *et al.* (1998) describe changes that are low in depth, but high in pervasiveness as 'far-reaching' change; they affect many people, even if in small ways. Changes that are both high in depth and pervasiveness are termed 'transformational'; these are the kinds of changes that many have in mind when they call for curriculum innovation and reform. In contrast, curricular changes that are both low in depth and pervasiveness are considered 'adjustments' while those that are high in depth but low in pervasiveness are considered 'isolated' instances of change. We are concerned with decisions to engage in transformational changes, but also with more isolated changes since these may still require significant effort on the part of faculty; we assume that decisions that have clear implications for faculty members' expenditures of time and energies require thought and decision-making.

The name of Stark and Lattuca's model, the 'academic plan-in-context', signals the situated nature of every curriculum; many factors, both internal and external to higher education institutions, may influence faculty as they engage in curriculum planning. The model can thus serve as a heuristic for thinking about influences on faculty decisions regarding curriculum change. Following the model's broad categories of influences, and our review of the relevant literatures, we propose a model of faculty decision-making about curricular change (Figure 5.1) that we will elaborate in the following sections (and reflect in more detail in Figure 5.2).

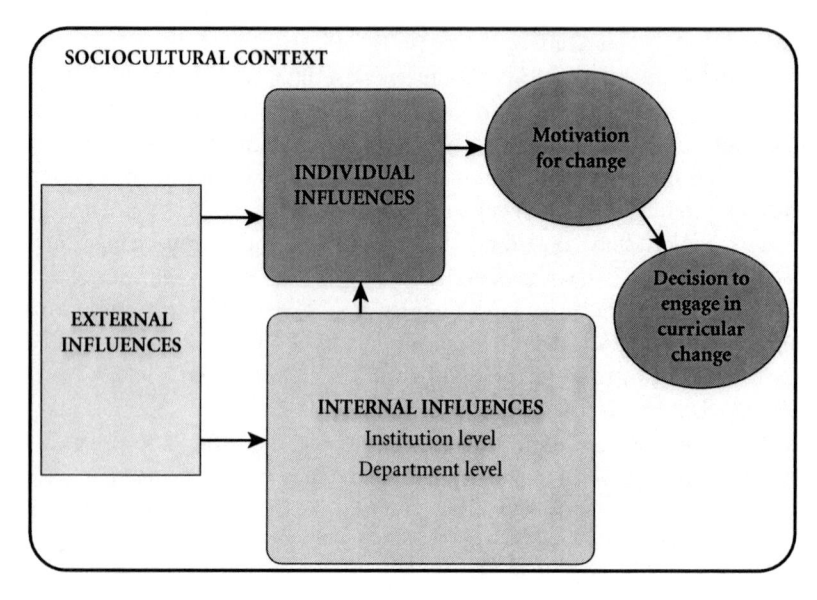

Figure 5.1 Initial model of faculty decision-making about curricular change

Following Figure 5.1, the discussion that follows begins by examining research and theory related to three types of contextual influences that may affect faculty members' thinking about their curricular responsibilities: sociocultural, external, and internal. We define *sociocultural factors* as larger social, cultural, and historical conditions that shape, sometimes surreptitiously, faculty thinking and behaviour related to curricular change. *External influences* are more proximal in time and space to higher education institutions (e.g. quality assurance processes, workforce needs). As indicated by the arrows in Figure 5.1, external factors can exert their influences on institutions and/or on units within those institutions and, by doing so, may have an indirect influence on individual faculty members' thinking and behaviour as well. *Internal influences* are those organizational factors – for example, institutional resources or departmental cultures – that may also affect faculty members' considerations regarding whether to engage in curriculum change. The *individual influences* component of the model recognizes that individual faculty have agency to act, or not to act, with regard to a particular influence. Our model also recognizes that an individual's motivation to engage in change is situational rather than a static trait or attitude. It is this situational motivation that results in a decision about whether or not to engage in a particular change effort. As the discussion that follows will show, the distinctions between these levels are less clear than Figure 5.1 suggests, but the refined model we will present later in this chapter reflects the current state of the research on curricular change and is helpful for purposes of analysis.

Sociocultural and external influences on change

Models of organizational change do not always take into account the larger social and cultural forces that shape work life in a given time and place, but social movements can have profound effects on our social institutions. In fact, Rojas (2012) notes that, in the literature on social movements in higher education, the emergence of new academic programmes is one of the most frequently studied topics. These studies focus on the interactions of external and internal actors surrounding curricular change as well as the changes produced by these interactions (Celis, 2014).

The social movement literature suggests a progression of changes that occurs in university curricula as social movements influence the work of higher education (ibid.). In the USA, two examples of social movements that eventually altered the post-secondary curriculum are the Civil Rights movement, which challenged discriminatory laws and behaviours that disenfranchised and disadvantaged African-Americans, and the women's movement, which took its inspiration from the Civil Rights movement and sought to empower women. As Celis notes, these movements not only produced significant changes in US society, they also substantially altered the college and university curriculum as new ideas and new educational resources were incorporated into courses and programmes in many fields and disciplines. Focusing on the development of women's studies, he points to the work of Boxer (1998) and Messer-Davidow (2002), who observed that, after the first women's studies programmes were established in US institutions, advocates formed national academic networks through which they could share resources and ideas and legitimize the new programmes. Both scholars further argue that the discipline that takes the lead in introducing a new field gives shape to the main characteristics of the curriculum and its supporting rationale, which in turn influence attitudes towards the adoption of new curricular programmes.

Social movements are but one type of sociocultural influence. Lattuca and Stark (2009) noted that the sociocultural context in which colleges and universities operate shapes the curriculum decisions that are made within them – although sometimes without conscious attention. For example, faculty rarely think twice today about using electronic resources – laptops, tablets, digital collections, full-text journal articles, clickers, smartphones, and many others – in their courses, but until the advent of digital communication, such choices were not possible, let alone plausible. Today, widespread technology use is reflected in the vast professional staff that supports instructors using new technologies in their teaching.

In addition to societal-level trends, Lattuca and Stark (ibid.) included external influences such as student demand, market forces, professional organizations, and quality assurance requirements in their model of academic plans in context. The salience of external influences may vary by field as well as by time period. In fields that are considered to be pathways to specific occupations, changes in labour market needs and student demand may have a significant impact on faculty decisions to engage in curricular change efforts to improve graduates' employability. Professional associations of scholars may also influence thinking about tertiary curriculum and necessary changes. For example, in the USA, a report called the *Framework for Success in Postsecondary Writing*, jointly published by the Council of Writing Program Administrators, the National Council of Teachers of English, and the National Writing Project (2011), describes the rhetorical and twenty-first-century skills, as well as habits of mind and experiences, thought to be critical for college success, and has been influential in many writing programmes in two- and four-year institutions. In countries with education ministries and other agencies that coordinate curriculum, government-level initiatives may mandate curricular changes that affect teaching and learning. For example, some studies suggest that curricula designed to emphasize creative thinking affected elementary, middle, and secondary school students' scores on tests of creativity (see Cheung and Lau, 2013, for a review).

Quality assurance is another example of an external influence that can catalyse faculty engagement in change efforts. In fields where accreditation of the baccalaureate institution is a requirement for professional licensure (e.g. medicine, dentistry, nursing, engineering, teaching), the influence of accreditation requirements will be strongly felt. In a large-scale study of the influence of accreditation on academic programmes, Lattuca *et al.* (2006) used survey data from a nationally representative sample of engineering faculty, administrators, students, and graduates in more than 200 engineering programmes in 40 US colleges and universities to assess the extent to which the implementation of outcomes-based accreditation criteria was associated with curricular change at the course and programme levels. The study used multiple data points to show that faculty had made changes in their undergraduate programmes in six of the largest engineering fields after the implementation of the new accreditation model. The analysis also linked these changes to a variety of external influences, including accreditation, but also to employer and student feedback and funding agency activity. Many engineering deans interviewed for the study also noted that the new criteria had improved faculty practices related to curriculum planning. In some institutions, the new criteria encouraged faculty to formalize or systematize the decision-making process for new courses, reduce duplication in curricula, and improve coordination with other engineering disciplines when making curricular changes.

Internal influences

Faculty work is shaped by the institutions in which it occurs. Organizational features and infrastructure – for example, institutional mission, finances, and governance practices – affect the ways in which faculty think about their roles and responsibilities for curriculum development, instruction, and assessment (Lattuca and Stark, 2009). Institutional influences are further complicated, however, by the existence of unit-level influences – department cultures and practices also influence how groups of faculty think about and engage the educational missions of their institutions and programmes.

Organizational culture

The challenge of assessing organizational culture in higher education institutions is that while the organization as a whole may have some distinguishing cultural features, each academic programme or unit within an institution has its cultural norms as well (Braxton, 2010). Some of these norms are based in disciplinary affiliations (Becher and Trowler, 2001; Gaff and Wilson, 1971; Ruscio, 1987); others are rooted in institutional norms (Clark, 1970, 1971); still others may be the results of geography, history, and sociocultural time. Consequently, while the norms of, for example, the college of education and the college of business in a large research university overlap to some extent (e.g. both value research productivity and grant-getting), they also may diverge in substantive ways (e.g. pedagogical research is valued in promotion and tenure in the school of education but not in the school of business). Culture, then, has local variants and faculty members' perceptions of what they perceive to be salient organizational cultures may affect (although not necessarily determine) their interest in, and willingness to engage in, curricular change efforts – whether these efforts are their own or require collaboration with colleagues.

One of the most salient organizational influences on faculty may be the relative value that their institutions and their departments place on research and teaching in decisions regarding tenure and promotion and merit salary increases (Fairweather, 2008). There is, however, little generalizable research that verifies the presumed link between faculty engagement in curricular change and their perceptions of their institutional and/or departmental reward system. Using data from approximately 17,000 faculty who responded to the National Survey on Postsecondary Faculty in 1992–3 and 1998–9, Fairweather showed that the more time a faculty member spends in the classroom, the lower his or her salary, regardless of the type of four-year institution (Fairweather, 2005). He also found that the differential cost/benefit of one hour teaching or publishing 'in the mean' shows that time spent teaching costs a faculty member money whereas time spent publishing is rewarded with higher pay (Fairweather, 2008). This kind of evidence suggests that faculty make rational decisions, based on presumed rewards, when faced with the option of engaging in curricular innovation or reform. To some extent, theories of motivation support the emphasis on faculty members' perceptions of the cost of a particular activity, but also present a more complex conceptualization of the motivation that reveals the interaction of personal and contextual features of faculty members' motivations to engage in change.

Theories of motivation suggest that faculty would have expectations about the perceived value and cost associated with a particular activity such as a course revision. Eccles and Wigfield (2002) explained that motivations to work towards a given goal are affected by four factors: the perceived utility value of the task in facilitating either the individual's short- or long-range goals or the attainment of desired external rewards; the individual's intrinsic interest in, and enjoyment of, the activity itself; the value the activity has for manifesting the individual's social or personal identity/ies and core values; and the perceived cost of engaging in the activity. As Fairweather's research suggests, cost can be understood in terms of lost time and energy for other activities. Henderson and Dancy (2007) and Hora (2012) identify insufficient resources, workloads, and/or time as barriers to successful educational change efforts in science and engineering fields. One study of science faculty found that 60 per cent of respondents cited inadequate resources, time and turf conflicts as barriers to course-level curricular change (Sunal et al., 2001). As Hora (2012) notes, normative expectations regarding research productivity will differentially affect the decision-making of faculty who are in different social positions in the university (e.g. untenured faculty, instructors).

Eccles (2011), however, argues that motivation to engage in a task like curricular reform may also be influenced by factors such as fear of failure or the social consequences of success (which depending on one's perspective could be positive or negative). Faculty members' perceptions of their ability to enact curricular change successfully, and to persuade their colleagues that such change is needed and should be institutionalized, can thus influence decisions to embark on – or avoid – a curricular change effort.

We will discuss motivation again with regard to individual-level characteristics, but here we note that each of the four components of this motivation model, which has been applied in studies of students and faculty in US academic settings (e.g. Eccles, 2011; Matusovich *et al.*, 2014; Matusovich *et al.*, 2010), can be influenced by contextual features – both past and present – that shape beliefs about costs, values, and expectations about the results of engagement in curricular change. In the US context, the latest national survey of postsecondary faculty members, faculty in all types of four-year colleges and universities perceived an increased emphasis on research productivity in faculty rewards (Schuster and Finkelstein, 2006). A more recent report by Cashmore *et al.* (2013), based on a survey of 55 institutions in the UK, suggests a similar cultural condition in which teaching appears to be undervalued in relation to research. The report further suggests a related problem rooted in the lack of 'robust criteria' to measure teaching excellence compared to the available criteria for assessing research productivity (e.g. publications and grant income).

Graham (2012) noted that communications and explanations from institutional leaders about educational visions and change may also be influential in shaping faculty beliefs about the value and costs of engaging in curricular change. Visions and rhetoric, however, must be accompanied by resources to motivate faculty buy-in. Henderson and Dancy (2007) observe that insufficient time and resources can impede educational changes, and Wieman *et al.* (2010) argue that the process of change requires institutions to provide additional resources to support change efforts. In the absence of visible supports faculty are likely to opt out of the change process.

Disciplinary and departmental cultures

Although there are exceptions, the departmental structure of most institutions reflects the disciplinary organization of knowledge, grouping faculty in the same field or specialization areas into organizational units. Departments, then, continue to socialize faculty members in disciplinary ways of thinking begun in graduate programmes. Academic discipline appears to be one of the strongest influences on the professional behaviours and attitudes of US faculty members (Smart *et al.*, 2000). Yet, as Smart *et al.* (ibid.) show in their analyses, variations in specialization areas create faculty sub-environments within larger disciplinary groupings such as biology, sociology, and engineering.

Building on these findings, Lattuca *et al.* (2010) speculated that different groups of faculty might vary in their receptiveness to particular educational reforms based on differences in a number of their beliefs and preferences – for example, their beliefs about the purpose of education, educational goals they perceive to be important in their fields, and their preferred teaching practices. Using data from more than 1,200 engineering faculty, they asked whether engineering faculty in different academic environments (defined by Holland's typology) varied in their responses to changing curricular and pedagogical requirements imposed by a new set of outcomes-based accreditation requirements phased into practice from 1997–2000 and mandated for all US engineering programmes in 2001.

The study found that, despite pressures to respond to the accreditation mandates, faculty did so to varying degrees; moreover, these variations in responses were consistent with expectations based on their Holland type. For example, engineering faculty in Enterprising and Investigative fields reported the greatest increases in emphasis on professional and ethical responsibilities, and the societal and global implications of engineering solutions, in their courses. This finding is consistent with Holland's description of individuals in Enterprising fields as tending to view problems in terms of their social influence and to value the development of leadership qualities. Investigative engineers reported somewhat less change than Enterprising engineers, but more than Realistic engineers, who reported the least change in their emphasis on professional and contextual knowledge and abilities, and who Holland described as preferring structured solutions to problems.

Similar findings have come from the National Survey of Student Learning, which has been implemented by more than 600 US colleges and universities since its inception. Nelson-Laird *et al.* (2008), for example, found that faculty in a variety of disciplines place different levels of emphasis on 'deep approaches' to learning.[2] Faculty in disciplines and fields characterized by more codified bodies of knowledge rated these approaches lower than their colleagues in fields characterized by less codified bodies of knowledge.

The need to develop faculty ownership of proposed organizational and educational changes is a constant theme in the literature on curricular change. In a discussion of why educational reform efforts succeed and fail, Kezar (2012) notes that research shows that deliberation and discussion among professionals commonly leads to authentic change. While individual understanding of change is needed for change to occur (discussed later in this chapter), research suggests that faculty also need opportunities 'to engage in ongoing discussion within the context of a deliberative learning process that helps them understand the necessity for change' (ibid., para. 13). In the case of programme-level change, such processes are necessarily communal. Ramsden *et al.* (2007) view a collegial commitment to student learning as a foundation for effective and coherent educational programmes, while Fisher *et al.* (2003) further specify the need for a sense of collective responsibility for curricular change on the part of department members. Bouwma-Gearhart (2012) suggests that collegial relationships of trust and mutual respect can inspire risk-taking in the classroom, while O'Meara (2005) notes that a culture of experimentation appears to empower faculty to try new approaches and share their experiences of these trials.

Individual-level factors: knowledge, beliefs, experiences, and motivations

In a review of the literature on the influence of rewards on faculty behaviour, O'Meara *et al.* (2008) acknowledge the interaction of individual and institutional influences, but argue that studies of faculty behaviours are dominated by a 'narrative of constraint' that focuses attention on structural and cultural barriers in the academic workplace that prevent faculty from engaging in particular kinds of work (p. 155). Such accounts overlook the agency that faculty exhibit when they make decisions about their professional lives (see Blackburn and Lawrence, 1995, for an extended discussion), and particularly with regard to decisions about curriculum and teaching (e.g., Henderson and Dancy, 2007; Stark, 2000).

Faculty motivation and agency

While institutional structures can constrain the extent to which faculty engage in curricular and pedagogical reform, research has revealed that intrinsic motivation and faculty agency play critical roles in faculty's engagement in curricular and pedagogical change. Faculty members *do* take the initiative in seeking strategic curricular and pedagogical reform assistance with appropriately knowledgeable and skilled peers within their departments and/or institutions (Akerson *et al.*, 2002; Bailey and Nagamine, 2012). Decisions to engage in change efforts may result from discontent with outcomes for one's students (e.g. Akerson *et al.*, 2002; Bailey and Nagamine, 2012). Dissatisfaction may also arise because poor student outcomes contribute to a diminished sense of efficacy. Such reactions may become motivators for individuals for whom teaching is an intrinsic value or important to their identity as academics (Akerson *et al.*, 2002; Bailey and Nagamine, 2012).

Faculty experiences and beliefs shape their curricular and instructional decisions including those regarding reform (Brown *et al.*, 2006; Gess-Newsome *et al.*, 2003; Hutchins and Friedrichsen, 2012). While experiences and beliefs can be treated separately, this separation is useful primarily for analytical purposes; practically, the two are inextricably linked as experiences shape beliefs and vice versa. In addition, our review of the relevant literature suggests that not only are experiences and beliefs shaped by knowledge of, for example, instructional practices, curriculum design principles, and student learning, but such knowledge may also alter beliefs and subsequent experiences. Oleson and Hora (2014) observe, however, that there is little research on the origins of faculty knowledge and beliefs about teaching or the role that their experiences play in the development of teaching practices.

Faculty beliefs and knowledge

Existing research indicates that a variety of beliefs emerge out of faculty experiences, and these either augur well for or militate against a faculty member's choices to engage in curricular or instructional change. Faculty hold conceptions about the nature of teaching within their respective disciplines (e.g. Donald, 2002; Smart *et al.*, 2000); the critical components of the faculty role in terms of the teaching to research balance (e.g. Janke and Colbeck, 2008; Luft *et al.*, 2004); and the role of the student in teaching (e.g. Major and Palmer, 2006). A lack of knowledge presents both conceptual (e.g. Brown *et al.*, 2006; Hutchins and Friedrichsen, 2012) and implementation barriers to change (e.g. Henderson, 2005; Hutchins and Friedrichsen, 2012).

While some faculty may engage in many approaches consistent with effective teaching practice, some aspects of their implicit instructional models or frameworks may be discordant with significant aspects of research-based reformed teaching approaches (Henderson, 2005). Several studies demonstrate frequent discrepancies between faculty members' conceptions of their teaching and their actual practice (Ebert-May *et al.*, 2011; Gess-Newsome *et al.*, 2003; Henderson and Dancy, 2007). In this regard, faculty appear to hold the ideal of reformed or student-centred teaching in mind and are able to implement certain – but not all – features of such models (Brown *et al.*, 2006; Gess-Newsome *et al.*, 2003; Hutchins and Friedrichsen, 2012). Often beliefs go unquestioned (Henderson, 2005) and, when firmly held, can be resistant to change (Henderson, 2005; Gess-Newsome *et al.*, 2003). For example, Sunal *et al.* (2001) found that faculty members who described their role as disseminator of the discipline, lecturer, or information provider were less likely than those who saw themselves as facilitators of learning 'to plan and implement significant change[s] in their courses' (p. 252).

Prior experiences

Research on teaching practices reveals a number of faculty experiences that appear to influence decisions about how and what to teach. We argue, by extension, that many of these experiences will have an impact – positive or negative – on faculty members' decisions about whether to engage in particular kinds of educational innovation and change because experiences affect individuals' sense of self-efficacy (Bandura, 1997) and their motivation (Eccles and Wigfield, 2002; Weiner, 2010).

A number of studies indicate that faculty rely on both formal and informal student feedback to guide their teaching (e.g. Hativa and Goodyear, 2001; Oleson and Hora, 2014) and that student feedback is associated with decisions to make changes in their courses (Lattuca et al., 2006). While some studies suggest that student feedback can encourage change (e.g. ibid.), others suggest how it can discourage change. Henderson et al. (2012) found that instructors often feel constrained by students' unfavourable responses and attitudes to new instructional approaches. Such responses need not be personally experienced to deter faculty from changing their courses; learning about the experiences of colleagues who have had negative experiences when engaging in educational innovations and reforms may be sufficient to dissuade faculty from engaging in change efforts. This contention is supported by theory and research on social learning, which indicates that experiences need not be direct to be influential; social learning can occur vicariously through observation (e.g. Bandura, 1997).

Intentional efforts to build faculty knowledge and beliefs about teaching, learning, and assessment may be particularly effective in countering misconceptions, altering feelings of efficacy, and providing needed understandings and experiences (O'Meara, 2005). Participation in professional development activities, in particular, may alter beliefs about teaching and learning as well as enhance faculty knowledge of effective practices (Felder and Brent, 2010; Oleson and Hora, 2014). Studies find that training and knowledge gains in student-centred pedagogies enhance faculty confidence to try new methods in the classroom (Major and Palmer, 2006; O'Meara, 2005). Training has also resulted in commitments to pedagogical change on a personal level (Bouwma-Gearhart, 2012; Major and Palmer, 2006). Several studies have linked instructional development activities with the use of evidence-based teaching practices. Lattuca et al. (2014) found a positive relationship between faculty members' attendance at a workshop on teaching or assessment and the use of student-centred teaching practices, in particular the use of active learning pedagogy and activity-based learning assessments such as group presentations and peer and self-assessments. Sunal et al. (2001) similarly found that faculty members 'with greater knowledge of effective teaching strategies and clearer ideas about planning and carrying out change in college courses were significantly more likely to implement change in their courses' (p. 252). Major and Palmer (2006) observed that an institutional-wide, multi-disciplinary initiative to encourage problem-based learning facilitated shifts in faculty's understanding of their roles as teachers to 'guides' or 'facilitators' and led to more use of student-centred approaches. Professional development activities that develop robust pedagogical content knowledge (see Shulman, 1986) will likely provide the most reliable knowledge for making decisions about curricular and instructional change.

Synthesis and conclusion: an emerging conceptualization of faculty decision-making about curricular and instructional change

In the preceding sections we have combined and considered findings from research on curricular and organizational change, faculty beliefs and attitudes, teaching practices, and curriculum planning in an effort to understand the various influences that may shape faculty members' decisions to engage (or not) in curricular and/or instructional change efforts. In this final section, we seek to clarify and explain how these categories of influences may interact. Our conceptualization is rooted in the US higher education context and, for the most part, in the research literature conducted in this context. Its applicability to other national and cultural contexts depends to a large extent on the resemblances between the US and other contexts.

Our conceptualization responds to calls for nuanced thinking about faculty decision-making processes (Hora, 2012) by focusing on the decision-making, whether intentional or subconscious, that necessarily precedes an actual curricular and/or instructional change process. Our conceptualization recognizes that the expectation that systemic educational improvements in undergraduate academic programmes will naturally occur as a result of a diffusion of innovation process (in which individuals learn about new, evidence-based innovations and adopt them – or not – for use in their disciplines and home institutions based on a rational assessment of their suitability) is largely unmet. Educators and funding agencies alike recognize that diffusion of innovations has not occurred with any frequency or regularity (see Kezar, 2001, 2010; Graham, 2012). New conceptualizations of faculty decision-making regarding curricular and instructional changes are consequently needed.

Our synthesis of research reveals that there is little direct evidence of decision-making related to curricular and/or instructional change to inform the development of a conceptualization of faculty decision-making in this area; as a result, we suggest, tentatively, the factors and conceptual linkages to be explored by researchers. The model we depict in Figure 5.2 is grounded in a situative perspective that assumes decision-making will be strongly shaped by the contexts in which it occurs; researchers should expect variations in salient factors as well as in linkages among factors, depending on the faculty member involved and the potential change effort under study.

Still, we make several assumptions. First among these is the assumption (above) that faculty decision-making about curricular and instructional change is situated in a complex of intersecting contexts – sociocultural, organizational, and departmental/disciplinary – that vary in salience for a given innovation or change for a given faculty member at a particular point in time

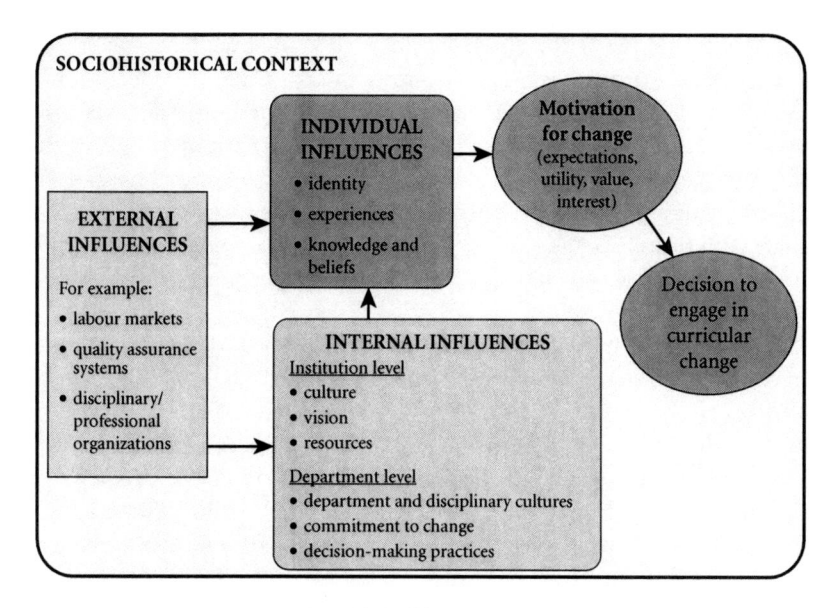

Figure 5.2 Proposed model of faculty decision-making about curricular change

and in a particular setting. This situative perspective argues that one cannot specify a set of identity characteristics that will be relevant in all curricular/instructional change decisions; researchers instead seek to understand how the decision-making process surrounding a particular curricular and/or instructional change evokes particular identity characteristics for a given faculty member.

For example, rather than assuming rank or gender is always important in decision-making about curricular and/or instructional change, we suggest that researchers instead seek to understand if, when, and why academic rank is or is not salient for a faculty member faced with the question of engaging in a specific educational change. Is rank highly salient for a junior faculty member asked to participate in a curricular overhaul of an introductory biology course she teaches because she perceives that participation in this effort may affect both her research productivity and her teaching evaluation – and thus her upcoming tenure bid? Is it any less salient for the senior male faculty member with a long history of research productivity but little experience in curricular innovation? Does rank dissuade the junior faculty member from engaging in change but create in the senior member a sense of autonomy that augurs participation without fear of negative consequences?

Second, we argue that identity must play a central role in our conceptualization of faculty response to change. For purposes of analysis, our review fragmented faculty into a number of component parts – beliefs, knowledge, experiences, and motivations. Our situative perspective, however, suggests a more holistic understanding of the 'self' whose prior knowledge and experiences shape their values, attitudes, and motivations and inform their decision-making. Following Holland and Lave (2009), who build on Vygotsky's work, we define identity as 'psychological formations ... complexes of memories, sentiments, knowledge and ideas' that once established become 'a ground for agency both in guiding one's behavior in cultural activities and in avoiding behaviors that are not compatible with the self-assigned identity' (p. 8). In this perspective, one's identity is socially produced and culturally constructed through one's activities in the world (Holland et al., 1998).

Thus, identity is not synonymous with or determined by sociodemographic characteristics; instead, it must be understood as reflecting multifaceted and evolving perceptions of the self. For faculty, academic identity may change over time as individuals progress through different career stages (see, for example, Neumann, 2009) or as a result of experiences that happen alongside, but not as a result of, one's academic and professional life. Such a conceptualization assumes that identity is defined by the individual-in-context, and reflects research findings, cited in this chapter, suggesting that the salience of one's identity as a teacher may shape one's receptivity to information about teaching and learning and participation in instructional development activities (e.g. Brownell and Tanner, 2012). Finally, our conceptualization of identity allows for the possibility that different identities may become salient in response to sociohistorical events or trends, as the rise of ethnic studies and women's studies programmes in the USA suggests (see Boxer, 1998; Messer-Davidow, 2002; Rojas, 2012).

While identity is a central concept in our conceptualization of faculty decision-making about curricular change, research suggests that faculty do not act solely on the basis of salient identities, particularly when acting in ways consonant with one's identity may perceived to be disadvantageous. Feelings of efficacy with regard to needed knowledge and skills related to curricular and/or instructional change, as well as estimates of the value, utility, and costs of engagement in change efforts, may also influence decision-making. Discussions of self-efficacy and motivation, either explicit or implied in the research we reviewed, again reveal the interactive nature of personal characteristics and organizational contexts, and suggest that a complex and non-linear understanding of decision-making with regard to engagement in curricular change efforts is needed. In some situations, identity may take the forefront in decision-making; in other situations, contextual variables may take precedence in faculty members' minds and thus have greater influence on their decisions.

The conceptualization we offer does not seek to predict behaviour but rather to enhance understanding of the complexity of faculty decision-making regarding curricular and instructional change. It thus has the potential to answer researchers' question about 'why' and 'when' faculty decide to risk change and to assist practitioners who hope to encourage and support educational innovation.

Notes

1 Although some individuals consider instruction separate from curriculum, this definition makes it clear that instruction is a critical element of every curriculum plan.
2 Following Marton and Saljo (1976), Entwistle and Ramsden, 1983, and Ramsden (2003), Nelson Laird *et al.* (2008) describe deep learning as reflecting 'a personal commitment to understand the material which manifests itself in the use of various strategies such as reading widely, combining a variety of resources, discussion of ideas with others, reflecting on how individual pieces of information relate to larger constructs or patterns, and applying knowledge in real world situations…. integrating and synthesizing information with prior learning in ways that become part of one's thinking and approaching new phenomena and efforts to see things from different perspectives' (p. 470).

References

Akerson, V. L., Medina, V. F. and Wang, N. (2002) 'A collaborative effort to improve university engineering instruction'. *School Science and Mathematics*, 102(8), pp. 405–19

Bailey, J. M. and Nagamine, K. (2012) 'Experiencing conceptual change about teaching: a case study from astronomy'. *American Journal of Physics*, 80 (6), pp. 542–51

Bandura, A. (1997) *Self-efficacy: The Exercise of Control*. New York: Freeman

Becher, T. and Trowler, P. R. (2001) *Academic Tribes and Territories: Intellectual Enquiry and the Cultures of Disciplines* (2nd edn). Buckingham: SRHE and Open University Press

Blackburn, R. T. and Lawrence, J. H. (1995) *Faculty at Work: Motivation, Expectation, Satisfaction*. Baltimore, MD: Johns Hopkins University Press

Bouwma-Gearhart, J. (2012) 'Research university STEM faculty members' motivation to engage in teaching professional development: building the choir through an appeal to extrinsic motivation and ego'. *Journal of Science Education and Technology*, 21 (5), pp. 558–70

Boxer, M. J. (1998) *When Women Ask the Questions: Creating Women's Studies in America*. Baltimore, MD: Johns Hopkins University Press

Braxton, J. M. (2010) 'Norms and the work of colleges and universities: introduction to the special issue – norms in academia'. *The Journal of Higher Education*, 81 (3), pp. 243–50

Brown, P. L., Abell, S. K., Demir, A. and Schmidt, F. J. (2006) 'College science teachers' views of classroom inquiry'. *Science Education*, 90 (5), pp. 784–802

Brownell, S. E. and Tanner, K. (2012) 'Barriers to faculty pedagogical change: lack of training, time, incentives, and tensions with professional identity?' *CBE-Life Sciences Education*, 11(4), pp. 339–46

Cashmore, A., Cane, C. and Cane, R. (2013) *Rebalancing Promotion in the HE Sector: Is Teaching Excellence Being Rewarded?* York: Higher Education Academy.

Celis, S. G. (2014) 'How intellectual movements among external and internal actors shape the college curriculum: the case of entrepreneurship education in engineering'. Unpublished dissertation. University of Michigan, Ann Arbor

Cheung, P. C. and Lau, S. (2013) 'A tale of two generations: creativity growth and gender differences over a period of education and curriculum reforms'. *Creativity Research Journal*, 25 (4), pp. 463–71

Clark, B. R. (1970) *The Distinctive College: Antioch, Reed, and Swarthmore*. Chicago: Aldine

Clark, B. R. (1971) 'Belief and loyalty in college organization'. *Journal of Higher Education*, 42 (6), pp. 499–515

Council of Writing Program, Administrators National Council of Teachers of English and National Writing Project. (2011) *Framework for Success in Postsecondary Writing*. Mountain View, CA: Creative Commons

Donald, J. G. (2002) *Learning to Think: Disciplinary Perspectives*. San Francisco: Jossey-Bass

Ebert-May, D., Derting, T. L., Hodder, J., Momsen, J. L., Long, T. M. and Jardeleza, S. E. (2011) 'What we say is not what we do: effective evaluation of faculty professional development programs'. *BioScience*, 61 (7), pp. 550–8

Eccles, J. S. (2011) 'Gendered educational and occupational choices: applying the Eccles et al. model of achievement-related choices'. *International Journal of Behavioral Development*, 35, pp. 195–201

Eccles, J. S. and Wigfield, A. (2002) 'Motivational beliefs, values, and goals'. *Annual Review of Psychology*, 53, pp. 109–132

Eckel, P., Hill, B. and Green, M. (1998) 'En route to transformation'. On Change: An Occasional Paper Series of the ACE Project on Leadership and Institutional Transformation. Washington, DC: American Council on Education (ERIC Document Reproduction Service No. ED435293)

Entwistle, N. J. and Ramsden, P. (1983) *Understanding Student Learning*. London: Croom Helm

Fairweather, J. (1996) *Faculty Work and Public Trust: Restoring the Value of Teaching and Public Service in American Academic Life*. Needham Heights, MA: Allyn and Bacon

Fairweather, J. (2005) 'Beyond the rhetoric: trends in the relative value of teaching and research in faculty salaries'. *Journal of Higher Education*, 76, pp. 401–22

Fairweather, J. (2008) *Linking Evidence and Promising Practices in Science, Technology, Engineering, and Mathematics (STEM) Undergraduate Education: A Status Report for the National Academies National Research Council Board of Science Education*. Washington, DC: National Academies

Felder, R. M. and Brent, R. (2010) 'The national effective teaching institute: assessment of impact and implications for faculty development'. *Journal of Engineering Education*, 99 (2), pp. 121–34

Fisher, P. D., Fairweather, J. S. and Amey, M. (2003) 'Systemic reform in undergraduate engineering education: the role of collective responsibility'. *International Journal of Engineering Education*, 19 (6), pp. 768–76

Gaff, J. G. and Wilson, R. C. (1971) 'Faculty cultures and interdisciplinary studies'. *Journal of Higher Education*, 42 (3), pp. 186–201

Gess-Newsome, J., Southerland, S. A., Johnston, A. and Woodbury, S. (2003) 'Educational reform, personal practical theories, and dissatisfaction: the anatomy of change in college science teaching'. *American Educational Research Journal*, 40 (3), pp. 731–67

Graham, R. (2012) *Achieving excellence in engineering education: the ingredients of successful change*. London: Royal Academy of Engineering

Hativa, N. and Goodyear, P. (Eds) (2001) *Teacher Thinking, Beliefs, and Knowledge in Higher Education*. Norwell, MA: Kluwer Academic

Henderson, C. (2005) 'The challenges of instructional change under the best of circumstances: a case study of one college physics instructor'. *American Journal of Physics*, 73 (8), pp. 778–86

Henderson, C. and Dancy, M. H. (2007) 'Barriers to the use of research-based instructional strategies: the influence of both individual and situational characteristics'. *Physical Review: Special Topics – Physics Education Research*, 3, 020102-1–020102-14

Henderson, C., Dancy, M. and Niewiadomska-Bugaj, M. (2012) 'Use of research-based instructional strategies in introductory physics: where do faculty leave the innovation-decision process?' *Physical Review Special Topics-Physics Education Research*, 8, 020104-1–020104-15

Holland, D. and Lave, J. (2009) 'Social practice theory and the historical production of persons'. *International Journal of Human Activity Theory*, 2, pp. 1–15

Holland, D., Lachicotte, W., Skinner, D. and Cain, C. (1998) *Identity and Agency in Cultural Worlds*. Cambridge, MA: Harvard University Press

Hora, M. T. (2012) 'Organizational factors and instructional decision-making: a cognitive perspective'. *The Review of Higher Education*, 35 (2), pp. 207–35

Hutchins, K. L. and Friedrichsen, P. J. (2012) 'Science faculty belief systems in a professional development program: inquiry in college laboratories'. *Journal of Science Teacher Education*, 23 (8), pp. 867–87

Janke, E. M. and Colbeck, C. L. (2008) 'Lost in translation: learning professional roles through the situated curriculum'. *New Directions for Teaching and Learning*, 113, pp. 57–68

Jaschik, S. (2010) 'Constant curricular change'. *Inside Higher Education*, 8 November. Retrieved from https://www.insidehighered.com/news/2010/11/08/pod

Kezar, A. (2001) *Understanding and Facilitating Organizational Change in the 21st Century: Recent Research and Conceptualizations*. Washington, DC: ASHE-ERIC Higher Education Reports

Kezar, A. (2010) 'Faculty and staff partnering with student activists: unexplored terrains of interaction and development'. *Journal of College Student Development*, 51 (5), pp. 451–80

Kezar, A. (2012) 'The path to pedagogical reform in the sciences: engaging mutual adaptation and social movement models of change'. *Liberal Education*, 98(1). Retrieved from http://www.aacu.org/liberaleducation/le-wi12/kezar.cfm

Lattuca, L. R. and Stark, J. S. (2009) *Shaping the College Curriculum: Academic Plans in Context*. San Francisco: Jossey-Bass

Lattuca, L. R., Bergom, I. and Knight, D. B. (2014) 'Professional development, departmental contexts, and the use of instructional strategies'. *Journal of Engineering Education*, 103 (4), pp. 549–72

Lattuca, L. R., Terenzini, P. T. and Volkwein, J. F. (2006) *Engineering Change: Findings from a Study of the Impact of EC2000*. Baltimore, MD: Accreditation Board for Engineering and Technology

Lattuca, L. R., Terenzini, P. T., Harper, B. J. and Yin, A. C. (2010) 'Academic environments in detail: Holland's theory at the subdiscipline level'. *Research in Higher Education*, 51 (1), pp. 21–39

Luft, J. A., Kurdziel, J. P., Roehrig, G. H. and Turner, J. (2004) 'Growing a garden without water: graduate teaching assistants in introductory science laboratories at a doctoral/research university'. *Journal of Research in Science Teaching*, 41 (3), pp. 211–33

Major, C. H. and Palmer, B. (2006) 'Reshaping teaching and learning: the transformation of faculty pedagogical content knowledge'. *Higher Education*, 51 (4), pp. 619–47

Marton, F. and Saljo, R. (1976) 'On qualitative differences in learning I: outcome and process'. *British Journal of Educational Psychology*, 46, pp. 4–11

Matusovich, H. M., Streveler, R. A. and Miller, R. L. (2010) 'Why do students choose engineering? A qualitative, longitudinal investigation of students' motivational values'. *Journal of Engineering Education*, 99 (4), pp. 289–303

Matusovich, H. M., Paretti, M. C., McNair, L. D. and Hixson, C. (2014) 'Faculty motivation: a gateway to transforming engineering education'. *Journal of Engineering Education*, 103 (2), pp. 302–30

Messer-Davidow, E. (2002) *Disciplining Feminism: From Social Activism to Academic Discourse*. Durham, NC: Duke University Press

Nelson-Laird, T. F., Shoup, R., Kuh, G D. and Schwarz, M.J. (2008) 'The effects of discipline on deep approaches to student learning and college outcomes'. *Research in Higher Education*, 49, pp. 469–94

Neumann, A. (2009) *Professing to Learn: Creating Tenured Lives and Careers in the American Research University*. Baltimore, MD: Johns Hopkins University Press

Oleson, A. and Hora, M. T. (2014) 'Teaching the way they were taught? Revisiting the sources of teaching knowledge and the role of prior experience in shaping faculty teaching practices'. *Higher Education*, 68 (1), pp. 29–45

O'Meara, K. (2005). 'The courage to be experimental: how one faculty learning community influenced faculty teaching careers, understanding of how students learn, and assessment'. *The Journal of Faculty Development*, 20 (3), pp. 153–60

O'Meara, K., Terosky, A. L. and Neumann, A. (2008) 'Faculty careers and work lives: a professional growth perspective'. *ASHE Higher Education Report*, 34(3). San Francisco: Jossey-Bass

Ramsden, P. (2003) *Learning to teach in higher education*. London: Routledge Falmer

Ramsden, P., Prosser, M., Trigwell, K. and Martin, E. (2007) 'University teachers' experiences of academic leadership and their approaches to teaching'. *Learning and Instruction*, 17 (2), pp. 140–55

Rojas, F. (2012). 'Social movements and the university' in Bastedo, M. N. (Ed.), *The Organization of Higher Education: Managing Colleges for a New Era*. Baltimore, MD: Johns Hopkins University Press, pp. 256–77

Ruscio, K. (1987) 'Many sectors, many professions' in Clark, B. (Ed.), *The Academic Profession: National, Disciplinary, and Institutional Settings*. Berkeley: University of California Press

Schuster, J. H. and Finkelstein, M. J. (2006) *The American Faculty: The Restructuring of Academic Work and Careers*. Baltimore, MD: Johns Hopkins University Press

Shavelson, R. J. (2010) *Measuring College Learning Responsibly: Accountability in a New Era*. Stanford, CA: Stanford University Press

Shulman, L. (1986) 'Those who understand: knowledge growth in teacher'. *Educational Researcher*, 15 (2), pp. 4–31

Smart, J. C., Feldman, K. A. and Ethington, C. A. (2000) *Academic Disciplines: Holland's Theory and the Study of College Students and Faculty*. Nashville, TN: Vanderbilt University Press

Stark, J. S. (2000) 'Planning introductory college courses: content, context, and form'. *Instructional Science*, 28, pp. 413–38

Sunal, D. W., Hodges, J., Sunal, C. S., Whitaker, K. W., Freeman, L. M., Edwards, L. and Odell, M. (2001) 'Teaching science in higher education: faculty professional development and barriers to change'. *School Science and Mathematics*, 101 (5), pp. 246–57

Trowler, P., Knight, P. and Saunders, M. (2003) *Change Thinking, Change Practice*. York: Higher Education Academy

Weiner, B. (2010) 'The development of an attribution-based theory of motivation: a history of ideas'. *Educational Psychologist*, 45 (1), pp. 28–36

Wieman, C., Perkins, K. and Gilbert, S. (2010) 'Transforming science education at large research universities: a case study in progress'. *Change*, 42, pp. 6–14

6
Institutional (teaching) entrepreneurs wanted! – Considerations on the professoriate's agentic potency to enhance academic teaching in Germany

CHRISTIAN J. SCHMID AND SABINE LAUER

Introduction: how to make teaching count

German state-controlled universities have to satisfy two, at best, equally valued tasks: research and teaching. Due to the emergence of multiversities, the status-ranked hierarchization of scientific disciplines, the massification of higher education, and New Public Management (NPM) reforms, the interrelation of academic research *and* teaching (see Neumann, 1996) is posing serious challenges for the management of universities and the professoriate. How does one teach effectively while simultaneously being highly productive in research? Or vice versa. The doxa of the academic field (see Bourdieu, 1975), however, predisposes academics and universities alike to seek scientific authority through research and *not* teaching. Professors, particularly junior academics, must constantly readjust preferences about how much time and effort to spend on one at the cost of the other. Other than research, which is embedded in scientific communities and transcends the membership at a specific university, academic teaching exclusively occurs within the local confinements of universities. Teaching is more directly administered by and accountable to a particular university organization. It is thus the task of academic teaching where a university's leadership may have some decision-making leeway to purposefully coordinate its members' activities via (hierarchized) authority relations. But, what are the chances for the universities to help emancipate academic teaching and thereby equilibrate the skewed nexus of research and teaching?

In this chapter, we present selected intermediate findings from research that originally set out to investigate into four award-winning German universities' endeavours to 'make teaching count'. Eventually, our empirical data prompted us to strongly argue the significance of individual, highly committed professors as indispensable initiators and key drivers of organizational change: institutional (teaching) entrepreneurs. We will therefore delineate exemplary vignettes of such distinct actors in the main section of this article by sketching

109

their professional trajectories, personal characteristics, motives, and strategies of action to implement institutional change: when, why, and how did they take on their mission to make teaching count at their university? We will conclude with lessons to be learned considering how the universities can effectively create conditions that trigger and support individual bottom-up commitment in an organization where the power of top-down *hierarchical* management is distinctively weak (see Hüther and Krücken, 2013).

The institutional status quo of teaching in German academia: a short situation report

Before arguing the specifics of our cases, we want to give a broad-brush sketch of the status quo and recent developments pertaining to the practice of academic teaching in German higher education institutions (HEIs).

Why teaching does not count within (German) academia

In the last decade, national policy-makers pushed hard to promote top-level research and thereby further intensified the predatory competition between research and teaching. Most notably, the *German Federal Ministry of Education and Research* (*Bundesministerium für Bildung und Forschung;* BMBF), together with the *German Research Foundation* (*Deutsche Forschungsgemeinschaft;* DFG), launched the so-called 'Excellence Initiative' in 2005 (see OECD, 2014). This multi-billion competitive funding programme is designed to leverage selected German universities into world-class research institutions. Only a small oligopoly of German universities was destined ever to get the 'research-excellent' label and, thus, all the prize money (Hartmann, 2009). However, this omnipresent, nationwide initiative awaked deluded desires throughout German HEIs to further expand their research capacities.

Universities are primarily rated and ranked on the basis of their research output (see Marginson and van der Wende, 2007). According to our own survey data, in which we asked the rectorates of all state-controlled German universities (N = 192; Schmid and Wilkesmann, 2015, p. 85) about their strategic development, we can confirm universal aspirations towards more research-intensive profiles. When asked about their future plans, the rectorates (n = 100) had to locate themselves on a five-point Likert-scale continuum between either *unambiguously* research- or teaching-centred. Of the respondents, 46 per cent clearly want to go into the direction of research; only 13 per cent aim for a more teaching-intensive university. Not a single German university strives for an exclusively teaching-centred profile. German state-controlled universities can afford to strategically neglect academic teaching because they do not have to worry about attracting students. They, rather, try to ward off a

Institutional (teaching) entrepreneurs wanted! • 111

record-breaking flood of students (Destatis, 2014), for which they have not enough capacity and from whom they are also not allowed to collect any tuition fees.

Academic teaching could almost be seen as the German professor's stepchild, neglected in favour of research or other side activities (see Kamenz and Wehrle, 2007). As in other countries, the German professoriate feels increasingly pressured to conform to the strong currency of research indicators, such as citation indices or the amount of third-party funding (Drennan et al., 2013).[1] For the individual academic, salary structures, promotions, and tenure depend more on research productivity than instructional performance. Unlike in other countries, where teaching is held in higher esteem and where there are well-established optional career tracks based on teaching activities, careers are still exclusively and widely dependent on research productivity in German academia (see Hilbrich and Schuster, 2014). For example, in German sociology, 'the chances of getting tenure increase by about 10 percent with every published SSCI article' (Lutter and Schröder, 2014, p. 19). In particular, German early career academics tend to emphasize their research rather than teaching when building an academic career (Wosnitza et al., 2014). In one of our own nationwide surveys (see Wilkesmann and Schmid, 2014, p. 12), 51 per cent of the responding professors (n = 1518) claim that, besides other qualifications, their 'teaching beliefs and attitudes' did not play any role in getting appointed as a tenured professor (*Professur*). Other than the students' in situ reactions and largely ignored student evaluations, teaching is a 'sacred affair' behind closed classroom doors that is shielded from collegial criticism. German professors do not visit and peer review each other's lectures and/or seminars. Only 17 per cent of the respondents (n = 1539) in the aforementioned survey would 'agree' or 'totally agree' that there is 'lively collegial exchange about teaching practice'.

To conclude with a bold claim: in German academia, only research really counts!

Efforts to make teaching count (too)

Obviously, there is enough 'taste for research (productivity)', but how to develop more 'appetite for teaching'? In recent years, increasing numbers of campaigns and public criticism have put the issue of teaching back on the agenda of higher education politics. Most of these intermittent calls and recommendations by students, academics, the *German Council of Science and Humanities* (*Wissenschaftsrat*), politicians responsible for education, employers' associations or media representatives remained without significant consequences. However, the Bologna reform had an unexpectedly dramatic initial impact, necessitating a revived awareness of the *why* and *how* of academic teaching, with universities being forced to redesign their curricula. Yet, only a few universities systematically took advantage of this occasion by seriously reflecting on their teaching styles, formats, and course designs. The majority of the professoriate skilfully forced their extant programmes into the new corset. It was not until 2010 that the German Federal Government would ultimately manifest its political intention to substantially improve study conditions and teaching performance by ratifying the so-called *Quality Pact for Teaching* (*Qualitätspakt Lehre*; BMBF, 2015a). Between 2011 and 2020, this initiative will fund over 90 per cent of public German HEIs, with grants totalling about €2 billion. To apply for this funding programme, universities were obliged to reconsider organizational policies, elaborate operational strategies, and suggest concrete measures to improve academic teaching.

In addition to government agencies, other interest groups have already been engaged in important groundwork for the advancement of academic teaching. Probably best known is the sponsorship of the *Donors' Association for the Promotion of Science and the Humanities in Germany* (*Stifterverband*), which collaborated with the *Conference of Ministers of Education* (*Kultusministerkonferenz*). In 2009, they launched a national *Competition for Teaching Excellence* (*Wettbewerb exzellente Lehre*), with grants totalling €10 million (Brockerhoff *et al.*, 2014). Furthermore, since 2006, they have been offering the most prestigious annual teaching award in Germany, which is endowed with €50,000: the 'ars legendi Preis'.

To conclude: at present, there is a climate of heightened political awareness and contested public debate about the many ills of higher education instruction in Germany. With the availability of previously non-existent funds, there is a real window of opportunity to make teaching count, *too*!

In search of best practice managerial governance of academic teaching

The crucial question, however, is how to best allocate resources and managerial efforts to most effectively improve the 'quality' of academic teaching and study conditions? This is where our ongoing research project, *Transformational Governance of Academic Teaching* (acronym: *TeachGov*; BMBF, 2015b), funded by the German BMBF, comes into play. Our research agenda is to find out how state-controlled German universities can systematically upgrade the overall prestige and, hence, the performance[2] of academic teaching. What can a university's senior management do to make teaching count?

We therefore explore, try to understand, and scrutinize award-winning teaching initiatives at various German universities to eventually provide policy-makers and management practitioners with *applicable knowledge* in the form of management interventions and/or organizational design templates. Theoretically speaking, our current research assignment is concerned with proposing solutions in the 'managerial self-governance' dimension of HEIs (see de Boer *et al.*, 2007). We prefer to talk about the *managerial governance* of academics, which we define as all deliberately induced, top-down management interventions to (re)design, establish, further cultivate or irritate (in)formal organizational arrangements so specified groups of members are (in)directly inclined to share predefined meanings and/or value-prescribed preferences that make them commit to designated areas of activity or objectives and (re/inter)act in desired behavioural patterns.

Methodology

Purposive sampling of award-winning HEIs

To begin with, we confronted the challenge of identifying universities with 'extraordinary' teaching performance. In contrast to academic research, there are no consolidated definitions that allow for indicators to nationally compare and rank German universities with respect to overall teaching performance or 'quality'.[3] The nationwide statistics on HEIs that are available from the *Federal Statistical Office* (Destatis, 2014) are limited to such indicators as the total number of students and passed examinations, average length of study, percentage of first-degree qualifiers, or completion rates. These data rather capture the efficiency of processing *quantities* of students than the *quality* of teaching and learning. Other than that, all German universities systematically conduct teaching evaluations as part of their mandatory quality assurance procedures. However, these evaluations do not conform to a single, nationally comparable standard (Schmidt, 2009). Anyway, we were looking for extraordinarily supportive *organizational frameworks* (see Feldman and Paulsen, 1999), which cannot be adequately captured with simplistic key performance indicators such as drop-out quotas.

We eventually found exemplary 'best practice' cases by taking advantage of the already mentioned national *Competition for Teaching Excellence*, which was started in 2010 to promote 'excellence of teaching' initiatives at German universities (see Brockerhoff et al., 2014). Of 108 submitted proposals from 110 universities, a pre-selection of 24 institutions were judged in a public hearing. The jury was composed of an advisory board and an international jury of 200 representatives from universities and politics. The ten winners were awarded with up to €1 million each to reward and further support their extraordinary institutional efforts on behalf of excellent academic teaching.

After thoroughly reviewing the publicly available documentation of this competition, we consulted project managers from the executing *Donors' Association*. They helped us to pre-select and recruit a 'purposive sample' (Flick, 2009, p. 122) of four state-controlled universities and the respective contact persons. Our limited sample of n = 4 universities nonetheless represents a welcome heterogeneity ranging from two small, teaching-intensive universities of applied sciences to two large universities that are known for their internationally competitive research excellence. For the base year 2015, the

German system of higher education (see HRK, 2015) can be generally divided into 88 *state-controlled* universities (*Universitäten*), 104 universities of applied sciences (*Fachhochschulen*) and 46 universities of art and music (*Kunst- und Musikhochschulen*). In contrast to the research-oriented universities shaped by the Humboldtian idea of detached study and scholarship, the German universities of applied sciences were founded to provide job-specific, needs-based vocational training, and application-oriented research.[4] The teaching load of professors at universities of applied sciences (18 hours per week) is twice as much as at universities, with a lower faculty–student ratio and fewer or no academic staff. In addition to a PhD degree, applicants for professorship at a university of applied sciences are required to have work experience of at least five years (including a minimum of three years outside academia).

A directed approach to the qualitative content analysis of expert interviews

After a prior screening of the *Competition for Teaching Excellence* documentation, university websites, and press releases, we conducted semi structured face-to-face 'expert interviews' (Flick, 2009, pp. 165–9; Littig and Pöchhacker, 2014, pp. 1087–9). Our aim was to understand and learn from each university's first-hand experiences about their journey to and institutional continuation of 'teaching excellence'. Therefore, we singled out various 'experts' (Littig and Pöchhacker, 2014, p. 1088) at each institution who are characterized by their privileged knowledge resources about the investigated initiatives.

Our interviewees can be categorized as follows:

- high-ranking organizational decision/policy-makers (members of the rectorate; n = 4),
- award-winning and/or recommended teaching practitioners/advocates (n = 9 full professors/faculty deans; n = 1 academic senior councillor [*akademischer Oberrat*]),
- higher education management professionals (n = 7; e.g. heads of centres for the enhancement of teaching and learning, quality assurance staff, project managers).

The n = 21 interviews lasted somewhere between 60 and 90 minutes, totalling over 1,760 minutes of audiotaped and fully transcribed verbal data.[5]

To elucidate the role of the institutional teaching entrepreneurs' agency, we chose a theory-guided 'directed approach to content analysis' (Hsieh and Shannon, 2005, pp. 1281–3). We therefore reconsidered striking empirical observations, which then informed our consultation of theory – institutional entrepreneurship/chordal triad of human agency (see next paragraph) – to develop a frame of coding categories[6] and apply it to our material. After the computer-assisted coding procedure was completed, we systematically compared the content of our interviews in a last stage of contextual analysis in which we interpreted commonalities and differences within (triangulation and cross-validation of perspectives) and across our cases (sample of HEIs).

Theoretical considerations: the agentic potency of 'teaching entrepreneurs'

In accordance with our research agenda, we began by asking the rectorates about their *managerial governance* to 'make teaching count'. These, however, would not in any way credit themselves. They readily admitted that the success – that would later be attributed to the 'university' and its highest representatives – hugely benefited from preliminary efforts of individual actors. Most rectorates would forward us to these key players, without whom nothing would and/or could have been achieved. We soon grew aware of the vital role of the 'institutional entrepreneurs' (see DiMaggio, 1988) within these universities who made use of their social skills and resources to significantly impact and push through a redefinition of the status quo ante of academic teaching: institutional change agents, 'who, whether or not they initially intended to change their institutional environment, initiate, and actively participate in the implementation of changes that diverge from existing institutions' (Battilana *et al.*, 2009, p. 70). This understanding of institutional entrepreneurship quite adequately characterizes the protagonist trailblazers of quality teaching found in our study in two respects. First, these agents almost always began reflecting on and altering their immediate teaching (environment) for no other reason than their very own personal concerns. Unlike most of their colleagues, they reflect on, educated themselves about and experimented with their teaching practices and formats. They did so without any *direct* institutional support or inducement (e.g. teaching sabbaticals, workshops, mission statements, incentives, or directives). Second, these 'teaching entrepreneurs' thereby consequently deviate from the existing modus operandi by making the obligation to teach more important than a 'conscientious fulfilment of duty'.[7] It is certainly not the norm to make teaching a big deal. It is an illicit – and almost 'heroic' – act, moreover, to violate the informal collegial non-aggression pact by openly denouncing grievances in others' approaches to teaching at the departmental level.

To capture the organizational impact of these 'teaching entrepreneurs', we will – as prominently proposed by Battilana (2004) – consult Emirbayer and Mische's (1998) concept of 'human agency':

> as a temporally embedded process of social engagement, informed by the *past* (in its *habitual aspect*), but also oriented toward the future (as a *'projective' capacity* to imagine alternative possibilities) and toward the present (as a *'practical-evaluative'* capacity to contextualize past habits and future projects within the contingencies of the moment).
>
> (p. 962, emphasis added)

In the next section, we will commence with our findings in the form of four vignettes of outstanding personalities and their crusade to advance teaching within their universities: *the* originating entrepreneurs and champions of the awarded teaching initiatives. We will investigate *why* and *how* they achieved their agency to eventually change their institutional environments. In doing so, we will refer to the 'chordal triad' (ibid., p. 970) of human agency by analytically disaggregating the iterative from the practical-evaluative and projective element of our teaching entrepreneurs' reflections and strategies of action (see ibid.).

- The *iterational element* is understood as a kind of inertial habitus that describes 'the selective reactivation by actors of past patterns of thought and action, as routinely incorporated in practical activity, thereby giving stability and order to social universes and helping to sustain identities, interactions, and institutions over time' (ibid., p. 971).
- The *practical-evaluative element* 'entails the capacity of actors to make practical and normative judgement among alternative possible trajectories of action, in response to the emerging demands, dilemmas, and ambiguities of presently evolving situations' (ibid.).
- The *projective element* 'encompasses the imaginative generation by actors of possible future trajectories of action, in which received structures of thought and action may be creatively reconfigured in relation to actors' hopes, fears and desires for the future' (ibid.).

Theoretically and empirically, these interrelated orientations always occur simultaneously but in different configurations. Contingent on specific and ever-evolving socio-structural contexts or the progress of change processes, action is either more dominantly oriented towards the past, the present, or the future ('dominant tone'; ibid., p. 972).

Findings: vignettes of exemplary cases

We want to note that, due to limited space, the presentation of our findings lacks in-depth description and contextualization of all relevant interrelations and dynamics as they evolved throughout the different stages of change.

The dynamic (manager) duo

The first vignette portrays two male professors of economics who – as a 'dynamic duo' – turned their small university of applied sciences upside down. After their mission was accomplished, the now award-winning university offers regular didactics workshops, well-established learning communities, professionalized didactics support, and a 'teaching and learning' service centre. At this university, academic teaching is no longer everyone's 'private affair' but an openly discussed and generally valued common agenda. We would most convincingly witness this spirit when we covertly participated at the annual 'Teaching Day' celebrations and workshops. As documented on the university website and in interview statements, the rectorate intends to capitalize on the unique selling point of superior *'quality* teaching and learning' in its strategic (impression) management to attract students and acquire additional external funds.

Iterational dimension: top management professionals qua habitus

Both economics professors had defining careers as top managers in international companies before they decided to apply for professorships. They opted for academia because they liked the idea of settling down and exchanging their stressful expatriate life for a new challenge. They are still very much influenced by their manager habitus formed in the private sector. In their narrations, they strikingly made constant use of management rhetoric and metaphoric. Their professional past life is apparent in their many judgements about the idiosyncrasies of organizing universities and their exemplary references of how things were performed much more efficiently in the management of for-profit companies. In their 'economic reasoning' about the 'many ills' of academia, these professors would – unlike higher education researchers (see Musselin, 2007) – not hesitate to compare universities with businesses.

> However, we are financed by taxpayers' money; we have to fulfil educational responsibilities, which ought to be measured by the very same criteria of efficiency just as private sector companies …. how to most efficiently organize this enterprise for what specified outcomes. Looking at our [university] figures, I am prompted to say, we would be bankrupt long ago. A driving school that must admit that only 60 per cent of its customers get a driver's licence would not survive the competition.
> (Interviewee 2, dynamic duo)

Practical-evaluative dimension: frustration made them do it!

The most dominant reason why these two professors took on responsibility and made a difference was the nagging frustration with the conditions under which they had to perform their teaching. After re-entering academia, they felt 'thrown into cold water'. As novices with no prior training or any institutional support, they had to 'learn the hard way' how to cope with the immense work overload of teaching at universities of applied sciences.

> Maybe my willingness to suffer was just not high enough to endure this frustration. Therefore, I told myself, if I must teach 18 hours, that is two days for 30 weeks per year; this adds up to 60 days of suffering and 300 days

of joy. When this equation won't work out for me, then I'll have to seriously reconsider my teaching job. That [thought] was the main cause for my dissatisfaction.... It became very clear that, in this culture, within these structures, I just cannot go on like this until my retirement.

(Interviewee 2, dynamic duo)

Both professors could also not adapt to a culture of 'academic loners', where everyone minds his own business and where there is no collegial exchange about academic teaching. In their former management careers, they were habituated to a culture of daily corridor talks, ongoing collegial discussions, and intensive exchange of work and/or organization-related narrations. This reticence made them even more suspicious of the attitude of indifference they experienced at their university. No one seemed to seriously care about the alleged core task of this institution: academic teaching. They were bewildered about the 'non-confrontational climate' at universities, where neither colleagues nor the rectorate would intervene in the case of obviously poor teaching performance (e.g. above-average student drop-out rates or below-average student evaluations of teaching scores).

In contrast to their peers, however, they would not allow themselves to put up with their dissatisfaction and compromise their self-expectation to provide quality teaching. First, they independently strived to manage their situation for the better. One day, these two professors engaged in the first of their sporadic chats about their common misery. From then on, they joined forces to embark on their mission. Characteristic of their managerial habitus and training, they thoroughly analysed their situation before collaboratively working out possible strategies for organizational change. For example, one of them conducted an in-depth network analysis based on a survey to map the structures of collegial communication about teaching experiences. After spotting an opportunity to bring their efforts into effect, they worked out a pilot project informed by their prior diagnosis and consultations. Long before submitting their proposal to the *Competition for Teaching Excellence*, they, first, advocated their plans before the rectorate to ensure full top-down support. After successfully acquiring the funding, they skilfully managed and continued to relentlessly propagate their project, so it did not lose momentum. They invested serious efforts in branding and marketing their initiative by designing a catchy logo and editing a newsletter. They negotiated reductions of teaching load for the participants of 'teaching and learning' communities, hosted workshops, and initiated and organized a large annual conference (Teaching Day) to report and advertise the progress of their project.

Projective dimension: striving for constant change

On a personal level, both professors are still driven by their managerial aspirations for constant change, task-oriented self-optimization, and the entrepreneurial lust of 'getting things done' and 'creating something of value'. On an institutional level, they strived to achieve some profound change in the larger organizational environment.

Being the ideal type of project manager always in search of new challenges, one partner of this 'dynamic duo' decided to step back, little by little, to take on new projects. He would withdraw his *full* engagement as soon as follow-up financing was ensured to reappoint didactics service personnel who would continue the extant achievements. Not being a higher education researcher in the first place, the other professor would, nonetheless, capitalize on his practical experiences and study of the academic field to eventually publish articles and obtain a second doctoral degree. In the near future (at the time of writing), he will even take a sabbatical to further intensify his new scholarly interest in HEIs, with a research stay abroad.

The managerialist dean

The second vignette portrays a former businessman in the engineering sector turned 'managerialist dean' at the faculty of mechanical engineering at a large university of applied sciences. His main merit is having invented and presided over a university-wide procedure to systematically assess, develop, and improve the quality of study programmes. In the course of negotiating the implementation of his initiative, he was – as reported by the rectorate – also instrumental in involving and *redefining* faculty deans as responsible leaders instead of mere representatives inhibited by the doctrine of 'pleasing collegiality'.

Iterative dimension: free, at last!

In his past life, this entrepreneur established a thriving firm. His final decision to give up his *full-time* engagement in the private economy was triggered by informal requests to apply for professorship. Coincidentally, he was in the fortunate situation of being able to choose between two attractive offers: a chair at a research-intensive university of technology (*Technische Universität*) and another chair at a large university of applied sciences. He turned down the first option because he anticipated significantly less administrative bureaucracy or annoying committee work and more freedom of self-determined action at a university of applied sciences. At the beginning of his professorship, he retained his company, but he eventually sold it to former employees. Thus, income and any existential hardships were no longer an action-guiding, motivational concern for him. What has remained, however, is his entrepreneurial spirit and assertive leadership personality.

Practical-evaluative dimension: just do it (yourself)!

In contrast to the 'dynamic duo' of the previous vignette, this 'teaching entrepreneur' was less of an *employee* adhering to a pre-existing social order, but rather a recalcitrant *self-employed* character. He passionately led his chair (institute) much like his very own 'company'. He also made full use of his formal authority as a dean to overrule previous (informal) conventions. For example, he arbitrarily upgraded the part-time position of the vice dean for teaching and learning (*Studiendekan*) to a full-time job.

His motivation to initiate change was not so much spurred by the personal despair he experienced in his own teaching activities. He was primarily motivated to 'optimize a product' in such ways as he was accustomed to from his days as the owner of a firm.

> Then came Bologna, the chance to create something different, new study programmes, and, at that time, I said to myself, if I must do it anyway, prepare an accreditation [of study programmes], then I will make the most out of this obligation and invent new curricula. Not just as a necessary evil. But rather just like a good engineer would go about such a task. To create a product and not a graduate. And when I have to launch a new product, then I have to follow a certain procedure, which I am very familiar with because of my former career. And this is exactly how I did it ... I let my staff members define the product in advance. I asked my colleagues [professors at his institute] who wanted to contribute. I let them take a look at it, consulted with them. I did a benchmark, product analysis and, accordingly, defined a graduate profile. Later on, we would discuss how to best implement these predefined competencies, as a product: a process instruction.
>
> (Interviewee 8, managerialist dean)

Not typical of German faculty deans, he admittedly commited himself to a *task-oriented* 'authoritarian' leadership style. He was willing to engage in open confrontation to enforce reflection and get things accomplished.

> Confrontation is positive. I can handle that ... A conflict wherein the involved parties are honest with each other. There may be people who say 'I am not interested. I became a professor [not manager]. I fulfil my duties, teach 18 hours per week and, apart from that, I want to be left alone'. That's okay with me as long as these colleagues do not disrupt our efforts .... In such a case I make the message very clear: 'Stay at home' [do not come to our project meeting].
>
> (Interviewee 8, managerialist dean)

In general, this professor does not conform to the 'professorial attitude' of putting up with all the alleged limitations of operating within the bureaucratic, petty-minded culture of German universities. Instead, he tries to circumvent inflexible regulations and compensate scarcity by seeking out alternative resources to finance or cross-subsidize ventures. As a self-confident teaching 'entrepreneur/intrapreneur' (see Hisrich, 1990, p. 209), he demonstrates initiative and assumes full responsibility for potential failure.

> This is not the sort of thinking I need here [at our faculty]. Money is not a thing. To give a classical example of universities: there is a total of €5 million of external funds. Then, people immediately start thinking about how to cut this overall budget into small pieces. My approach is entrepreneurial. When a colleague proposes 'I have a great idea', then I will do my best to somehow raise the money. Or I will pre-finance research assistants for a colleague who wants to push his research and raise external grants .... That is the risk I will readily take [as the faculty dean].
> (Interviewee 8, managerialist dean)

Projective dimension: elitist pioneering role

This 'managerialist dean' is driven by his competitive spirit to further establish his department as a best practice role model within his university. In doing so, he is a welcome 'key player' who is in frequent contact with the rectorate, which he regularly advises by request. In the end, all of his aspirations and efforts at the faculty level are to nurture a 'culture of excellence' and provide an elitist institutional environment to attract the best future students and colleagues.

> As a faculty we have a leading role [in this university]. We are at the forefront of demonstrating what is possible and the others follow the lead ... I imagine we will establish quite an elitist club [at our faculty] where only those can join who strive for ... [or] who perform, peer-reviewed research, cooperation with prestigious research universities ... highly accomplished colleagues. Where it is an honour to be a member of this institution.
> (Interviewee 8, managerialist dean)

The didactic-/technophile engineer

Unlike the previous vignettes, where manager personalities would dominantly act out their entrepreneurial vitality, the following case portrays a male professor of ecological engineering who is genuinely concerned with the *didactics* of teaching itself. He can be credited with introducing, promoting, and guiding the large-scale implementation of e-learning techniques in a research-excellent technical university.

Iterative dimension: technological affinity

After graduating with a PhD in engineering, this 'teaching entrepreneur' took over the position of the managing director in a private sector planning office, which is a job he still holds to this day. Prior to his current appointment in academia, he spent a three-year stint at a university of applied sciences. After he tired of the 'school-like' teaching culture and became annoyed by his former colleagues' dispassionate work attitude, he applied for a vacant chair. This chair was formerly held by his doctoral supervisor and pertains to one of the best German research universities, with excellent research staff, superior facilities, and privileged financial resources.

Socialized as an engineer, this professor self-reportedly had no awareness and expertise about the didactics of teaching at the very beginning of his academic career. However, he would build on his technical affinity with the solution-oriented pragmatism typical of 'German engineering' to get his endeavours started: 'As an engineer one has not cut one's teeth on didactic methods. We are all auto-didactics.... And engineers favour practicable applications [and not theory talk]' (interviewee 7, technophile engineer).

Practical-evaluative dimension: getting the students' attention

Aside from his strong value-rational conviction about the absolute worth of the Humboldtian idea of the 'unity of research *and teaching*', his main motivation to engage in the didactics of teaching was the ambition to get all his students' full attention. As a distinguished technophile, he was quickly drawn to the promises of technology-enhanced teaching and learning. After becoming sufficiently acquainted with the methodology of blended learning, he would pioneer this approach to teaching within his faculty. To cite the appreciative vice-rector for teaching and learning: 'If we just had more of his kind in each and every faculty ... we would be doing even better now. With little money, he has pushed this topic right from the start by constantly putting the issue of blended learning back on the agenda' (interviewee 6, vice-rector).

In addition to his engineering capacities and technical competences, his intrapreneurial actions are also shaped by his managerial habitus. Strategically smart, he advertised his inventions and aspirations as the means to excel in competition. At his elitist university, all staff compete within a distinctive and generally valued 'culture of high performance'. For example, there is a public ranking of individual teaching performances. Low performers are 'symbolically' punished with a slight reduction of their basic funds (*Grundmittel*) at the level of individual chairs. Such 'neo-liberal' performance-discriminating managerialism is broadly rejected as highly dysfunctional in German academia. At this university, however, professors actually seem to be more inclined to observe, compare, and mimic each other's achievements. Showing us the most recent ranking of student evaluations of teaching, this professor commented as follows:

> Look at the scores, the folks at the bottom. For the most part, these are senior professors who will retire sooner or later, anyway. This is where biology

[extinction] will resolve the problem. The case is somewhat different for all newly appointed, junior colleagues. Nobody within this cohort wants to take a place down below [bottom of ranking]. Again, we are part of a highly competitive environment here. We literally fight for resources. And when you trigger this competitive spirit in such ways, then it will actually work. I am quite convinced that this works for engineers but also philosophers. Does not matter. This is not dependent on socialization in engineering. It has to do with appealing to the competitive spirit of humans.

(Interviewee 7, technophile engineer)

We were told many tales indicative of this competitive spirit; for example, one professor envied his colleague's new online learning platform in which excited students simulated business scenarios (serious gaming). He then copied this innovation and took it one step further, with even more features. Obviously, the competitive quest for teaching excellence has become contagious. It did not lead to a 'winner take all' mentality, in which the jealous or indifferent member of staff resigns; it caused more of an 'elevator effect', enhancing the general status and prestige of academic teaching to higher levels.

Projective dimension: pushing the agenda for his university

In the meantime, this professor heads a task force of like-minded peers comprising distinguished experts for specific blended learning methods and tools. As a 'rectorate's delegate', he also presides over a commission that is in charge of a seven-digit sum (in euros) to support future blended learning projects. The 'technophile engineer' has established himself as a 'competent authority' (Wrong, 1995, p. 52) for blended learning didactics. He is often referred to for consultation, interviews or expert talks within, but also outside, his university.

The rebel ambassador of academic teaching

The last vignette reflects on a professor of electrical engineering and information technology at a large, top-performing research university. Among his many accomplishments, he has been granted considerable funds from a nationally recognized fellowship for teaching excellence to further realize his mission. He is also a member of the rectorate where he, against expectation, does *not* preside over the 'teaching and learning' devision.

Iterative dimension: the deviant serial entrepreneur/manager

Before joining his university, this professor pursued a multi-faceted career in several private sector companies. Among other jobs, he worked as a research engineer, consultant, project manager, chief technological officer (CTO), and managing director. He still runs his privately owned consultancy firm. Possibly due to his former experience in corporate business, he features a deviant, sometimes cynical attitude towards some logics (or illusions) constitutive of the academic field. The subsequent excerpt from an interview with him exemplarily illustrates his distinctively 'disillusioned' attitude:

> I believe, with a background in the private sector you internalized a certain canon of values. And that canon of values is different from the one in academia .... There are many pseudo-values, pseudo-metrics in academia .... In the private industry sector there is a clear-cut value function, which is not always the most ethical and fair one. But you cannot manipulate it. I'm talking about profit [only]. And if my customers pay for my products then I was successful ... And after a successful career in business you are socialized differently. In various regards. And you go back to university for other reasons than pecuniary ones or to make a career.
>
> (Interviewee 18, rebel ambassador)

This late-ordained professor's amazement about the idiosyncrasies of life in academia pertains to many issues, such as leadership or human resource development: 'Sometime in the Middle Ages we abolished serfdom, except within universities' (interviewee 18, rebel ambassador). In our judgement, he mimics the superordinate *anti-hero* among his pure-bred academic colleagues, who subordinate themselves to the mainstream norms of accomplishing or safeguarding 'academic prestige'.

Practical-evaluative dimension: a man of action/conviction

Deeply shaped by his entrepreneurial 'go-getter' habitus, this professor puts his ideas into action, even if his decisions are not very popular with every one of his colleagues or staff members.

> I prompted my chair's whole staff to come join me into retreat for a weekend. Where we would let ourselves be inspired by pedagogues. To not always harp on the same string. And other campaigns, which would not make me friends in my faculty. The same goes for my term as dean of studies, where there was a lot of bloodshed during the implementation of the Bologna reform... This is doer-mentality. It's a good thing to just do it. To make things happen. I am not overly concerned with pleasing everybody.... They [colleagues] will surely get upset about this, lament about me introducing [a specific curricula design]. I'm like: 'if you don't like it, leave me alone'. The students decide what they will favour. And I provide them with more practice-oriented courses.
>
> (Interviewee 18, rebel ambassador)

As attested by other interviewees and informants, an idea-charismatic authority, charming demeanour, and social skills come to his aid to win over colleagues for his endeavours and prevent or overcome collegial resistance. He operates with the determination and persuasiveness of a *man of conviction*. In this way, he successfully launched many new and sometimes unusual formats of teaching and learning. His popular student-activating teaching style builds on his extroverted, inventive personality. He thrives on intensive interaction with his students and is not afraid of risking a loss of face or professorial, status-hierarchized authority.

> Over the years we have tested many things [in teaching], just because, like 'I don't give a damn. Let's do it'. It's amazing. You can do much more than you might imagine.... We did gymnastic exercises in the lecture hall and all kinds of gimmicks. Filmed it. Uploaded it to YouTube and showed it to our surprised pedagogues, who were like 'What? You do this with 500 students?' Of course. Why not? I can't stand this blocking attitude.... It's a matter of authenticity. I'm very aware of the fact that this is not for everybody. If colleagues imitate my style of teaching dressed in suit and tie, students will be like 'This bloke is out of his mind'. I must admit, those things are related to attitude and personality. However, I still won't tolerate that negative, refusing attitude. Impossible is nothing.
> (Interviewee 18, rebel ambassador)

Projective dimension: representing

On a personal level, this professor continues to try to enjoy himself as much as possible in teaching. Therefore, he keeps experimenting with new 'exiting' methods of interacting with his students, always preserving his curious 'white belt' mentality. On an institutional level, he has evolved into an ambassador for 'teaching excellence' within – but also outside – his university. He remains a bustling advocate for academic teaching. Because of his widely acknowledged expertise and entertaining qualities, he is in high demand as a keynote speaker or invited guest contributor at various symposia for academic teaching. On a more political side, he now presents his vision and exerts influence as a member or advisor in national higher education committees.

Conclusion: the 'triple s' strategy to (help) make teaching count

> That teaching mission should appear as a resounding priority throughout every institution involved in the delivery of higher education – a daily lived priority and not just worthy words in a mission statement. The truth about that daily lived reality, however, is an embarrassing disappointment. For research shows that serious commitment to best practice in the delivery of

this core teaching mission is not universal, is sporadic at best and frequently *reliant on the enlightened commitment of a few individuals.*
(Higher Level Group, 2013, p. 14, emphasis added)

This overall assessment of European Union's HEIs resonates well with our specific findings based on the study of best practice institutions. The achievements made at all the investigated universities were dependent on highly committed and socially skilled actors to bring about change. They are the merit of institutional teaching entrepreneurs who quasi-voluntarily – for whatever reason – take on the personal responsibility for systematic or organizational failures. Although the wording might be unduly exaggerated, it takes some 'heretic heroism' to initially step outside the mainstream, possibly or actually stigmatize oneself by openly criticizing the prevailing 'illusio' of the field: 'understood as a fundamental belief in the interest of the game and the value of the stakes which is inherent in that membership' (Bourdieu, 2000, p. 11). The portrayals of the 'teaching entrepreneurs' liberatingly demonstrate that it is possible to break with the extant 'working consensus' (Goffman, 1959, p. 9) not to touch on the issue of (poor quality) teaching. These professors renounce the 'bad faith' (see Berger, 1990, p. 56) in German academia, which suggests that there is no alternative other than to stick with the default choices and strategies of making or maintaining research-only 'careers'(!?) in academia. It is debatable how privileged and in what relevant aspects the actors within our sample are distinctively free to do so.[8] However, we must consider why vast numbers of equally privileged peers with comparable levels of frustration continue with their teaching obligations, and remain (stoically) indifferent in regards to deficient organizational support structures. Are they consciously 'gaming the system', being pimped by the system or serving as slaves to the game without really knowing?

To return to our initial research question: is there anything to be learned from these cases in regards of the *managerial governance* of universities? What can a university's senior management do other than helplessly hope for the initiative and managerial savvy of such exceptional personnel? If we once again bring to mind the vignettes of our study, we may draw some careful conclusions for top-down management interventions to enhance academic teaching. Thus, we pay tribute to the circumstance that leadership qua formal authority is rather impotent or delicate at universities where strategies of effective workplace resistance are very likely and manifold (see Anderson, 2008). In alignment with the three temporal dimensions of human agency, we propose a *'triple s' strategy* of interrelated measures: scouting, supporting, and scaling.

Scouting predominantly accounts for the iterative dimension of the professoriate's individual agency. Our most pragmatic advice would thus be to select or scout professors who already feature the desired qualities. If they are really serious about importing new impulses, rectorates might want to risk the recruitment of unorthodox and critically reflective actors different from the mainstream, pure-bred 'homo academicus' (Bourdieu, 1988). Rather than wait for the fortunate to come, a university's leadership may also benefit from already existing human resources. They must actively try to *systematically* identify professors who are extraordinarily engaged in some form of teaching activities but have remained unnoticed so far. Additionally, the rectorates can directly impact the status of academic teaching by consciously supervising or vetoing the decision-making process during appointment procedures or tenure tracks. This stage is where they can most effectively define some minimum standard of teaching qualifications that must not be compromised for (excellent) research performance. At the gates of organizational entry, they can clearly signal their appreciation of academic teaching to external and internal audiences. Some universities already demand mandatory participation in didactics workshops for newly appointed professors.

Supporting predominantly accounts for the practical-evaluative dimension of human agency. By focusing on individual agency, our empirical findings strongly suggest that the task of successfully making teaching count at German universities is the sole accomplishment of individual 'teaching heroes'. Of course, we are very aware of the 'individualist-managerial bias' (Weik, 2011, p. 471) within our argumentation. The institutional teaching entrepreneurs' agency is necessarily instrumental but not sufficient in bringing about substantial organizational change. As embedded agents (see Delbridge and Edwards, 2013), their institutional work (in progress) profits from windows of opportunity (e.g. external funding), depends on cooperation from colleagues, and thrives on support from the rectorate. Other than the willingness to provide mostly minor human or financial resources to help realize the professors' plans, the rectorate must openly express its support before the rest of the professoriate. By publicly acknowledging behaviours that exceed the job requirements, the senior management encourages institutional entrepreneurs to endure setbacks and keep going. They can decisively help the faculty to gain the 'symbolic power' which 'is typically deployed to further entrench the reality that defines as valuable the practices that are the basis of [their very own] legitimacy' (Hallett, 2003, p. 133). In our study, we could easily sense how serious the senior management of universities was in promoting and valuing efforts to improve teaching and study conditions. Nothing can be achieved by a rectorate whose contribution is *only* to show up at official events to deliver obligatory lip service and sweet talk. Much (more) can be accomplished if the rectorate credibly and consistently engages in ongoing collegial negotiations to help push through projects by carefully mediating and moderating vested interests.

Scaling predominantly accounts for the projective dimension to human agency. Pilot projects or initiatives at the level of individual chairs or departments cannot expand university-wide without the approval and appreciation of the senior management. The latter can significantly support extant, early stage developments with concrete and practical help (practical-evaluative dimension), but also by offering prospective trajectories. In our cases, the rectorates would involve, consult, and upgrade the teaching entrepreneurs as competent or 'expert authorities' (Wrong, 1995, p. 52). By publicly sharing and disseminating their mission or promoting those key players into some formal positions (e.g. vice-rector for teaching and learning, head of a commission), the rectorates manifest and potentiates their *future* agency on a larger scale.

In worst-case scenarios of no institutional support or obstructionist policy, previous achievements and personal willingness remain untapped potential for the organization, or completely dissolve. Not only are the universities dependent on the skilful engagement of entrepreneurial professors, the managerial governance of a university is also similarly facilitated or restricted by the leadership qualities of its decision-making authorities. Whatever sort of the above-proposed management intervention is to be executed, it is always a question of authenticity, commitment, style, and substance that predetermines its success or failure. After some years of studying the organization of German HEIs, we claim that insufficient hierarchical power over academics (see Hüther and Krücken, 2013; Musselin, 2007) is also a function of personal characteristics, management (in)competences, leadership styles, and a lack of will, accountability, and risk-taking of the 'powers to be'. With this in mind, it is up to the rectorates to decide if they *really wish* (at all!) and how skilfully they *actually can* manage to 'make teaching count'!

Notes

1 In contrast to research, teaching is a domain of scholarly activity for which there still are no standardized, comparable metrics that may be accounted for as individual performance indicators.
2 By teaching performance, we mean active deliberations about and real efforts invested into any form of preparing or conducting academic teaching (see also Wilkesmann and Schmid, 2012, p. 41). As organizational scholars, we do not intend to suggest any definition of (measurable) teaching *quality*.
3 We are very aware of the fact that research/publications indicators are controversially discussed (Osterloh and Kieser, 2015, pp. 307–12). In contrast to teaching indicators, well-established research indicators and performance-based funding schemes do inform individual research practices and strategies as well as decision-making in higher education policy (see, e.g., Biester and Flink, 2015).
4 In the meantime, they aspire to overcome their stigma as 'vocational schools' by intensifying and expanding their research activities to gradually converge into full-fledged doctoral-granting universities (Vogel, 2009, pp. 876–7).
5 In the process of translating interview passages that were originally conducted in the German language, the verbatim data have been stripped of colloquial language and filler words to present readable extracts to our readers.
6 The theory-driven categories of our coding procedure are broad and vague enough to not predetermine precariously strong biases imposed on the text (definitive concepts). We rather understand our categories as 'sensitizing concepts' (see Bowen, 2008) to organize our data analysis and still allow for some 'naturalistic' specification with narrations of lived experience as they are expressed by our indigenous informants.
7 We do not suggest that a routinized fulfilment of job obligations is *per se* of low quality.

Institutional (teaching) entrepreneurs wanted! • 129

8   Without going into further detail, we can affirm that our teaching entrepreneurs are anything but failures in research. Their extraordinary commitment to teaching is not caused by pressures to compensate for poor research performance. It seems like they want to excel in everything they turn their hands to.

References

Anderson, G. (2008) 'Mapping academic resistance in the managerial university'. *Organization*, 15 (2), pp. 251–70

Battilana, J. (2004) *Foundations for a Theory of Institutional Entrepreneurship: Solving the Paradox of Embedded Agency*. Retrieved from http://www.insead.edu/facultyresearch/research/doc.cfm?did=1412

Battilana, J., Leca, B. and Boxenbaum, E. (2009) 'How actors change institutions: towards a theory of institutional entrepreneurship'. *The Academy of Management Annals*, 3 (1), pp. 65–107

Berger, P. L. (1990) 'Sociological perspectives: society as drama' in Brissett, D. (Ed.), *Communication and Social Order: Life as Theater. A Dramaturgical Sourcebook* (2nd edn). New York: de Gruyter, pp. 51–61

Biester, C. and Flink, T. (2015) 'The elusive effectiveness of performance measurement in science: insights from a German university' in Welpe, I. M., Wollersheim, J., Ringelhan, S. and Osterloh, M. (Eds), *Incentives and Performance*. Wiesbaden: Springer, pp. 397–412

BMBF [Federal Ministry of Education and Research]. (2015a) *Quality Pact for Teaching: Championing Ideal Study Conditions*. Retrieved from http://www.qualitaetspakt-lehre.de/en/index.php

BMBF [German Federal Ministry of Education and Research]. (2015b) *TeachGov: Analyzing the Effects of the Transformational Governance of Academic Teaching*. Retrieved from http://www.hochschulforschung-bmbf.de/de/1711.php

Bourdieu, P. (1975) 'The specificity of the scientific field and the social conditions of the progress of reason'. *Social Science Information*, 14 (1), pp. 19–47

Bourdieu, P. (1988) *Homo academicus*. Stanford, CA: Stanford University Press

Bourdieu, P. (2000) *Pascalian meditations*. Stanford, CA: Stanford University Press

Bowen, G. (2008) 'Grounded theory and sensitizing concepts'. *International Journal of Qualitative Methods*, 5 (3), pp. 12–23

Brockerhoff, L., Stensaker, B. and Huisman, J. (2014) 'Prescriptions and perceptions of teaching excellence: a study of the national "Wettbewerb Exzellente Lehre" initiative in Germany'. *Quality in Higher Education*, 20 (3), pp. 235–54

de Boer, H., Enders, J. and Schimank, U. (2007) 'On the way towards New Public Management? The governance of university systems in England, the Netherlands, Austria, and Germany' in Jansen, D. (Ed.), *New Forms of Governance in Research Organizations: Disciplinary Approaches, Interfaces and Integration*. Dordrecht: Springer, pp. 137–54

Delbridge, R. and Edwards, T. (2013) 'Inhabiting institutions: critical realist refinements to understanding institutional complexity and change'. *Organization Studies*, 34 (7), pp. 927–47

Destatis (2014) '2.7 Millionen Studierende im Wintersemester 2014/2015'. *Statistisches Bundesamt*, 26 November. Retrieved from https://www.destatis.de/DE/PresseService/Presse/Pressemitteilungen/2014/11/PD14_419_213pdf.pdf?__blob=publicationFile

DiMaggio, P. J. (1988) 'Interest and agency in institutional theory' in Zucker, L. G. (Ed.), *Institutional Patterns and Organizations: Culture and Environment*. Cambridge, MA: Ballinger, pp. 3–21

Drennan, J., Clarke, M., Hyde, A. and Politis, Y. (2013) 'The research function of the academic profession in Europe' in Teichler, U. and Höhle, E. A. (Eds), *The Work Situation of the Academic Profession in Europe: Findings of a Survey in Twelve Countries*. Dordrecht: Springer, pp. 109–36

Emirbayer, M. and Mische, A. (1998) 'What is agency?' *American Journal of Sociology*, 103 (4), pp. 962–1023

Feldman, K. A. and Paulsen, M. B. (1999) 'Faculty motivation: the role of a supportive teaching culture'. *New Directions for Teaching and Learning, 1999*, 78, pp. 69–78
Flick, U. (2009) *An Introduction to Qualitative Research* (4th edn). Los Angeles: Sage
Goffman, E. (1959) *The Presentation of Self in Everyday Life*. Garden City/New York: Doubleday
Hallett, T. (2003) 'Symbolic power and organizational culture'. *Sociological Theory*, 21 (2), pp. 128–49
Hartmann, M. (2009) 'The excellence initiative: a change of paradigm of German university policy'. *Roczniki Nauk Społecznych*, 1 (37), pp. 171–93
Higher Level Group on the Modernisation of Higher Education. (2013) *Improving the Quality of Teaching and Learning in Europe's Higher Education Institutions*. Retrieved from http://ec.europa.eu/education/library/reports/modernisation_en.pdf
Hilbrich, R. and Schuster, R. (2014) 'Qualität durch Differenzierung? Lehrprofessuren, Lehrqualität und das Verhältnis von Lehre und Forschung'. *Beiträge zur Hochschulforschung*, 36 (1), pp. 70–89
Hisrich, R. D. (1990) 'Entrepreneurship/intrapreneurship'. *American Psychologist*, 45 (2), pp. 209–22
HRK [German Rectors' Conference]. (2015) *German Higher Education System*. Retrieved from http://www.hrk.de/uploads/media/GERMAN_HIGHER_EDUCATION_SYSTEM.pdf
Hsieh, H.-F. and Shannon, S. E. (2005) 'Three approaches to qualitative content analysis'. *Qualitative Health Research*, 15 (9), pp. 1277–88
Hüther, O. and Krücken, G. (2013) 'Hierarchy and power: a conceptual analysis with particular reference to new public management reforms in German universities'. *European Journal of Higher Education*, 3 (4), pp. 307–23
Kamenz, U. and Wehrle, M. (2007) *Professor Untat. Was faul ist hinter den Hochschulkulissen*. Berlin: Econ
Littig, B. and Pöchhacker, F. (2014) 'Socio-translational collaboration in qualitative inquiry: the case of expert interviews'. *Qualitative Inquiry*, 20 (9), pp. 1085–95
Lutter, M. and Schröder, M. (2014) 'Who becomes a tenured professor, and why?: Panel data evidence from German sociology, 1980–2013'. MPIfG Discussion Paper 14/19, Max Planck Institute for the Study of Societies, Cologne. Retrieved from http://www.mpifg.de/pu/dp_abstracts/dp14-19.asp
Marginson, S. and van der Wende, M. (2007) 'To rank or to be ranked: the impact of global rankings in higher education'. *Journal of Studies in International Education*, 11 (3–4), pp. 306–29
Musselin, C. (2007) 'Are universities specific organisations?' in Krücken, G., Kosmützky, A. and Torka, M. (Eds), *Towards a Multiversity? Universities Between Global Trends and National Traditions*. Piscataway, NJ: Transcript; distributed in North America by Transaction, pp. 63–84
Neumann, R. (1996) 'Researching the teaching-research nexus: a critical review'. *Australian Journal of Education*, 40 (1), pp. 5–18
OECD. (2014) *Promoting Research Excellence. New Approaches to Funding*. Retrieved from http://www.oecd-ilibrary.org/science-and-technology/promoting-research-excellence_9789264207462-en;jsessionid=ec0nkasih8ac7.x-oecd-live-03
Osterloh, M. and Kieser, A. (2015) 'Double-blind peer review: How to slaughter a sacred cow' in Welpe, I. M., Wollersheim, J., Ringelhan, S. and Osterloh, M. (Eds), *Incentives and Performance*. Dordrecht: Springer, pp. 307–21
Schmid, C. J. and Wilkesmann, U. (2015) 'Perspectives on managerialism in German academia: an empirical situation report and explanations'. *Beiträge zur Hochschulforschung*, 2, pp. 54–85
Schmidt, U. (2009) 'Evaluation an deutschen Hochschulen – Entwicklung, Stand und Perspektiven' in Widmer, T., Beywl, W. and Fabian, C. (Eds), *Evaluation - Ein systematisches Handbuch*. Wiesbaden: Springer, pp. 163–9
Vogel, M. P. (2009) 'The professionalism of professors at German Fachhochschulen'. *Studies in Higher Education*, 34 (8), pp. 873–88
Weik, E. (2011) 'Institutional entrepreneurship and agency'. *Journal for the Theory of Social Behaviour*, 41 (4), pp. 466–81
Wilkesmann, U. and Schmid, C. J. (2012) 'The impacts of new governance on teaching at German universities: findings from a national survey'. *Higher Education*, 63 (1), pp. 33–52

Wilkesmann, U. and Schmid, C. J. (2014) 'Intrinsic and internalized modes of teaching motivation'. *Evidence-based HRM: A Global Forum for Empirical Scholarship*, 2 (1), pp. 6–27

Wosnitza, M., Helker, K. and Lohbeck, L. (2014) 'Teaching goals of early career university teachers in Germany'. *International Journal of Educational Research*, 65, pp. 90–103

Wrong, D. H. (1995) *Power: Its Forms, Bases and Uses*. New Brunswick, *et al.*: Transaction

7
Organizing teaching in Chinese universities

SHUANGYE CHEN

Introduction

The higher education system in China started to expand in 1999 and has recently become the largest in the world based on the size of its student population. The gross enrolment ratio in China's higher education reached 34.5 per cent in 2013, while it was merely 3.5 per cent in 1991 (MOE, n.d.). Given the enormous size and the speed of expansion in the Chinese higher education system, few organizational studies have addressed how university teaching is organized as one of the technical cores and how it is adapted throughout higher education massification and the catch-up race in the global ranking game.

Along with the phenomenal development of the Chinese higher education system, there were rising discussions of higher education models in Asia (Altbach and Umakoshi, 2004; Marginson, 2011), particularly in China (Hayhoe et al., 2011; Li, 2012; Zha et al., 2015). Systematic and ostensive features of Chinese universities have been explored and defined from the historical-cultural and the sociopolitical approaches (Zha et al., 2015), while the performative aspect has not been given adequate attention in previous studies. University teaching is a 'soft' technical core that is usually practised in the organizational activities but is rarely manifested. Organizing (Weick, 1979; Bengtsson et al., 2007; Czarniawska, 2008) provides a powerful analytical lens to look into the rules of the activities beyond the structure. Identifying the latent 'grammar' (Weick, 1979; Bengtsson et al., 2007) of teaching in the Chinese higher education system would be helpful to illuminate how teaching, as an overlooked and under-addressed aspect of the university organization, has been structured and coordinated in practice. Contextualized in its historical legacy and the current changing trajectory, university teaching in Chinese universities equally offers a rich illustrative case. Therefore, this chapter outlines how teaching has been organized and governed in Chinese universities over the past five decades.

Analytical anchors

Organizing provides a distinctive conceptual perspective to differentiate constructed processes from the structural entity of organization (Bakken and Hernes, 2006; Czarniawska, 2008). In contrast with organization as a noun, organizing as both a noun and a verb suggests a shifted interest in the rules underlying activities, process, and ongoing, changing dynamics (Bengtsson *et al.*, 2007).

Organizing was theorized by Weick (1979) as a social grammar to make separate variables and individual behaviours into a meaningful whole.

> Organizing is like a grammar in the sense that it is a systematic account of some rules and conventions by which sets of interlocked behaviors are assembled to form social processes that are intelligible to actors. It is also a grammar in the sense that it consists of rules for forming variables and causal linkages into meaningful structures (later called cause maps) that summarize the recent experience of the people who are organized. The grammar consists of recipes for getting things done when one person alone can't do them and recipes for interpreting what has been done.
> (pp. 3–4)

Following this line of thinking, an activity-community model of organizing was developed by Bengtsson and her colleagues (2007) to renew the grammar of organizing. At the activity level, organizing is defined as 'coordinative measures taken to deal with the orientation of activities in time and space' (Bengtsson *et al.*, 2007, p. 6). At the community level, organizing is regarded as 'the attempts to form what we call imagined communities' (ibid.). Although the interplay of activities and communities may facilitate a richer understanding of the complicity of organizing, as the researchers claimed (ibid.), this chapter focuses on the activities of teaching, instead, of the people and communities of Chinese universities. Because this chapter provides a critical review of how teaching has been organized in the past five decades in such a large Chinese higher education system, the analytical level of the activity-related aspects of organizing is appropriate and feasible for the discussion.

This chapter will frame the analysis of organizing teaching in Chinese universities from the suggested polarized coordination dimension of activities as a 'loosely coupled form of organizing' or a 'integrated form of organizing' (ibid.). As conceptualized in the activity dimension of coordination (ibid.), a loosely coupled form of organizing entails a complex context 'where time needs to be coordinated continuously', 'boundary spanning happens in an entrepreneurial pattern', and 'challenges, possibilities and problems occur persistently and are impossible to avoid'. In contrast, an integrated form of organizing indicates a simple context 'where time is linear and easily planned or scheduled', 'the local distinct factory setting dominates the context of the activities', and 'things go as planned or can easily be adjusted to fit with an expected course of action' (ibid., p. 146).

Coupling is an established concept in examining the institution of schools and their relationship with the external environment (Weick, 1976; Meyer and Rowan, 1977). Tight coupling describes a system that consists of interdependent components in close responsiveness but without distinctiveness (Orton and Weick, 1990; Spillane *et al.*, 2011). In the previous English literature, as reframed in its social context of schooling, schools are regarded as 'loosely coupled' or 'decoupled' from the external environment (Weick, 1976; Meyer and Rowan, 1977). Recent educational reforms of high-stakes accountability in the western contexts have tightened the loose coupling and increased the responsiveness of schools to external demands, especially from the government (Spillane *et al.*, 2011). However, no study has ever examined the unique case of coupling in Chinese universities. The context of centralized bureaucracy and planned society has bred a distinctive grammar of tight coupling and strong coordination mechanisms, with their particular political and economic measures.

Throughout the last five decades, the higher education system in China has experienced tremendous restructuring and contextual changes. In addition to its internal reforms, the external changes from a simple context to a complex one are illuminating for elucidating how organizing has been formed and shaped in China.

Historical and empirical anchors

To envision the elusive activity of university teaching in the changing Chinese universities, this section sketches out the historical and empirical situations of university teaching from the educational statistics data available from the Chinese Ministry of Education.

The temporal anchors are selected from 1949–2013 and intentionally pinpointed at 1978, 1985, 1993, and 1999. The year 1949 marked the beginning of the Chinese higher education system under the new communist regime. The universities recorded in 1949 were essentially the missionary universities, private universities, and public universities from the 'old' Republican regime. In 1952, the 'new' system of Chinese higher education was being established from the revolution, and the 'old' universities continued to be restructured in the new China (Hayhoe, 1987). The 'new' system is regarded as a lasting institutional archetype for the Chinese higher education (Hu, 2001).

The year 1978 celebrated a new era for Chinese universities when the Cultural Revolution ended and the open-door policy was announced. Chinese university operations returned to normal after the social and educational turmoil and set down a path of accelerated development (Hayhoe, 1989). In 1985, a foremost educational reform was launched by the policy paper *Decision of Reforming Educational System*. This policy triggered deep and sweeping reforms in Chinese higher education. In line with the societal change from the planned economy to the market, another far-reaching educational reform was introduced in 1993 by the policy paper *Outline of Chinese Education and Development*. The year 1999 marked a new stage of higher education development in China based on the decision to expand university enrolment, starting in 1999, and the launch of the national strategic project Building World-class Universities in 1998. Finally, the latest educational statistics data released by the Ministry of Education in 2013 have informed the most recent higher education landscape in China.

For each temporal anchor, ten indicators were estimated in Table 7.1 to scaffold a rich and dimensional depiction of the teaching context of Chinese universities. The chosen indicators include the number of higher education institutions (HEIs) (including four-year bachelor's degree-granting universities and associate degree-granting colleges and vocational institutions), the number of undergraduate students (including bachelor's degree and associate degree programmes), the number of postgraduate students, the average undergraduate population size at each institution, the number of full-time teaching staff, the number of all working staff (including teaching staff), the student–teacher ratio (undergraduate students to full-time teaching staff), the average teaching staff and all working staff population sizes at each institution, and the ratio of teaching to non-teaching staff.

Based on the empirical data shown above, the context of organizing teaching in Chinese universities has visibly evolved from simple to complex. Within a time span of 64 years, the number of HEIs has increased 12-fold. The number of students has expanded more than 200 times, while the number of postgraduate students has risen over 2,000-fold.

The 1949 system was small in its scale in every sense. A typical 1949 Chinese university, if there was such a thing, had approximately 80 teaching staff serving 500–600 undergraduate students. There were very few postgraduate students to be supervised. A teacher typically needed to teach in small classes and could develop frequent interactions with students out of class, based on the student–teacher ratio, which was as low as 7.2:1. Simultaneously, a teaching staff member had an average of two non-teaching staff members to support teaching and organizational operations. Given the organizational size and the human resources sustaining teaching, the context of organizing teaching in this period was simple for an integrated coordination.

The period from 1978–85 exhibited rapid development in the scale of the Chinese higher education system. The student number doubled within seven years, and the student–teacher ratio dropped to 4.2:1. Between 1978 and 1999, the average teacher population was stable still, and a typical pre-1999 university accommodated 2,500–3,000 persons, with quickly expanding numbers of

Table 7.1 Selected educational statistics describing the context of organizing teaching in Chinese universities

Year Indicators	1949	1978	1985	1993	1999	2013
1. HEIs	205	598	1,016	1,065	1,071	2,491
2. Undergraduate students	116,500	856,300	1,703,100	2,535,500	4,134,200	24,680,726
3. Postgraduate students	629	10,934	87,331	106,771	233,513	1,793,953
4. Average institutional undergraduate population	568	1,432	1,676	2,074	3,815	9,814
5. Full-time teaching staff	16,100	206,300	344,300	387,800	425,700	1,496,865
6. All staff	46,000	518,000	870,600	1,021,300	1,065,100	2,296,262
7. Student–teacher ratio	7.2:1	4.2:1	4.9:1	6.5:1	9.7:1	16.5:1
8. Average institutional teaching staff population	79	345	339	364	397	601
9. Average institutional working staff population	224	866	857	959	994	922
10. Ratio of teaching to non-teaching staff	1:1.9	1:1.5	1:1.5	1:1.6	1:1.5	1:0.5

Sources: Raw data are from Educational Statistics in 1999 and 2013 (MOE, n.d.)

undergraduate and postgraduate students. As in all western countries, China has embarked on the similar developmental stage of higher education massification.

However, the average post-1999 university is large, with an institutional size of over 100,000 students and teachers. Based on the growing number of students, teachers needed to teach in large classes while having less time for more students with diverse needs. The student–teacher ratio increased, while the teaching to non-teaching staff ratio decreased. Teaching was intensified in the post-1999 university.

Based on the limited statistics data, a new but complex organizational context for university teaching surfaced. The organizational size alone indicates persistent challenges and problems that could not be avoided. Similarly, the grammar of organizing or the coordination mechanisms shifted from an integrated form to a loosely coupled form.

Chinese genre of organizing teaching

The educational statistics roughly describe the changing contexts of organizing teaching. What substantial happenings and what features underlie the organizing teaching in Chinese universities will be explored in this part. Following the analogy of grammar, genre is used to indicate substantial features of the activities and the specific contexts.

Because organizational research concerning teaching in Chinese universities is limited, few rigorous empirical studies can be found (Wang, 1999; Chen and Hu, 2012). Based on these limited historical and empirical studies, the following analyses have largely drawn from the empirical data and conclusions from my PhD dissertation study (Chen, 2006). In line with the patterns that have emerged from the educational statistics in the previous section, three distinctive periods demonstrate the changing genre of organizing teaching in Chinese universities. The periodization is only analytically differentiated.

Genre is closely related to the historical development and the external institutional environments. Ever since the founding of 'new' China, Chinese universities have adopted and ingrained the institution of academic specializations (zhuanye), which are usually understood as academic majors or academic programmes in other higher education systems. Academic specializations are the keyword of the university teaching and define the organizing and organization of people, material, and symbolic resources, knowledge and identity (Lu and Chen, 2002; Chen and Lo, 2006). In the Chinese context, academic specializations have gone far beyond a concept of curriculum and became institutionalized as the core mechanism or the grammar of organizing university teaching in China (Zhou, 2002; Hu, 2001; Lu and Chen, 2002; Chen, 2006). In the last 15 years, there has been an increasing trend to de-institutionalize academic specializations in university teaching (especially at the undergraduate level). However, the embedded logic and mechanisms remain.

Specialization-centred, tightly coupled organizing of teaching: pre-1985 stage

The three decades on this stage witnessed drastic restructuring, founding, collapsing, and reviving of the Chinese higher education system through the establishment of a new educational system that was in line with the socialist state, the Cultural Revolution, and the reform and open-door policy.

Since 1950, private and missionary universities in China have been transformed into public institutions. The liberal arts college mode of teaching, which used to flourish in those colleges and universities, disappeared as people were lost and the universities were dismantled and merged into other institutions. Certain disciplines, such as sociology, were no longer allowed.

At the same time, two exemplary socialist universities, Renmin University of China and Harbin Institute of Technology, were founded after the Soviet model of the university (Hu, 2001). Renmin University of China represented a mode of arts and social sciences, but those disciplines were mostly grounded on Marxism and socialism. As a science and technology counterpart, Harbin Institute of Technology became a prototype of the new university, which served the construction of the new China and was quickly copied and scaled up in other places.

By the end of 1953, the historical restructuring within the system achieved a highly centralized and specialized governance structure, in which comprehensive universities were reduced to 7 per cent of all institutions and overseen by the Department of Higher Education, while over 90 per cent institutions were specialized colleges and were attached to and supervised under the corresponding ministries or departments (ibid.).

Beyond this structural reshaping, the introduction of specialization-centred educational planning was key to internally reengineering the system. In an article published in *People's Education* in 1952 by then Vice-minister Mr Zeng Zhaolun, specialization (zhuanye) was regarded as pivotal to connecting university curriculum and university organizational structure (i.e. faculty and department) with the 'new' planned economy (Zeng, 1999). This article was frequently referenced in later research and became a classic historical document that unambiguously described the design logic and rules led by specialization for reorganizing the Chinese higher education system. What happened after the article was published provided strong and real evidence of how those rules and design in writing were truthfully and successfully implemented and materialized. For example, specialized colleges of agriculture, iron and steel, mining, and petroleum were quickly established to align with the industries' needs and to address personnel shortages. The strong and tight coupling mechanism between university teaching and external environments was realized through specialization-centred design under socialist planning. In Figure 7.1, the loop illustrates how the tight coupling corresponded and matched in the system.

Organizing teaching in Chinese universities • 139

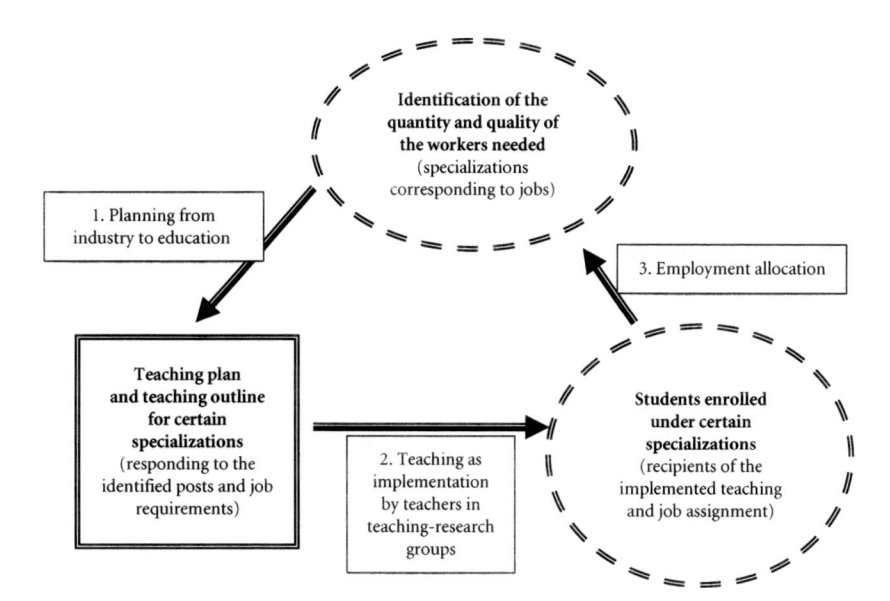

Figure 7.1 Loop of specialization-centred, tightly coupled organizing of teaching

In the adopted Soviet model of higher education, specializations were developed out of the aggregated 'real' and individual needs of each factory in every industry. An established catalogue of specializations was designed according to the established vocations and industrial development. Updates and minor revisions were made at certain times. The code of each specialization was identical to the corresponding industry (Chen, 2006). The catalogue of specializations nearly represented the human resource planning in the planned economy system. The aims of specializations were closely aligned with the job requirements for specific posts in all industries.

The planning department would collect and identify the quantity and quality of personnel that were needed each year. The educational planning would carefully follow the mandated common Teaching Outline (учебная программа) and Teaching Plan (учебный план) of respective specializations, which were informed by the planning departments and a national specialist committee (Chen, 2006). Textbooks designed to implement the teaching plan were standardized and used nationally across institutions. Faculties and schools disappeared from the university structure, and teaching-research groups (jiaoyan zu) were widely established to work under the departments to ensure truthful delivery of the teaching plan through teaching for certain core courses or specializations. Because the role of research was separated and moved to research institutions outside of the university – for example, the Chinese Academy of Science (CAS) and Chinese Academy of Social Science (CASS) – the teaching staff in the university were expected to focus on teaching and research related to teaching within the teaching-research groups (Chen, 2012).

The total number of enrolments and the specific number of students in each specialization were strictly regulated by human resource forecasting and the planning system administered by the planning departments. Students decided their specializations of study during enrolment and were allowed little room to make changes irrespective of their personal interests or later discovered orientations. Every enrolled student was supposed to fulfil a planned vacancy in four years through the employment allocation system. At that time, higher education was free for eligible members, and the state even provided each student with a monthly living allowance. In this tightly coupled system, students lost the freedom to choose as an individualistic agent but gained free higher education leading to a secured decent tenured job. At the system-wide level, the visible and invisible costs of supporting such a form of organizing were very high. As Hayek (1991) criticized socialism as 'the fatal conceit', this integrated design of organizing teaching centred on 'magic' specializations was rooted in incorrect premises of social conditions and policy support. Aligning the technical core of the university with the external demand in such a corresponding form was logically appealing but practically invalid. The simple context supporting the specialization-centred, tightly coupled organizing was 'designed' to be a close and reduced environment for social experiments. However, the design was vulnerable to the challenges of individual interests, social interaction, bounded rationality, and imperfect information (Hayek, 1991).

Social complexity is a hard reality that cannot be avoided or romanticized. Therefore, the context for organizing opened up from the designed simple context in a planned society. The end of the Cultural Revolution and the launch of the economic open-up policy were joined with calls for reform within the Chinese higher education system in 1985. The market as an idea and a mechanism had been urged to enter the planned socialist society since the 1980s. The contextual changes posed problems and challenges to the previous tightly coupled form of organizing teaching.

De-specialization-oriented, loosely coupled organizing of teaching: post-1985 and post-1999 stages

In this section, 1999 was chosen to mark a contextual difference of reactive de-specialization and proactive de-specialization when the system was expanding from an elite system to mass higher education.

Reactive de-specialization

During the post-1985 stage, before the 1999 expansion movement, universities had recovered from the destruction caused by the Cultural Revolution, but external contextual turbulences and organizing university teaching in various ways posed challenges to the system.

As discussed in the previous section, the simple context for tightly coupled organizing was constructed to design an order of coordination systems. The economic reform in China functioned as a 'destructive' force that shook the loop, starting from the employment and labour market. Enterprises were not coordinated by planning departments but were responsive to the market of demand and supply. Given the uncertainty and ambiguity faced, how could enterprises send information regarding the quantity and quality of employees needed in four years? No such information was available in the spontaneously ordered market (ibid.). Thus, the Teaching Outline and Teaching Plan for respective specializations was lost as the reference point for decisions, as shown in Figure 7.2.

Moreover, the employment allocation system had been phased out since the mid-1990s. Students could choose jobs from the labour market instead of waiting for official assignments. Although certificates and specializations were still useful during the first screening in the job market, the changing economy and the opportunities in the labour market also favoured capable students who liked to take a risk and may not have the corresponding specialized experience from a university. Due to external changes, the supportive conditions that had strengthened the loop of tightly coupled organizing were weakening or diminishing while, in the internal university system, specializations remained robust from their ostensive entities – for example, the catalogue, the basic organization of teaching-research groups, the teaching plan and outline, textbooks, and established curriculum structures.

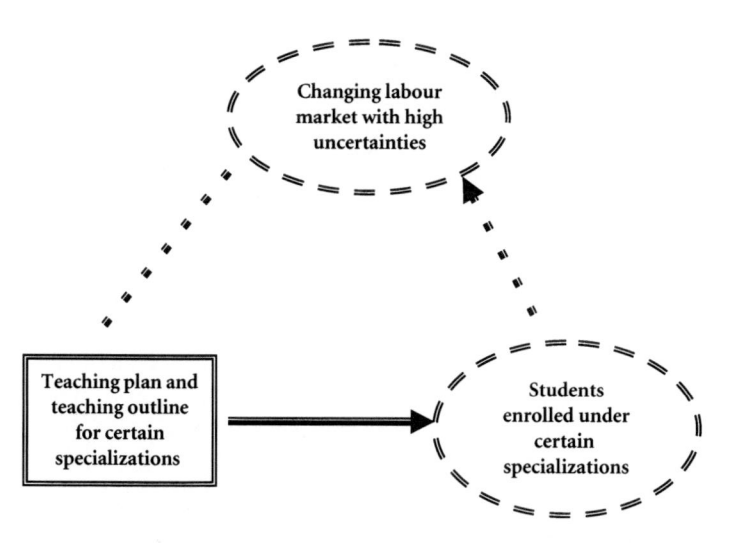

Figure 7.2 Context for reactive de-specialization during the post-1985 stage

In the late 1990s, another trend of reversed institutional restructuring emerged. By 1953, 8.5 per cent of all universities within the Chinese higher education system were comprehensive universities (ibid., p. 5). Starting in the mid-1990s, universities and specialized colleges were urged to merge to increase their internal efficiency. By 2005, 20 per cent of all bachelor's degree institutions were comprehensive universities (MOE, n.d.). The comprehensive universities became more encompassing, with medical schools or other missing disciplines. The specialized institutions, such as the old normal universities, were expanded and became more inclusive with new disciplines, while the university names were retained – for example, Beijing Normal University and East China Normal University. The organizational expansion and disciplinary diversification were essentially negating the 1950s restructuring and facilitated de-specialization in the internal contexts.

However, teachers and institutions were not active in teaching reforms during this stage (Wang, 1997). Although some new specializations were fashioned after the 'market' among the universities, the inherent grammar of specializations was sustained (Chen, 2006). There was a rising awareness of needing to broaden the narrow focus of specializations and weaken the constraints by allowing flexibility in the adjusted curriculum structure (Wen, 2000). Nevertheless, the rules and templates for organizing specialization-centred teaching were entrenched in the regulative, normative, and cognitive aspects of the institutionalized university context (Chen, 2006). Before a new grammar of organizing teaching was established, the general reformed measures to de-specialize were reactive and inconsequential.

Proactive de-specialization

The post-1999 stage is a rough demarcation of periodization. Some organizing teaching changes occurred in the late 1990s, but the impacts became visible in the 2000s. For example, pioneering universities such as Peking University, Nanjin University, and Sun Yat-sen University experimented with undergraduate education reforms in the mid-1990s, while the larger and wider organizing changes surfaced in the 2000s (Chen and Lo, 2012).

In this period, the higher education expansion decision in 1999 triggered a series of profound changes throughout the system. Concerning teaching, national evaluation of undergraduate teaching was implemented in the 2000s to assess the teaching quality of degree-granting institutions. In the last decade, the Ministry of Education has established a wide range of projects to support innovations in teaching and reward exemplary cases. Along with further economic development and the changing labour market, the external context for organizing teaching has become more complicated, with conflicting demands and rich incentives. The coordination rules for organizing teaching should be renewed in practice instead of by design.

Universities, especially top universities, were motivated to initiate teaching reforms. In this stage, the old grammar from specialization-centred organizing was increasingly challenged and tested with alternative practices and experiments. In general, principles of releasing temporal space, allowing more freedom, and creating flexibility were practised to remove the constraints of the original specialization-centred system (Lu, 2015). Using students' workloads as an example in Table 7.2, by comparing the course structure and workloads among Northeast Normal University in 1954, a national key comprehensive university (K) in 2003, and a local ordinary college (L) in 2004, de-specialization resulted in a looser course structure, with more elective courses, fewer required courses, and reduced workloads. Of note, the top university was more aggressive in releasing more learning space to the students, with reduced workloads, while increasing the proportion of elective courses outside of the specialization. University K was among the first group of comprehensive universities in the 1990s to introduce general elective courses, which were essential for establishing common practices in Chinese university teaching to break through the specialization-centred curriculum (Liu, 2006) (see Table 7.2).

To moderate the lasting effects of over-specialization in Chinese universities, general education as an idea and as a locally explored practice was introduced after 1999 (Li, 2006). Beyond general elective courses, small colleges that advocated more general foundation courses across disciplines were boldly established within the relaxed frame of curriculum, which departed from the specialization-centred structure. Yuanpei College of Peking University is an example of such early proactive explorations. This college was named after a well-respected former president, Mr Cai Yuanpei, and aimed to create a new organization to cultivate creative interdisciplinary talents (Xie et al., 2011). Students' autonomous choices were respected, and their learning initiatives were encouraged and supported (Jin, 2006). Limited in scale as Yuanpei College was, this emerging mode suggested a new forming grammar of organizing teaching to centre on students' learning instead of specializations. In the case of Yuanpei College, students might develop their individualized specializations without a given teaching outline or teaching plan. Their specialized learning experiences were uniquely organized. No predetermined required courses or corresponding textbooks could be identified. However, this new grammar may not be valid for other non-elite institutions.

Therefore, the national evaluation of university undergraduate teaching played a role in institutionalizing what rules and conditions should be followed when organizing teaching in the university. In the last issue of the System of Evaluation Indicators for Undergraduate Teaching (MOE, 2011), specializations became one of 19 indicators under seven categories, which included visions, teaching staff, instructional environment and usages, specialization

Table 7.2 Comparison of course structures and workloads

Categories	Contents	Northeast Normal University in 1954	University K in 2003	University L in 2004
Common compulsory courses (or common foundation courses)	Politics	18%	8–10%	9%
	PE	4%	2.8%	5%
	English	6%	5.8%	6%
	Computer skills or Military theories	—	5.8%	2%
Compulsory courses for specialization	Foundational courses	18%	36–40%	37%
	Specialized courses	50%		
Elective courses for specialization		—	24%	23%
Other elective courses		—	12%	5%
Practicum	Graduate thesis	—	4.3%	6%
	Social service	4%	—	7%
Total		230 credits or 3094 study hours	140–50 credits	170–80 credits or 2400–500 study hours

Sources: The data for Northeast Normal University are adapted from Hu (2001); the data for the other two case universities are adapted from Chen (2006). K is a national key comprehensive university. L is a local ordinary college

development and teaching reforms, governance of teaching, learning culture, teaching effect and impacts. These broad indicators suggest a trend of assessing undergraduate teaching from a wide and comprehensive perspective. This system also helped Chinese universities to better practise organizing with codified rules and expectations.

Conclusion and coda

The past five decades of higher education development in China have witnessed a unique trajectory of organizing university teaching, which has shifted from a tightly coupled form to a loosely coupled form. Internal and external contexts for organizing teaching experienced a dramatic change from simple to complex.

As a local concept, specialization has defined the old grammar of organizing teaching in the planned society and during the transition period to the market society. The current rules governing the organizing contrast with the previous grammar. The new grammar of organizing teaching is oriented towards despecialization.

Interestingly, this trend has also been accompanied with changes from teacher-centred teaching to student-centred teaching and to the latest student-centred learning. Teaching and learning are more integrated than ever. For example, the very recent movement of MOOCs in the Chinese universities, newly established teaching and learning centres and the proliferation of surveys on students' learning engagement and performance signify a new era of organizing teaching towards students' learning in the Chinese universities. However, university teachers and academics are confronted with a renewed but difficult job to teach in the Chinese universities.

References

Altbach, P. G. and Umakoshi, T. (2004) *Asian Universities: Historical Perspectives and Contemporary Challenges*. Baltimore, MD: Johns Hopkins University Press

Bakken, T. and Hernes, T. (2006) 'Organizing is both a verb and a noun: Weick meets Whitehead'. *Organization Studies*, 27 (11), pp. 1599–616

Bengtsson, M., Mullern, T., Soderholm, A. and Wahlin, N. (2007) *A Grammar of Organizing*. Cheltenham and Northampton: Edward Elgar

Chen, S. Y. (2006) 'When universities meet the market: Emergence of new undergraduate programs in the two Chinese universities'. Unpublished PhD dissertation. Chinese University of Hong Kong.

Chen, S. Y. (2012) 'Contributing knowledge and knowledge worker: the role of Chinese universities in the knowledge economy'. *London Review of Education*, 10 (1), pp. 101–12

Chen, S. Y. and Hu, L. F. (2012) 'Higher education research as a field in China: its formation and current landscape'. *Higher Education Research and Development*, 31 (5), pp. 655–66

Chen, S. Y. and Lo, N. K. L. (2006) 'Forms of organized knowledge in universities: four analytical perspectives of academic programs in Chinese universities'. *Peking University Education Review*, 4 (4), pp. 18–28

Chen, S. Y. and Lo, L. N. K. (2012) 'The trajectory and future of the idea of the university in China' in Barnett, R. (Ed.), *The Future University: Ideas and Possibilities*. London: Routledge, pp. 50–8
Czarniawska, B. (2008) *A Theory of Organizing*. Cheltenham and Northampton: Edward Elgar
Hayek, F. A. (1991) *The Fatal Conceit: The Errors of Socialism*. Chicago: University of Chicago Press
Hayhoe, R. (1987) 'China's higher curricular reform in historical perspective'. *The China Quarterly*, 110, pp. 196–230
Hayhoe, R. (1989) 'China's universities and western academic models'. *Higher Education*, 18 (1), pp. 49–85
Hayhoe, R., Li, J., Lin, J. and Zha, Q. (2011) *Portraits of 21st Century Chinese Universities: In the Move to Mass Higher Education*. Dordrecht and Hong Kong: Springer and Comparative Education Research Center
Hu, J. (2001) *Origin of the Modern Institution of the Chinese Higher Education: University Reform in the Early 1950s*. Nanjin: Nanjin Normal University Press
Jin, D. (2006) 'Practice of autonomous choice of undergraduate majors in the Chinese institutional environments'. *Higher Education Research*, 9, pp. 88–93 (in Chinese)
Li, J. (2012) 'World-class higher education and the emerging Chinese model of the university'. *Prospects*, 42 (3), pp. 319–39
Li, M. (2006) 'Reflection on the philosophy and the operational system of general education in Chinese universities: 1995–2005'. *Peking University Education Review*, 4 (3), pp. 86–99
Liu, J. (2006) 'General education or a supplement to professional education: study of liberal optional courses in Peking University'. *Fudan Education Forum*, 4 (1), pp. 8–13 (in Chinese)
Lu, X. (2015) 'On academic workload'. *China's Higher Education Research*, 6, pp. 38–48
Lu, X. and Chen, X. (2002) 'Connotation of majors in the university'. *Educational Research*, 7, pp. 47–52
Marginson, S. (2011) 'Higher education in East Asia and Singapore: rise of the Confucian model'. *Higher Education*, 61 (5), pp. 587–611
Meyer, J. and Rowan, B. (1977) 'Institutionalized organizations: formal structure as myth and ceremony'. *American Journal of Sociology*, 83 (2), pp. 340–63
MOE (Ministry of Education of China) (n.d.) *Educational Statistics in 2013*. Retrieved from http://www.moe.edu.cn/s78/A03/moe_560/s8492/s8493/201412/t20141216_181724.html
MOE (Ministry of Education of China). (2011) *System of Evaluation Indicators for Undergraduate Teaching*. Retrieved from http://www.moe.edu.cn/publicfiles/business/htmlfiles/moe/s7168/201403/165457.html
Orton, J. D. and Weick, K. E. (1990) 'Loosely coupled systems: a reconceptualization'. *Academy of Management Review*, 15, pp. 203–23
Spillane, J. S., Parise, L. M. and Sherer, J. Z. (2011) 'Organization routines as coupling mechanisms: policy, school administration, and the technical core'. *American Educational Research Journal*, 48 (3), pp. 586–619
Wang, W. (1997) 'History, status quo and prospect of systematic reform of higher education curriculum in China'. *Youse Jinshu Higher Education Research*, 4, pp. 56–60
Wang, W. (1999) 'Review of research on curriculum and teaching in universities and colleges in 50 years' in Chen, X. (Ed.), *Higher Education Research in China for 50 Years (1949–1999)*. Beijing: Educational Science Press, pp. 237–42
Weick, K. (1976) 'Educational organizations as loosely coupled systems'. *Administrative Science Quarterly*, 21 (1), pp. 1–19
Weick, K. (1979) *The Social Psychology of Organizing* (2nd edn). Reading: Addison-Wesley
Wen, F. (2000) 'Mode of specialized education and its reform in China'. *Higher Education*, 2, pp. 5–11 (in Chinese)
Xie, X., Qi, L. and Lu, X. (2011) 'Autonomous choice of majors and practice of cross-disciplinary specializations: case of Yuanpei College at Peking University'. *Chinese Higher Education Research*, 1, pp. 54–7 (in Chinese)

Zeng, Z. L. (1999) 'Issues of academic specializations in higher education' (original from 1952), in Chen, X. (Ed.), *Higher Education Research in China for 50 Years (1949–1999)*. Beijing: Educational Science Press, pp. 299–302
Zha, Q., Shi, J. and Wang, X. (2015) 'Is there a Chinese model of a university?' *International Higher Education*, 80, pp. 27–9
Zhou, C. (2002) 'Understanding of the institution of the university from organizational study'. *Educational Research*, 6, pp. 68–71 (in Chinese)Acknowledgement: This is to acknowledge the funding support from Basic Research Fund for Universities in China (SKZZX2013016)

III
Organizing learning

8
Learners and organizations
Competing patterns of risk, trust, and responsibility

RAY LAND

Introduction

This chapter attempts to addresses one of the central concerns of this volume, namely how discernible trends in teaching and learning might change organizational structures and behaviours. The principal research question of this chapter is to consider how shifts towards a corporatist consumer discourse of learning, arising from intensified global competitiveness, combined with a changed tempo of organizational life driven by technological speed, are creating tensions within traditional modes of organization of teaching and learning.

In considering this issue it is necessary to examine the discursive shift that has occurred over the last three decades from a language of *education* and *learning* to one concerned with *the student experience*. Teaching in higher education is increasingly rendered as the facilitation of learning and the provision of learning opportunities or experiences. This shift has come about through a range of factors including the erosion of welfarism, and a move to a marketized notion of higher education as principally a private good (and a primarily economic rather than educational transaction) (Apple, 2000). Learning increasingly gains prominence in policy documents as a far more individualistic activity (Field, 2000), with the learner rendered as a consumer of services, 'a situation in which the learner has certain needs and where it is the business of the educator to meet these needs' (Biesta, 2005). A consumer logic of value for money, accountability and the need for increasingly rigorous protocols and standards of inspection then ensues. The corporatist discourse of the 'student experience' becomes, to a great extent, an empty signifier which is difficult to argue against. It can easily be deployed to put students and teaching staff in an oppositional stance, through the use, for example, of consumer satisfaction student surveys in which the student-as-consumer 'rates' the professor-as-service-provider. In public and marketing documentation the discourse becomes interwoven with narratives of excellence, images of graduate success and student happiness, a sense of student entitlement, and the friendliness and helpfulness of (providing) staff. In its strongest rendition this representation can depict learning within the organization as an undertaking that is non-problematic, without any significant incurring of risk. It does not entail deep personal change or transformation, troublesome challenge or even, at times, engagement.

This chapter begins by examining the state higher education currently finds itself in, economically, politically, pedagogically, and technologically. It then explores the contradictions and competing discourses that arise for the organization, and how it might choose to behave, when it is simultaneously required to produce satisfied consumers as well as graduates for the wider society who can act in complex, uncertain, risk-laden, and unpredictable environments. The latter, of course, entails radically different forms of curriculum, student–staff relationships, and student encounters. Finally, it attempts to bring these competing discourses into some form of tension through a four-fold analytic model.

The state we are in

Barnett (2000) has characterized the state that higher education finds itself in at the beginning of the twenty-first century as being one of 'supercomplexity'. While, on the one hand, this might prove to be a source of important opportunities for academics and other higher educational 'new professionals' (Gornall, 2004), as new academic identities and roles emerge in the spaces opened up by this changing environment, this same environment has, on the other hand, brought tensions and difficulties in terms of competing priorities, particularly regarding the intensification of academic labour and expectations of greater research productivity. The new environment is also characterized by qualities of epistemological contestability (Barnett, 2000) and organizational ambiguity (Alvesson, 2002) in which both academics and learners find themselves caught. There is an increasing sense of borderlessness or the blurring of boundaries – what Bergquist (1995, p. 11) terms 'boundariless anxiety' – which both academics and learners find themselves negotiating. It is therefore worth considering particular aspects of the changing conditions of the higher education landscape in a little more detail before we move on to analyse the experience of learners and their varied reactions to such a changing and protean organizational environment.

Organizations beset by risk

The discursive shift mentioned above would appear to be one kind of organizational response to a perceived climate of risk (Adam *et al.*, 2000). The sources of such a perception are multiple. The implications of the steep increases in participation rates in the last three decades occasioned by the changed conditions of higher education, particularly in terms of the increased entry of non-traditional students into the HE system, are alone sufficient to have had a profound impact upon the conditions of academic work in higher education institutions around the world. These implications included declining units of resource necessitating stringencies in staff–student ratios and infrastructure, and a much less homogeneous student body. These elements in turn occasioned subsequent effects: significant changes in student expectations; the redesign of curricula and changed pedagogy; shifts in the balance of priorities for staff in relation to teaching and research roles; and confused public perceptions about the role and status of both universities and their graduates in modern society (Barnett, 2000). Scott (1995) emphasizes that the transition from elite to mass must be interpreted not just in terms of the expansion of numbers and ensuing resource pressures, but also 'in the context of the restless synergy between plural modernisations – of the academy, polity, economy, society and culture' (pp. 9–10). Nixon (1996) argues that the 'significant shift' during this period of crisis 'is at the level of values and underlying structures of belief; structures that are in new and vital interplay with emergent forms of professional agency' (p. 93).

Speed, the digital, and new modes of organizing learning and teaching

The supercomplexity noted earlier is compounded by the speed of the digital age, the proliferation of knowledge and information that the latter brings in its wake, and the risks that arise from behaviours within unpredictable and seemingly ungovernable social media networks. By destabilizing and seemingly 'disordering' the academic text, digital media enable alternative academic discourses, new literacies, and multimodal forms of knowing to emerge. Blogs are about posts, not pages. Wikis are streams of conversation, revision, amendment, and truncation (Alexander, 2006, p. 32). In doing so they alter the traditional roles of teacher and learner and, by extension, the nature of the academic institution itself. Digital technologies, predicated on 'fast time' (Eriksen, 2001) and time–space compression, are already transforming the ways in which knowledge is both generated and disseminated in a manner quite different from that of traditional print culture (predicated on 'slow time') with which universities have been imbricated for centuries. These changes give rise to new temporalities and the changing nature of knowledge, which in turn foster new digital pedagogies and new forms of educational institution (Land, 2011). They also temporally 'recalibrate' the working patterns of online learners (Sharma, 2014). Sheail (2015) observes 'how temporal narratives are used to drive organizational change and how organizational change, in turn, affects temporal experience' (p. 7), warning that:

> understanding the dominant times and spaces of the university campus as central, and those accessing the campus in asynchronous or asymmetric ways as peripheral, may not just lead to spatially biased practices of distancing, but to a lack of recognition of emergent inequalities which are digitally reconfigured and potentially invisible. (p. 5)

Moreover, open access to digital learning environments and digital scholarship, through its unprecedented capacity for infinite reuse, revision, remixing, and redistribution, can deliver qualitatively different practices both in research and in pedagogy. Given the unique characteristic of digital items – that the marginal cost of their storage, reproduction, and distribution is, effectively, zero – this affords an opportunity to satisfy everyone's right to get as much education as they desire and to reclaim the original purpose of scholarship – that it be built upon and not locked up behind paywalls. They also offer opportunities to radicalize the way feedback and other data on quality of provision may be gathered. Compared with the sophisticated digitized consumer response-gathering of other business organizations, such as Amazon, eBay, Facebook and Tesco, the use of such 'analytics' data in quality improvement is in its infancy.

Challenge to academic authority

The new media, characterized by their volatility, multivocality, and radical contestability, become implicated in the twenty-first-century university's difficulty in maintaining and asserting its traditional authority. The endless incompleteness of open digital text, its permanent state of new ideas and emergence, its endless revisability and mutability, the networked nature of its knowledge, seem to undermine the authority of academic knowledge, which has traditionally been necessary as the foundation of research evidence, and hence of veracity and the verifiable. As Barnett (2005) observes:

> we now live in a world of radical contestation and challengeability, a world of uncertainty and unpredictability. In such a world, all such notions – as truth, fairness, accessibility and knowledge – come in for scrutiny. In such a process of continuing reflexivity, fundamental concepts do not dissolve but, on the contrary, become systematically elaborated. (p. 789)

In this respect the changing nature of digital media exposes the university's inability to claim universality in its pursuit of truth, and is characterized by the 'supercomplexity' Barnett sees as integral to the twenty-first-century academy, and a changing relationship between the organization and the learners within it.

At the practical level of the organization of teaching and learning, the digital technologies have implications for the design and delivery of courses, and offer new models of delivery. They transform the spatial and temporal relationships of learning in two powerful ways. The first is through new forms of online distance learning which may expand the reach of organizations to the other side of the world (ushering in new pedagogical, cultural, and ethical issues of dealing with online and international students). The second is through the capacity of the Bring Your Own Device (BYOD) phenomenon to bring the wider world into the traditional classroom through simultaneously opening up other channels of communication as well as that with the classroom teacher (Bradford Networks, 2015). Apart from the complex security issues that arise from 'onboarding' vast numbers of devices within an organization's information system, new learning technologies provide opportunities as well as challenges to enhance our understanding of the learning process and the potential to improve course design. A recent Universities UK Report (Universities UK, 2013) provides examples of emerging technologies with far-reaching implications for the organization of learning and teaching (see Table 8.1).

Table 8.1 Emergent learning technologies

Emergent learning technologies

Analytics: most virtual learning environments involve some basic analysis of learner behaviours such as the volume of engagement with an online resource. Increased engagement with digital learning environments and resources increases the amount of data that can be collected, allowing analytic techniques to be applied in more sophisticated ways to improve the feedback to students and structure their learning	• Adaptive learning develops a model of a learner's understanding of topics and concepts, allowing detailed feedback on progress and providing personalized pathways to reach learning outcomes • Social network analysis provides tools to make online class and student networks more visible in order to help guide more effective learning, linkages, and engagement • Discourse analytics enables better assessment of the quality of contributions and connections that a student may make during their time on a course, including outside formal class structures
Semantic web technologies: automation of personalized support to construct knowledge by enabling technologies to make informed linkages across the web on the basis of labels and tags. Applied to education, this technique may enable programmes to identify resources of interest to students enrolled on a particular course in a more targeted and automated way	
Virtual problem-based learning: development of procedural skills by using technologies to enhance problem-based learning approaches through immersive, experiential learning environments. These models can bring students and educators together from multiple locations	

Source: Adapted from Universities UK, 2013, p. 27

Global competition

The speed and reach of digital technologies has ushered in a globalized world in which huge amounts of data, including financial data, cross vast distances instantly. Globalization emerges from digitization, and is dependent upon its speed. Knowledge, work, and jobs can be easily outsourced, to the other side of the world, in such an accelerated environment. In the midst of this supercomplexity, as nations compete for market share and economic growth, there has been an escalating global demand for higher education. Enhanced technologies for the transfer of huge flows of data and information, and the transportation of goods and people, coupled with liberalization and deregulation of markets worldwide, has resulted in the complex phenomenon of global competition, one significant effect of which would appear to be the exposure of domestic economic life to influences or control from corporations in other countries, and a greater inter-penetration of markets. Higher education, in this regard, is now exposed as much as any other industry, and global positioning has become a significant factor for university senior managers.

Learning in a risk society: the organization's hold on quality and order

The foregoing tendencies give us some sense of the state higher education finds itself in. As higher education systems become massified, or universalized, costs rise exponentially and public demands for transparency and accountability increase. The greater the number of stakeholders in a higher education sector, the greater the call for the improvement of provision. Unsurprisingly this same power of information and communication technologies (operating through fibre-optic cables quite literally at the speed of light) has also been harnessed by organizations to render their practices more visible and accountable, and to appropriate and repurpose the potentially 'disordering' practices of digital culture (Hemmi et al., 2009) towards a more orderly function. This is taking place through the more efficient analysis of diverse forms of evaluation data ('data mining') and the emerging field of learner analytics (Buckingham Shum and Ferguson, 2012). The implementation of new national systems of quality assurance – requiring institutions to undergo academic audit, and the assessment of both teaching and research quality at unit level (Trow, 2010) – has come into existence within a climate of increasingly global institutional competition and consumer-oriented marketization where student satisfaction ratings become a powerful, if not *the* most powerful, factor. Through the discourse of 'excellence', manifest initiatives such as national teaching fellowship schemes, centres of excellence in teaching and learning, and the research excellence gradings of various national and international league table rankings (Land and Gordon, 2015), such regulatory practice can be identified as a more domesticating tendency in tension with the emancipatory but unruly and potentially transgressive capacity of the digital.

The question then arises of what kind of learners we need to cope, and hopefully thrive, in such a supercomplex social, economic, and technological environment, what kinds of learning they should undertake, and what forms of higher education organization might be in a position to offer such provision. It is at this point that we find strong competing (and at times seemingly irreconcilable) discourses on the nature of learning in higher education institutions. The following sections consider the tensions between these discourses.

Powerful knowledge: disciplines as an organizing principle

Though access and participation have increased markedly in the recent decades of massification and expansion, commentators such as Morrow (2009) have argued that they are not an end in themselves and are not, per se, more important than 'epistemic access' (ibid.) and 'transformation as a knower' (Bernstein, 1975). Epistemic access, Morrow (2009, p. 37) suggests, refers to how we 'shape and guide enquiry ... to discover the truth'. Such epistemic access, Young (2012) maintains, is an 'inarguable' basis of the curriculum. Learners need access to what he terms 'powerful knowledge' in order to have understanding of, and to participate in, the principal debates and arguments of the time. And where better to look for guides to enquiry, Young suggests, than the disciplinary communities, the 'communities of enquiry':

> Their distinctiveness as institutions is the unique value they place on innovation and the creation and defence of new knowledge. It is primarily through the peer review system, [sic] that the institution of science distributes rewards, shapes research priorities and, albeit indirectly, influences the school and university curriculum. (para. 2)

It is these characteristics of disciplines, Young argues, that makes them fundamentally modern. 'Without them we would not have had any of the economic and social progress of the last two centuries' (ibid.). The communities of enquiry, which act as gatekeepers of disciplinary knowledge, are both 'reproducers' and 'disrupters' in that they conserve knowledge (and inequalities it must be said), but also provide tools to 'think the un-thinkable'. Disciplinary knowledge has been (and currently remains) the main structuring principle of how higher education institutions tend to be organized.

Transformation and ontological shift

Meyer and Land (2003, 2005), however, through their analytical framework of 'threshold concepts', take the view that the gaining of epistemic fluency also entails significant 'ontological shifts', or changes in the subjectivity of the learner.

In effect, you *become* what you know. If you gain access to powerful knowledge, you are empowered and *transformed* by that access. Without this ontological dimension, powerful knowledge would resemble little more than Freire's 'banking' notion of education (Freire, 1970). Precious conceptual 'jewels' would be deposited and accumulated in one's account in the Bank of Episteme. Powerful knowledge, Meyer and Land contend, is frequently 'troublesome knowledge' (Perkins, 2006) and, in a transformative model of learning, knowledge is necessarily troublesome in order to unsettle learners from their prevailing, often entrenched, understanding. As Dewey (1986) observed back in 1933: 'The path of least resistance and least trouble is a mental rut already made. It requires troublesome work to undertake the alteration of old beliefs' (p. 136).

The encounter with troublesome knowledge provokes a 'liminal' state. Liminality is viewed as a 'betwixt and between state', a space of transformation in the process of learning in which there is a reformulation of the learner's meaning frame (Schwartzman, 2010) and an accompanying shift in the learner's subjectivity (Meyer and Land, 2005). A state of comparative uncertainty is encountered 'in which the learner may oscillate between old and emergent understandings' (Cousin, 2006, p. 4). Learning thresholds are often the points at which students experience difficulty and are often uncomfortable for the learner, as they require a letting go of customary ways of seeing things, of prior familiar views. Barnett maintains that a higher education should be 'subversive in the sense of subverting the student's taken-for-granted world'. This, he believes, will allow students to realize that no matter how much effort is put in 'there are no final answers' (1999, p. 155). Thus, understanding comes to be seen as an iterative practice as opposed to an isolated process with a clear beginning and end point.

Liminality

The liminal state can be seen to perform a progressive function which begins with the encountering and integration of something new. This subsequently entails a recognition of shortcomings in the learner's existing view of the phenomenon in question and an eventual letting go of the older prevailing view. At the same time, this requires a letting go of the learner's earlier mode of subjectivity. There then follows an envisaging (and ultimate accepting) of the alternative version of self which is contemplated through the threshold space, the learner's 'emergent being' as Blackie *et al.* (2010) portray this. This involves a 'reauthoring' of self, according to Ross (2011), or 'undoing the script'. As the French novelist Marcel Proust once observed: 'The only real voyage of discovery consists not in seeing new landscapes, but in having new eyes, in seeing the universe with the eyes of another' (Shattuck, 1974, p. 131).

Learning in the liminal space further entails the acquisition and use of new forms of written and spoken discourse and the internalizing of these. In its more frustrating manifestations it can be experienced as a suspended state in which understanding approximates to mimicry or lack of authenticity. It can be unsettling, experienced often as a sense of loss, as prevailing earlier conceptual views, and earlier states of subjectivity, are relinquished.

Lee Shulman, former Director of the Carnegie Foundation for the Advancement of Teaching, observed that 'without a certain amount of anxiety and risk, there's a limit to how much learning occurs. One must have something at stake. No emotional investment, no intellectual or formational yield' (Shulman, 2005, p. 1). In a similar vein, Schwartzman (2010) maintains that real learning requires 'stepping into the unknown, which initiates a rupture in knowing' (p. 38). Such a view of learning, as an *educational* transaction, is concerned not so much with the student's acquisition of knowledge or consumption of services as with their 'coming into presence' (Biesta, 2005) which entails 'being challenged by otherness and difference', what Derrida terms a 'transcendental violence' (Derrida, 1978) that is persistent, presenting difficult demands and situations. In this mode the learner is not in a position to identify and state their learning needs, which are emergent and contingent, and require an altered relation of *trust* with their teachers and fellow learners. In this transformative approach to learning, students, as organizational actors, are rendered differently, as co-enquirers, co-creators, co-producers (Neary and Amsler, 2012). Teachers, in turn, have to assume a different form of responsibility, operating within risk and uncertainty, which cannot be predicated on the assumed certainties of a conventional accountability protocol.

The providing organization: learner as consumer

In contradistinction to this sentiment, a powerful discursive shift has occurred within higher education globally over the last three decades in which higher education teaching is rendered as the facilitation of the 'student learning experience', and as a primarily economic rather than educational transaction (Apple, 2000). Teaching in higher education is increasingly rendered as the *facilitation* of learning and the 'delivery' of learning opportunities or experiences (Barber *et al.*, 2011). Of course, on the one hand, if higher education is viewed as a qualitative personal transformation of the learner, this becomes difficult to commodify. A 'student experience', on the other hand, can be rendered and marketed as various forms of commodity, and costed accordingly.

In this pervasive discourse of new managerialism the learner is constructed as a consumer of services, 'a situation in which the learner has certain needs and where it is the business of the educator to meet these needs' (Biesta, 2005). As Charles Kettering of General Motors once observed, 'The key to economic prosperity is the organised creation of dissatisfaction' (cited in Rifkin, 1995, p. 19). The advent of global communications and media, it might be argued, has intensified the production of 'dissatisfied consumers' through increased opportunity for targeted and personalized advertising. In a digital era, marketing becomes more and more important in the creation of need, and this has now become a permanent feature of the higher education landscape. As new public management emphasizes the nature of higher education as a private good, the notion of higher education moves from being one career option to an obligation that (at least in middle-class families) becomes de rigueur, the lack of which comes to be viewed almost as socially deviant. In this regard, higher education can be commodified and, theoretically at least, market choices made regarding its purchase. Through the use of consumer satisfaction surveys and module evaluation scores, such corporatist discourse can, on occasion, be deployed to place students and their teachers in an oppositional stance, and to intensify internal market competition between colleagues and courses. In this way teaching to satisfaction ratings sets different parameters for what counts as education, and as quality. The discourse is antithetical to critical or transformative notions of pedagogy. It is frequently interwoven with signifiers of excellence, narratives of graduate success, representations of student happiness, a sense of student entitlement, and the unfailing friendliness and helpfulness of (providing) staff. There is a danger that teaching, and the organization of learning, become risk averse, formulaic, and comfortable in order to minimize the possibility of receiving unfavourable ratings. In the worst scenario, learning may be depicted as non-problematic, without risk, requiring minimal commitment.

Clearly such a transformative approach to learning sits uneasily with a new managerialist rendering of the learner as consumer of educational services. The obligation and commitment to be provoked into liminal states of learning, to experience troublesome knowledge, to undergo uncomfortable ontological shifts which can lead to different ways of thinking, different modes of knowledge, and deep personal change are less easy to present as a consumer entitlement (and perhaps even less so in a fee-paying environment). Indeed, in this approach the learner may be viewed less as the consumer than as the product, or even the raw material.

The learner's pedagogic rights

Competing models of quality in higher education clearly come into play amid these tensions. On the one hand, there are concerns for student satisfaction and the learner's entitlement, particularly in environments where the learner is expected to make a contribution to the costs of their higher education, if not meet the entire cost. On the other hand, there is a commitment to the idea of higher education as a *reinvention* of the learner:

> For apart from inquiry, apart from the praxis, individuals cannot be truly human. Knowledge emerges only through invention and re-invention, through the restless, impatient, continuing, hopeful inquiry human beings pursue in the world, with the world, and with each other.
>
> (Freire, 1970, p. 58)

Jenkins and Barnes (2014) view the emphasis on consumption and entitlement to services as a misplaced curtailment of students' *pedagogic rights* of transformation, confusion, hard work, and challenge, where liminality and uncertainty trigger different ways of thinking, different modes of knowledge, and deep personal change. Barnett, similarly, has observed that, in a time of supercomplexity:

> The student is perforce required to venture into new places, strange places, anxiety-provoking places. This is part of the point of higher education. If there was no anxiety, it is difficult to believe that we could be in the presence of a higher education.
>
> (Barnett, 2007, p. 147)

Moreover, pedagogy, he has argued elsewhere, 'must be founded on openness, mutual disclosure, personal risk and disturbance' (Barnett, 2004, p. 258). The notion of pedagogic rights originates in the work of Bernstein (2000) who envisioned learners' as deserving a three-fold entitlement to enhancement, inclusion, and participation (see Table 8.2).

Conclusion: competing patterns of risk, trust, and responsibility

The US educator Harlan Cleveland once wryly observed that 'the outsiders want the students trained for their first job out of university, and the academics inside the system want the student educated for 50 years of self-fulfilment.

Table 8.2 The learner's pedagogic rights

Enhancement	Individual	'the right to the means of critical understanding and to new possibilities' (Bernstein, 2000, p. xx)	Confidence
Inclusion	Social	'The right to be included socially, intellectually, culturally and personally [including] the right [to be] autonomous' (ibid., p. xx)	'Communitas' Belonging in group(s)
Participation	Political	'The right to participate in discourse and practices that have outcomes: to participate in the construction, maintenance and transformation of social order' (ibid., p. xxi)	Civic discussion and action

Source: Bernstein, cited in Mclean *et al.*, 2011

The trouble is that the students want both' (Cleveland, cited in Schwartz, 2003, para. 3).

We have seen earlier how competing discourses currently render the experience of learners within higher education organizations in radically different ways. These discourses present the pattern of responsibilities and obligations of stakeholders in the learning process in similarly different fashion (with the learner as consumer, as client with obligations, as subject to be transformed) and for different ends. These discourses can both inspire or undermine the trust of learners, of academics, of employers, and of the public at large, and we know from the work of Stensaker and Harvey (2011) how, when the quality of institutions is under scrutiny, trust becomes a critical factor in the establishment of legitimacy, autonomy, and accountability. To conclude, it might be helpful to view the tensions between these different visions of how learners and higher education organizations should engage with each other through the lens of Land and Gordon's four 'contexts of enhancement'. This model suggests that quality enhancement in higher education organizations may take one, or a blend of, the following modes: 1) a high-fidelity mode (with the priority on consistency to a set of principles and standards); 2) a low-fidelity mode (with greater latitude allowed according to local contexts); 3) a consumerist approach (based on student satisfaction) or 4) a managerialist approach (where efficient resourcing is key). We might represent these choices diagrammatically as shown in Table 8.3.

High-fidelity mode

In terms of meeting the demands, within a massified system, of intakes of large numbers of students from increasingly varied educational backgrounds, it might be argued that adopting a high-fidelity approach (Saunders, 2009) would assist an organization to comply with the requirements of a stated policy or strategy, either at sectoral level or at institutional level. The approach typically expects an evidence-based response – which might be at institutional, departmental or programme level, depending upon circumstances – that can demonstrate fulfilment of, and alignment with, a set of declared objectives, outputs or standards. The informing notions of a high-fidelity approach are likely to be those of convergence, alignment, and consistency. The intended gains of this approach include reassurance to user groups and other stakeholders regarding the coherence, consistency, and reliability of provision and practice. The potential risks or weaknesses in the approach are that too great a concern with prescription might dampen down innovation, that one size will be deemed to fit all, with a distinct possibility that a high degree of fidelity may be illusory, with colleagues at various levels within an organization engaging in 'impression management' behaviours. The organizational approach generally operates on the basis of low trust of other stakeholders such as students and academics.

Table 8.3 Contexts of enhancement

Context	Informing notion	Idea of quality	Gains	Risks	Trust
High fidelity	convergence and alignment	consistency, conformity to standard	coherence, consistency, and reliability	stifles innovation, insufficiently context-sensitive, tokenism, compliance	low trust of variation
Low fidelity	importance of context, tolerance of variation	engagement, innovation, variation	taps into how architects prefer to work, fosters motivation, sense of ownership, relevance	restricted to specific pockets, practice fragmented	high trust of local practice
Managerial	effective resource deployment, 'joined-upness'	transformed practice	better matching of resources to strategies, greater efficiencies	resistance, conflict, 'noise', non-compliance, judicious subversion	low trust of local practice
Consumerist	market competitiveness, institutional positioning, strong brand competition	fitness for purpose, value for money, excellence	student-centred provision, consumer satisfaction, improvement of student learning	distortion by the market, stifling of innovation, reputational damage	high trust of the market

Source: Land and Gordon, 2013

Low-fidelity mode

Conversely, for colleagues concerned to provide a *transformative* higher education experience that can address the individual variability of learners in different disciplinary cultures and with varying levels of educational and cultural experience, then the attractions of a low-fidelity approach (Saunders, 2009) may become more pronounced. The informing notion of this mode is the importance of *context* and the need for both recognition and tolerance of the *variability* that arises within and between contexts. The potential gains of this approach are that it can tap into the grain of situated change and can have substantial impact. It can foster engagement and reach down to the point of action, or street level (Lipsky, 1980). Through genuine engagement of academics and other key staff it can stimulate development and transforming action within communities of practice, such as disciplinary 'tribes' (Becher and Trowler, 2001), whose behaviour is often difficult to influence. However, a potential drawback of this approach is that innovative enhancement activity may well remain restricted to the specific pockets or enclaves within departments and that practice may well become diffuse or fragmented. A low-fidelity approach has to acknowledge that control will have to be relinquished to a certain extent and, therefore, requires a degree of *trust* at practitioner level and with other stakeholders, and a tolerance of variation and heterogeneity in solutions and approaches. For this reason, it may be troublesome for policy-makers wishing to impose some form of standardization over practice or a system-wide shift. This raises the issue of scale. A recurrent concern with this mode is how to scale an initiative upward without corroding the trust that was necessary to its original development.

Consumerist mode

The policy decision of governments increasingly to transfer a proportion of the cost of university financing to tuition fees and a growth in the number of private universities in many countries give rise to an increasing concern with consumerist approaches. A significant element of the consumerist approach is a more student-centred provision and the pursuit of consumer satisfaction. There is frequently an emphasis on quality enhancement activity in the student experience and a continuing focus on the improvement of student learning as a legitimate purpose and concern of a university's activity. The approach also signals that 'one size does not fit all' and opens up opportunities for new forms of offering to innovative institutions (distance learning organizations, online courses, private universities, collaborative international partnerships). A significant tool of enhancement recruited to this purpose has increasingly been that of the student survey. The National Student Survey (NSS) in the UK, the Course Experience Questionnaire (CEQ) in Australia and the National Student

Survey of Student Engagement (NSSE) in the USA have all proved influential. It should be noted, however, that such surveys can be predicated on quite different premises. Whereas the NSS, for example, primarily seeks to elicit student *satisfaction* with the provision they are currently experiencing, the NSSE seeks less to elicit student opinion than to assess the nature, quality, and extent of their *engagement*, which includes the extent of the student's personal involvement and effort as well as aspects of institutional provision. The former approach, as discussed above, does not always sit comfortably with transformative approaches to learning which may push students beyond their comfort zones, while the latter may be more aligned with 'pedagogies of uncertainty' in which students encounter troublesome knowledge.

A managerial approach

All of the foregoing modes are, to a great extent, dependent upon the quality of management operating in the organization. Good management is dependent, in the last resort, on effective learning taking place, and a managerial approach will be informed primarily by notions of effective resource deployment and the pursuit of greater 'joined up-ness'. The gains of such an approach, when it succeeds, are likely to be a better alignment of activities across an institution or sector, greater efficiencies in the use of resourcing and firmer control of policy direction. There is, generally, a better matching of resources to institutional strategies for teaching and learning. In the notoriously protean environments of higher education organizations, once characterized as 'organized anarchies' (Cohen *et al.*, 1972), insensitive, poorly communicated or poorly timed managerial interventions can provoke adverse effects that take the form of open resistance, unhelpful noise within the system or more guarded and covert non-compliance, or judicious subversion.

Towards partnership with learners

The old adage of working *with* people rather than working *on* people would apply to all these modes of intervention, whether with learners or their teachers. In practice, the pursuit of effective learning practices within higher education organizations is likely to involve a hybrid blend of these different modes that is appropriate to a given institution and context. Recent emphases in the sectors of many countries on the principles of recognition of diversity, the importance of collaborative endeavour, and the idea of staff–student partnerships would indicate promising ways forward.

References

Adam, B., Beck, U. and van Loon, J. (2000) *The Risk Society and Beyond: Critical Issues for Social Theory*. London: Sage

Apple, M. W. (2000) *Official Knowledge: Democratic Education in a Conservative Age*. New York and London: Routledge

Alexander, B. (2006) 'Web 2.0: a new wave of innovation for teaching and learning?' *Educause Review*, 41 (2), pp. 32–44. Retrieved from http://www.educause.edu/ir/library/pdf/ERM0621.pdf

Alvesson, M. (2002) *Understanding Organisational Culture*. London: Sage

Barber, M., Moffit, A. and Kihn, P. (2011) *Deliverology 101: A Field Guide for Educational Leaders*. Thousand Oaks, CA: Corwin Press

Barnett, R. (1999) *The Idea of Higher Education*. Buckingham: Open University Press

Barnett, R. (2000) *Realising the University in an Age of Supercomplexity*. Buckingham: SRHE and Open University Press

Barnett, R. (2004) 'Learning for an unknown future'. *Higher Education Research and Development*, 23 (3), pp. 247–60

Barnett, R. (2005) 'Recapturing the universal in the university'. *Educational Philosophy and Theory*, 37 (6), pp. 783–95

Barnett, R. (2007) *A Will to Learn: Being a Student in an Age of Uncertainty*. Buckingham: SRHE and Open University Press

Becher, T. and Trowler, P. (2001) *Academic Tribes and Territories* (2nd edn). Buckingham: SRHE and Open University Press

Bergquist, W. H. (1995) *Quality Through Access, Access with Quality: The New Imperative for Higher Education*. San Francisco: Jossey-Bass

Bernstein, B. (1975) *Class, Codes and Control, vol. III*. London: Routledge

Bernstein, B. (2000) *Pedagogy, Symbolic Control and Identity*. Oxford: Rowman and Littlefield

Biesta, G. (2005) 'Against learning: reclaiming a language for education in an age of learning'. *Nordisk Pedagogik*, 25, pp. 54–66

Blackie, M. A. L., Case, J. M. and Jawitz, J. (2010) 'Student-centredness: the link between transforming students and transforming ourselves'. *Teaching in Higher Education*, 15 (6), pp. 637–46

Bradford Networks. (2015) *The Impact of BYOD in Education*. Cambridge, MA: Bradford Networks. Retrieved from http://www.bradfordnetworks.com/resources/whitepapers/the-impact-of-byod-in-education/

Buckingham Shum, S. and Ferguson, R. (2012) 'Social learning analytics'. *Educational Technology and Society*, 15 (3), pp. 3–26. Retrieved from http://oro.open.ac.uk/34092

Cohen, M. D., March, J. G. and Olsen, J. P. (1972) 'A garbage can model of organisational choice'. *Administrative Science Quarterly*, 17 (1), pp. 1–25

Cousin, G. (2006) 'An introduction to threshold concepts'. *Planet*, 17, pp. 4–5

Derrida, J. (1978) 'Violence and metaphysics: an essay on the thought of Emmanuel Levinas' in Bass, A. (trans.), *Writing and Difference*. Chicago: Chicago University Press, pp. 79–153

Dewey, J. (1986) 'How we think: a restatement of the relation of reflective thinking to the educative process' (original from 1933) in Boydston, J. A. (Ed.), *John Dewey, The Later Works, 1925–1953: 1933 Essays and How We Think*. Carbondale: Southern Illinois University Press

Eriksen, T. H. (2001) *Tyranny of the Moment: Fast and Slow Time in the Information Age*. London: Pluto Press

Field, J. (2000) *Lifelong Learning and the New Educational Order*. Stoke on Trent: Trentham

Freire, P. (1970) *Pedagogy of the Oppressed*. New York: Herder and Herder

Gornall, L. (2004) '"new professionals": academic work and occupational change in higher education'. Unpublished doctoral thesis. School of Social Sciences, Cardiff University

Hemmi, A., Bayne, S. and Land, R. (2009) 'The appropriation and repurposing of social technologies in higher education'. *Journal of Computer Assisted Learning*, 25 (1), pp. 19–30

Jenkins, C. and Barnes, C. (2014) 'Student satisfaction negates pedagogic rights: theirs and ours!' 13th Learning and Teaching Symposium, June. University of Westminster

Land, R. (2011) 'Speed and the unsettling of knowledge in the digital university' in Land, R. and Bayne, S. (Eds), *Digital Difference: Perspectives on Online Learning*. Rotterdam, Boston, and Taipei: Sense, pp. 61–72

Land, R. and Gordon, G. (Eds) (2013) *Enhancing Quality in Higher Education: International Perspectives*. New York and London: Routledge International Higher Education Series

Land, R. and Gordon, G. (2015) *Teaching Excellence Initiatives: Modalities and Operational Factors*. York: Higher Education Academy. Retrieved from https://www.heacademy.ac.uk/sites/default/files/resources/Teaching%20Excellence%20Initiatives%20Report%20Land%20Gordon.pdf

Lipsky, M. (1980) *Street-level Bureaucracy: Dilemmas of the Individual in Public Services*. New York: Russell Sage Foundation

Mclean, M., Abbas, A. and Ashwin, P. (2011) *The Use and Value of Basil Bernstein's Theory and Concepts to Illuminate the Nature of (In)Equalities in Undergraduate Social Science Education*. Retrieved from http://www.pedagogicequality.ac.uk/documents/Bernstein_and_inequality_JUNE_25_2011_001.pdf

Meyer, J. H. F. and Land, R. (2003) 'Threshold concepts and troublesome knowledge: linkages to ways of thinking and practising' in Rust, C. (Ed.), *Improving Student Learning: Ten Years On*. Oxford: OCSLD, pp. 1–16

Meyer, J. H. F. and Land, R. (2005) 'Threshold concepts and troublesome knowledge (2): epistemological considerations and a conceptual framework for teaching and learning'. *Higher Education*, 49 (3), pp. 373–88

Morrow, W. (2009) *Bounds of Democracy: Epistemological Access in Higher Education*. Pretoria, South Africa: HRSC Press

Neary, M. and Amsler, S. (2012) 'Occupy: a new pedagogy of space and time?' *Journal for Critical Education Policy Studies*, 10 (2), pp. 106–38

Nixon, J. (1996) 'Professional identity and the restructuring of higher education'. *Studies in Higher Education*, 21 (1), pp. 5–16

Perkins, D. N. (2006) 'Constructivism and troublesome knowledge' in Meyer, J. H. F. and Land, R. (Eds), *Overcoming Barriers to Student Understanding: Threshold Concepts and Troublesome Knowledge*. London: Routledge, pp. 33–47

Rifkin, J. (1995) *The End of work: The Decline of the Global Labor Force and the Dawn of the Post-market Era*. New York: G. P. Putnam's Sons

Ross, J. (2011) 'Unmasking online reflective practices in higher education'. Unpublished PhD thesis. University of Edinburgh

Saunders, M. (2009) 'Theme 2 commentary' in Bamber, V., Trowler, P. and Saunders, M. (Eds), *Enhancing Learning, Teaching, Assessment and Curriculum in Higher Education: Theory, Cases, Practices*. Maidenhead: Open University Press, pp. 91–9

Schwartz, S. (2003) 'The higher purpose'. *Times Higher Education*, 16 May. Retrieved from https://www.timeshighereducation.co.uk/comment/columnists/the-higher-purpose/176727.article

Schwartzman, L. (2010) 'Transcending disciplinary boundaries: a proposed theoretical foundation for threshold concepts' in Meyer, J. H. F., Land, R. and Baillie, C. (Eds), *Threshold Concepts and Transformational Learning*. Rotterdam, Boston, and Taipei: Sense, pp. 21–44

Scott, P. (1995) *The Meanings of Mass Higher Education*. Buckingham: SRHE and Open University Press

Sharma, S. (2014) *In the Meantime: Temporality and Cultural Politics*. Durham, NC: Duke University Press

Shattuck, R. (1974) *Proust*. London: Fontana Modern Masters

Sheail, P. (2015) 'Time-shifting in the digital university: temporality and online distance education'. Unpublished PhD thesis. University of Edinburgh

Shulman, L. (2005) 'Pedagogies of uncertainty'. *Liberal Education*, 91 (2). Retrieved from https://www.aacu.org/publications-research/periodicals/pedagogies-uncertainty

Stensaker, B. and Harvey, L. (Eds) (2011) *Accountability in Higher Education: Global Perspectives on Trust and Power*. London: Routledge

Trow, M. (2010) 'Managerialism and the academic profession: the case of England' in Burrage, M. (Ed.), *Martin Trow: Twentieth-century Higher Education. Elite to Mass to Universal*. Baltimore:

Johns Hopkins University Press, pp. 269–98. (First published as: Trow, M. (1993) *Managerialism and the Academic Profession: The Case of England*. Stockholm: Council for Studies of Higher Education)

Universities UK (2013) *Massive Open Online Courses: Higher Education's Digital Moment?* London: Universities UK

Young, M. (2012) *The Curriculum: 'An entitlement to powerful knowledge': A Response to John White*. Retrieved from http://www.newvisionsforeducation.org.uk/2012/05/03/the-curriculum-%E2%80%98an-entitlement-to-powerful-knowledge%E2%80%99-a-response-to-john-white/

9
Organizing teaching in project teacher teams across established disciplines using wearable technology
Digital didactical designing, a new form of practice

ISA JAHNKE, EVA MÅRELL-OLSSON, AND THOMAS MEJTOFT

Introduction

In the internet-driven world, one factor has changed that has an enormous impact on our current understanding of the nature of teaching and learning and its organization in education. This changing factor is ubiquitous access to information through mobile technology. More people have better access to information with easy-to-use mobile devices, any time and anywhere; we have potentially all information always at hand, via our media devices. Such a simple-sounding development has a tremendous impact on learning. Traditionally, information and communication technology (ICT) was segregated from the teaching classroom, for example, in computer labs. This segregation has changed with the advent of smaller flexible devices. There is a shift from separating ICT and education to co-located settings where mobile technology becomes part of the classroom; both have merged into new teaching spaces that expand the space for communication and social interaction into multi-existing co-located communication spaces: CrossActionSpaces (Jahnke, 2016). These new spaces, which have emerged from sociotechnical actions, provide new possibilities for teaching and learning.

The chapter explores how teachers meet the new challenges that these new situations pose to their field. Adopting the digital didactical design approach and design-based research methods, we studied, how three different study programmes were involved in the redesign and reorganization of a course at a Swedish university. The reorganization of the courses led to a new form of teaching practice leading towards learning expeditions. More specifically, the teachers redesigned the course from the view of a 'process' instead of starting with the organization of when and where students meet. Teaching becomes process design – designing for learning expeditions.

The findings illustrate a change in organizing teaching. The traditional course-based teaching has moved away from a common routine activity and turned into a design project. We argue that to plan courses along processes, a *digital didactical design thinking* is required that combines different knowledge areas. Today, universities are organized along existing disciplines, but the established boundaries are blurring in future teaching practices. In the university of the future, teaching will be organized in project teacher teams in which different teachers with different expertise across disciplines plan and conduct teaching as a project within a given time frame, where the driving force will be teaching by *topic* and not teaching by subject as it is today.

Theoretical lens: technology-enhanced designs for deeper and meaningful learning expeditions

When teachers consider integrating new or existing forms of technology into their designs for teaching and learning, they need to rethink the existing course design. With new technology, different opportunities for learning will be available that would not be available without technology. For example, mobile and wearable technology in learning situations allows the possibility for sharing content and supporting discussions among learners independent of their location. However, without integration-specific technology in the course designs, learning will not be successful because the learner does not see the benefit of using it (Jahnke et al., 2014a).

In the redesign of the courses that we studied, students had the opportunity to use mobile technology, especially wearable technology, such as smart glasses with an internet connection. Therefore, the theoretical view described below shows what is already known about mobile and wearable technology adoption in teaching and learning.

Emerging mobile and wearable technology enables real-time monitoring and support for collaborative processes. When using small flexible devices, such as media tablets, in teaching and learning, this usage fosters collaboration, creativity, and deeper learning (Jahnke et al., 2014b). Learners in tablet classrooms express learning as an activity that is engaging, with interaction and collaboration with peers (Norqvist et al., 2014). The learners expressed that the creation, making, and sharing of products is a useful activity in supporting learning progress. Students adopt technology to express their learning process in different ways. They become 'makers' in 'maker spaces' (Hatch, 2013), as shown in a study of tablet classrooms where learning expeditions happened in reflective and co-located maker spaces (Jahnke and Kumar, 2014).

Learning in those dynamic co-located situations, where wearables meet learning, can be characterized as deeper and meaningful learning expeditions, designed as a process, in which students 'make meaning' while creating something and reflecting on it. Such a design helps students engage in problem-solving; they are active, constructive, and cooperative in an authentic (real-life) situation by guided reflections ('meaningful learning', by Jonassen et al., 2003).

This kind of new learning design is especially relevant for engineering education. In such a maker space, collaborative learning is inherent. A maker space in engineering education provides a situation where interaction occurs among students. This interaction is of high relevance for engineering students because different participants can typically provide different valuable inputs during the design process (Klein et al., 2006).

Digital didactical designing (DDD)

Digital didactical designing (DDD) is the act of modelling and forming the teaching practice for different designs for learning. The focus of design lies on specific educational components. A design is the act of giving a *form*; it shapes a focus and key points for doing teaching; it is process and product at once. The course design makes a specific teacher's actions and activities visible. It puts certain elements of a classroom in the centre but does not take the whole reality into consideration.

There is a difference between teaching processes and learning designs. Teaching is the design act of modelling the learning processes. In detail, teaching 'defines' sociotechnical-pedagogical processes in which the enablement of student learning is the central purpose. It is not possible to *deliver* learning, but teaching may create conditions for that learning to take place. Many different designs exist for different learning processes. Teaching can restrict or enable learning by applying different designs to help increase the likelihood that learning occurs. This understanding has its foundation in the learning-centred paradigm, where students construct meaning rather than have teachers deliver knowledge (Jonassen et al., 2003).

The term 'didactics' (didactical) comes from the Scandinavian and German concepts of 'Didaktik' (Klafki, 1963; Wildt, 2007), and this concept shifts understanding from teaching to learning and emphasizes intended learning outcomes and student competence development. Didaktik does not only include methods – that is, 'how' to teach – but also embraces the questions of 'what' to learn (curriculum and content), 'why', 'when/where', in what kinds of situations and locations, and how it can be reached (e.g. resources, institutional, and academic staff development). One central component in Didaktik is the cultivation of social relationships and interactions, which are crucial for learning; an example of this cultivation is the formation of collaboration and active engagement with other learners' resources and knowledge. Without a design that includes social relations, a didactical design would be mainly teacher-led instead of learner-centred.

We call this method 'digital' because, in an internet-driven world, teaching practices are always technology-based, but these practices range in their support of different forms of learning, where the quantity and the quality of the technology integration vary. The term 'digital' is also relevant because it makes visible what is usually neglected. When new technology is launched for learning processes, the didactical design is usually changing. The pure addition of technology in the practice of teaching affects the existing didactical designs and vice versa.

In a dream world, a teacher aligns the following components to create a *form* for learning processes (Jahnke et al., 2014a, 2014b):

- Intended learning outcomes are clear and visible for students. The teacher communicates the learning criteria. Such criteria are relevant, so the students know how they will affect their learning progress.
- Learning activities are provided – for example, in terms of assignments that help students to achieve the intended learning outcomes.
- Assessment is designed as a process-based evaluation – for example, students receive guided reflections within the learning process to affect their performance or skill development.
- Social relations and multiple social roles are supported – for example, teachers are experts but also process mentors and learning companions, and they design for learning processes in which students are not only consumers but also producers, meaningful makers, reflectors, and co-designers of learning.
- Web-enabled mobile technology is part of the didactical design and gives access to multi-existing co-located communication spaces that support different student activities, such as documenting the student learning products, learning as a work-in-process, creating and collecting artefacts (e.g. information), sharing, reflecting, and presenting the student's learning process.

How do the teachers 'design' for learning in their practice? What *forms* do they give to their teaching practice? What learning designs do they apply in the 'classroom'? Five elements build the frame for modelling the DDD in practice; the DDD links teaching processes to learning.

This view on didactics, technology, and design placed studies on technology-enhanced teaching and learning in a new light. Learning is not only a cognitive effort, and teaching is not a delivery activity to reach the cognitive dimension. Instead, teaching is an activity-driven design (Lund and Hauge, 2011), and learning is an ongoing activity of meaningful and reflective knowledge production instead of consumption.

In this chapter, we focus on the designs for social relationships. Social relations embrace all kinds of human interaction in which the state of the social relationship between actor and situation changes based on interaction and crossreaction (Jahnke, 2015). Performed patterns of relationships, known as roles, are one way to 'see' the state of social relations between learners and between teacher and learners, in ways in which the social relations have been solidified (Jahnke, 2016, Chapter 3 on roles).

Organizational prerequisites

The organizational prerequisites for DDD are illustrated in Figure 9.1. A main prerequisite is how institutions look at the teacher's role. Teachers are experts and, when they develop new designs for learning, they are also learners. The model of teachers as collaborative learners at the workplace (Goggins et al., 2013) is a promising concept that institutions could implement.

The ways in which institutions can support this change are described below.

The DDD is illustrated as the middle layer in Figure 9.1 called Digital didactical design (layer no. 2). The middle layer is affected by the interaction of teachers, students, and content (Klafki, 1963), which is illustrated in layer no. 1 (Didactical interactions). In earlier years, content was in the textbook. Educational resources and the uses of other content and materials are much more widespread in the digital age than in previous years (Hyman, 2012). The materials range from podcasts, videos, slide-share, and social networking sites to publications, which are increasingly available online. The organizational prerequisite for a design that tends towards 'design for learning' lies in the ability of the university personnel to promote such a change (they want, they can, they do, and others do not hinder them).

- Educational institutions require an open mind towards using other forms of content, not only textbooks or traditional forms of published

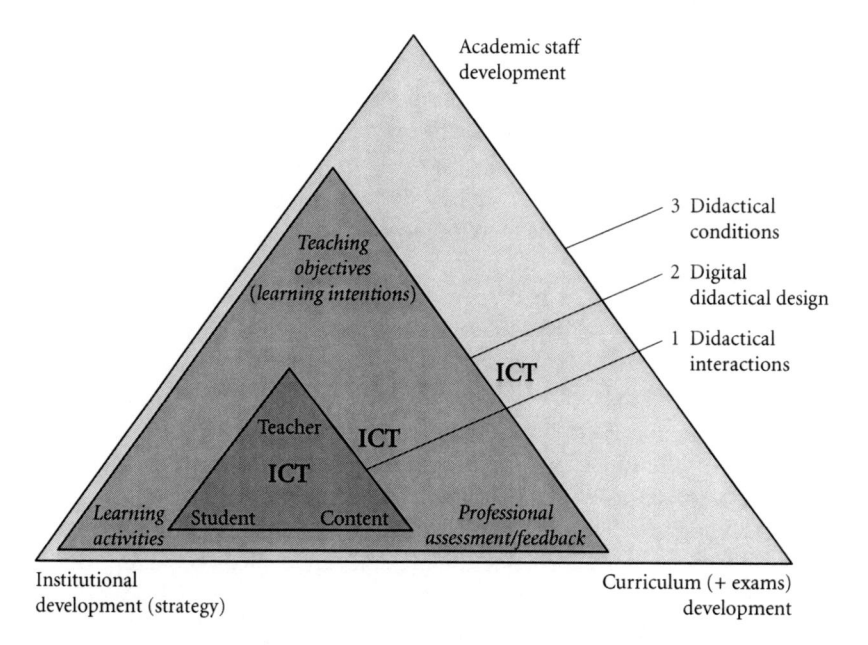

Figure 9.1 Digital didactics from a broad view: organizational prerequisites
Source: Jahnke, 2016

material. In addition, when content is made by students, then the organizational prerequisite is that teachers have the freedom and support from different actors to develop new designs for creating collaborative content. Support can include time allocation, financial benefits, and other resources (e.g. assistants).
- Second, the institution requires a 'reflection model' for teachers. Teachers obtain space and time to design for learning in a teacher team, but they also need a method to reflect together about their practice. Nice examples include Odder in Denmark and its reflection model (Norqvist et al., 2014) and the P. K. Yonge Developmental Research School at the University of Florida. The institution has creatively rebuilt new spaces for learners and teachers with the slogan 'classrooms without borders', and teachers are seen as collaborative learners at the workplace (Jahnke, 2016). A German example is the University of Mainz and its Gutenberg Teaching Council (GLK; Gutenberg Lehrkolleg), where the change has been institutionalized and has moved from traditional teaching towards 'designs for learning'. The GLK supports teachers and students to conduct new teaching and learning practices in a variety of different activities (see, e.g., the GLK's annual report), such as teacher exchanges, awards for teaching heroes, and benefits for new learning concepts (e.g. learning through reflective making, in which students are not only consumers of knowledge, but also producers and reflective makers).

Figure 9.1 also illustrates an outer layer (layer no. 3, Didactical conditions) that embraces three elements: institutional strategies, curriculum development (study programmes), and academic staff/teacher professional development. The elements point to further organizational prerequisites for conducting DDD:

a) In regard to professional development for teachers and instructors, usually universities offer workshops from pedagogical university centres. These workshops are also relevant but do not help teachers solve problems when they occur within their classroom. Workshops are often conducted separately and need external days; they are not connected to the teachers' workplaces. In addition, teachers need a community of reflecting peers. To overcome a teacher–students–loneliness constellation, open communities of practice could be cultivated and are an organizational prerequisite for reflecting on existing teaching cultures. The Scholarship of Teaching and Learning (SOTL) in the UK is an approach for teaching reflections. These approaches are often loosely coupled and could be more strongly connected to the teaching practice by providing support from institutional leaders and improving institutional framing.
b) The issue of 'organizational and institutional strategies' points to existing structures in educational institutions. The prerequisite for DDD lies in the

institutional strategy. Does the strategy support a change towards 'design thinking', or does it rather hinder such a development? What existing traditions support or hinder teachers in performing new creative pedagogies?

c) 'Curriculum development' scrutinizes existing structures of study programmes, including exams. For example, what if existing study programmes focus on content but neglect the integration of creativity? Are the university and decision-makers prepared to go in a new direction and try something new? For instance, teachers can create new forms of learning expeditions where students are creative, but the curriculum does not ask for creativity, and the written exams do not reflect on student creativity. This situation can be interpreted as a mismatch between layer 2 and layer 3 (Figure 9.1). In such a case, either the curriculum or the teacher's applied designs need to be changed.

Study context

In a study programme in higher education at Umeå University, instructors and teachers reorganized an existing course. Within this, they created a new form of a project in which student groups from three different study programmes collaborated to solve a problem and present a challenge. The overall challenge required students to design a learning expedition using wearable technology for pupils in school (seventh graders).

The course redesign was conceptually inspired by the design-based research approach. The study aimed to explore new forms of innovative pedagogy, particularly how smart glasses may support student learning when they walk through a flexible learning process. The problem-solving task was to design a learning expedition for end-users (pupils) adopting wearables. Such a learning expedition can be characterized as a treasure hunt. It is important to stress that the teacher team *did not* design the learning expeditions *for* the students; rather the teachers provided an open situation, environment, and support.

The new course included a two-level interaction with three groups.

- Level 1. The *first group* of university students (Group 1) consisted of six students from the Masters of Science Study Programmes in Engineering Physics and in Industrial Engineering and Management. They focused on *pedagogical and social design*. The *second group* of university students (Group 2) consisted of three students in the Masters of Science Study Programme in Interaction Technology and Design. This group focused on developing the *technical application* for delivering location-based information through smart glasses.
- Level 2. The *third group* (Group 3) involved the participants from schools: two young school pupils, including a girl (a 13-year-old) and a boy (a 15-year-old).

The students in our research case came from different master'm programmes. The classes belonged to different modules in different Master's programmes. However, they have one module, 'Planning and organizing work', in a project in common that fits all programmes. This commonality points to an organizational prerequisite. To create a 'design for learning' across existing study programmes, one needs to identify (or create) a module that belongs to, or suits all involved in study programmes.

Students designing a sociotechnical-pedagogical design

Student groups 1 and 2 were assigned to create a learning expedition for pupils. The students developed an application for Google Glass using location-based information. The learning expedition design also required pupil collaboration to solve the task within the expedition. The design should involve challenges that require the pupils to collaborate to complete one level of the expedition and move forward to the next. For example, the pupils obtained different pieces of information and needed to put them together to solve the puzzle.

Thus, the students needed to create a design that involved the social, technical, and pedagogical dimension – what we call a sociotechnical-pedagogical design. The students planned and conducted the design. They developed a design for a learning expedition and developed a practical application of the design. The pupils were the end-users of the sociotechnical-pedagogical design.

Three criteria were crucial for learning progress. Criterion 1 was that the learning expedition should be engaging and motivating for the young school pupils. Criterion 2 was that the pedagogical challenges and clues should not be too easy but also not too difficult for the pupils (Figures 9.2a and 9.2b). The third criterion was that the clues should be connected to functionalities of Google Glass.

The overall content frame for the learning expedition was connected to the topic of 'culture', such as art, sculpture, music, and poems. The culture theme was chosen because Umeå was the European Capital of Culture in 2014. The students were not only challenged by developing a technical solution, but also by creating a pedagogically meaningful design. More specifically, they were requested to create a learning expedition that connected the general content/ theme of *culture*. The topic provided them with questions and information about the city's culture. For example, one task for the pupils was to find words in poems printed on a big wall. The pupils had to combine the words they found to figure out the clue to the next challenge.

The pupils (Group 3) participated during a field test of the learning expedition in mid-May 2014. They used Google Glass to walk through the learning expedition outside the school environment by solving challenges and pedagogical tasks that the university students had created for them. For example,

> Ur "Dagbok 3:e feb 1977", välj 6:e bokstaven ur ett globalt ord.
>
> hennes svar stänkte högt
> som salt skum
> medan den söta sippen
> föll till jorden
>
> just now

Place 2: Umea The Heart

Notification: First Challenge!

Title: Experiment

Card 1: Beware of dihydrogen monoxide! Get the coin out of the bowl without touching the liquid. Take the help of Elvira materials and Axel's instructions.

Card 2 (Elvira): Get the material outside the insurance company at the corner of Nygatan. Axel has the instructions! Meet him in the middle of the park afterwards.

Card 3: (Full View) http://s23.postimg.org/y6r8uvym3/awdowakd.png

Card 4: Film and tweet the result. Tweet "Help" for lifeline and ask the Oracle.

Card 2 (Axel): Go to the salon Clipto get the instructions pushed to you. Meet then Elvira in the middle of the park.

Figure 9.2 a) Technical application: seeing the real world, 'the wall in a tunnel' with the Swedish text added through Google Glass; b) Pedagogical design example

Figure 9.3 Pupils' learning situation

when the school pupils approached a specific area, they received location-dependent information through Google Glass. The expedition was held in the city centre of Umeå, outside buildings, where it was possible to use GPS (Figure 9.3).

Method

The exploratory study (Stake, 2005; Yin, 1994) is inspired by the approaches of design-based research (Wang and Hannafin, 2005) and participatory action research (Lewin, 1946), where real-life situations (not in a laboratory) are created to provide a platform for studying and exploring how emerging technology can support learning processes, organizing teaching, and reorganizing courses.

The course was held in the spring of 2014 with 11 participants, including nine university students, divided into two groups, and the two young school pupils (three groups in total). The study data were collected through observations and group discussions with both the university students and the school pupils. The two university student groups wrote evaluation reports that were included in the data collection. The reports describe the work process, collaborations, and reflections on problems and challenges throughout the semester for each group. Every second week during the semester, the two student groups discussed together the project and the students' own experiences with regard to communication and collaboration within and across the groups.

The empirical material was analysed through an inductive thematic analysis (Ely, 1991) to identify key concepts and emerging patterns based on the theory of DDD (Jahnke et al., 2014a). In this study, we used three criteria to analyse the reorganization of teaching and learning: a) challenging students by topic not by subject, b) interaction and communication and c) designing for processes.

Empirical findings: reported experiences

In this section, we provide empirical findings, experiences, and insights into new conditions for teachers' innovative pedagogy and how teachers may reorganize courses by topic while considering existing subjects. This study can serve as an example of new forms of course organization in educational settings to enhance teacher and student collaborative creativity (Herrmann, 2009). The findings are grounded on the analysis of a triangulated data set.

a) *The teachers' design for challenging students to become designers*
When developing the assignment for the students, the teachers considered that the two student groups were from three different study programmes with different course plans and curricula but that all were registered for the same mandatory course of the Master of Science Programme. The combination of the two courses was designed as a project-based learning approach. Combining the two different courses created a situation that offered a design for learning that aimed at solving a real-world problem, where the topic and not the subjects guided the learning process.

The course design and assignments for the university students were created with the learning intention that the students could develop skills to become designers in 'making' a sociotechnical-pedagogical design-in-practice (planning and construction). To solve the problem given by the teacher group, the students had to collaborate within each group and between the two groups of university students; each group also worked with the university teacher who was responsible for the project. The communication included face-to-face meetings, emails, and online communication through a group-management system.

This form of bridging and integrating different courses required a negotiation of the group responsibilities to avoid misunderstanding and to make the complex 'design situation' more understandable and clearer for everyone involved. For example, it was useful to create and facilitate a learning community where all participants could receive the same information at the same time to ease the communication between the two groups and the teacher. Thus, a shared Google+ group was used for the project. Communication and collaboration within the groups and between the groups and the project leader occurred most often as regular face-to-face meetings, approximately every second week, for brainstorming or for solving problems that occurred during the project.

In this situation, the students needed to learn to organize the collaboration – both within the group (collaboration) and between the two groups (cooperation) – when designing the learning expedition activity and the application using new technology (smart glasses). A challenge for this complex situation was that the participants (students) had different knowledge and conditions such as Industrial Engineering and Management, Engineering Physics and Interaction Design. In a situation like this one, it is hard to foresee what specific communication types are needed, which increases the complexity for teachers and students (Jahnke et al., 2014b). Another challenge was to create a learning environment where all the learners participated on an equal footing, using every person's competence, so every student felt that they were helping to solve a *joined and not an individual assignment*.

b) *Interaction within and between groups*

The teachers organized learning in which the student groups created channels and platforms for communication, such as Google+, text messages, Facebook groups, Google drive, and Bitbucket. However, the design for interaction within each student group was approached differently.

Group 1 (students from the Masters of Science Programmes in Engineering Physics and in Industrial Engineering and Management) had no problem communicating or making decisions. The members organized themselves as a project using project management tools such as defining formal roles, rules, and contracts (they alternated roles). Decisions were made without any misunderstanding according to the students (interview data). Conflicts were successfully avoided because the groups created a common ground, shared understanding, and developed a strategy on what to create, how to solve the assignment, and how to make decisions that included everyone. This student group described the collaboration as that they were all equal members, and they took every group member's thoughts and suggestions into consideration when making decisions within the group.

Group 2 (students from the Master of Science Programme in Interaction Technology and Design) faced more challenges when interacting and making joint decisions. Individually, they described their problems of interaction as due to personal chemistry. Two of the group members had trouble when communicating; consequently, the third group member negotiated and, in the end, she/he made the decisions to ensure progress. This student group did not formally organize their interactions. They had a rather ad-hoc communication strategy. For this group, the project was more of a cooperation than a collaboration because they divided responsibilities and work tasks among themselves to avoid further conflicts.

One explanation for why Group 1 did not have interaction trouble is that they organized themselves without negative group dynamics. They negotiated roles at the beginning of the project and assigned tasks, functions, and responsibilities to each role. In other words, this kind of group and role organization is important for students to be successful in learning. The effect of the negotiation of roles is studied in empirical studies by Strijbos *et al.* (2003), who noted that the allocation of roles helps student teams perform better. Their results show that roles can increase the participants' awareness of interactions and efficiency through cohesion and responsibility. Their study involved 57 persons, separated into ten teams. Five teams 'were instructed to use roles' and the other five were 'instructed to rely on their intuition and previous experiences'.

Group 1 in our study also focused on content and solving the assignment, which Group 2 did not do in the same way. Group 2 described that they had personal problems that affected their learning process of solving the problem and their phase of idea finding. When both groups met, the formally organized Group 1 helped the bigger group meeting in synergizing the ideas of both groups.

One reason for the two different approaches to solving the communication and interaction problems is that Group 1 consisted of students from two different study programmes that, hence, did not know each other very well before this project. Thus, formal directives and roles needed to be established before the project started. Group 2, however, consisted of students from the same study programme with a good prior knowledge of each other. This situation made this group believe that formal roles and directives were not necessary. Consequently, when problems arose in the groups, Group 2 was less ready to face these problems than Group 1.

For the school pupils (Group 3), interaction and collaboration occurred during the event when they walked together through the learning expedition using Google Glass. The interactions were designed by the university students to avoid conflicts between the pupils because they did not know each other in advance. The activity should be experienced as joyful for the pupils. Therefore, it was important to avoid designing interaction tasks that could lead to conflicts and affect learning. Both of the school pupils described the activity as fun and challenging, and they learned a lot. They also mentioned that the activity will be a memory for life for them.

The result of the relationship level's importance in learning is supported by previous studies. For example, Herrmann *et al.* (2004) and Jahnke (2010) extended the theory of roles as important design criteria in learning; learning is understood as a form of reflective communication (Jahnke, 2016). Their studies show the relationships of formal and informal roles and indicate that these relationships enable and constrain learning and knowledge sharing. When students expect the teacher to deliver all information to the students, they see themselves in a consumer role where the teachers solve all of the problems. When teachers want students to overcome this state and turn into active agents, the design for learning requires offering learning activities in which the students need to be active and reflect on their roles. Learning through reflection sounds like a promising approach.

c) *Processes that support a shared understanding*

The students in Group 1 reflected on topic, problem-solving, and group organization. They had a flow of creativity in terms of a large number of ideas when creating the learning expedition (Figure 9.4).

In contrast, Group 2 focused more on the assignment but neglected the group organization. This group of students struggled with finding ideas, and they did not reflect on the processes of creating ideas and synergizing them. Consequently, Group 2 did not go beyond existing ideas and were not as creative as Group 1.

Even if the organization of interaction and communication varied within the groups, similar phases of asynchronous contributions and synchronous meetings occurred. For example, discussions and decision-making involved extra activities such as explanation, disagreement and agreement, shared understanding, and strategies on how to solve the assignment. The design for learning processes also required the students to create a shared understanding of formal and informal 'contracts' or regulations between group members. This design is different from individual learning, where students mainly work on the assignment without dealing with unexpected occurrences during a social process.

The designed situation and interaction during the learning expedition and the design-in-practice for the pupils also included shared understanding. They had to explain and discuss to share a mutual understanding on the best way to solve the learning expeditions. When a shared understanding occurred, they made an agreement or a decision on how they should progress. The answer to the question on how effective their shared understanding of a problem was could be observed in whether the pupils solved the challenge. These results were used as feedback for the students regarding whether their sociotechnical-pedagogical design was useful in the practice.

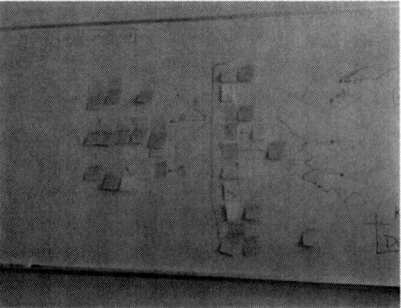

Figure 9.4 Phases of finding ideas and synergizing (Group 1)

Discussion, conclusions, and implications

This study provides insights into new forms of innovative pedagogy and how to reorganize teacher teams across existing study programmes. The aim was to support a new form of a learning opportunity for students to become *designers of learning expeditions*. The process and the results of this study have increased the knowledge of the opportunities and pitfalls when developing sociotechnical-pedagogical applications for emerging technologies such as wearable technology. When teachers give students assignments that include new technologies that are not widespread in society, collaborative creativity is required on every level due to the lack of knowledge about the technology.

The results clearly show that this project is pushing the limits of new forms of innovative pedagogy for collaborative learning and the conditions for creative teaching and learning situations and also contributes to the debate of the digitalization of educational institutions. The question remains: how does an initiative such as DDD change existing organizational structures?

The DDD initiative shows that teachers bridged existing study programmes and that they specifically created new forms of designs for learning through learning expeditions. Those learning expeditions not only contribute to surface learning, textbook or content learning, but also foster deeper (Jahnke et al., 2014a), meaningful learning (e.g. Buchem et al., 2013; Jonassen et al., 2003), in which students are pro-sumers and 'reflective makers' (Jahnke, 2016). The teachers' practice of collaboration has created a new understanding of teacher roles and student roles. The involved teachers worked as collaborative learners and are designers; while collaborating in a new form across existing structures, they affected the organization 'university' in terms of rethinking existing practices. Whether there will be a long-term effect is unknown and depends on several factors – for example, how the faculty and departments react to this initiative. However, because this course was in the local newspaper and on TV and because the cross-listed course is repeated this year, the likelihood is high that the teachers started a change. In addition, we observed another initiative in chemistry education where teachers, together with the Pedagogical Centre at the same university, changed a traditional course from lectures to an enquiry-based learning course, where students are active in groups supported by Wikis and other forms of technology.

The reorganization of teacher teams provides an opportunity to design for teaching and learning in new ways where:

- the teacher is the facilitator for creating an open environment that supports students in becoming collaborative designers across existing study programmes (the sociotechnical application design and the pedagogical design) and
- the students develop 'design-in-use experiences' for a real audience and end-users.

Such a design for learning, where students become designers and makers of a design for others, is similar to the real world and motivates students to learn. Instead of differentiating learners in different study programmes, it might be useful to bring them together in a design learning approach as we presented in this study. Teaching then occurs:

- across existing departments and established boundaries (e.g. different study programmes are involved)
- when connecting different places and spaces
- through the connection to a real-world problem (e.g. the process and product designed by the university students are connected to real end-users).

This design for learning can be called a 'learning expedition'. Such learning expeditions can be characterized as rather open-ended, problem-based learning paths that include aims-oriented learning to master X or explore and understand the implications of N. In these expeditions, the learning methods and instruments are very open and occur in maker spaces with reflecting peers, where process-based assessment and guided reflections support the learning progress (Jahnke *et al.*, 2014a).

A design for learning expedition also requires skills such as reflection, analysing, and creating synthesis (Bloom, 1956). With this example of how to redesign teaching and assignments created by teachers, the course allowed the students to practise these skills.

Working with emerging technologies in educational institutions has the potential to create new designs for teachers' collaboration among and across existing groups. Such a design requires collaborative creativity. Teachers then create designs for learning by topic and not by subject. This approach might be promising for the universities of the future.

References

Bloom, B. S. (1956) *Taxonomy of Educational Objectives, Handbook I: The Cognitive Domain*. New York: David McKay

Buchem, I., Jahnke, I. and Pachler, N. (2013) 'Mobile learning and creativity: current concepts and studies. Guest editorial preface'. *International Journal of Mobile and Blended Learning (ijMBL)*, 5 (3), pp. 1–3

Ely, M. (1991) *Doing Qualitative Research: Circles Within Circles*. London: Falmer Press

Goggins, S., Jahnke, I. and Wulf, V. (2013) *CSCL@work, Computer-supported Collaborative Learning at the Workplace*. New York: Springer

Hatch, M. (2013) *The Maker Movement Manifesto: Rules for Innovation in the New World of Crafters, Hackers, and Tinkerers*. New York: McGraw-Hill Education

Herrmann, T. (2009) 'Design heuristics for computer supported collaborative creativity'. Proceedings of the 42nd Hawaii International Conference on System Sciences, January. Waikoloa, Hawaii

Herrmann, T., Jahnke, I. and Loser, K. U. (2004) 'The role concept as a basis for designing community systems' in Darses, F., Dieng, R., Simone, C. and Zackland, M. (Eds), *Cooperative Systems Design*. Amsterdam: IOS Press, pp. 163–78

Hyman, P. (2012) 'In the year of disruptive education'. *Communications of the ACM*, 55 (12), pp. 20–2. doi: 10.1145/2380656.2380664

Jahnke, I. (2016) *Digital Didactical Designs. Teaching and Learning in CrossActionSpaces*. New York: Routledge

Jahnke, I. and Kumar, S. (2014) 'Digital didactical designs: teachers' integration of iPads for learning-centered processes'. *Journal of Digital Learning in Teacher Education*, 30 (3), pp. 81–8. doi:10.1080/21532974.2014.891876

Jahnke, I., Norqvist, L. and Olsson, A. (2014a) 'Digital didactical designs of learning expeditions' in Rensing, C., de Freitas, S., Ley, T. and Munoz-Merino, P. J. (Eds), *Open Learning and Teaching in Educational Communities. The 9th EC-TEL2014, European Conference on Technology-Enhanced Learning*. LNCS vol. 8719, September. Graz, Austria, and New York: Springer, pp. 165–78

Jahnke, I., Svendsen, N. V., Johansen, S. K. and Zander, P. O. (2014b) 'The dream about the magic silver bullet: the complexity of designing for tablet-mediated learning'. ACM Group 2014 conference proceedings, November. Florida

Jahnke, I. (2010) 'Dynamics of social roles in a knowledge management community'. *Computers in Human Behavior*, 26 (4), pp. 533–46. doi: 10.1016/j.chb.2009.08.010

Jonassen, D. H., Howland, J., Moore, J. and Marra, R. M. (2003) *Learning to Solve Problems with Technology: A Constructivist Perspective*. Merrill, Prentice Hill: Pearson

Klein, M., Sayama, H., Faratin, P. and Bar-Yam, Y. (2006) 'The dynamics of collaborative design: insights from complex systems and negotiation research' in Braha, D., Minai, A. A. and Bar-Yam, Y. (Eds), *Complex Engineered Systems*. New York: Springer, pp. 158–74

Klafki, W. (1963) *Studien zur Bildungstheorie und Didaktik* (Studies of education theory and didactics). Weinheim: Beltz

Lewin, K. (1946) 'Action Research and minority problems'. *Journal of Social Issues*, 2 (4), pp. 34–46

Lund, A. and Hauge, T. E. (2011) 'Designs for teaching and learning in technology-rich learning environments'. *Nordic Journal of Digital Literacy*, 4, pp. 258–72

Norqvist, L., Jahnke, I. and Olsson, A. (2014) 'The learners' expressed values of learning in a media tablet learning culture' In Rensing, C., de Freitas, S., Ley, T. and Munoz-Merino, P. J. (Eds), *Open Learning and Teaching in Educational Communities. The 9th EC-TEL2014, European Conference on Technology-Enhanced Learning*. LNCS vol. 8719, September. Graz, Austria, and New York: Springer

Stake, R. E. (2005) 'Qualitative case studies' in Denzin, N. K. and Lincoln, Y. S. (Eds), *The Sage Handbook of Qualitative Research* (3rd edn). Thousand Oaks, CA: Sage, pp. 695–727

Strijbos, J.-W., Martens, R. and Jochems, W. (2003) 'The effect of roles on group efficiency' in Wasson, B., Baggetun, R., Hoppe, U. and Ludvigsen, S. (Eds), *Proceedings of International Conference on Computer Support for Collaborative Learning 2003*. Bergen: Intermedia

Wang, F. and Hannafin, M. J. (2005) 'Design-Based research and technology-enhanced learning environments'. *ETR&D*, 53(4), pp. 5–23

Wildt, J. (2007) 'On the way from teaching to learning by competences as learning outcomes' in Pausits, A. and Pellert, A. (Eds), *Higher Education Management and Development in Central, Southern and Eastern Europe*. Münster: Waxmann, pp. 115–23

Yin, R. K. (1994) *Case Study Research* (2nd edn). Thousand Oaks, CA: Sage

10
Changing organizational structure and culture to enhance teaching and learning
Cases in a university in Hong Kong

SAMUEL K. W. CHU AND SANNY S. W. MOK

Introduction

Advancements in social media and digital technologies have transformed the current spread of information and knowledge. On the forefront of knowledge creation and new discoveries, the university is no exception. To keep pace with the fast-changing times, universities must embrace these new technologies in their teaching and learning. As Albert Einstein once said, 'The world as we have created it is a process of our thinking. It cannot be changed without changing our thinking.' We see that how the 'thinking' of members of a university in general can be changed through the introduction of new teaching and learning initiatives by individual lecturers with the support of top management. We argue that teaching and learning can be enhanced by a combination of organizational structural and cultural change: the process starts with structural changes, such as funding opportunities and performance evaluation, which offer incentives for pedagogical innovations. Once the initial innovations begin and yield positive effects, a gradual spread and diffusion of innovative pedagogies will follow, which changes the university's organizational culture in the area of teaching and learning.

To begin this chapter, we first briefly review the existing literature on organizational change in the context of higher education, highlighting the importance of understanding one's institution and the sustainability of changes. The second section presents three case studies from our perspective of university lecturers, drawing on our specific experience in applying new technologies and innovative pedagogies at the course/programme level. The first case involves the use of Wiki, an online collaborative platform, to facilitate group project work in a course. The second case discusses and compares two types of social media, blogs and Facebook, on their effectiveness in facilitating knowledge management (KM) and promoting a culture of mutual support in the context of students' summer internships. The third case discusses a newly accepted proposal that combines face-to-face lectures and online classes to cater to students' increasingly diversified off-campus learning experiences and any difference in individual students' learning paces in two undergraduate programmes. The effectiveness of the project or the conditions that contribute to desirable teaching and learning outcomes will be discussed in each case. After discussing the details of the three projects, in the third section we will look at organizational change from an etic perspective, relating the significance of structural change in bringing about such cultural changes.

Organizational change in higher education teaching and learning

Situated on the edge of knowledge, universities constantly face the challenge of keeping pace with knowledge change. This challenge is especially prominent in the twenty-first century because information spreads quickly and easily through the internet. In light of this challenge, organizational change has been recommended, among others, as a method for universities to adapt to the ever fast-changing world (for a review, see Fumasoli and Stensaker, 2013). This recommendation involves both structural and cultural changes within the institution (Cameron, 1984; Gumport, 2000; Clark, 2004a, 2004b; Browne, 2005). Not only do universities have to change, but such transformations should be sustainable, or as Clark (2004a, p. 356) put it 'the altered practices [should be] turned into a steady state of change'. With sustainability of change in mind, organizational change in teaching and learning deserves the attention of policy-makers, university administrators, and educators because the processes of teaching and learning provide institutions with their life blood (Browne, 2005). Readers should note that, although the case studies in this chapter focus on teaching and learning in courses/programmes, existing literature organizational studies in the field of higher education typically discuss change on a large scale – for example, policy change on an institutional (Amaral *et al.*, 2003; Locke *et al.*, 2011) or even national level (Schwarz and Teichler, 2000; Amaral *et al.*, 2002).

Organizational change involves both structural and cultural aspects. Organizational structure depends on three factors: its surrounding environment and the organization's interactions with it, the operational (i.e. the workflow employed) and material (i.e. the physical and information materials used) technologies, and the organization's size (Child, 1972). To put this definition into context, structural organization changes in higher education touch on the issues of university governance, the role of academic leadership, the relationship between academics and administrators within the university, and their relationship with state and policy-makers, as revealed by Fumasoli and Stensaker (2013) after analysing 25 years' worth of literature on this topic. In contrast, cultural organizational change can be considered as changes in the organizational members' shared ideas, beliefs, assumptions, asserted values, and visions of the organization or its work (Peterson and Spencer, 1991; Eckel *et al.*, 1998; Clark, 2004a). It is a change in the symbolic aspects of the material components found in the organizational structure. Though ephemeral, such symbolic qualities are reflected in the members' concrete practices or 'the way in which organizational members go about their work', as stated by Fidler *et al.* (1997, p. 35).

Three case studies of organizational change in university teaching and learning

In section 2, we present three cases of implementing organizational change in the area of university teaching and learning: the first and second cases are completed and the third is in progress. The pedagogy and technologies involved differ in each case – a wiki is used in a group project work in case 1, social media is used for out-of-class communication in case 2, whereas a blended mode of lecture delivery is adopted in case 3 – but they all involve the introduction of a new practice on the course/programme level. The section focuses on the process and evaluation of cultural organizational change at the front line of teaching and learning, with all changes directly exerting an effect on students and lecturers.

Case 1: applying an online collaborative authoring tool to facilitate students' group project work

Wikis have been commonly used as KM tools to facilitate the creation, sharing, discussion, and revision of knowledge artefacts in group projects (Da Lio *et al.*, 2005). Wiki software has also been applied in various ways in education, including the support of individual and group writing projects, course management, and distance education (Bold, 2006; Parker and Chao, 2007). The wiki has risen to popularity because of its open-source nature; its capacity for simultaneous editing, content organization, and edit history features; and its flexibility in allowing private or public access (Lamb, 2004; Engstrom and Jewett, 2005; Raman, Ryan and Olfman, 2005).

In case 1 (Chu, 2008), TWiki was introduced in an undergraduate course on KM. Students were required to write a chapter for a wikibook[1] in groups of four to five. Instead of writing the chapter using Microsoft Word, the more conventional word processing software, students performed their projects using the open-source online collaborative groupware. The lecturer designed wiki templates for draft reports, discussions, and finalized reports (see Figure 10.1), so students could start up their project and modify to suit their needs. The usability and effectiveness of TWiki in facilitating group project work was evaluated.

Changing organizational structure and culture • 189

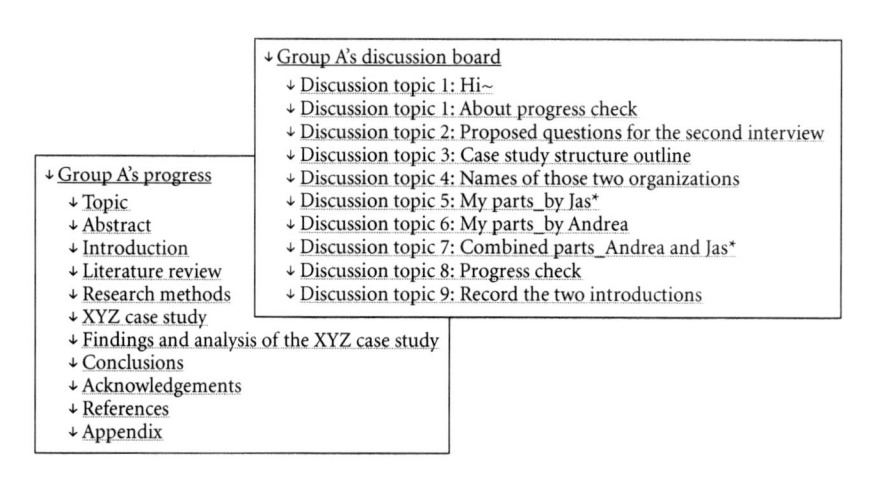

```
                        ↓ Group A's discussion board
                            ↓ Discussion topic 1: Hi~
                            ↓ Discussion topic 1: About progress check
                            ↓ Discussion topic 2: Proposed questions for the second interview
                            ↓ Discussion topic 3: Case study structure outline
↓ Group A's progress        ↓ Discussion topic 4: Names of those two organizations
    ↓ Topic                 ↓ Discussion topic 5: My parts_by Jas*
    ↓ Abstract              ↓ Discussion topic 6: My parts_by Andrea
    ↓ Introduction          ↓ Discussion topic 7: Combined parts_Andrea and Jas*
    ↓ Literature review     ↓ Discussion topic 8: Progress check
    ↓ Research methods      ↓ Discussion topic 9: Record the two introductions
    ↓ XYZ case study
    ↓ Findings and analysis of the XYZ case study
    ↓ Conclusions
    ↓ Acknowledgements
    ↓ References
    ↓ Appendix
```

Figure 10.1 TWiki templates for 'group progress' and 'group discussion'
Source: Chu, 2008

Overall, the results from the questionnaires and interviews were generally positive regarding the effectiveness of TWiki in facilitating student group projects and as a tool for KM in terms of knowledge creation, capturing, sharing, and transferring (see Table 10.1). Students agreed that the use of the wiki improved their collaboration because it allowed different members to simultaneously work on different parts of the report, to keep track of each other's work progress, and to respond to groupmates' work in the form of comments. The perceived improved level of collaboration had a significant moderate correlation to a perceived improved quality of work. The open-source nature of TWiki also contributed to the students' increased efforts. Opening the product to public access motivated students to put in more effort in the wiki-based assignment compared with conventional assignments – the wiki editing history showed that a student edited her own chapter six months after the assignment submission. The post-submission edit showed that students did not merely treat the project as an assignment but as their own creation, freely available on the internet, contributing to knowledge building, sharing, and transfer.

Of note in Table 10.1, the group of more frequent TWiki users consistently gave lower ratings to the survey questions, although the difference was not significant as shown by the Mann-Whitney test. This finding suggests that when students had limited experience with TWiki, they had confidence that it was a useful tool for online collaborative projects. However, as students gained more experience with TWiki, they found it a less useful tool than their original impression; thus, they rated it less favourably in all five aspects listed in Table 10.1. Nevertheless, for both groups of students, all five aspects had a mean rating above the mid-point three (out of five), meaning that TWiki was still positively received among students.

Table 10.1 Student responses on the use of TWiki

Survey questions	Group 1: more frequent users mean; median (95% CI) ($N_1 = 19$)	Group 2: less frequent users mean; median (95% CI) ($N_2 = 19$)	Results from Mann-Whitney test: p-value
1. Improved collaboration using wiki[a]	3.3; 3.0 (3.0–3.6)	3.4; 4.0 (2.9–3.8)	0.752^
2. Improved quality using wiki[a]	3.1; 3.0 (2.7–3.4)	3.3; 3.0 (2.9–3.7)	0.345^
3. Ease of using TWiki [b]	3.2; 3.0 (2.8–3.5)	3.3; 3.0 (2.9–3.6)	0.671^
4. Enjoyment in using TWiki[a]	3.1; 3.0 (2.7–3.4)	3.4; 3.0 (2.9–3.8)	0.306^
5. TWiki as a suitable tool[a]	3.4; 3.0 (3.0–3.8)	3.7; 4.0 (3.3–4.0)	0.168^

Notes:
[a]The respondents answered according to a five-point Likert scale, with 1 as 'not at all' and 5 as 'very much so'
[b]The respondents answered according to a five-point Likert scale, with 1 as 'very difficult' and 5 as 'very easy'
^Ratings from Group 1 and 2 were not significantly different as shown by the Mann-Whitney test at a 5% significance level

Source: Chu, 2008, p. 753

This finding leads to the observation that, while students were generally positive about the use of TWikis, they experienced difficulty in formatting and other technical problems, partly due to the imperfections interface design and partly because of their unfamiliarity with the software's editing tool. The students' concerns demonstrated the importance of sufficient training when new technology is introduced in teaching and learning. For example, brief training during regular class hours should be supplemented by in-depth training in an additional lab session if necessary. Apart from training students to use the software, it is important to help students overcome any social obstacles they face in editing each other's work. Students reported that they felt uncomfortable editing or commenting on the work of other groups because they were unfamiliar with the topic or the situation of the other groups. To improve students' ease of using collaborative platforms such as TWiki, guidelines and instructions on how to edit or comment on others' work could be given, so students may feel more at ease in the practice of peer reviewing/editing. Alternatively, user-friendly platforms for collaboration could be considered, especially with the maturation of online collaboration technology. In the years that followed this study, the first author offered students more user-friendly wiki tools such as PBworks (Law *et al.*, 2014) and the flexibility of choosing from a range of online collaboration platforms to suit their own needs (Chu and Kennedy, 2011).

Case 2: using blogs and Facebook to support learning during internship

This section summarizes findings from two studies (Chu *et al.*, 2012; Chan *et al.*, 2013) and illustrates how two popular types of social media, blogs and Facebook, could facilitate KM and scaffold tertiary students' learning processes during their internship experience. Building on Chu *et al.*'s (2012) study on the use of blogs to support students' internship learning experiences, Chan *et al.* (2013) compared three cohorts of students who communicated through blogs and one cohort who communicated through Facebook. During the two- to three-month internship period, students communicated with their peers and supervisors through the aforementioned social media platforms. Blogs and Facebook are two pre-eminent social technologies that have emerged in recent years. Both tools act as a platform to allow the sharing of information, such as texts, pictures, and sound files, so a community of browsers could interact (Gonczi, 2004). The decision to use blogs and Facebook was made in hopes of offering students emotional and work support from their peers and teachers, particularly when they were newcomers to an organization without someone familiar to confide in. Qualitative content analysis was applied to categorize students' posts according to their themes. Students were also interviewed to understand their perceptions of the social media used. The results showed that both blogs and Facebook facilitated KM, as we will explain below.

In this section, we adopt the KM cycle to explain the role social media plays in students' learning. Scholars have proposed that KM could be represented by the KM cycle, which is a cyclic process that encompasses knowledge capturing, creating, sharing, disseminating, acquiring, and applying by individuals or groups (Meyer and Zack, 1996; McElroy, 1999; Bukowitz and Williams, 2000). Relating KM to organizational culture and technologies, Dalkir (2011) summarized the KM cycle as a three-stage process: 1) knowledge capture and/or creation, 2) knowledge sharing and dissemination, and 3) knowledge acquisition and application. Information and knowledge sharing can be promoted with a favourable organizational culture and adequate technology support.

Results from both studies showed that both blogs and Facebook served as effective platforms to facilitate KM, express their feelings, and provide mutual support. They engaged in regular activities on these social media, including writing entries or posts, reading their peers' postings, and providing and receiving comments. In Chan *et al.* (2013), student engagement was compared across the two platforms. The study found that the students engaged actively in

Organizational culture

Knowledge capture
- knowledge reflection
- experience capture

KM Technologies

Update • Assess • Contextualize

Knowledge acquisition and application
- knowledge construction
- problem solving

Knowledge sharing and dissemination
- knowledge sharing
- posting questions
- providing feedback

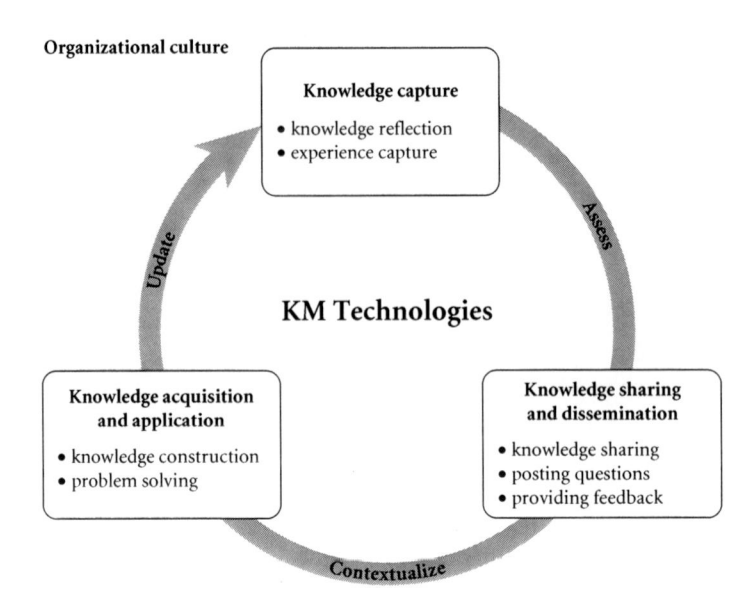

Figure 10.2 An integrated KM cycle
Source: Adapted from Dalkir, 2011, p. 270

knowledge capture and knowledge sharing and dissemination, but they were significantly less active in knowledge acquisition and application, as observed from the low proportion of posts under this theme (see Table 10.2). Under the theme of knowledge capture, there were significantly more posts in Facebook than blogs in the subthemes knowledge reflection and experience capture. Under the theme of knowledge sharing and dissemination, a significant contrast was observed in the users' feedback provision behaviour: Facebook users posted more feedback than blog users: the subtheme of 'providing feedback' had an average of 4.38 posts more than blogs, meaning that they shared and disseminated knowledge more often on Facebook than on blogs.

Students also used blogs and Facebook to express their positive and negative feelings (see Table 10.3). They appeared to share emotions more often on blogs, with an average of 1.36 more posts on blogs. With regards to social support from peers, while students agreed that both platforms facilitated emotional support and that they had received support from peers through commenting, they gave much higher ratings to the perceived support they received from peers on Facebook than on blogs (see Table 10.4). Students' preference for Facebook could be explained by its higher everyday usage outside of any educational purposes, which echoes an earlier study showing that students' study media usage partially reflects their general media usage (Schuster *et al.*, 2014).

Table 10.2 Distribution of coded blogs and Facebook entries in the theme of KM processes

	Blogs (n = 53) Mean	Facebook (n = 20) Mean
Knowledge capture	5.25	25.35
Knowledge reflection	3.19	10.6
Experience capture	2.06	14.75
Knowledge sharing and dissemination	2.20	7.4
Information sharing	1.7	1.4
Posting questions	0.19	1.3
Providing feedback	0.32	4.7
Knowledge acquisition and application	3.96	2.25
Knowledge construction	2.3	0.8
Problem solving	1.66	1.45

Note: The figures represent the average number of blog entries or Facebook posts each participant contributed

Source: Chan et al., 2013, p. 5

Interviews with students reviewed difference in usage between blogs and Facebook. While both were effective in facilitating KM processes, blog users valued the platform's function in facilitating knowledge capture, sharing, and dissemination, which was achieved by posting on and reading other's entries (Chu et al., 2012). In contrast, Facebook users appreciate the platform's more advanced group features for collaborative interaction, which supports a bottom-up building of communities and networks (Chatti et al., 2007; Group Features, n.d.). Such interactive features, including group notifications, private messaging, and the 'like' function provide more channels to demonstrate social support. This difference explains why Facebook users are more willing to express support on the platform. Blogs do support mutual support, but it occurs outside the platform – for example, in telephone calls or face-to-face conversations.

Table 10.3 Distribution of coded blogs and Facebook in the theme of socio-emotional expressions

	Blogs (n = 53)	Facebook (n = 20)
Emotional expressions	4.96	3.6
Positive emotions	2.42	3
Negative emotions	1.57	0.6
Social support	0.98	5.55

Source: Chan et al., 2013, p. 6

Table 10.4 Students' perceived support received on blogs and Facebook

Survey items	Blogs (n = 53)		Facebook (n = 20)		Sig. Mann–Whitney
	Mean (SD)	Median	Mean (SD)	Median	
Perceived support from classmates via commenting	2.67 (0.65)	3.00	3.00 (0.32)	3.00	**0.03***
Perceived support from supervisor via mutual interactions	1.92 (0.84)	3.00	2.85 (0.59)	3.00	**<0.01***

Notes: Ratings are based on a four-point Likert-type scale: 1 – 'Strongly disagree', 2 – 'Disagree', 3 – 'Agree', and 4 – 'Strongly agree' (with a mid-point of 2.5)
*Significant at $p < 0.05$

Source: Chan *et al.*, 2013, p. 7

Various types of social media have been employed for this purpose since 2006, using blogs in the earlier years and gradually shifting to Facebook for the more recent cohorts. Data have been collected annually to review the platforms' usability, effectiveness, and user perception. The comparison studies show that, with the use of appropriate social media technologies, social motivation to pursue KM can be enhanced. Each type of social media has its own potentials and weaknesses, as discussed above. In general, with its user-friendly and easy-to-learn collaborative features, Facebook is more effective in promoting an organizational culture of mutual support and thus facilitating the social-collaborative process of KM. Individuals are more willing to connect, communicate, and reflect on their knowledge and experiences on the platform. Through regular review, the lecturer was able to choose the most suitable platform to connect students with their peers and teachers during the internship period, thus improving the pedagogy.

Case 3: introducing BSTL pedagogy to provide flexibility for both teachers and students and maximize learning

Case 3 discusses the recently accepted proposal for the implementation of a blended synchronous teaching and learning (BSTL) pedagogy (see Figure 10.3) in two undergraduate programmes. By employing rich media technologies, this mode of teaching and learning combines face-to-face and online classes (Collopy and Arnold, 2009), so various advantages can be attained without

Figure 10.3

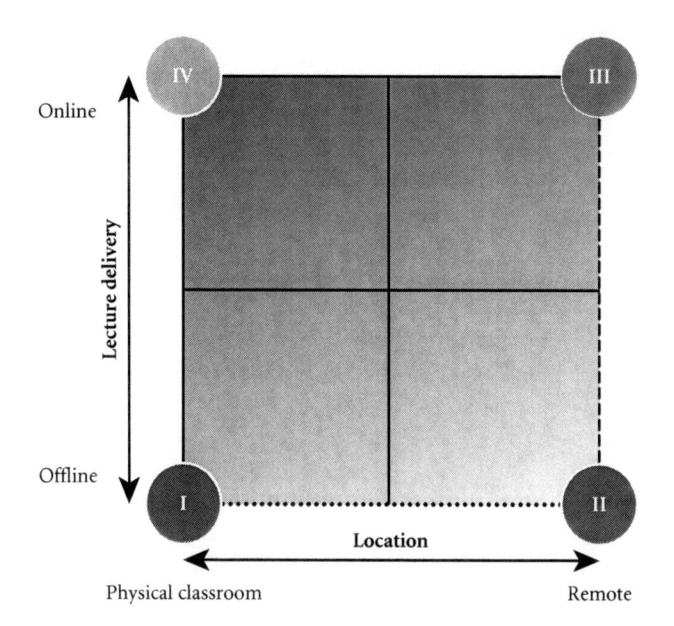

Point	Mode	Example
I	Traditional	Traditional classroom lecture
II	Traditional	Offline distance learning
III	Could be traditional or blended	Traditional: MOOCs (Massive Open Online Courses)
		Blended: cyber programs with some face–to–face elements
IV	Blended	Lectures in physical classroom with online exercises
	Blended	Learning through a mix of online–offline and physical classroom/remote modes

Figure 10.3 A two-dimensional BSTL model with examples of different matrix points

Source: Adapted from Staker *et al.*, 2011, p. 6

sacrificing the valuable interactions between course instructors and students and among students.

The learning space for university students in the twenty-first century is no longer limited to lecture rooms. One of the educational aims of the university is to cultivate intercultural understanding and global citizenship, in which students are encouraged to join academic exchange programmes overseas. However, many students give up their wish to go overseas for academic exchange because certain courses cannot be taken when they are abroad. Those who are determined to participate in the exchange may need to extend their study for a semester or even a year. Other reasons for students' absence include physical injury, sickness, or time conflicts. Thus, they must catch up by doing self-learning at home without the course instructors' support. They also lose the opportunity to participate in group discussion and interaction during classes. In light of the above problems, the project proposed to improve on the present mode of teaching and learning, so students could maximize their learning both inside and outside the classroom.

BSTL offers both live broadcasts of classes (synchronous learning) and the reviewing of classes that have been videotaped online (asynchronous learning). This combination caters to the students' individual needs – particularly for deep or slower learners – they could re-watch the videos at home to revise and consolidate the lecture contents at a self-designed pace. The slower or deep learners could take the opportunity to view or listen to these recorded lectures at their own time for self-paced learning or reviewing purposes. The flexibility in delivering lectures addresses the personal needs of students to overcome spatial constraint. With all lectures archived in the form of video or audio files, students who are not present to join the face-to-face classes or live broadcast may watch the videos later to catch up with the progress. This technology maintains the teacher–student interactions in class, so bilateral communication could take place effectively. The BSTL approach is hoped to, first, relieve students' concerns when they decide whether to pursue other types of learning experiences overseas (thus encouraging them to enrich their university education) and, second, promote a culture of understanding and catering to individual students' learning pace and needs.

Because the project will be implemented in spring 2016, we do not have any results available as yet. Instead, we would like to emphasize the importance of funding for such innovations for teaching and learning. Funding to encourage such an innovative scheme is of exceptional importance because technological and infrastructural support is needed to bring the plan into real practice. Human resources, such as teaching assistants, are needed to control and monitor the video-recording (for live online broadcast of the lecture and for the subsequent archiving of the lecture) while the lecturer conducts the lesson with students in a physical classroom. Various aspects require funding to purchase the materials and equipment needed. For instance, an open-source web conferencing system (e.g. BigBlueButton), equipment (e.g. network camera), classroom set-up (e.g. cost of renovation, cabling, etc.), and the buy-in of staff (project assistants, etc.) require funding to support.

Supporting organizational change with funding

In section 2, we have discussed three cases of introducing innovative technology to change organizational culture. All three cases were made possible because of a structural change – the support of either university-level or faculty-level teaching-related funding, some of which established more recently than others. Such funding welcome applications from lecturers who would like to try innovative pedagogies. The university-level teaching development grant (TDG) was the university's initiative to promote the quality of teaching and learning in specific areas. Cases 1 and 2 were relevant to some of the grant's focus, including curriculum or pedagogical innovations, e-learning, and experiential learning, and hence gained support from the grant. Apart from the university-level grant, the faculty-level teaching development fund offers additional support for teaching-related projects that are beneficial at the faculty level. For example, based on the work done with the university-level TDGs, the first author applied for a faculty-level fund to conduct the additional work mentioned in Case 2 regarding automating the assessment of students' collaborative learning on social media.

Funding for the BSTL implementation in case 3 came from a new source called the Dean's Innovation Fund (DIF). This fund differs from the above two funding sources in the sense that it expects applicants to make a direct contribution to innovation within the faculty – pedagogy innovation in the case of BSTL implementation – or in other aspects including curriculum, research, and knowledge exchange. Like the faculty-level teaching development fund, it is intended to complement other sources of funding that are available at the university level, and much of this funding would be spent on aspects that the university-level funds do not support (e.g. buying out the teaching load for a project team member or equipment costs). However, with a cap of HK$ 250,000 for each project – three times the usual amount offered in other faculty-level funds – the DIF allows project teams to try pedagogies that require a larger budget. Additional funding could also be awarded to support the improvement of infrastructure such as renovation, cabling, installation, and integration of equipment. With this funding, the authors will be able introduce innovative online teaching and learning pedagogy, as mentioned above.

Top management support is essential when promoting organizational change. With a vision for the organization's future and an understanding of the need for change, leaders will establish internal support for change and reduce any resistance or obstacles to change (Fernandez and Rainey, 2006). Thus, the allocation of funding is a means for university leaders to promote the introduction of innovative pedagogy through a structural change in the organization. Each fund prompts lecturers to improve specified areas of interest and simultaneously provide them with the financial resources to realize these improvements. Lecturers are thus encouraged to experiment with innovative pedagogical ideas. For example, the three case studies discussed in section 2 are examples of the lecturer taking initiative to integrate technology in courses to enhance teaching and learning. When such projects prove to be effective, more and more lecturers will engage in these innovative practices (with or without funding), which, in turn, promote organizational change (see Figure 10.3).

The structural change of providing more funding opportunities is one of the supporting factors for organizational cultural change. One other motivation is the emphasis placed on teaching staff's performance evaluations, as related to innovative and effective pedagogies. These performance evaluations are essential to both lecturers and students because the evaluation results may be used in personnel decisions and for providing feedback to improve teaching (Goldschmid, 1978). In the area of teaching, lecturers are often encouraged to be classroom researchers who gather measures of student learning to improve their teaching (Centre for Research on Learning and Teaching, 2014). That is, whether lecturers employ new methods of teaching that improve student learning has become an indicator of their performance. To become a classroom researcher, resources are needed for lecturers to hire an assistant to help design research instruments, collect and analyse data to evaluate the effectiveness of the new pedagogy. Therefore, through applying for funding, lecturers on the front line of teaching and learning could obtain resources to realize their plans of pedagogical improvement. Because the needs of one course may vary from the next, having funding available for individual lecturers' applications allows for a bottom-up organizational change in culture, so the changes suit each cohort of students involved. At the same time, administrators could encourage more effort and input on certain areas of interest; the faculty-level teaching development fund requires project proposals to align with the faculty's visions, allowing individual faculties to emphasize development in key aspects as they see fit. Additional funding (e.g. the DIF in case 3) could be created to promote the faculty's key development areas. With this structure, university administrators could outline a general direction for change, while those on the front line have the flexibility to tailor plans to suit their own situation.

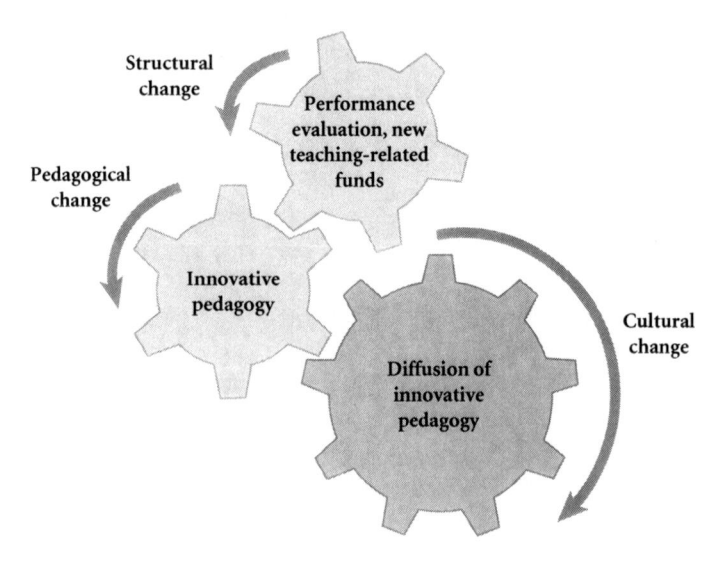

Figure 10.4 The process of organization change

Conclusion

We have reviewed both structural and cultural changes in the first part of the chapter. Most cases point to two important criteria for a successful implementation and smooth transition in the organization: understanding and sustainability. We then presented three cases based on our own experience in introducing organizational changes in university teaching and learning at the course/programme level. The first case presents and evaluates the use of TWiki to facilitate group project work. The second discusses and compares the effectiveness of blogs and Facebook as tools to promote KM and the culture of mutual support. The third discusses a proposal to use a BSTL approach in lectures to break the physical and temporal constraints of the classroom, enabling students to continue to participate in classes outside of the classroom to carry out their other learning experiences and to learn at their own pace. For the first two cases, the students' use and perception of the new technology and pedagogy used was the focus of evaluation. Because students make up the majority of end-users in both cases, the change would not be sustainable without students' favourable reception and, hence, motivation to engage in the new initiatives. Additionally, by analysing the students' behaviour on the platforms, we gathered information on the technology's effectiveness in achieving the project goals and its potential and weakness, and we then improved the practice based on our understanding of the situation.

After examining organizational change from the perspective of a course/programme for students and lecturers, we looked at the process on a university-wide level. Initiatives for improvement are essential in promoting organizational change. These changes start with the university's decision on funding availability and its allocation and performance evaluations that carry expectations of teaching staff contributing to innovative and effective pedagogy. By making funding available on all possible structural levels (e.g. university level, faculty level) and providing additional support on emphasized aspects (e.g. technological innovative pedagogy), lecturers are offered substantial motivation to implement new teaching practices in their own classes. Eventually, with increasing successful cases, more lecturers will engage in new practices, thus inducing a culture of change in the institution.

Note

1   Wikibook – an eBook constructed on an online wiki platform.

References

Amaral, A., Jones, G. and Karseth, B. (Eds.) (2002) *Governing Higher Education: National Perspectives on Institutional Governance*. Dordrecht: Kluwer Academic

Amaral, A., Meek, V. L., and Larsen, I. M. (Eds) (2003) *The Higher Education Managerial Revolution?* Dordrecht: Kluwer Academic

Bold, M. (2006) 'Use of wikis in graduate course work'. *Journal of Interactive Learning Research*, 17 (1), pp. 5–14

Browne, E. (2005) 'Structural and pedagogic change in further and higher education: a case study approach'. *Journal of Further and Higher Education*, 29 (1), pp. 49–59

Bukowitz, W. and Williams, R. (2000) *The Knowledge Management Fieldbook*. London: Prentice Hall

Cameron, K. S. (1984) 'Organizational adaptation and higher education'. *The Journal of Higher Education*, 55 (2), pp. 122–44

Centre for Research on Learning and Teaching (2014) *Guidelines for Evaluating Teaching*. University of Michigan. Retrieved from http://www.crlt.umich.edu/tstrategies/guidelines

Chan, R. C. H., Chu, S. K. W., Lee, C. W. Y., Chan, B. K. T. and Leung, C. K. (2013) 'Knowledge management using social media: a comparative study between blogs and Facebook'. Proceedings of the ASIS&T 2013 Annual Meeting. Montreal, Quebec

Chatti, A., Klamma, R., Jarke, M. and Naeve, A. (2007) 'The Web 2.0 driven SECI model based learning process'. International Conference of Advanced Learning Technologies (ICALT-2007), July. Niigata, Japan

Child, J. (1972) 'Organizational structure, environment and performance: the role of strategic choice'. *Sociology*, 6 (1), pp. 1–22

Chu, S. (2008) 'TWiki for knowledge building and management'. *Online Information Review*, 32, pp. 745–58

Chu, S. K. W. and Kennedy, D. M. (2011) 'Using online collaborative tools for groups to co-construct knowledge'. *Online Information Review*, 35 (4), pp. 581–97

Chu, S. K. W., Chan, C. K. K. and Tiwari, A. F. Y. (2012) 'Using blogs to support learning during internship'. *Computers and Education*, 58 (3), pp. 989–1000

Clark, B. R. (2004a) 'Delineating the character of the entrepreneurial university'. *Higher Education Policy*, 17 (4), pp. 355–70

Clark, B. R. (2004b) *Sustaining Change in Universities*. Berkshire: SHRE/Open University Press

Collopy, R. M. B. and Arnold, J. (2009) 'To blend or not to blend: online-only and blended learning environments'. *Issues in Teacher Education*, 18 (2), pp. 85–101

Da Lio, E., Fraboni, L. L. and Leo, T. (2005) 'TWiki-based facilitation in a newly formed academic community of practice'. Paper presented at the 2005 International Symposium on Wikis, 16–18 October. San Diego, CA

Dalkir, K. (2011) *Knowledge Management in Theory and Practice* (2nd edn). London: MIT Press

Eckel, P., Hill, B. and Green, M. (1998) *On Change: En Route to Transformation*. Occasional Paper, No. 1. Washington, DC: American Council on Education

Engstrom, M. E. and Jewett, D. (2005) 'Collaborative learning: the wiki way', *TechTrends*, 49 (6), pp. 12–68

Fernandez, S. and Rainey, H. G. (2006) 'Managing successful organizational change in the public sector'. *Public Administration Review*, 66 (2), pp. 168–76

Fidler. B., Russell, S. and Simkins, T. (Eds) (1997) *Choices for Self-managing Schools: Autonomy and Accountability*. London: Paul Chapman

Fumasoli, T. and Stensaker, B. (2013) 'Organizational studies in higher education: a reflection on historical themes and prospective trends'. *Higher Education Policy*, 26 (4), pp. 479–96

Goldschmid, M. L. (1978) 'The evaluation and improvement of teaching in higher education'. *Higher Education*, 7 (2), pp. 221–45

Gonczi, A. (2004). 'The new professional and vocational education' in Foley, G. (Ed.), *Dimensions of Adult Learning: Adult Education and Training in a Global Era*. Crows Nest, NSW: Allen and Unwin, pp. 19–34

Group Features (n.d.) *Help Center* [Facebook page]. Retrieved 2 April 2015 from https://www.facebook.com/help/265435626889287/

Gumport, P. J. (2000) 'Academic restructuring: organizational change and institutional imperatives'. *Higher Education*, 39 (1), pp. 67–91

Lamb, A. (2004) 'Wide open spaces wikis ready or not'. *Educause Review*, 39 (5), pp. 36–48

Law, W. W. T., King, R. B., Notari, M., Cheng, E. W. L. and Chu, S. K. W. (2014) 'Why do some students become more engaged in collaborative wiki writing? The role of sense of relatedness'. Paper presented at the OpenSym 2014. Berlin

Locke, W., Cummings, W. K. and Fisher, D. (2011) *Changing Governance and Management in Higher Education: The Perspectives of the Academy*. Dordrecht: Springer

McElroy, M. (1999) 'The knowledge life cycle'. Proceedings of the ICM Conference on KM, April. Miami

Meyer, M. and Zack, M. (1996) 'The design and implementation of information products'. *Sloan Management Review*, 37 (3), pp. 43–59

Parker, K. and Chao, J. (2007) 'Wiki as a teaching tool'. *Interdisciplinary Journal of e-learning and Learning Objects*, 3 (1), pp. 57–72

Peterson, M. and Spencer, M. (1991) 'Understanding academic culture and climate' in Petereson, M. (Ed.), *ASHE Reader on Organization and Governance*. Needham Heights, MA: Simon and Schuster, pp. 140–55

Raman, M., Ryan, T. and Olfman, L. (2005) 'Designing knowledge management systems for teaching and learning with wiki technology'. *Journal of Information Systems Education*, 16 (3), pp. 311–20

Schwarz, S. and Teichler, U. (2000) *The Institutional Basis of Higher Education Research. Experiences and Perspectives*. Dordrecht: Kluwer Academic

Schuster, K., Thöing, K., May, D., Lensing, K., Grosch, M., Richert, A., Tekkaya, A. E., Petermann, M. and Jeschke, S. (2014) 'Status quo of media usage and mobile learning in engineering education'. European Conference on e-Learning ECEL 2014, October. Copenhagen

Staker, H., Chan, E., Clayton, M., Hernandez, A., Horn, M. and Mackey, K. (2011) 'Blended-learning models' in Staker, H. (Ed.), *The Rise of K-12 Blended Learning*, pp. 7–9. Retrieved from http://www.christenseninstitute.org/wp-content/uploads/2013/04/The-rise-of-K-12-blended-learning.emerging-models.pdf

IV
Organizing identities

11
Multiversities and academic identities
Change, continuities, and complexities

MARY HENKEL

Introduction

For much of the twentieth century, universities were regarded as relatively stable, bounded institutions with important but distinctive functions, fulfilled through distinctive forms of organization and substantial degrees of autonomy, as least as far as their core tasks of research, scholarship, and teaching were concerned. They were academic institutions operating under academic regimes, of value to society but within a defined field. It is true that in the USA, conceptions of the university were changing but they remained contested.

In the last two decades, changes on a global scale have taken place in the governance, functions, and workforces of these institutions that raise questions about what kind of organizations they now are and what that means for what has been their defining profession.

Recent international research on the academic profession seems to endorse the argument that what has emerged is a 'duality' between organization and profession that needs to be bridged (Noordegraaf and Schinkel, 2010; Leišytė, 2014). It suggests that academics have become 'distanced from their institutional and departmental homes' (Locke et al., 2011, p. 3); they perceive the university as an organization in which 'the periphery has become ... the centre' (Rhoades and Sporn, 2002, p. 24). The discipline remains a strong force in academic identity formation and development. However, the ideal, perhaps most cogently expressed by Burton Clark (1983, p. 32), of a mutually reinforcing dynamic between discipline and institution, with the basic unit or department 'melding the two and drawing strength from the combination' seems to have little resonance in many contemporary academic working lives (Archer, 2008; Clegg, 2008; Fredman and Doughney, 2012; Schimank and Lange, 2009; Ylijoki, 2013).

This chapter will draw on empirical findings and normative and theoretical analyses in some recent studies of organizational change in European universities to look more closely at the characterization of the relationships between institutions and the academic profession in terms of duality, distance, and alienation. The primary aim is to address questions about the actual and potential capacity of universities in the early twenty-first century to be a positive force in academic identity formation and development. How far is it possible for academics to find individual and collective meaning in their membership of a contemporary university? Are universities organizations with whose values, aspirations, and conceptions of work academics can identify? If so, how is this to be achieved?

We will begin with a brief review of the new social, political, and economic demands and pressures on universities that have led to major transformations, prompting some to suggest their characterization as 'new multiversities' (Krücken *et al.*, 2011). It will go on to outline one narrative of the consequences for the relations between universities and the academic profession, the dominant theme of which is a weakening of the bonds between them that is attributable to the adoption of New Public Management (NPM) models: 'organizational management logic' (Leišytė, 2014, p. 63) threatens to drive out academic values and modes of governance. However, it will then explore some alternative interpretations of organizational change. For the most part, they move away from a polarization of managerial and academic modes of coordination and control, drawing primarily on institutionalist theories and concepts of organizational identity development to suggest that 'new multiversities' have not substituted one dominant organizational model or culture for another, but rather recognized possibilities for accommodation between the two. The final narrative considered takes more account of change as a continuing feature of the world in which multiversities work, the diversity and fluidity of new multiversity workforces, and the opportunities they provide for the construction of new or reconfigured professional identities. It reflects a broader context in which many professions are reappraising their roles and relationships with organizations, other occupational groups, and their clients, and in consequence finding themselves making some shifts in their norms and values.

Secular changes and the emergence of the 'new multiversity'

Transformations of universities can, at least in part, be understood as an inevitable consequence of changes that have been increasing in intensity and in scope throughout the second half of the twentieth century, albeit in different degrees and at different speeds in different national contexts. More recently they have been understood as global phenomena. Not only have they had a profound effect upon a range of institutions, including universities, but they also have implications for constructions of identity.

The scale and diversity of the interests and populations served by universities have greatly expanded and their boundaries have become more permeable. They 'are now more than ever central institutions of modern society' (Krücken *et al.*, 2011), pivotal organizations in a global context substantially informed and shaped by neo-liberal ideology. They are thus increasingly held publicly accountable for their performance in and contributions to market economies, predominantly characterized as knowledge economies, in which the keys to success are innovation and responsiveness to change. Many universities are themselves active competitors in global markets for higher education and research customers and funding, markets of which global evaluative and reputational ranking systems are important drivers (Sahlin, 2012). At the same time, their performance in the production of new knowledge, including basic, strategic, and applied research, in knowledge transfer with businesses, public service, and third sector organizations and in the development of highly skilled workforces is widely perceived as critical for the competitiveness of their regions, nations, and localities in broader global markets.

In the face of changing conditions for their social and political legitimacy, universities have had to transform themselves. Fifty years after Clark Kerr argued that 'the logic of history' in the form of industrialization had created a new model, 'an imperative, rather than a reasoned choice among elegant alternatives' (Kerr, 1963, p. 6), that is the multiversity, it seems that global changes have brought us to a similar, and no more comfortable, conclusion: the defining characteristic of the 'new multiversities' is diversity (Krücken *et al.*, 2011) and the concept can still be seen as centred in paradoxes, conflicts, constant interaction, and flux (Rothblatt, 2012). They are institutions with multiple purposes, serving multiple interests; they incorporate multiple communities and multiple values. Not only do they educate increasingly large and varied student populations, but they also require an increasingly diverse workforce to fulfil their functions.

Meanwhile, the multi-dimensional dynamics of globalization are increasingly evident: not just economic and political but also technical, structural, and temporal. They create a still more challenging context for the 'new multiversity' than that of the 1960s. New technologies, notably in communications, information, and knowledge, have brought about a dramatic compression of time and space and 'a new age of borderlessness' (Urry, 1988, p. 5). Social theorists argue that we are now in an era of 'reflexive modernization' (Beck, 1992; Giddens, 1991) in which change is conceived as a continual, reiterative feature of social life (Henkel, 2012). There has been an 'expansion of disembedding mechanisms, which prise social relations free from the hold of specific locales' (Giddens, 1991, p. 2). Individuals are less constrained by ties with and dependence upon dominant, stable communities or organizations in the construction of identity. Identity has become 'a reflexively organised endeavour' (Giddens, 1991; cf. Jenkins, 1996; Taylor, 2008) orchestrated primarily by the individual and individual choices; a process of individual construction (Beck, 1992), deconstruction, and reconstruction (Barnett and Di Napoli, 2008).

It has thus become increasingly clear that academics cannot be assumed to be pursuing their careers in tightly connected stable structures and mutually reinforcing cultures, separated from other sectors of society. Rather they are working in shifting, multi-level or 'glonacal' (Marginson and Rhoades, 2002) and multi-dimensional (collaborative and competitive; public and private) environments (Henkel, 2012). They are likely to be involved in working relationships organized in networks, consortia, 'hybrid communities' (Gibbons et al., 1994) that may form and reform within relatively short time frames. They may cross geo-political boundaries and organizational fields. They may be inter- or intra-institutional. There are more possibilities for individual choices but not necessarily for freedom of choice.

New Public Management and multiversities

It is in this context of complexity and change that the 'new multiversities' are not only licensed, but also under increasing pressure to become strong, strategic actors, nationally and internationally (Krücken and Meier, 2006), expected to take corporate responsibility for their own futures. An increasingly important dimension of this responsibility is financial. Institutional autonomy has become a central plank of national higher education policies. However, it is, for the most part, a 'bounded autonomy' (Sahlin, 2012; cf. Enders et al., 2013). Governments have sought to establish it on their own terms, often, though not universally, within the broader framework of NPM (Shattock, 2014). This has had major implications for higher education institutions.

NPM can be seen as perhaps the most influential and comprehensive of the 'generalized scripts' (Krücken and Meier, 2006) or 'templates' that have been diffused globally in recent decades for organizational reform of public sector institutions, including higher education. Developed over time but centred on management, it represents a broadly coherent but not fixed set of principles and mechanisms (many of which are shared with other scripts, such as 'modernization'). They include the adoption of private sector or business management structures and instruments; clearer institutional accountability, internal and external, for output and performance; strong emphasis on the efficient use of resources, human, as well as financial; reduced dependence on public funding; competition, including competitive performance-based resource allocation; external and internal quality assurance systems.

A prerequisite for 'organizational actorhood' (Krücken and Meier, 2006) is strong organizational integration, a significant challenge for new multiversities in a globalized world. Within NPM approaches integration demands structural change: the replacement of academic, collegial forms of governance, through leadership understood within the 'primus inter pares' principle and the 'loose coupling' of basic units, by corporate management. This entails a combination of hierarchical structure to ensure clearly defined authority and accountability at the top and down through the organization (centralized delegation), and structural elaboration to accommodate multiple functions, as distinct from multiple disciplinary cultures. Key decision-making powers are now in the hands of university rectors or presidents and their senior management teams. Concomitantly, in most if not all European systems, formal academic power as reflected in strong academic senates and councils has been weakened (Shattock, 2014). Most university leaders are academics, but not all are and recruits from a new range of professionals outside academe may also be sought for the greater variety of second-tier strategic management posts that have now been created in higher education institutions. Shifts are occurring, too, away from the election by peers of university leaders, senior academics, deans, and heads of department towards appointment; managerial skills have a new place in the criteria for these posts, which has prompted reappraisal of the concept and role of academic leadership (Meek et al., 2010b).

Meanwhile, the universities' workforces are undergoing major expansion and reconfiguration. As new tasks and responsibilities are introduced into universities and some previously perceived as subordinate and at the periphery of the university (Krücken and Meier, 2006; cf. Rhoades and Sporn, 2002) are brought nearer to the centre, new professions and occupational groups have been introduced and changes have been made in academic work and its organization. New skills and knowledge are required, for example, for the development of academic capitalism, technology transfer, information and communication systems, widening participation and student employability policies, and for the diversification of funding. More elaborated management structures are needed to organize them. In the UK, the European country where some of these changes have been taken furthest, the number of professional managers in higher education institutions increased by 30 per cent between 2004–5 and 2008–9 (Shattock, 2014).

These developments raise questions about academic authority and the relationships between academics themselves in universities. While universities remain knowledge-centred organizations, there has been a significant redistribution of formal power in universities away from those fully engaged in research and teaching. Universities are 'managed institutions', required to give greater priority to values of corporate accountability, economy, and efficiency. Those who become managers might be coming to be perceived by academics as members of a different profession, with different interests and focus, even if the extent to which university management is now professionalized varies widely between institutions and nations (Krücken and Meier, 2006).

Substantial changes in the employment status and conditions of academics add to a picture of weakening bonds between academics and their institutions. They also mean changes in academic work and in values that have informed how that is understood. Both of these developments have strong significance for the key question addressed in this chapter.

Massification has meant an increase in the demand for academics: between the years 2003 and 2012, there was a 23.5 per cent increase in the number of academic staff in the UK, for example (Equality Challenge Unit, 2014). However, competition to join the academic profession remains intense. Constraints on public funding, the advent of marketization and the growing complexity and volatility of public and private demands and expectations have put a new premium on flexible academic labour markets. In the UK tenure was effectively abolished in 1988. More generally, in both the USA and Europe the balance between tenured staff and fixed-term appointments has seen a dramatic shift towards the latter (Enders and de Weert, 2009). By 2004 it was estimated that between 20 per cent and 50 per cent of academic staff were contingent (Leišytė and Dee, 2012). The academic profession has become segmented. A key development has been the growth of the secondary market, which aspiring academics can no longer assume or even expect to provide a route to an established academic post.

At the same time, the incentives to compete for the highest academic talent have increased; in some countries universities have more freedom to individualize academic contracts and are exercising it (de Weert, 2009; Musselin, 2013; Leišytė and Hosch-Dayican, 2014). In consequence, there are new inequalities within the academic staff of universities. They include growing disparities of financial reward but there are other differences, more critical to academic identity. First are those between, at one end, academics with little stake in or perceived value to the institution and, at the other, a highly valued elite group on whose commitment universities see themselves as strongly dependent. Second are differences in the nature and control of academic work. There is now a substantial literature on the demise of holistic concepts of academic work. Academic contracts may now not only be time limited (often to a year or less), but also restricted in the scope of the work entailed. While the research–teaching nexus remains as an ideal model and, indeed, a strong track record in the two is still commonly a necessary condition of promotion towards the professoriate (see, e.g., Leišytė and Hosch-Dayican, 2014, p. 473), there is a growing trend towards research-only and teaching-only contracts.

National and international policies have also tended to support the separation of research from teaching and expect their organization to be a matter for institutional management (Enders and de Weert, 2009; Musselin, 2005, 2013; Leišytė and Hosch-Dayican, 2014) rather than individual academic decision or intra-departmental negotiation. Career progression is increasingly structured within the time lines and criteria set by a combination of external evaluation and internal monitoring and performance appraisals. With the growing dependence on research excellence for reputation and income generation, institutions are likely not only to privilege research output, the securing of research funding, and prestigious forms of technology transfer and research entrepreneurialism in promotion criteria, but also to punish academics whose records on such dimensions fall short of expectation (Harley, 2002). The immediate implications for individual academic identities may be severe (Henkel, 2000; Lucas, 2006). There are also longer-term consequences for how teaching is organized.

Changes in conceptions and the organization of teaching have significant implications for academic identities. Evidence abounds, particularly in the case of teaching, of the 'unbundling' of academic work and the rise of the 'para-academic', amounting, in some eyes, to the 'hollowing out' of academic professional practice (Macfarlane, 2010): through definition of distinctive tasks seen as dependent on new technologies and specialist practitioners to meet widening interpretations of student needs, new media of teaching and learning, and new methods of assessment of student's work (see also Musselin, 2005; Enders and de Weert, 2009). Academic competence in teaching has been challenged with the shift in emphasis towards student learning, student employability, and students as consumers and away from teaching content and academic (provider) definitions of quality and excellence.

Some research on early career academics in the UK and in Finland finds them strongly critical of the institutional regimes within which they are working (Archer, 2008; Ylijoki, 2013). Ylijoki cites their perception that much of the activity undertaken by themselves but also by senior professors is 'wasted time', leaving them disillusioned about academic careers. Archer, whose study was carried out in various types of UK universities, found widespread condemnation of 'new managerial' impacts on academic work: the dominance of audit and 'counting', a culture of competitiveness, careerism, and the stifling of creativity in teaching and research. She saw her respondents as largely constructing their identities as 'personal principled projects' (Archer, 2008, p. 270), informed by 'core' values of intellectual endeavour, criticality and professionalism, collegiality, and collaboration. However, a predominant feature of these projects was struggle against institutional regimes. All 'were engaged to some extent in resisting, challenging and/or protecting themselves from the insatiable demands of higher education, with its fast tempo and incessant requirement to produce' (ibid., p. 275); they were constantly trying to 'squeeze out' more 'critical' intellectual work.

This narrative is one in which reforms designed to enable 'multiversities' to become effective organizational actors, with enhanced capacity to accommodate complexity and respond to continuous change, have resulted in substantial academic alienation from their institutions: division between managers and academics; damage to core conceptions of academic work and the values that underpin it; loss of academic power and authority in the university. It also raises questions about universities as distinctive organizations. How far do they continue to provide 'a distinctive organizational format within which teaching and research can evolve' in the twenty-first century (Krücken *et al.*, 2011, p. 9)?

All of these are critical concerns for addressing the relationship between universities and academic professional identities. The rest of the chapter will offer some alternative narratives of change that move away from polarization and duality and attempt to engage with the complexities of the universities' and individuals' responses to change and their implications for academic identity construction.

Change and continuity in organizational reforms

Recent research on organizational reforms in European universities offers a more nuanced picture of their current structures and modes of coordination and control (Bleiklie *et al.*, 2011; Bleiklie *et al.*, 2015; Meek *et al.*, 2010b; Sahlin, 2012; Stensaker, 2004; Clark, 1998), reflecting an institutionalist perspective on organizational change, one that emphasizes the influence of existing organizational models and cultures on reform processes and outcomes.

Structural complexities and intra-institutional relationships

First, we will look again at the hierarchization of universities. Hierarchical structures are not new to them, even if they have now been given a more central function in the organization and control of academic work and within a different configuration of values, concepts, and principles. Academics who have become managers have, at least until very recently, acquired their new designations with little preparation or formal training for a managerial role (Henkel, 2000; Meek *et al.*, 2010a). Their modus operandi are shaped by, if not imbued with, conceptions of academic governance oriented towards debate, consultation, negotiation, and mediation rather than command and control. Communication with multiple actors, including those further up the hierarchy, is central to their role. Studies in different national contexts suggest that they are not captives of the ideologies of neo-liberalism or NPM (Santiago *et al.*, 2006; Deem *et al.*, 2007; Trowler, 2010). Moreover, although there is still not a great deal of research on middle managers in European universities, recent examples suggest that strong academic achievements are an increasingly important criterion for appointment. There is early and more current evidence that deans and heads of department in changing regimes take their academic leadership responsibilities very seriously (Henkel, 2000; Meek *et al.*, 2010a) and that their professional academic identities are of critical importance to them as they address the new challenges of management.

Bleiklie *et al.* (2011) suggest that analyses of structural change in higher education institutions have often been over simplified. They argue that universities should be understood as 'penetrated hierarchies', penetrated, that is, by network governance. Networking, always a strong feature in academic work, can be seen as impacting significantly on university governance, cutting into vertical lines of decision-making. Network governance is an increasing dimension of national and international policy-making in higher education, as elsewhere (Paradeise *et al.*, 2009), and academics who are members of prestigious scientific organizations, research funding bodies or evaluative agencies are likely to have significant influence in their universities, as well as in the wider arena. Elite scientists remain important carriers of trends and innovation in the organization of knowledge (see, e.g., Schiene and Schimank, 2007; Whitley *et al.*, 2010; Leišytė and Dee, 2012), with the political power to influence their coordination with various models of management. As academics engage in a greater variety of networks, including with businesses, local and regional government, and cultural organizations, the distinctions between their universities and the environment may become less clear.

The implications of such emerging structural complexities for the relationship between academics and their institutions are not straightforward. Elite academic networks may succeed in reinforcing academic values in some universities but they may also be implicated in the decline of holistic conceptions of academic work and the devaluation of teaching observed across a range of institutions, with the consequences noted above for academic professional identities. Academics who have come into the university with strong roots in other professions or in business and finance may belong to networks likely to bring different influences to bear. They may be carriers of different organizational traditions and practices and have different conceptions of their professional selves, and different expectations of the institutions in which they now work, grounded in different organizational models.

Multiple organizational models, collegiality, and identities

The need for universities to engage with multiple organizational models is important for Sahlin (2012), albeit within an understanding that they are distinctive organizations, with distinctive functions substantially grounded in their own histories of national and international legitimacy. From this perspective, however powerful and far-reaching the new models of governance and management impacting upon 'new multiversities' are and however clearly articulated, relative to the earlier models that have with time become more implicit and taken for granted, they do not obliterate those organizational and governance ideals that previously informed faculty and other staff's working lives. She argues that the challenge for university leaders is 'to translate all those pressures, demands and expectations that bound the university autonomy and to mix the many diverse organizational ideals that frame universities into a meaningful and working structure' (ibid., p. 199). However, it seems clear that, for Sahlin, making space for collegiality is of overriding importance. She proposes not only that collegiality can be sustained in contemporary universities, but also that, if the challenge is to be met, it is needed at every level of the organization. At the heart of collegiality are two ideas: the first, and most generally relevant, is 'a work process' (ibid., p. 210), entailing critical engagement with others: peer review, dialogue, questioning, testing of research findings, and openness to critique and refutation; second is a mode of organization that makes the space and provides the freedom for actors, individually and collectively, to manage the uncertainties involved in sustaining the role of universities in contemporary societies.

The importance and feasibility of ensuring that collegial principles and academic values and standards remain fundamental to universities in the entrepreneurial and managerial age are underlined by Dill (2012). The reasons for this lie not only in the introduction of multiple organizational models and priorities, but also in the diversification of epistemic cultures in universities. He argues that 'the rapid expansion and fragmentation of academic knowledge' may make it more difficult than ever to sustain common academic standards, norms and values across the university (p. 229). But it is also more important, in the light of the growth in multidisciplinary and interdisciplinary programmes of both research and teaching. Academics must, in his view, take more collective responsibility for the management of academic culture 'understood as the communication and control of the values and norms affecting teaching and research' in their institutions (ibid.). It is a matter, partly, of establishing collegial structures and work processes of debate, argument, negotiation, and mediation in which this responsibility can be undertaken.

He cites examples of where senior academics, rather than administrators, have set up and run institution-wide collective mechanisms for the definition and maintenance of academic standards and the improvement of academic quality based on collegial engagement between faculty members. Here he can be understood as drawing on traditional holistic concepts of academic work in which research, teaching and service, and, indeed, governance are integrally connected and suggesting a concrete way in which a collegial model of university governance maintains a strong and visible presence. It could arguably be conceptualized as a form of network governance, in which intra-institutional networks are extended or created and the external networks of the participants are also drawn upon and have an influence in the institution.

It could also be seen as a counterforce to the trends towards the 'unbundling', fragmentation, and compartmentalization arising from the scope and complexity of contemporary academic work. Such mechanisms and forums, set up with a clear focus on a search for common academic values, can arguably ensure attention to the intellectual developmental purposes for which new educational and research methodologies and technologies can be used in higher education.

However, most important for the concerns of this chapter, is that the kind of structures and mechanisms proposed are designed to invoke collegiality across the institution and so to underline collective academic responsibility and capacity to contribute to the good of the institution as a whole and, in so doing, strengthen academics sense of identity with it.

Organizational identity and academic identity

The idea that academic institutions themselves may have or construct an identity has emerged as important for universities as strategic actors in the current context and perhaps could be more fully exploited for the study of the relationship between universities and the professional identities of their members. Its potential lies partly in the complexity and ambiguity of the concept, incorporating, as it does, two sets of interconnecting ideas: the first involving the juxtaposition between a predominantly external orientation, to do with reputation and image, and a predominantly internal one, to do with what the organization is or is believed to be by its members. The second juxtaposes difference or distinctiveness alongside sameness or identification: changing demands may provoke questions both about what is special about this organization and what makes it part of a wider collective that is also distinctive.

The place of organizational identity in higher education studies and the interconnections of the concepts encapsulated by it owe much to Burton Clark, and particularly his study of liberal arts colleges in the USA, although it contains little explicit mention of identity (Clark, 1970). Firmly located in 'old institutionalist' organization theories in which values and norms are central to what an organization is, Clark's research explores how distinctive institutional cultures (values, norms, central character) were constructed over time from within (in some cases strongly shaped by responses to crises) and found expression in organizational myths, symbols, and sagas that represented a powerful reality for their members, while also contributing to a public institutional reputation.

Since then two sets of pressures have brought with them greater emphasis on the external aspects of university identities that meant a rise in the influence of new institutionalist theory, a fundamental assumption of which is that organizations depend for their survival on the legitimacy accorded them by their environment (Stensaker, 2004), now expanded and more multi-faceted. Universities, under pressure to respond, look outside for new ways to define themselves, new templates within which to secure legitimacy. Second, the increasing need to be active participants in a range of markets means that distinctive mission statements, external image, and, increasingly now, 'brand' (Enders and de Weert, 2009; Dill, 2012) become more critical factors for universities' success, together with evidence of organizational adaptability. A consequence is that identity, instead of 'emerging from deep inside the organization, ... is located in the formal structure' and other visible features. It is 'transformed from a stable, distinct, and enduring characteristic to a fluent entity' (Stensaker, 2004, pp. 24–5).

However, Stensaker's own work, drawing on Scott (1994), suggests that it is possible to bring together 'old' and 'new' institutional theory in a framework (neo-institutionalism) that takes account of a perception that organizations such as universities derive their legitimacy from both the environment of which they are part and the meaning they have for their members, on whose work they rely. In a study of the response of six Norwegian higher education institutions to the quality reforms of the 1990s, Stensaker (2004) shows how, in some cases, they found it possible to make an integrated, institution-wide response to national reforms through processes of translation and reinterpretation: translating new organizational ideals (including more bureaucratization) and new conceptions of quality and its improvement entailed in the reform policies into ideas for taking forward pre-existing academic agendas, such as curriculum reform and innovation; and reinterpreting the existing organizational identities of their institutions and the ideals and organizational myths in which they were expressed in such a way as to accommodate different concepts and practices from different organizational cultures without a fundamental loss of meaning. Moreover, while they did look outside themselves for specific ideas and approaches to implementing reform, they went beyond imitation, the selection of new templates and their reproduction, to develop programmes for change that were distinctive and reinforced their organizational identities.

Stensaker gives a high profile to the role of leadership in the development of structural and conceptual frameworks for such organizational change. Institutional leaders and senior staff were the prime sources of the qualitative data informing his research and while there was evidence of a degree of critical engagement by academic staff in the process of reform, at least in some of the institutions, the question as to how far that was seen as having a real influence on the reinterpretation of organizational identity that emerged remained open. And if it had, was this enough for academics to recognize and embrace the reconstructed organizational identity of their institutions, as a source of strength and support for what most mattered to them as professionals in the task of responding to new needs and demands?

Stensaker found some positive answers to this second question, notably in institutions where bottom-up initiatives accompanied top-down initiatives for quality improvement and there was space for the exercise of academic freedom to test, adapt, develop, and create approaches to teaching, curriculum development, and programme evaluation within institution-wide frameworks, and so to sustain professional alongside bureaucratic organizational models.

The narrative that might be distilled from these accounts of work by Sahlin, Dill, and Stensaker suggests that contemporary higher education institutions are seeking a number of ways in which to combine organizational models in the context of a need to manage new pressures, demands, and functions; and that accommodations to be made with the new regimes primarily involve academics, some occupying new roles, and institutional leaders. This reflects basic assumptions that universities remain distinctive organizations with core functions of research and teaching requiring the sustenance of academic values and collegial modes of working. Relationships between institutions and their academic staff are not necessarily weakened; indeed, they may be strengthened. The idea of what incorporating a diversity of organizational models and multiple occupational groups would mean is not, however, given much substance.

Multiversities: new spaces, new choices?

The definition of academic work and what it involves is now more uncertain, not only because of the changes already discussed, specialization and unbundling, and the introduction of academic management. Universities' research and educational aims have expanded and diversified at an unprecedented rate, as have perceptions of the resources, structures, and modes of organization needed to meet them. Reframing education to foreground student learning, as distinct from academic teaching, has, for example, given a higher profile to educational theory, as well as to the role of technological advances. Further still, it has introduced a quite radical change of perspective to academics, many of whom were socialized into their profession within a master–apprentice model.

Policy pressures on universities in some countries to take more responsibility for student employability have meant a new focus on skills and work experience and reappraisal of the role of and structures for careers advice. New conceptions of educational quality have been incorporated along with systems for its improvement. One consequence is that the boundaries between academic and other forms of work have become less stable and more difficult to define. Students, particularly now that they come from more diverse backgrounds, need help from a greater variety of staff, which in turn implies more communication and collaboration, and less clear distinction, between academics and others. In some institutions, new structures, staffed by 'para-academics' (Macfarlane, 2010), are established to accommodate newly perceived needs: academic development units or centres, for example, for students and sometimes for academics, for whom professional development needs are being redefined. This can generate new forms of intra-institutional and inter-professional competition, resentment, and anxieties (Land, 2008), as well as boundary blurring, with negative consequences for the relationships between academics and their institutions.

However, redefinitions of the educational and research functions of the new multiversities of the twenty-first century also open up new possibilities for professional identity construction, not least for academics. At the same time as universities are institutionalizing rather standardized career paths to the professoriate (Musselin, 2013; Leišytė and Hosch-Dayican, 2014), predominantly in terms of research outputs, research grants and research management, which may exclude and be a source of identity loss for some, they are also creating new roles that may provide new opportunities for reframing career aspirations in higher education and research or knowledge production.

There is a growing body of research offering more comprehensive analysis and reconceptualization of the patterns of role distribution and role change in higher education institutions and their implications for academic and other professional identities (see, particularly, Whitchurch, 2008, 2009, 2013). Members of established professions in well-defined roles, financial, legal, estate management, human resources, are more visible and more important for the institution as strategic actor. However, a greater challenge is to be found in the variety of new roles filled by a much wider range of staff that includes academics but also some from other professions, some from business or public service, some from higher education or research administration, many with postgraduate qualifications. Some of these roles, for example in quality assurance, equity policies or technology transfer, are becoming institutionalized, but many are still emergent, fluid, and subject to redefinition. Whitchurch's research in three 'Anglo-Saxon' systems (Whitchurch, 2009) has suggested that while some roles can be fairly clearly categorized as professional or academic, others might be located near the 'perimeters' of these areas. These may often 'converge in *third spaces* around broadly based projects' (italics original), such as widening participation initiatives or business/technology incubation or, more ambitiously, extending the university's role in regional economic development (Whitchurch, 2008, p. 384). They might be relatively short or long term, with relatively narrow or broad objectives. A characteristic of *third space* is that it is occupied by mixed staff teams or partnerships, members of which might move in and out. Different projects may require leadership from different members throughout or at different times. Work in *third space* may demand new levels of attention to and understanding of different perspectives, and mean moving out of epistemic, institutional, and even sector boundaries. It might also entail review and reappraisal by individuals of familiar normative frameworks, professional goals, criteria of success, and esteem – and so also of identities.

This is a very different context from that in which many of the academics involved might have begun their academic lives: one in which professional identities were formed out of social embeddedness in a disciplinary culture with relatively stable norms, values, and practices. It is more in tune with the disembedding processes generated in late capitalism and the dynamics of globalization (Giddens, 1991). There are few scripts. Career building and professional identity construction are more individualized and uncertain projects (Whitchurch, 2008). But the institution might have an important place in them. Work in the *third space* is likely to be institution-centred: to do with the institution as strategic or organizational actor, taking or at least accepting responsibility for its own future. Professional identity construction might be strongly interconnected with continuing institutional development and, arguably, organizational identity.

Conclusion

Universities in Europe, as elsewhere, have long been understood as highly complex organizations (Clark, 1983), accommodating an ever increasing range of epistemologies and epistemic cultures. However, for much of the twentieth century, their aims and dominant values were defined, and their work substantially orchestrated, by one distinctive if rather loosely coordinated profession.

The last two decades have seen them reaching a different order of complexity, as they have become 'ever more central institutions' in their societies. They can be said to have become 'multiversities' with multiple purposes, serving multiple interests and dependent upon increasingly diverse workforces. The balance of coordinating influences upon them as between the state, the market, and the academic profession has changed significantly in a now global environment of perpetual change. The pressures upon them are great and in many ways conflicting. They are required by governments within a framework of bounded autonomy, to become strategic actors, more responsible for their own viability and their own direction, and more publicly accountable, but in a world in which market forces are increasingly powerful. In this context there is a premium on institutional integration.

The application of organizational management logic provides one route towards integration in terms of the enhancement of organizational capacity to make collective or corporate decisions and more coherent and efficient use of resources and to strengthen institutional accountability. Almost universally the 'new multiversities' have resorted in some degree to managerial models of governance, more hierarchical structures, and more vertical decision-making.

However, integration depends on other factors, more relevant to the questions addressed by this chapter. They are to do with organizational identity. What sort of institution is this? In part, this is a question given higher priority in the context of marketization. Multiversities are encouraged to produce mission statements, and so to give their institution a distinctive and coherent external image. However, it is also a question of internal meaning and value, for those on whose work it depends. The ideal is a strong interaction between the two.

The various narratives outlined in this chapter suggest that there is no easy way to achieve integration and, indeed, that it is, rather, a continuing project. Managerial solutions based on a dominant organizational model are likely to generate alienation. They are also unrealistic, if their implementation depends upon key actors socialized within different organizational models or cultures. The argument for strengthening identity by building on past history but renewing it by translation and reinterpretation is not straightforward either, even if it is embarked upon just with academics, given the collegial culture of critical engagement and argument.

It is true that multiversities remain knowledge-based and knowledge-centred organizations. Their capacity to produce multiple advanced forms of knowledge and to equip new generations with the knowledge and skills to meet new social and economic demands has relied heavily on the work processes and space for diversity and creativity entailed in collegial academic practices, values, and organization. Academics have also demonstrated that they have been able to extend the networking that has long been an important dimension of their organization into some of the new collaborations needed for a more diverse contribution to societies.

However, academic models are not necessarily sufficient and while some academics may be able to maintain the pursuit of their academic identities within a framework in which academic values and conceptions of knowledge are dominant, others, and perhaps the majority, will work with more uncertainty and less control of their boundaries. There is more space and more need not only for a greater diversity of expertise and personnel, but also for experiment with different organizational models and for more individuals willing to adapt and make new choices and modes of working in the task of helping their institutions to keep pace with the changes confronting them. While some may wish or be content to move between institutions in this context, others may find one institution playing a substantial part in their identity projects.

References

Archer, L. (2008) 'The new neo-liberal subjects? Younger academics' constructions of professional identity'. *Journal of Education Policy*, 23 (3), pp. 265–85

Barnett, R. and Di Napoli, R. (2008) *Changing Identities in Higher Education: Voicing Perspectives.* Abingdon: Routledge

Beck, U. (1992) *Risk Society: Towards a New Modernity.* London: Sage

Bleiklie, I., Enders, J., Lepori, B. and Musselin, C. (2011) 'Universities as penetrated hierarchies: organizational rationalization, hierarchization and networking in higher education'. EGOS Conference Paper. 27th EGOS Colloquium. Reassembling Organisations, July. Gothenburg

Bleiklie, I., Enders, J. and B. Lepori (2015) 'Organizations as penetrated hierarchies: institutional pressures and variations in patterns of control in European universities'. *Organization Studies*, 36 (7), pp. 873–96

Clark, B. R. (1970) *The Distinctive College: Antioch, Reed and Swarthmore.* Chicago: Aldine

Clark, B. R. (1983) *The Higher Education System: Academic Organization in Cross-national Perspective.* Los Angeles: University of California Press

Clark, B. R. (1998) *Creating Entrepreneurial Universities: Organizational Pathways of Transformation.* Oxford: Pergamon

Clegg, S. (2008). 'Academic identities under threat?' *British Educational Research Journal*, 34 (3), pp. 329–45

Deem, R. Hillyard, S. and Reed, M. (2007) *Knowledge, Higher Education and the New Managerialism: The Changing Management of UK Universities.* Oxford: Oxford University Press

Dill, D. (2012) 'The management of academic culture revisited: integrating universities in an entrepreneurial age' in Stensaker, B., Välimaa, J. and Sarrico, C. (Eds), *Managing Reform in Universities: The Dynamics of Culture, Identity and Organisational Change.* Basingstoke: Palgrave Macmillan, pp. 222–37

de Weert, E. (2009) 'The organised contradictions of teaching and research' in Enders, J. and de Weert, E. (Eds), *The Changing Face of Academic Life: Analytical and Comparative Perspectives.* Basingstoke: Palgrave Macmillan, pp. 134–54

Enders, J. and de Weert, E. (2009) 'Towards a T-shaped profession: Academic work and career in the knowledge society' in Enders, J. and de Weert, E. (Eds), *The Changing Face of Academic Life: Analytical and Comparative Perspectives*. Basingstoke: Palgrave Macmillan

Enders, J., de Boer, H. and Weyer, E. (2013) 'Regulatory autonomy and performance: The reform of higher education re-visited'. *Higher Education*, 65 (1), pp. 5–23

Equality Challenge Unit (2014) *Equality in Higher Education: Statistical Report 2014*. London: Equality Challenge Unit

Fredman, N. and Doughney, J. (2012) 'Academic dissatisfaction, managerial change and neo-liberalism'. *Higher Education*, 64, pp. 41–58

Gibbons, M., Limoges, C., Nowotny, H., Schwartzman, S., Scott, P. and Trow, M. (1994) *The New Production of Knowledge: The Dynamics of Science and Research in Contemporary Societies*. Thousand Oaks, CA: Sage

Giddens, A. (1991) *Modernity and Self-Identity*. Cambridge: Polity Press

Harley, S. (2002) 'The impact of research selectivity on academic work and identity in UK universities'. *Studies in Higher Education*, 27 (2), pp. 187–205

Henkel, M. (2000) *Academic Identities and Policy Change in Higher Education*. London: Jessica Kingsley

Henkel, M. (2012) 'Exploring new academic identities in turbulent times' in Stensaker, B., Välimaa, J. and Sarrico, C. (Eds), *Managing Reform in Universities: The Dynamics of Culture, Identity and Organisational Change*. Basingstoke: Palgrave Macmillan, pp. 156–76

Jenkins, R. (1996) *Social Identity*. London: Routledge

Kerr, C. (1963) *The Uses of the University*. Cambridge, MA: Harvard University Press

Krücken, G. and Meier, J. (2006) 'Turning the university into an organisational actor' in Drori, G., Meyer, J. and Hwang, H. (Eds), *Globalization and Organization*. Oxford, New York: Oxford University Press, pp. 241–57

Krücken, G., Kosmützky, A. and Torca, M. (2011) *Towards a Multiversity: Universities Between Global Trends and National Traditions*. Bielefeld: Transcript

Land, R. (2008) 'Academic development: identity and paradox' in Barnett, R. and Di Napoli, R. (Eds), *Changing Identities in Higher Education: Voicing Perspectives*. Abingdon: Routledge, pp. 134–44

Leišytė, L. (2014) 'Changing academic identities in the context of a managerial university: bridging the duality between professions and organizations. Evidence from the US and Europe' in Cummings, W. and Teichler, U. (Eds), *The Relevance of Academic Work*. Dordrecht: Springer, pp. 59–73

Leišytė, L. and Dee, J. R. (2012) 'Changing academic practices and identities in Europe and the US: critical perspectives' in Smart, J. C. and Paulsen, M. B. (Eds), *Higher Education: Handbook of Theory and Research*. Dordrecht: Springer, pp. 123–206

Leišytė, L. and Hosch-Dayican, B. (2014) 'Changing academic roles and shifting gender inequalities: a case analysis of the influence of the teaching–research nexus on the academic career prospects of female academics in the Netherlands'. *Journal of Work-based Rights*, 17 (3–4), pp. 467–90

Locke, W., Cummings, W. and Fisher, D. (Eds) (2011) *Changing Governance and Management in Higher Education: The Perspectives of the Academy*. Dordrecht: Springer

Lucas, L. (2006) *The Research Game in Academic Life*. Maidenhead: Open University Press and McGraw Hill

Macfarlane, B. (2010) 'Morphing of academic practice: unbundling and the rise of the para-academic'. *Higher Education Quarterly*, 65 (1), pp. 59–73

Marginson, S. and Rhoades, G. (2002) 'Beyond national states, markets and systems of higher education: a glonacal agency heuristic'. *Higher Education*, 43, pp. 281–309

Meek, V. L., de Boer, H. and Goedegebuure, L. (2010a) 'The changing role of academic leadership in Australia and the Netherlands' in Meek, V. L., Goedegebuure, L., Santiago, R. and Carvalho T. (Eds), *The Changing Dynamics of Higher Education Middle Management*. Dordrecht: Springer, pp. 31–54

Meek, V. L., Goedegebuure, L., Santiago, R. and Carvalho, T. (Eds) (2010b) *The Changing Dynamics of Higher Education Middle Management*. Dordrecht: Springer

Musselin, C. (2005) 'European academic labour markets in transition'. *Higher Education*, 49, pp. 135–54

Musselin, C. (2013) 'Redefinition of the relationships between academics and their university'. *Higher Education*, 65, pp. 25–37

Noordegraaf, M. and Schinkel, W. (2010) 'Professional capital contested: a Bourdieusian analysis of conflicts between professionals and managers'. *Comparative Sociology*, 10 (1), pp. 1–29

Paradeise, C., Reale, E., Bleiklie, I. and Ferlie, E. (Eds) (2009) *University Governance: Western European Comparative Perspectives*. Dordrecht: Springer

Rhoades, G. and Sporn, B. (2002) 'New models of management and shifting modes and costs of production: Europe and the United States'. *Tertiary Education and Management*, 8, pp. 3–28

Rothblatt, S. (2012) *Clark Kerr's World of Higher Education Reaches the 21st Century: Chapters in a Special History*. Dordrecht: Springer

Sahlin, K. (2012) 'The interplay of organizing models in higher education: what room is there for collegiality in universities characterized by bounded autonomy?' in Stensaker, B., Välimaa, J. and Sarrico, C. (Eds), *Managing Reform in Universities: The Dynamics of Culture, Identity and Organisational Change*. Basingstoke: Palgrave Macmillan, pp. 198–221

Santiago, R., Carvalho, T., Amaral, A. and Meek, V. (2006) 'Changing patterns in the middle management of higher education institutions: the case of Portugal'. *Higher Education*, 52 (2), pp. 215–50

Schiene, C. and Schimank, U. (2007) 'Research evaluation as organisational development: the work of the academic advisory council in Lower Saxony' in Whitley, R. and Gläser, J. (Eds), *The Changing Governance of the Sciences: The Rise of Evaluative Systems*. Dordrecht: Springer, pp. 171–90

Schimank, U. and Lange, S. (2009) 'Germany, a latecomer to New Public Management' in Paradeise, C., Reale, E., Bleiklie, I. and Ferlie, E. (Eds), *University Governance: Western European Comparative Perspectives*. Dordrecht: Springer, pp. 51–75

Scott, W. R. (1994) 'Institutions and organizations: towards a theoretical synthesis' in Scott, W. R. and Meyer, J. W. (Eds), *Institutional Environments and Organizations: Structural Complexity and Individualism*. London: Sage, pp. 55–80

Shattock, M. (Ed.) (2014) *International Trends in University Governance: Autonomy, Self-government and the Distribution of Authority*. London: Routledge

Stensaker, B. (2004) 'The transformation of organisational identities: interpretations of policies concerning the quality of teaching and learning in Norwegian higher education'. Dissertation. University of Twente

Taylor, P. (2008) 'Being an academic today' in Barnett, R. and Di Napoli, R. (Eds), *Changing Identities in Higher Education: Voicing Perspectives*. Abingdon: Routledge, pp. 27–39

Trowler, P. (2010) 'UK higher education: captured by new managerialist ideology?' in Meek, V. L., Goedegebuure, L., Santiago, R. and Carvalho T. (Eds), *The Changing Dynamics of Higher Education Middle Management*. Dordrecht: Springer, pp. 197–212

Urry, J. (1988) 'Contemporary transformation of time and space' in Scott, P. (Ed.), *The Globalization of Higher Education*. Buckingham: SRHE: Open University Press, pp. 1–17

Whitchurch, C. (2008) 'Shifting identities and blurring boundaries: the emergence of third space professionals'. *Higher Education Quarterly*, 62 (4), pp. 377–96

Whitchurch, C. (2009). 'The rise of the blended professional in higher education: a comparison between the UK, Australia and the United States'. *Higher Education*, 58 (3), pp. 407–18

Whitchurch, C. (2013) *Reconstructing Identities in Higher Education: The Rise of Third Space Professionals*. London and New York: Routledge

Whitley, R., Gläser, J. and Engwall, L. (Eds) (2010) *Reconfiguring Knowledge Production: Changing Authority Relationships in the Sciences and their Consequences for Intellectual Innovation*. Oxford: Oxford University Press

Ylijoki, O.-H. (2013) 'Boundary-work between work and life in the high-speed university'. *Studies in Higher Education*, 38 (2), pp. 242–55

12
Boundary crossing and maintenance among UK and Dutch bioscientists
Towards hybrid identities of academic entrepreneurs

LIUDVIKA LEIŠYTĖ AND BENGÜ HOSCH-DAYICAN

Introduction

Recent changes in the institutional environment, namely the New Public Management-inspired reforms and increasing requirements for commercialization and student employability, may lead to blurring boundaries between science and industry and lead towards conflicts in academic responses. Further, the traditional 'scholar' notion of an academic is shifting towards that of an academic entrepreneur (Lam, 2010, 2011; Link and Siegel, 2007). Despite ample recent evidence that academics' commercial and entrepreneurial activities, such as patenting and starting spin-off companies (especially in biosciences and engineering), are increasing, it is still unclear to what extent traditional academic work and output are combined with services and entrepreneurship in these disciplines. In other words, whether life scientists have given up their academic roles or have retained them and, if so, to what extent, needs to be explored.

Building on the literature on symbolic boundaries (Lamont and Molnar, 2002) and the notion of academic identities (Henkel, 2000), we ask the following research questions:

- What type of boundary crossing or maintenance can be identified among bioscientists in regard to academic entrepreneurship?
- How are teaching and research roles combined with entrepreneurship roles?
- What does this boundary crossing mean for the academic identities of bioscientists in the context of managerial universities?

Biosciences are known, on the one hand, for their big advances in fundamental research and, on the other hand, for their strong links to the biotechnology industry. In this field, some evidence suggests that the boundaries between academia and industry and between fundamental and applied research are rather blurred (Link and Siegel, 2007). Bioscientists rely heavily on external funding for their work at universities, especially in regard to research; thus, their likelihood of boundary maintenance of academic norms and practices may be limited due to the need to attract various types of funding from industry. This makes it interesting to focus on bioscience groups in the context of managerial universities in the current study.

This study[1] starts with the conceptual background of the research, followed by a literature review. Further, we introduce the study methods and present our findings. We conclude with a discussion and conclusion.

Conceptual background

The concept of symbolic boundaries is helpful in understanding whether and to what extent academics become involved in new work roles and adopt practices. Symbolic boundaries are 'conceptual distinctions made by social actors to categorize objects, people, practices, and even time and space' (Lamont and Molnar, 2002, p. 168). They generate feelings of similarity and group membership through which people acquire status and monopolize resources. The concept is also applied to professional disciplines and scientific activity. Among professional disciplines, boundary setting can occur in several formats, including the protection of autonomy, resources, and privileges against outside challenges (Gieryn, 1999; Lamont and Molnar, 2002). This type of boundary work is evident when scientists seek to protect their autonomy from attempts by legislators, managers or other stakeholders to control aspects of scientific work. This response suggests that the greater the scientists perceive the challenge from the outside, the more likely they would be inclined towards protective behaviour by maintaining their academic boundaries, which would mean sticking to traditional teacher and researcher roles and practices instead of adjusting to new values and engaging in new work roles (Leišytė et al., 2010; Teelken, 2012).

Traditionally, teaching and research have been at the core of the holistic view of an academic, as noted in the Humboldtian model (Schimank and Winnes, 2000), whereas being an academic also means belonging to a disciplinary community and adhering to a set of scientific norms and values. Disciplinary communities have the features of the classic Tönnies' Gemeinschaft, such as commonality, limited interaction with people outside the community (boundary maintenance), closeness via shared beliefs, norms, and traditions that presuppose a clear pattern of behaviour (Leišytė, 2015).

However, economic developments and the promotion of innovation systems in recent decades have prompted the loosening of the traditional academic boundaries in several different ways. On the one hand, disciplinary boundary crossing can be observed via the increase in interdisciplinary work (e.g. Land,

2012). On the other hand, the academic-scientific boundaries have become crossed, as evidenced by increasingly blurred boundaries between science and industry (e.g. Owen-Smith and Powell, 2001; Lam, 2010). This latter type of boundary crossing, in particular, involves a differentiation of traditional academic work roles. In the context of the demands of external funding agencies and university managers, academics are increasingly expected to adjust their work roles to the mission and profile of the organizations in which they work and thus adapt more hybrid work roles (Leišytė and Dee, 2012). This hybridization can be expressed either in structurally differentiated work roles (i.e. separation of teaching and research), or academics may choose from a more diversified pallet of roles from teaching to academic entrepreneurship and are offered the chance to build credibility in multiple arenas (Enders and de Weert, 2009; Henkel, 2005).

The extent to which academic-scientific boundary crossing occurs can vary among different contexts and disciplines. For instance, while boundary maintenance generally remains more common among humanities, it is less evident among life scientists (Leišytė, 2007; Leišytė et al., 2010. Traditional academic roles still matter for life scientists, but they are more open to embracing the new work roles than other disciplines, such as the humanities, and thus experience less clash or conflict with the non-academic spheres. The present study builds upon the insights of previous research (Jansen, 2010; Leišytė et al., 2010) and aims to provide empirical evidence on the symbolic boundary work of scientists in the field of biosciences. Previous study of British and Dutch bioscientists (Leišytė, 2007) has shown that academics react to changes in their institutional environment by symbolic compliance, compliance, and proactive manipulation. They have a certain amount of freedom to pursue their own research agendas by symbolically complying with prioritized research agendas and, to a large extent, prioritize academic output over commercial output (ibid.). However, the previous study did not identify how boundary blurring and maintenance influence the role mixes of academics and what this blurring of the boundaries means for their academic identities.

Knowledge commercialization in biosciences

Among the various channels available for establishing links between university and knowledge users, the commercialization of academic knowledge, such as patenting and licensing of inventions, and consulting for industry have attracted major attention both within the academic literature and the policy community (O'Shea et al., 2008; Phan and Siegel, 2006; Rothaermel et al., 2007). Commercialization is considered a prime example for generating academic impact because it constitutes immediate, measurable market acceptance for the output of academic research and provides opportunities for industrial actors to participate in training students (Leišytė and Westerheijden, 2014; Markman *et al.*, 2008).

Policy discourses have significantly advanced, with most policy-makers now understanding that there is no simple pipeline from university research to industrial development and economic growth. New models of university–enterprise cooperation have been internalised, such as the importance of Mode 2 knowledge production and the Triple Helix relationships among universities, enterprises and government (Etzkowitz, 2008; Harloe and Perry, 2008). Researchers investigating the commercialization efforts of universities at the institutional and individual levels have explored the entrepreneurship characteristics of academics and the factors that facilitate their entrepreneurial activities, including collaborations with enterprises and industry. These studies have mostly examined the institutional and input factors rather than the characteristics of the personnel involved (Etzkowitz, 2003; Rasmussen *et al.*, 2006).

Recent studies have often conceptually distinguished between collaboration and commercialization and have shown that engagement in collaboration is far more frequent than engagement in patenting and academic entrepreneurship (D'Este and Patel, 2007; Perkmann and Walsh, 2007). Recently, Perkmann *et al.* (2013) distinguished between activities that they call 'academic engagement' (i.e. collaboration with non-academic actors, most notably companies, by student placements or contract research and consulting and other forms of knowledge exchange) and commercialization (i.e. academic entrepreneurship and IP-related activities). Unlike academic engagement, research on commercialization has been systematically documented and synthesised in published reviews (Geuna and Muscio, 2009; Larsen, 2011; Phan *et al.*, 2005; Rothaermel *et al.*, 2007).

Recent studies have found that knowledge commercialization activities are driven by different individual characteristics, motivations, and values, and by institutional factors (Bercovitz and Feldman, 2008; D'Este and Perkmann, 2011; Haeussler and Colyvas, 2011; Link and Siegel, 2007). The systemic factors that have been identified include the incentive schemes within their institutional environment, such as governmental programmes to foster university–industry collaboration; the perceived need of the companies in the vicinity to collaborate with the groups; incentive schemes within the university, such as technology transfer offices and science parks; financial incentives, such as subsidies, tax reductions, and matching funds; the networks it has in the field; and possible conflicting interests that arise between academic research and existing commercialization activities (D'Este and Patel, 2007). Suggested individual factors include the motivations, capacities, and credibility of the individual researchers and their networks.

There is ample evidence of increased academic commercial activities at universities, especially in the USA, in the past decades (ibid.; Siegel *et al.*, 2007). However, commercialization tendencies differ strongly across different disciplines, as noted in the technology entrepreneurship literature. Perkmann *et al.* (2013) found that biosciences are more likely to become involved in commercialization activities (i.e. patenting and spin-off creation) because the fundamental research in this field is quite close to application, as observed in the biotechnology sector (Link and Siegel, 2007). These studies have shown that, given the right contextual conditions and incentives and the relevant motivations, academics will pursue commercialization of their knowledge in one or another form (Lam, 2011; Leišytė, 2011). These studies support the notion of boundary crossing in biosciences in which academics can be strongly identified as academic entrepreneurs.

However, some authors note that the boundaries between public and private knowledge and between the university and the marketplace are blurring only to some extent (Gieryn, 1983; Shapin, 1994). As noted by Owen-Smith and Powell (2001), the academic responses to commercial opportunities in biosciences also show patterns of conflict and agreement. For example, research productivity studies have noted the conflicts between publishing and patenting that bioscientists experience (Leišytė *et al.*, 2009). Bioscientists maintain their boundaries by prioritizing science and scientific output over the commercialization of their knowledge, even though they engage with industry via funding doctoral student research, student placements, and some patenting activity. In such cases, the academic identity of a scientist and a teacher may be more pronounced than that of an academic entrepreneur. For bioscientists, for example, such boundary maintenance would mean teaching in bioscience programmes, pursuing their research lines from previous unanswered questions, and publishing research in high-impact factor journals such as *Nature*.

In light of these previous findings, we can formulate the following hypotheses on the conditions under which life scientists would be more inclined towards boundary crossing versus boundary maintenance:

H1: The prospects of generating academic impact and/or credibility has an influence on academics' strategies of boundary crossing and maintenance;
H2: Managerialism as a systemic-level factor provides incentive structures to build academic credibility through the commercialization of research and academic entrepreneurialism;
H3: In the case of conflicting interests between managerialist imperatives and academic credibility, traditional academic roles and identities will be more emphasized than academic entrepreneurship to ensure credibility.

Methods

We studied academics from biosciences departments in four research universities in two national contexts: the UK and the Netherlands. The UK has been a leader in Europe in adopting managerial imperatives in universities since the early 1990s and has introduced a range of performance criteria that follow the research and teaching evaluation demands and a distinct performativity discourse (Leišytė *et al.*, 2010). In this context, academics would be expected to be more inclined towards boundary-crossing behaviour.

The study includes documents, a website, and archival material analysis with 16 semi-structured interviews with academics from biosciences and eight managers that were performed in 2008/9. The interviews have been conducted at two universities in the UK and two universities in the Netherlands. The interviewees were chosen to ensure an even distribution between senior and junior academic positions. Interviews were face-to-face and lasted 45–60 minutes each. They were transcribed and coded according to the themes that emerged from the data and the main themes determined a priori of changing academic work based on a literature review. The analysis was performed using NVIVO software. The interview data were complemented by the relevant strategic documents and institutional statistics from the studied universities and national policy documents.

In both countries, a strong and a weak department have been selected based on the results of external research evaluation results to account for different levels of productivity and quality. The case studies in both systems differ in terms of the level of managerialism at the universities and the strength of the performance-based funding of the universities.

At the organizational level, one can observe higher accountability demands, stronger hierarchy, and a stricter definition of the academic job profiles in the UK. Performance assessment and accountability, which occurs at the national, university, faculty, and departmental levels, is much more complex. Additionally, the Research Excellence Framework (REF, and its predecessor Research Assessment Exercise, RAE) pressured university management and individual researchers to produce a certain quantity, type, and quality of research outputs because the research funding allocation depended on the performance ranking of the higher education institution according to the REF criteria. The RAE and later REF have increasingly emphasized not only academic excellence, but also the impact of the research on society and the economy.

In the Netherlands, the national research evaluation regime is less strict because the research evaluation results are mainly used as information for the university management and are not directly linked to the funding of research or teaching (Leišytė and Westerheijden, 2014). Relevance to society is one of the criteria upon which the research quality is evaluated. Further, a number of national policy documents in the past decades have indicated the need to 'valorize' knowledge emanating from Dutch universities. These policies have been strongly reflected in the funding scheme requirements of the research funding agencies. At the same time, both systems of higher education share similarities that are likely to influence boundary blurring between the university and industry.

In both contexts, universities have become more centrally managed organizations with streamlined decision-making in which performance monitoring has become increasingly important (Whitley *et al.*, 2010). Strategic priority setting by the management has become a routine part of managerial activity with an emphasis on positioning universities within the global higher education market (de Boer *et al.*, 2007). In this setting, research commercialization and the attraction of external funding, contracts, and income from industry have become vital. Thus, the university management has put forward performance indicators that are related to knowledge commercialization alongside indicators such as the number of high-impact publications and teaching quality results (Leišytė, 2011).

Further, the importance of students and teaching has been increasingly emphasized by national policies and universities in both countries. Student numbers generate income for universities either through governmental funding based on student numbers, as in the Netherlands, or through student fees, as in the UK. The number of students graduated each year is among the university performance indicators and influences their ranking. The resulting focus on attracting larger student numbers means potentially increasing teaching and administrative workloads for staff in the case of stable staff numbers or even reduced staff numbers due to budget cuts. As part of this trend, teaching 'relevant' subjects that would increase the employability of students is becoming increasingly emphasized at universities in the UK and the Netherlands. This trend often manifests itself in the managerial initiatives to improve teaching at universities by including external industry stakeholders in the curriculum committees and quality assurance instruments of universities and requirements to provide student placements in industry. Thus, tapping into alternative sources of funding from industry and engaging in fee-generating contracts or teaching activities have become a managerial expectation towards academics in both studied contexts.

Findings

In the following section, we present the empirical evidence from the four case studies in the UK and the Netherlands. We first show how the studied bioscientists experience managerialism in their organizational context in regard to knowledge commercialization imperatives. Further, we present the patterns of boundary-crossing and boundary-maintenance behaviour among the studied biotechnology scientists by focusing on their collaborative behaviour. We aim to determine to what extent academics cooperate with non-academic actors in the commercialization of their teaching and research. Next, we focus on how academics maintain their academic freedom, which is one of the core values of academia, by exploring their research output and the selection of research topics. We aim to understand the extent to which bioscientists preserve their academic values and prioritize their academic roles or to what extent academic entrepreneurship has become central or peripheral to their academic work.

Reaching this aim allows us to draw conclusions on the 'holistic' academic identity of bioscientists in the studied organizational contexts.

Managerial imperatives from universities as experienced by the studied academics

The UK academics mentioned that the universities are pressed by the funding bodies to perform in terms of knowledge commercialization, especially in terms of research commercialization. (The abbreviations used below (e.g. SBSR1II) are anonymous to avoid identifying institutions or people.) However, in the view of the academics, the costs outweigh the benefits of this enterprise:

> Now, research councils would love to be able to say, 'We do this, we do this, this is this discovery, and this is how many millions you are earning from that and therefore give us more money.' But it doesn't work that way. The pressure to make it work that way has increased the demand for universities to measure their spin-out companies and to measure their licensing agreements and to measure their patents and all these sorts of stuff. And most of those are going up, but, of course, if you work out the total costs and the money that is coming back, I mean, they just don't add up at all.
> (SBSR1II)

Similarly, in the Dutch cases, academics are concerned that the pressure to patent is not lined up with the arrangements to facilitate patenting and increase the income of the research groups; thus, they are quite sceptical of the university's imperatives to commercialize the knowledge:

> It is not my primary thing, and part of that is that I think the benefit for patenting for a research group at least here is not well thought out. And it is a lot of work. So I have been disappointed by patenting sometimes. That you do a lot of work and you do not get any benefit back from it, apart from ownership. It is sometimes the industry and – we have about 15 patents or so in the group, but some are sold by others. I do not know. We never get the real revenues out of it, so ... But if a part of that money, the revenues, would stream back to the research group, I would be more willing to consider. But I think it is not well arranged yet. I think they are trying to improve that.
> (RBSR1II)

In addition, a paradox of expectations is observed in the UK in regard to teaching outcomes among the expectations of the university, government, and industry, as noted by the interviewed academics. The clash of understandings of what skills and knowledge graduates should have confuses academics in what the key goals are of their teaching, although academics clearly prefer the reasoning that is less linked to entrepreneurship and transferable skills and more to the real science:

> So, how it has been interpreted in government circles is we should be turning out graduates who are science-aware, they are business-aware, know about IT, and start-up companies and all this sort of stuff. And accordingly, you put lots of effort for business training in your science team, but what you are doing isn't worth a damn in science, right? ... Now, the big industry – so when I talked to big industry, big pharma, the biotech concept, they haven't said this at all. They just want us to really train hard scientists who are independent thinkers. However, I think in consulting them, the language has gone wrong, and I suppose essentially what they've said is they want people who could innovate. Well, I can see how you could take innovation, and in government circles say that is the same as an entrepreneur because you might think that's what business means, but actually what business means basically is a bloody good scientist who can free think and run for themselves and – well, I think it has been misinterpreted in government circles. When it comes down from the government end to the universities in our senior management groups, they think they know what entrepreneurial means, and they just mean business modules, MBA-type stuff, right.
>
> (SBSR1II)

In this sense, government and management are perceived as creating confusion through the variety of commercialization expectations for academics. On the one hand, academics are supposed to commercialize their knowledge and 'produce' entrepreneurial scientists; on the other hand, the biotechnology industry demands graduates with solid scientific background. The pressure from the universities to produce patents and license them does not seem to be fully supported with the procedural arrangements, which would favour academics, and creates an adverse effect in the long run.

These findings show that managerialism provides incentives for boundary crossing in terms of knowledge commercialization to some extent, thus confirming H1. However, as predicted in H3, conditions for conflict between managerialist demands for commercialization and academic values exist, which may lead towards boundary maintenance.

Boundary-crossing behaviour: academic entrepreneurship roles

In general, the importance of the commercialization of knowledge is widely recognized by the interviewed biotechnology scientists from both countries. The potential applicability of research has become an important factor in the selection of research topics. However, the extent of entrepreneurship activities differs between the analysed countries and departments.

In the UK, the commercialization activities of the interviewed academics are rather limited and are prioritized after research and teaching. Teaching relevant to industry is mentioned as being important in this regard:

> So, that will suggest … our major role is to actually train people to go out into industry and actually keep those companies running and keep them ahead, and of course, economically, it is much more difficult to put your finger on that.
>
> (SBSR1II)

At the same time, the studied UK bioscientists mention some entrepreneurial activities. Two of eight interviewed researchers indicated that they are currently involved in patenting research or creating spin-off companies. The factors that account for the involvement of these researchers in both activities are either intrinsic motivations or financial aspects. With respect to patenting, the weak department appears to have a strong culture of patenting, transferring results to industry, and other commercialization activities. Although only one junior researcher from this department is currently involved in commercialization, many others reported filing patents in the past. However, they do not seem to be driven by management demands to patent; rather, it is 'an incidental thing that might arise occasionally' (QBWR4II). Instead of responding to managerial pressures, this academic thinks that a patent results out of the normal flow of the academic work. In contrast, the creation of spin-off companies is motivated by the financial limitations of universities because the revenues from these companies help finance the research of the scientists. Moreover, having a spin-off company is a practical aspect in patenting research. If the research product is developed jointly with the company or the research outcome is useful for the company, the patent will be jointly filed by the research group and the spin-off company.

Collaborations with industry are also not very common in the UK biotechnology departments, even though such collaboration is inherent to the nature of bioscience research:

> I think you need to put in place opportunities for people from industry and university to get together, but actually, they've got an awful lot in common, and in the biological sciences, most of what you are doing, even industry, is fundamental research. I mean there are some things that are purely applied.
>
> (SBSR1II)

Companies infrequently approach the research groups for their expertise to solve a problem in a particular area. Although the applicability of research is also an important goal, this contact often drives researchers to collaborate with other disciplines instead of industry, especially if their research topic is not particularly suitable for offering solutions for a specific industry problem. This preference can be explained because external collaboration, especially in terms of interdisciplinary or international academic research cooperation, is encouraged by university management to bring in external funding because many grant schemes support such collaborative research projects. Funding programmes that emphasize industrial collaboration were not addressed by any of the interviewed researchers in either department.

In contrast, the research departments in the Netherlands report more commercialization activities, and their bioscientists are more involved in entrepreneurial roles than in teaching and research. As noted by the interviewed academics, part-time academics who are teaching now work in daily practice in the industry, hospitals or pharmacies. Their role is important in making sure that the programme quality is high and relevant to industry (UBWR1II).

With respect to industry collaborations, contacts with large-scale and small spin-off companies with several different projects can be observed. One of the main motivations mentioned for such collaborations is the need to obtain industry funding to finance patents, which is a very costly process:

> Sometimes we keep the patents ourselves for two years. But after 2.5 years, you are really going to make big costs because then it goes to – in Europe it goes to the national phases, and you have to do the translation, not you but other guys, and these are very expensive procedures. So, if you do not have a candidate, a partner willing to collaborate based on the patents, then we drop the patents…. If we find an industrial partner who is interested in this patent and the technology, then a kind of contract should be signed, but all contracts are different, but always three elements that are important. That we arrange that the industrial partner will take over all the costs associated with the patents. We should be in agreement on royalties, so when the patent comes to commercialization and products that we get some money back. But, most importantly, for these pharmaceutical products, the development time is ten to 15 years.
>
> (UBWR1II)

Industry is thus approached as a contract partner for patents and a financial source to perform further R&D. Grants from companies are used to hire a PhD or postdoctoral student to further work in collaboration with the company on the technology covered by the patent. This kind of collaboration is seen as providing mutual benefits, as stated by a junior researcher from the strong department:

> We are very independent, and we have a long tradition of collaboration with companies. So they come to us and ask our help to develop this or that. So, we help each other, I guess. The companies want to know how to produce something, or they want to know to characterize whatever, and

you can make it a postdoc project or a PhD project. So, in the end, a person is educated in this way, and the company also gets what it wants.

(RBSr3II)

Finally, another incentive for collaborating with companies is to guarantee external funding by third-party research funders, such as European grant programmes that specifically reward collaboration with academic groups and companies. Therefore, many European projects that involve research groups from other disciplines and/or universities and companies in the consortium can be found at the biotechnology groups of Dutch universities. In this respect, the Dutch interviewed academics are strongly entrepreneurial in pursuing consortium-building activities with other European partners and industry and being able to attract European research projects.

In the Dutch context, we observe patenting differences between the research groups. The weak group shows keen interest in patenting; sometimes this activity is even preferred over publishing journal papers, which is still the most important research output for biotechnology scientists. In the strong group, however, the attitudes towards and involvement in patenting activity are mixed. One interviewed professor from this department is not so involved in research commercialization, whereas another professor is significantly more active in patenting, industry collaboration, and building spin-offs and strongly encourages his assistants and students to follow his example. In this sense, he is an example of an academic entrepreneur who successfully combines teaching, research, and commercialization. Commercialization activities are very common in the group of this professor, in terms of PhD students starting spin-off companies or other junior scientists applying for Dutch Technology Foundation (STW) valorization grants to exploit further commercial possibilities for the technology they are working on. Their major motivations are the urge to show that the university is not doing just basic science and that the technology can also be applied; additionally, they hope that these small companies will collaborate with the university once they grow.

Altogether, knowledge commercialization roles among studied bioscientists are more pronounced in the Netherlands than in the UK. The common factors driving these activities in both countries are the belief that research in this field should be applicable and the need to attract external funding due to financial constraints from the university. In addition, commercialization is strongly supported by some funding schemes in the Netherlands and in the EU, which is an additional motivation for Dutch bioscientists to engage in such activities.

Boundary maintenance: biotechnologists upholding traditional academic roles

The previous section has shown that commercialization activities occur in the studied departments in both countries, but they are not central to the academic work of the bioscientists. Thus, some boundary maintenance is occurring in which academic identities are strongly defined by traditional academic values and academics focus on the teaching and research roles. What is the reason for this maintenance? What factors foster this maintenance in both countries?

Emphasis on publications

First of all, traditional academic output is still highly emphasized in both contexts. In the UK, academic journal publications, especially in high-impact factor, peer-reviewed journals, are still the most highly valued research output because the quality of the work is centrally assessed by the number of articles published in such journals. Additionally, publishing research is seen as a moral obligation:

> I'm sure your obligation if you do research is that, particular if it is public funding, you should put it out to the public domain. And that, what that does mean is that they're pieces of work which, to be frank, might not be the highest quality, but I think should find a home to be published. To go out there.
>
> (QBWR4II)

In the Netherlands, researchers from both universities also stated that publications are indispensable in their work. Journal articles are particularly important, given the background of performance indicators used at their universities and the credibility-building norms of academia. Just as in the UK context, the publication record is the first thing that is considered when assessing how good a department is. Therefore, researchers tend to set strict regulations to guarantee that their freedom to publish is not hampered when they collaborate with companies; if they see a setback, they prioritize the publication, not the collaboration or patenting:

> The research should fit in our research programme, and if you talk about selection, sometimes we get grants from industry to do projects, and one of the criteria, in the long run, we should be able to publish the results. If industry is not willing to do that, then we say, well, then we do not start the collaboration. So, at the end, it should end in publications.
>
> (UBWR1II)

Obstacles for publishing while collaborating with industry can arise in many other ways. It is important for companies that competitors do not steal the idea, so they try to guarantee that the results will not be published or in some other way disclosed before they becomes the company's property. This necessity has negative consequences for PhD students, in particular, who work under contracts with industry or work in companies. The collaboration and patenting can delay the publication procedure, or the company can announce that they do not want the data to be published. Here again, though, the priority is given to the academic research and the publication:

> I have seen a lot of disasters there that students work for three or four years on projects, and then the company says, 'No, we do not want to publish it.' And then, well, I do not have a problem, but my PhD students will have, and, of course, I have to guide these students like a father. It can also be – sometimes they ask for one year, which is not acceptable, but I can give them three months or so, and then they can judge whether the patent can be applied for or not. However, they cannot influence either the contents or block publication of data.
> (UBWR1II)

Academic freedom

Research freedom and autonomy are still very important for the studied bioscientists, even in the cases of strong orientation towards research commercialization and industry collaboration. In the UK, problem choice follows naturally from one's own research interest for most biotechnology scientists. The decision about which area to study is mostly influenced by the academic community itself. What is medically or industrially important is not very significant. Company demands can lead researchers to deviate from their research line and adjust themselves to the specific request of the company, but this adjustment is seen as an opportunity rather than a limitation because it 'opens up a total new sort of horizon' (QBWR3II).

There is enough room to manoeuvre when selecting research topics, but getting these topics funded is the tricky part. Everyone wants innovative research, but, at the same time, they want to know that it is a safe bet. Additionally, one must act strategically to obtain funding from grant organizations – the influence of this strategizing varies from simply adjusting the language and ticking boxes to completely adopting the priority topics set by the funders:

> I mean, if anybody actually believes that the themes they dream – I mean, okay, how does the theme emerge? The theme usually emerges because there is a committee of ten people who are on some sort of grants committee, and the director will come down to research council, give us the themes that they think will be important for the next – so we can bid for the convent [sic]. So, what do you get? You might get the buzzwords; you get the latest buzzwords; that's all you are getting. Yet, we know in science that the major changes have come from left field. They have come from something obscure; by that I mean, recombinant DNA technology, antibodies, DNA fingerprints, you

name it. Everything that's happened in biology has come from something that you could not have predicted, that that research was not going to lead to that. And so what do I believe that [you get] by throwing all your eggs into the latest buzzword? No, it's not like that. So, that's not how it happens, but government does not understand. The government does not understand. So, that's how it happens, and the research councils are not brave enough to tell government clearly enough 'that is not how it happens' and because saying 'Let's get on to do our own thing' sounds as if you don't want any control and you are not responsible, that's why you are in the situation you are in.

(SBSR1II)

Some researchers express concern about the quality of research when the freedom to select research topics is limited due to the funding situation. Simultaneously, although industrial or medical relevance does not directly determine topic choice, they play a role in funding applications and therefore indirectly influence research topics. One must clearly demonstrate the impact of the proposed research in these applications.

In the Netherlands, researchers also report having a high level of freedom. There is some influence of company funding on research, but it is minimal. Topic selection is adjusted to industry needs, but it is not too restrictive. Thus, there is always room for publishing results, as demonstrated above. Just as in the UK, topic selection can depend on the topic priorities set by the call for proposals. In some cases, topic selection starts with the idea, and then the researchers look for a grant programme that would be suitable to submit their proposal (e.g. UBWR4II). In some other cases, scientists try to fit their research question into the area of calls for proposals (e.g. RBSR1II). The EU funding tends to have predefined topics that restrict the researchers in the possibilities, but national funding schemes (NWO) offer more freedom. The type of research is important for getting funding. Applied research attracts industry funding, but more fundamental research is only likely to be funded by national funding councils – even they do not offer many possibilities because industry is sometimes involved in the funding committees (e.g. in the STW) (RBSR1II). Additionally, there is the problem of buzzword/fashionable topics (RBSR4II).

Senior researchers at the strong department report being able to keep a red line of research. They build upon existing research questions and findings but stress that funding is an important factor. A project can 'die down because of funding problems' (RBSR1II). Money is an important factor to keep the scientific work going, to obtain new equipment and to hire new staff. Therefore, industry funding becomes an important driving force for the selection of research themes, but they still try to focus on their own interests. As shown in the previous section, there is a mutual trade-off between scientific research and the industry. Scientists can select a topic in which companies have an interest, so they can get it financed; then, for example, they can take on a new PhD student and decide together about the further course of the research and expand the scope of their expertise (RBSR2II).

In the strong department, the academic freedom, especially in applied research, is more restricted by industry collaborations (and funding), and the researchers seem to be more worried about the need to adjust topic selection to industry needs and funding priorities. Junior researchers are particularly affected by this restriction; they think that in applied research, or in projects in which they collaborate with the industry, they are more restricted, although they can negotiate about what needs to be done:

> We had the project meeting every half year and also from the company; they checked the project, how it was going. It was through the university but paid by the company. So they had the role – in that respect, they could say what I work on exactly, what direction I should go during that period.
> (RBSr3II)

They experienced more freedom in basic research, in which they collaborated with other academic departments and universities because a mutual understanding of what was interesting was more likely to come about. In applied research, however, if research is financed by a company, then pursuing topics of own interest becomes more difficult – the researcher is not encouraged to follow whatever is interesting to him or her, and the company has a strict idea in mind (RBSR4II). Industry is very sharply shaping choices and can even be decisive on the course of research for an entire discipline, as in the case of molecular biology, where departments allegedly tweak their subjects and focus on one certain type of bacteria to sustain their scientific activity because there is no money otherwise.

In the weak department, researchers reported having more freedom for the selection of their research topic; their selection depends largely on whether they consider the area as important and interesting. This freedom applies to both senior and junior researchers and is highly appreciated. Even in projects that are conducted in collaboration with industry, researchers want to sustain their red line of research, but they have to make it look like a short-term project to secure industry funding:

> Yeah, it is a red line going through, and I have one project in which there is a year-by-year financing, but we know that the work is much more than one year, but this is like money directly from industry, so they are not waiting to commit themselves for four years. It would be much easier first, if they would just say, okay, we pay for the complete PhD because then you do not have this unresolved [sic] financial contract and with experiments still going on all the time.
> (UBWR3II)

Discussion and conclusion

This study has shown that bioscientists are crossing the boundaries of academia and industry when they commercialize their research results via patenting and spin-off company creation. They also do so by contract research with industry, which is especially used to support PhD students who perform research in industry. The Dutch bioscientists who were studied seemed to be more engaged in this type of boundary crossing. In teaching activities, bioscientists mainly uphold the view of boundary maintenance where the belief of educating students in solid science is deeply rooted and is rationalized because this foundation is what industry wants as well – good-quality science graduates rather than entrepreneurs. Further, boundary maintenance is observed among all studied bioscientists in regard to preferring fundamental research, preserving academic freedom and ensuring their academic credibility as built via publications in good journals.

However, among the Dutch bioscientists, we observed some boundary crossing in this regard when it comes to accepting publication delays because first patent needs to be granted, or tweaking the research proposal topics so it is acceptable to the industrial partners.

We observed a slight difference between the higher- and lower-performing departments in terms of their boundary-maintenance behaviour. The lower-performing groups were more engaged in partnerships with industry, and they were active in the commercialization of their own research results because they needed to ensure they acquired funding from industry.

Overall, we noted differences between the responses of the UK and Dutch universities, which imply that the difference in governance regimes and managerial context matters for boundary crossing in academia. The pressure to cross boundaries and attract external funding, whether it will be EU or national funding, seems to be more pronounced at Dutch universities. Further, the organizational aspects, such as performance indicators, matter in both contexts, but more traditional outputs matter a lot in the UK due to the dominance of national evaluation in the managerial discourse and performance measurements at the studied UK universities. In the Dutch context, academics were more aware of managerial imperatives to 'valorize' their research results and get involved in commercialization, which are closely linked to the requirements of funding agencies. These findings are very much in line with the findings of Laudel (2006), Whitley et al. (2010) and Leišytė (2007). Simultaneously, there is support for the boundary-maintenance thesis of biosciences as noted by the studies of Shapin (1994) and Owen-Smith and Powell (2001).

Further, this study revealed that bioscientists find it challenging to combine entrepreneurship roles with teaching and research roles. Sometimes, this combination leads to conflicts in terms of producing timely research output or determining the focus of teaching programmes. We have also observed that personal motivations and financial incentives are strong drivers for combining the roles and acquiring the hybrid identity of an academic entrepreneur (also see Lam, 2011). This is especially noted in the cases where boundary crossing is pronounced and academics created their own companies and recruited their students to work in those companies. Thus, this study supports the notion that bioscientists can combine a variety of roles and that, in this sense, the identity of academic entrepreneurs can become part and parcel of the hybrid academic identity given the right motivations and appropriate organizational conditions and funding demands. However, the blending of roles seems to happen in cases when the main core role of research is still preserved.

Note

1   This research was funded by the German Research Foundation (DFG) 2006–9. The project, entitled 'Management and Self-government of Universities: Comparison of Decision-making Processes and Consequences for Research' was coordinated by Professors Schimank, Enders and Kehm. The data used in this chapter was collected by the first author.

References

Bercovitz, J. and Feldman, M. (2008) 'Academic entrepreneurs: organizational change at the individual level'. *Organization Science*, 19 (1), pp. 69–89

D'Este, P. and Patel, P. (2007) 'University–industry linkages in the UK: what are the factors underlying the variety of interactions with industry?' *Research Policy*, 36, pp. 1295–313

D'Este, P. and Perkmann, M. (2011) 'Why do academics engage with industry? The entrepreneurial university and individual motivations'. *The Journal of Technology Transfer*, 36, pp. 316–39

de Boer, H., Enders, J. and Leišytė, L. (2007) 'On striking the right notes: shifts in governance and the organizational transformation of universities'. *Public Administration*, 85 (1), pp. 27–46

Enders, J. and de Weert, E. (2009) *The Changing Face of Academic Life: Analytical and Comparative Perspectives*. Basingstoke: Palgrave MacMillan

Etzkowitz, H. (2003) 'Research groups as "quasi-firms": the invention of the entrepreneurial university'. *Research Policy*, 32 (1), pp. 109–21

Etzkowitz, H. (2008) *The Triple Helix: University–Industry–Government Innovation in Action*. London: Routledge

Geuna, A. and Muscio, A. (2009) 'The governance of university knowledge transfer: a critical review of the literature'. *Minerva*, 47, pp. 93–114

Gieryn, T. F. (1983) 'Boundary-work and the demarcation of science from non-science: strains and interests in professional ideologies of scientists'. *American Sociological Review*, 48, pp. 781–95

Gieryn, T. F. (1999) *Cultural Boundaries of Science: Credibility on the Line*. Chicago: University of Chicago Press

Haeussler, C. and Colyvas, J. A. (2011) 'Breaking the ivory tower: academic entrepreneurship in the life sciences in UK and Germany'. *Research Policy*, 40, pp. 41–54

Harloe, M., and Perry, B. (2008). 'Universities, localities and regional development: the emergence of the "mode 2" university?' *International Journal of Urban and Regional Research*, 28 (1), pp. 212–23

Henkel, M. (2000) *Academic Identities and Policy Change in Higher Education*. London: Jessica Kingsley

Henkel, M. (2005) 'Academic identity and autonomy in a changing policy environment'. *Higher Education*, 49 (1–2), pp. 155–76

Jansen, D. (Ed.) (2010) *Governance and Performance in the German Public Research Sector*. Dordrecht: Springer

Lam, A. (2010) 'From "ivory tower traditionalists" to "entrepreneurial scientists"? Academic scientists in fuzzy university-industry boundaries'. *Social Studies of Science*, 40, pp. 307–40

Lam, A. (2011) 'What motivates academic scientists to engage in research commercialization: "gold", "ribbon" or "puzzle"?' *Research Policy*, 40, pp. 1354–68

Lamont, M. and Molnar, V. (2002) 'The study of boundaries in the social sciences'. *Annual Review of Sociology*, 28 (1), pp. 167–95

Land, R. (2012) 'Crossing tribal boundaries: interdisciplinarity as a threshold concept' in Trowler, P., Saunders, M. and Bamber, V. (Eds), *Tribes and Territories in the 21st Century: Rethinking the Significance of Disciplines in Higher Education*. London: Routledge

Larsen, M. T. (2011) 'The implications of academic enterprise for public science: an overview of the empirical evidence'. *Research Policy*, 40, pp. 6–19

Laudel, G. (2006) 'The art of getting funded: how scientists adapt to their research conditions'. *Science and Public Policy*, 33, pp. 489–504

Leišytė, L. (2007) *University Governance and Academic Research: Case Studies of Research Units in Dutch and English Universities*. Enschede: University of Twente, CHEPS

Leišytė, L. (2011) 'Research commercialization policies and their implementation in the Netherlands and in the US'. *Science and Public Policy*, 38 (6), pp. 437–48

Leišytė, L. (2015) 'Changing academic identities in the context of a managerial university: bridging the duality between professions and organizations' in Cummings, W. and Teichler, U. (Eds), *The Relevance of Academic Work in Comparative Perspective*. Dordrecht: Springer, pp. 59–73

Leišytė, L. and Dee, J. (2012) 'Changing academic practices and identities in Europe and the US: critical perspectives' in Smart, J. C. and Paulsen, M. B. (Eds), *Higher Education: Handbook of Theory and Research*. Dordrecht: Springer, pp. 123–206

Leišytė, L. and Westerheijden, D. F. (2014) 'Research evaluation and its implications for academic research in the United Kingdom and the Netherlands'. Discussion paper no. 01-2014, TU Dortmund: Zentrum für Hochschulbildung. Retrieved from http://www.zhb.tu-dortmund.de/wb/Wil/Medienpool/Downloads/DP_paper-01-2014.pdf

Leišytė, L., Enders, J. and de Boer, H. (2009) 'The balance between teaching and research in Dutch and English universities in the context of university governance reforms'. *Higher Education*, 58 (5), pp. 619–35

Leišytė, L., Enders, J. and de Boer, H. (2010) 'Mediating problem choice: academic researchers' responses to changes in their institutional environment' in Whitley, R., Gläser, J. and Engwall, L. (Eds), *Reconfiguring Knowledge Production: Changing Authority Relationships in the Sciences and their Consequences for Intellectual Innovation*. Oxford: Oxford University Press, pp. 291–324

Link, A. N. and Siegel, D. S. (2007) *Innovation, Entrepreneurship, and Technological Change*. Oxford: Oxford University Press

Markman, G. D., Siegel, D. S. and Wright, M. (2008) 'Research and technology commercialization'. *Journal of Management Studies*, 45 (8), pp. 1401–23

O'Shea, R., Chugh, H. and Allen, T. (2008) 'Determinants and consequences of university spinoff activity: a conceptual framework'. *Journal of Technology Transfer*, 33, pp. 653–66

Owen-Smith, J. and Powell, W. (2001) 'Careers and contradictions: faculty responses to the transformation of knowledge and its uses in the life sciences'. *Research in the Sociology of Work*, 10, pp. 109–40

Perkmann, M. and Walsh, K. (2007) 'University–industry relationships and open innovation: towards a research agenda'. *International Journal of Management Reviews*, 9, pp. 259–80

Perkmann, M., Tartari, V., McKelvey, M., Autio, E., Broström, A., D'Este, P., Fini, R., Geuna, A., Grimaldi, R., Hughes, A., Krabel, S., Kitson, M., Llerena, P., Lissoni, F., Salter, A. and Sobrero, M. (2013) 'Academic engagement and commercialisation: a review of the literature on university–industry relations'. *Research Policy*, 42, pp. 423–42

Phan, P. H. and Siegel, D. S. (2006) 'The effectiveness of university technology transfer: lessons learned from qualitative and quantitative research in the US and UK'. *Foundations and Trends in Entrepreneurship*, 2, pp. 66–144

Phan, P. H., Siegel, D. S. and Wright, M. (2005) 'Science parks and incubators: observations, synthesis and future research'. *Journal of Business Venturing*, 20, pp. 165–82

Rasmussen, E., Moen, Ø. and Gulbrandsen, M. (2006) 'Initiatives to promote commercialization of university knowledge'. *Technovation*, 26, pp. 518–33

Rothaermel, F. T., Agung, S. and Jiang, L. (2007) 'University entrepreneurship: a taxonomy of the literature'. *Industrial and Corporate Change*, 16, pp. 691–791

Schimank, U. and Winnes, M. (2000) 'Beyond Humboldt? The relationship between teaching and research in European university systems'. *Science and Public Policy*, 27 (6), pp. 397–408

Shapin, S. (1994) *A Social History of Truth: Civility and Science in Seventeenth-Century England*. Chicago: University of Chicago Press

Siegel, D. S., Wright, M. and Lockett, A. (2007) 'The rise of entrepreneurial activity at universities: organizational and societal implications'. *Industrial and Corporate Change*, 16 (4), pp. 489–504

Teelken, J. C. (2012) 'Compliance or pragmatism: how do academics deal with managerialism in higher education? A comparative study in three countries'. *Studies in Higher Education*, 37 (3), pp. 271–90

Whitley, R., Gläser, J. and Engwall, L. (Eds) (2010) *Reconfiguring Knowledge Production: Changing Authority Relationships in the Sciences and their Consequences for Intellectual Innovation*. Oxford: Oxford University Press

13
University academic promotion system and academic identity
An institutional logics perspective

YUZHUO CAI AND GAOMING ZHENG

Introduction

In the past two or three decades, universities around the world have been pressurized by both government mandates and societal needs to assume an increasing economic role for making more direct contributions to economic development and innovation (Clark, 1998; Etzkowitz, 1990; Etzkowitz et al., 2000). In response to these pressures, universities have tended to become more efficient, productive, and even entrepreneurial, and, in turn, to accordingly expect their academics to change their practices. For example, under the global isomorphism of emulating practices of private sectors, a growing number of countries have introduced 'new public management' (Hood, 2000) or 'new managerialism' (Clarke and Newman, 1994; Clarke and Newman, 1997) into higher education (Maassen, 2003). Following policies addressing performance-based funding, corporation models of university governance and marketization, many universities' higher-level administrators have adopted structures and practices 'commanding ideological overtones of efficiency and effectiveness' (Townley, 1997, p. 265). All of these studies imply changes and challenges in academic work.

However, because higher education is a highly institutionalized field (Meyer et al., 2007), changing the discourses of higher education institutions (HEIs) and specifically the behaviours of academics is rather challenging (Clark, 1983; Musselin, 2007). They often either resist changes or decouple their practical work from formal structural changes (Krücken, 2003; Townley, 1997). The reluctance of academics to change/reform is to a large extent due to the heavy inertia of traditional academic identity, which has originated and been sustained throughout universities' historical development (Townley, 1997). Academic identities influence academic behaviours because they affect academics' 'sense of purpose, self-efficacy, motivation, commitment, job satisfaction and effectiveness' (Day et al., 2006, p. 601), which largely determine individuals' behaviours.

Regardless of academics' efforts to avoid coercive pressures that impose a norm of managerialism, the New Public Management (NPM) reform in higher education has resulted in academic identity conflicts or multiple identities (Winter and O'Donohue, 2012). The multiple identities of academics are aligned with different 'institutional logics' (Friedland and Alford, 1991; Thornton *et al*., 2012), such as the logic of professionalism, the logic of managerialism, the logic of the liberal academy, and the logic of the market (Townley, 1997; Winter and O'Donohue, 2012).

While numerous empirical studies in higher education have addressed the higher education reforms and their impact on academic work (Cheng, 2012; Hoecht, 2006; Lai, 2013), few studies have examined the impact of policy changes on academic work from an academic identity perspective. The few studies that have addressed academic identities during higher education reform (for example, Billot, 2010; Henkel, 2005a; Leišytė, 2015; Leišytė and Dee, 2012; Leišytė *et al*., 2010; Townley, 1997; Winter, 2009; Winter and O'Donohue, 2012) have mainly studied academic identity as a key factor that influences the academics' responses to government reforms or analysed the identity changes and conflicting values in the context of higher education transformation. How policy changes in an institution, as a regulative aspect of an organization's changes, may theoretically and empirically affect academic identities remains unknown. Leišytė (2015) discussed the changes (including policy changes) in the institutional environment of academics in American and European contexts and changes of academic identities in the dynamic institutional environment. Her study has, to some extent, bridged the gap and presented a typology to understand academic identities in a managerial context. However, her study did not explore in what way or why the changes of policies will change academic identities. Moreover, her study focused on American and European systems, which are both advanced and mature academic communities. The status of academics in comparatively less developed systems, such as Chinese academia, remains unexplored.

This chapter is an effort to fill the gaps by constructing an analytical framework for understanding the relationships between changes of policies and identities from the institutional logics perspective (Friedland and Alford, 1991; Thornton *et al*., 2012) and then applying this framework in a case study of a Chinese research university to understand how the changes/reforms of academic promotion policy in an institution affect academic identity.

Methodology

Case studies is the preferred method when 1) 'how' or 'why' questions are being posed, 2) the investigator has little control over events, and 3) the focus is on a contemporary phenomenon within a real-life context (Yin, 1994).

In our study, the research question is a 'how' research question, we have little control over the effects of the university academic promotion policy, and the research is focused on a contemporary phenomenon within a real-life context. Hence, a case study is an appropriate research method for our study. Thus, one important step is to select the case. We found a representative or typical case that can represent a common situation of a community of academics in China. Following this logic, an academic community in a research university (B University) in Beijing was selected as our analysis unit. B University is a typical research university in China, and it has been granted the promotion authority of full professors and associate professors by the Chinese Ministry of Education (MoE) since 1986, which means it can develop its own university academic promotion policy and individually promote academics. Furthermore, to avoid the interference of disciplinary impact, our study only focused on academics in one school, named Faculty E (in the field of Social Sciences). Faculty E was selected instead of other faculties for two reasons: 1) each faculty performs academic promotion individually but under the same university guidance, which makes the situation in each faculty similar, and Faculty E can represent other faculties; 2) we have some personal relations with the management in Faculty E to allow entry to the field, which is a very important step to ensure the feasibility and possibility of the research. Furthermore, to increase the likelihood of the case being understood from various perspectives, we collected data from multiple sources, including documents, literature, and semi-structured interviews. Documents of national academic promotion policy in China and the relevant policy studies, as well as documents of university and faculty promotion policy and the existing literature, which are relevant to the topic, were evaluated. Regarding the interviewees, both university managers and academics were considered. In the latest round of academic promotion in Faculty E in 2013, 18 academics were recommended by their departments for promotion. We invited all of them to be interviewed; we received 11 replies, of whom seven agreed, including one newly promoted full professor (A6), three newly promoted associate professors (A1, A2, and A3), one un-promoted associate professor (A7), and two un-promoted lecturers (A4 and A5). Moreover, three managers in Faculty E (M1, M2, and M3) who were involved in organizing academic promotion and one university policy-maker (P1) who participated in the university academic promotion policy-making process were interviewed. Interviews were mainly conducted via face-to-face communication, skype meetings, and emails depending on the agreement with the interviewees. Then, all collected data were coded and categorized manually by the researchers. The code categories were based on our analytical framework, and the data were coded accordingly. Later, we examined all entries with the same code, made generalizations based on the coded and categorized data, and evaluated the plausibility of some hypotheses that had evolved during the analysis.

Analytical framework

Definitions of academic promotion policy and academic identity

Following Jenkins' (1978, p. 15) definition that policy is 'a set of interrelated decisions ... concerning the selection of goals and the means of achieving them within a specific situation', we understand *academic promotion policy* as a set of interrelated decisions, from different levels of authorities, concerning the criteria and procedures for promoting academics to higher ranks.

Identity, as a collective identity or a social identity, refers to 'our understanding of who we are and who other people are, and, reciprocally other people's understanding of themselves and others' (van Stekelenburg, 2013, p. 1). Identity is shaped by personal values and beliefs and the context of social institutions and social relations (Billot, 2010; Henkel, 2005a, 2005b). The construction of social identity is realized in the community (Henkel, 2005a, 2005b) and, in the case of defining academic identity, communities refer to disciplines and institutions (Clark, 1987; Henkel, 2005a, 2005b). Academic identity has been commonly understood as the extent to which academics perceive themselves primarily as members of an enterprise or a higher education institution (administrative identity) and/or members of an academic profession/discipline (professional identity) (Billot, 2010; Clark, 1983; Henkel, 2005a, 2005b; Winter, 2009). Academic identity is often more related to discipline than institution (Harris, 2005). In this study, we follow the understanding that academic identity is defined as 'the values and beliefs' that academics 'hold regarding their work' (Leišytė and Dee, 2012, p. 125), and the analysis of changes and construction of academic identities should be considered in the context of institutions and disciplines (Clark, 1987; Henkel, 2005a, 2005b).

While academic identity possesses the characteristics of stability, it is also a dynamic construct (Billot, 2010). It can be shifted due to structural changes in higher education (Henkel, 2005a), emerging local practices (Lee and Boud, 2003), coercive forces, and incentives (Billot, 2010). Thus, changing academic identities are concerned with changing institutional environment or institutional logics.

Institutional logics perspective

The primary motivations for developing the institutional logics approach are to use institutional logics to concretely define the content and meaning of institutions (Thornton and Ocasio, 2008) and to better explain how institutions both enable and constrain action by incorporating macro structure, local culture, and human agency (Thornton et al., 2012). Institutional logic is defined as 'a set of material practices and symbolic constructions' that constitute an institutional order's 'organizing principle' and are 'available to organizations and individuals to elaborate' (Friedland and Alford, 1991, p. 248). For example, institutional orders at the societal level can be a family, a community, a religion, a state, a market, a profession, or a corporation (Thornton et al., 2012). The concepts of institutional logics can be applied in an organizational field (Greenwood et al., 2011) or even within an organization (McPherson and Sauder, 2013). Nevertheless, institutional logics at all levels 'are ... embedded in societal-level logics' (Thornton et al., 2012, p. 17). One central argument of the institutional logics perspective is that multiple and contending logics provide the dynamic for potential change in both organizations and societies. Fundamental to this process are shifts and interplays among institutional logics, identities, and practices (ibid.), which will be further explained below.

Influence of policy on identities, as explained from the institutional logics perspective

The governance and management reforms in higher education are intended to change academic work or the behaviours of academics (Maassen, 2003) by disrupting the equilibrium of the existing institutional environment where the actors are embedded (Howlett et al., 2009). The reforms mainly exert changes on the regulative dimension (Scott, 2008) by setting new policies and regulative procedures. From the institutional logics perspective (Friedland and Alford, 1991; Thornton et al., 2012), policy often introduces new institutional logics (Bastedo, 2009; Townley, 1997). However, one must realize that new logics in higher education are not merely introduced by policies but also emerge through other means – for example, the activities of professional networking and emulation of best practices in a global context, as implied by Cai (2010) in his study on governance reforms in Chinese higher education. Although we acknowledge other practices, especially academics' and managers' emanating from the 'best practices' from advanced higher education systems, may play a key role in the changes of logics, our analysis in this chapter remains focused on policy only because we believe that 'learning from others' can be largely reflected in policy design.

When evaluating changes of institutional logics, the concept of identity is central. As noted by Meyer and Hammerschmid (2006, p. 1000), '[s]hifts in institutional logics can be analysed by the extent to which actors draw on the social identities derived from the competing logics'. Indeed, identities are shaped by institutional logics (Friedland and Alford, 1991). Meanwhile, 'shifts in these identities can also catalyse changes in logics' (Thornton et al., 2012, p. 130). When individuals are embedded in a context with pluralistic institutional logics, their identities can be shaped by different logics differentially or by a hybrid of logics (ibid.). To approach the issue of how promotion policies affect academic identities by catalysing changes in institutional logics, we formulated the following analytical framework (Figure 13.1).

```
                    Historical dependency, strategies and practices
    ┌─────────────────┬──────────────────────┬─────────────────┐
    │ Historical path │ Other practices (e.g.│ Policies in the │
    │ of academic     │ learning from best   │ reform on       │
    │ promotion       │ practices elsewhere) │ academic        │
    │ system dev.     │                      │ promotion       │
    └─────────────────┴──────────────────────┴─────────────────┘

        Traditional              New              Multiple/contesting
        institutional  ◄────►    institutional    institutional logics
        logics                   logics

        Traditional    ◄────►    Hybrid    ◄────► Emerging
        identities               identity         identities
                         Academic identities

        Academics' attitudes to changes in the institutional environment
```

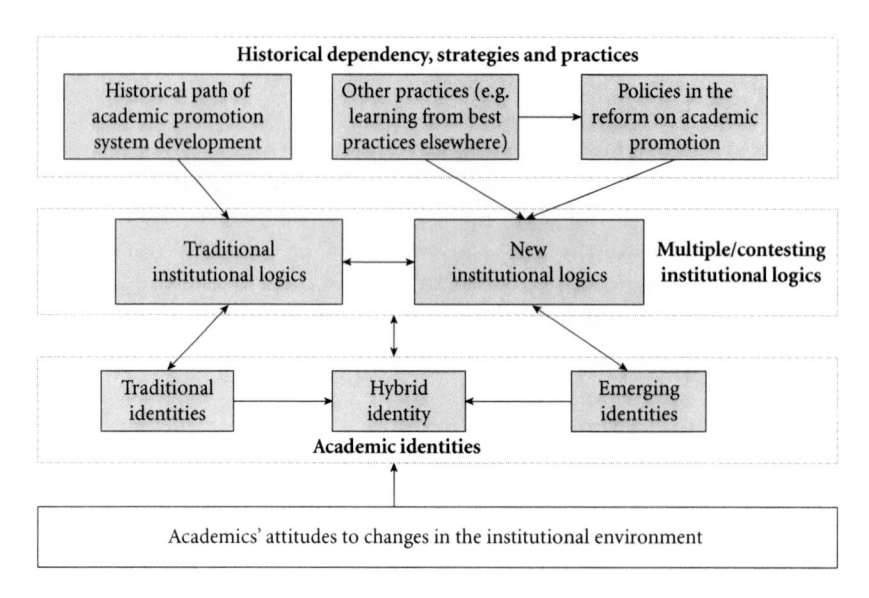

Figure 13.1 Analytical framework for understanding influences of policies on identities

Specifically, our analysis follows three steps. First, we look closely at the historical path of the academic promotion system and recent reforms of academic promotion policies in the case. Second, we analyse what institutional logics aligned with the traditional academic promotion system and what new logics were introduced by the reforms in the case. Third, we discuss how the mingling of institutional logics influences academic identities. To discern academic identities in this case, we relied on the interviewees' responses on their attitudes towards external institutional changes. Thus, academic identity construction could be described 'in terms of either internalisation of values, aspirations, sense of meaning and worth, language, theories and knowledge' or as the 'internal–external dialectic of identification' and 'individuation' (self-identification) of academics within the changing institutional environment (Henkel, 2005b, p. 148). In other words, by studying academics' perception or understanding of what they do and their response to the impact of institutional logics, we can learn how they identify themselves. By combining institutional theory with resource dependence, Oliver (1991) suggested that a strategic response to institutional pressures towards conformity will vary from conforming to resisting (including five strategies: acquiescence, compromise, avoidance, defiance, and manipulation), depending on the institutional antecedents of the institutional pressures. Other studies (Leišytė, 2007; Leišytė et al., 2010; Teelken, 2012) have further examined Oliver's proposition in empirical studies. The institutional logics derived from either the tradition or reform policies can be seen as institutional pressures. Although Oliver's focus on the responses is at the organizational level, the five strategies might also be useful for understanding individual academics' strategies to cope with different logics within their working environment.

Academic promotion system: traditions and reforms

Academic promotion policy changes are part of and consistent with the overall higher education reforms in China, which basically can be understood as responses to the growing market economy and open society in China (Cai and Yan, 2015). The university academic promotion system in China has gone through three developmental stages since 1949, respectively called the politics-oriented stage (1949–66), the transformation stage (1977–85), and the market-oriented stage (1986–present) (Mao and Cai, 2010). The period from 1967–76 was the decade of the 'Cultural Revolution', in which the entire higher education system could be considered as closed down, regardless of its reopening in the early 1970s for admission of politically qualified students only (Cai, 2004). In the first stage, the university academic promotion system was highly government-controlled, and academics' political performance was highly weighted in their academic appointments. In the second stage, market mechanisms were gradually introduced in Chinese universities; consequently, the central government started to transfer the administration of academic appointment to the hands of provincial governments. Along with marketization, the reforms of academic promotion in the third stage are characterized by the following two fundamental changes. One is the shift from academic appointment to academic promotion. Second, more and more Chinese HEIs can independently conduct academic promotion and develop their own institutional policies. By 2012, 175 HEIs have been granted autonomy in promoting full professors, and 123 HEIs can evaluate and promote associate professors.

Today, academic work (primarily teaching and research) has generally become the main performance indicator in Chinese academic promotion. Comparably, research performance, particularly research publication, has greater weight in promotion assessment (Ma and Wen, 2012; Mohrman et al., 2011). The assessment criteria at the institutional level are largely influenced by relevant policies at both the national and regional levels (Zhang, 2013). For instance, the MoE provides the structure for academics' population at each university, such as: full professor (20 per cent), associate professor (30 per cent), lecturer (40 per cent), and assistant lecturer (10 per cent).

Against the background of the state-led academic promotion reform at national level, Chinese universities individually reform their own systems. In our case, the academic promotion system has undergone profound reforms since 2002, with the main efforts to standardize the promotion process and

250 • Yuzhuo Cai and Gaoming Zheng

enhance academic outcomes. Our study focuses on the more recent university academic promotion policy since 2009, which can be briefly described as follows.

Currently, academic promotion is conducted annually at B University. The university's human resource office decides the quota of academics to be promoted in each academic rank, based on the structure of the academic population provided by the MoE and the demands proposed by academic units. The main assessment consideration lies in research output, teaching commitment, and administrative responsibilities. The promotion process consists of three steps: 1) evaluation and recommendation by faculties; 2) assessment by disciplinary-based committee, as organized by the university; and 3) evaluation and approval/rejection by a committee of the university (see Figure 13.2). Among the three steps, the first one is the most crucial.

Institutional logics associated with the academic promotion system and its reforms

Until the 1980s, the whole higher education system in China was a national *danwei*, which was a unique organization form in China without counterparts in western countries (Yan, 2010). A *danwei* was a public, non-governmental organization (ibid.), a multi-functional, self-sufficient, closed small society (Zhang, 2012). The institutional environment of *danwei* had familial characteristics – that is, universities created family-like surroundings to provide emotional and economic support for academics, and academics inside HEIs connected with each other like family members (ibid.). However, the *danwei* was an extension and affiliation of the state's administration sector (Dong, 2008; Pu, 2001) and a tool to realize the state's redistribution of resources and central control (Song, 2006). As such, traditionally, the institutional logics aligned with Chinese academia

Evaluation at faculty level	Evaluation at discipline's level	Evaluation at university's level
• academics' application • evaluation and recommendation at department's level • evaluation at faculty HR Committee meeting	• based on the evaluation result of faculties vote and decide the final list of candidates	• vote and approve the evaluation result at discipline's level • announce the result

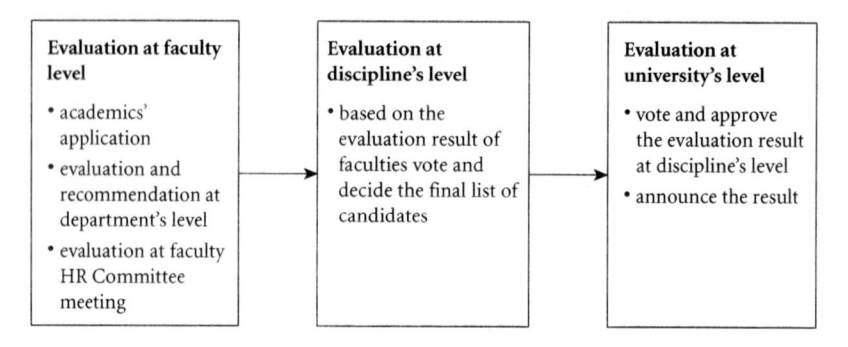

Figure 13.2 Process of academic promotion at B University

in the past (1949–86) was a hybrid of family logic and state logic; these terms were defined by Thornton *et al.* (2012).

Since the 1980s, the market mechanism has been largely introduced in Chinese higher education (Cai, 2010), and universities are thus becoming more open and independent organizations (Yan, 2010). Such change facilitates the rise of professionalism in Chinese higher education. Meanwhile, the development of the academic profession tends to be influenced by corporation logic, even though other logics, such as the rising logic of professionalism and the traditional logics of state and family, tend to prevent academics from internalizing corporation logic.

Basically, the institutional logics aligned with the traditional academic promotion system and the reforms can be summarized in Table 13.1. The categories of institutions logics are based on Thornton *et al.* (2012).

The above discussion can be best echoed in the case, in which new logics such as profession logic and corporation logic tend to prevail around academic work. Data analysis shows that the recent policy reflects profession logic and motivates academics to prioritize research, particularly international research activities, such as publications in international citation indices, involvement in international research projects, and participation in international conferences. This prioritization is aligned with a worldwide belief in the academic community that 'research is supposed to be a prominent focus of academic work … reputation is established by national and international peer groups of scholars' (Enders and Musselin, 2008, p. 145).

Another reflection of profession logic is the emphasis on research quality, which follows the belief that reputation is established by enhancing the quality of activities. For example, Interviewee A7 believed,

> ideally, academics' promotion should depend on the quality of academic activities, but not the quantity … In some foreign universities, usually good ones, though an academic may probably have only two to three academic papers, often higher quality but not necessarily being SCI [Science Citation Index] or SSCI [Social Sciences Citation Index] papers, the work will be judged by peer reviewers for academic promotion. As long as the quality is recognized, the person could get promoted for career advancement.
> (A7, personal communication, 18 April 2014)

The recent academic promotion policy in the case advocates effectiveness and productivity, which is a consequence of the introduction of managerialism (Abromov, 2012) or corporation logic into higher education. Similar to that in the USA and Continental Europe (Leišytė and Dee, 2012), quantification of academic output has been increasingly expected in academic work in the case. Meanwhile, to increase effectiveness, the new policy encourages academics to collaborate with other academics within or across institutions. This policy is

Table 13.1 Institutional logics aligned with changes of university academic promotion system

Categories	Traditions		Reforms	
	State logic	Family logic	Corporation logic	Profession logic
Root metaphor	State as redistribution mechanism	Family (*danwei*) as firm	Hierarchy as corporation	Profession as relational network
Sources of legitimacy	Compulsory compliance	Unconditional loyalty	Position of HEIs in the market	Academics' expertise
Sources of authority	Bureaucratic domination	Patriarchal domination	University management	Professional association
Sources of identity	Social class	*Danwei* reputation	Bureaucratic roles revealed by quantity of production	Personal reputation, established by quality of activities
Basis of norms	Citizenship in the nation	Membership in *danwei*	Employment in universities	Membership in guild and association
Basis of attention	Status of interest group	Status in *danwei*	Status in hierarchy	Status in profession
Basis of strategy	Increase public good	Increase *danwei*'s honour	Increase size and diversification of HEIs	Increase personal reputation
Informal control mechanism	Backroom politics	Family politics	Organizational culture	Academic celebrity
Economic system	Welfare socialism	Family capitalism	Managerial capitalism	Personal capitalism

Source: Based on Thornton et al., 2012

based on the belief that collaborative work likely increases effectiveness. Interviewee A7 maintained,

> doing research in collaboration is learnt from foreign countries. It is a more productive way to multiply research outputs... Of course, collaborative work does have its advantages: it enables people to use limited resources to produce more and in a quicker way.
> (A7, personal communication, 18 April 2014)

Another phenomenon reflecting corporation logic is the demand for academics to perform administrative duties (such as serving as deans and departmental directors) and social services (such as knowledge transfer, training, and consultancy). This phenomenon is also in line with a global trend that academics are to be more closely bound to institutions' missions (Enders and Musselin, 2008; Kolsaker, 2008).

In regard to the relationships among the multiple logics, it is difficult to simply define the type of relationship because these relationships are dynamic and constantly changing. For example, as presented above, both the quantity and quality of research, which reflect the demand of corporation logic and profession logic, respectively, are considered important in academic promotion. However, the two can hardly be reconciled in practice. Academics might struggle between the choices of conducting high-quality research and publishing more; putting more efforts on one may hamper the performance/output of the other. Nevertheless, a clear tendency reflected in the case university is that quality is valued more during the promotion assessment, though quantity remains as a threshold. Thus, in the case, corporation logic and profession logic are contesting each other, but profession logic seems to have the advantage and might become more dominant in the future.

We also found that traditional institutional logics are at work in the case. For instance, the encouragement of research collaboration is a product of the impact of not only corporation logic, but also family logic. As A7 said, 'usually the formation of research groups in China would combine the authoritarian paternalistic leadership, the hierarchical relationship between supervisors and students, and some drawbacks of authoritarian management from Chinese tradition and culture' (A7, personal communication, 18 April 2014). Another interviewee, A1, described her research group to be a big 'family' for her (A1, personal communication, 17 April 2014). Both logics drive academics to align their academic activities closely with the institution's interest.

Based on the analysis above, we argue that, under the impact of academic promotion reforms, new institutional logics such as corporation logic and profession logic have been introduced into Chinese academia. Instead of replacing the traditional logics, they, together with the traditional ones, constitute a new constellation of institutional logics. The relationships among logics in this new constellation of institutional logics are complex and dynamic. Under the impact of the constellation of institutional logics, a new hybrid identity is shaped and developed, which will be further explained in the next section.

Influence of multiple logics on academic identities

Here, we will first examine the traditional identity of academics, which is aligned with traditional institutional logics, and then discuss the changes of academic identities due to the changing institutional logics. Our analysis will demonstrate and explain why academics in Chinese universities do not become 'academic managers' or 'managed academics' as in western universities (Kolsaker, 2008; Winter, 2009). Instead, a new hybrid identity for Chinese academics is formed.

From the 1950s to the 1980s, under the impact of family logic and state logic, academics in China were *danwei men* in the national *danwei* (system), which featured a unified identity, a similar income, and a limited scope of activities (Yan, 2010). In that system, the relationship between the state, universities, and academics was strongly hierarchical 'control-depend[ent]' (Zhang, 2012) or a 'patronage relationship', as described by Yan (2010).

Since the 1980s, with the introduction of corporation logic, academics have gradually changed from *danwei men*, whose activities are constrained to *danwei*, to social men in a market-based system, who are characterized by a more independent identity, a diversified income, and a broader scope of activities (ibid.). Academics are no longer family members in a *danwei* but employees in universities (Zhang, 2012). Meanwhile, under the impact of profession logic, academics tend to consider themselves as 'a group of professionals with certain skills in academia and human resources in a free academic market, who are capable of performing research, teaching and social service, and earning their livings by doing that' (Wang and Chen, 2014). Academics focus more on their development within disciplines rather than within institutions (Zhang, 2012), giving the highest priority to research (Li et al., 2013).

Current research on changes of academic identities in the European context usually focuses on how new management practices that follow the logic of managerialism challenge traditional academic identity, as underlined by the logic of professionalism (Abromov, 2012; Billot, 2010; Kolsaker, 2008; Leišytė, 2015). These studies have shown that the constructive interaction and interdependence between managerialism and academic professionalism often result in an academic identity schism: an identity of 'academic managers' and that of 'managed academics' (Kolsaker, 2008; Winter, 2009). Academic managers have internalized the values of managerialism (Winter, 2009), which is congruent with corporation logic. Managed academics have defended the values of academic professionalism (ibid.) and traditional professional identity (Kolsaker, 2008), which is aligned with professional logic.

In China's context, the effects of corporation logic would lead academics to become 'academic managers'; however, other logics, such as the profession logic and traditional logics of the state and family, tend to decouple its effects. Partially for this reason, academics in China have not become 'managed academics'. Chinese academics did not carry on professional identity in the same tradition as their western counterparts. Instead, professional identity is a new product for them after the 1980s. Meanwhile, features of *danwei men*, the real legacy from tradition in the Chinese context, remain in the vein of academic identity. Thus, under the impact of the constellation of institutional logics (including family logic, corporation logic, state logic, and profession logic), a new hybrid identity of academics has developed in the Chinese academia.

This new hybrid identity compounds features of professional identity, corporate identity, and *danwei men* identity (family identity and state identity). Compared with *danwei men*, academics with the new hybrid identity are more likely to perceive themselves as members of a profession instead of an institution. When compared with 'managed academics' and 'academic managers', they retain some features of *danwei men* in their beliefs and values. Academics with this new hybrid identity are facing institutional pressures from four different institutional logics, and the dynamic interaction of theses institutional logics constructs an academic identity in a different direction.

As stated when explaining the analytical framework, the construction of an academic identity could be described by analysing the academics' perceptions or understanding of their work and their response to the impact of institutional logics. Following this approach, we reveal the main characteristics of the new hybrid identity. First, academics with the new hybrid identity embrace the values and beliefs of their professional identity. The interview data show that most academics appreciated values of professional identity and held supportive attitudes towards the elements of the academic promotion policy that are aligned with profession logic, such as prioritizing research over teaching, paying more attention to the quality of research, and internationalizing academic work. Though one interviewed academic mentioned that he was more inclined to do teaching, in practice he closely complied with the current policies. While the interviewed academics tended to apply 'acquiescence strategic responses' (Oliver, 1991) to the institutional pressure of profession logic, not all of the academics were content with the pressure for more international publications. Some challenged the idea of evaluating academics' achievement based primarily on publication in internationally indexed (i.e. SSCI) journals and the rationales behind it. For example, Interviewee A1 criticized the emphasis of using SSCI papers as a key evaluation criterion:

> SSCI is created mainly for the American system. Even some good-quality European journals are not included in the citation indices list .... The values orientation of SSCI might be not in favour Chinese researchers .... There is a business group to promote its popularity for profit.
>
> (A1, personal communication, 17 April 2014)

Second, academics with the new hybrid identity selectively adopt the values aligned with corporate identity. Regarding activities imposed by corporation logic, the interviewees' response varied. For instance, most academics thought it unnecessary to take up administrative tasks. As Interviewee A4 stated, 'Putting some academics who would like to concentrate on academic development in the position of management is actually a waste of their gift for research' (A4, personal communication, 14 April 2014). As a response, the academics applied an 'avoidance strategy' (Oliver, 1991), trying their best to preclude the necessity of doing administrative tasks.

Negative responses can also be seen in their attitude towards collaborative work. As A4 complained, 'Once the research group gets tasks or research projects, we have to do that; we only have limited autonomy in doing research' (A4, personal communication, 14 April 2014). Some interviewees even noted that research activities in research groups were mainly pragmatic and made little contribution to the knowledge pool. Nevertheless, most academics compromised and joined research groups. As A7, the only individual researcher among our interviewees who claimed to be a 'recluse', said:

> [Regarding the attitude towards collaborative work] Chinese academics can be divided into three groups currently. One group is 'compliants', which is the majority; the second is 'resistants'; the third is 'recluses'. Recluses neither comply with the norms or rules, nor revolt. Instead, they escape and exile themselves by 'jumping into a speedy train, allowing it to take them to the wild woods'.
>
> (A7, personal communication, 18 April 2014)

Therefore, most academics applied 'comply strategic responses' (Oliver, 1991) in this aspect. As mentioned before, collaborative work is underlined by family logic as well. This example shows that traditional values sometimes support corporate values and demand that academics adopt activities that are imposed by corporation logic. This example also implies that features of traditional identity remain in the new hybrid identity, which will be discussed further in the third point.

However, commonly academics agreed on the importance of social engagement. Academics' 'acquiescence strategic responses' (Oliver, 1991) can be observed, as demonstrated by A7, 'I am willing to do these activities... Only after you see how the research outcomes are applied in the society, you get to know what you've studied is connected to society' (A7, personal communication, 18 April 2014). Thus, academics applied different strategic responses to activities imposed by corporation logic, depending on whether other logics contested or supported the activities.

Third, some features of the traditional identity remain in the new hybrid identity. As mentioned before, some interviewed academics believed that the formation of research groups in universities occurs under the impact of family logic and combines the authoritarian paternalistic leadership and some other traditional elements. Interviewees maintained that the relationship between the research group leader and its research fellows is a patronage relationship, while that between the university and group leaders it is a hierarchical relationship. The patronage model is different from the contractual partnership model, which is a common phenomenon in the corporate environment and often observed in many European universities (Leišytė and Dee, 2012). The two models can be distinguished as follows:

> In a patronage model, the research group leader is a professor who takes care of the group within a hierarchical governance mode. The partnership model, in contrast, refers to a flatter group hierarchy, where the group leader is more of a manager and a colleague.
>
> (Leišytė and Dee, 2012, p. 157)

Values aligned with the corporate identity tend to form research groups in the model of the contractual partnership; however, in China's reality, the remaining features of the traditional academic identity lead research group leaders to form their research groups in a patronage model.

Readers might notice that a discussion of state identity is absent here; however, because academic promotion reform is a top-down and state-led approach in China, we believe the impact of state logic on Chinese academia remains. However, its impact seems to be felt in a more subtle and indirect way.

Conclusion

This chapter is an effort to construct an analytical framework for understanding the relationships between policies and identities from the institutional logics perspective and then to apply this framework to a case of a Chinese research university to explore the impact of academic promotion policy on academic identity changes. The case analysis is summarized in Figure 13.3.

As the Figure 13.3 demonstrates, under the impact of family logic and state logic in an institutional environment, Chinese academics were traditionally *danwei men*, with a unified identity, a similar income, and a limited scope of activities, and the relationship between the state, universities, and academics was a hierarchical patronage. With reforms in academic promotion system, profession logic and corporation logic have been introduced into Chinese academia. Under the impact of the new constellation of institutional logics, consisting of family logic, state logic, corporation logic, and profession logic, a new hybrid identity of academics has been developed in China's context. With the new hybrid identity, academics have accepted some activities imposed by academic promotion policy, which are aligned with values of professional identity,

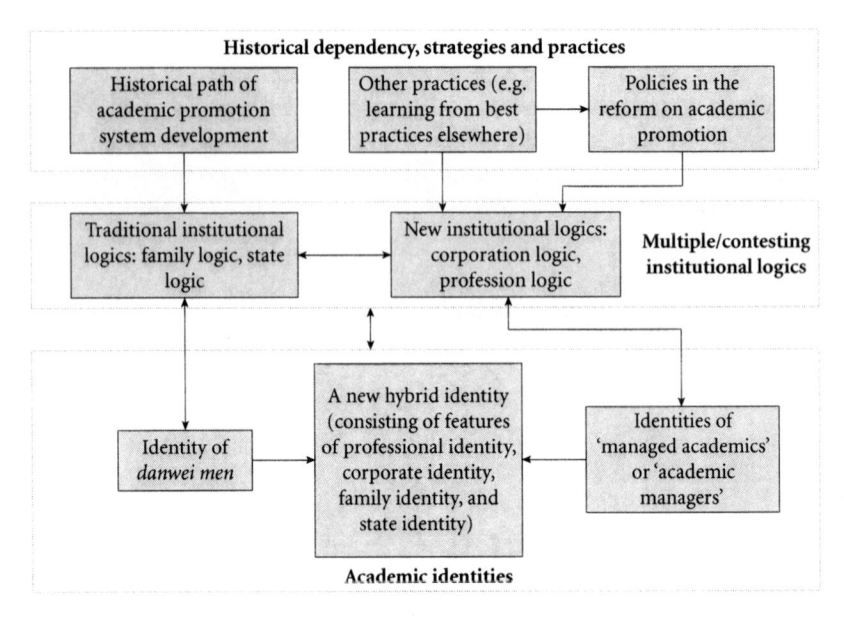

```
                    Historical dependency, strategies and practices
┌─────────────────┐   ┌─────────────────┐   ┌─────────────────┐
│ Historical path │   │ Other practices │   │  Policies in the│
│  of academic    │   │ (e.g. learning  │──▶│ reform on       │
│   promotion     │   │ from best       │   │ academic        │
│ system          │   │ practices       │   │ promotion       │
│ development     │   │ elsewhere)      │   │                 │
└─────────────────┘   └─────────────────┘   └─────────────────┘
                                                     │
┌─────────────────┐   ┌─────────────────┐            ▼
│  Traditional    │   │ New institutional│  ┌─────────────────┐
│ institutional   │◀─▶│ logics:          │  │ Multiple/        │
│ logics: family  │   │ corporation      │  │ contesting       │
│ logic, state    │   │ logic,           │  │ institutional    │
│ logic           │   │ profession logic │  │ logics           │
└─────────────────┘   └─────────────────┘  └─────────────────┘
                              ▲
                              │
                     ┌────────────────┐
                     │ A new hybrid   │
                     │ identity       │   ┌─────────────────┐
┌─────────────────┐  │ (consisting of │   │ Identities of   │
│  Identity of    │  │ features of    │   │ 'managed        │
│  danwei men     │  │ professional   │◀──│ academics'      │
│                 │  │ identity,      │   │ or 'academic    │
└─────────────────┘  │ corporate      │   │ managers'       │
                     │ identity,      │   └─────────────────┘
                     │ family         │
                     │ identity, and  │
                     │ state identity)│
                     └────────────────┘
                        Academic identities
```

Figure 13.3 Changes of academic identities in China from an institutional logics perspective

such as prioritizing research and the quality of research and internationalization. Academics' beliefs and values, which are aligned with professionalism, decouple the impact of corporation logic on the formation of academic identity. Therefore, academics have shown their concerns regarding activities imposed by corporation logic and selectively adopted them. They have avoided administrative responsibilities while actively participating in social service and passively participating in collaborative research. The formation of research groups and the patronage relationship within research groups reveal that features of the traditional academic identity remain in the new hybrid identity and influence academic work.

In addition to contributing to the knowledge pool by providing empirical findings revealing the Chinese academics' changing identity under the academic promotion system reforms, another significance of the study is the construction of an analytical framework for understanding the policies' impact on identities using the insights of institutional logics. The framework is novel, particularly in the context of higher education studies. Our case analysis also proves the usefulness of the analytical framework, which we constructed for this study.

Nevertheless, the framework is still in the developmental stage and on the conceptual level. To materialize the analytical framework, more empirical studies are necessary to further validate its applicability in broader contexts. This validation will be addressed in future theoretical studies and empirical tests.

References

Abromov, R. N. (2012) 'Managerialism and the academic profession: conflict and interaction'. *Russian Education and Society*, 54 (3), pp. 63–80. doi: 10.2753/RES1060-9393540304

Bastedo, M. N. (2009) 'Convergent institutional logics in public higher education: state policymaking and governing board activism'. *Review of Higher Education*, 32 (2), 209–34

Billot, J. (2010) 'The imagined and the real: identifying the tensions for academic identity'. *Higher Education Research and Development*, 29 (6), pp. 709–21. doi: 10.1080/07294360.2010.487201

Cai, Y. (2004) 'Confronting the global and the local: a case study of Chinese higher education'. *Tertiary Education and Management*, 10 (2), pp. 157–69

Cai, Y. (2010) 'Global isomorphism and governance reform in Chinese higher education'. *Tertiary Education and Management*, 16 (3), pp. 229–41

Cai, Y. and Yan, F. (2015) 'Supply and demand in Chinese higher education' in Schwartzman, S., Pillay, P. and Pinheiro, R. (Eds), *Higher Education in the BRICS Countries: Investigating the Pact Between Higher Education and Society*. Dordrecht: Springer, pp. 149–69

Cheng, M. (2012) 'Accountability and professionalism: a contradiction in terms'. *Higher Education Research and Development*, 31 (6), pp. 785–95

Clark, B. R. (1983) *The Higher Education System: Academic Organization in Cross-national Perspective*. Berkeley: University of California Press

Clark, B. R. (1987) *The Academic Life: Small Worlds, Different Worlds. A Carnegie Foundation Special Report* (vol. ISBN-O-931050-32-4). Princeton, NJ.: Carnegie Foundation for Advancement of Teaching

Clark, B. R. (1998). *Creating Entrepreneurial Universities: Organizational Pathways of Transformation*. Oxford: Pergamon

Clarke, J. and Newman, J. (1994) 'The managerialisation of public service' in Clarke, J. H., McLaughlin, J. C. A. C. E., Cochrane, A. D. and McLaughlin, P. E. (Eds), *Managing Social Policy*. London: Sage, pp. 13–31

Clarke, J. and Newman, J. (1997) *The Managerial State: Power, Politics and Ideology in the Remaking of Social Welfare*. London: Sage

Day, C., Kington, A., Stobart, G. and Sammons, P. (2006) 'The personal and professional selves of teachers: stable and unstable identities'. *British Educational Research Journal*, 32 (4), pp. 601–16. doi: 10.1080/01411920600775316

Dong, X. (2008) 'The institutional effects of universities as danwei: an analysis based on the new institutionalism in sociology'. *Journal of Heilongjiang College of Education*, 27 (8), pp. 44–6

Enders, J. and Musselin, C. (2008) 'Back to the future? The academic professions in the 21st century'. *Higher Education to 2030*, 1, pp. 125–50

Etzkowitz, H. (1990) 'The second academic revolution: the role of the research university in economic development' in Cozzens, S., Healey, P., Rip, A. and Ziman, J. (Eds), *The Research System in Transition*, vol. 57. Dordrecht: Springer, pp. 109–24

Etzkowitz, H., Webster, A., Gebhardt, C. and Terra, B. R. C. (2000) 'The future of the university and the university of the future: evolution of ivory tower to entrepreneurial paradigm'. *Research Policy*, 29 (2), pp. 313–30. doi: 10.1016/s0048-7333(99)00069-4

Friedland, R. and Alford, R. R. (1991) 'Bringing society back in: symbols, practices, and institutional contradictions' in Powell, W. W. and DiMaggio, P. (Eds), *The New Institutionalism in Organizational Analysis*. Chicago: University of Chicago Press, pp. 232–63

Goodrick, E. and Reay, T. (2011) 'Constellations of institutional logics: changes in professional work of pharmacists'. *Work and Occupations*, pp. 1–45. doi: 10.1177/0730888411406824

Greenwood, R., Raynard, M., Kodeih, F., Micelotta, E.R. and Lounsbury, M. (2011) 'Institutional complexity and organizational responses'. *The Academy of Management Annals*, 5 (1), pp. 317–71. doi: 10.1080/19416520.2011.590299

Harris, S. (2005) 'Rethinking academic identities in neo-liberal times'. *Teaching in Higher Education*, 10 (4), pp. 421–33. doi: 10.1080/13562510500238986

Henkel, M. (2005a) 'Academic identity and autonomy in a changing policy environment'. *Higher Education*, 49 (1/2), pp. 155–76. doi: 10.1007/s10734-004-2919-1

Henkel, M. (2005b) 'Academic identity and autonomy revisited' in Bleiklie, V. and Henkel, M. (Eds), *Governing Knowledge: A Study of Continuity and Change in Higher Education: A Festschrift in Honour of Maurice Kogan*. Dordrecht: Springer, pp. 145–65

Hoecht, J. (2006) 'Quality assurance in UK higher education: issues of trust, control, professional autonomy and accountability'. *Higher Education*, 51, pp. 541–63

Hood, C. (2000) 'Paradoxes of public-sector managerialism, old public management and public service bargains'. *International Public Management Journal*, 3 (1), pp. 1–22. doi: http://dx.doi.org/10.1016/S1096-7494(00)00032-5

Howlett, M., Ramesh, M. and Perl, A. (2009) *Studying Public Policy: Policy Cycles and Policy Subsystems* (3rd edn). Don Mills, Ontario, and Oxford: Oxford University Press

Jenkins, W. I. (1978) *Policy Analysis: A Political and Organizational Perspective*. New York: St Martin's Press

Kolsaker, A. (2008) 'Academic professionalism in the managerialist era: a study of English universities'. *Studies in Higher Education*, 33 (5), pp. 513–25

Krücken, G. (2003) 'Learning the "new, new thing": on the role of path dependency in university structures'. *Higher Education*, 46 (3), pp. 315–39

Lai, M. (2013) 'The changing work life of academics: a comparative study of a renowned and a regional university in the Chinese mainland'. *The Australian Association for Research in Education*, 40, pp. 27–45

Lee, A. and Boud, D. (2003) 'Writing groups, change and academic identity: research development as local practice'. *Studies in Higher Education*, 28 (2), p. 187

Leišytė, L. (2007) 'University governance and academic research, case studies of research units in Dutch and English universities'. PhD dissertation. University of Twente

Leišytė, L. (2015) 'Changing academic identities in the context of a managerial university – bridging the duality between professions and organizations: evidence from the US and Europe' in Cummings, W. K. and Teichler, U. (Eds), *The Relevance of Academic Work in Comparative Perspective: The Changing Academy – The Changing Academic Profession in International Comparative Perspective* 13. Switzerland: Springer International, pp. 59–73

Leišytė, L. and Dee, J. R. (2012) 'Understanding academic work in a changing institutional environment: faculty autonomy, productivity, and the identity in Europe and the United States' in Smart, J. C. and Paulsen, M. B. (Eds), *Higher Education: Handbook of Theory and Research*, 27. Dordrecht: Springer, pp. 123–206

Leišytė, L., Enders, J. and de Boer, H. (2010) 'Mediating problem choice: academic researchers' responses to changes in their institutional environment' in Whitley, R., Gläser, J. and Engwall, L. (Eds), *Reconfiguring Knowledge Production: Changing Authority Relationships in the Sciences and their Consequences for Intellectual Innovation*, vol. 3. Oxford: Oxford University Press, pp. 266–90

Li, L., Lai, M. and Lo, N. (2013) 'Academic work within a mode of mixed governance: perspectives of university professors in the research context of western China'. *Asian Pacific Education Review*, 14, pp. 307–14

Ma, W. and Wen, J. (2012) 'A study on academic salary and remunerations in China' in Altbach, P. G., Reisberg, L., Yudkevich, M., Androushchak, G. and Pacheco, I. F. (Eds), *Paying the Professoriate*. Oxford: Routledge, pp. 94–103

Maassen, P. (2003) 'Shifts in governance arrangement: an interpretation of the introduction of new management structures in higher education' in Amaral, A., Meek, V. L. and Larsen, I. M. (Eds), *The Higher Education Managerial Revolution? Higher Education Dynamics*. Dordrecht, London: Kluwer Academic, pp. 31–53

Mao, Y. and Cai, Z. (2010) 'A survey of the professional development system of teachers in university since the foundation of the People's Republic China'. *Research on Education Txinghua University*, 31 (6), pp. 27–34. doi: 10.3969/j.issn.1001-4519.2010.06.003

McPherson, C. M. and Sauder, M. (2013) 'Logics in action: managing institutional complexity in a drug court'. *Administrative Science Quarterly*, 58 (2), pp. 165–96. doi: 10.1177/0001839213486447

Meyer, J. W., Ramirez, F. O., Frank, D. J. and Schofer, E. (2007) 'Higher education as an institution' in Gumport, P. J. (Ed.), *Sociology of Higher Education: Contributions and Their Contexts*. Baltimore: Johns Hopkins University Press, pp. 187–221

Meyer, R. E. and Hammerschmid, G. (2006) 'Changing institutional logics and executive identities: a managerial challenge to public administration in Austria'. *American Behavioral Scientist*, 49 (7), pp. 1000–14. doi: 10.1177/0002764205285182

Mohrman, K., Geng, Y. Q. and Wang, Y. J. (2011) 'Faculty life in China'. Retrieved from http://www.nea.org/assets/docs/HE/H-Mohrman_28Feb11_p83-100.pdf

Musselin, C. (2007) 'Are universities specific organisations?' in Krücken, G., Kosmützky, A. and Torka, M. (Eds), *Towards a Multiversity?: Universities Between Global Trends and National Traditions*. Bielefeld: Transcript, pp. 63–84

Oliver, C. (1991) 'Strategic responses to institutional processes'. *The Academy of Management Review*, 16 (1), pp. 145–79

Pache, A. C. and Santos, F. (2013) 'Inside the hybrid organization: selective coupling response to competing institutional logics'. *Academy of Management Journal*, 56 (4), pp. 972–1001. doi: 10.5465/amj.2011.0405

Pu, X. (2001) 'Impact of "Danwei" logics on universities' organizational behaviours'. *Liaoning Education Research*, 12, pp. 31–3

Scott, W. R. (2008) *Institutions and Organizations: Ideas and Interests* (3rd edn). London: Sage

Song, J. (2006) 'The institutional environment for knowledge innovation in Chinese research universities: an interpretation of the 'work–unit' system'. *Tsinghua Jounal of Education*, 27 (4), pp. 48–52

Teelken, J. C. (2012) 'Compliance or pragmatism: how do academics deal with managerialism in higher education? A comparative study in three countries'. *Studies in Higher Education*, 37 (3), pp. 271–90. doi: 10.1080/03075079.2010.511171

Thornton, P. H. and Ocasio, W. (2008) 'Institutional logics' in Greenwood, R., Oliver, C., Sahlin, K. and Suddaby, R. (Eds), *The SAGE Handbook of Organizational Institutionalism*. Los Angeles and London: Sage, pp. 99–129

Thornton, P. H., Ocasio, W. and Lounsbury, M. (2012) *The Institutional Logics Perspective: A New Approach to Culture, Structure and Process*. Oxford: Oxford University Press

Townley, B. (1997) 'The institutional logic of performance appraisal'. *Organization Studies*, 18 (2), pp. 261–85

van Stekelenburg, J. (2013) 'Collective identity' in Snow, D., della Porta, D., Klandermans, B. and McAdam, D. (Eds), *The Wiley-Blackwell Encyclopedia of Social and Political Movements*. Oxford: Blackwell

Wang, C. and Chen, P. (2014) 'Crisis behind porisperity: analysis of deep problems with Chinece academics profession'. *Tsinghua Jounal of Education*, 35 (2), pp. 35–43

Villani, E. and Phillips, N. W. (2013) 'Beyong institutional complexity: the case if different organizational successes in confronting multiple institutional logics'. Paper presented at the 35th DRUID Celebration Conference 2013, June. Barcelona

Winter, R. P. (2009) 'Academic manager or managed academic? Academic identity schisms in higher education'. *Journal of Higher Education Policy and Management*, 31 (2), pp. 121–31. doi: 10.1080/13600800902825835

Winter, R. P. and O'Donohue, W. (2012) 'Academic identity tensions in the public university: which values really matter?' *Journal of Higher Education Policy and Management*, 34 (6), pp. 565–73. doi: 10.1080/1360080X.2012.716005

Yan, F. (2010) 'The academic profession in China in the context of social transition: an institutional perspective'. *European Review*, 18, pp. 99–116

Yin, R. K. (1994) *Case Study Research: Design and Methods* (2nd edn). Thousand Oaks, CA: Sage

Zhang, J. (2013) 'Promotion criteria, faculty experiences and perceptions: a qualitative study at a key university in China'. *International Journal of Educational Development*, 33, pp. 185–95. doi: http://dx.doi.org/10.1016/j.ijedudev.2012.04.004

Zhang, Y. (2012) 'From danwei affiliation to contractual employment: qualitative analysis of the personnel reform in higher education institutions in Mainland China'. *Remin University of China Education Journal*, 4, pp. 5–14

Conclusion

ROSEMARY DEEM

In writing this final part of Leišytė and Wilkesmann's book, I am not going to rehearse again or attempt to synthesize the contents of the chapters, which can speak very well for themselves. Instead, I want to reflect a little on some of the broader issues raised by the book in relation to academic staff, universities as organizations, and teaching and learning in higher education. Some of these matters are already addressed by the editors in their introduction, in emphasizing how they want to try to explore both how managers of teaching and learning can influence teaching, learning and academic identities and how teaching and learning initiatives can change organizational structures. But here I want to combine some of the major themes of the book with suggesting how these might be further developed in the future. The five themes in question are the differences between managing and leading teaching, new technologies in teaching and learning and the myth of the student 'digital native', the relationship between the changing work and identities of academics and those other university staff who support teaching, how external drivers sometimes force us to do strange things in relation to the quality of teaching (using the example of the 2015 introduction to the UK of a Teaching Excellence Framework), and, finally, possible future alternative organizational structures for higher educational institutions.

I am sure that many readers of this book will be academics themselves, interested in knowing more about the findings of recent research on higher education teaching and learning, whether as researchers or teachers or both. But another audience will be those (some of them combining this work with other aspects of being an academic) who are responsible for overseeing teaching and learning in their department, faculty or institution. Increasingly such roles are vital to complex universities with broad curricula, many academic departments, multiple modes of delivery, and a diverse student body. Unlike research, face-to-face teaching, in particular, can be viewed as a very routinized activity, tightly scheduled, the content and assessment heavily specified, the outcomes (as modern quality assessment requires) carefully set out. Managing it can often be a matter of keeping the show on the road and dealing ad hoc with crises and complaints. But there is, as Gibbs *et al.* have noted in a cross-cultural comparative study of how heads of department lead teaching in a variety of disciplines and working in research-intensive contexts, a big difference between *managing* teaching and *leading* teaching (Gibbs *et al.*, 2009). The former is a routine activity whereas the latter is much more engaged and seeking to change, develop, and nurture teaching as an important part of university and academic life, not just something which has to be done to bring in money. If, as Land points out in this volume, there is now increased emphasis on 'the student experience' as a whole (which can, as he observes, tend to deflect attention from purely educational discourses), then simply *managing* teaching (rather than *leading* it with imagination and inspiring people), is not enough. But we cannot assume that people who undertake roles that involve the management and leadership of teaching will know in advance how to do those tasks in imaginative and non-bureaucratic ways. Learning about this needs to be an integral part of how managers and leaders are inducted and trained, as well as being a theme in their continuing professional development. There are still a good many countries where such preparation and continuing professional development for university managers and leaders does not exist or only in minimal form. Even where it does exist, some may regard it as an experience to be endured or a rite of passage (Deem, 2013) rather than as serious thought-provoking life-long learning. This book will be immensely helpful to those who want to lead teaching rather than just manage it.

Technologies of various kinds have long supported teaching and learning, even before the days of the internet. There are now some amazing ways in which this can be done, as, for example, in the Swedish case study in this volume by Jahnke, Mårell-Olsson and Mejtoft, which examines the organizational effects of using tablets and Google Glass for teaching. Also in this book, Chu and Mok consider, using case studies drawn from Hong Kong, how funding and a supportive culture in universities can enable technology to be used in innovative ways in the classroom. But we do need to remember that, however good the technology, poor teaching can wipe out the advances offered by technology. The rise of social media, as Chu and Mok observe, has also had significant effects on teaching as a teaching tool. But social media can be utilized for a variety of other purposes, including as a vehicle through which academics can exchange ideas about teaching and learning or communicate with their students, as well as a means by which students can share their views of teaching through institution or HE system-wide social media groups or via internet-based fora such as RateMyProfessor. The ease with which all this can be done and the need to 'manage' social media, both as a marketing tool and as a pedagogic device, has itself led to a number of organizational and staffing changes in universities including, in those countries where fees are charged for even public higher education, considerable emphasis on selling HE 'brands', media promotion, and other public relations management. New technologies also pose challenges to some of the issues raised in the book about the interconnections between academics, teaching, and organizations, particularly in relation to the phenomenal growth of varied forms of distance learning (see Coates and Bexley, this volume), which do not just refer to the rather over-hyped use of MOOCS (Massive Open Onine Courses), most of which cost more money to produce than they can ever give back, but also to other forms of asynchronous or remote learning, some of which are now routinely combined with face-to-face learning. Distance learners may be exposed to different forms of higher education organizations than conventional universities, such as publishers, and, with so many other ways of acquiring new knowledge, not everyone now regards universities as a major organizational means of acquiring post-school education, as the meaning of to being 'educated' continues to change (Evans-Greenwood et al., 2015). A lot of discussion in the new technology and teaching field has also emphasized for some time how a new generation of higher education students termed 'digital natives' are both demanding change in how digital and other new technologies inform teaching (which will have both organizational effects and affect the teaching and identities of academics too) and showing up considerable gaps between the knowledge the 'digital natives' have of technologies and the technological knowledge of the people who teach those students. But as some recent work on this topic shows, the digital gap between students and teachers is not necessarily as wide and as significant as sometimes portrayed (Jones and Shao, 2011; Margaryana et al., 2011). Maybe just being aware of this correction to a widespread myth about students and digital technologies might itself provoke both bottom-up and top-down changes in the ways that universities and academics support and use new technologies in their teaching.

There is in the volume, as might be expected, and as already noted, a considerable focus on talking about those who teach, or manage/govern teaching in higher education. But a concern for organizational interdependencies ought also to include those who support teaching from a variety of perspectives. As indicated in several chapters in the book (Schmid and Lauer; Henkel; Leišytė and Hosch-Dayican), the situations and identities of academics are in considerable flux, whether they are acting as institutional entrepreneurs for teaching innovations, operating in and deriving identity from the 'multiversity' as well as their disciplines, or engaging in symbolic boundary crossing of the borders of different disciplines. But other changes are also occurring to the nature of academic work, not only due to organizational changes of various kinds as evidenced in this volume and elsewhere (Nyhagen and Baschung, 2013), including reduced public funding, massification, of undergraduate entry, the introduction of new technologies, changes to academic labour markets (Musselin, 2008, 2012), and changes in work pace (Ylijoki, 2011). These developments have led to some significant changes in the work itself and who does it, such as casualization (Courtois and O'Keefe, 2015; Lama and Joullié, 2015), where in some HE systems the percentage of academics in precarious jobs exceeds 50 per cent of the total academic staff. There is also some evidence of greater collectivization in research as well as teaching (Nyhagen and Baschung, 2013). Though, as the editors note in the introduction, teaching as an organizational activity tends to be more collectivized than research, it is also the case many academics still teach alone. Other changes include more specialization (ibid.) and greater job and between-country mobility (Kenway and Fahey, 2008), as well as speeding-up of the job, the latter particularly affecting the extent to which academics see a sharp, blurred or no boundary between their academic work and the rest of their lives (Ylijoki, 2011). The consequences of some of these changes affect not just academics, particularly those who prefer research to teaching, perhaps giving them what Leišytė calls in the introduction, a more 'normal' job identity rather than that of a vocation, but also affecting many other staff who work in universities. Administrative staff or those academics who only teach every so often now have to cover the other work (student contact, assignment return, unpopular courses) of research-engaged academics while they are working at home, roaming the globe or buying themselves out of teaching. Furthermore, teaching by academics does not take place in a vacuum (Deem, 2015b) but is supported by an array of other staff from cleaners, audio-visual technicians, and timetablers to laboratory technicians and student counsellors. This also has profound organizational implications not always acknowledged by academics and is a significant dimension that needs taking into account when we discuss the relationship between higher education organizations and teaching.

Of course, some changes to academic work – particularly teaching – take place as a result of external drivers and this is evident in several chapters in the book, including Coates and Bexley, and Leišytė and Hosch-Dayican. This may comprise, among other things, various forms of quality assessment and audit. As someone responsible for leading teaching and learning at my university, the most recent initiative to hit my desk in the UK as I write this chapter has been the idea of a Teaching Excellence Framework (or TEF). This is an ideologically driven initiative being introduced with what appears to be unseemly haste in autumn 2015, after being mentioned in the Conservative Election Manifesto in spring 2015. It has apparently been sparked off by the desire of the government to have something to regulate 'lazy academics', deal with 'coasting students' (those believed not to be making enough effort in their studies), rival the periodic Research Excellence Framework, which can trace its roots back to 1986, and to address concern about value for money for UK undergraduate students who are now paying very high tuition fees. Interestingly, no politician ever suggested a TEF in return for the very high fees that the UK has been charging international students since the early 1980s. Though just prior to the May 2015 UK General Election, there was a bit of an academic debate in the UK about teaching excellence initiatives (Deem, 2015a; Land and Gordon, 2015; Tsui, 2015), this was soon bypassed as impractical and irrelevant. The current idea is that the TEF should be run using existing metrics (which may include the annual final-year undergraduate National Student Satisfaction Survey, contact hours, percentage of academic staff with a teaching qualification, percentage of first-class degrees and first job destinations of new graduates), some of which have no evident connection to excellence in teaching. It may be that this initiative will lead to teaching having a more equal status with research and to academics being keener to achieve high standards of teaching and develop more new initiatives, but almost certainly it will involve a lot of organizational angst, new costs, and game-playing, as institutions figure out how to work the new system. The only reward available for TEF success seems to be the ability to charge higher fees, something to which the National Union of Students has already objected.

Finally, I would just like to focus very briefly on what kinds of future organizational structures in universities might be needed in order to facilitate high-quality teaching and learning. Dee's chapter looks, at among other things, some of the organizational obstacles to reforming and reshaping teaching. Wilkesmann, also in this volume, has talked about how different forms of governance may result in the differential valuing of teaching in higher education institutions. Leišytė explores how institutional logics can create some protected spaces for academics and their teaching if negotiated carefully. The editors, in their introduction, suggest that the typical German university, lying somewhere between a company and a German club, democratic and consultative albeit with accountability and some elements of hierarchy, might provide a model for other countries seeking new organizational forms for their higher education institutions. This is obviously worth exploring. So too is the example of a university in northern Spain run as a cooperative. This is Mondragon University, which has hardly any administrative staff and a very flat structure, but good relationships with other local organizations, strong teaching, and a high record of student employment after graduation (Wright et al., 2011). There is, despite big variations in culture and other aspects of local context, a lot of copying, policy borrowing by politicians, and evidence of isomorphism in many institutions of higher education. A sustained effort to look at alternative organizational models and how they could facilitate higher-quality teaching could be one excellent outcome from reading this book.

References

Courtois, A. and O'Keefe, T. (2015) 'Precarity in the ivory cage: neoliberalism and casualisation of work in the Irish higher education sector'. *Journal for Critical Education Policy Studies*, 13 (1), pp. 43–56

Deem, R. (2013) 'Universities under New Labour: senior leaders' responses to government reforms and policy levers – findings from an ESRC project on public service leadership' in Teelken, C.,

Ferlie, E. and Dent, M. (Eds), *Leadership in the Public Sector: Promises and Pitfalls*. London: Routledge, pp. 155–73

Deem, R. (2015a) *A Critical Commentary on Ray Land and George Gordon 'Teaching Excellence Initiatives: Modalities and Operational Factors*. York: Higher Education Academy

Deem, R. (2015b, August) 'Who is actually working in the contemporary university and who values that work? A rethinking of new meanings of valuable work in the academy'. Plenary address to the WORK2015 New Meanings of Work Conference. University of Turku, Finland

Evans-Greenwood, P., O'Leary, K. and Williams, P. (2015). 'The paradigm shift: redefining education', September. Retrived from http://www2.deloitte.com/au/en/pages/public-sector/articles/redefining-education.html

Gibbs, G., Knapper, C. and Piccinin, S. (2009) *Departmental Leadership of Teaching in Research-Intensive Environments*. London: Leadership Foundation for Higher Education

Jones, C. and Shao, B. (2011) *The Net Generation and Digital Natives: Implications for Higher Education*. Milton Keynes: Open University/Higher Education Academy

Kenway, J. and Fahey, J. (2008) *Globalizing the Research Imagination*. New York and London: Routledge

Lama, T. and Joullié, J. E. (2015) 'Casualization of academics in the Australian higher education: is teaching quality at risk?' *Research in Higher Education Journal*, 28, pp. 1–11

Land, R. and Gordon, G. (2015) *Teaching Excellence Initiatives: Modalities and Operational Factors*. York: Higher Education Academy

Margaryana, A., Littlejohn, A. and Vojt, G. (2011) 'Are digital natives a myth or reality? University students' use of digital technologies'. *Computers in Education*, 56 (2), pp. 429–40

Musselin, C. (2008) 'Towards a sociology of academic work' in Amaral, A., Bleiklie, I. and Musselin, C. (Eds), *From Governance to Identity. A Festschrift for Mary Henkel*. Dordrecht: Springer, pp. 47–56

Musselin, C. (2012) 'Redefinition of the relationships between academics and their university'. *Higher Education*, 65, pp. 25–37

Nyhagen, G. M. and Baschung, L. (2013) 'New organizational structures and the transformation of academic work'. *Higher Education*, 66, pp. 409–23

Tsui, A. B. M. (2015) *A Critical Commentary on Ray Land and George Gordon 'Teaching Excellence Initiatives: Modalities and Operational Factors*. York: Higher Education Academy

Wright, S., Greenwood, D. and Boden, R. (2011) 'Report on a field visit to Mondragón University: a cooperative experience/experiment'. *Berghahn Journals*, 4 (3), pp. 38–56. Retrived from https://docs.google.com/viewerng/viewer?url=http://community-wealth.org/sites/clone.community-wealth.org/files/downloads/article-wright-et-al.pdf

Ylijoki, O.-H. (2011) 'Boundary-work between work and life in the high-speed university'. *Studies in Higher Education*, 38 (2), pp. 242–55

Index

Page numbers in *italic* refer to figures and tables. Added to a page number, 'n' refers to notes.

academic capitalism 209
academic departments: academics' perceived distance from 205; cross-departmental linkages 21–2; innovation in 27; structural differentiation 14, 21; subcultures 25
academic development units 217
academic disciplines: as an organizing principle 157; effects on teaching and learning *17–18*, *see also* disciplinary communities; disciplinary culture
academic engagement 164, 226
academic entrepreneurs: hybrid identities 223–40
academic exchange 195–6
academic freedom 236–8
academic identity(ies) 61–2, 211; change and implications for 211; changes in 2, 80, 104, 265; and curricular change 103–4; dominance of the academic logic of governance 60; influence on academic behaviours 243; organizational conditions 5; organizational identity 215–17; as 'personal principled projects' 211; as a 'reflexively organized endeavour' 207; reluctance to change/reform 243, *see also* academic promotion system, and academic identity (study)
academic lobby 59
academic logic of governance 56, 58, 60
academic loners 118
academic managers 254
academic networks 94
academic power 209
academic profession 4; competition to join 210; hollowing out of 211; segmentation 210; as threatened by quasi-market logics 59
academic promotion system, and academic identity (study) 243–58; analytical framework 246–9; conclusion 257–8; influence of multiple logics 254–7; institutional logics 250–4; methodology 244–5; policy/policy changes 246, 249–50

'academic quarter' institutions 34
academic reform: case study 28–30; China 135, 142; fostering 25–8; organizational culture and 24–5, *see also* innovation; university transformation
academic roles: importance/upholding of, biosciences 225, 234–5; performance indicators and 5; splintering of 2
academic self-governance 57, 58
academic standards 50, 214
academic values *18*, 28, 80, 214
academic work: changes in 75; differentiation of 225; holistic concepts 210, 214; in third space 218; unbundling of 211; uncertainty of definition 217, *see also* learning; teaching
academic writing 3
academic-plan-in-context model 91, *92*
academic-scientific boundary crossing (study) 223–40, 264; conceptual background 224–5; findings 229–40; knowledge commercialization 225–7; methods 227–9
academics: critical of institutional regimes 211; differing beliefs 14; employment status and conditions 209; engagement in curricular change *see* faculty decision-making, curricular change; function-based descriptors 79; inequalities 210; influence 213; leverage of institutional strategies 20; massification and demand for 210; perceived distance from their institutional and departmental homes 205; reactions to changes in the institutional environment 225; reluctance to change/reform 243; responses to commercialization 227; responses to managerialism 61–4; role in reform *26*, 27, 28, *see also* institutional entrepreneurs; managed academics; para-academics
accountability 55, 60, 134, 151, 156, 162, 207, 209, 219
accreditation: and curricular change 94–5, 98

268

Index

accreditation associations *18*
'acquiescence strategic responses' 255, 256
active learning 101
activity community model of organizing 133
activity-based typologies 79
adaptive learning *155*
adjustments (curricular) 92
administrative duties: corporation logic and 253
agency: concept of 115; creation and maintenance of protected spaces 59; curricular change 99–100; institutional entrepreneurs 114, 115, 116, 127; transactional governance 50–1
alienation 14, 25, 206, 211, 219
alignment 162
analytics 154, *155*, 156
Anglo-American universities 1
anti-hero (entrepreneur) 124
Apollo Education Group 70
applied research 237, 238
Archer, L. 211
assessment(s) *18*, 72, 81, 172
asynchronous learning 196, 264
attitudes 97
Australia: organizing and managing university education 68–82
Australian Catholic University 77–8
authentic change 98
authentic pedagogy 72
authoritarian leadership 120, 257
authority 73–4; challenges to 154–5; NPM, multiversities and 209; power dynamics and shared 24, *see also* conjoint authority; disjoint authority
autonomous units: responses to threats to professional autonomy 63–4
autonomy 162; boundary setting 224; in research 236, *see also* bounded autonomy; institutional autonomy; professional autonomy
Avolio, B. 35, 36

'banking' notion of education 158
Barber, M. 71
Barnes, C. 161
Barnett, R. 152, 154, 158, 161
basic research 238
Bass, B.M. 35, 36
Battilana, J. 115
Baumol, W.J. 69
Beijing Normal University 142
beliefs 14, 99–100, 153, 188, 258
Bengtsson, M. 133

Bergquist, W. 28, 152
Bess, J. 16
best practice 113, 121, 125
biosciences, academic-scientific boundary crossing (study) 223–40
Blackie, M.A.L. 158
Bleiklie, I. 212
blended learning 122, 123
blended synchronous teaching and learning *see* BSTL pedagogy
blogs 191–4
Bologna reform 111, 120
Bond, C. 80
bottom-up initiatives 3, 14, 35, 51, 198
boundariless anxiety 152
boundary blurring 1, 5, 24, 65, 152, 170, 217, 223, 225, 227, 265
boundary crossing *see* academic-scientific boundary crossing (study)
boundary expansion 62
boundary maintenance 225, 227, 234–6, 239
boundary setting 224
boundary spanning 133
bounded autonomy 208
Bouwma-Gearhart, J. 99
Boxer, M.J. 94
brand 215
bricolage 62
bridging study programmes 179, 183
Bring Your Own Device (BYOD) 155
BSTL pedagogy 194–6, 197
budget process 23
Building World-class Universities 135
bureaucratic control 56–7, 134
bureaucratic organizational culture 24
Bush, V. 60
business pressures 71–2

Cai, Y. 247
capability requirements 75
capstone projects 13
capstone subjects 81
career progression 210
career track 49
careers advice 217
Cashmore, A. 97
casual labour 78–9
Celis, S.G. 93
centralization 1, 22, 24, 27, 56–7, 134, 228
Centres for Excellence in teaching and learning (CETL) 50
Chan, R.C.H. 191
China: higher education 132, 250, 251

Chinese Academy of Science (CAS) 139
Chinese Academy of Social Sciences (CASS) 139
Chinese culture: teaching-learning nexus 43–4
Chinese universities: academic promotion system 249–57; organizing teaching in *see* organizing teaching in Chinese universities
chordal triad of human agency 116
Chu, S.K.W. 191, 263
Civil Rights movement 93–4
clarity: and innovation 14
Clark, B. 16, 187, 215
classroom researchers 198
'classrooms without borders' 174
Cleveland, H. 161
co-located communication spaces 169, 172
co-located learning situations 170
Coates, H. 69, 70, 79
cognitive science 13
Coleman, J.S. 33
collaboration 217; academic engagement in 226; Chinese academics 253, 256; encouragement of 251–3; external pressures as drivers of 16; wikis and improved 190, *see also* industry collaboration; research collaboration
collaborative authoring tools 188–92
collaborative learners 173, 183
collaborative learning 170, 171, 179, 183
collective action 4, 33, 52
collective identity 246
collective responsibility: curricular change 99
collectivization 265
collegiality 56, 70, 99, 213–15
'coming into presence' 159
commercial pressures 70, 74
commercialization 225–7, 231, 232
commitments 35, 36
communication 22, 27, 97, 180–2, 212, 217
communities of enquiry 157
communities of practice 62, 164, 174
community level organizing 133
community membership 51–2
community stakeholders 18
competence 211
competent authority 128
competing discourses: student learning 162
competition: inter-professional and intra-institutional 217; for resources 23, 55, 57, 58, 60; teaching and learning, Hong Kong 43; to join the academic profession 210; and university transformation 55, *see also* global competition; market-based competition
Competition for Teaching Excellence 112, 113, 114
competitiveness 60, 123
compliance 225
'comply strategic responses' 256
comprehensive universities (Chinese) 142
Conference of Ministers of Education (Germany) 112
conflict(s) 13, 16–19, 24, 227, 244
conflicting goals 23
conflicting subcultures 25
conformity 248
conjoint authority 33, 36, 51
consensus 3, 14, 23, 80
consistency 162
consulting firms 76
consumer discourse 151
consumer satisfaction 164
consumer satisfaction surveys 151, 160
consumerism 17, 156, 163, 164–5
consumers: learners as 151, 159–60
control 20, 56–7, 134, 164
convergence 162
cooperation 36, 226
coordination *see* loose coupling; tight coupling
corporate identity 255, 256, 257
corporation logic 251, 252, 253, 254, 255, 257, 258
corporatist discourse 151, 160
cost pressures 69–70
cost-benefit: curricular change 96, 97, 104
Council of Writing Program Administrators 94
coupling *see* loose coupling; tight coupling
Course Experience Questionnaire (CEQ) 164
critical reflection 26
cross-departmental linkages 21–2
CrossActionSpaces 169
cultural organizational change 187–8, 198; innovation technology (case studies) 188–96
Cultural Revolution 134, 138, 140, 249
cultural values 1, 14, 24, 25
curricular and instructional change: an emerging conceptualisation of faculty decision-making 102–4; defining 91–3; internal influences 95–102; realization of 90; sociocultural and external influences 92, 93–5; successful 90
curriculum development: digital didactical designing 175
customization 24

Dalkir, K. 191
Dancy, M.H. 96, 97
danwei 250, 254
danwei men 254, 255, 257
data mining 156
de-institutionalization 137
de-specialization 140–5
Deakin University (Victoria) 77
deans 212
Dean's Innovation Fund (DIF) 197
decentralization 21, 24, 57
decision points: academic plans 91
Decision of Reforming Educational System (China) 135
decision-making: academic participation in 57; centralized 1, 228–9; governance and 35, 38; intersection of academic and managerial 24; power and politics 23, 209; teaching and learning 21; top-down 2, *see also* faculty decision-making
Dee, J.R. 16
deep(er) learning 98, 105n2, 170, 183
deliberative learning 98
departmental culture 97–9
depth of change 91, 92
Derrida, J. 159
design for learning 172, 173, 174, 176, 181–2, *see also* 'learning expeditions' study
'deviant resistor' response 63, 64
deviant serial entrepreneur/manager 123–4
Dewey, J. 158
didactic/technophile engineer 121; iterative dimension 121–2; practical-evaluative dimension 122–3; projective dimension 123
didactics 171
Didaktik 171
difference: finding and establishing 71
digital age 153–4, 159–60, 173
digital didactical designing (DDD) 171–2; organizational prerequisites 173–5, *see also* 'learning expeditions' study
digital media 153, 154
digital natives 264
digital scholarship 154
Dill, D. 214, 216
direct governance 74
disaggregation 79, 80, 116
disciplinary boundary crossing 224
disciplinary communities 61, 157, 224
disciplinary culture 97–9
discourse analytics *155*

discretion: response to threats to professional autonomy 62–4
discursive shift: in teaching and learning 151, 152, 159, 162
disembedding mechanisms 207, 218
disengagement 81
disjoint authority 33, 34, 37, 51
dissatisfied consumers 159
disseminators: likelihood of curricular change 100
distance learning (online) 154, 264
divergent perspectives 15, 26–8
diversity 15, 165
Dobson, I.R. 75
doer-mentality 124
Donors' Association for the Promotion of Science and the Humanities in Germany *see Stifterverband*
dynamic manager duo 116–17; iterational dimension 117; practical-evaluative dimension 117–18; projective dimension 118–19

e-learning 72
East China Normal University 142
Eccles, J.S. 96, 97
Eckel, P. 91, 92
economic reform: China 141
economic tensions 78–9
education service firms and providers 70
educational planning: China 139
effectiveness 243, 251
efficacy 104
efficiency 80, 209, 243
Einstein, A. 186
Eisenberg, E. 27
elite academic group 210
elite academics 60, 62
elite managers 63, 64, 65
elite oligopolistic clubs 70
elite scientists 213
elite system of education 71, 78, 80, 140
elitist pioneering role 121
emergent being 158
emergent learning technologies *155*
Emirbayer, M. 115
emotions 192
employability 81, 94, 209, 217, 229
employer influence *18*
employment allocation system (China) 141
employment status 209
energizing context 27
engagement *see* academic engagement; social engagement; student(s), engagement

enhancement *see* individual enhancement; quality enhancement
enrolment-based budgeting 23
entrepreneurial researcher 79
entrepreneurialism: in biosciences 231–4; institutional strategy 19–20; organizational culture 24, *see also* academic entrepreneurs; institutional entrepreneurs
environmental scanning 28–9
epistemic access 157
epistemological contestability 152
Ernst and Young 76
ethical issues 154
ethical responsibilities: responses to accreditation mandates 98
Europe: balance between tenured staff and fixed-term appointments 210; change and continuity in organizational reforms 212–17
evidence-based approaches 101, 162
'excellence' discourse 156
Excellence Initiative 110
Excellence in Teaching 39
expectations 80, 96–7
experiences: and curricular change 99–102, *see also* industry experience; student experience
experimentation 21, 99
expert authority 128
external environment 15, 16–19
external image 215, 219
external influences: curricular change 93–5
extrinsic motivation 2

Facebook 191–4
facilitation of learning: teaching as 151, 159, 183
faculty decision-making, curricular change 89–104; an emerging conceptualization of 102–4; internal influences 95–102; situative perspective 102–3; socio-cultural and external influences 92, 93–5
Fairweather, J. 96
family logic 250, 251, *252*, 253, 254, 255, 256, 257
far-reaching change 92
Finland 211
first-year experience (FYE) programmes 29–30
Fisher, P.D. 99
flexibility: pedagogy for 194–6
flexible academic labour markets 210

flexible reforms 15, *26*, 27–8
Framework for Success in Postsecondary Writing 94
Freire, P. 158
Full Range Leadership Model 35
Fumasoli, T. 187
funding 42, 43, 48–9, 57, 60, 70, 196–8, 229, 237

Gemeinschaft 61, 224
German Council of Science and Humanities 111
German Federal Government 112
German Federal Ministry of Education and Research 40, 110
German Research foundation 110
German universities: 'academic quarter' institutions 34; efforts to making teaching count 111–12; macro-level governance 37–8, 38–9, 40–1; managerial governance *see* Transformation Governance of Academic Teaching study; meso-level governance 44–7; neglect of teaching in 110–11; organizational structure 3; sabbatical teaching 51; typology 114, *see also* University of Mainz
Gibbs, G. 263
global citizenship 195
global competition 151, 156, 207
globalization 43, 156, 207, 218
goals 14, 15, 21, 23, 28, 33, 74
Goedegebuure, L. 79
Gordon, G. 162
governance *see* university governance
government policies *17*
government-level initiatives: curricular change 94
Graham, R. 90, 97
grassroots innovation 15, 26–7
Gutenberg Teaching Council (GLK) 174

Hammerschmid, G. 247
Harbin Institute of Technology 138
Harvey, L. 162
Hayek, F.A. 140
Henderson, C. 96, 97, 101
Herrmann, T. 181
hierarchies 71, 81, 212
high-fidelity mode 162, *163*
high-stakes accountability 134
higher education: as an obligation 160; current state of 152–6; as reinvention of the

learner 160–1, *see also* university education
higher education institutions: hold on quality and order 156–60, *see also* universities
holistic concepts: academic work 210, 214
Holland, D. 98, 104
Hong Kong: macro-level governance 38, 39, 42–4; meso-level governance 47–51
Hora, M.T. 90, 96
horizontal structures 15, *26*, 27
hybrid alliances 75–6
hybrid communities 208
hybrid identities 223–40, 254, 255–7
hybrid work roles 75
hyper-internationalization 68

idealized influence 35
ideas: organizational cultural change 188
identity *see* academic identity(ies); hybrid identities; professional identity(ies); student(s), identity
incentives 14, 25, 38
inclusion-exclusion dynamic 14, 25
indirect governance 74
individual behaviour: and organizational structure 3–4
individual enhancement: as learner's pedagogic right *161*
individual factors: commercialization 226; curricular change 98, 99–102
individualized consideration 36
individualized specializations 143
industry collaboration 232–4; academic freedom 238; obstacles to publishing 235–6
industry experience 74
industry funding 237
inequalities: academic staff 210
informal communication 22, 27
informal networks 22
information and communication technology (ICT) 81, 156, 169
information sharing technology 191
innovation 14, 21, 27, 52, 102, 123
innovative enhancement 164
innovative technology 188–96, 197
inspirational motivation 35, 45, 51
institutional accountability 219
institutional architectures (emergent) 75–8, 81
institutional autonomy 38, 56, 60, 208

institutional cultures 215
institutional entrepreneurs: agency 114, 115, 116, 127; exemplary cases 116–25; preserving protected spaces 62
institutional logics: academic promotion system and academic identity (study) 243–58; governance change 56–8; protected spaces and their nestedness under different 59–61
institutional orders (societal) 247
institutional strategy *see* strategy
institutional work 4, 34, 35, 47, 62, 127
institutions 34–5
instructional change *see* curricular and instructional change
integrated form of organizing 133
integrated learning 21
intellectual property 70
intellectual stimulation 36, 44–5, 51
intended learning 171, 172
inter-personal interactions 22
inter-professional competition 217
interaction(s) 22, 171, 172, 175, 180–1, 196
intercultural understanding 195
interdisciplinarity 13, 19, 22, 224
interest groups 112
internal influences: curricular change 95–102
international ecosystem 71
internationalization 19, 25
internship(s) 13; using blogs to support learning during 191–4
intra-institutional competition 217
intra-institutional relationships 212–13
intrinsic motivation 2, 46
'isolated' instances of change 92
isomorphism 71
iterational dimension (institutional entrepreneurs) 116; didactic/technophile engineer 121–2; dynamic duo 117; managerialist dean 119; rebel ambassador 123–4; scouting 126–7

Jahnke, I. 181, 263
Jenkins, C. 161
Jenkins, W.I. 246

Kennie, T. 71
Kerr, C. 207
Kettering, C. 159
Kezar, A. 24, 98
knowledge: acquisition and application 191, 192, *193*; changing nature of 153; commercialization 225–7;

creation/capture 55, 62, 70, 186, 189, 191, 192, *193*; curricular change 101; disciplinary 157; dissemination 14, 55, 71, 75, 153, 191, 192, *193*; expansion and fragmentation 214; keeping pace with change in 187; powerful 157, 158; troublesome 158, 165, *see also* prior knowledge
knowledge architectures (new) 72
knowledge management 191–4

Land, R. 157, 158, 162
'later-career' senior academic 79
Lattuca, L.R. 90, 91, 92, 94, 95, 98, 101
Laudel, G. 239
Laureate Education 70
Lave, J. 104
Lawrence, T.B. 3, 35, 47
leadership 212; authoritarian 120, 257; changes in 74; faculty engagement in curricular change 97; new forms of 82; new institutional architectures 76–7; and organizational change 216; training 74, 82; transformational governance 35, 45, 46
leading teaching 263
learner analytics 156
learners: addressing variability 164; changing relationship between organizations and 154; as consumers 151, 159–60; partnership with 165; pedagogic rights 160–1; teachers as collaborative 173, 183, *see also* students
learning: as an individualist activity 151; in a risk society 156–60, *see also* teaching and learning
learning activities 172
learning communities 13, 27, 28, 116, 118, 179
'learning expeditions' study 169–84; challenge of co-located communication spaces 169; discussion, conclusions and implications 183–4; empirical findings 179–82; method 178–9; study context 175–9; teaching as process design 169; theoretical lens 170–5
learning management systems 72
learning thresholds 158
lecturers 197, 198
legitimacy 162, 215, 216
Leišytė, L. 62, 239, 265
liminality 158–9
loose coupling 1, 22, 133, 134, 140–5, 174
low-fidelity mode *163*, 164

macro-level governance 34, 35, 37–44, 61
Mahat, M. 69, 70
mainstream actors 50–1
Major, C.H. 101
makers/maker spaces 170, 171, 183
managed academics 254, 255
management: displacement of traditional values 80; structure and workforce 75; support, organizational change 197, *see also* new public management; senior management
management by objectives 38
managerial habitus 117, 118, 122
managerial role 212
managerial self-governance 38, 57, 58; in search of the best *see* Transformation Governance of Academic Teaching study
managerial values 28, 80
managerial-type universities 59
managerialism 2; academic responses 61–4; alienation 219; boundary crossing 230–1, 239; learner as consumer 159; performance discrimination 122; professionalism and academic identity schism 254; quality enhancement *163*, 165; reduced protected spaces 61, *see also* new public management
managerialist dean 119; iterative dimension 119; practical-evaluative dimension 119–21; projective dimension 121
managers: beliefs, as a difficulty for change 14; leverage of institutional strategies 20; role in reform 26, 27, *see also* academic managers; elite managers; middle managers; professional managers
managing teaching 263
Mårell-Olsson, E. 263
market forces 94, 219, 251
market-based competition *17*, 19, 42
marketing 159–60
marketization 1, 151, 156, 210
massification 2–3, 210
Massive Open Online Course (MOOC) 81, 91, 145, 264
mechanistic coordination 22
Meijtoft, T. 263
Merton, R.K. 56
meso-level governance 34, 35, 37, 38, 39, 44–51, 61
Messer-Davidow, E. 94

Meyer, J.H.F. 157, 158
Meyer, R.E. 247
micro-level governance 34, 35, 39
middle managers 212
Ministry of Education (China) 142
Mische, A. 115
mission/mission statements 15, 20–1, 74, 79, 215, 219
mobile technology 2, 169, 170, 172
Mode 2 knowledge production 226
Mok, S.S.W. 263
Mondragon University 266
monitoring 2
Morrow, W. 157
motivation: faculty engagement in curricular change 96, 97, 99–100; governance and 35, 36, 46; institutional (teaching) entrepreneurs 120, 122; intrinsic versus extrinsic 2; teaching reform, China 143
multiple identities 244
multiple logics: influence on academic identities 254–7
multiple organizational models 213–14
multiversities 219; new public management and 208–12; new spaces, new choices? 217–18; secular changes and the emergence of the new 206–8
mutual learning 27
mutual respect 99

Nanjin University 142
National Council of Teachers of English 94
national funding schemes 237
National Student Satisfaction Survey 266
National Student Survey 38, 41, 48, 164
National Student Survey of Student Engagement 164–5
National Survey on Postsecondary Faculty 96
National Survey of Student Learning 98
National Writing Project 94
Nelson Laird, T.F. 98
neo-institutionalism 34, 215, 216
neo-liberalism 59, 122, 207, 212
Netherlands: academic-scientific boundary crossing (study) 223–40
network governance 213
networks/networking 22, 27, 94, 212–13, 220
new professionals 63, 64, 65, 152
new public management (NPM) 3, 36; academic identity conflicts 244; blurring of boundaries between science and industry 223; disaggregation of work roles 80; government pressure and adoption of 243; macro-level (case study) 37–44; marketization of education 160; and multiversities 208–12, *see also* managerialism
New Steering Instruments (NSIs) 38
niche dominators 76, 77–8
Nixon, J. 153
non-academic staff 75, 79
'normal' job identity 2, 265

obligation(s): higher education as an 160; private finance and new 70
O'Byrne, D. 80
OECD countries 2, 79
old institutional theory 215, 216
Oliver, C. 248–9
O'Meara, K. 99
on-the-job training 74
onboarding 155
'one size does not fit all' 164
online course management 91
online education 19, 72, 77, 154, 188–92, 264
Online Education Services 78
'only research matters' institutions 33, 34, 38, 39, 41, 43
ontological shift: transformative model of learning 157–8
open access: digital learning 154
open communities of practice 174
'open resistor' response 63–4
open-source nature: of wikis 188, 189
organizational actorhood 208
organizational ambiguity 152
organizational change 89; cultural values 24; faculty ownership 98; funding 196–8; leadership 216; teaching and learning 187–99; temporal narratives 153
organizational context: teaching and learning 15–16, 19–25
organizational culture: and academic reform 24–5; and curricular change 95–7
organizational identity: and academic identity 215–17, 218
organizational integration 208, 219
organizational interdependencies 264
organizational learning 26
organizational management logic 219
organizational performance 22
organizational power 23
organizational prerequisites: for digital didactical designing 171–2, 173–5

organizational reforms: change and continuity in 212–17
organizational structure(s): academic identity 5; German universities 3; and individual behaviour 3–4; new consensus about appropriate 3; teaching and learning 4–5, 15, 19–25, 266, see also structural change
organizing 133
organizing teaching, in Chinese universities 132–45; analytical anchors 133–4; changing
contexts 135–7, 145; de-specialization 140–5; historical and empirical anchors 134–7; specializations 137, 138–40; typology 134
Outline of Chinese Education and Development 135
Owen-Smith, J. 227
ownership: complexity of organizational 73; of organizational and educational change 98

Palmer, B. 101
para-academics 211, 217
participation: in course change 91; in decision-making 57; learner's pedagogic right 161
partnership: with learners 165; public-private 73, 78
partnership model (research) 257
patronage model (research) 257
Pawlak, K. 28
pedagogy(ies): authentic 72; BSTL 194–6, 197; change 101; for improving teaching and learning 13; learners' rights 160–1; MOOCs and transformation of 81; of uncertainty 165
peer coaching 50
peer review 56
peer support 192, 193, *194*
Peking University 142, 143
penetrated hierarchies 212
People's Education 138
perceived value: curricular change 96, 97, 104
performance: -based funding 38, 57; criteria 41, 57, 60, 227–8; culture of high 122; indicators 5, 113, 229, 235, 239, 249; measurement 55, 60, 61; monitoring 228–9; and reward/incentive 36, 38, see also organizational performance; teaching, evaluation(s)

performativity 228
Perkmann, M. 226, 227
'personal principled projects': academic identities as 211
pervasiveness of change 91, 92
pioneering universities (Chinese) 142
P.K. Yonge Developmental Research School 174
politics 23–4
portfolio positions 75
portfolio-style assessments 81
Powell, W. 227
power 23–4, 127, 209
powerful knowledge 157, 158
practical-evaluative dimension (institutional entrepreneurs) 116; didactic/technophile engineer 122–3; dynamic duo 117–18; managerialist dean 119–21; rebel ambassador 124–5; supporting 127
precarious employment 265
prestige 19, 56, 57, 63
Price, I. 71
price pressures 70
price-makers/takers 70
principal agent relations 2
prior experiences: and curricular change 100–2
prior knowledge 13
priorities 14, 15, 20, 21, 23, 33, 152, 229
private finance 70
private institutions 73, 78, 81
privatization 73
proactive de-specialization 142–5
proactive manipulation 63–4, 225
problem choice: bioscience research 236
problem-based learning 13, 24, 27, 43, 44, 101, 155, see also 'learning expeditions' study
process design: teaching as 169
process-based evaluation 172
profession logic 251, *252*, 253, 254, 255, 257
professional associations: and curricular change 94
professional autonomy 2, 22, 41, 46, 56, 59, 61–4, 89
professional behaviours: academic discipline and 97
professional development 27, 30, 39, 101, 174, 217, 263
professional identity(ies) 61, 218, 255
professional managers 2, 57, 60, *63*, 64, 65, 209
professional responsibilities: response to accreditation mandates 98

Index • 277

profiling 62
programme-level change 98
programmed learning 72
project teacher teams, organizing teaching in (study) 169–84
projective dimension (institutional entrepreneurs) 116; didactic/technophile engineer 123; dynamic duo 118–19; managerialist dean 121; rebel ambassador 125; scaling 127–8
promotion 210, *see also* academic promotion system
protected spaces: multi-level nestedness 59; responses to threats to 61–4; under different institutional logics 59–61, 65
Proust, M. 158
public institutions 73
public-private partnerships 73, 78
publications: biosciences and emphasis on 235–6

quality: analytics data 154; collegial engagement 214; new conceptions of 217; research 237, 251, 253; standardization 72; teaching 1, 266; teaching development grants 197; wikis and improved *190*
quality assurance *17*, 57, 94–5, 113, 156, 218
quality enhancement 162–5
Quality Initiative for Teaching 40
Quality Pact for Teaching 112
quantification: academic output 251
quasi-market governance 37, 41, 55, 56–7; academic responses to the threat to protected spaces 61–4; at macro-level 38; mechanisms *58*; protected spaces 59, 60, 65

Ramsden, P. 98
rank/ranking: curricular change 103, 104; German universities 110; global evaluative 207; macro-level governance and 41, 42, 44; market-based competition *17*; and research funding, UK 228; student evaluations of teaching 122–3; transparency and 70
rating (student) 151, 263
reactive de-specialization 140–2
rebel ambassador 123; iterative dimension 123–4; practical-evaluative dimension 124–5; projective dimension 125
receptiveness to change 98
recursive relationships 3–4, 34–5

reflection model 174
reflective communication 181
reflexive modernization 207
reform *see* academic reform; organizational reform
regulation 70
reinterpretation: of new organizational ideals 216
reinvention of the learner 160–1
Renmin University of China 138
reputation 210, 251
research: China 139, 257; collaboration 253; collectivization 265; funding 60, 228; governance 4; literature and understanding of university transformation 4; orientation, German universities 110–11; productivity 96–7, 103, 111, 152, 227, 251; profession logic and prioritization of 251; quality 237, 251, 253; quantity 253; tied to income streams 79, *see also* teaching-research nexus
Research Assessment Exercise (RAE) 228
Research Excellence Framework (REF) 38, 41, 228, 265
research universities 20, 23, 27, 33–4, 77
research-only contracts 210
resource allocation 20, 23
resources: competition for 23, 55, 57, 58, 60; in the digital age 173; insufficient, as barrier to educational change 96, 97
'return to professionalism' 59
revenue generation 19, 20, 210, 229
reversed institutional restructuring (China) 142
reward/reward systems 1, 14, 25, 36, 96
Rhoades, G. 23, 27
Riggio, R.E. 35, 36
risk 152–3
risk aversion 160
risk society 156–60
Rojas, F. 93
roles: change and distribution in institutional 218; as important design criteria in learning 181–2; negotiation of, learning expedition study 180–1, *see also* academic roles; work roles
Ross, J. 158

sabbatical teaching 51
Sahlin, K. 213, 216
sanction 2, 48
scaling 127–8

scholarly openness 70
Scholarship of Teaching and Learning (SOTL) 174
schoolification 2
Schwartzman, L. 159
Science the Endless Frontier 60
Scott, P. 153
Scott, W.R. 216
scouting 126–7
secondary market 210
secular changes: and the emergence of the new multiversity 206–8
SEEK 70, 78
self-employed character (managerialist dean) 120
self-governance 2, 3, *see also* academic self-governance; managerial self-governance
semantic web technologies *155*
semi-autonomous units: responses to threats to professional autonomy *63*, 64
senior management 112, 127, 156, 209, 231; 'teaching matters too' study 38, 42, 44–5, 48, 50, 51
service institutions 76
service learning 13, 24, 27, 28
shared authority 24
shared governance 24
shared understanding 182
Sheail, P. 153
Shulman, L. 159
Smart, J.C. 97–8
social engagement 256
social identity 246
social inclusion (learner's pedagogic right) *161*
social learning 101
social media 191–4, 263
social movements 93–4
social network analysis *155*
social relations 171, 172, 207, 246
social support 192, 193, *194*
societal-level logics 247
sociocultural influences *92*, 93–5
soft-governmental regime 37, 51
Soviet model of education 138, 139
Spain 266
specialization 1; Chinese universities 137, 138–40, 143
speed of the digital age 153
staff-student ratios *136*, 153
stakeholder guidance 58, 60–1
standardization *17*, *18*, 24, 57, 72, 139, 164, 249
Stark, J.S. 90, 91, 92, 94

state logic 251, *252*, 254, 255, 257
state regulation 37, 38, 57–8
status hierarchies 81
Stensaker, B. 162, 187, 216
Stifterverband 39, 40, 41, 112
strategic ambiguity 27–8
strategic capability 80
'strategic gamer' response *63*, 64
strategic plans/planning 20, 28, 29
strategic responses: institutional pressures 248, 255, 256
strategy: commercial pressures and change in 74; digital didactical designing 174–5; teaching and learning 15, 19–20
stratification pressures 71
'streamlined status quo' institutions 76, 77
Strijbos, J.-W. 181
structural change 187, 197, 198, 208, 212, 246
structural complexities 212–13
structural differentiation 1, 14, 21
student(s): demand, curricular change 94; as designers of learning expeditions 169–84; disengagement 81; engagement 165, 191–4; experience 151, 159, 164; feedback 101; identity 75; new institutional architectures and choice for 81; numbers, Chinese universities 135, *136*, 140; numbers and income generation 229; rating by 151, 263; satisfaction 1, 156, 160, 162, 165; use of wikis to facilitate group project work 188–92, *see also* learners; staff-student ratios
Student Evaluation of Teaching and Learning (Hong Kong) 48
student-centred approaches 101
student-centred provision 164
subcultures 25
substantive autonomy 59
subversive education 158
Suddaby, R. 47
Sun Yat-sen University 142
Sunal, D.W. 100, 101
supercomplexity 152, 153, 154, 156, 161
supporting 127
surface learning 2
sustainability of change 187
Sweden: organizing teaching in project teacher teams 169–84
Swinburne Online 78
Swinburne University 78
symbolic boundaries 223, 224
symbolic compliance 225

Index • 279

symbolic power 127
synchronous learning 196
System of Evaluation Indicators for Undergraduate Teaching 143–5
systemic factors: of commercialization 226

teacher-student interaction 196
teacher-student loneliness 174
teachers: as collaborative learners 173, 183
teaching: in Chinese universities *see* Chinese universities; collectivization 265; difference between managing and leading 263; discrepancies between practice and conceptions of 100; evaluation(s) 41, 47–8, 49, 113, 142, 143–5, 198, 228; in German universities *see* German universities; and learning *see* teaching and learning; and research *see* teaching-research nexus
teaching development grants 43, 48–9, 197
teaching entrepreneurs *see* institutional entrepreneurs
Teaching Excellence Framework (TEF) 265, 266
teaching excellence initiatives 265–6
teaching and learning: digital media and new modes of 153–4; discursive shift in 151, 152, 159, 162; divergent perspectives as a resource for improving 15, 26–8; external environment 15, 16–19; literature on 4, 30; organizational change in 187–99; organizational structure 4–5, 15, 19–25, 266; pedagogical practices for improving 13; as risk averse 160; as secondary activities 55; technologies and 3, 43, 81, 154–5, 263–4; university transformation and implications for 78–81
'teaching matters, too' (study): discussion 51–2; empirical results 39–51; methodology 37–9; theoretical framework 34–7
Teaching Outline (China) 139, 141
Teaching Plan (China) 139, 141
teaching staff: Chinese universities 136, 139–40
teaching-only contracts 210
teaching-research nexus 33, 79, 96, 97, 109, 210
technology(ies): curricular change 94; and global competition 156; teaching and learning 3, 43, 81, 154–5, 263–4; university transformation 3, *see also* information and communication technology; mobile technology; wearable technology
technology transfer 209, 210, 218, 226
Temple, P. 23
temporal narratives: organizational change 153
tenure 111, 210
third spaces 218
Thornton, P.H. 251
threshold concepts 157
tight coupling 22, 134, 138–40, 141
time: as a barrier to educational change 96, 97
time-space compression 153, 207
Tönnies 61, 224
top-down decision-making 2, 35
top-down initiatives 3, 14, 27
training: and curricular change 101; leadership 74, 82
transaction: learning as an educational 159
transactional governance 2, 36–7, 47–51, 52
transcendental violence 159
Transformation Governance of Academic Teaching study 112–13; findings 116–25; potency of teaching entrepreneurs 115–16; purposive sampling of award-winning HEIs 113–14; qualitative content analysis of expert interviews 114–15; triple strategy to (help) make teaching count 125–8
'transformation as a knower' 157
transformational change 92
transformational governance 2, 35–6, 44–7, 51–2
transformative model of learning 157–8, 160, 164, 165
'transformer' institutions 76, 78
translation: of new organizational ideals 216
transnational hierarchies 71
transparency 70, 156
Triple Helix relationships 226
troublesome knowledge 158, 165
Trow, M. 78
trust 99, 162, 164
tuition fees 17, 38, 41, 42, 45, 70, 111, 164, 265
TWiki 188–92

Umeå University 175
unbundling of academic work 211
uncertainty 158
'undoing the script' 158
United Kingdom: academic-scientific boundary crossing (study) 223–40; macro-level governance (case study) 38, 39, 41–2; meso-level governance 47–51

United States: academic commercial activities 226–7; academic reform (case study) 28–30; balance between tenured staff and fixed-term appointments 210; decrease in state provision to higher education 1; faculty decision-making, curricular change 89–105
units integrated in institutional structures and agendas: response to threats to professional autonomy 63
universities: Anglo-American 1; as change averse 1; Chinese *see* Chinese universities; German *see* German universities; as loosely coupled 1; stratification 72, *see also* multiversities; research universities
Universities UK Report (2013) 155
university education 68–82; China 132, 250, 251; contexts shaping 69–75; demand for 68; emergent institutional architectures 75–8; emerging organizational forms 73–5, *see also* learning; teaching
university governance: change from the institutional logics perspective 56–8; complexity of 56; direct and indirect 74; imaginary contradictions 2–3; recursive process 34–5; shared 24; structural organizational change 187; university transformation 2, 4, 56, *see also* self-governance; transactional governance; transformational governance
University Grants Committee (Hong Kong) 42, 43
University of Mainz 174
University of Melbourne 77
university transformation 1–2; competition and 55; external pressures as drivers of 16–19; governance literature/ studies 4, 56; implications for teaching and learning 78–81; organizational conditions and difficulties of large-scale 13–14; reasons/ causes 2–3, *see also* academic reform
utility value: curricular change 96, 97, 104

value: bureaucratic control 57; faculty engagement in curricular change 96, 97, 104; peer review and 56
value for money 151
value-added 82
values: academic reform and 28; aligned with professionalism 258; commercial pressures and shift in 74; corporate identity 257; cultural organizational change 188; hybrid identities 256; significant shift in 153, *see also* academic values; cultural values; managerial values
variability of learners 164
virtual learning environments *155*
virtual problem-based learning *155*
virtual universities 72, 77
vision 19, 36, 44, 51, 74, 97, 188
Vught, F. van 71

wearable technology: student design of learning expedition using 169–84
web-enabled mobile technology 172
Weick, K. 133
Whitchurch, C. 218
Whitley, R. 239
Wieman, A. 97
Wigfield, A. 96
wikis 153, 188–92
Winter, R. 80
women's movement 93–4
women's studies 94
work roles 75, 79, 80
work-integrated learning 81
work-simulated learning 81
workforce 75, 209
working conditions 4, 5
workload 96
World University Ranking 44

Ylijoki, O.-H. 211
Young, M. 157
Yuanpei College of Peking University 143

Zhaolun, Z. 138

A GARLAND SER

THE ENGLIS
WORKING CLA

A Collection of
Thirty Important Titles
That Document and Analyz
Working-Class Life before
the First World War

Edited by

STANDISH MEACHAN
University of Texa

East London

Walter Besant

Garland Publishing, Inc.
New York & London
1980

For a complete list of the titles in this series,
see the final pages of this volume.

The volumes in this series are printed on acid-free,
250-year-life paper.

This facsimile has been made from a copy in
the British Art Reference Library
of Yale University.

Library of Congress Cataloging in Publication Data

Besant, Walter, Sir, 1836–1901.
East London.

(The English working class)
Reprint of the 1901 ed. published by Chatto & Windus,
London.
Includes index.
1. London. East End—Description. 2. London.
East End—Poor. 3. London. East End—Social life and
customs. 4. London—Description—1901–1950. 5. London
—Poor. 6. London—Social life and customs. I. Title.
II. Series: English working class.
DA685.E1B5   1980   942.1'4   79-56945
ISBN 0-8240-0100-1

Printed in the United States of America

EAST LONDON

PRINTED BY
SPOTTISWOODE AND CO. LTD., NEW-STREET SQUARE
LONDON

Traitors' Gate, Tower of London.

EAST LONDON

BY

WALTER BESANT, M.A., F.S.A.

AUTHOR OF
'LONDON' 'WESTMINSTER' 'SOUTH LONDON' 'FIFTY YEARS AGO'
'SIR RICHARD WHITTINGTON' ETC.

WITH AN ETCHING BY FRANCIS S. WALKER, R.E.
AND 54 ILLUSTRATIONS BY PHIL MAY, JOSEPH PENNELL
AND L. RAVEN HILL

LONDON
CHATTO & WINDUS
1901

Copyright, 1899, 1900, 1901, by
THE CENTURY CO.

CONTENTS

		PAGE
I	WHAT EAST LONDON IS	1
II	THE CITY OF MANY CRAFTS	19
III	THE POOL AND THE RIVERSIDE	39
IV	THE WALL	101
V	THE FACTORY GIRL	114
VI	THE KEY OF THE STREET	153
VII	THE ALIEN	185
VIII	THE HOUSELESS	209
IX	THE SUBMERGED	227
X	THE MEMORIES OF THE PAST	253
XI	ON SPORTS AND PASTIMES	285
XII	THE HELPING HAND	317
	INDEX	359

ILLUSTRATIONS

	PAGE
Traitors' Gate, Tower of London	*Frontispiece*
A Street Row in the East End	2
Map of East London	5
London Street, Limehouse	11
A Typical Street in Bethnal Green	15
An East End Wharf	25
An East End Factory	31
Barge-Builders	36
The Water-Gate of London: Tower Bridge Looking Toward St. Paul's	43
The Bank of "The Pool." Looking Toward Tower Bridge	49
In the Docks	53
The Tower of London	57
The Water-Gate of London: Tower Bridge from the East Side of the Tower	63
The Turn of the Tide on the Lower Thames	69
Coming Up the Lower Thames with the Tide	75
Off Shadwell	80
Ratcliffe-Cross Stairs	83
Limehouse Basin and Church	89
The Thames Side at Limehouse	93
Greenwich Hospital	97
Wade Street, Limehouse	117
In an East End Gin-Shop	125
The British Workman in Epping Forest	131
Brook Street, Limehouse	139

ILLUSTRATIONS

	PAGE
AN AUGUST BANK-HOLIDAY IN THE EAST END	145
A MUSIC-HALL	150
THE WEST INDIA DOCK GATES	157
THE BARGES THAT LIE DOWN THE THAMES	163
EAST LONDON LOAFERS	169
THE "HOOLIGANS"	175
SUNDAY GAMBLING	179
WHITECHAPEL SHOPS	190
A CORNER IN PETTICOAT LANE	197
A "SCHNORRER" (BEGGAR) OF THE GHETTO	200
EAST AND WEST HAM	215
EAST AND WEST HAM, FROM THE MARSHES	215
SALVATION ARMY SHELTER	232
SANDWICH-MEN	245
"A QUIET DULLNESS"	259
THE STREET AND OLD CHURCH TOWER, HACKNEY	262
AN EAST LONDON SUBURB, OVERLOOKING HACKNEY MARSHES	265
CLAPTON	269
THE OLD CHURCH, STOKE NEWINGTON	272
A STREET IN STOKE NEWINGTON	274
HOUSE IN STOKE NEWINGTON IN WHICH EDGAR ALLAN POE LIVED	277
HAMPSTEAD HEATH, LOOKING "HENDON WAY"	293
THE SHOOTING-GALLERY	299
ON MARGATE SANDS	305
TOYNBEE HALL AND ST. JUDE'S CHURCH	312
THE NEW WHITECHAPEL ART GALLERY	322
THE EAST LONDON MISSION	329
THE NEW MODEL DWELLINGS	336
DR. BARNARDO'S HOME, STEPNEY CAUSEWAY	340
MILE END ALMSHOUSES	347
"THE BRIDGE OF HOPE," A WELL-KNOWN EAST END NIGHT REFUGE	355

I

WHAT EAST LONDON IS

A Street Row in the East End.

EAST LONDON

I

WHAT EAST LONDON IS

IN my previous books on London I have found it necessary to begin with some consideration of the history and antiquities of the district concerned. For instance, my book on Westminster demanded this historical treatment, because Westminster is essentially an old historical city with its roots far down in the centuries of the past: once a Roman station; once the market-place of the island; once a port; always a place of religion and unction; for six hundred years the site of the King's House; for five hundred years the seat of Parliament; for as many the home of our illustrious dead. But with East London there is no necessity to speak of history. This modern city, the growth of a single century,—nay, of half a century,—has no concern and no interest in the past; its present is not affected by its past; there are no monuments to recall the past; its history is mostly a blank—that blank which is the history of woods and meadows, arable and pasture land, over which the centuries pass, making no more mark than the breezes of yesterday have made on the waves and waters of the ocean.

It is, however, necessary that the reader should understand exactly what I mean by East London. For this purpose I have prepared a small map showing the part of Greater London, which in these pages stands for East London. I include all that area which lies east of Bishopsgate Street Without and north of the river Thames; I include that area newly covered with houses, now a densely populated suburb, lying east of the river Lea; and I include that aggregation of crowded towns, each large enough to form an important city by itself, formed of the once rural suburban villages called Hackney, Clapton, Stoke Newington, Old Ford, Stepney, Bow and Stratford.

In order to save the trouble of a long description, and because the reader ought to know something of the natural features of the ground on which East London stands, I have presented on the map certain indications by which the reader, with a little study, may make out for himself as much of these natural features as are necessary. He will see, for instance, that the parts now lying along the bank of the river were formerly either foreshore or marshland, overflowed at every high tide, and lying below a low, natural cliff, which receded inland till it met the rising ground of the bank of the river Lea. The figures on the map mark the sites of villages successively reclaimed from the river by a dyke or sea-wall; if the reader were to visit these riverside parishes he would find in many places the streets actually lower than the high tide of the river, but protected by this sea-wall, now invisible and built over. North of the cliff was a level expanse of cultivated farms, woods and orchards, common ground and pasture land.

This level ground was a manor belonging to the Bishop of London; the farmers, huntsmen, fowlers, and fishermen occupying it were his tenants; he was jealous over encroachments, and would not permit the City to stretch out its arms over his domain. The history of the manor belongs to the antiquary: to the East Londoner himself it has no interest; and indeed, there is very little to tell. That Captain Cour-

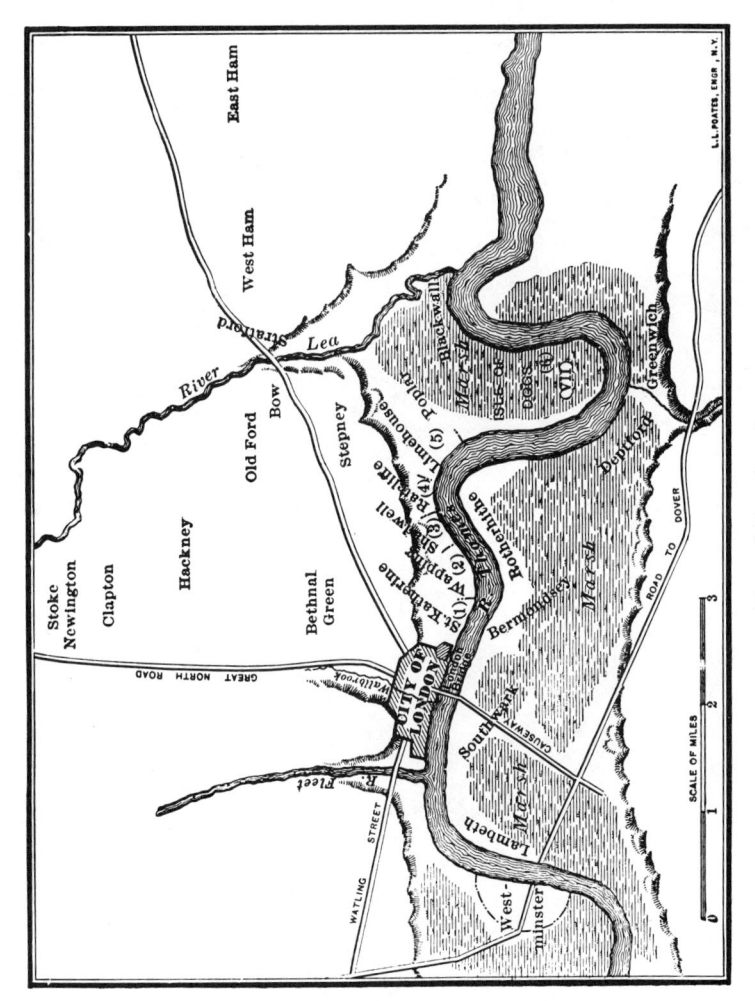

Map of East London.

ageous, Wat Tyler, marched his men across this manor. They came by the road marked "To Bow." One of our kings held a Parliament in the Bishop's Palace; heretics were occasionally burned here; there were one or two monastic houses; a bishop's palace there was; and there was one parish church, for the large parish called Stebenhithe, now Stepney. Farmhouses were scattered about; there were orchards and gardens, lovely woods, broad pastures, acres of waving corn. The citizens of London, though this place belonged to the bishop, had the right of hunting and fishing in its woods and over its low-lying levels; it was a right of the most valuable kind, for the marshes were full of wild birds and the woods were full of creatures fit for man's food. In the year 1504, Sir Thomas More, writing to his friend Dean Colet, then Vicar of Stepney, says: "Wheresoever you look, the earth yieldeth you a pleasant prospect; the temperature of the air fresheth you, and the very bounds of the heavens do delight you. Here you find nothing but bounteous gifts of nature and saint-like tokens of innocency."

The whole of the area between the northern road, which is our western boundary, and the river Lea is now covered with houses and people; the peninsula, marked on the map by the number "VII," consisting of low and malarial ground, long stood out against occupation, but is now almost entirely covered over and absorbed by factories and workmen's residences; what is more, the people of the original East London have now overflowed and crossed the Lea, and spread themselves over the marshes and meadows beyond. This population—not to speak of the suburban villas, which now cover many square miles—represents a movement and a migration of the last twenty years. It has created new towns which were formerly rural villages. West Ham, with a population of nearly 300,000; East Ham, with 90,000; Stratford, with its "daughters," 150,000; and other "hamlets" similarly overgrown. Including, therefore, as we must include, these new populations, we have an aggregate of nearly two millions of people, living all together in what ought to be a single city under one rule. This should be a very remarkable city for its numbers alone; the population is greater than that of Berlin or Vienna, or St. Petersburg, or Philadelphia. As a crowded mass of humanity alone it should demand serious consideration. In other respects, however, it is more remarkable still. You will acknowledge with me that in these respects and from these points of view, no other city in the world is like East London.

To begin with, it is not a city by organization; it is a collocation of overgrown villages lying side by side. It had, until this year (1900), no center, no heart, no representative body, no mayor, no aldermen, no council, no wards; it has not inherited Folk's Mote, Hustings, or Ward Mote; it has therefore no public buildings of its own. There are vestry halls and town halls, but they are those of the separate hamlets—Hackney or Stratford—not East London. It has no police of its own; the general order is maintained by the London County Council. It is a city full of churches and places of worship, yet there are no cathedrals, either Anglican or Roman; it has a sufficient supply of elementary schools, but it has no public or high school, and it has no colleges for the higher education and no university; the people all read newspapers, yet there is no East London paper except of the smaller and local kind; the newspapers are imported from Fleet Street; it has no monthly magazines nor any weekly popular journals, not even penny comic papers—these also are imported; it has no courts of law except the police courts; out of the one hundred and eighty free libraries, great and small, of London, only nine or ten belong to this city—two of these are doubtful, one at least is actually falling to pieces by neglect and is in a rapid state of decay. In the streets there are never seen any private carriages; there is no fashionable quarter; the wealthy people who live on the northeast side near Epping Forest do their shopping in the City or the West End; its places of amusement are of the humbler kind, as we shall learn in due course; one meets no ladies in the principal thoroughfares; there is not visible, anywhere, the outward indication of wealth. People, shops, houses, conveyances—all together are stamped with the unmistakable seal of the working-class.

Perhaps the strangest thing of all is this: in a city of two millions of people there are no hotels! Actually, no hotels! There may be, perhaps, sprung up of late, one or two by the docks, but I think not; I know of none. No hotels. That means, of course, that there are no visitors. Is there anywhere else in the world a great city which has no visitors? It is related of a New Zealander that he once came over intending to make a short stay in London. He put up at a hotel in the City of London itself, on the eastern side; his wandering feet took him every day into Whitechapel and Wapping, which, he imagined, constituted the veritable London of which he had read. After three or four weeks of disappointed monotony in search of London's splendors he sought a returning steamer at the docks. "London," he said, "is a big place; but for public buildings and magnificence and rich people, give me Canterbury, New Zealand."

There are no visitors to demand hotels; there are also none to ask for restaurants. Consequently there are none. Dining-rooms, coffee-rooms, and places providing for the working-men, places of the humbler kind where things to eat may be had, there are in plenty. Most of the working folk take their dinners in these places; but the restaurant of the better kind, with its glittering bars and counters, its white tables, its copious catering, and its civil waiters, does not exist in East London. Is there any other city of the world, with even a tenth part of this population, of which these things would be said? This crowded area, this multitude of small houses, this aggregation of mean streets—these things are the expression and the consequence of an expansion of industries during the last seventy years on a very large and unexpected scale; East London suddenly sprang into existence because it was unexpectedly wanted. A map of London of the year 1830 shows a riverside fringe of hamlets—a cluster of houses outside the City of London and along the two principal roads marked on my map. For the whole of the district outside and around there are lanes and paths through fields and orchards and market gardens, with occasional churches and clusters of houses and detached country residences.

I have said that there is no municipality, that there are no mayor, aldermen, or wards; one reason is that it is a manufacturing, not a trading, city; the wharves and docks are for the use and convenience of the merchants of the great trading city, their neighbor; manufacturers are not a gregarious folk; they do not require a bourse or exchange; they can get along without a mercantile center; they do not feel the want of a guildhall; they do not understand that they have any bond of common interest except the necessity of keeping order. The city sprang up so rapidly, it has spread itself in all directions so unexpectedly, it has become, while men, unsuspecting, went about their daily business, suddenly so vast that there has been no opportunity for the simultaneous birth or creation of any feeling of civic patriotism, civic brotherhood, or civic pride.

The present condition of East London suggests to the antiquary, in certain respects, the ancient condition of the City of London before the people obtained their commune and their mayor. For as the City was divided into wards, which were manors owned and ruled by aldermen, with no central organization, no chief or leader of the citizens, so East London, until the changes in last year's Act of Parliament, consisted of parishes, vestries, boards of guardians, and

London Street, Limehouse.

other boards, with no cohesion, no central government, and, in important matters, such as fire, water, sanitation, police, education, law, subject to external authority.

There are no newspapers, but then their newspapers are published in Fleet Street, only two or three miles away. But their books—where do they get their books? There are no book-shops. Here is a city of two millions of people, and not a single bookseller's shop. True, there are one or two second-hand book-shops; there are also a few shops which display, among other goods, a shelf or two of books, mostly of the goody kind—the girls' Sunday-school prize and the like. But not a single place in which the new books of the day, the better literature, the books of which the world is talking, are displayed and offered for sale. I do not think that publishers' travelers ever think it necessary to visit East London at all. Considering the population, I submit that this is a very remarkable omission, and one that can be observed in no other city in the world a tenth part so thickly populated.

Some twelve years ago I was the editor of a weekly sheet called the "People's Palace Journal." In that capacity I endeavored to encourage literary effort, in the hope of lighting upon some unknown and latent genius. The readers of the "Journal" were the members of the various classes connected with the educational side of the place. They were young clerks chiefly—some of them very good fellows. They had a debating society, which I attended from time to time. Alas! They carried on their debates in an ignorance the most profound, the most unconscious, and the most self-satisfied. I endeavored to persuade them that it was desirable at least to master the facts of the case before they spoke. In vain. Then I proposed subjects for essays, and offered prizes for verses. I discovered, to my amazement, that, among all the thousands of these young people, lads and girls, there was not discoverable the least rudimentary indication of any literary power whatever. In all other towns there are young people who nourish literary ambitions, with some measure of literary ability. How should there be any in this town, where there were no books, no papers, no journals, and, at that time, no free libraries?

Another point may be noted. Ours is a country which has to maintain, at great cost, a standing army of three hundred thousand men, or thereabouts, for the defense of the many dependencies of the Empire. These soldiers are all volunteers; it is difficult, especially in times of peace, to get recruits in sufficient numbers; it is very important, most important, that the martial spirit of our youth should be maintained, and that the advantages which a few years' discipline with the colors, with the subsequent chances of employment, possess over the dreary life of casual labor, should be kept constantly before the eyes of the people. Such is the wisdom of our War Office that the people of East London, representing a twentieth part of the population of the whole country, have no soldiers quartered on them; that they never see the pomp of war; that they never have their blood fired with the martial music and the sight of men marching in order; and that in their schools they are never taught the plain duties of patriotism and the honor of fighting for the country. In the same spirit of wisdom their country's flag, the Union Jack, is never seen in East London except on the river; it does not float over the schools; the children are not taught to reverence the flag of the country as the symbol of their liberties and their responsibilities; alone among the cities of the world, East London never teaches her children the meaning of patriotism, the history of their liberties, the pride and the privilege of citizenship in a mighty empire.

What appearance does it present to the visitor? There is, again, in this respect as well, no other city in the world in the least like East London for the unparalleled magnitude of its meanness and its monotony. It contains about five hundred miles of streets, perhaps more—a hundred or two may be thrown in; they would make little difference. In his haste, the traveler who walks about these streets for the first time declares that they are all exactly alike. They contain line upon line, row upon row, never-ending lines,

A Typical Street in Bethnal Green.

rows always beginning, of houses all alike—that is to say, there are differences, but they are slight; there are workmen's houses of four or five rooms each, all turned out of the same pattern, as if built by machinery; there are rows of houses a little better and larger, but on the same pattern, designed for foremen of works and the better sort of employees; a little farther off the main street there are the same houses, but each with a basement and a tiny front garden—they are for city clerks; and there are dingy houses up squalid courts, all of the same pattern, but smaller, dirty, and disreputable. The traveler, on his first visit, wanders through street after street, through miles of streets. He finds no break in the monotony; one street is like the next; he looks down another, and finds it like the first two. In the City and in the west of London there are old houses, old churches, porches that speak of age, courts and lanes that have a past stamped upon them, though the houses themselves may be modern. Here there seems to be no past; he finds no old buildings; one or two venerable churches there are; there is one venerable tower—but these the traveler does not discover on his first visit, nor perhaps on his second or his third.

As are its streets, so, the hasty traveler thinks, must be the lives of the people—obscure, monotonous, without ambition, without aims, without literature, art or science. They help to produce the wealth of which they seem to have so little share, though perhaps they have their full share; they make possible splendors which they never see; they work to glorify the other London, into which their footsteps never stray. This, says the traveler, is the Unlovely City, alike unlovely in its buildings and in its people—a collocation of houses for the shelter of a herd; a great fold in which the silly sheep are all alike, where one life is the counterpart of another, where one face is the same as another, where one mind is a copy of its neighbor.

The Unlovely City, he calls it, the City of Dreadful Monotony! Well, in one sense it is all that the casual traveler understands, yet that is only the shallow, hasty view. Let me try to show that it is a city full of human passions and emotions, human hopes and fears, love and the joys of love, bereavement and the sorrows of bereavement; as full of life as the stately City, the sister City, on the west. Monotonous lines of houses do not really make or indicate monotonous lives; neither tragedy nor comedy requires the palace or the castle; one can be human without a coronet, or even a carriage; one may be a clerk on eighty pounds a year only, and yet may present, to one who reads thought and interprets action, as interesting a study as any artist or æsthete, poet or painter.

Again, this city is not, as our casual observer in his haste affirms, made up entirely of monotonous lives and mean houses; there are bits and corners where strange effects of beauty can be seen; there is a park more lovely than that of St. James's; there are roads of noble breadth; there is the ample river; there are the crowded docks; there are factories and industries; there are men and women in East London who give up their lives for their brothers and their sisters; and beyond the city, within easy reach of the city, there are woods and woodlands, villages and rural haunts, lovelier than any within reach of western London.

It will be my task in the following pages to lay before my readers some of the aspects of this city which may redeem it from the charges of monotony and unloveliness. Do not expect a history of all the villages which have been swallowed up. That belongs to another place. We have here to do with the people; humanity may be always picturesque; to the philosopher every girl is beautiful because she is a girl; every young man is an object of profound interest because he is a man, and of admiration because he is young. You have no idea how many girls, beautiful in their youth; how many women, beautiful in their lives; how many young men of interest, because they have their lives before them; how many old men of interest, because their lives are behind them, are living in this city so monotonous and so mean.

II

THE CITY OF MANY CRAFTS

II

THE CITY OF MANY CRAFTS

SOME time ago I compiled a list of the various crafts carried on in London during the fourteenth and fifteenth centuries, simply using for the purpose the more accessible books. It was a time when everything wanted for the daily use of the people was made or prepared by the craftsmen of the City, always excepting the things of luxury in demand only by the richer sort, such as foreign wines, silks, velvets, fine weapons, inlaid armor, swords of tempered steel, spices and oil and carpets. The London weaver sat at his loom, the London housewife sat at her spinning-wheel, the London cutler made knives for the Londoner, the "heaumer" made helmets, the "loriner" made bits and spurs, and so on. Yet the number of the crafts was only between two and three hundred, so simple was the life of the time. Then I made another compilation, this time for the eighteenth century. In the interval of four hundred years many new inventions had been made, many new arts had come into existence, many new wants had been created—life had become much more complex in character. My list of crafts and trades had actually doubled, though many things were made out of London. At the present moment even, when dependence is largely necessary on outside industrial centers and when no great city is sufficient to herself in manufactures, when whole classes of manufactures have been localized in other parts, when one might fairly expect a large reduction in the number of trades, we find, on the other hand, a vast increase. Especially is this increase remarkable in East London, which, as a home of industries, hardly existed seventy years ago. It is now especially a city of the newer wants, the modern crafts, the recent inventions and applications.

East London is, to repeat, essentially and above all things a city of the working-man. The vast majority of the people work at weekly wages, for employers great or small. But the larger employers do not live near their factories, or among their people; you may find at Mile End and elsewhere a few houses where wealthy employers have once lived, but they have long since gone away. The chief difference between the present "City," properly so called, and East London is that in the City everybody—principals, clerks, servants, workmen, all go away as soon as the offices are closed, and no one is left; in East London the employers go away when the factories are closed, but the employees remain. There is therefore no sensible diminution in the population on Saturdays and Sundays; the streets are never deserted as in the City. The manufacturers and employers of East End labor live in the country or at the West End, but for the most part in the suburbs beyond the river Lea, on the outskirts of Epping Forest, where there are very many stately houses, standing in their gardens and grounds, occupied by a wealthy class whose factories and offices are somewhere about East London.

The distribution of the trades curiously follows the old mediæval method, where the men of each trade inhabited their own district for purposes of work and had their own place recognized and assigned to them in the great daily fair or market of Chepe. In Whitechapel, for instance, we may find gathered together a very large percentage of those, men and women—Polish Jews and others—who are engaged in making clothes. In Bethnal Green and in Shoreditch are found the followers of the furniture and woodwork trade; the riverside gives lodging to those who live by work in the docks; bootmakers are numerous in Mile End, Old Town, and Old Ford; the silk trade still belongs especially to Spitalfields and Bethnal Green. The large factories which turn out such a boundless collection of useful, if unlovely, things line the riverside of the Isle of Dogs, and the factory hands have their houses in newly built streets near their work; in Hoxton there is carried on an entirely different class of industries, chiefly of the smaller kind, such as fur and feather dressing; their number and the number of their branches and subdivisions are simply bewildering when one begins to investigate the way in which the people live. In watchmaking, which belongs to Clerkenwell, a man will go through life in comfort knowing but one infinitesimal piece of work—how to make one small bit of a watch; so in these East End trades a man or a woman generally knows how to do one thing and one thing only, and if that one piece of work cannot be obtained the man is lost, for he can do nothing else. In cigar-making, for instance, there are many women who do nothing all their lives but take out of the tobacco-leaf the mid rib; this must be done so that the stalk will be pulled out readily without disturbing or abrading the surface of the leaf. It is work, too, which is well paid, a "stripper" getting from twenty-three to twenty-five shillings a week.

The division of labor among the population can be arrived at from a study of certain tables prepared by Mr. Charles Booth for his great work on the "Life and Labor of the People of London." For his purpose he takes a population of nearly a million—to be accurate, 908,958—inhabiting the area which he defines as East London and Hackney. My own definition of East London, however, includes a much larger area, and when we add West Ham, with its large population of 270,000, nearly all sprung up in the last quarter of a century; that of East Ham, with 90,000, where, twenty years ago, there was but a hamlet and a church in the fields; and Stratford, with Bow, Bromley, and Forest Gate, with about 200,000 more, and Walthamstow, with Leyton and the suburbs south of Epping Forest, we have a population nearly amounting to two millions. Nor does he include the Isle of Dogs, now very thickly populated. Let us, however, take Mr. Booth's figures as applicable to his district, which is that with which we are most nearly concerned. He has ascertained, partly from the last census and partly from independent research and investigation, the main divisions of the various industries and the number of people dependent upon each. Thus, out of his solid million he could find only 443 heads of families, representing 1841 souls, and 574 women, representing 1536 souls, who were independent of work— that is to say, only one person in 600 lived on accumulated savings either of himself or his father before him. This percentage in an industrial town is extremely small. The whole of the rest live by their own work, the greater part by industries, but a few by professions. Thus, of the latter there are 4485 persons—a very small proportion—supported by the professions, meaning the clergy, the medical men, the lawyers, the architects, etc. Of clerks and subordinates in the professions there are 79,000 persons maintained, there are 34,600 persons supported by shops of all kinds, there are 9200 persons supported by taverns and coffee-houses; this accounts for less than 140,000. The whole of the remaining 726,000 live on the wages earned by the breadwinner.

It is, in fact, altogether an industrial population. If, again, we take Mr. Charles Booth's figures in greater detail there are seventy-three thousand who depend upon casual employment; there are the railway servants, the police, the road service, the sailors, and the officials. There are, next, those employed in the main divisions of trade—dress, furniture, building, and machinery—and there are the significant items of "sundry artisans," "home industries," "small trades,"

An East End Wharf.

and "other wage-earners," amounting in all to the support of about eighty-five thousand persons. It is among these "sundries" that we are to look for the astonishing variety of industries, the strange trades that our complex life has called into existence, and the minute subdivisions of every trade into branches—say, sprigs and twigs—in which one man may spend his whole life. We are now very far from the days when a shoemaker sat down with the leather and his awl and worked away until he had completed the whole shoe, perfect in all its parts, a shoe of which he was proud as every honest workman should be, with no scamping of work, no brown paper instead of leather for the heel. The modern system leaves no room for pride in work at all; every man is part of a machine; the shoe grows without the worker's knowledge; when it emerges, not singly but by fifties and hundreds, there is no one who can point to it and say, "Lo! I made it. I—with my right hand. It is the outcome of my skill." The curse of labor, surely, has never been fully realized until the solace of labor, the completion of good work, was taken away from the craftsman. Look at the list, an imperfect one, of the subdivisions now prevailing in two or three trades. Formerly, when a man set himself to make a garment of any kind he did the whole of it himself, and was responsible for it and received credit for it, and earned wages according to his skill. There is now a contractor; he turns out the same thing by the score in half the time formerly required for one; he divides the work, you see; he employs his "baster, presser, machinist, buttonholer, feller, fixer, general hand," all working at the same time to produce the cheap clothing for which there is so great a demand. In bootmaking the subdivision is even more bewildering. There are here the manufacturers, factors, dealers, warehouse men, packers, translators, makers of lasts, boot-trees, laces, tips and pegs—all these before we come to the bootmaker proper, who appears in various departments as the clicker, the closer, the fitter, the machinist, the buttonholer, the table hand, the sole maker, the finisher, the eyeletter, the rough-stuff cutter, the laster, the cleaner, the trimmer, the room girl, and the general utility hand. Again, in the furniture and woodwork trade there are turners, sawyers, carvers, frame makers, cabinet-makers, chair makers, polishers, upholsterers, couch makers, office, bedroom, library, school, drawing-room, furniture makers; upholsterers, improvers, fancy-box makers, gilders, gluers, and women employed in whichever of these branches their work can be made profitable.

If we turn to women's work as distinct from men's, we find even in small things this subdivision. For instance, a necktie seems a simple matter; surely one woman might be intrusted with the making of a single tie. Yet the work is divided into four. There is the woman who makes the fronts, she who makes the bands, she who makes the knots, and she who makes the "fittings." And in the match-making business, which employs many hundreds of women and girls, there are the splint makers, the dippers, the machinists, the wax-vesta makers, the coil fillers, the cutters down, the tape cutters, the box fillers, the packers, and so on.

It is not my intention in this book to enter into detail concerning the work and wages of East London. To do so, indeed, with any approach to truth would involve the copying of Mr. Charles Booth's book, since no independent single investigator could hope to arrive at the mass of evidence and the means of estimating and classifying that evidence with anything like the accuracy and the extent of information embodied in those volumes. I desire, however, to insist very strongly upon the fact that the keynote of East London is its industrial character; that it is a city of the working-classes; and that one with another, all except a very small percentage, are earners of the weekly and the daily wage. I would also point out that not only are the crafts multiplied by the subdivisions of contractors, but that every new invention, every new fashion, every new custom, starts a new trade and demands a new set of working folks; that every new industrial enterprise also calls for its new workmen and its skilled hands—how many thousands during the last twenty years have been maintained by the bicycle? As for wages, they speedily right themselves as the employer discovers the cost of production, the possible margin of profit, and the level of supply and demand, tempered by the necessity of keeping the work-people contented and in health.

Another point to observe is the continual demand for skilled labor in new directions. A walk round the Isle of Dogs, whose shores are lined with factories producing things new and old, but especially new, enables one to understand the demand, but not to understand the supply. Early in this century the general application of gas for lighting purposes called for an army of gas engineers, stokers, and fitters and makers of the plant required. The development of steam has created another army of skilled labor; the new appliances of electricity have called into existence a third army of workingmen whose new craft demands far more skill than any of the older trades. Consider, again, the chemical developments and discoveries; consider the machinery that is required for almost every kind of industry; the wonderful and lifelike engine of a cotton mill, which deals as delicately as a woman's fingers with the most dainty and fragile fiber, yet exercises power which is felt in every department of the huge mill; consider the simple lathe driven by steam; consider the new materials used for the new industries; consider the machinery wanted to create other machinery; and consider, further, that these developments have all appeared during the nineteenth century, that East London is the place where most of them, in our country, were first put into practice. If, I say, we consider all these things we shall understand something of the present population of East London.

Again referring to Mr. Charles Booth's book, there you

may learn for yourself what is paid to men, women, and children for every kind of work; there you may learn the hours employed and all the conditions—sanitary, insanitary, dangerous, poisonous—of all the industries. It must be enough here to note that there are, as might be expected, great variations in the wages of the work-people. High skill, whatever may be the effect, in certain quarters, of sweating, still commands high wages; those trades which make the smallest demand for skill and training are, as might be expected, poorly paid. For instance, there is no work which calls for more skill than that of the electrical or mechanical engineer, or the engineer of steam or of gas. Therefore we observe without astonishment that such a man may receive £3 or £4 a week, while the wage of the ordinary craftsman ranges, according to the skill required, from 18s. to 35s. a week. In the work of women it is well to remember that the lower kinds of work are worth from 7s. to 12s. in ordinary seasons, and that there are some kinds of work in which a woman may make from 15s. to 25s. a week. In thinking of East London remember that the whole of the people (with certain exceptions) have to live on wages such as these, while the clerks, who belong to a higher social level and have higher standards of comfort, are not in reality much better off with their salaries ranging from £80 a year to £150.

It might be expected that in speaking of trade and industry we should also speak of the sweating, which is so largely carried on in this city of industry. There is, however, nothing on which so much half-informed invective has been written—and wasted—as on the subject of sweating. For my own part, I have nothing to say except what has been already said by Mr. Charles Booth, who has investigated the subject and for the first time has explained exactly what sweating means. The sweater is either the small master or the middleman; the employer practically resigns the responsibility of his workmen and makes a contract with a middleman, who

An East End Factory

relieves him of trouble and makes his profit out of the workmen's pay. Or the employer finds a middleman who distributes the work and collects it, does part of it himself, and sweats others, being himself sweated. Or sometimes it is a "chamber master" who employs "greeners"—new hands—for long hours on wages which admit of bare subsistence—sweating, in fact, is the outcome in all its shapes of remorseless competition. Many experiments have been tried to conduct business on terms which will not allow the sweater's interference. These experiments have always ended in failure, often because the work-people themselves cannot believe in the success of any system except that with which they are familiar. Some twelve or fifteen years ago my friend Mrs. H—— started a workshop at St. George's-in-the-East on coöperative principles. She made shirts and other things of the kind. At first she seemed to be getting on very well; she employed about a dozen workwomen, including a forewoman in whom she placed implicit confidence. Her successful start, she said, was due entirely to the enthusiasm, the zeal, the devotion, of that forewoman. Then a dreadful blow fell, for the devoted forewoman deserted, taking with her the best of the workwomen, and started a sweating shop herself—in which, I dare say, she has done well. My friend got over the blow, and presently extended her work and enlarged her premises. The enlargement ruined her enterprise; she had to close. Her experience was to the effect that it is only by the sweated farthing that in these days of cut-throat competition shops which sell things made by hand or by the sewing-machine can pay their expenses, that the sweater is himself sweated, and that the workwoman, starving under the sweating system, mistrusts any other and is an element of danger in the very workroom which is founded for her emancipation.

She also discovered that the workgirl requires constant supervision and sharp—very sharp—admonition; she found that the system of fines adopted by many workshops saves a great deal of trouble both in supervision and in admonition; that a gentle manner is too often taken for weakness and for ignorance. And she impressed upon me the really great truth that the working girl is never employed out of sentimental kindness, but as a machine, by the right and judicious use of which an employer may make a livelihood or even perhaps a competence. In other words, when we talk about miserable wages we must remember all the circumstances and all the conditions, and, she insisted, we must set aside mere sentiment as a useless, or even a mischievous, factor. For my own part, I do not altogether agree with my friend. I believe in the power and uses of sentiment. Let us by all means ascertain all the facts of the case, but let us continue our sentiment—our sympathy—with the victim of hard conditions and cruel competition.

A remarkable characteristic of East London is the way in which the industrial population is constantly recruited from the country. I shall speak of the aliens later on. I mean, in this place, the influx from the country districts and from small country towns of lads or young men and young women who are always pouring into East London, attracted by one knows not what reports of prosperity, of high wages, and greater comforts. If they only knew—most of them—what awaits them in the labyrinthine city!

Long ago it was discovered that London devours her own children. This means that city families have a tendency to die out or to disappear. All the city families of importance—a very long list can be drawn up—of the twelfth and thirteenth centuries—the Bukerels, Basings, Orgars, Battes, Faringdons, Anquetils—have disappeared in the fifteenth. All the great names of the fifteenth—Whittington, Philpot, Chichele, and the rest—are gone in the sixteenth; all the great names of the sixteenth century have disappeared in the eighteenth, and we may ask in vain, "Where are those families which were leaders of the City in the beginning of the nineteenth?"

The same thing seems true of the lower levels. I cannot here inquire into the reasons; the fact remains that London demands the continual influx of new blood, whether for the higher or the lower work. At the same time, there is also the continual efflux. I should like if it were possible, but it would entail an enormous amount of work and research, to ascertain how far the descendants of the old London families, the rich merchants of the last three or four hundred years, are still to be found among our county families. There are descendants of Henry Fitz Ailwyn, first mayor of London, and there are also descendants of the Thedmars, the Brembres, the Philpots, the Walworths. Are there descendants of the Boleyns and the Greshams? Are there descendants among the county families and the nobility of those city merchants who made their "plum" in the last century, and were so much despised by the fashion of the day? Further, I should like to ascertain, if possible, how far the old London families are represented by descendants in America. It would, again, be interesting to learn how many firms of merchants still remain of those which flourished in London a hundred years ago. And it would also be interesting if we could learn, in a long-settled parish of working folk, such as Bethnal Green or Spitalfields, how many names still survive of the families who were baptized, married, and buried at the parish church in the year 1800. The last would be an investigation of great and special interest, because no one, so far, has attempted to ascertain the changes which take place in the rank and file of a London parish, and because the people themselves keep no record of their origin, and the grandchildren, as a rule, neither ask nor seek to know where their grandfathers were born; they care nothing for the rock from which they were digged.

Again I venture to borrow two or three simple figures

from Mr. Booth. He tested a small colony called an "Irish" neighborhood; it consisted of 160 persons. I presume that he means 160 heads of families; of these 57 were Londoners by birth; out of London, but in the United Kingdom, 88 were born; the remaining 15 were foreigners by birth. And out of 693 applicants for relief to the Charity Organization

Barge-Builders.

Society in Mile End, Old Town, and St. George's-in-the-East, 486, or seventy per cent., were Londoners by birth; 207, or thirty per cent., were born out of London.

It may be added that if we take the whole of London it is roughly estimated that 630 in the thousand of the population are natives of London, that 307 come from other parts of England and Wales, that 13 are Scotch, 21 Irish, 8 colonists, and 21 of foreign birth. This estimate may have been slightly altered by the recent influx of Russian Jews,

THE CITY OF MANY CRAFTS 37

but the difference made by a hundred thousand or so cannot be very great. The settlements of the alien, especially in East London, will be considered in another chapter. Meantime, to one who lives in the suburbs of London—to one who considers the men of light and leading in London: its artists, men of letters, architects, physicians, lawyers, surgeons, clergy, etc.—it seems at first sight as if no one was born in London. The City merchants, however, can, I believe, point to a majority of their leaders as natives of London. It would be easy to overstate the case in this respect.

The statistics, so far as they can be arrived at, as to religion are startling. On October 24, 1886, a census was taken of church attendance. The results were as follows: Over an area including 909,000 souls there were 33,266 who attended the Church of England in the morning, and 37,410 who attended in the evening. This means 3.6 per cent. in the morning and 4.1 per cent. in the evening, so that out of every 100 persons 96 stayed away from church. Taking the nonconformist chapels, it was found that 3.7 per cent. attended some chapel, while 3.3 per cent. attended the mission halls in the evening. These mission halls, with their hearty services, the exhortations of the preacher, and the enthusiasm of the singing, are crowded. So that, taking all together, there were between seven and eight per cent. of the population who went to some religious service in the evening. This leaves about ninety-two per cent., men and women, boys and girls and infants, who did not attend any kind of worship. This does not indicate the hatred of religion which is found among Parisian workmen; it is simply indifference and not hostility, except in special cases and among certain cranks. And although he does not go to church the East Londoner is by no means loath to avail himself of everything that can be got out of the church; he will cheerfully attend at concerts and limelight shows; his wife will cheerfully get what she can at a rummage sale; and they will cheerfully send their children to as many picnics in the country, feasts, and parties as may be provided for them by the clergy of the parish. But they will not go to church. To this rule there are certain exceptions, of which I shall perhaps speak in due time.

These few notes will not, I hope, be thought out of place in a volume whose object it is to present the reader with some kind of portraiture of the people of East London, the only study in that city which is curious and interesting. I want, once more, these facts to be borne in mind. It is a new city, consisting of many old hamlets whose fields and gardens have been built upon chiefly during this century. It is a city without a center, without a municipality, and without any civic or collective or local pride, patriotism, or enthusiasm. It is a city without art or literature, but filled with the appliances of science and with working-men, some of whom have acquired a very high degree of technical skill. It is a city where all alike, with no considerable exceptions, live on the weekly wage; it is a city of whose people a large percentage were born elsewhere; and it is a city which offers, I suppose, a greater variety and a larger number of crafts and trades than any other industrial center in the world—greater even than Paris, which is the home of so many industries. And it is not a city of slums, but of respectability. Slums there are; no one can deny them; there are also slums in South London much worse in character, and slums in West London, where the "Devil's Acre" occupies a proud preëminence in iniquity; but East London is emphatically not a city of slums.

III

THE POOL AND THE RIVERSIDE

III

THE POOL AND THE RIVERSIDE

EAST LONDON, then, is a collection of new towns crammed with people; it is also a collection of industries; it is a hive of quiet, patient, humble workers; all its people live by their own labor; moreover, it is a busy port with a population of sailors, and those who belong to sailors, and those who make their livelihood out of sailors, and such as go down to the sea in ships. Its riverside is cut up with docks; in and about among the houses and the streets around the docks rise forests of masts; there is no seaport in the country, not even Portsmouth, which is so charged and laden with the atmosphere of ocean and the suggestion of things far off as this port of London and its riverside. The port and the river were here long before East London was begun. The port, however, was formerly higher up, below London Bridge. It was one of London's sturdy mayors who bluntly reminded a king, when he threatened to take away the trade of London, that, at least, he would have to leave them the river. For, you see, while the river runs below London Bridge, it is not much harm that any king, even a mediæval monarch, can do to London trade.

And now come with me; let us walk quietly about this strange city which has so little to show except its people and their work.

We will begin with the riverside, the port and the Pool and the "hamlets" which lie beside the river.

There is one place in London where, at any time of day and all the year round, except in days of rain and snow, you may find a long line of people, men and women, boys and girls—people well dressed and people in rags, people who are halting here on their errands or their business, and people who have no work to do. They stand here side by side, leaning over the low wall, and they gaze earnestly and intently upon the river below. They do not converse with each other; there is no exchange of reflections; they stand in silence. The place is London Bridge; they lean against the wall and they look down upon the Pool—that is to say, upon the reach of the river that lies below London Bridge. I have never crossed the bridge without finding that long line of interested spectators. They are not in a hurry; they seem to have nothing to do but to look on; they are not, apparently, country visitors; they have the unmistakable stamp of London upon them, yet they never tire of the prospect before them; they tear themselves away unwillingly; they move on slowly; when one goes another takes his place. What are they thinking about? Why are they all silent? Why do they gaze so intently? What is it that attracts them? They do not look as if they were engaged in mentally restoring the vanished past; I doubt whether they know anything of any past. Perhaps their imagination is vaguely stimulated by the mere prospect of the full flood of river and by the sight of the ships. As they stand there in silence, their thoughts go forth; on wings invisible they are wafted beyond the river, beyond the ocean, to far-off lands and purple islands. At least I hope so; otherwise I do not understand why they stand there so long, and are so deeply wrapped in thought.

To those who are ignorant of the fact that London is one of the great ports of the world the sight of the Pool would not convey that knowledge. What do we see? Just below us on the left is a long, covered quay, with a crane upon

The Water-Gate of London: Tower Bridge Looking Toward St. Paul's.

it. Bales and casks are lying about. Two steamers are moored beside the quay; above them are arranged barges, three or four side by side and about a dozen in all; one is alongside the farther steamer, receiving some of her cargo; on the opposite shore there are other steamers, with a great many more barges, mostly empty; two or three tugs fight their way up against the tide; heavily laden barges with red sails, steered by long sweeps, drop down with the ebb; fishing smacks lie close inshore, convenient for Billingsgate market; there is a two-masted vessel, of the kind that used to be called a ketch, lying moored in midstream—what is she doing there?

The steamers are not the great liners; they are much smaller craft. They run between London and Hamburg, London and Antwerp, London and Dieppe. The ships which bring the treasures of the world to London port are all in the docks where they are out of sight; there is no evidence to this group of spectators from the bridge of their presence at all, or of the rich argosies they bear within them.

You should have seen this place a hundred years ago. Try to carry your imagination so far back. Before you lie the vessels in long lines moored side by side; they form regular streets, with broad waterways between; as each ship comes up-stream it is assigned its place. There are no docks; the ships receive or discharge their cargo by means of barges or lighters, of which there are thousands on the river; there are certain quays at which everything is landed, in the presence of custom-house officers, landing surveyors, and landing masters. All day long and all the year round, except on Sunday, the barges are going backward and forward, lying alongside, loading and unloading; all day long you will hear the never-ending shouting, ordering, quarreling, of the bargees and the sailors; the Pool is as full of noise as it is full of movement. Every trade and every country are represented in the Pool; the rig, the lines, the masts of every ship proclaim her nationality and the nature of her trade. There are the stately East and West Indiamen, the black collier, the brig and the brigantine and the schooner, the Dutch galliot, the three-masted Norwegian, the coaster, and the multitudinous smaller craft—the sailing barge, the oyster boat, the smack, the pinnace, the snow, the yacht, the lugger, the hog boat, the ketch, the hoy, the lighter, and the wherries, and always ships dropping down the river with the ebb, or making their slow way up the river with the flow.

Steam is a leveller by sea as well as on land; on the latter it has destroyed the picturesque stage-coach and the post-chaise and the Berlin and the family coach; by sea it banishes the old sailing craft of all kinds; one after the other they disappear; how many landsmen are there who at the present day know how to distinguish between brig and brigantine, between ketch and snow?

I said that there is no history to speak of in East London. The Pool and the port must be excepted; they are full of history, could we stop for some of it—the history of shipbuilding, the expansion of trade, the pirates of the German Ocean; when one begins to look back the things of the past arise in the mind one after the other and are acted again before one's eyes. For instance, you have seen the Pool in 1800. Look again in 1400. The Pool is again filled with ships, but they are of strange build and mysterious rig; they are short and broad and solidly built; they are not built for speed; they are high in the poop, low in the waist, and broad in the bow; they roll before the wind, with their single mast and single sail; they are coasters laden with provisions; they are heavily built craft from Bordeaux, deep down in the water with casks of wine; they are weather-beaten ships bringing turpentine, tallow, firs, skins, from the Baltic. And see, even while we look, there come sweeping up the river the long and stately Venetian galleys, rowed by

THE POOL AND THE RIVERSIDE

Turkish slaves, with gilded masts and painted bows. They come every year—a whole fleet of them; they put in first at Southampton; they go on to Antwerp; they cross the German Ocean again to London. Mark the pious custom of the time. It is not only the Venetian custom, but that of every country; when the ship has reached her moorings, when the anchor is dropped and the galley swings into place, the whole ship's company gather together before the mainmast —slaves and all—and so, bareheaded, sing the Kyrielle, the hymn of praise to the Virgin, who has brought them safe to port.

Of history, indeed, there is no end. Below us is the custom house. It has always stood near the same spot. We shall see Geoffrey Chaucer, if we are lucky, walking about engaged in the duty of his office. And here we may see, perhaps, Dick Whittington, the 'prentice lad newly arrived from the country; he looks wistfully at the ships; they represent the world that he must conquer—so much he understands already; they are to become, somehow, his own ships; they are to bring home his treasures—cloth of gold and of silver, velvet, silk, spices, perfumes, choice weapons, fragrant woods; they are to make him the richest merchant in all the City; they are to enable him to entertain in his own house the King and the Queen, and to tear up the King's bonds, amounting to a princely fortune. You may see, two hundred years later on, one Shakspere loitering about the quays; he is a young fellow, with a rustic ruddiness of countenance, like David; he is quiet and walks about by himself; he looks on and listens, but says nothing. He learns everything, the talk of sailors, soldiers, working-men—all, and he forgets nothing. Later on, again, you may see Daniel Defoe, notebook in hand, questioning the sailors from every port, but especially from the plantations of Virginia. He, too, observes everything, notes everything, and reproduces everything. As to the Pool and the port and their history one could go on forever. But the tale of London Town contains it all, and that must be told in another place.

Come back to the Pool of the eighteenth century, because it is there that we get the first glimpse of the people who lived by the shipping and the port. They were, first, the sailors themselves; next, the lightermen, stevedores, and porters; then the boat builders, barge builders, rope-makers, block-makers, ships' carpenters, mast- and yard-makers, ship-wrights, keepers of taverns and ale-houses, dealers in ships' stores, and many others. Now, in the eighteenth century, the shipping of London port increased by leaps and bounds; in 1709 there were only five hundred and sixty ships belonging to this port; in 1740 the number was multiplied by three; this number does not include those ships which came from other British ports or from foreign ports. With this increase there was, naturally, a corresponding increase of the riverside population. Their homes were beyond and outside the jurisdiction of the City; they outgrew the inefficient county machinery for the enforcement of order and the prevention and punishment of crime. As years went on the riverside became more densely populated, and the people, left to themselves, grew year by year more lawless, more ignorant, more drunken, more savage; there never was a time, there was no other place, unless it might have been some short-lived pirate settlement on a West Indian islet, where there was so much savagery as on the riverside of London—those "hamlets" marked on my map—toward the close of the eighteenth century. When one thinks of it, when one realizes the real nature of the situation and its perils, one is amazed that we got through without a rising and a massacre.

The whole of the riverside population, including not only the bargemen and porters, but the people ashore, the dealers in drink, the shopkeepers, the dealers in marine stores, were joined and banded together in an organized system of plunder and robbery. They robbed the ships of their cargoes

The Bank of "The Pool." Looking Toward Tower Bridge.

as they unloaded them; they robbed them of their cargoes as they brought them in the barge from the wharf to the ship. They were all concerned in it—man, woman, and child; they all looked upon the shipping as a legitimate object of plunder; there was no longer any question of conscience; there was no conscience left at all; how could there be any conscience where there was no education, no religion, not even any superstition? Of course the greatest robbers were the lightermen themselves; but the boys were sent out in light boats which pulled under the stern of the vessels, out of sight, and received small parcels of value tossed to them from the men in the ships. These men wore leathern aprons which were contrived as water-tight bags, which they could fill with rum or brandy, and they had huge pockets concealed behind the aprons which they crammed with stuff. On shore every other house was a drinking-shop and a "fence" or receiving-shop; the evenings were spent in selling the day's robberies and drinking the proceeds. Silk, velvets, spices, rum, brandy, tobacco—everything that was brought from over the sea became the spoil of this vermin. They divided the work, they took different branches under different names, they shielded each other; if the custom-house people or the wharfingers tried to arrest one, he was protected by his companions. It was estimated in 1798 that goods to the value of £250,000 were stolen every year from the ships in the Pool by the men who worked at discharging cargo. The people grew no richer, because they sold their plunder for a song and drank up the money every day. But they had, at least, as much as they could drink.

Imagine, then, the consternation and disgust of this honest folk when they found that the ships were in future going to receive cargo and to discharge, not in the open river, but in dock, the new wet docks, capable of receiving all; that the only entrance and exit for the workmen was by a gate, at which stood half a dozen stalwart warders; that the good old leathern apron was suspected and handled; that pockets were also regarded with suspicion and were searched; and that dockers who showed bulginess in any portion of their figures were ignominiously set aside and strictly examined. No more confidence between man and man; no more respect for the dignity of the working-man. The joy, the pride, the prizes of the profession, all went out as if at one stroke. I am sorry that we have no record of the popular feeling on the riverside when it became at last understood that there was no longer any hope, that honesty had actually become compulsory. What is the worth of virtue if it is no longer voluntary? For the first time these poor injured people felt the true curse of labor. Did they hold public meetings? Did they demonstrate? Did they make processions with flags and drums? Did they call upon their fellow-workmen to turn out in their millions and protest against enforced honesty? If they did, we hear nothing of it. The riverside was unfortunately considered at that time beneath the notice of the press. After a few unfortunates had been taken at the dock gates with their aprons full of rum up to the chin; after these captives had been hauled before the magistrate, tried at the Old Bailey, without the least sympathy for old established custom, and then imprisoned and flogged with the utmost barbarity, I think that a general depression of spirits, a hitherto unknown dejection, fell upon the quarter and remained, a cloud that nothing could dispel; that the traders all became bankrupt, and that the demand for drink went down until it really seemed as if from Wapping to Blackwall the riverside was becoming sober.

Billingsgate, the great fish-market, is down below us, just beyond the first wharves and the steamers. This is one of the old harbors of London; it was formerly square in shape, an artificial port simply and easily carved out of the Thames foreshore of mud and kept from falling in by timber piles driven in on three sides. It was very easy to construct such a port in this soft foreshore; there were two others very much like this higher up the river. Of these one remains to this day, a square harbor just as it was made fifteen hundred —or was it two thousand?—years ago.

The first London Bridge, the Roman bridge built of wood, had its north end close beside this port of Billingsgate. My own theory—I will not stop to explain it, because you are

In the Docks.

not greatly interested, friendly reader, in Roman London—is that the square harbor was constructed with piles of timber on three sides and wooden quays on the piles, in order to provide a new port for Roman London when those higher up the river were rendered useless for sea-going craft by the building of the bridge. If you agree to accept this theory without question and pending the time when you may possibly take up the whole subject for yourself, you may stand with me at the head of the present stairs and see for yourself what it was like in Roman times, with half a dozen merchantmen lying moored to the wooden quays; upon them bales of wool, bundles of skins, bars of iron, waiting to be taken on board; rolls of cloth and of silk imported, boxes containing weapons, casks of wine taken out of the ships and waiting to be carried up into the citadel; in one corner, huddled together, a little crowd of disconsolate women and children going off into slavery somewhere—the Roman Empire was a big place; beside them the men, their brothers and husbands, going off to show the Roman ladies the meaning of a battle, and to kill each other, with all the grim earnestness of reality, in a sham fight for the pleasure of these gentle creatures. One does not pity gladiators; to die fighting was the happiest lot; not one of them, I am sure, ever numbered his years and lamented that he was deprived of fifty, sixty, seventy, years of life and sunshine and feasting. Perhaps—in the other world, who knows?—in the world where live the ghosts whose breath is felt at night, whose forms are seen flitting about the woods, there might be—who knows?—more battle, more feasting, more love-making.

They have now filled up most of the old port of Billingsgate, and made a convenient quay in its place. They have also put up a new market in place of the old sheds. With these improvements it is said to be now the finest fish-market in the world. Without going round the whole world to prove the superiority of Billingsgate, one would submit that it is really a very fine market indeed. Formerly it was graced by the presence of the fishwomen—those ladies celebrated in verse and in prose, who contributed a new noun to the language. The word "Billingsgate" conveys the impression of ready speech and mother-wit, speech and wit unrestrained, of rolling torrent of invective, of a rare invention in abuse, and a give-and-take of charge and repartee as quick and as dexterous as the play of single stick between two masters of defense. The fishwomen of the market enjoyed the reputation of being more skilled in this language than any other class in London. The carmen, the brewers' draymen, the watermen, the fellowship porters were all skilled practitioners,—in fact, they all practised daily,—but none, it was acknowledged, in fullness and richness of detail, in decoration, in invention, could rise to the heights reached by the fishwomen of the market. They were as strong, also, physically, as men, even of their own class; they could wrestle and throw most men; if a visitor offended one of them she ducked him in the river; they all smoked pipes like men, and they drank rum and beer like men; they were a picturesque part of the market, presiding over their stalls. Alas! the market knows them no more. The fishwoman has been banished from the place; she lingers still in the dried-fish market opposite, but she is changed; she has lost her old superiority of language; she no longer drinks or smokes or exchanges repartee. She is sad and silent; we all have our little day; she has enjoyed her's, and it is all over and past.

If you would see the market at its best you must visit it at five in the morning, when the day's work begins—the place is then already crowded; you will find bustle and noise enough over the sale of such an enormous mass of fish as will help you to understand something of hungry London. Hither come all the fishmongers to buy up their daily supplies. If you try to connect this vast mass of fish with the mouths for which it is destined you will feel the same kind of bewilderment that falls upon the brain when it tries to realize the meaning of millions.

Next to Billingsgate stands the custom house, with its noble terrace overlooking the river and its stately buildings. This is the fifth or sixth custom house; the first of which we have any record, that in which Chaucer was an officer, stood a little nearer the Tower. After keeping the King's accounts and receiving the King's customs all day, it was pleasant for him to sit in the chamber over the Gate of Ald, where he lived, and to meditate his verses, looking down upon the crowds below.

Next to the custom house you see the Tower and Tower

Hill. I once knew an American who told me that he had been in London three years and had never once gone to see even the outside of the Tower of London. There are, you see, two varieties of man—perhaps they are the principal divisions of the species. To the first belongs the man who understands and realizes that he is actually and veritably compounded of all the generations which have gone before. He is consciously the child of the ages. In his frame and figure he feels himself the descendant of the naked savage who killed his prey with a club torn from a tree; in his manners, customs, laws, institutions, and religion, he enjoys, consciously, the achievements of his ancestors; he never forgets the past from which he has sprung; he never tires of tracing the gradual changes which made the present possible; like the genealogist, he never tires of establishing a connection. I am myself one of this school. I do not know any of my ancestors by sight, nor do I know whether to look for them among the knights or among the men at arms, but I know that they were fighting at Agincourt and at Hastings, beside Henry and beside Harold. If I consider the man of old, the average man, I look in the glass. When I sit upon a jury I am reminded of that old form of trial in which a prisoner's neighbors became his compurgators and solemnly swore that a man with such an excellent character could not possibly have done such a thing. When I hear of a ward election I remember the Ward Mote of my ancestors. I think that I belong more to the past than to the present; I would not, if I could, escape from the past.

But, then, there is that other school, whose disciples care nothing about the past. They live in the present; they work for the present, regardless of either past or future; their faces are turned ever forward; they will not look back. They use the things of the past because they are ready to hand; they would improve them if they could; they would abolish them if they got in the way of advance. They are the practical

The Tower of London.

men, the administrators, the inventors, the engineers. For such men the laws of their country, their liberties, the civic peace and order which allow them to work undisturbed, all are ready made; they found them here—they do not ask how they came. If they come across any old thing and think that it is in their way, they sweep it off the earth without the least remorse; they love a new building, a new fashion, a new invention; they are the men who only see the Tower of London by accident as they go up and down the river, and they think what a noble site for warehouses is wasted by that great stone place. This is a very large school; it embraces more than the half of civilized humanity.

Let me speak in this place of the Tower to the former school—the lesser half.

Three hundred years ago Stow wrote of the Tower of London in these words: "Now to conclude in summary. The Tower is a citadel to defend or command the city, a royal palace for assemblies or treaties, a prison of state for the most dangerous offenders, the only place of coinage for all England, the armory for warlike provision, the treasury of the ornaments and jewels of the Crown, the general conserves of the most ancient records of the king's courts of justice at Westminster."

The history of the Tower would cover many sheets of long and gloomy pages. There is no sadder history anywhere. Fortunately, we need not tell it here. When you think of it, remember that it is still, as it always has been, a fortress; it has been in addition a palace, a court, a mint, a prison; but it has always been a fortress, and it is a fortress still; at night the gates are shut; no one after dark is admitted without the password; to the lord mayor alone, as a compliment and a voluntary act of friendliness on the part of the Crown, the password is intrusted day by day. The Tower was surrounded by a small tract of ground called the Tower Liberties. Formerly the City had no jurisdiction over this district. Even now the boundaries of the Liberties are marked out again every three years by a procession including the mayor of the Tower, the chief officials, including the gaoler with his axe of office, and the school children carrying white wands. They march from post to post; at every place where the broad arrow marks the boundary the children beat it with their wands. In former times they caught the nearest bystander and beat him on the spot, in this way impressing upon his memory, in a way not likely to be forgotten, the boundaries of the Tower Liberties. In such fashion, "by reason of thwacks," was the barber in the "Shaving of Shagpat" made to remember the injunctions which led him to great honor. In every London parish to this day they "beat the bounds" once a year with such a procession. I know not if the custom is still preserved outside London. But I remember such a beating of the bounds, long years ago, beside Clapham Common, when the boys of the procession caught other boys, and, after bumping them against the post, slashed at them with their wands. We were the other boys, and there was a fight, which, while it lasted, was brisk and enjoyable.

There are two places belonging to the Tower which should be specially interesting to the visitor. These are the chapel, called "St. Peter ad Vincula," and the terrace along the river. The history, my American friend, which this chapel illustrates is your property and your inheritance, as much as our own. Your ancestors, as well as ours, looked on while the people buried in the chapel were done to death. Look at those letters "A. B." They mark the grave of the hapless Anne Boleyn, a martyr, perhaps: a child of her own bad age, perhaps—who knows? Beside her lies her sister in misfortune,—no martyr, if all is true, yet surely hapless,—Katherine Howard. Here lies the sweetest and tenderest of victims, Lady Jane Gray; you cannot read her last words without breaking down; you cannot think of her fate without tears. Here lies Sir Walter Raleigh—is there anywhere in America a monument to the memory of this illustrious man? For the rest, come here and make your own catalogue; it will recall, as Macaulay wrote, "whatever is darkest in human nature and in human destiny, with the savage triumph of implacable enemies, with all the miseries of fallen greatness and of blighted fame."

The other place, the terrace along the river, is fit for the musing of a summer afternoon. In front you have life—the life of the day; behind you have life, but it is the life of the past. Nowhere in England can you find such a contrast. Sit down upon this terrace, among the old, useless cannon, among the children at play, and the contrast will presently seize you and hold you rapt and charmed.

It is also the best place for seeing the gray old fabric itself, with its ancient walls and towers of stone, its barbican, its ditch, its gates, its keep, and the modern additions in brick and wood that have grown up among the mediæval work—incongruities which still do not disfigure. On the east of the Tower a new road has been constructed as an approach to the Tower Bridge. From this road another and quite a new view can now be obtained of the Tower, which from this point reveals the number and the grouping of its buildings. I have not seen represented anywhere this new side of the Tower.

I have said nothing all this time of London's new gate. Yet you have been looking at it from London Bridge and from the terrace. It is the new Water Gate, the noblest and most stately gate possessed by any city: the gate called the Tower Bridge. It is, briefly, a bascule bridge—that is, a bridge which parts in the middle, each arm being lifted up to open the way, like many smaller bridges in Holland and elsewhere, for a ship to pass through. It was begun in 1884 and finished in 1894.

It consists of two lofty towers communicating with either shore by a suspension bridge. There is a permanent upper bridge across the space between the towers, access being gained from the lower level by lifts. The lower bridge, on the level of the two suspension bridges, is the bascule, which is raised up by weights acting within the two towers, so as to leave the space clear.

The width of the central span is 200 feet clear; the height of the permanent bridge is 140 feet above high-water mark, and the lower bridge is 29 feet when closed. The two great piers on which the towers are built are 185 feet long and 70 feet wide; the side spans are 270 feet in the clear.

The bascule may be described as a lever turning on a pivot; the shorter, and therefore the heavier, end is within the Tower. The weight at the end of the lever is a trifle, no more than 621 tons. That of the arm, which is 100 feet long, is 424 tons. If you make a little calculation you will find that the action of one side of the pivot very nearly balances that of the other, with a slight advantage given to the longer side. You are not perhaps interested in the construction of the bridge, but you must own that there is no more splendid gate to a port and a city to which thousands of ships resort than this noble structure. The bascule swings up about seventeen times a day, but the ships are more and more going into the docks below, so that the raising of the arms is becoming every day a rarer event. It is a pleasant sight to see the huge arms rising up as lightly as if they were two deal planks, which the great ship passes through; then the arms fall back gently and noiselessly, and the traffic goes on again, the whole interruption not lasting more than a few minutes—less time than a block in Cheapside or Broadway.

Beyond the Tower are the docks named after St. Katherine. They are so named to commemorate an ancient monument and a modern act of vandalism more disgraceful perhaps than any of those many acts by which things ancient and precious have been destroyed.

The Water-Gate of London: Tower Bridge from the East Side of the Tower.

THE POOL AND THE RIVERSIDE 65

On the site of those docks there stood for seven hundred years one of the most picturesque and venerable of City foundations. Here was the House called that of St. Katherine by the Tower. Its first foundress was Matilda, queen of Stephen. She created the place and endowed it, in the spirit of the time, in grief for the loss of two children who died and were buried in the Church of the Holy Trinity Priory, Aldgate. Later on, Eleanor, Queen of Edward I, added certain manors to the little foundation, which had hitherto been but a cell to the Holy Trinity Priory. She appointed and endowed a master, three brethren, three sisters, the bedeswoman, and six poor clerks. Fifty years later, a third Queen, Philippa, wife of Edward III, increased the endowments. We should hardly expect this ancient foundation to survive to the present day, but it has done so. The house was spared at the Dissolution; it was considered peculiarly under the protection of the Queen consort, since three queens in succession had endowed it. Therefore, while all the other religious houses in the country were swept away this was spared; it received a Protestant form; it was called a college, a free chapel, a hospital for poor sisters. The warden, who received the greater part of the endowment, became a dignified person appointed by the Queen, the brethren and sisters remained, the bedeswoman remained, the endowment for the six poor clerks was given to make a school. The precinct became a Liberty, with its own officers, court, and prison; the buildings were retired and quiet, in appearance like a peaceful college at Cambridge; the warden's house was commodious; the cloisters were a place for calm and meditation; there was a most beautiful church filled with monuments; there was a lovely garden, and there was a peaceful churchyard. Outside, the precinct was anything but a place of peace or quiet. It was a tangle of narrow lanes and mean streets; it was inhabited by sailors and sailor folk. Among them were the descendants of those Frenchmen who had fled across the Channel when Calais fell; one of the streets, called Hangman's Gains, commemorated the fact in its disguise, being originally the Street of Hammes and Guisnes, two places within the English pale round Calais.

This strange place, mediæval in its appearance and its customs, continued untouched until some eighty years ago. Then—it is too terrible to think of—they actually swept the whole place away; the venerable church was destroyed; the picturesque cloister, with the old houses of sisters and of brethren, the school, the ancient court house, the churchyard, the gardens, the streets and cottages of the precinct, were all destroyed, and in their place was constructed a dock. No dock was wanted; there was plenty of room elsewhere; it was a needless, wanton act of barbarity. They built a new church, a poor thing to look at, beside Regent's Park; they built six houses for the brethren and sisters, a large house for the warden; they founded a school, they called the new place St. Katherine's. But it is not St. Katherine's by the Tower, and East London has lost the one single foundation it possessed of antiquity; it has also lost the income, varying from £10,000 to £14,000 a year, which belonged to this, its only religious foundation.

In the modern chapel at Regent's Park you may see the old monuments, the carved tombs, the stalls, the pulpit, taken from the ancient church; it is the putting of old wine into new bottles. Whenever I stand within those walls there falls upon me the memory of the last service held in the old church, when, amid the tears and lamentations of the people who loved the venerable place, the last hymn was sung, the last prayer offered, before the place was taken down.

Outside the docks begins the place they call Wapping. It used to be Wapping in the Ouze, or Wapping on the Wall. I have spoken of the embankment on the marsh. All along the river, all round the low coast of Essex stands "The Wall," the earthwork by which the river is kept from over-

THE POOL AND THE RIVERSIDE

flowing these low grounds at high water. This wall, which was constantly getting broken down, and cost great sums of money to restore, was the cause of the first settlement of Wapping. It was in the reign of Queen Elizabeth that people were encouraged to settle here, in order that by building houses on and close to the wall this work would be strengthened and maintained.

Stow says that about the year 1560 there were no houses here at all, but that forty years later the place was occupied and thickly settled by "seafaring men and tradesmen dealing in commodities for the supply of shipping and shipmen." If this had been all, there would have been no harm done, but the place was outside the jurisdiction of the city, and grave complaints were made that in all such suburbs a large trade was carried on in the making and selling of counterfeit goods. The arm of the law was apparently unable to act with the same vigor outside the boundaries of the lord mayor's authority. Therefore the honest craftsman was encouraged by impunity to make counterfeit indigo, musk, saffron, cochineal, wax, nutmegs, steel and other things. "But," says Strype, "they were bunglers in their business." They took too many apprentices; they kept them for too short a time, and their wares were bad, even considered merely as counterfeits. The making of wooden nutmegs has been, it will be seen, unjustly attributed to New England; it was in vogue in East London so far back as the sixteenth century. The craftsmen of the City petitioned James I. on the subject; a royal commission was appointed who recommended that the City companies should receive an extension of their power and should have control of the various trades within a circle of five or six miles' radius. Nothing, however, seems to have come of the recommendation.

Before this petition, and even in the lifetime of Queen Elizabeth, there was alarm about the growth of the suburbs; it was argued that there were too many people already; they

F

were too crowded; there were not enough provisions for so many; if the plague came back there would be a terrible mortality, and so on. Therefore orders were issued that no new buildings should be erected within three miles of the City, and that not more than one family should live in one house. Nothing could be wiser than these ordinances. But nature is not always so wise as human legislators. It is therefore credible that children went on being born; that there continued to be marrying and giving in marriage; that the population went on increasing; and, since one cannot, even in order to obey a wise law, live in the open air, this beneficent law was set at defiance; new houses were built in all the suburbs, and if a family could not afford a house to itself it just did what it had always done—took part of a house. In the face of these difficulties East London began to create itself, and riverside London not only stretched out a long arm upon the river wall, but threw out lanes and streets to the north of the wall.

Not much of Wapping survives. The London docks cut out a huge cantle of the parish; the place has since been still further curtailed by the creation of a large recreation ground of the newest type. Some of the remaining streets retain in their name the memory of the gardens and fields of the early settlements; there is Wapping Wall, Green Bank, Rose Lane, Crabtree Lane, Old Gravel Lane, Hermitage Street, Love Lane,—no London suburb is complete without a Love Lane or a Lovers' Walk,—Cinnamon Street: does this name recall the time of the wooden nutmegs?

Let me, at this point, introduce you to Raine's Charity. Did you know that in our East London, as well as in the French village, we have our Rosière? The excellent Raine, who flourished during the last century, built and endowed a school for girls who were trained for domestic service; he also left money for giving, once a year, a purse containing a hundred golden sovereigns, upon her wedding day, to a girl coming from his own school who could show four years'

The Turn of the Tide on the Lower Thames.

domestic service with unblemished character. On the occasion when I assisted at this function there was observed—I do not think that the custom has since been abolished—a quaint little ceremony. The wedding was held in the church of St. George's-in-the-East. This church, a massive structure of stone, built a hundred and fifty years ago, stands a little off a certain famous street once called Ratcliffe Highway. They have changed its name, and shamed it into better ways. When the marriage was celebrated the church was crowded with all the girls, children, and women of the quarter. This spontaneous tribute to the domestic virtues, in a place of which so many cruel things have been alleged, caused a glow in the bosom of the stranger. Indeed, it was a curious spectacle, this intense interest in the reward of the Rosière. The women crowded the seats and filled the galleries; they thronged the great stone porch; they made a lane outside for the passage of the bridal party; they whispered eagerly, without the least sign of scoffing. When the bride, in her white dress, walked through them they gasped, they trembled, the tears came into their eyes. What did they mean—those tears?

After the service the clergyman, with the vestrymen, the bridal party, and the invited guests, marched in procession from the church through the broad churchyard at the back to the vestry hall. With the procession walked the church choir in their surplices. Arrived at the vestry hall, the choir sang an anthem composed in the last century especially for this occasion. The rector of St. George's then delivered a short oration, congratulating the bride and exhorting the bridegroom; he then placed in the hands of the bridegroom an old-fashioned, long silk purse containing fifty sovereigns at each end. This done, cake and wine were passed round, and we drank to the health of the bride and her bridegroom. The bride, I remember, was a blushing, rosy maiden of two and twenty or so; it was a great day for her,—the one day of all her life,—but she carried herself with a becoming modesty; the bridegroom, a goodly youth, about the same age, was proposing, we understood, something creditable, something superior, in the profession of carter or carman. It is more than ten years ago. I hope that the gift of the incomparable Raine—the anthem said that he was incomparable—has brought good luck to this London Rosière and her bridegroom.

The church of St. George's-in-the-East stands, as I have said, beside the once infamous street called the Ratcliffe Highway. It was formerly the home of Mercantile Jack when his ship was paid off. Here, where every other house was a drinking den, where there was not the slightest attempt to preserve even a show of deference to respectability, Jack and his friends drank and sang and danced and fought. Portugal Jack and Italy Jack and Lascar Jack have always been very handy with their knives, while no one interfered, and the police could only walk about in little companies of three and four. Within these houses, these windows, these doors, their fronts stained and discolored like a drunkard's face, there lay men stark and dead after one of these affrays —the river would be their churchyard; there lay men sick unto death, with no one to look after them; and all the time, day and night, the noise of the revelry went on—for what matter a few more sick or dead? The fiddler kept it up, Jack footed it, one Jack after the other, heel and toe with folded arms, to the sailors' hornpipe; there were girls who could dance him down, there was delectable singing, and the individual thirst was like unto the thirst of Gargantua.

The street, I say, is changed; it has now assumed a countenance of respectability, though it has not yet arrived at the full rigors, so to speak, of virtue. Still the fiddle may be heard from the frequent public house; still Mercantile Jack keeps it up, heel and toe, while his money lasts; still there are harmonic evenings and festive days, but there are changes;

one may frequently, such is the degeneracy, walk down the street, now called St. George's, without seeing a single fight, without being hustled or assaulted, without coming across a man too drunk to lift himself from the kerb. It is a lively, cheerful street, with points which an artist might find picturesque; it is growing in respectability, but it is not yet by any means so clean as it might be, and there are fragrances and perfumes lingering about its open doors and courts which other parts of London will not admit within their boundaries.

There are two squares lying north of this street; in one of them is the Swedish church, where, on a Sunday morning, you may see rows of light-haired, blue-eyed mariners listening to the sermon in their own tongue. In a corner, if you look about, you may come upon the quaintest little Jewish settlement you can possibly imagine; it is an almshouse, with a synagogue and all complete; if you are lucky you will find one of the old bedesmen to show you the place. St. George's Street, also, rejoices in a large public garden; no street ever wanted one so badly; it is made out of the great churchyard, where dead sailors and dead bargemen and dead roysterers lie by the hundred thousand. And one must never forget Jamrack's. This world-wide merchant imports wild beasts; in his place—call it not shop or warehouse— you will find pumas and wildcats of all kinds, jackals, foxes, wolves, and wolverines. It is a veritable Ark of Noah.

In the very heart of Wapping stands a group of early eighteenth century buildings, with which every right-minded visitor straightway falls in love; they consist of schools and a church; to these may be added the churchyard—I suppose we may say that a churchyard is built, when it is full of tombs. This sacred area is separated from the church by the road; it is surrounded by an iron railing, and within there is a little coppice of lilac, laburnum, and other shrubs and trees which have grown up between the tombs, so that in the spring and summer the monuments become half-revealed and half-concealed; the sunshine, falling on them, quivering and shifting through the light leaves and blossoms, glorifies the memorials of these dead mariners. The schools are adorned with wooden effigies of boy and girl—stiff and formal in their ancient garb; the church is not without a quiet dignity of its own, such a dignity as I have observed in the simple meeting-house of an American town. In some unexplained manner it seems exactly the sort of church which should have been built for captains, mates, quartermasters, and bo's'uns of the mercantile marine in the days when captains wore full wigs and waistcoats down to their knees. The master boat-builder and master craftsman, in all the arts and mysteries pertaining to ships and boats, their provision and their gear, were also admitted within these holy walls. The church seems to have been built only for persons of authority; nothing under the rank of quartermaster would sit within these dignified walls. You can see the tombs of former congregations; they are solid piles of stone, signifying rank in the mercantile marine. The tombs are in the churchyard around the church, and in the churchyard on the other side of the road. As you look upon the old-fashioned church, this Georgian church, time runs back; the ancient days return: there stands in the pulpit the clergyman, in his full wig, reading his learned and doctrinal discourse in a full, rich monotone; below him sit the captains and the mates and the quartermasters, with them the master craftsman, all with wigs; the three-cornered hat is hanging on the door of the high pew; for better concentration of thought, the eyes of the honest gentlemen are closed. The ladies, however, sit upright, conscious of the Sunday best; besides, one might, in falling asleep, derange the nice balance of the "head." When the sermon is over they all walk home in neighborly conversation to the Sunday dinner and the after-dinner bottle of port. The tombs in the churchyard belong to the time when

Coming Up the Lower Thames with the Tide.

a part of Wapping was occupied by this better class, which has long since vanished, though one or two of the houses remain. Of the baser sort who crowded all the lanes I have spoken already. They did not go to church; always on Sunday the doors stood wide open to them if they would come in, but they did not accept the invitation; they stayed outside; the church received them three times—for the christening, for the wedding, for the burial; whatever their lives have been, the church receives all alike for the funeral service, and asks no questions. After this brief term of yielding to all temptations, after their sprightly course along the primrose path, they are promised, if in the coffin one can hear, a sure and certain hope.

Here are Wapping Old Stairs. Come with me through the narrow court and stand upon the stairs leading down to the river. They are now rickety old steps and deserted. Time was when the sailors landed here when they returned from a voyage; then their sweethearts ran down the steps to meet them.

> "Your Polly has never been faithless, she swears,
> Since last year we parted on Wapping Old Stairs."

And here, when Polly had spent all his money for him, Jack hugged her to his manly bosom before going aboard again. Greeting and farewell took place in the presence of a theater full of spectators. They were the watermen who lay off the stairs by dozens waiting for a fare, at the time when the Thames was the main highway of the City. The stairs were noisy and full of life. Polly herself had plenty of repartee in reply to the gentle badinage of the young watermen; her Tom had rivals among them. When he came home the welcome began with a fight with one or other of these rivals. The stairs are silent now; a boat or two, mostly without any one in it, lies despondently alongside the stairs or in the mud at low tide.

Sometimes the boats pushed off with intent to fish; the river was full of fish, though there are now none left; there were all kinds of fish that swim, including salmon; the fishery of the Thames is responsible for more rules and ordinances than any other industry of London. The boatmen were learned in the times and seasons of the fish. For instance, they could tell by the look of the river when a shoal of roach was coming up stream; at such times they took up passengers who would go a-fishing, and landed them on the sterlings—the projecting piers of London Bridge—where they stood angling for the fish all day long with rod and line.

Next to the Wapping Old Stairs is Execution Dock. This was the place where sailors were hanged and all criminals sentenced for offenses committed on the water; they were hanged at low tide on the foreshore, and they were kept hanging until three high tides had flowed over their bodies—an example and an admonition to the sailors on board the passing ships. Among the many hangings at this doleful spot is remembered one which was more remarkable than the others. It was conducted with the usual formalities; the prisoner was conveyed to the spot in a cart beside his own coffin, while the ordinary sat beside him and exhorted him. He wore the customary white nightcap and carried a prayer-book in one hand, while a nosegay was stuck in his bosom; he preserved a stolid indifference to the exhortations; he did not change color when the cart arrived, but it was remembered afterward that he glanced round him quickly; they carried him to the fatal beam and they hanged him up. Now, if you come to think of it, as the spot had to be approached by a narrow lane and by a narrow flight of steps, while the gallows stood in the mud of the foreshore, the number of guards could not have been many. On this occasion, no sooner was the man turned off than a boat's company of sailors, armed with bludgeons, appeared most unexpectedly, rushed upon the constables, knocked down the hangman, hustled the chaplain, overthrew the sheriff's officers, cut down the man, carried him off, threw him into a boat, and were away and in midstream, going down swiftly with the current before the officers understood what was going on.

When they picked themselves up they gazed stupidly at the gallows with the rope still dangling—where was the man? He was in the boat and it was already a good way down the river, and by that kind of accident which often happened at that time when the arrangements of the executive were upset, there was not a single wherry within sight or within hail.

Then the ordinary closed his book and pulled his cassock straight; the hangman sadly removed the rope, the constables looked after the vanishing boat, and there was nothing to be done but just to return home again. As for the man, that hanging was never completed and those rescuers were never discovered.

As an illustration of the solitude of this place, before its settlement under Queen Elizabeth, one observes that there was a field called Hangman's Acre, situated more than a quarter of a mile from the river, where in the year 1440 certain murderers and pirates were hanged in chains upon a gallows set on rising ground, so that they should be seen by the sailors in the ships going up and down the river. There was not therefore at that time a single house to obstruct this admonitory spectacle.

The "hamlet" of Shadwell is only a continuation of St. George's or Ratcliffe Highway; its churchyard is converted into a lovely garden, one of the many gardens which were once burial grounds; the people sit about in the shade or in the sun; along the south wall is a terrace commanding a cheerful view of the London docks, with their shipping. There is a fish-market here, the only public institution of Shadwell; there are old houses, which we may look at and

Off Shadwell.

perhaps represent, but there is little about its people that distinguishes them from the folk on either hand.

In the year 1671 the church was built; Shadwell was already a place with a large population, and the church was built in order to minister to their spiritual wants. What could be better? But you shall learn from one example how the best intentions were frustrated and how the riverside folk were suffered to go from bad to worse, despite the creation of the parish and the erection of the church. The first rector was a nephew of that great divine and philosopher, Bishop Butler. He was so much delighted with the prospect of living and working among this rude and ignorant folk, he was so filled and penetrated with the spirit of humanity and the principles of his religion, that his first sermon was on the text, "Woe is me that I sojourn in Mesech, that I dwell in the tents of Kedar!" This good man, however, received permission from the bishop to live in Norfolk Street, Strand, about three miles from his church. And so, with a nonresident clergy, with no schools, with no restraints of example or precept, with little interference from the law, what wonder if the people reeled blindly down the slopes that lead to death and destruction?

The name of Ratcliffe or Redcliff marks a spot where the low cliff which formerly rose up from the marsh curved southward for a space and then receded. It is a "hamlet" which at first offers little to interest or to instruct. It consists of mean and dingy streets—there is not a single street which is not mean and dirty; none of the houses are old; none are picturesque in the least; they are rickety, dirty, shabby, without one redeeming feature; there is a church, but it is not stately like St. George's-in-the-East, nor venerable like that of Stepney; it is unlovely; there are "stairs" to the river and they are rickety; there are warehouses which contain nothing and are tumbling down; there are public houses which do not pretend to be bright and attractive— low-browed, dirty dens, which reek of bad beer and bad gin. Yet the place, when you linger in it and talk about it to the clergy and the ladies who work for it, is full of interest. For it is a quarter entirely occupied by the hand-to-mouth laborer; the people live in tenements; it is thought luxury to have two rooms; there are eight thousand of them, three quarters being Irish; in the whole parish there is not a single person of what we call respectability, except two or three clergymen and half a dozen ladies; there are no good shops, there are no doctors or lawyers, there is not even a newsvender, for nobody in Ratcliffe reads a newspaper. But the place swarms with humanity; the children play by thousands in the gutters: and on the door-steps the wives and mothers sit all day long and in all weathers, carrying on a perpetual parliament of grievance. Here once—I know not when—stood Ratcliffe Cross, and the site of the cross—removed, I know not when—was one of the spots where, in 1837, Queen Victoria was proclaimed. Why the young Queen should have been proclaimed at Ratcliffe Cross I have never been able to discover. I have asked the question of many persons and many books, but I can find no answer. The oldest inhabitant knows nothing about it; none of the books can tell me if the accession of the Queen's predecessors was also proclaimed by ancient custom at Ratcliffe Cross. Unfortunately, it is now extremely difficult to find persons who remember the accession of the Queen, not to speak of that of William IV.

Ratcliffe has other historical memories. Here stood the hall of the Shipwrights' Company. This was a very ancient body; it existed as the Fraternity of St. Simon and St. Jude from time immemorial; the Shipwrights' Company formerly had docks and building yards on the south of the Thames; then they moved their hall to this place on the north bank, and seem to have given up their building yards.

Here was a school, founded and maintained by the Coopers' Company, where Lancelot Andrewes, the learned bishop, was educated.

There is another historical note concerning Ratcliffe. It belongs to the year 1553. It was in that year that Admiral

Ratcliffe-Cross Stairs.

Sir Hugh Willoughby embarked on that voyage of discovery from which he was destined never to return. He was sent out on a roving commission to "discover regions, dominions, islands, and places unknown," and he began by an attempt to discover the northeast passage. Remember that geographers knew nothing in those days of the extent of Siberia. Willoughby had three ships; their tonnage was, respectively, 160 tons, 120, and 90. His crews consisted of 50, 35, and 27 men, respectively. With such tiny craft they put forth boldly to brave unknown Arctic seas. It was from Ratcliffe Stairs that Willoughby went on board on May 10, 1553. Half a mile down the river the flotilla passed Greenwich Palace, where the young King, Edward VI, was residing. It was within a few weeks of his death; consumption had laid him low. When the ships passed the palace they "dressed" with flags and streamers, they fired cannons of salute, they blew their trumpets. The young King was brought out to see them pass. It was his last appearance in public; on July 6th he was dead. As for Willoughby, he parted with one of his ships, and after being tossed about off the coast of Lapland he resolved to winter at the mouth of the river Argina. Here, in the following spring, he was found with his companions, all dead and frozen. A strange story of English enterprise to be connected with these forlorn and ramshackle stairs.

Here is another story about Ratcliffe. In a street by the river, beside the stairs, are two or three big ruinous warehouses, mostly deserted. One of these has a double front, the left side representing a private house, the right a warehouse. What was stored in the warehouse I know not; the whole riverside is lined with warehouses and stores. The place is now for a third time deserted, and stands with broken windows. It has been deserted, so far as the original purpose was concerned, for many years. Some thirty years ago a young medical man began to live and to practise in Ratcliffe. He became presently aware that the death-rate among the children was frightful. There was no hospital nearer than the London Hospital in the Whitechapel Road, and that was two miles away; there were no nurses to be obtained and there were no appliances; if a child was taken ill it had to lie in the one room occupied by the whole family, without ventilation, without proper food, without skilled care, without medicines. Therefore in most cases of illness the child died.

He found this rickety old warehouse empty; he thought that he would do what he could, being quite a poor man, to make a hospital for children. He did so; with his slender funds he got a few beds and quickly filled them. He was physician, surgeon, dispenser, druggist, everything; his wife was nurse and everything else. Together these two devoted people started their hospital. Well, it grew; it became known; money began to come in; other doctors and nurses were taken on; all the rooms, there were many, were filled; the children began to recover. Presently the house became so prosperous that it was resolved to build a separate Children's Hospital, which was done, and you may see it—a noble place. But for the founder this crown of his labors came too late. The work killed him before the new hospital was completed; one of the wards, the Heckford Ward, is named after the man who gave all his strength, all his mind, all his knowledge, all his thoughts; who gave his life and his death; who gave himself, wholly and ungrudgingly, to the children. His patients recovered, but their physician died. He gave his own life to stay the hand of death.

Then the house stood empty for a time; it was presently taken over by the vicar of the parish and made into a playhouse for the little children in the winter after school hours, from four to seven; I have told you how the children swarm in the Ratcliffe streets. After seven the house was converted into a club for the rough riverside lads, where they could box and play single stick and subdue the devil in them, and so presently could sit down and play games and listen to reading and keep out of mischief. But the house is condemned; it is really too ramshackle; it is empty again, and is now to be pulled down.

There is still another story whose scene is laid at Ratcliffe. There is a house beside the church which is now the vicarage. It is a square, solid house, built about the end of the seventeenth century. It is remarkable for a dining-room whose walls are painted with Italian landscapes. The story is that there lived here, early in the eighteenth century, a merchant who rode into London every day, leaving his only daughter behind. He desired to decorate his house with wall-paintings, and engaged a young Italian to stay in the house and to paint all day. Presently he made the not unusual discovery that the Italian and his daughter had fallen in love with each other. He knew what was due to his position as a City merchant, and did what was proper for the occasion—that is to say, he ordered the young man to get out of the house in half an hour. The artist obeyed, so far as to mount the stairs to his own room. Here, however, he stopped, and when the angry parent climbed the stairs after the expiration of the half hour to know why he was not gone, he found the young lover, dead, hanging to the canopy of the bed. His ghost was long believed to haunt the house, and was only finally laid, after troops of servants had fled shrieking, when the wife of the vicar sat up all night by herself in the haunted chamber, and testified that she had neither seen nor heard anything, and was quite willing to sleep in the room. That disgusted the ghost, who went away of his own accord. I wish I could show you one room in the house. It was the old powdering-room. When your wig had been properly curled and combed you threw a towel or dressing-gown over your shoulders and sat in this little room, with your back to the door. Now, the door had a sliding panel, and the barber on the other side was provided with the instrument which blew the white powder through the panel upon the wig. The operation finished, you arose, slipped off the dressing-gown and descended to your coach with all the dignity of a gold-laced hat, a wig white as the driven snow, lace ruffles, a lace tie, and a black velvet coat—if you were a merchant—with gold buttons, and white silk stockings. A beautiful time it was for those who could afford the dignity and the splendor which made it beautiful. For those who could not— Humph! Not quite so beautiful a time.

After Ratcliffe we pass into Limehouse. It was at Limehouse Hole that Rogue Riderhood lived.

The place is more marine than Wapping; the public houses have a look, an air, a something that suggests the sea; the shops are conducted for the wants of the merchantmen; the houses are old and picturesquely dirty; the streets are narrow; one may walk about these streets for a whole afternoon, and find something to observe in every one, either a shop full of queer things or a public house full of strange men, or a house that speaks of other days—of crimps, for instance, and of press gangs, and of encounters in the streets; there are ancient docks used for the repair of wooden sailing ships; there are places where they build barges; a little inland you may see the famous church of Limehouse, with its lofty steeple; it was only built in 1730. Before that time there was no church at Limehouse; since that time nobody has gone to church at Limehouse, speaking of the true natives, the riverside folk, not of those who dwell respectably in the West India Dock Road. It is, however, doubtless a great advantage and benefit to a sea-going population to have a churchyard to be buried in.

At Limehouse the river suddenly bends to the south, and then again to the north, making a loop within which lies a peninsula. This is a very curious place. It occupies an area of a mile and a half from north to south, and about

Limehouse Basin and Church.

THE POOL AND THE RIVERSIDE 91

a mile from east to west. The place was formerly a dead level, lower than the river at high tide, and therefore a broad tidal marsh; it was, in fact, part of the vast marsh of which I have already spoken, now reclaimed, lying along the north bank of the river. This marsh was dotted over with little eyots or islets, sometimes swept away by the tide, then forming again, composed of rushes, living and dead, the rank grasses of the marsh, and sticks and string and leaves carried among the reeds to form a convenient and secure place where the wild birds could make their nests. When the river wall was built the marsh became a broad field of rich pasture, in which sheep were believed to fatten better than in any other part of England. Until recently it had no inhabitants; probably the air at night was malarious, and the sheep wanted no one to look after them; the river wall was adorned with half a dozen windmills; dead men, hanging in chains, preached silent sermons by their dolorous example to the sailors of the passing craft; there was instituted at some time or other before the seventeenth century a ferry between its southern point and Greenwich, a road to meet the ferry running north through the island. Pepys crossed once by this ferry in order to attend a wedding. It was in the plague year, when one would have thought weddings were not common and wedding festivities dangerous things. But there was still marrying and giving in marriage. He was with Sir George and Lady Carteret; they got across from Deptford in a boat, but found that their coach, which ought to have met them, had not come over by ferry, the tide having fallen too low. "I being in my new colored silk suit and coat trimmed with gold buttons and gold broad-lace round my hands, very rich and fine, . . . so we were fain to stay there in the unlucky Isle of Dogs, in a chill place, the morning cool, the wind fresh, to our great discontent." Why does he call the Isle of Dogs unlucky?

In the middle of the island stood, all by itself, a little

chapel. Nothing is known about its origin. I am inclined to think that, like many other chapels built on this river wall, on town walls, and on bridges, it was intended to protect the wall by prayers and masses, sung or said "with intention." We have already found a hermitage by, or on, the wall at Wapping, another place of prayer for the maintenance of this important work.

Why this peninsula was called the Isle of Dogs no one knows. One learned antiquary says that the King kept his hounds there when he stayed at Greenwich Palace. Perhaps. But the antiquary produces no proof that the royal kennels were ever set up here, and the person who trusts a little to common sense asks why the King should have sent his hounds across a broad and rapid river by a dangerous ferry when he had the whole of Greenwich Park and Black Heath in which to build his kennels. "Drowned dogs," suggests another, but doubtfully. No. I have never heard of drowned dogs being washed ashore in any number, either here or elsewhere. Drowned dogs, it is certain, were never an appreciable factor in the flotsam and jetsam of the Thames. "Not the Isle of Dogs," says another, "but the Isle of Ducks. Ducks, you see, from the wild ducks which formerly—" No; when the wall was built, which was probably in the Roman time, the wild ducks vanished, and as no tradition of any kind can be traced among the Saxons concerning the Roman occupation they never heard of these ducks. For my own part, I have no suggestion to offer, except a vague suspicion that, as Pepys thought, there was a tradition of bad luck attaching in some form to the place, which was named accordingly. If a man on the downward path is said to be going to the dogs, a place considered as unlucky might very well have been called the Isle of Dogs. Now a level marsh without any inhabitants and adorned by gibbets and dangling dead bodies would certainly not be considered a lucky place. You must not expect anything in the place of the least

THE POOL AND THE RIVERSIDE 93

antiquity. Yet a walk round the Isle of Dogs is full of interest. To begin with, the streets are wide and clean; the houses are all small, built for working-men; there are no houses of the better sort at all; the children swarm, and are healthy, well fed, and rosy; the shops are chiefly those of

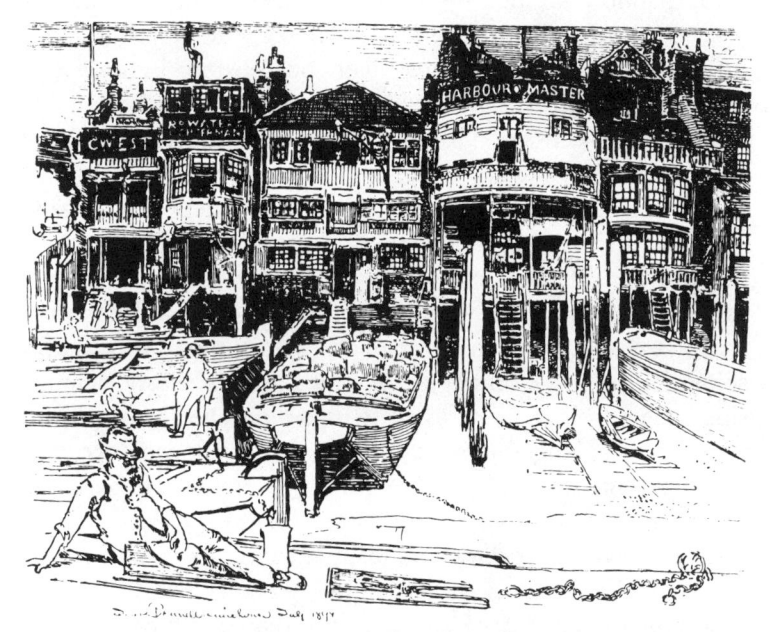

The Thames Side at Limehouse.

provisions and cheap clothing. All round the shore there runs an unbroken succession of factories. These factories support the thousands of working-men who form the population of the Isle of Dogs. All kinds of things are made, stored, received, and distributed in the factories of this industrial island; many of them are things which require to be carried on outside a crowded town, such as oil storage, oil, paint, color, and varnish, works; disinfectant fluid works, boiler-makers, lubricating-oil works; there are foundries of brass and iron, lead-smelting works, copper-depositing works, antimony and gold-ore works. All kinds of things wanted for ships are made here—cisterns and tanks, casks, steering-gear, tarpaulin, wire rope, sails, oars, blocks, and masts; there are yards for building ships, barges, and boats.

Of public buildings there are few: two churches and one or two chapels. There are Board-schools and church schools; there are no places of amusement, but posters indicate that theaters and music-halls are within reach. On the south of the island the London County Council has erected a most lovely garden. It is four or five acres in extent; there are lawns, trees, and flower-beds; there is a stately terrace running along the river; there are seats dotted about, and on certain evenings in the summer a band plays. Above all, there is the view across the river. All day long that pageant, of which we have already spoken, goes up and down, never ending; the ships follow each other—great ships, small ships, splendid ships, mean ships; the noisy little tugs plow their way, pulling after them a long string of lighters heavily laden; the children, peeping through the iron railings, know all the ships, where they come from and to what "line" they belong. Beyond the river is Greenwich Hospital, once a splendid monument of the nation's gratitude to her old sailors, now a shameful monument of the nation's thanklessness. Would any other country so trample upon sentiment as to take away their hospital from the old sailors, to whom it belonged and to whom it had been given? The old pensioners are gone, and the people have lost the education in patriotism which the sight and discourse of these veterans once afforded them.

It is needless to say that there is not a single book-shop in the Isle of Dogs; we do not expect a book-shop anywhere in East London; there are also very few news-agents. I saw one, the whole of whose window was tastefully decorated with pictures from the "Illustrated Police Budget." These illustrations are blood-curdling: a lady bites another lady, such is the extremity of her wrath; a burglar enters a bedroom at night; a man with a revolver shows what revenge and jealousy can dare and do, and so on. I am sure that the people read other things; the "Police Budget" is not their only paper, but I confess that this was the only evidence of their favorite reading which I was able to discover when I was last on the island. There are no slums, I believe, on the Isle of Dogs. I have never seen any Hooligans, Larrikins, or any of that tribe—perhaps because they were all engaged in work, the harder the better. You will not see any drunken men, as a rule, nor any beggars, nor any signs of misery. We may conclude that the Isle of Dogs contains an industrious and prosperous population; the air that they breathe, when the fresh breeze that comes up with the tide has dropped, is perhaps too heavily charged with the varied fragrance of the multitudinous works, with the noise of various industries: as for the hammering of hammers, the grinding and blowing and whirring of engines, to these one gets accustomed. It is a place where one might deliberately choose to be born, because, apart from the general well-being of the people and the healthfulness of the air, there is a spirit of enterprise imbibed by every boy who grows up in this admirable island. It is engendered by the universal presence of the sailor and the ship; wherever the sailor and the ship are found there springs up naturally in every child the spirit of adventure.

A large part of the island is occupied by docks—the West India docks, the Blackwall Basin, and the Millwall Dock. We need not enter into the statistics of the tonnage and the trade; it is sufficient to remember that the docks are always receiving ships, and that the sailors are always getting leave to go ashore, and that some of them have their wives and families living in the Isle of Dogs. That would be in itself sufficient to give this suburb a marine flavor; but think what it means for a boy to live in a place where at every point his eyes rest upon a forest of masts, where he is always watching the great ships as they work out of dock or creep slowly in; think what it means when, in addition to living beside these great receiving docks, he can look through doors half open and see the old-fashioned repairing dock, with the wooden sailing ship shored up and the men working at her ribs, while her battered old figure-head and her bowsprit stick out over the wall of the dock and over the street itself. The Tritons and the Oceanides, the spirits of the rolling sea, open their arms with invitation to such a boy. "Come," they say, "thou too shalt be a sailor, it is thy happy fate; come with a joyful heart; we know the place, deep down among the tiny shells of ocean, where thou shalt lie, but not till after many years. Come. It is the sweetest life of any; there is no care or cark for money; there is no struggle on the waves for casual work and for bare food; no foul diseases lurk on the broad Atlantic; the wind of the sea is pure and healthy, the fo'c'sle is cheerful, and the wage is good." And so he goes, this favorite of fortune.

For some strange reason the gates of the docks are always bright and green in spring and summer with trees and Virginia creepers, which are planted at the entrance and grow over the lodge. Within, flower-beds are visible. Outside, the cottages for the dock people also have bright and pleasant little front gardens. To the forest of masts, to the bowsprit sticking out over the street, to the ships that are warped in and out the dock, add the pleasing touch of the trees and flowers and the creepers before we leave the Isle of Dogs—that "unlucky" isle, as Pepys called it.

The last of the East London riverside hamlets is Blackwall. Where Blackwall begins no one knows. Poplar Station is in the middle of the place, included in the map within the letters which spell Blackwall. And where are the houses of Blackwall? It is covered entirely with docks. There are

Greenwich Hospital.

THE POOL AND THE RIVERSIDE

the East India docks and the Poplar docks and the basin. There are also half a dozen of the little old repairing docks left, and there is a railway station with a terrace looking out upon the river; there is a street running east, and another running north. Both streets are stopped by Bow Creek; the aspect of both causes the visitor to glance nervously about him for a protecting policeman. And here, as regards the riverside, we may stop. Beyond Bow Creek we are outside the limits of London. There follow many more former hamlets—West Ham, East Ham, Canning Town, Silverton, and others—now towns. These places, for us, must remain names.

IV

THE WALL

IV

THE WALL

I DO not mean the old wall of London, that which was built by the Romans, was rebuilt by Alfred, was repaired and maintained at great cost until the sixteenth century, when it began to be neglected, as it was no longer of any use in the defense of the City. For two hundred years more the gates still stood, but the wall was pulled down and built upon, no one interfering. That wall is gone, save for fragments here and there. I speak of another wall, and one of even greater importance.

No one knows when this other wall was first built. It was so early that all record of its building has been lost. It is the wall by which the low-lying marshes of the Thames, once overflowed by every high tide, were protected from the river and converted into pastures and meadow-land and plow-land. It is the wall which runs all along the north bank of the river and is carried round the marshy Essex shores and round those Essex islands which were once broad expanses of mud at low tide, and at high tide shallow and useless stretches of water. It protects also the south bank wherever the marsh prevails. It has been a work of the highest importance, to London first, and to the country next. It has converted a vast malarious belt of land into a fertile country, and it has made East London possible, because a great part of East London is built upon the reclaimed marsh, now drained and dry. In order to understand what the wall means, what it is, what it has done, and what it is doing, we must get beyond the houses and consider it as it runs along the riverside, with fields on the left hand and the flowing water many feet higher than the fields on the right.

In order to get at the wall, then, we must take the train to Barking, about eight miles from London Bridge. This ancient village, once the seat of a rich nunnery, some remains of which you may still see there, is on the little river Roding; we walk down its banks to its confluence with the Thames. There, after suffering a while from the fumes of certain chemical works, we find ourselves on the wall, with no houses before us; we leave the works behind us, and we step out upon the most curious walk that one may find within the four seas that encompass our island.

No one ever walks upon this wall; once beyond the chemical works we are in the most lonely spot in the whole of England; no one is curious about it; no one seems to know that this remarkable construction, extending for about a hundred and fifty miles, even exists; you will see no one in the meadows that lie protected by the wall; you may walk mile after mile along it in a solitude most strange and most mysterious. Even the steamer which works her noisy way up the broad river, even the barge with its brown sail, crawling slowly up the stream with the flowing tide, does not destroy the sense of silence or that of solitude. We seem not to hear the screw of the steamer or even the scream of the siren; overhead the lark sings; there are no other birds visible about the treeless fields; the tinkle of a sheep-bell reminds one of Dartmoor and its silent hillsides.

Presently there falls upon the pilgrim a strange feeling of mystery. The wall belongs to all the centuries which have known London; it is a part of the dead past; it speaks to him of things that have been; it reminds him of the Vikings and the Danes when they came sweeping up the river in their long, light ships, the shields hanging outside, the fair-haired, blue-eyed fighting men thirsting for the joy of battle; they are on their way to besiege London; they will pull down part of the bridge, but they will not take the City. The fresh breeze that follows with the flood reminds him of the pageant and procession, the splendid pageant, the never-ending procession, of the trade which is the strength and the pride and the wealth of London, which has been passing before this wall for all these centuries, and always, as it passes now, unseen and unregarded, because no one ever stands upon the wall to see it.

A strange, ghostly place. If one were to tell of a murder, this would be a fitting place for the crime. Perhaps, however, it might be difficult to persuade his victim to accompany him. The murderer would choose the time between the passing of two ships; no one could possibly see him; he would conduct his victim along the wall, conversing pleasantly, till the favorable moment arrived. The deed accomplished, he would leave the wall and strike across the fields till he found a path leading to the haunts of man. Any secret or forbidden thing might be conveniently transacted on the wall; it would be a perfectly safe place for the conjuration of conspirators and the concoction of their plans, or it would be a place to hide a stolen treasure, or a place where a hunted man could find refuge.

Let us stand still for a moment and look around. The wall is about fifteen feet high; at the base it is perhaps thirty feet wide; the sides slope toward the path on the top, which is about seven feet across; the outside is faced with stone; the inside is turfed. Looking south the river runs at our feet, the broad and noble river which carries to the port of London treasures from the uttermost ends of the earth and sends out other treasures in exchange. There are many rivers in the world which are longer and broader,—for instance, the Danube and the Rhine, even the Oronoco and the Amazon,—but if we consider the country through which the river flows, the wealth which it creates, the wealth which it distributes, the long history of the Thames, then, surely, it is the greatest of all rivers. As we stand over it we mark how its waters are stirred into little waves by the fresh breeze which never fails with the flood of the tide; how the sun lights up the current rolling upward in full stream, so that we think of strong manhood resolved and purposed; it is not for nothing that the tide rolls up the stream. Then we mark the ships that pass, ships of all kinds, great and small; the ships and the barges, the fishing smacks and the coasters, some that sail and some that steam; the heavy timber ship from the Baltic, the Newcastle collier, the huge liner; they pass in succession along the broad highway, one after the other. This splendid pageant of London trade is daily offered for the admiration of those upon the wall. But it is a procession with no spectators; day after day it passes unregarded, for no one walks upon the wall. And if a stray traveler stands to look on, the pageant presently becomes a thing of the imagination, a dream, an effect of animated photographs.

On the land side lie the fields which have been rescued from this tidal flow; they are obviously below the level of the river; one understands, looking across them, how the river ran of old over these flats, making vast lagoons at high tide. It is useful to see the fact recorded in a book or on a map; but here one sees that it really must have been so. Gradually, as one passes along the wall and looks landward, the history of the reclamation of the marsh unfolds itself; we see in places, here and there, low mounds, which are lines of former embankments; these are not all parallel with the river; they are thrust forward, protected by banks at the side, small pieces rescued by some dead and gone farmer, who was rewarded by having as his own, with no rent to pay, the land he had snatched from the tide. Perhaps it was long before rent was thought of; perhaps it was easier to build the bank and to take a slip of the foreshore and the marsh, with its black and fertile soil, than it was to cut down the trees in the forest and to clear the land; perhaps these embankments were constructed by the lake dwellers, who made their round huts upon piles driven into the mud, and after many thousands of years made the discovery that it was better to be dry than wet, and better to have no marsh fevers to face than to grow inured to them.

When was this wall built? How long has it been standing? Is it the first original wall? Have there been rebuildings? Learned antiquaries have proved that long before the advent of the Romans the south of Britain was occupied by people who had learned such civilization as Gauls had to teach them. This was no small advance, as you would acknowledge if you looked into the subject; they knew many arts; they already had many wants; they had arrived at a certain standard of comfort; they carried on an extensive trade.

How long ago? It is quite impossible to answer that question. But there are other facts ascertained. Let us sum them up in order.

1. South Britain, at least, and probably the Midland as well, had the same religion, the same arts, the same customs, the same forms of society, as Gaul.

2. There was an extensive trade between Britain and Gaul —of what antiquity no one knows.

3. When we first hear of London it was a place of resort for many foreign merchants.

4. Tessellated pavements of Roman date have been found in Southwark at a level lower than that of the river.

5. Tacitus made Galgacus, the British leader, indignant because the Britons were compelled by the Romans to expend their strength and labor on fencing off woods and marshes.

6. Roman buildings are found behind the wall in Essex. To this point I will return immediately.

7. No settlement or building or cultivation whatever was

possible beside the river anywhere near London until the wall had been built.

8. Are we to believe that a city possessing a large trade, attracting many foreign merchants, would have continued to stand in the midst of a vast malarious swamp?

9. Indications have been found of an older wall, consisting of trunks of trees laid beside each other, the interstices crammed with small branches. Such a rude wall might be effective in keeping back the great body of water.

10. In order to arrive at the civilization represented by a large foreign trade and a trading city there must have been many years of communication and intercourse. In fact, I see no reason why London should not have existed as a trading-place for centuries after Thorney was practically deserted, having ferries instead of a bridge, and centuries before the coming of the Romans.

These considerations show the conclusion to which I have arrived. For centuries there had been a constant intercourse between the Gauls and the southern Britons; trading centers had been established, notably in Thorney Island, at Southampton, at Lymne, which was afterward an important Roman station, and at Dover. When the ships began to sail up the Thames the superior position of London was discovered, and that port quickly took over the greater part of the trade by the Thorney route. When London grew, it became important to reclaim the malarious marsh and the wasted miles of mud. Some kind of embankment, perhaps that old kind with trunks of trees, was constructed. At first they put up the wall on the opposite side, which the Saxons afterward called the South Work (Southwark), meaning the river wall and not a wall of fortification; then they pushed out branches on the north side and they carried the wall gradually, not all at once, but taking years, even centuries, over the work, down the Thames, along the Essex shores and round the mud islands, but the last not till modern times.

At the end of the Essex wall there is an instructive place at which to consider its probable date.

It is a very lovely and deserted place, about a mile and a half from a picturesque little village, five or six miles from a railway station, called Bradwell—I suppose the meaning of the name is the broad wall. When the visitor reaches the seashore he finds the wall running along, a fine and massive earthwork; but behind the wall, and evidently built after the wall, there are the earthworks of a Roman fortress; you can still trace the ramparts after all these years though the interior is now plowed up; this was one of the forts by means of which the count of the Saxon shore (Comes littoris Saxonici) kept the country safe from the pirates, always on the watch for the chance of a descent; his ships patrolled the narrow seas, but always, up the creeks and rivers, all the way from Ostend to Norway, lay the pirate,—Saxon, Dane, Viking,—watching, waiting, ready to cross over if those police ships relaxed their watchfulness, ready to harry and to murder. You may stand on the wall, where the Roman sentinel kept watch; you may strain your eyes for a sight of the pirate fleet, fifty ships strong and every ship stout, clinker built, sixty feet long and carrying a hundred men. As soon as the Romans took their ships away they did come, and they came to stay, and as soon as the Saxons forgot their old science of navigation the Danes came, and after the Danes, or with them, the men of Norway. Long after this Roman fortress had been deserted and forgotten, so that to the people it was nothing more than a collection of mounds round which clung some vague tradition of terror, a person, whose very name is now unknown, built here a chapel dedicated to St. Peter; the chapel, still called St. Peter's on the Wall, is now a barn. Ruined chapel, ruined fortress, both stand beside the wall, which still fulfils its purpose and keeps out the waters from the lowlands within.

Why do I mention this chapel? What has it to do with

East London? Well, consider two or three facts in connection with this chapel. If you walk along the wall you presently come to a little village church; it is called the Church of West Thurrock; the church, like that old chapel of St. Peter, stands beside, or on, the wall; it is a venerable church; it has its venerable churchyard; it is filled with the graves of rustics brought here to lie in peace for a thousand years and more. And there is no village, or hamlet, or farm, or anything within sight. It was built beside the wall. Again, they built two churches at least, beside, or on, the wall of London City, not to speak of the churches built at five gates of the City; they built a hermitage beside the wall at Wapping; another by the city wall at Aldgate; on London Bridge they built a chapel; on the wall in Essex, as we have seen, they built a chapel. I see in all these churches and chapels built beside, or on, a wall, so many chapels erected for prayers for the preservation of the wall; at West Thurrock the people of the farmhouses made the chapel their parish church, and so it has continued to the present day. But it was originally a chapel on the wall, intended to consecrate and protect the wall. Perhaps there are others along the wall, but I do not know of any.

I have said that it is possible that the wall stands upon the site of earlier attempts to rescue the land and to keep out the water. For instance, when the excavations were made for the foundation of the new London Bridge, three separate sets of piles for rescuing more and more of the foreshore were laid bare, and lower down the river, as I have said, the workmen found, in repairing the wall, a very curious arrangement of trunks of trees laid one upon the other, with branches and brushwood between, evidently part of a wooden work meant for a dam or tidal wall.

The maintenance of the wall has always been a costly business; the tides find out the weak places, and bore into them and behind them like a gimlet that grows every day larger and longer and more powerful. For instance, there was a flourishing monastery near the junction of the Lea with the Thames; it was called the House of Stratford Langthorne. One morning the brethren woke to find that the river wall had given way and that their pastures and meadows, their cornlands and their gardens were all three feet deep in water. They had to get away as fast as they could and to remain in a much smaller and more uncomfortable cell, on higher ground, until the wall could be patched up again. In the fifteenth century the pious ladies of Barking Nunnery made a similar discovery; their portion of the river wall had broken down. They had no funds for its repair. Then King Richard, the third of that name, came to their assistance. This pious monarch had got through with most of his enemies and nearly all his relations, and was just then going off to settle matters with his cousin, Henry the Welshman, when this misfortune to the Barking nuns happened.

Fifty years later the Plumstead marshes were "drowned" by the breaking of the wall. In 1690 the Grays Marsh, lower down the river, was overflowed by the same accident; in 1707 the wall gave way at a place called Dagenham; it took nearly twenty years to repair the wall, which was carried away time after time; the receding tide carried out into the bed of the river so much earth that a bank was formed in mid-channel, and it seemed as if the river would be choked. At last, however, it was found possible to construct a wall which would stand the highest tide. If we walk along this part of the wall we observe a large black pool of water; this was left behind when the wall shut out the river; the lake still remains and is full of fish, and on Sundays it is surrounded by anglers, who stand all day long intent upon expectations which are seldom rewarded. Out of this lake and its fishing originated the ministerial white-bait dinner. It began when the occupant of a house beside this lake invited William Pitt to dine with him in order to taste the eels of the pond and the white-bait of the river. Pitt brought other members of the Cabinet, the dinner became a yearly institution, the place was presently transferred from Dagenham to Greenwich, and the ministerial white-bait dinner was held every year, in June or July, until ten or twelve years ago, when the pleasant institution was stopped.

To return to the date of the wall. We have seen that nobody knows when it was put up, that it must have been there in some form or other for a very long time. It is tolerably certain that the wall was either built by the Romans or that it existed before their time. My own belief is, as I have stated, that it was put up here and there as occasion or necessity served, that some of the land was rescued strip by strip, each time by a new wall advanced before the others. Embankments, mounds, and traces of a more ancient wall can be observed, as I have said, at many points; it is worthy of note that in the county of Lincoln, where there is also the necessity of a sea-wall, there are two, one standing at a distance of half a mile in advance of the other. And I think that this process of rescuing the land has gone on at intervals to the present day. Even now there are broad stretches of mud along the Essex shore which might be reclaimed; at the present moment there are projects afloat for reclaiming the whole of the Wash, but the conditions of agriculture in England are no longer such as to encourage any attempts to add more acres to estates which at present seem unable to pay either landlord or farmer.

I have said enough, however, to show that this earthwork, so much neglected and so little known, is really a most important structure; that it has made East London possible, and London itself healthy, while it has converted miles and miles of barren swamp into smiling meadows and fertile farms.

V

THE FACTORY GIRL

V

THE FACTORY GIRL

EAST LONDON—one cannot repeat it too often—is a city of working bees. As we linger and loiter among the streets multitudinous, we hear, as from a hive, the low, contented murmur of continuous and patient work. There are two millions of working-people in this city. The children work at school; the girls and boys, and the men and women, work in factory, in shop, and at home, in dock and in wharf and in warehouse; all day long and all the year round, these millions work. They are clerks, accountants, managers, foremen, engineers, stokers, porters, stevedores, dockers, smiths, craftsmen of all kinds. They are girls who make things, girls who sew things, girls who sell things. There are among them many poor, driven, sweated creatures, and the sweaters themselves are poor, driven, sweated creatures, for sweating once begun is handed on from one to the other as carefully and as religiously as any holy lamp of learning. They work from early morning till welcome evening. The music of this murmur, rightly understood, is like the soft and distant singing of a hymn of praise. For the curse of labor has been misunderstood; without work man would be even as the beasts of the field. It is the necessity of work that makes him human; of necessity he devises and discovers and invents, because he would die if he did not work; and because he has to subdue the animal within him. The animal is solitary; the man must be gregarious. He must make a friend of his brother, he must obey the stronger, he must make laws, he must fight with nature, and compel her to give up her secrets. It is only by means of work that man can rise; it is his ladder; in the sweat of his face he eats his bread—yea, the bread of life. It is not with any pity that we should listen to this murmur. It should be with pure contentment and gratitude, for the murmur, though it speaks partly of the whirr of ten thousand wheels and partly of those who stand and serve those wheels, speaks also of this blessed quality of work, that it enables men to use the body for the sake of the soul. Man must work.

Imagine, if you can, what would follow if you held up your hand and said: "Listen, all. There will be no more work. You may stop the engines, or they may run down of their own accord. You may take off your aprons and wash your hands. You may all sit down for the rest of your lives. Your food will be waiting for you when you want it. Eat, drink, and be happy if you can." If they can! But can they, with nothing to do—no work to do, only, like the sheep in the field, to browse, or, like the wolves of the forest, to rend and tear and slay?

If you can use your eyes as well as your ears, look about you. It is really like looking at a hive of bees, is it not? There are thousands of them, and they are all alike; they are all doing the same thing; they are all living the same lives; they wake and work and rest and sleep, and so life passes by. If you look more closely you will observe differences. No two human creatures, to begin with, are alike in face. More closely still, and you will discover that in the greatest crowd, where the people are, like sheep in a fold, huddled together, every one is as much for himself—there is as much individuality here—as in the places where every one stands by himself and has room to move in and a choice to make.

Let us take a single creature out of these millions. Perhaps if we learn how one lives, how one regards the world,

Wade Street, Limehouse.

we may understand, in some degree, this agitated, confused, restless, incoherent, inarticulate mass.

I introduce you to a baby. Her name is Liz. She has as yet but a few days of life behind her. She is hardly conscious of hunger, cold, or uneasiness, or any of the things with which life first makes its beginning apparent to the half-awakened brain. She opens eyes that understand nothing—neither form, nor distance, nor color, nor any differences; she sees men, like trees, walking. When she is hungry she wails; when she is not hungry she sleeps. We will leave the child with her mother, and we will stand aside and watch while the springs and summers pass, and while she grows from an infant to a child, a girl, a woman.

The room where the baby lies is a first-floor front, in a house of four rooms and a ruinous garret, belonging to a street which is occupied, like all the streets in this quarter, wholly by the people of the lower working-class. This is London Street, Ratcliffe. It is a real street, with a real name, and it is in a way typical of East London of the lower kind. The aristocracy of labor, the foremen and engineers of shipyards and works, live about Stepney Church, half a mile to the north. Their streets are well kept, their doorsteps are white, their windows are clean, there are things displayed in the front windows of their houses. Here you will see a big Bible, here a rosewood desk, here a vase full of artificial flowers, here a bird-cage with foreign birds,— Avvadavats, Bengalees, love-birds, or a canary,—here a glass case containing coral or "Venus's fingers" from the Philippines, here something from India carved in fragrant wood, here a piece of brasswork from Benares. There is always something to show the position and superiority of the tenant. It is the distinctive mark of the lower grades of labor that they have none of these ornaments. Indeed, if by any chance such possessions fell in their way they would next week be in the custody of the pawnbroker; they would "go in."

We are, then, in a first-floor front. Look out of the window upon the street below: meanwhile the baby grows. The street contains forty houses. Each house has four rooms, two or three have six; most of the people have two rooms. There are, therefore, roughly speaking, about one hundred families residing in this street. The door-steps, the pavement, and the roadway are swarming with children; the street is their only playground. Here the little girl of six bears about in her arms, staggering under the weight, but a careful nurse, her little sister, aged twelve months; here the children take their breakfast and their dinner; here they run and play in summer and in winter. It seems to be never too hot or too cold for them. They are ragged, they are bareheaded, they are barefooted and barelegged, their toys are bits of wood and bones and oyster-shells, transformed by the imagination of childhood into heaven knows what of things precious and splendid. Of what they have not they know nothing; but, then, they mind nothing, therefore pity would be thrown away upon them. It is the only world they know; they are happy in their ignorance; they are feeling the first joy of life. By their ruddy faces and sturdy limbs you can see that the air they breathe is wholesome, and that they have enough to eat.

The room is furnished sufficiently, according to the standards of the family. There is a table, with two chairs; there is a chest of drawers with large glass handles. On this chest stands a structure of artificial flowers under a glass shade. This is the sacred symbol of respectability. It is for the tenement what the Bible or the coral in the window is for the house. So long as we have our glass shade with its flowers we are in steady work, and beyond the reach of want. On each side of the glass shade are arranged the cups and saucers, plates and drinking-glasses, belonging to the family. There are also exhibited with pride all the bottles of medicine recently taken by the various members.

It is a strange pride, but one has observed it among people of a more exalted station. There are also set out with the bottles certain heart-shaped velvet pincushions, made by the sailors, and considered as decorations of the highest æsthetic value. The chest of drawers is used for the clothes of the family—the slender supplement of what is on the family back. It is also the storehouse for everything that belongs to the daily life. There is a cupboard beside the chimney, with two shelves. Any food that may be left over, and the small supplies of tea and sugar, are placed on the upper shelf, coals on the lower. On the table stands, always ready, a teapot, and beside it a half-cut loaf and a plate with margarine, the substitute for butter. Margarine is not an unwholesome compound. It is perhaps better than bad butter; it is made of beef fat, clarified and colored to resemble butter. I am told that other people eat it in comfortable assurance that it is butter.

When the child grows old enough to observe things she will remark, from time to time, the absence of the chest of drawers. At other times she will discover that the drawers are empty. These vacuities she will presently connect with times of tightness. When money is scarce and work is not to be got things "go in" of their own accord; the pawnbroker receives them.

She will learn more than this; she will learn the great virtue of the poor, the virtue that redeems so many bad habits—generosity. For the chest of drawers and the best clothes are more often "in" to oblige a neighbor in difficulties than to relieve their own embarrassments. The people of Ratcliffe are all neighbors and all friends; to be sure, they are frequently enemies, otherwise life would be monotonous. Always some one is in trouble, always some of the children are hungry, always there is rent to pay, always there is some one out of work. Liz will learn that if one can help, one must. She will learn this law without any formula or written code, not out of books, not in church, not in school; she will learn it from the daily life around her. Generosity will become part of her very nature.

You will perceive, however, that this child is not born of the very poor; her parents are not in destitution; her father is, in fact, a docker, and, being a big, burly fellow, born and brought up in the country, he gets tolerably regular employment and very fair wages. If he would spend less than the third or the half of his wages in drink his wife might have a four-roomed cottage. But we must take him as he is. His children suffer no serious privation. They are clothed and fed; they have the chance of living respectably, and with such decencies as belong to their ideals and their standards. In a word, Liz will be quite a commonplace, average girl of the lower working-class.

The first duty of a mother is to "harden" the baby. With this view, Liz was fed, while still a tiny infant, on rusks soaked in warm water, and when she was a year old her mother began to give her scraps of beefsteak, slightly fried, to suck; she also administered fish fried in oil—the incense and fragrance of this delicacy fills the whole neighborhood, and hangs about the streets day and night like a cloud. For drink she gave the baby the water in which whiting had been boiled; this is considered a sovereign specific for building up a child's constitution. Sometimes, it is true, the treatment leads to unforeseen results. Another child, for instance, about the same age as Liz, and belonging to the same street, was fed by its mother on red herring, and, oddly enough, refused to get any nourishment out of that delightful form of food. They carried it to the Children's Hospital, where the doctor said it was being starved to death, and made the most unkind remarks about the mother—most unjust as well, for the poor woman had no other thought or intention than to "harden the inside" of her child, and all the friends and neighbors were called in to prove that plenty of herring had been administered.

As soon as Liz was three years of age she had the same food as her parents and elder sisters. You shall dine with the family presently. For breakfast and tea and supper, and for any occasional "bever" or snack, she had a slice of bread and margarine, which she cut for herself when, like Mrs. Gamp, so disposed. It was indeed terrifying to see the small child wielding a bread-knife nearly as big as herself. She got plenty of pennies when work was regular; nobody is so generous with his pennies as the man who needs them most. She spent these casual windfalls in sweets and apples, passing the latter round among her friends for friendly bites, and dividing the former in equal portions. This cheap confectionery for the children of the kerb and the door-step supplies the place of sweet puddings, for the mystery of the pudding is unfortunately little known or understood by the mothers of Ratcliffe.

In the matter of beer, Liz became very early in life acquainted with its taste. There is a kind of cheap porter, sold at three farthings a pint, considered grateful and comforting by the feminine mind of Ratcliffe. What more natural than that the child should be invited to finish what her mother has left of the pint? It would not be much. What more motherly, when one is taking a little refreshment in a public house, than to give a taste to the children playing on the pavement outside? And what more natural than for the children to look for these windfalls, and to gather round the public house expectant? It seems rough on the little ones to begin so early; it is contrary to modern use and custom, but we need not suppose that much harm is done to a child by giving it beer occasionally. Formerly all children had beer for breakfast, beer for dinner, and beer for supper. In Belgium very little children have their bock for dinner. The mischief in the case of our Liz and her friends was that she got into the habit of looking for drink more stimulating than tea, and that the habit remained with her and grew with her.

At three years of age Liz passed, so to speak, out of the nursery, which was the door-step and the kerb, into the schoolroom. She was sent to the nearest Board-school, where she remained under instruction for eleven long years. She began by learning certain highly important lessons; first, that she had to obey; next, that she had to be quiet; and, thirdly, that she had to be clean. As regards the first and second, obedience and order were not enforced in the nursery of London Street. They were, it is true, sometimes enjoined with accompaniment of a cuff and a slap, not unkindly meant, in the home. As for cleanliness, one wash a week, namely, on Sunday morning, had hitherto been considered sufficient. It was, however, a thorough wash. The unkempt locks, brown with the dust and grime of a week's street play, came out of the tub a lovely mass of light-brown, silky curls; the child's fair skin emerged from its coating of mud; her rosy cheeks showed their natural color; her round, white arms fairly shone and glowed in the sunshine. On Sunday morning Liz presented the appearance of a very pretty child, clean and fair and winsome. As soon as she went to school, however, she had to undergo the same process every morning except Saturday. If she appeared in school unwashed she had to go home again; not only that, but there was often unpleasantness in the matter of pinafore. Saturday is a school holiday, therefore no one washes on Saturday, and face and hands and pinafore may all go grimy together.

Liz remained at school from three to fourteen years of age. What she learned I do not exactly know. Some years ago I looked through some "readers" for Board-schools, and came to the conclusion that nothing at all could be learned from them, counting scraps as worth nothing. But I hear that they have altered their "readers." Still, if you remember that no one has any books at all in London Street, that even a halfpenny paper is not often seen there, that no talk goes on which can instruct a child in anything, you will

In an East-End Gin-Shop.

own that a child may be at school even for eleven years and yet learn very little. And since she found no means of carrying on her education after she left school, no free libraries, no encouragement from her companions, you will not be surprised to hear that all she had learned from books presently dropped from her like a cloak or wrapper for which she had no further use. Let us be reasonable. The Board-school taught her, besides a certain small amount of temporary and short-lived book-lore, some kind of elementary manners—a respect, at least, for manners; the knowledge of what manners may mean. The clergy and the machinery of the parish cannot teach these things. It can be done only at the Board-school. It is the school, and not the church, which softens manners and banishes some of the old brutality, because, you see, they do not go to church, and they must go to school. How rough, how rude, the average girl of Ratcliffe was before the Board-schools were opened, Liz herself neither knows nor comprehends. These schools have caused the disappearance of old characteristics once thought to be ingrained habits. Their civilizing influence during the last thirty years has been enormous. They have not only added millions to the numbers of those who read a great deal and perhaps—but this is doubtful—think a little, but they have abolished much of the old savagery. I declare that the life of this street as it was thirty or forty years ago simply could not be written down with any approach to truth in these pages.

Let me only quote the words of Professor Huxley, who began life by practising as a medical man in this quarter. "I have seen the Polynesian savage," I once heard him say in a speech, "in his primitive condition, before the missionary or the blackbirder or the beach-comber got at him. With all his savagery, he was not half so savage, so unclean, so irreclaimable, as the tenant of a tenement in an East London slum." These words open the door to unbounded flights of imagination. Leave that vanished world, leave the savage slum of Huxley's early manhood, to the region of poetry and fancy, to the unwritten, to the suggested, to the half-whispered. It exists no longer; it has been improved.

Liz passed through school, then, from one standard to the next. We have seen that she learned manners, order, obedience, and the duty of cleanly clothes and cleanly language. She learned also to love teacher and school. Teacher came to see her when she was ill, and brought her nice things. Teacher kissed her. There were others, however, who took a mean advantage of her affectionate nature, and used it as a means of keeping her out of mischief—ladies who went in and out of the streets and houses, not afraid of anything; who gathered the children together on Sundays, and sang with them and talked to them, and gave them oranges. These ladies knew all the children. When they walked down the streets the very little ones ran after them, clinging to their skirts, catching at their hands, in the hope of a word and a kiss. Liz, among the rest, was easily softened by kindness. She had two schools,—that provided by the country and that provided by these ladies, who taught her more than books can teach,—and both schools, if you please, were provided for nothing. Whatever may happen to Liz in after life, her respect for manners and for the life of order will remain. And sometimes, when things look very black and there is real cause for sadness and repentance, this respect may be the poor girl's most valuable asset.

At the age of fourteen, when she had to leave school, she was a sturdy, well-built girl, square-shouldered, rather short, but of a better frame than most of her companions, because her father was country-born; her features were sharp, her face was plain, but not unpleasing; her gray eyes were quick and restless, her lips were mobile; her cheek was somewhat pale, but not worn and sunken. She looked abounding in life and health; she was full of fun, and quick to laugh on the smallest provocation; she was ready-witted and prompt with repartee and retort; she danced as she went along the street, because she could not walk sedately; if a barrel-organ came that way she danced in the road, knowing half a dozen really pretty steps and figures. She had something in her quick movements, in the restlessness of her eyes, in the half-suspicious turn of the head, of the street sparrow, the only bird which she knew. If you grow up among street sparrows there is every reason for the adoption of some of their manners; the same resemblance to the sparrow, which is an impudent, saucy bird, always hungry, always on the lookout for something more, may be observed in other street children. She was affectionate with her companions, but always watchful for her own chance.

In her views of the conduct of life she was no strict moralist. She was ready to condone some things which more rigid maidens condemn. She would not, for instance, bear malice because her brother, for one of the smaller crimes, such as gambling on the pavement, got into trouble; nor would she judge him harshly if he was found in the possession of things "picked up"—unconsidered trifles; nor would she resent being knocked down by her brother when in drink. She had too often seen her mother cuffed by her father when he came home drunk to feel any resentment about such a trifle. In sober moments her brother did not use his fist upon her, nor did her father, except under the provocation of drink, drive the whole family flying into the street by "taking the strap" to everybody.

What did she know about the outer world? From her books and her school little enough. Her own country, like every other country, was to her a geographical expression. Even of London she knew nothing, though from the river stairs and foreshore she could see a good deal of it. Once a year, however, she had been taken for a day in the country, either by train to the nearest seaside place, or by brakes and wagonettes to Epping Forest. She was therefore by no means ignorant of green fields. Why, there was the "Island Garden," in the Isle of Dogs, close at hand. But of trees and flowers and birds individually she knew nothing, and she never would know anything. A bird was a bird, a tree was a tree to her. On the whole of nature her mind was a blank. About her own country, its history, its position, its achievements, she had learned something, but it was rapidly becoming a vague and dim memory; of literature she knew nothing. She had learned a little singing, and had an ear for melody. She never read either newspapers or books, not even penny story-books, therefore she added nothing to her scanty knowledge.

What did she think about and what did she talk about? When one lives in a crowded street, where every family lives in one room, or in two at the most, there is an unfailing, perennial stream of interest in the fortune and the conduct, the good luck and the bad luck, of the neighbors. Liz and her companions did exactly what other people do in country towns much duller than London Street—they talked about one another and the people about them. They talked also of the time when they, like their elder sisters, would go about as they pleased: to the Queen's Music-hall and to the Pavilion Theatre; when they could enjoy the delights of walking up and down their favorite boulevard—it is called Brook Street —all the long winter evening, each with her young man. The young girls always talk about the life before them. They know perfectly what it is going to be; they see it all round them. Who are they that they should expect anything but the common round, the common lot? They also, like their elder sisters, talk of dress. Already they plan and contrive for some extra bit of finery. Let us not believe that Liz was ever troubled with vacuity of mind or with lack of interest in her thoughts and conversation. There is in London Street even too much incident. Where there are

The British Workman in Epping Forest.

always in the street men out of work, families whose "sticks" are all "in," children who are kept alive by the generosity of other people, only not quite so poor as themselves; where there is always sickness, always violence, always drunkenness, always lads taken away by the man in blue, and always the joy of youth and the animation of children and young girls—why, Piccadilly is a waste by comparison, and Berkeley Square is like unto Tadmor in the desert.

In the case of Liz and her friends there was an additional interest in the river and the craft of all kinds. The children would stand on Ratcliffe Cross Stairs and gaze out upon the rushing tide and upon the ships that passed up and down. At low tide they ran out upon the mud, with bare feet, and picked up apronfuls of coal to carry home. Needs must that a child who lives within sight of ships should imagine strange things and get a sense of distance and of mystery. And sometimes a sailor would find his way to London Street—a sailor full of stories of strange lands across the seas, such as would make even the dullest of Ratcliffe girls launch out in imagination beyond the dim and dusty street.

Once, for instance, a cousin came. It was at Christmas. Never was such a Christmas. He was a sailor. He came from the West India docks—or was it from Limehouse Basin? It was the only time; he never came again. But could any one privileged to be present ever forget the celebration of that home-coming? He had money in his pocket—lots of money. He threw it all upon the table—nine pounds in gold, Liz remembered, and a heap of silver and copper. On Christmas eve the feast began. Relations and far-off cousins were found and invited. The family had two rooms. The company, with the guests, numbered twenty-one. A barrel of beer and any quantity of whisky and gin were laid in for the occasion. No more joyful family reunion was ever known. Outside, there were the usual Christmas rejoicings. In the street the drunken men reeled about; there was an occasional fight; the houses were all lighted up, but nowhere was a nobler spread or a longer feast or a more joyous Christmas known than in those two rooms. It took three days and three nights. From Friday, which was Christmas eve, till Monday, which was Boxing-day, this feast continued. During all this time not one among them, man, woman, or child, undressed or went to bed. The children fell asleep, with flushed faces and heavy heads, in corners, on the landing, anywhere; the others feasted and drank, danced and sang, for three days and three nights. Now and then one would drop out and fall prone upon the floor; the others went on regardless. Presently the sleeper awoke, sat up, recovered his wandering wits, and joined the revelers again.

For plenty and profusion it was like unto the wedding-feast of Camacho. There were roast geese and roast ducks, roast turkey and roast beef, roast pork and sausages and ham, and everything else that the shops at this festive season could supply.

On the third day, toward three in the afternoon of Monday, lo, a miracle! For the money was all gone, and the barrel of beer was empty, and the bottles were empty, and the bones of the geese and the turkeys were all that was left of the feast. The company broke up, the cousin departed, the family threw themselves upon the beds and slept the clock twice round. Who could forget this noble Christmas? Who could forget a feast that lasted for three whole days and three long nights?

Liz had got through her school-time; she must go to work.

Of course, she knew all along what awaited her. She must do as the others did, she must enter a factory. She contemplated the necessity without any misgiving. Why should she not go into a factory? It was all in the natural order of things, like getting hungry or waking up in the morning. Every girl had to be cuffed, every girl had to get out of the way when her father was drunk, every girl had to go to work as soon as she left school.

There is apparently a choice of work. There are many industries which employ girls. There is the match-making, there is the bottle-washing, there is the box-making, there is the paper-sorting, there is the jam-making, the fancy confectionery, the cracker industry, the making of ornaments for wedding-cakes, stockings for Christmas, and many others. There are many kinds of sewing. Virtually, however, this child had no choice; her sisters were in the jam factory, her mother had been in the jam factory, she too went to the jam factory.

There are many branches of work more disagreeable than the jam factory. Liz found herself at half-past seven in the morning in a huge building, where she was one among a thousand working women and girls, men and boys, but chiefly girls. The place was heavily laden with an overpowering fragrance of fruit and sugar. In some rooms the fruit was boiling in great copper pots; in some girls were stirring the fruit, after it had been boiled, to get the steam out of it; in some machinery crushed and ground the sugar till it became as fine as flour. The place was like a mill. The flour of sugar hung about the room in a cloud of dust; it lay in such dust on the tables and the casks; it got into the girls' hair, so that they were fain to tie up their heads with white caps; it covered their clothes, and made them sticky; it made tables, benches, floor, all alike sticky. There were other developments of sugar; sometimes it lay on tables in huge, flat cakes of soft gray stuff like gelatine; they turned this mass, by their craft and subtlety, into innumerable threads of fine white silk; they drew it through machines, and brought it out in all the shapes that children love. Then there were rooms full of cocoanut. They treated casks full of dessicated cocoanut till that also became like flour. There were other rooms full of almonds, which they stripped and bleached and converted also into fine flour; or they turned boxes of gelatine into Turkish delight and jujubes. All day long and all the year round they made crackers; they made ornaments for wedding-cakes; they made favors; they made caramels; they made acidulated drops; they made things unnamed except by children. In all these rooms girls worked by hundreds, some sitting at long tables, some boiling the sugar, filling the pots with jam, stirring the boiling fruit, feeding machinery, filling molds; all were as busy as bees and as mute as mice. Some of them wore white caps to cover their hair, some wore white aprons, some wore coarse sacking tied all round for a skirt to keep off stickiness. All day long the machinery whirred and pulsed an accompaniment to the activity and industry of the place.

"I like the smell," said Liz. First impressions are the best; she continued to like the smell and the factory and the work.

She was stouter and stronger than most girls. They gave her a skirt of sacking, and put her where her strength would be of use. She liked the movement, she liked the exercise of her strong arms, and she liked the noise of the place; she liked the dinner-hour, with its talking and laughing; she liked the factory better than the school; she liked the pay-day, and the money which she kept for herself.

I say that she liked the work and the sense of society and animation. About a year afterward, however, a strange and distressing restlessness seized her. Whether she was attracted by the talk of the other girls, or whether it was an instinctive yearning for change and fresh air, I know not. The thing was infectious. Many other girls compared their symptoms, and found them the same. Finally, the restlessness proving altogether too much for the children, they took hands, thirty of them, and one Saturday afternoon, without bag or baggage, they ran away.

They ran through Wapping and along Thames Street, which is empty on Saturday afternoon; they ran across London Bridge, they poured into London Bridge Station. One of the girls knew the name of the station they wanted; it was in Kent. They took tickets, and they went off.

They had gone hopping.

Thousands of Londoners in the season go hopping. I wish I could dwell upon the delights of the work. Unfortunately, like the summer, it is too soon over. While it lasts the hoppers sleep in barns, they work in the open, they breathe fresh air, they get good pay, they enjoy every evening a singsong and a free-and-easy. The beer flows like a rivulet; everybody is thirsty, everybody is cheerful, everybody is friendly.

When it was over Liz returned, browned and refreshed and strengthened, but fearful of the consequences, because she had deserted her work. But she was fortunate. They took her back into the factory, and so she went on as before.

Let us follow her through a single day. She had to be at the factory at half-past seven in the morning, and, with an hour off for dinner, to work till six. She made her breakfast on tea, bread and margarine, and a "relish." The relish included many possibilities. It depended mainly on the day of the week. It is obvious that what one can afford on a Monday is unattainable on a Friday. On Monday it might be a herring or a haddock, an egg or a rasher of bacon. On Friday and Saturday it would be a sprig of water-cress or a pickle.

With all factory girls dinner is a continual source of anxiety and disappointment, for the ambitions of youth are lofty, and the yearnings of youth are strong, and the resources of youth are scanty. Within the factory there were, for those who chose to use them, frying-pans and a gas-stove. The girls might cook their food for themselves. There was also hot water for making tea; but the factory girl detests cooking, and may be trusted to spoil and make unfit for human food whatever cooking is intrusted to her. Besides, there were the eating-houses. Here, if you please, were offered to the longing eyes of Liz, always hungry at half-past twelve, daily temptations to extravagance. Just think what the bill of fare every day offered to a girl of discernment in the matter of dinner.

Saveloy and Pease Pudding
German Sausages and Black Pudding
Fried Fish and Pickles
Meat-pie
Pie-crust and Potatoes
Fagots and Mustard Pickle
Beans, Potatoes, Greens, Currant Pudding
Jam Pudding

The mere choice between these delicacies was bewildering, and, alas! on many days only the cheapest were attainable. Every day Liz pondered over the list and calculated the price. The meat-pie at twopence—glorious! But could she afford twopence? The jam pudding at one halfpenny! It seems cheap, and a good lump too, with a thick slab of red jam—plum jam—laid all over the top. But yet, even a halfpenny is sometimes dear. You see that dinner is wanted on seven days in the week. It was impossible to afford jam pudding every day. Fagots, again. They are only a penny hot, and three farthings cold. A fagot is a really toothsome preparation. In appearance it is a square cake. In composition it contains the remnants and odd bits of a butcher's shop—beef, veal, mutton, lamb, with fat and gristle contributed by all the animals concerned. The whole is minced or triturated. It is treated with spices and shreds of onion, and is then turned out in shapes and baked. No one in the position of our Liz can withstand the temptation of a fagot. The rich people who keep the shops, she believes, live ex-

Brook Street, Limehouse.

clusively on fagots. Wealth cannot purchase anything better than a fagot.

To begin with, she had only five shillings a week. When we consider the Sunday dinner, her clothes and her boots, her share of the rent, her breakfast, her amusements, her clubs, of which we shall speak immediately, I do not think that she was justified in laying out more than twopence, or at the most twopence halfpenny, on her daily dinner. A meat-pie with potatoes, a fagot with mustard pickles and greens, and a jam pudding would absorb the whole of her daily allowance. It left this growing girl hungry after eating all of it.

Meantime, the factory people are as careful about their girls as can be expected. They insist on their making a respectable appearance and wearing a hat. In many other ways they look after them. There is a good deal of paternal kindliness in the London employer, especially when he is in a large way.

The factory girls of East London have shown a remarkable power of looking after themselves. Once or twice they have even had a strike. On one occasion they made a demonstration which made the government give in. It is old history now. Once there was a certain statesman named Lowe—Bob Lowe, he was irreverently called. He made a considerable stir in his day, which was about five-and-twenty years ago. He was then Chancellor of the Exchequer. To-day I doubt if there are many young people in England under five-and-twenty who could pass an examination in the political career of Bob Lowe. He was a very fine scholar. He had been a fellow and lecturer of his college at Oxford; he had been a barrister practising in Australia, and he was believed to hold in contempt our colonial empire, and to hunger after the time when Great Britain would become a second Holland. Once he conceived the idea of a tax on matches. His scholarship supplied him with a punning motto, "Ex luce lucellum" ("from light a little profit"). The match-makers rebelled. They marched down to Westminster in their thousands. They demonstrated: they stated their grievance. Bob Lowe quailed, and the government withdrew the bill.

Our young friend Liz had nothing to do with this prenatal business, which, had it happened in her own time, she would have greatly enjoyed. Where she showed her native ability was in the establishment of clubs. They were practical clubs; they were organized upon an entirely new and original method. I can best explain it by giving an illustration. Thus, there is the one-pound club. Twenty girls agree to get up a one-pound club. For twenty weeks they have to subscribe each a shilling. To determine the order of taking the money they draw numbered tickets. The girl who draws No. 1 receives twenty shillings in a lump the first week; the girl who draws No. 2 takes the second week's money, and so on. It is obvious that this method can be applied to anything, provided the girls who draw the earlier numbers play fair. It seems that they generally do. Should they shirk their duty, there are "ructions." The girl Liz could not, at first, aspire to the one-pound club. But there were humbler clubs—sixpenny, even penny, clubs. Thus, there were boot clubs, calico clubs, petticoat clubs, tea-fight clubs, jewelry clubs, and, but secretly and among the older girls who had sweethearts to consider and to please, there were spirit clubs, for gin and whisky, not for supernatural manifestations. A girl cannot belong to all these clubs at once, but the convenience of belonging to two or three at a time is very great. It enables a provident girl to keep her wardrobe in order by small weekly savings which are not much felt. In the matter of boots, now; if one draws No. 1 there is a new pair at once; suppose the pair lasts for three months, after six weeks another boot club might give the same girl the last number instead of the first, and so on.

Her days were not spent wholly in the factory. At seven

in the winter and at six in the summer she was free; she had also her Saturday afternoons and her Sundays. In other words, she had a fair five hours of freedom every day, ten hours of freedom on Saturdays, and the whole of Sunday. Now, five hours a day of continuous freedom from work is as much as in any working community can be expected. It is a third of the waking day. How did Liz get through that time?

She very soon got beyond her mother's control. It is not, indeed, the custom with many mothers to exercise authority over a girl at work. Liz did what other girls did. She therefore spent most of her evenings in the boulevard of her quarter, a place called Brook Street. Here she walked about, or ran about, or danced arm in arm with other girls, chaffing the lads, whom she treated, if she had the money, to a drink. She went sometimes to a music-hall, where some of the factory girls "did a turn" or danced in the ballet. She wore no hat or bonnet in the street, and she retained the apron which is the badge of her class. She looked on with interest when there was a fight. She listened with a critical mind when there was an exchange of reproaches between two women.

Then a girls' club got hold of her and persuaded her to come in. The club was run by some of those ladies of whom I have spoken, the same who trade on the affection of the children for their own purposes, which may be described as a mean and underhand attempt to make the little ones learn to prefer good to evil. At this club there was singing every night, there was dancing with one another, there was reading, there was talking; everybody behaved nicely, and for two or three hours it was a restful time, even though young girls do not feel the need of rest or understand its use.

When the club closed, the girls went away. If it was a fine night and not too cold they went back for a while to Brook Street, where there was neither rest nor quiet nor godly talk.

Besides her evenings, the girl had the four bank-holidays, and the holidays of Christmas and Easter. Nobody in London does any work between Thursday in Passion Week and Easter Tuesday, nor does any one work much between Christmas eve, when that falls on Thursday or Friday, and the following Tuesday.

These days and seasons are not only holidays, they are days reserved for weddings and christenings. It is necessary, of course, that a girl who respects herself should make a creditable appearance at such a time. She must therefore save, and save with zeal. Saving up for bank-holiday becomes a passion. Dinner is reduced to the lowest possible dimensions, even to a halfpenny lump of currant pudding, which is as heavy as lead and the most satisfying thing for the money that can be procured.

Bank-holiday demands a complete change of clothes, from the hat to the boots. Everything must be new. There must not be an old frock with a new hat, nor an old pair of boots with a new frock. This means a great deal of saving. It must also be accompanied by a general cleaning up of the windows, the door-steps, the stairs, the rooms. All over London Street before bank-holiday there is unusual movement. Chairs are brought out, and girls stand upon them to clean the ground-floor windows.

I have already spoken of the change that has come over this quarter. Formerly a holiday was celebrated after the manner of the ancient Danes, by long and barbaric drinking bouts. Early in the morning girls would be seen lying helpless on the pavement. Lads ran about carrying bottles of gin, which they offered to every one. These are customs of the past, though complete soberness is not yet quite achieved.

Still, however, the Ratcliffe girl likes to keep her bank-holiday at home among her own people, in her beloved Brook Street. She cheerfully saves up all she can, so that there may be a good sum for bank-holiday, enough for new clothes

An August Bank-Holiday in the East End.

THE FACTORY GIRL

and something over, something to treat her friends with. And when the day is over she must go back to her work with an empty purse. Well for her if it is not also with an aching head.

When Liz was approaching the age of seventeen she had learned, from every point of view, all that she would ever learn; she had risen as high as she could rise in the factory; she made as good wages as she would ever make; she lived at home, sharing a room with two sisters; she paid her mother sixpence a week for bed and lodging; her character was formed; her acquaintance with good and evil was deep, wide, and intimate; she was steady, as girls of her class go, thanks to those ladies; if she ever drank too much she was ashamed of herself, and as yet she had no sweetheart. She was affectionate and responded to kindness, but she was self-willed, and would bear no thwarting. She was deficient on the side of imagination. She could not enter into the thoughts or the position of any one except herself; that was the natural result of her narrow, groove-like life. She had rules of conduct and of behavior; of religion she had little, if any, discoverable. She never went to church or chapel. She was fond of every kind of excitement, yet the emotional side of religion touched her not. The Irish girls, of whom there are many at Ratcliffe, were Catholics, and sometimes went to church. Once Liz went there, too, and seemed to like the music and the lights, but she did not repeat her visit.

This was her life all through the week. On Sunday, however, she made a difference.

On that morning she lay in bed till ten or eleven. She spent the time before dinner over her wardrobe; at one o'clock she sat down with the family to the most important ceremony of the week, the Sunday dinner. To other people besides the working-folk of Ratcliffe the Sunday dinner is an institution. Pope's retired citizen, on Sundays, had, we know, two puddings to smoke upon the board. To all people of the middle class the Sunday dinner is the occasion for a little indulgence, for a glass of wine after dinner. To the resident in Ratcliffe it means a big feed, as much as a man can eat, and that of a popular and favorite dish. There are many dishes dear to the heart of the working-man. He loves everything that is confected with, or accompanied by, things of strong taste. If he knew of the delicacy called lobscouse he would have it nearly every Sunday; if he knew of that other delicacy called potato-pot he would order it frequently. As it is, he relies for the most part upon some portion of pig—that creature of "fine miscellaneous feeding." He loves roast pork, boiled pork, fried pork, baked pork, but especially he loves pig's head. His wife buys this portion of the animal, stuffs the ears and eyes thereof with sage and onions,—a great deal of sage and much onion,—and sends it to the bakehouse. Pig's head thus treated and done to a turn is said to have no fellow. It is accompanied by beer, and beer in plenty. The family sit down to this meal when it is brought in from the baker, and continue eating until they can eat no longer. So, in Arabian deserts, if you would win the hearts of the Bedouin you give them a sheep, and they will eat until they can eat no longer. It is part of the Sunday dinner that there is to be no hint or suspicion of any limit, except that imposed by nature. They eat till they can eat no more.

When she was seventeen Liz found a sweetheart.

He was a young fellow of twenty or thereabouts. He had come out of his native village, some place in the quiet country, a dull place, to enjoy the life of London. He was a highly skilled agricultural laborer; there was nothing on the farm that he could not do. He knew the fields and the woods, the wild creatures and the birds; he knew how to plow and to reap; he could keep an allotment full of vegetables all the year round; he understood a stable and a dairy, a paddock and sheepfold. Yet with all this knowledge he came to London, where it was of no earthly use to him. He threw over the best work that a country lad can have, and he became nothing but a pair of hands like this girl's father. He was a pair of hands; he was a strong back; his sturdy legs were fit to do the commonest, the heaviest, the most weary work in the world. One evening Liz was standing alone on the pavement, looking at something or other—a barrel-organ, a cheap Jack, one of the common sights and sounds—when this young fellow passed along, walking heavily, as one who has walked chiefly over plowed fields. He looked at her. Something in her face,—it was an honest face,—something in her attitude of alertness and the sharp look of her eye struck his imagination. He hitched closer. In Brook Street it is permissible, it is laudable, to introduce yourself. He said huskily: "I've seen you here before. What's your name? Mine is George."

That was the beginning of it. Presently the other girls met Liz walking proudly along Brook Street with a big, well-set-up young fellow. They moved out of her way. Liz had got a chap. When would their turn come?

Next night they met again. On Sunday she walked with him along the Mile End Road without her apron and in her best hat. It was a parade and proclamation of an engagement. She told her mother, who was glad. "A man," she said, "is a better friend than a woman. He sticks." Liz did not tell the ladies of the club, but the other girls did, and the ladies looked grave and spoke seriously to her about responsibilities.

George did stick to her. He was an honest lad; he had chosen his sweetheart, and he stuck to her. When he had money he gave her treats. He took her by train to Epping Forest, to North Woolwich Gardens, to the theater, to the music-hall. In his way he loved the girl. She would not leave the club, but she gave him part of every evening. He talked to her about the country life he had left behind him. He told her the stories about poachers which belong to every village ale-house. It pleased him to recall the past he had thrown away. All day long he carried heavy bales and boxes and burdens backward and forward. It was monotonous

A Music-Hall.

work, cheered only by the striking of the hours and the thought of the coming evening. The poor lad's day was hallowed by his evening walk.

Six months later Liz was married. It was on the August bank-holiday. The wedding took place at St. James's Church, Ratcliffe. It was celebrated in a style which did honor to the quarter. The bride was dressed in heliotrope satin. She wore a large hat of purple plush. The bridesmaids were brilliantly attired in frocks of **velveteen, green** and crimson and blue. They too wore hats of plush. After

THE FACTORY GIRL

the ceremony they adjourned to the residence of the bride, where a great feast was spread. The rejoicing lasted all day and all night. When the young couple began their wedded life it was with an empty purse and a week of borrowed food. I hope that George will not get drunk, will not knock his wife down, and will not take the strap to her. If he does, we must comfort ourselves with the thought that to Liz it will be no new thing, hitherto unknown in the land, not an unnatural thing when the drink is in a man, and, unless repeated in soberness, a trifle to be endured and forgotten and forgiven, even seventy times seven.

Here we must leave our girl. She is now a wife. For a little while she will go on at the factory; then she will stay at home. London Street will be enriched by half a dozen children all her own. Like their mother, these children will play in the dust and the mud, like her, they will go to school and be happy; like her, they will go to work in the factory. Liz will be repeated in her children. As long as she lives she will know and enjoy the same life, with the same pleasures, the same anxieties, the same luck. She will "do" for her girls when they grow up. Now and then she will be taken on as a casual at the old factory. London Street will always be her whole world; she will have no interests outside, and when she dies it will be only the vanishing of one out of the multitudes which seem, as I said at the beginning, to be all alike, all living the same life, all enduring, hoping, loving, suffering, sinning, giving, helping, condoling, mourning, in the same kindly, cruel, beneficent, merciless, contradictory, womanly fashion that makes up the life of London Street.

VI
THE KEY OF THE STREET

VI

THE KEY OF THE STREET

DURING our walk along the riverside we passed here and there small groups of men, either two and three together or in companies of ten or a dozen. They were "hanging around," hands in pockets, an empty pipe between their lips, with a slouching, apathetic air; in every case a public house was within very easy reach; in most cases the public house afforded them door-posts and walls against which to lean. They were observed in large numbers around the dock-gates and in long lines leaning against the dock-walls. There was no alertness or activity in the look or the carriage of any of these men; on the other hand, there was no dejection or unhappiness. Had we stopped to ask any of them what they were doing they would have assumed for the moment an imitation of readiness indicated by a slight stiffening of the knee-joints, the withdrawal of the hands from the pocket, and the attitude of attention by which they gave the inquirer to understand that they were waiting for a job.

This is their trade—waiting for a job; it appears to be a trade which takes the spirit out of a man, which makes him limp, which makes him unwilling to undertake that job when it arrives, which tempts him to look for any other way of getting food than the execution of that job, which narrows his views of life so that the haven where he would be is nothing but the bar of the public house, and the only joy he desires is the joy of endeavoring to alleviate a thirst that nothing can assuage.

This manner of life can hardly be reckoned among the more noble. It demands no skill and no training. What they mean by a job is the fetching or carrying something, either in the way of transferring cargo from ship to quay or carrying something from one house to another. If it is the former, if one of these fellows gets taken on at the docks, he enters with a sigh; his work is not worth a fourth part of that done by one of the regular staff, and as soon as he has earned enough for the day's wants he retires, he goes back to his street corner and his public house, he once more seizes on the momentary rapture of a drink, and he rejoins his limp companions.

I have considered the daily life of the factory girl. Let me now consider that of the casual hand, almost as important an element on the riverside as the girl.

In most cases he is a native of the place; he was born on the riverside; he has been brought up on the riverside; he was born and brought up conveniently near the public house, beside which he wastes the leaden hours of his dreary life. A country lad cannot easily become a creature so weak and limp; the father of the casual hand was himself in the same profession, his mother was a factory girl like her of whom we have been speaking.

This man—he never seems to be more than five-and-thirty, or less than thirty—is one of the very few survivors of a numerous family; the riverside families are very large if you count the graves, for the mortality of the young fills the graveyards very rapidly; most of this man's brothers and sisters are dead—one can hardly, looking at the man himself and his surroundings, say that they are "gone before"; it is best to say only that they are gone, we know not whither. He himself has been so unfortunate, if we may put the case plainly, as to escape the many perils of infancy

The West India Dock Gates.

and childhood. He has not been "overlaid" as a baby, nor run over as a child, nor carried off with diphtheria, scarlatina, croup, or any other of the disorders which continually hover about these streets, nor has he been the victim of bad nourishment and food which was unsuited to him. He has become immune against contagion and infection; wet feet and cold and exposure have been unable to kill him; the close and fetid air of the one-family living room has carried off his brothers and sisters, but has not been able to strike him down; he is like a soldier who has come unscathed through a dozen battles and a malarious campaign. Surely, therefore, this man ought to be a splendid specimen of humanity, strong and upright. The contrary is the case, however. You observe that he is by no means the kind of Briton we should like to exhibit; he hath a sallow complexion, his shoulders are sloping and narrow, his chest is hollow, his walk is shambling, he has no spring in his feet, his hands betray by their clumsiness his ignorance of any craft, he is flat-footed, his eye lacks intelligence, he is low-browed, the intellectual side of him has not been cultivated or even touched; if you talked with him you would find that he has few ideas, that his command of language is imperfect, and that he is practically inarticulate. The best thing that could happen to such a man would be compulsory farm work, but no farmer would have him on any terms, and he himself would refuse such work; he means to go on as he always goes on, to wait outside the public house for the casual job.

As a child and as a boy he was made to attend school—indeed, he liked nothing better than the hours of school. His mother, who found that in order to send the children off clean and tidy to school she had herself to get up early, and, besides, had to assume for herself some outward appearance of cleanliness, threw every possible obstacle in the way of school attendance. But she was firmly overruled by the school-board visitor and by the magistrate. Therefore she abandoned opposition and acquiesced, though with sadness too deep for words, in the inevitable.

The boy remained at school until his fourteenth year, when he was allowed to leave, on passing the fourth standard. If you ask what he had learned one might refer you to any of the "readers" used in London Board-schools, but probably these interesting and valuable works are not within easy reach. It must suffice, therefore, to explain, as in the case of Liz, that the elementary school readers, as a rule, contain selections, snippets, and scraps of knowledge, and that if a boy who passed the fourth standard remembered them all, from the first to the fourth inclusive, they would carry him a very little way indeed toward the right understanding of the round world and all that is therein.

Now comes the question, What good will the boy's education be to him in the life that lies before him? Truly, in the case of the casual hand, little or none. For, you see, although, apart from the encyclopedic snippets and the scraps, the boy has learned to read and to write, he never needs the latter accomplishment at all, and, as regards the former, he has no books; his father had no books, his friends have no books. But all the world read newspapers. Not all the world; there is a considerable section, including the casual hand and certain others whom we shall meet immediately, who never read the papers. This boy is not going to read the papers; his father never did, his friends never do, he will not. Why should he? The papers contain nothing that is of the least importance to him; they are apparently in a conspiracy to make it impossible for such as himself to drink unless they work. He speedily forgets his scraps of information, and he gets no more from the usual sources.

You must not, however, imagine that he never learns anything. It is impossible for any boy to grow up in a crowded street in complete ignorance. Something he must learn; some views of life he must be forced to frame, though unconsciously. He will grow up in ignorance of the things which form actual life in other circles, but it is with a riverside lad as with a village lad. The latter, brought up in the country, acquires insensibly a vast mass of information and knowledge about the things of the country—the fields, the hedges, the woods, the birds, the creatures—without book, without school, without master; so the riverside lad, by running about on the Stairs and the foreshore, acquires a vast mass of information about the port and the river and the ships and the ways of those who go down to the deep. He knows the tides, he knows the jetsam and the flotsam of the tides, he trudges and wades in the mud of the foreshore to pick up what the tide leaves for him; he knows all the ships, where they come from, whither they are bound, the great liner which puts in at the West India docks, the packet boats, the coasters, the colliers, the Norwegian timber ships, he knows them all; he knows their rig, he knows their names and when to expect them—the river and all that floats upon it are known to him as a book is known to the student. Were it not for the work, the physical activity, the discipline, the obedience, expected of the man before the mast, he would be a sailor. Concerning the imports and the exports of London he knows more than any official of the Board of Trade—that is to say, figures concern him not, but he knows the bales and the casks and the crates and the boxes: are not his friends engaged every day in discharging cargo and taking it in? All this, you will acknowledge, means a good, solid lump of knowledge which may occupy his brain and give him materials for thought and conversation—if he ever did think, which is doubtful, and if he could converse, which is not at all doubtful.

There is another kind of knowledge which the riverside lad picks up. It is the knowledge of the various ways, means, tricks, craft, and cunning by which many of his friends and contemporaries get through life without doing any work. It is with him as with men in other lines; he knows how things are done, but he cannot do them himself; he lacks courage, he lacks the necessary manner, he lacks the necessary quickness; he would be a rogue if he could; he admires successful roguery, but he is unable to imitate or to copy or to practise roguery. Not everyone can defy the law even for a brief spell between the weary periods of "stretch."

From picking up trifles unguarded and unwatched on the shore to doing the same thing in the streets is but a step. There are plenty of these lads who learn quite early to prey upon the petty trader. I have been told by one of his victims how to watch for and to observe the youthful prowler. You place yourself in one of the busy streets lined with shops in some position, perhaps at a shop-door, where you may observe without being suspected; it is like Jefferies' rule for observing the wild creatures; assume an attitude of immobility; the people pass up and down, all occupied with their own affairs, unobservant; presently comes along a boy, long-armed, long-legged; his step is silent and slouching, his eyes beneath the peak of his cap glance furtively round; the stall is unprotected; the goods exposed for sale are only guarded by a child, who is looking the other way; then, in a moment, the hand darts out, snatches something, and the lad with the long and slouching step goes on without the least change in his manner, unsuspected. He is ready to pick up anything—a loaf from the baker, an apple from the coster's cart, an onion from the green-grocer; nothing comes amiss. And he does it for the honor and the glory of it and the joy in the danger. He is not going to become an habitual criminal, not at all; that career requires serious work; he is going to become a casual hand, and he will remember pleasantly in his manhood the cunning and the sleight-of-hand with which as a boy he knew how to lift things from shop and stall and barrow.

The Barges that Lie Down the Thames.

I have spoken of the unguarded things upon the foreshore at low tide. There are still lingering by the riverside survivals of the good old days when the whole people lived in luxury on the robberies they committed from the ships loading and unloading in the river. There are barges which go up and down with the tide. At ebb tide they lie in the mud; the men in charge go ashore to drink; the boys then climb on board in search of what they can get. If the barge is laden with sugar they cut holes in the bags and fill their pockets, their hats, their boots, their handkerchiefs with the stuff, which they carry ashore and sell. They get a halfpenny a pound for their plunder. If the barge is laden with coals they carry off all that their clothes will hold; one goes before to warn the rest of danger; plenty of houses on the way are open to them; it is a comparatively safe and certainly a pleasant way of earning a penny or two. It is also a way which brings with it its own punishment. For the great and ever present temptation with the riverside lad is to shirk work; a physical shrinking from hard work is his inheritance; every way by which he can be relieved from work strengthens this physical shrinking; not at one step, not suddenly, does a young man find work impossible for him; the casual hand grows slowly more casual; the waiter on fortune's jobs grows steadily more inclined to wait; he finds himself tied to the lamp-post opposite the public house; chains bind him to the doors; within is his shrine, his temple, his praying place, his idol; he keeps his hands in his pockets while he keeps his eyes on the swinging door and suffers his mind to dwell all day long on the fragrance of the beery bar.

Every year there are thousands of boys who leave the London Board-schools, their "education" completed, with no chance of an apprenticeship to any trade, their hands absolutely untrained, just a hanging pair of hands, prehensile, like the monkey's tail. It is indeed lucky that they are prehensile, otherwise what would be the lot of their owners?

They leave school; they have to face the necessity of making a livelihood for themselves, of earning their daily bread, perhaps for sixty long years to come, without knowing any single one of the many arts and crafts by which men live and provide for their families and themselves. At the outset it appears to be a hopeless task. Of course, it is the greatest possible misfortune for a lad to learn no trade. If we consider the waste of intellectual power alone, where there is no training to skilled labor, it must be acknowledged to be the greatest misfortune that can befall a boy at the outset. Still, all is not lost. For a steady lad, willing to work, this misfortune may be partly overcome. There are many openings for such a boy. Let us consider, for instance, what lines of work he may attempt, keeping only to those which require no previous training and no skill.

He hears of these openings from other boys; he has heard of such openings all his life. For instance, he would very much like to enter the service of the City of London, as one of the boys whose business it is to keep the streets clean. You may see these boys, in a red uniform, running about among the horses and omnibuses in Cheapside; they are always under the horses' feet, but they never get run over; they are active and smart lads; they seem to take a pride in doing their humble work rapidly and thoroughly. They receive very good pay, which helps to keep up their spirits— 6s. 6d. a week, rising to 9s. or 10s. Even better than this is the railway service, where a smart lad may very soon get 9s. a week. He may then rise to the position of a railway porter. Now, at the great London stations, in which the trains are coming in and going out all day long, and every passenger with luggage is good for a tip of threepence or sixpence, no one knows what the weekly earnings of a railway porter may be. Things are whispered; nothing is known for certain; the position, however, is recognized as one of the prizes in the profession of the unskilled hand.

Then there are the factories—matches, jam, all kinds of factories—into which, if a boy is fortunate enough to be taken, he may make at the outset 5s. or 6s. a week. It is, however, generally felt that there is a lack of interest about factory work. A much more enviable occupation is that of a van boy, whose very simple duty is to sit behind among the boxes and parcels, in order to take care that none of them are stolen and that none drop off into the street. One is expected to assist in loading and unloading, which means somewhat heavy work, but the greater part of the day is spent in being pleasantly carried up and down the streets of London and enjoying a moving panorama of the town in all its quarters. There are great possibilities for the van boy; if he is ambitious he may hope to become, in course of time, even driver of the van, a post of real distinction and responsibility, with "good money," although the hours may be long.

Some boys, without taking thought for the future, jump at the post of beer boy to a barge. It is attractive, it is light work, it is well paid, but it leads to nothing. One would not recommend any young friend to accept this post. Generally a barge is loaded and unloaded by one or two gangs of men, seven in a gang. Each of these men pays the beer boy twopence a day, so that if there are two gangs to the barge he will make 2s. 4d. a day, or 14s. a week, his simple duty being to carry beer to the men at work from the nearest public house. The work seems easy, but it requires activity; the gangs are thirsty, tempers are quick, and cuffs are frequent.

This kind of errand situation is very easy to get; in every trade an errand boy is wanted. I am surprised that no one has magnified the post and preached upon the necessity, for the conduct of the internal trade of the country, of the errand boy. As yet he has not found his prophet. Thus a greengrocer is lost without his errand boys; a suburban greengrocer in a flourishing way of business will have twenty boys in his employ; every small draper, every shopkeeper, in fact, small or great, must have his errand boy—but this is a post reserved for older lads. Some one must carry round the things; it is the boy who has learned no trade; the carriage of the basket is the first use to which he puts his unskilled hands. I believe that five shillings a week is the recognized pay for the situation. In one way or another, however, the boy finds some kind of place and begins to earn a living.

As a rule, these boys live well. For breakfast they have bread and butter and tea, with a "relish," such as an egg or a piece of bacon; at twelve they take their dinner at one of the humbler coffee-houses which abound in the streets of East London; it consists of more bread and butter and tea, with half a steak and potatoes. For tea they go to another coffee-house; they can get two thick slices of bread for a halfpenny each; butter or jam costs another halfpenny; a cup of coffee costs a halfpenny, or a whole pint may be had for a penny. In the evening their favorite supper is the dish familiarly known as "ha'porth and ha'porth"—that is, fish and potatoes at a halfpenny each. So far their life is healthy, with plenty of work and plenty of food, and, in most cases, strong drink is neither desired nor taken. The craving for drink comes later. The dangerous time of life is the age when the boy passes into manhood. Then the simple meals at the coffee-house no longer suffice. Then it becomes necessary to have beer, and beer in ever-increasing quantities. Then the boy grows out of his work; he becomes too big to carry beer for the bargees or to go round with the newspapers, or to sit at the back of the van, or to carry about cabbages in a basket.

What is he to do next?

There are, even for a grown man, many situations which demand no training and no apprenticeship. In all the warehouses, in the great shops, in offices of every kind, there are wanted men to fetch and carry, to load and unload, to pack

East London Loafers.

and unpack. In the docks there are wanted troops of men to load and to unload. In the markets and on the railways there are wanted men to carry and to set out the goods. In every kind of business servants must be had to do that part of the work which requires no skill. Unfortunately the supply is greater than the demand. There are many lads who get into the service of companies, railways, or factories, and remain in steady work all their working lives in the same employment. There are, on the other hand, a great number who have to hang about on the outskirts of regular work, who are taken on in times of pressure and find it difficult to get work when times are slack; these are the men who become the casual hands; these are the men who hang about the dock-gates and loaf round street corners.

The process of degeneration by which the promising lad sinks into the casual hand is easy to follow.

The work, whatever it may be, is finished at half-past six or seven. The lads have, therefore, like the factory girl already considered, four or five solid hours every evening to get through. The other day I was looking through some statistics of work in the eighteenth century. It then began at six, sometimes at half-past five; it left off at eight in the evening, with the exception of those trades which could not be carried on by the light of tallow candles. The people went to bed before ten. The time for supper, rest, and recreation was therefore reduced to two hours. There was no Saturday afternoon holiday. All through the pre-Reformation time there had been a Saturday half-holiday, because Saturday was reckoned as the eve of a saint's day, and every eve of an important saint's day was a half-holiday. The Reformation swept away this grateful respite from work. Therefore, except for Sunday, the craftsman's working-day was practically the whole day long.

We have changed these long for shorter hours; the people

have now a long evening to themselves and the Saturday half-holiday, as well as Sunday.

Consider what this means to a lad of sixteen, one of the riverside lads. He has, we have seen, no books and no desire for reading; a free library offers no attractions to him; he has no study or pursuit of any kind; he does not wish to learn anything; and he has four hours, perhaps five, to get through every evening, except Saturday, when he has nine hours, and Sunday, when he has the whole day—say sixteen hours. In every week he has actually forty-five long hours in which to amuse himself as best he can. What is that boy to do? He must do something which brings with it excitement and activity; his blood is restless; he knows not what he wants; it is an age which has its ideals, and his are of the heroic kind, but too often of a perverted heroism.

A few of them, but in proportion very few indeed, belong to the boys' clubs which are scattered about East London. They are the fortunate boys; they contract friendships with the young men—gentlemen always—who run the club; they can learn all kinds of things if they like; they work off their restlessness and get rid of the devil in the gymnasium with the boxing-gloves and with the single stick; they contract habits of order and discipline; they become infected with some of the upper-class ideals, especially as regards honor and honesty, purity and temperance; the fruits of the time spent in the club are seen in their after life; these are the lads who lead the steady lives and become the supporters of order and authority. A few again, but very few, get the chance of polytechnic classes and continuation schools, but these things are mostly above the riverside folk. Here and there a class is formed and taught by ladies in one or other of the minor arts, such as wood-carving, in which the lads quickly take great delight.

Setting aside these, what becomes of all the rest?

They have the music-hall; there are half a dozen music-halls in which the gallery is cheap; they go to one of these places two or three times a week in winter; they have the public house, but these lads are not, as a rule, slaves to drink so early in life; their own lodgings are not inviting either for comfort or for rest or for society. They have, however, the street.

It is the street which provides the casual hand; it is also the street which produces the drunkard, the loafer, the man who cannot work, the man who will not work, the street rough, the street sneak, and the street thief. The long evening spent in the street nourishes and encourages these and such as these of both sexes.

It is of course the old story—the abuse of liberty. We shorten the hours of work, and we offer nothing in the place of work, except the street; we leave the lads, whom we thought to benefit, to their own devices, and to discover, if they can, the way to turn the hours thus rescued from drudgery into a means of climbing to a higher life. We leave them, even, in complete ignorance as to any higher life at all. Their own idea of employing their idle time is to do nothing, to amuse themselves, and, as the street is the only place where they can find amusement for nothing, they go into the street.

They begin by walking about in little companies of two and three; by way of asserting their early manhood the boys smoke cheap cigarettes, called, I believe, "fags"; also, by way of asserting their own importance—no one knows the conceit and vanity of lads of fifteen and sixteen, the age between the boy and the man—they occupy a great deal of the pavement, they hustle each other, regardless of other people; they get up impromptu fights and sham fights; they wrestle; they make rushes among the crowd; they push about the girls of their own age, who are by no means backward in appreciating and returning these delicate attentions; they whistle and sing, and practise the calls of the day and the locality. A very favorite amusement, in which they are joined and assisted by the girls, is to get up a little acting in dumb show; some of them are excellent mimics. I have, for instance, read more than once in the columns of temperance organs or the letters of philanthropists, tearful or indignant, most melancholy accounts of precocious drunkenness among the boys and girls of East London—that poor East London! "I have seen," writes the visitor to Ratcliffe and Shadwell, "with my own eyes, boys and girls, quite young boys and girls, reeling about drunk,—actually drunk, hopelessly drunk,—the girls, poor creatures, worse than the boys. I spoke to one. She was no more than thirteen or so—a pretty child, but helplessly intoxicated. When I spoke to her she tried to reply, but became inarticulate; she gasped, she laughed—the awful laugh of a drunkard! She made a gesture of helplessness, she fell sideways on the pavement, and would not rise. Her companions, as far gone as herself, only laughed. A sad sight, truly, in a civilized country!"

A very sad sight, indeed! This observer, however, did not understand that the personation of drunken people is one of the favorite amusements of the boys and girls in the evening streets. They have every day opportunities of studying their subject. A life school exists in every street, and is thrown open every night, and the fidelity with which every stage of drunkenness is represented by these young actors would be remarkable even on the boards of Drury Lane. Had the indignant writer of that letter known so simple a fact his pity and his wrath would have been reserved for a more worthy object.

Acting and running and shouting are amusing as far as they go, but they are not enough. The blood is very restless at seventeen; it wants exercise in reality. This restlessness is the cause of the certain street companies of which the London papers have recently spoken with indignation. They are organized originally for local fights. The boys

The "Hooligans"

of Cable Street constitute themselves, without asking the permission of the War Office, into a small regiment; they arm themselves with clubs, with iron bars, with leather belts to which buckles belong, with knotted handkerchiefs containing stones—a lethal weapon—with sling and stones, with knives even, with revolvers of the "toy" kind, and they go forth to fight the lads of Brook Street. It is a real fight; the field is presently strewn with the wounded; the police have trouble in putting a stop to the combat; with broken heads, black eyes, and bandaged arms, the leaders appear next day before the magistrate.

The local regiment cannot always be meeting its army on the field of glory; the next step, therefore, to hustling the people in the street is natural. The boys gather together and hold the street; if any one ventures to pass through it they rush upon him, knock him down, and kick him savagely about the head; they rob him as well. In the autumn of last year (1899) an inoffensive elderly gentleman was knocked down by such a gang, robbed, kicked about the head, and taken up insensible; he was carried home, and died the next day. These gangs are the modern Mohocks; South London is more frequently favored with their achievements than the quarter with which we are here concerned; they are difficult to deal with because they meet, fight, and disperse with such rapidity that it is next to impossible to get hold of them. It is an ugly feature of the time; it is mainly due to the causes I have pointed out, and it will probably disappear before long. Meantime, the boys regard the holding of the street with pride; their captain is a hero, as much as the captain of the Eleven at a public school.

Sometimes they devise other modes of achieving greatness. A year or two ago half a dozen of them thought that it would be a good thing if they were to attend Epsom races on the Derby Day, the great race of the year. One can go to Epsom by road or rail; the latter is the cheaper and the easier way, but the more glorious way is to go by road, as the swells go. They hire a carriage and pair, and get a luncheon hamper from Fortnum and Mason's, and pay for a stand on the hill—the thing can be done for about £25. These boys thought to emulate the swells; they would drive to Epsom. They therefore helped themselves to a baker's horse and light cart, and, all in the gray of the morning, drove the whole way in the greatest glory to the race-course. Arrived there they sold the horse and cart to a Gipsy for three pounds, and spent the day in watching the races, in betting on the events, and in feasting. When the glorious day was over and their money all gone they found an outhouse near the common, and there lay down to sleep, intending to walk home in the morning. Now, the baker, on discovering his loss, had gone to the police, and the police, remembering the day and suspecting the truth, for the lads' thirst for sport was well known, telegraphed to Epsom; the horse and cart were recovered, and in the middle of the night the boys themselves were found. They did return to town in the morning, but not as they left. It was in the roomy vehicle commonly called "Black Maria" that they were taken to the police court, and from the court to the Reformatory, where they still languish.

The boys are great gamblers. As gambling and betting are strictly forbidden in the streets, they have to find places where they can play undisturbed. Sunday is the day devoted to gambling. The boys get on board a barge, where they sit in the hold and play cards—locally called "darbs"—all day long; sometimes they find an empty house, sometimes a room in a condemned row of crazy tenements. The favorite game, the name of which I do not know, is one in which the dealer holds the bank; he deals a card to every player and one to himself. Each player covers his card with a stake, generally a penny; the cards are turned up; the players pay the dealer for cards below, and are paid for cards above

Sunday Gambling.

the dealer's card. It is quite a simple game, and one in which a boy may lose his Saturday wages in a very short time. They also play "heads and tails," and they are said to bet freely among each other.

At this period of their career some of them begin to read a good deal. Not the newspapers, not any books; their reading is confined to the penny novelette; for them Jack Harkaway performs incredible feats of valor; it is not for them that the maiden of low degree is wedded by the belted earl—that is for the girls; for these lads, to whom a fight is the finest thing in the world, the renowned Jack Harkaway knocks down the wicked captain on the quarter-deck, rescues a whole ship's company from pirates, performs prodigies at Omdurman. His feats are described in the amazing sheets which he calls "ha'penny bloods" or "penny dreadfuls." If the boys buy a paper it is one of like mind, such as are written and printed especially and exclusively for him.

They go often, I have said, to the music-hall; there are three or four in their own quarter—the Paragon, Mile End Road; the Foresters, Cambridge Road; and the Queen's, Poplar. But they go farther afield, and may be found in the galleries of even West-End music-halls to see a popular "turn." As for concerts and lectures and entertainments given at the Town Hall or other places, they will not go to them. There is too much "class."

At this time, namely, at sixteen or seventeen, the boys commonly take a sweetheart; they "keep company" with a girl; night after night they walk the streets together; what they talk about no one knows, what vows of constancy they exchange no man hath ever heard or can divine; they take each other, the boy paying when he can, to the music-hall or to the theater; they stand drinks—it is at this period that the fatal yearning for drink begins to fasten itself upon the lad. The "keeping company" is perhaps a worse evil than the growing thirst for drink; it ends, invariably, in the early marriage, which is one of the most deplorable features in the lower life; the young girl of sixteen or seventeen, ignorant of everything, enters upon the married life, and for the rest of her days endures all the wretchedness of grinding poverty, children half-nourished and in rags, a drunken husband and a drunken self. The boys' clubs, the girls' clubs, the settlements, of which I shall speak again presently, do all in their power to occupy the young people's minds with other things; but the club closes at ten, and the street remains open all night.

None of these street boys and girls—or very few, as I have said already—are country-born; the country lads come up to London Town, to the city paved with gold, in thousands, but they are older than these children of the street; they have not learned the fascination which the street exercises upon those who have always lived in it and always played in it.

Their martial tastes should make them enlist, but the discipline forbids enlistment. Many of them, however, belong to the Tower Hamlets Militia, a regiment called out for drill for six weeks every year. They enjoy sporting the uniform; they like marching; they like the band and the mess in barracks, but they cannot endure the discipline for more than six weeks, even in return for the grandeur and the glory of the thing.

What, then, is the connection between the casual hand and the lads of the street? This: the life of the street is an ordeal through which these lads must pass, since we give them no other choice; some of them emerge without harm; for them the craving for drink has not become a demoniac possession; they have never been haled before the police court; they know not the interior of prison or reformatory; they have not married at seventeen; these are the young fellows who get, and keep, permanent places with "good money," they are hewers of wood and drawers of water like the children of Gideon, yet they live not in the slums; their homes are in the Monotonies; theirs is a four- or six-roomed house, one of a row, one of a street, a flat in a barrack; their houses and dwelling-places stand side by side miles around. But the life that is led in these streets is not monotonous, because every man has his own life and his own experience, his birth and childhood, his manhood and his age, and these can never be monotonous.

There remain, alas! those with whom we began, the company of two or three who hang around the corner outside the public house or lean against the walls of the docks. They are the men whom the ordeal of the street, more than any other cause, has broken down. They have emerged from that ordeal with a confirmed habit of taking the Easy Way, that of no self-restraint, that which temptation indicates with beckoning finger and false smiles; at nineteen they have lost any possible joy of work, pride in work, desire for work—they know not any work which can afford the workman joy or pride; to them the necessity tor work is an ever-present curse which corrupts and poisons life. Were it not for this cruel necessity they might pass through the allotted span with no more effort and no more ambition than the common slug of the hedge.

Alas! work must be done if they would drink; they do not mind being badly fed; it is wonderful to think of the small amount of solid food they get, but they must drink. In their single room they have wife and children, but they must drink; they hang about waiting for work, in the hope that no work may come, yet that food will appear; they have neither honesty, nor self-respect, nor any sense of duty or responsibility at all. But they must drink.

What to do for, or with, these unfortunates is the most difficult and the most pressing question of the slums. The only hope seems to be to get hold of the boys and girls and to spare them, if possible, the cruel ordeal of the street.

And meantime, while we look and while we talk, lo! the company has melted away; the cold wind and the rain have fallen upon them; drink has robbed them of their immunity; the infirmary ward holds them to-day; to-morrow the pauper's funeral will wind up the sum and story of their sordid days.

VII

THE ALIEN

VII

THE ALIEN

LONDON has always held out hands of toleration, if not of welcome, to the alien. He has come to London from every part of Great Britain and Ireland, and from every country of Europe. Under the Plantagenets the country lad was as much an alien or a foreigner as the Hollander or the German. To country lads and the continental alike London was the city paved with gold. First came Saxon, Jute, and Angle; then came Dane; then Norman; after these came Fleming, French, German. The German, indeed, laid hands on our foreign trade and kept it for six hundred years; whenever one of our kings married a foreign princess the Queen's countrymen flocked over in swarms, to pick up what they could. William the Conqueror's consort brought over the weavers from her own country; when Eleanor of Provence married Henry III her people came with her, especially the ecclesiastics, seizing on dignities and benefices from the Archbishopric of Canterbury downward; when Queen Mary married Philip of Spain the streets of London were filled with Spaniards; when Charles I married Henrietta of France French priests, for the first time since the Reformation, paraded the streets by scores, offending the Protestant conscience. Italy and the South of France sent usurers with the pope's license to prey upon the land.

London was a city of refuge as well as a city where gold

was to be picked up in the streets. Many exiles have sought and found protection within its walls.

The most important of these arrivals was that of the French Huguenots after the revocation of the Edict of Nantes. An immense number came over; in one year 15,500 were relieved by the collection of a fund amounting to £63,713. A large colony of 13,500 of them settled in London, most of them in Spitalfields, at that time still a place of fields. Here they introduced the industry of silk-weaving, very much to the profit of the country and city of their adoption.

The next invasion of aliens was that of the unfortunate Palatines, in the year 1709. The Palatinate had been devastated by the French; it was a vast battle-field plundered during every incursion of the enemy; in despair, the people abandoned their country; they flocked over to England in companies and troops; the immigration continued for three years, during which time thirteen thousand thrust themselves upon the mercy of the City. A collection was made for them amounting to £22,038. These people, who seem to have been agricultural rather than industrial, contributed little to the population of London; three thousand of them were sent to Ireland; to each of the provinces of North and South Carolina six hundred were sent; to New York nearly four thousand, but seventeen hundred died on the voyage, no doubt enfeebled by their sufferings and privations before embarking; they seem not to have met with favor in New York; many of them emigrated to Pennsylvania, where, it is said, their descendants still preserve the memory of their origin. Those who settled in London got their names Anglicized, so that they were entirely absorbed and lost in the general population.

At the beginning of the French Revolution, when the madness of the revolutionaries fell upon the priests and nobles, there was an immense flight of the persecuted classes into

England. They did not however, as a rule, come to settle; as soon as circumstances permitted they returned to France; some, however, remained; it is not uncommon to find families descended from the *emigres* of 1792-93 who preserve the memory of their former nobility, though they have long since abandoned all intention of claiming a title which carries with it neither privilege nor property nor honor.

The *emigres* formed during their stay small colonies in and about London. One of them was at St. Pancras, in whose churchyard many of them are buried; another was a little further out, five or six miles out of the City, at Hampstead—the Roman Catholic chapel built for them still remains; there were other small settlements, and many of them remained in Westminster and in Soho. The hospitality offered them, the pity shown to them, the maintenance granted to them by our government, the cordial friendship extended to them by our people, were worthy of all praise. Yet it was remarked, with some bitterness, that when these refugees were enabled to return to their own country they ignored every obligation of gratitude, or even courtesy, and actually refused to admit their old friends of the English gentry to their salons in Paris. Partly, I believe, this apparent ingratitude was due to their poverty, of which they were ashamed.

Another political invasion of refugees was that of the Poles after their abortive rising in the thirties; they, too, were received by our government with a generosity unparalleled. There were many thousands of them. They were granted barracks to live in and a small pension to live upon; both were continued as long as they lived; they must now all be dead; some of them no doubt married here, and their children must now be part of the general population. A few of the most foolhardy ventured back again, to lead one more forlorn hope in another mad attempt at rebellion, and to die unprofitable patriots by the Russian bayonet.

In our own time there has been—it is still going on—a considerable influx of Russian Polish and German Jews flying from the Judenhetze of the continent. I will speak of them immediately.

Every year there is an immigration as from a barren and an unfertile soil to a land of promise. The immense strides made by industrial Germany during the last few

Whitechapel Shops.

years will probably check this immigration. Hamburg, Berlin, not to speak of Antwerp and Rotterdam, also rapidly growing centers of trade, will attract some of those who have been accustomed to look toward London as the land of promise. At present there appear to be about ten thousand new immigrants every year, without counting those who purpose going on to America. They consist of Russians, Poles, Germans, Dutch, Norwegians, Swedes, Danes, Belgians, French, Austrians, Hungarians, Italians, Swiss—but we have gone through the whole of Europe. I find no mention of Spain or Portugal or Turkey; nor are there, so far as I have heard, any aliens hailing from the smaller peoples—the Croats, Celts, Servians, or Bulgarians. What becomes of this array? What has become of the hundred thousand who have come over during the last ten years? Go up and down the streets of East London—over the shop-fronts you will see everywhere German and Jewish names, which seem to answer this question in part. Walk along the Whitechapel Road on a Sunday morning; there you will see most of the hundred thousand, there you will see the peaceful invaders who have occupied a large part of East London and have achieved for themselves, by dint of unconquerable patience and untiring work, a far better livelihood, with a far higher level of comfort, than could have been possible for them in their native lands. As for their children, you may look for them in the Board-schools; they have become English—both boys and girls: except for their names, they are English through and through; they accept our institutions, laws, and customs; they rejoice with our successes, they grieve with our misfortunes; never yet has it been known that the second generation of the alien has failed to become English through and through. I believe that our power of absorbing alien immigrants is even greater than that of the United States.

The foreign element, with the exception of the Polish Jews, and that only for mutual help and at the outset, does not seek to separate itself and to create its own quarter. In the West End, it is true, there are streets principally inhabited by Italians, French, and Swiss; that is because the people are employed in the restaurants as waiters and cooks, in the laundries, in the *charcuteries* and provision shops, which exist for the use of the foreigner. But their children will become English; you may see them playing on the asphalted pavements outside the schools; you fail to perceive any difference between the children of the German waiter and those of the English working-man. There are thousands of German clerks in London; they come over, some to stay, some to learn the conduct and the extent of English trade and to take back with them information about markets and prices and profits, which may be useful to their friends of Hamburg and Altona. In either case they learn English as quickly as they can, and live in the English fashion. Where, again, is the French colony? There are thousands of French people in London, but there is no French colony. There is a society of Huguenot families, there is a French hospital, there are two or three French Protestant churches, but there is no part of East London, or of any other quarter of London, where we may find French the prevailing speech. There are, again, a good many Dutch. Where are they? Some of them have a kind of colony in Spitalfields, where they make cigars; as for the rest, they are scattered. One may see some of them any Sunday morning in their church, all that is left of the great church of the Augustine Friars; in that old place a scanty congregation meets for service in the Dutch language and after the Dutch use. It is pleasant to sit among them and to look around upon the serious faces of the Hollanders, our former rivals, and to make believe to listen to the sermon, which sounds so much like English until you try to make out what it means. The feet of these honest burghers rest upon the dust of many great princes and lords and noble dames buried in the church of the Augustines, because it was so holy a place that sepulture here was a certain passport through purgatorial fires, without a stay in purgatory, to the gates of heaven. Hither, on the day after the battle of Barnet, which practically ended the Wars of the Roses, they brought, in the long, grunting country wagons, the bodies of the lords and knights who fell upon the field, and buried them within this church. That of Warwick the king-maker lay here, the face uncovered, for some days, so that the people might be assured of his death. But I doubt whether the Hollander cares much about the bones of ancient nobles. There are also Swedes in East London, but the only place where I have met them is in their church near St. George's-in-the-East, where you may see them any Sunday at the Swedish service. They are a pleasant-looking race, with brown hair and blue eyes; they appear to be largely composed of seafaring folk; one would like to be able to converse with them. However, they have no quarter of their own.

Of course, the most important foreign element in East London is that of the newly arrived Jewish immigrants. They are the poorest of the very poor; when they come over they have nothing. They are received by the Jewish Board of Guardians, which is, I believe, a model of a well-managed board; work is speedily found for them; their own people take them on at the lowest wage at which life can be sustained until they learn enough to move on and get higher pay. Their ranks are always recruited by new arrivals; there is talk of their taking work away from English workmen. Yet there seem to be no signs, as on the continent, of a Judenhetze, or any such wide-spread, unreasoning hatred of the Jew as we lately saw in France, and such as we have seen in Russia and in Germany.

The newly arrived Jews have their own colony. It has much increased of late years. They now occupy, almost to the exclusion of others, a triangular area of East London—without a map it is not easy to make the limits understood—lying north of the Whitechapel Road immediately without the city limits: it has a base of nearly half a mile and an altitude of three fourths of a mile. Here, for the time, the poorer Jews are all crowded together. It is alleged that they have ingenious ways of sweating each other; as soon as the Polish Jew has got his head a little above water he begins to exploit his countrymen; he acquires the miserable tenements of the quarter and raises the rent and demands a large sum for the "key"—that is to say, the fine on going in.

These Jews all succeed, unless they are kept down by their

favorite vice of gambling. It is perhaps as well for their own peace that for the first few years of their residence in London they should live in their own quarter, among their own people. For the transformation of the poor, starving immigrant, willing to do anything at any wage, to the prosperous master workman is unlovely. He succeeds partly because he is extremely industrious, patient, orderly, and law-abiding. But there are other reasons. It is sometimes pretended that the Jew is endowed naturally with greater intellectual power than is granted to men of other nationality. This I do not believe. The truth seems to be that advanced by Mr. Charles Booth, I think for the first time. "The poorest Jew," he says, "has inherited through the medium of his religion a trained intellect." This fact, if you consider it, seems quite sufficient, taken with those other gifts of industry and obedience to order and law, to explain the Jew's success among the poorer classes through which he works his way upward.

He is a person of trained intellect. What does this mean? Poor and miserable as he stands before you, penniless, ragged, half-starved, cringing, this man has been educated in the history of his own people, in the most ancient literature of the world, in a body of law which exercises all the ingenuity and casuistry of his teachers to harmonize with existing conditions. It is like putting into the works of an engineer, among the general hands, one who has been trained in applied mathematics. Into any kind of work which means competition, the Jew brings the trained intellect and the power of reasoning due to his religious training; he brings also the habit of looking about for chances and looking ahead for possibilities which long generations of self-defense have made hereditary. These faculties he brings into the market; with them he contends against the dull mind, untrained and simple, of the English craftsman. What wonder if he succeeds? Nothing but brute violence, which he will not meet with here, can keep him down.

This I believe to be the great secret of the Jew's success. It is his intellectual superiority over working-men of his own class. Observe, however, that we do not find him conspicuously successful when he has to measure his intellectual strength against the better class. In law, for instance, he has produced one or two great lawyers, but not more than his share; in mathematics and science, one or two great names, but not more than his share. I am inclined to think that in every branch of intellectual endeavor the Jew holds his own. But I doubt if it can be proved that he does more. So long as we can hold our own in the higher fields there will be no Judenhetze in this country. I am informed, however, that the leaders of the people in London are persistent in their exhortations to the new-comers to make themselves English—to make themselves English as fast as possible; to send their children to the Board-schools, and to make them English. It is the wisest advice. There should be no feeling as of necessary separation between Jew and Christian. We ought to live in amity beside each other, if not with each other; we should no more ask if a man is a Jew than we ask if a man who has just joined our club is a Roman Catholic or a Unitarian.

Yet, even in this country, it cannot be said that the Jew is popular; there are prejudices against him which are no longer those concerning his religion. Here, again, I turn to the authority who has made so profound a study of the question; the importance of the question is my excuse. This is how Mr. Charles Booth explains the dislike and suspicion with which the Jews are still regarded by many: "No one will deny that the children of Israel are the most law-abiding inhabitants of East London. . . . The Jew is quick to perceive that law and order, and the sanctity of contract, are the *sine qua non* of a full and free competition in the open market. And it is by competition, and by competition alone, that the Jew seeks success. But in the case of the foreign Jews it is a competition unrestricted by the personal dignity of a definite standard of life and unchecked by the social feelings of class loyalty and trade integrity. The small manufacturer injures the trade through which he rises to the rank of a capitalist by bad and dishonest production. The petty dealer suits his wares and his terms to the weakness, the ignorance, and the vice of his customers; the mechanic, indifferent to the interests of the class to which he belongs, and intent only on becoming a small master, acknowledges no limit to the process of underbidding fellow-workers except the exhaustion of his own strength. In short, the foreign Jew totally ignores all social obligations other than keeping the law of the land, the maintenance of his own family, and the charitable relief of coreligionists."

The place and time in which to see the poorer Jews of London collected together is on Sunday morning in Wentworth Street and Middlesex Street, Aldgate — the old Petticoat Lane. These streets and those to right and left are inhabited entirely by Jews; Sunday is their market-day; all the shops are open; the streets are occupied by a triple line of stalls, on which are exposed for sale all kinds of things, but chiefly garments — coats and trousers. There is a mighty hubbub of those who chaffer and those who offer and those who endeavor to attract attention. You will see a young fellow mounted on a pair of wooden steps, brandishing something to wear; with eloquence convincing, with gesture and with action, he declares and repeats and assures the people of the stoutness of the material and the excellence of the work. The crowd moves slowly along, it listens critically; this kind of thing may become monotonous; the oratory of the salesman, in order to be effective, continually requires new adjectives, new metaphors, new comparisons; among the crowd are other professors of the salesman's rhetoric. They know the tricks, they have learned the art. One wonders how many such fervid speeches this young man has to make before he effects a single sale. We need not pity

A Corner in Petticoat Lane.

him, although at the close of the market his voice is hoarse with bawling and the results are meager; he enjoys the thing; it is his one day of glory, and he has admirers; he knows that among the audience there are many who envy his powers and would fain take his place and deceive the people.

Not all the holders of stalls are so eloquent. Here, before a miserable tray resting on crazy trestles, stand a ragged old couple. They look very, very poor; they cast wistful eyes upon the heedless crowd; their wares are nothing but common slippers of bright red and blue cloth. Will you buy a pair because the makers are so old and so poor? Alas! they cannot understand your offer; their only language is Yiddish, that remarkable composite tongue which in one place is a mixture of Russian and Hebrew, in another of German and Hebrew, in another of Lettish and Hebrew. They stare, they eagerly offer their wares; a kindly compatriot from the crowd interprets. There is a little bargaining, and the slippers are in your pocket. Very well. It is a piece of good luck for the old pair; like unto him who had the splendid shilling "fate cannot harm them; they will dine to-day." True to their national instincts, which are Oriental, they have made you pay three times as much for the slippers as they would charge one of their own people. Going on slowly with the crowd one admires the variety of the wares laid out on trestles. Who wants these rusty iron things—keys, locks, broken tools, things unintelligible? Somebody, for there is noisy chaffering.

You observe that the newly arrived Polish Jew is for the most part a man of poor physique; he is a small, narrow-chested, pasty-faced person. "Is this," you ask, "a descendant of Joshua's valiant captains? Is this the race which followed Judas Maccabæus? Is this the race which defied the legions of Titus?" "My friend," replies a kindly scholar, one of their own people, "these are the children of the Ghetto. For two thousand years they have lived in the worst parts of a crowded city; they have been denied work, except of the lowest; they have endured every kind of scorn and contumely. Come again in ten years' time. In the free air of Anglo-Saxon rule they will grow; you will not know them again."

It is among these new-comers that one recognizes the Oriental note; there is among the women a love of bright colors; among the men, even with the poorest, a certain desire for display; an assertion of grandeur. Look at this little shop of one window on the ground floor. It is crowded with girls. Outside the proprietor stands. He is not tall, but he swells with pride; a large cigar is between his lips; it is a sign and a symbol. His poorer countrymen look with envy upon that very large cigar.

A "Schnorrer" (Beggar) of the Ghetto.

He condescends to talk because he is so proud that he must display the cause of his glory. "All the week," he says, "I study what to give them on Sunday. To-day it's bonnets. Last Sunday it was fichus. Next Sunday? That is my secret. My wife serves the shop. I furnish the contents. All the week my son Jacob keeps it, but there is no trade except on Sunday."

In a second-hand furniture shop, to which we have been directed, the proprietor sits among his tables and chairs. He also has a large cigar for the better display of his grandeur. He is conscious of the envy with which the man who has a shop is regarded by a man who must work with his own hands. This man has more—he has a father. You called on purpose to see that father. You would like to see him? You are invited to step up-stairs. There, in a high-backed chair, with pillows on either side, sits a little shriveled-up creature. His eyes are bright, for he has just awakened from the sleep which fills up most of the day and all the night. Beside him is the Book of the Law in Hebrew. Upon the open book there rests his pipe. Two girls, his great grandchildren, sit with him and watch him. For the old man is a hundred and three years of age. Yet he can still read his Hebrew Bible, and he can still take his pipe of tobacco.

"Last night," said one of the girls, "we carried him downstairs into the shop, and the people crowded round to see him. He drank a whole glass of beer—in their sight."

The patriarch nods and laughs, proud of the feat. He then talks about himself. He was born in the Ghetto of Venice—you can see the place to this day. His father came to London when he was a child. His occupation, he tells us, was formerly that of cook. He was employed as cook for the great banquets of the City companies; in that capacity he used to drink as much wine as he wished to have, and in those days he wished for a great deal. His lengthened years, therefore, are not due to abstinence from strong drink. He was also a follower of the Ring, and was constantly engaged as second or bottle-holder in the prize-fights so common in the first sixty years of the century. He remembers what was once considered a great political event, the committal of Sir Francis Burdett to the Tower of London in 1808. Sir Francis was at the time a leading Radical. He was afterward the father of Angela, Lady Burdett-Coutts, a leader in the noble army of philanthropists.

We are not allowed to talk too long to this ancient and venerable survival. After a quarter of an hour or so his watchful nurses dismiss us, and he promises to see us again —"if I live," he adds, with a sigh. "If I live." It is his constant refrain. He has outlived all his friends, all his companions, all his enemies, all his contemporaries. There is no pleasure left to him save that of being admired on account of extreme old age. It is enough. It binds him to life; he would not wish to die so long as that is left. "If I live," he says.

For my own part, I like sometimes to sit in the synagogue on the Sabbath and listen to the service, which I do not understand. For it seems to explain the people—their intense pride, their tenacity, their separation from the rest of the world. Their service—I may be mistaken; I have no Hebrew—strikes upon my ears as one long, grand hymn of praise and gladness. The hymns they sing, the weird, strange melodies of the hymns, are those, they allege, which were sung when Israel went out of Egypt; they are those which were sung when in the Red Sea the waters stood up like a wall on either side to let them through; they are those which were sung when Pharaoh's hosts lay drowning and the walls of water closed together. The service, the reading, the hymns, the responses—they are all an assertion that the choice of the Lord hath fallen upon this people; the Lord their God hath chosen them. Let no one speak of Jews until he has listened to their service. By their worship the mind of a people may be discerned.

I have already mentioned the settlement of the Huguenot silk-weavers at Spitalfields—the fields behind the old hospital and monastery called St. Mary's. There they have remained. Until quite recently, they carried on from father to son the trade of silk-weaving; there are silk-weavers in

Spitalfields and Bethnal Green. An attempt has been made to revive the trade; meantime many of the old houses remain with their wide windows on the first floor, and over the shops one may still see the French names, or these names rudely Anglicized. But the French settlement no longer exists; the French language has been forgotten, and the Huguenots are completely absorbed. They are now like all the rest of us, a mongrel blend of Celt, Saxon, Dane, Norman, Fleming, and everything else. It is the Anglo-Saxon blend, or, as we ought rather to call it, the Anglo-Celtic blend.

A small colony of Italians has settled in another part of London—not in East London. You would know the colony, which does not belong to these pages, if you were to stumble upon it accidentally, by the barrel-organs in the courts, by the barrows on which the Italian costers carry round their penny ices, by the bright-colored handkerchiefs and the black hair of the women, and by the cheap Italian restaurants, where the colonists can rejoice in Italian cookery and Italian wine.

In the West India Dock Road, before you reach the docks, there is a building on the north side which contains a colony always changing. It is the home of the Indian and Malay sailors—the Lascars and the Arabs. I remember spending a morning there with one who was afterward murdered by Cairene ruffians in the desert of Sinai. This man loved the place because he loved the Oriental folk who lodged there, and because he not only talked their languages, but knew their manners and customs, and would sit with them after their manner, talk with them on their own subjects, and become one of themselves. On this occasion he met a certain poor Persian scholar down on his luck. He was a man of great dignity and presence, insomuch that one realized the truth that in the East clothes do not make the man. He was in rags, but he had lost nothing of his dignity. It was pleasant to see them sitting down together on the floor, side by side, discussing and quoting Persian poetry, and still more pleasant to see the Persian quickly yielding to the charm of a common love of literature and treating the infidel as a friend and a brother. It is a strange place and full of strange people; no one can understand how strange it is, how great is the gulf between the Oriental and the Occidental, unless he can talk with them and learn how they think and how they regard us. My friend interpreted for me, afterward, something of what the Persian scholar had said. Colossal is the pride of the Oriental; inconceivable the contempt with which he regards the restless West.

> " Here as I sit by the Jumna bank,
>   Watching the flow of the sacred stream,
> Pass me the legions, rank on rank,
>   And the cannon roar and the bayonets gleam."
>
>   . . . .
>
> " When shall these phantoms wither away,
>   Like the smoke of the guns on the wind-swept hill,
> Like the sounds and colors of yesterday;
>   And the soul have rest and the air be still? "

Nearly opposite this house is a small street which contains the Chinese colony. Compared with the Chinese colony of New York, part of which I once visited, one sweltering night in July, that of London is a small thing and of no importance. Yet it is curious. There are not, I believe, more than a hundred Chinese, or thereabouts, in all; they occupy a few houses in this street; there are one or two small shops kept by Chinamen; it is considered quite safe to visit the place, at all events in the daytime; I was myself taken there by one who was personally known to the shopkeepers. There was not much that was attractive or interesting offered for sale, except Chinese playing-cards, which are curious; conversation in Pidgin-English is difficult at first, but one quickly acquires enough of the *patois*. There is a boarding-house for Chinese in the street; the ground floor we found furnished with a tiny joss-house, in one corner, and a large table which occupied nearly the whole of the room; the table was covered with Chinamen sitting and sprawling; they were wholly absorbed in a little gamble with dominoes and small Chinese coins; their absorption in the chances of the game was complete. One of them, the banker, manipulated the dominoes; nobody spoke; every time that a domino was turned there was the exchange of coins in silence. The eager, intent faces were terrifying; one recognized the passion which sees nothing, hears nothing, cares for nothing, feels nothing, but the fierce eagerness of play. We looked on for five minutes. No one spoke, no one breathed. Then I became aware that in a room, a cupboard at the back, there was a fire, with a great black pot hanging over it and a man with a spoon taking off the cover and stirring the contents and inspecting the progress of the stew. Presently he came out, ladle in hand, and bawled aloud, but in Chinese. I took his bawling for an announcement of dinner. But none of the players heard; the banker turned up another domino; there was another exchange of coins; no one heeded the call.

Yet it was the dinner-bell; down-stairs came chattering, laughing, and joking, half a dozen of the boarders, each with a basin in his hand. The cook filled every man's basin, and they went up-stairs again, and none of the players marked them or heeded them, or turned his head, and none of the boarders took the slightest notice of the players. Nobody meanwhile paid the least attention to the joss-house, where burned the candle which is said to be the Chinaman's sole act of worship. And nobody took the least notice of the stranger who stood at the door and looked on.

Across the road, in another house, was an opium den. We have read accounts of the dreadful place, have we not?

Greatly to my disappointment, because when one goes to an opium den for the first time one expects a creeping of the flesh at least, the place was neither dreadful nor horrible. The room was of fair size, on the first floor; it was furnished with a great bed, covered with a mattress; there was a bench against the wall, and there were half a dozen common cane chairs. Two men were lying on the bed enjoying the opium sleep, perhaps with the dreams that De Quincey has described—but one cannot, even the thought reader cannot, read another man's dreams. A third man was taking his opium by means of a long pipe. Half a dozen men were waiting their turn. One of them had a musical instrument. Except for the smell of the place, which was overwhelming, the musical instrument was the only horror of the opium den. When I think of it I seem to remember a thousand finger-nails scratching the window, or ten thousand slate-pencils scratching a schoolboy's slate. It is one of those memories which sink into the brain and never leave a man. Nor can I understand why, under the weird and wonderful torture of the intolerable music of that instrument, even the sleepers themselves did not awake, their dreams dissipated, their opium, so to speak, wasted and rendered of none account, and fly, shrieking, forswearing forever opium and the Chinese quarter.

There are small colonies and settlements of other foreigners. Anarchists make little clubs where murders are hatched, especially murders of foreign sovereigns; they think to overthrow a settled government by the assassination of a king; they succeed only in adding one more to the anxieties and the dangers that accompany a crown. There are Orleanists, Bonapartists, Carlists, and I know not what, who carry on their little intrigues and their correspondence with partizans in France and Spain and elsewhere, with a great show of zeal and much promise of results—the day after tomorrow. But with these we have nothing to do. It is enough for us to note the continual immigration into London of aliens who become in a few years English in manners, and in the next generation are English in speech and in thought, in will, as in manners. As it was in the days of Edward I, when the men of Rouen, the men of Caen, the men of the Empire, the Venetian, the Genoese, the Fleming, the Gascon, the Spaniard, the Hamburger, from every part of western Europe came as merchants to trade, and remained to settle. So it is in the days of Victoria. They come to the banks of the Thames by thousands every year, and they come to stay, and they are content to be absorbed.

VIII

THE HOUSELESS

VIII

THE HOUSELESS

AT the present moment nearly all those parts of East London which are inhabited by working-men of all kinds, from the foreman and the engineer and the respectable craftsman in steady employ at good wages down to the casual and the dock-hand and the children of the street, are suffering from a dearth of houses. In this vast labyrinthine maze of streets—all houses—there are not enough houses. The people are willing to incur discomfort; a respectable household, accustomed to the decencies of life and the wholesome separation of their children from themselves and from each other, will consent to pack them all into one room, or into a workman's flat of two rooms in a "model" barrack; they are ready to offer double the former rent, with a tremendous premium on the "key," but still there are no houses and no lodgings to be had even on those terms. The rents of the lowest tenements are mounting daily; there seems to be no limit in the upward tendency; the landlord is no longer doubtful as to the increased rent he can demand; the rise is automatic, it goes on without any stimulus or grinding on his part. A single room, in some quarters, is the very best that can be hoped for; the rent of that room, which was formerly from three to four shillings, is now six or more, while the charge for the "key,"—*i. e.*, the fine on taking the room,—which was formerly a few shillings, is now a pound or even more.

Meantime, although they are willing to pay the high rents,

people are everywhere found wandering in search of lodgings. A workman who has found employment must be within easy reach of his work; if he cannot find lodgings, what is he to do? The workhouse authorities have in some cases risen to the occasion. They agree to take in a man's wife and family and to keep them at a fixed charge until the breadwinner finds a lodging. He himself seeks a fourpenny bed at a "doss" house—*i. e.*, a common lodging-house.

In some parts it is reported that the overcrowding has actually led to the letting, not of rooms, but of beds; the children are put to sleep under the bed; men on night duty hire the bed for the day; nay, it is even said that beds are divided among three tenants, or sets of tenants. Of these one will occupy it from ten in the evening till six in the morning, another from six in the morning till two in the afternoon, and a third from two until ten. This Box and Cox arrangement would present difficulties with the children.

The situation, which has been growing worse for a long time, has now reached that acute stage in a social problem when it can no longer be neglected by statesmen or by philanthropists. Attention, at least, has been called to the evil—papers are read, articles are written, speeches are made; so far we have got little farther than an understanding of the difficulties which are such as to seem fatal to any proposed remedy that has been yet advanced. For my own part, I have no views except a conviction that something must be done, and that without delay, and that the best that can be done will only be the least dangerous of many proposed experiments.

The subject may appear technical and dry, but it is impossible to speak of work-a-day London without touching on the difficulty of housing the people. A speaker at a recent meeting took exception to the phrase "housing of the people." He said, which is quite true, that the people are not cattle. We are not, yet we must be housed whether we are rich or poor, or only middling. I am, myself, housed indifferent well, but I feel no comparison with an ox or a cow when I am told so.

The facts of the case were first ascertained by a commissioner for the "Daily News," and published in that paper early in 1899. The work was carried out by Mr. George Haw, a resident in one of the new settlements. The reader who wishes to consider the subject from every point of view is referred to the volume in which Mr. Haw has reprinted his valuable papers.

It is not probable that the difficulties which any one populous city has to encounter have no lesson to convey to other cities, though the circumstances in each case must vary with the conditions of site, access, and many other considerations. Overcrowding in New York or in Boston would certainly present many features differing widely from those in London. Moreover, the remedy or the alleviations which would serve in one case might be impossible in another.

The principal causes operating to produce this overcrowding are three—the vast and rapid increase of population, the extraordinary development of new industries in East London, with a consequent demand for more labor, and the flocking of country lads into the town.

For instance, there are two places, both lying outside the limits of the London County Council, which twenty or thirty years ago were mere villages or rural hamlets, the churches standing among market gardens and fields, having still their great houses and gardens, the residence of City merchants who drove in their own carriages to and from their offices. One of them, called East Ham, I remember, a quarter of a century ago, as a village spread about on a large area, as if land had no value. It was a flat expanse, fertile, and lying close to the Thames marshes. The map of that time shows farms and farmhouses, almshouses, and a few cottages. This place has now a population of ninety thousand, increasing every day, and consisting entirely of the working-class.

Its neighbor, formerly also a village a little nearer London and called West Ham, presents on the map of 1891 the aspect, familiar to the growing suburban town, of a small central area covered with streets, and with new streets running out north, south, east, and west. It is quite obvious from the map that West Ham was destined to be rapidly built over. It is now a huge town of two hundred and seventy thousand people, also, like East Ham, entirely consisting of working-people. It was at one time a place much loved by Quakers; evidence of their occupation still remains in certain stately old houses, now let out in lodgings; their gardens are built over; the character of the place is changed; the streets are crowded with people; trains and omnibuses run about all day; one of the Quaker's gardens still survives; it belonged to a member of the Gurney family; the house has been pulled down, but the lordly garden is kept up and the grounds around it have become the park for the West Ham folk. The quickened demand for lodgings has caused the whole of this town to be overrun with streets of small workmen's houses, containing four or six rooms each, most of which are let to families by two rooms or by single rooms. But the demand still continues; by-streets are run across, narrow lanes usurp the small backyard or little slip of garden; when the whole available space is built over, what will happen next? The crazy condition of these jerry-built houses, after a few years, opens up another and a different set of questions. The case of West Ham represents only on a more rapid scale what has been going on for many years over the whole of industrial London. And now we seem at last to have arrived at an end to the accommodation possible on the old method of small houses and narrow streets.

The results of the overcrowding are, as might be expected, deplorable in the extreme. Among other evils, it kills the infants; it dwarfs those who grow up among its evil influences; it poisons the air; it deprives the house of comfort, of cleanliness, of decency; it drives the man to drink; and it

East and West Ham.

East and West Ham, from the Marshes.

THE HOUSELESS

makes the life of their unhappy wives one long-continued misery of hopeless battle with dirt and disease. The late Sir Benjamin Richardson would allow, in his "City of Health," no more than twenty-five persons to an acre; in some of the outlying suburbs of London there are no more; in others there are, or have been, actually as many as 3000 people crowded together over a single acre of ground. Put them up all together in a solid square; each person will take 2 feet by 1½ feet—that is, three square feet. The whole company of 3000 will stand on 9000 square feet, or 1000 square yards. This is about a fifth of an acre, so that if we spread them out to cover the whole of the acre each person will have no more than a square yard and a half in which to stand, to sleep, and to breathe.

Of course, the first effect of the overcrowding is the vitiation of the air. The extent of this vitiation has been ascertained by chemical analysis. But, indeed, the senses of sight and smell do not require the aid of chemical analysis in order to prove that the air is corrupt and unwholesome. It is poisoned by the breathing of so many; by the refuse that will always be found lying about where a multitude of people are massed together; by all the contributions of all the unwashed. Sometimes the kindly rains descend and wash the pavements and the roads; sometimes the fresh breeze quickens and drives out the malodorous air from the narrow streets, but wind and rain cannot enter into rooms where the occupants jealously keep the windows closed, and fear cold more than they fear the fetid breath of diphtheria and fever; the wind drops; the warm sun comes out; then from the ground under and between the stones, from the saturated road, from the brick walls, from the open doors, the foul air steals back into the street and hangs over the houses invisible, yet almost as pestilential as the white mist of the morning that floats above the tropical marsh.

The magnitude of the evil may be estimated by the fact

that nearly a million people have to live in London under these conditions. A whole million of people are condemned to this misery and to the moral and physical sufferings entailed—the degradation of decent women, the death of children who might have grown up honest and respectable men and women! A whole million! We cannot think in millions; the magnitude of the number conveys no impression as to the magnitude of the evil. We can only realize it by taking a single case. Let us take the case of A. B. and his family. He was by trade a mechanical engineer; perhaps they called him a fitter, but it matters nothing; he was a decent and a sober man; he had a wife and five children, the eldest of whom was twelve and as "likely" a girl as one would see anywhere—but they were all likely children, clean and well kept and well fed and well mannered, the pride of their mother. The man had employment offered him in some works. It was absolutely necessary for him to live near his work. He broke up, therefore, his "little home"—they all delight in making a "little home"—and brought his children to live in the overcrowded quarter near his work. After a great deal of difficulty he secured one room. It was no more than ten feet square; in that room he had to pack all his children and his wife and all his effects. There was simply no room for the latter; he therefore pawned them; it would be only for a time, a few days, a week or two, and they would find a house, or at least better lodgings. Imagine, if you can, the change. This unfortunate family came from a decent flat of three rooms, in which the two boys slept in the living-room, the three girls in one bedroom and the parents in the other. They had on the staircase access to a common laundry; the roof was the place for drying the clothes; it was also a place where on a summer evening they could breathe fresh air. In place of this flat they had to accommodate themselves in a single small room. This had to contain all their furniture; to be at once the common bedroom, living-room, kitchen, wash-house, drying-room, dressing-room—think of it! There was, however, no choice. They pawned most of their "sticks"; they brought in nothing but absolute necessaries; they had a large bed, a table, a cupboard, two or three chairs, some kitchen things, and a washtub—little else. And so, uncomplaining, they settled down. It would only be for a week or two. Meantime, the rent of this den was 6s. 6d. a week, and a pound for the "key."

Outside, the pressure grew worse; the more the factories flourished, the more hands were wanted; new houses were run up with all the speed and all the scamping of work that a jerry-builder could provide, but still the pressure grew. For the man his home brought no comfort; he was not a drinking man, but he began to sit in the public house and to spend his evenings talking; his children could not sit at home; they ran about the streets; the eldest girl, who was so pretty and had been so sweet, began to assume the loud talk and rowdy habits of the girls around her; on the unfortunate woman lay the chief burden of all. She toiled all day long to keep things sweet and clean; alas! what can be done when seven people have to sleep in a room with little more than a thousand cubic feet of air between them all? She saw her husband driven away to the public house, she saw her children losing their bright looks and their rosy cheeks: what could she do? Many of the women around her, giving up the struggle, went in and out of the public house all day. This woman did not. But she was no longer the neat, clean housewife amid her clean surroundings. The stamp of deterioration was upon her and upon the others.

Then the summer came, with a week of hot weather to begin with, and the foundation of the house asserted itself; the house, you see, was built upon the rubbish of the dust-cart. You do not believe it possible? I can show you whole streets in the suburbs which I have myself seen built upon the rubbish of the dust-heap. It contains, among other things useful and beneficial to the occupants, quantities of cabbage stumps and other bits of vegetable matter. So when the hot weather came the cabbage stumps behaved accordingly; the foul air from the foundations crept through the floors and crawled up the stairs and poured under the doors.

First it was sore throat, then it was something else, and from house to house it was spread, and the doctor came and went, and in the broad bed of the little room lay four children sick at once; their soft, white skins were hard and dry and red; their brains wandered; the mother, with haggard face, bent over them.

It is all over now; three of the children lie in the new cemetery; the man has got a house at last; he will not get back his children, nor will the two who are left to him ever be again what they once were. This is one story out of the thousands which may be told of the people who live in the crowded quarters.

Another cause of overcrowding springs from the bad building of the workmen's houses. It is not only the foundation that is rotten: the house itself is built of bad brick laid in single courses, the woodwork is unseasoned and shrinks, zinc is used instead of lead, the stairs are of matchboard—only the cheapest and worst materials are used. There are laws, there always have been laws, against bad building; there are inspectors, yet the bad building continues. A man who had been an apprentice in the building trade told me how this surprising result of our laws and our inspectors used to be possible twenty-five years ago. "It is this way," he said; "I was a boy when these houses were built. For a house like this it was £15 to the inspector; for one of the smaller houses it was £10." We must not believe it possible for such a thing to happen now; one's faith in human nature would suffer too severe a blow, but when one looks around

THE HOUSELESS

in certain quarters that little transaction between the honest builder and the faithful inspector recurs to my unwilling memory.

In course of time authority interposes. The houses are condemned. Out go the people, with their sticks, into the street; the houses are boarded up, the boys throw stones at the windows; the place is deserted. But where are the people to go?

There is a riverside parish entirely inhabited by the lowest kind of working-people, chiefly dock laborers and casuals and factory girls. There are literally no inhabitants of a higher class, except the clergy and a few ladies who live and work among the people. There was until recently a population of eight thousand in this parish. But street after street has been condemned; the houses, boarded up, their windows broken by the boys, stand miserably waiting to be pulled down; the parish has lost three thousand of its population. Where have they gone? Nobody knows; but they must go somewhere, and they have certainly gone where the rents are higher and the crowding worse.

Or the London County Council, becoming aware of the insanitary condition of a whole area, condemns it all, *en bloc*, takes it over, pulls down the miserable tenements and erects new buildings in their place. Nothing could be better; everybody applauds this vigorous action. Yet what happens? I will show you from a single example.

There is an area of fifteen acres in Bethnal Green, one of the worst and most overcrowded parts of London. It contains twenty streets, all small; there were 730 houses, and there were 5719 people. About a third of this army lived in tenements of one room each; nearly a half lived in tenements of two rooms. This area has been entirely cleared away; the London County Council turned out the people, and built upon the site a small town whose streets are fifty feet wide, whose houses are five stories high; water and gas are laid on, workshops are provided, there are only thirty one-room tenements, there are only five hundred of two rooms, and so on; the rent of the two-room tenements is six shillings a week; the center of the area is occupied by a circular terraced garden. Nothing could be better. Moreover, to crown all, the cost of the whole will be repaid to the ratepayers by means of a sinking fund spread over sixty years.

BUT—what became of the five thousand while these fine palaces were being built? Did their condition improve? Or did it become worse during the period of construction? They were turned out; they had to go somewhere; they imposed themselves upon districts already overcrowded, their habits most certainly grew more careless and more draggled, their condition most certainly grew worse. How many of the five thousand will come back to the old quarters and enter upon the civilized life offered to them? I know not; but the experience is that the former occupants do not return.

London in all directions is now thickly planted with the huge, ugly erections called model lodging-houses, workmen's residences, and barracks. South London, across the river, is especially rich in these erections. Drury Lane, the historic Drury Lane, once the home of Nell Gwynne, the site of the National Theatre, accommodates a vast number of people in its barracks; it is favored also with two playgrounds for the children; both are disused burial grounds—one of them is the burial ground in "Bleak House."

Opinions vary as to the success of these buildings. Their advantages at first sight appear overwhelming. Step out of a Drury Lane block into one of the courts beside it and a dozen advantages will immediately be perceived by all your senses at once. It is a great thing to be clean if you like cleanliness; to have a sanitary house if you like fresh air; to have conveniences for washing if, unlike Dr. Johnson, you prefer your linen to be clean. But there are certain losses about the block building. I do not say that they are greater than the gains. It has always been the instinctive desire of the Englishman to have his own home, to himself, separate. It is a survival of the early Anglo-Saxon custom when each family formed a settlement to itself. The workingman would like to have his cottage and his bit of garden, and to enjoy his own individuality apart from the rest of the world. In the block he loses this distinction; his family is one of fifty, of a hundred; his children are part of a flock, there is no more distinction among them than in a flock of sheep. There are great dangers attending the loss of the individual; it tends to destroy ambition, to weaken the power of free thought, to injure the responsibility of self-government. This loss is a very great danger among a people whose whole history illustrates the value of a sturdy assertion of self, of personal independence, of responsibility, and of a continual readiness to revolt against any encroachments of authority. For these reasons many regard the barrack or block system with suspicion and dislike.

Other reasons there are which make these flats unpopular, even though they continue to be in great request. They are defects which might be managed by the exercise of a little organization. But it has not yet occurred to the managing bodies of these barracks that the tenants who are intrusted with the votes for the government of the country might also very well be intrusted with the government of their own dwellings. Thus it is complained that a whole staircase is sometimes terrorized by two or three roughs, that there are quarrels and drunken brawls on the stairs at night, that there are continual disputes concerning the day for using the laundry, that the stairs are not kept clean, that the children see and hear and learn things which they should not—but then the children of the streets learn things which they should not; I fear we cannot keep the children from the tree of knowledge. The presence of drunken rowdies, the objection of many to take their share in cleaning the stairs, and other scandals of the kind ought all to be remedied or, at least, attacked by the formation of committees of order composed of the tenants themselves. I have long been of opinion that the real remedy of most of the abuses of our streets and slums would be the organization of the respectable inhabitants into committees of order and the banishment of the police. Such committees in our barrack dwellings should have power of ejectment against evil-doers; they should be their own police.

It is characteristic of the Salvation Army that they sometimes attack a rowdy staircase in their own way by sending two girl lieutenants to take a flat and live there, setting an example of cleanly and orderly life, and bringing round the women to a better mind. I have heard that their success in this work has been marked, and I am prepared to believe it. At the same time, the committee would be a permanent police, while the appearance of the girls can only be occasional and only temporary.

Another result of the barrack life—one which the working-man himself does not perceive—is that the children grow up slow of sight, not short-sighted, but slow of sight. They have nothing to exercise their eyes upon; in the country there are a thousand things; children are always looking about them for the birds, the creatures, the flowers, the berries; in the barracks their playground is an asphalted pavement, with the high houses for boundary walls; there is nothing to look at. When they are taken out for a day in the country, once or twice a year, they see in a bank of flowers only a breadth of color, such as a house-painter might spread; it takes time for them to discern the flowers and the grasses which produce the pleasing effect; one bird is to them the same as another; they are not quick enough to catch the rapid flight of the swallow. One tree is the same as another; they do not discern differences of shape or color in the leaf or in the bough. A few summer days in the country cannot give to that child the training of sight which the country-bred child receives every time it goes out into the open.

Here, then, are the facts of the case: overcrowding, with results most dangerous to the community, and the principal causes—increase of population, rapid development of industries, the necessity of being near the work, the condemnation of insanitary streets and areas. There remain the remedies proposed. We have seen that the erection of blocks, while it provides decent accommodation for a vast number of working-men, turns out a large number into the streets to find what accommodation they can. Obviously, therefore, the further extension of this method would result in far worse overcrowding. The housing in big barracks has also, it has been seen, its own dangers.

We come, next, to the proposal which seems to meet with the greatest amount of favor. It is the creation and erection of industrial villages within easy reach of town—say not more than twelve miles out. The railways would have to sell cheap workmen's tickets; the villages should consist of three- or four-roomed cottages, each with a scullery and a garden. There should be a common garden as well; there should be no sale of drink in any of the villages; there should be in each a coöperative store; the rent of a cottage ought not to exceed three shillings a week.

This is the proposal advanced by General Booth of the Salvation Army ("Darkest England," p. 210).

It is announced ("Times," February 20, 1900) that the London County Council is about to ask of Parliament an increase of its powers, so that it may buy up land beyond its own limits, with a view of erecting some such industrial villages. We must therefore wait to see the result of this new experiment. We may be quite certain that it will prove to bring with it dangers and evils at present unsuspected, but I think that the gains will be greater than the losses. The country village will be as much better than the barrack as the barrack is better than the narrow and stinking court.

It is hoped that when the advantages of living in the country are understood the men will not mind living at a distance from their work. At the same time, the experiment must be on a very large scale, and if it fails will prove very costly. Objections are taken to the municipality acting as builder and landlord; it is urged that private companies might take up the question; but the experiment made by a private company, if it fails, costs the whole capital advanced by private persons, whereas if the experiment of the County Council fails it will be only the loss of the ratepayers' money. Whatever is done must be done quickly; mischiefs incalculable are inflicted upon the children by the present overcrowding. To neglect it is to make the evils far worse. The remedy requires a great mind and a clear vision and unlimited powers. As yet little practical attention has been paid to the cry of the houseless and the rack-rented, and to the sobs of the children poisoned physically by the air, corrupt and vitiated, which they have to breathe; poisoned morally by evil companionship, starved and cabined mentally for want of light and air and sunshine, for want of the breeze among the trees and the grass of the meadows and the flowers of the field and the creatures of the air and of the hedge.

IX

THE SUBMERGED

IX

THE SUBMERGED

THE word "submerged" likes me not. I have endeavored to find or to invent another and a better word. So far without success. The word must define the class. It is the unhappy company of those who have fallen in the world. There are many levels from which one may fall; perhaps there are many depths into which one may fall; certainly I have never heard of any depth beyond which there was not another lower and deeper still. The submerged person, therefore, may have been a gentleman and a scholar, an officer, a prodigal; or he may have been a tradesman, or a working-man, or anything you please; the one essential is that he must have stepped out of his own class and fallen down below. He is a shipwrecked mariner on the voyage of life, he is a pilgrim who has wandered into the dark and malarious valleys beside the way. We have read in the annals of luckless voyages how those who escaped with their lives wandered along the seashore, living by the shell-fish they could pick up, moving on when there were no more mussels, huddled together at night in the shelter of a rock for warmth. We know and are familiar with their tales of misery. As these shipwrecked mariners on the cold and inhospitable coast, so are the unfortunates whom we call submerged; in a like misery of cold and starvation do they drag on a wretched existence.

They have no quarter or district of their own; we come

upon them everywhere. In the wealthy quarters there are courts and alleys, lanes and covered ways, where they find shelter at night; they slouch along aimlessly, with vacant faces, in the most fashionable streets; they stand gazing with eyes which have no longer any interest or expression upon a shop-window whose contents would provide a dozen of them with a handsome income for life; in the warm summer evenings you may see them taking up their quarters for the night on the seats outside St. James's Park; if you walk along the Thames embankment you will see them sitting and lying in corners sheltered from the wind; they seek out the dry arches if they can find any, happy in the chance of finding them; they sit on door-steps and sleep there until the policeman moves them on; wherever a night watchman, placed on guard over an open excavation, hangs up his red lamp and lights his fire in the workman's grate you will find one or two of the submerged crouching beside the red coals; the watchmen willingly allow them their share of warmth and light. If you are walking in the streets late at night you will presently pass one of them creeping along looking about for a crust or a lump of bread. Outside the Board-schools, especially, these windfalls are to be found, thrown away by the children; it is a sign that food is cheap and work is abundant when one sees lumps of bread thrown into the gutter. These are the gifts of fortune to the submerged; the day has brought no jobs and no pence, not even the penny for a bare shelter with the Salvation Army; fate, relentless, has refused to hands willing to work—perhaps unwilling, for the submerged are sometimes incapable of work; like their betters, they have nerves. But in the night under the gas-lamps there are the gifts of the great goddess, Luck—the children's lumps of bread lying white in the lamplight on kerb or door-step.

Or, again, if you are in the streets early in the morning, at the hour when the cheap restaurants set out upon the pavement their zinc boxes full of the refuse and unspeakable stuff of yesterday, you will find the person submerged busy among this terrible heap; he finds lumps of food, broken crusts, bones not stripped clean; he turns over the contents with eager hands; he carries off, at last, sufficient for a substantial meal.

One would hardly expect to find history occupying herself with a class so little worthy of her dignity. Yet have I found some account of the submerged in the eighteenth century. They did not prowl about the streets at night nor did they search the dust-box in the morning, because there were no crusts of costly wheaten bread thrown away, and there were no dust-boxes. But they had their customs. And the following seems to have been the chief resource of the class.

There were no police walking about the streets day and night; there were night watchmen, who went home about five in the morning; then for an hour, before the workmen turned out on their way to the shops, the streets were quite deserted and quiet. At that hour the submerged had their chance; they were the early vultures that hovered over the City before the dawn; they went out on the prowl, carrying lanterns in the winter; they searched the streets; where the market carts had passed there were droppings of vegetables and fruit, there were bones thrown out into the streets, there were things dropped; drunken men were lying on door-steps, stretched out on the pavement between the posts, or propped up against the walls; the night watchmen paid no attention to these common objects of the night, the helplessly drunk; they cleared out their pockets of money no doubt, otherwise they left them. But the prowlers, after another investigation of the pockets, carried off everything portable—hat, wig, necktie, ruffles, boots, coat, everything. The cold air quickened the recovery of the patient; when he came to his senses and sat up he was ready to repent, not in sackcloth, but in shirtsleeves. Later on in the day the prowlers inveigled children into back courts, stripped them of their fine frocks, cut off their long curls, and so let them go. Or they lay in wait for a drunken man and led him carefully to some quiet and secluded spot, where he could be stripped of all. But

Salvation Army Shelter.

the submerged of George III were a ruder and a rougher folk than those of Queen Victoria.

The submerged do not, as a rule, give trouble to the police, nor are they a terror to the householder; they do not rob, they do not brawl, they do not get up riots, they do not "demonstrate," they endure in quiet. Their misery might make them dangerous if they were to unite; but they cannot unite, they have no leader, they have no prophet; they want nothing except food and warmth, they accuse nobody, they are not revolutionaries; they are quite aware —those of them who have any power of thought left—that no change in the social order could possibly benefit them. They live simply, each man clothed with his own misery as with a gaberdine. And they know perfectly well that their present wretchedness is due to themselves and their own follies and their own vices. They have lost whatever spirit of enterprise they may once have possessed; in many cases long habits of drink have destroyed their power of will and energy.

Many causes have made them what they are. As many men, so many causes. They cannot be reduced to a class; they come from every social station—many of them are highly educated men, born of gentle-folk, some of county families, some of the professional classes. Their tale of woe, if you ask it, is always the lamentation of the luckless; it should be the lamentation of a sinner. Incompetence, especially that kind of incompetence which belongs to an indolent habit of mind and body; the loss of one situation after another, the throwing away of one chance after the other, the shrinking from work either bodily or mental, which grows upon a man until for very nervousness he is unable to do any work; the worn-out patience of friends and relations, drink—always drink; dismissal which involves the loss of character, the habit begun in boyhood of choosing always the easier way; sickness, which too commonly drives a man out of work and sends him on to the streets in search of casual jobs; crime and the gaol—all these causes work in the same direction; they reduce the unfortunate victim to the condition of hopelessness and helplessness which is the note of the submerged.

I think that where the case is one in which the former social standing was good the most common cause is loss of character. This does not mean, necessarily, the taint of dishonesty. It means, in many cases, simply incompetence. How shall a clerk, a shop assistant, find another place when he can only give reference to a former employer who can say nothing in his praise? He goes down, he takes a worse place with lower pay, he continues in his incompetence; he is again dismissed. He falls lower still. In any country it is a terrible thing for a young man to lose his character; it is fatal in a country where laborers of his kind, at the only work he can do, are redundant; while men with good character can be obtained, who will employ a man without a character? For such a man it would seem as if a new country—a new name—were the only chance left for him. He tries the new country. Alas! Incompetence is no more wanted there than at home. If, as sometimes happens, such an one yields to the temptation that is always before the penniless and falls into crime, it is no longer a descent along the familiar easy slope; it is a headlong plunge which the unfortunate man makes, once for all, into the Male-bolge of the submerged.

I was once in a London police court looking on at the day's cases which were brought up one after the other before the magistrate. The drunk and disorderly came first; these were soon dismissed; indeed, there is a terrible monotony about them; the reporters do not take the trouble even to listen or to make a note of them unless the prisoner is a man of some note. Then followed the case of a young man, apparently four- or five-and-twenty years of age. He was described as a clerk; he was dressed in the uniform of his craft, with a black coat and a tall hat; it was the cold, early spring, and he had no overcoat or wrapper or collar or neckerchief of any kind, and he was barefooted. The sight of him filled one with a kind of terror. Now, the face of that poor wretch told its own story; it was a handsome face, with regular features, light hair, and blue eyes. As a boy he must have been singularly attractive; as a child, lovely.

But now the face was stamped and branded with the mark of one who has always followed the Easy Way; his weak mouth, his shifting eyes, the degradation of what had once promised to be a face of such nobility and beauty, proclaimed aloud his history. I could see the boy at school who would do no more work than he was obliged to do; the young clerk at five shillings a week, who would do no more than he was bidden, and that without intelligence or zeal; the lad rising, as even the junior clerk rises, by seniority; the billiard-room, the public house, the wasted evenings, the betting, the evil companions, the inevitable dismissal for incompetence, the difficulty of finding another place, the influence of friends not too influential, the second dismissal, the tramp up thousands of stairs in search of a vacant desk where character was not required, borrowing of small sums, with faithful promises of repayment, the consequent loss of friends, the alienation even of brothers, the inevitable destitution, the pawning of all but the barest necessaries of clothes, even at last parting with his boots—all this was revealed by the mere aspect of the man. He was charged with stealing a pair of boots to replace those which he had pawned. There was no shame in his face; the thing had come at last which he had felt coming so long. It was not shame, it was a look of resigned hopelessness; he was become the foot-ball of fate, he was henceforth to be kicked about here and there as fate in her gamesome moods might choose. Practically there was no defense; he had nothing to say; he only shook his head; the magistrate was lenient because it was a first offense. Leniency in such a case is only apparent, though the magistrate means well, for a fortnight in prison is as ruinous for the rest of a man's life as a twelvemonth. So he stepped out of the dock, and presently the wheels of Black Maria—sometimes called the Queen's omnibus—rolled out into the street with the day's freight of woe and retribution.

I met this poor creature afterward; I came upon him carrying a pair of boards; I stumbled over him as he sat in the sun in St. James's Park, monumental in shabbiness; I met him once or twice shambling about the Embankment, which was his favorite boulevard—a place where no work can be picked up, and for that reason, I suppose, dear to him. London is a very big city, but such men as this have their haunts; they are too weak of will to wander far from the way of habit; it requires an effort, a moment of energetic decision, to change his daily walk from the Embankment to the Strand. I never saw him, except on that one occasion when he was a sandwich man, doing any kind of work; I never saw him begging; I never saw him in a shelter at night; I know not how he lived or how, if ever, he procured a renewal of his rags when they fell off him. Presently it occurred to me that I had not seen him lately. I looked about for him. By this time I took an interest in the case; had he asked me for money I should have given him some, I dare say. Why not? The indiscriminate giving of alms is, one knows and has been taught for years, a most mischievous thing; but in this case money will not lift a man out of the slough, nor will it plunge him deeper; give him money and he will devour it; refuse him money and he will go on just in the same way. But I have never seen him since, and I am sure that in some workhouse infirmary he lay lingering awhile with pneumonia, which carries off most of the half-fed and the ill-clad, and that he died without murmuring against his fate, resigned and hopeless. I dare say that those who composed his limbs in death admired the singular beauty of the face. For lo! a marvel—when the debased soul, which has also debased the face, goes out of the body, the face resumes the delicacy and the nobility for which it was originally intended.

Another case of a submerged. I knew something of the man, not the man himself. He began very well; he was clever in some things; he could play more than one instrument, he was a companionable person; he got into the civil service by open competition very creditably; for some ten or twelve years he lived blamelessly. It was known by his friends that he was always thirsty; he would drink large quantities of tea for breakfast; he drank pints of cold water with his pipe. Presently his friends began to whisper—things. Then openly there were said—things. Then I was told that A. A. had been turned out of his place, and that meant a good many—things. For certain reasons I was interested in the man. One evening in July I strolled in St. James's Park after dinner; the air was balmy; the benches of the park were nearly full. I found a vacant seat and sat down. Beside me was a youngish man; by the light of the gas-lamp I observed that the brim of his hat was broken, and that in other respects rags were his portion. He entered into conversation by a question as to some race-horse, to which I pleaded ignorance. He then began to talk about himself. It was, as I have said above, the lamentation of the luckless. "One man," he said, "may steal a pig, another may not look over the garden-wall. I, sir, am what I am; in rags, as you see; penniless, or I should not be here; tormented by thirst, and no means of procuring a drink. I, sir, am the man who looked over the garden-wall." He went on; suddenly the story became familiar to me; he was the man of whose decline and fall I had heard so much.

He had not abandoned his grand air, for which he was always distinguished. I offered him a cigar. He examined it critically. "A brand of this kind," he said, "I keep in tea for three years." He lit it. "A gentleman," he reminded me, "is not lowered by bad luck, nor is he disgraced by having to do work belonging to the service—the menial service. The other day I was a sandwich man—in Bond Street. I met my brother face to face. I have a brother—" the poor man is a member of the Travelers and a few other clubs of that kind. "He will do nothing for me. At sight of me he winced; he changed color. Do you think I flinched? Not so, sir. The disgrace was his; he felt it." And so on; he was instructive. I believe his friends shipped him off somewhere.

Some of the submerged contrive to make their own livelihood; they are even able, as a rule, to take a bed at the Sixpenny Hotel. One of these institutions has, indeed, the credit of being the chosen haunt of the brokendown gentlemen. Here they are all broken down together; to meet here, to cook their own suppers, to rail at fortune like kings deposed is an agreeable diversion. At least they talk with each other in the language to which they are accustomed. And there is always something about the manner of the brokendown "swell" which distinguishes him from those of lower beginnings. There is something of the old gallantry left; he does not sit down and hang a head and moan like the poor bankrupt small trader; so long as the sixpence is forthcoming he is not unhappy.

It is a strange company; they were once soldiers, sportsmen, billiard players, betting men, scholars, journalists, poets, novelists, travelers, physicians, actors. One of the submerged of whom I heard had been a reader of some learned language at one of our universities; another was a clergyman—not, if the story about him was true, quite admirable professionally; both these gentlemen, however, found it best, after a time, to exchange the Sixpenny Hotel for the workhouse, where they are at least free from the anxiety about the sixpence.

One more illustration of the submerged who has been a gentleman. I met him once, only once. It was in Oxford Street; he was standing before the window of a very artistic and attractive shop—a china and glass shop. The window was most æsthetically "dressed"; it contained, besides Venetian glass and other glass of wondrous cunning and beauty, a small dinner-table set out with flowers, glass, silver plate, costly china of new design, some white napery, and those pretty little lights—called fairy lights—which were a few years ago fashionable.

The man was unmistakably a gentleman; his dress betrayed his extreme poverty; his boots showed a solution of continuity between the upper leather and the sole; his closely buttoned coat was frayed, his round hat was broken, apparently he had no shirt; he certainly had no collar; his red cotton handkerchief was tied round his neck; the morning was cold and raw, a morning in November. Evidently, a gentleman. The poor wretch was looking at the dinner-table; it reminded him of mess nights, of dinner parties, of clubs, of evenings abroad and at home, before he fell; of what else did that dinner-table remind him—of what light laughter and music of women's voices, while as yet he was worthy to sit among them? One knows not. He was absorbed in the contemplation of the table; as he gazed his face changed strangely; it went back, I know not how many years; it became the face of a hawk, the face of a man keen and masterful. How did he fall? How came the look of mastery and command to go out of his face?

I spoke to the man. I touched him on the arm; he started; I pointed to the fairy lights; "Do you remember," I asked him, "when those things came in?" "It was about ten years ago," he said, without hesitation. Then the present moment reasserted itself. He became again one of the submerged. "Lend me half a crown," he said. "On Monday morning I will meet you here, and I' ll return it." On the following Monday morning I repaired to the china and glass shop. My friend, however, had forgotten his appointment. Faith in my own expectations would have been shaken had he kept it. I have only to add that he took the half crown as one gentleman accepts, say, a cigar, from another. "Thanks, thanks," he said, airily, and he moved away with the bearing of one who is on his way to his club. It was pleasant to observe the momentary return to the old manner, though the contrast between the rags and the manner presented an incongruity that could not pass unobserved, and I regret to this day that I did not invite him to a chop-house and to a statement from his own point of view as to the turning of fortune's wheel.

I have said that the submerged do not, as a rule, give much trouble to the police. They may have had their lapses from virtue, their indiscretions, but they are not habitual criminals. The way of the latter, so long as he keeps out of prison, is much more comfortable; for transgressors the prison in which they pass most of their time is hard, but the intervals of freedom are often times of plenty and revelry. The submerged have no such intervals. The common rogue is generally a brazen braggart, while the submerged is timid and ashamed. Of course, too, it is by no means a common thing that he has been a gentleman; in East London there are over ten thousand of the homeless and the wanderers, loafers, and the casuals, with some criminals. I have before me twelve cases investigated by an officer of the Salvation Army. The men belonged to the following trades: confectioner, feather-bed dresser, tailor, riverside laborer, sawyer, distiller, accountant in a bank, builder's laborer, plumber's laborer, carman, match-seller, slater. Out of the twelve, one, you see, had been a gentleman. The cause of destitution was variously stated: age—it is very difficult in some trades to resist the pressure of the young; cataract in one eye; inability to find work, though young and strong; cut out by machinery; last place lost, by his own fault—an admission reluctantly made and not explained; arm withered; brought up to no trade, and so on.

As for their attempts to get work, the odd job appears to be the most common, if the most hopeless. It will be seen from the cases given above that the men can no longer get work at their own trades; now, they know no other; what, then, are they to try? One cannot expect much resource in an elderly man who has been making confectionery all his life, when he has lost his place and his work; nor in a feather-bed dresser, when feather-beds are no longer made. The former can do nothing in the world except make sugar plums according to certain rules of the mystery; the latter can do nothing but "dress" feather-beds. The ignorance and helplessness of our craftsmen outside their own branch of work are astonishing. So that the run after the odd job is explained. There is nothing else for them to try. A great many working hands are dock laborers, and fight every day for the chance of being taken on; but a man advanced in years, with the sight of one eye gone or with a withered arm—what chance has he of getting employment?

Sometimes they try to sell things—boot-laces and useful odds and ends. But capital is wanted, a few shillings that can be locked up, and the returns are deplorable. Sometimes they try matches; the man with the "box o' lights" is busy on Sundays and holidays outside the railway station or at the stopping places of omnibus or tram; I believe that threepence or so represents the average daily profit to be made in this branch of commerce. A few try to sell newspapers, but they are cut out by the boys who run and bawl and force their "specials" on the public. Newspaper selling in the streets is only good when one has a popular "pitch." For instance, at Piccadilly Circus, where the stream of life runs full and strong, a news-vender must do very well, but such "pitches" are rare. Sometimes they offer the latest novelty out for one penny. The trade in "novelties" depends on the attractiveness of the wares; they must be really novel to catch the eye, and they must seem desirable. The principal markets for the penny novelties are the kerb of Broad Street and that on the north side of Cheapside. There is generally a new "novelty" every week, and the ingenuity, the resource, the invention of the unknown genius who provides it are beyond all praise. When he hits the popular taste you may see the dealers selling their pennyworths as fast as they can lay them out on their trays. Sometimes there is a "frost"; the novelty does not "catch on." Then the poor dealer loses his little capital, and what happens to the inventor no one knows.

It is recorded of a certain collector, who spent his whole life in making a collection of the penny novelties, that at his death his museum, his life's work, was sold for the enormous sum of £12. I suppose he might have found comfort in the reflection that there are a great many men whose whole life's work would not fetch as many pence. But his soul must have felt a certain amount of dejection after so busy a pursuit—and one covering so many years—to find it valued at no more than £12. How many poets, novelists, preachers, journalists, could get as much as £12 for their contributions to literature? After all, he was above the average, this collector.

One would think that journalism would offer chances to the submerged. Here, at least, is a door always wide open. I know of one case in which a man just let out of prison met with a singular piece of good luck; he was a man whose character was hopelessly gone, and could never be retrieved, who had committed frauds and cheats innumerable upon all his old companions, whose friends had long since plainly told him that nothing, nothing more would be done for him, and that no mercy would be shown him in case of further frauds. The day came when he was released from prison; he stood outside and looked up and down and across the road; he saw a stony-hearted world; amid this multitude of people there was not one single person to whom he could turn for help; it was a cold, gray morning; he had concocted several little schemes of villainy in his cell; now, in the open air, he realized that they were hopeless; prison had somewhat reduced his strength of mind; he felt that just then he could not sit down and work out any one of his schemes; he saw no prospect before him but that of a casual loafer in the streets, submerged for life.

He turned to the east; he wandered away, he knew not where; he had a small sum of money in his pocket, enough for a short time. After that, the slouch along the streets.

Suddenly he came upon a street scene, a short, quick, dramatic scene enacted in a few minutes. It fired his imagination; he saw a chance; he bought paper and pen at a stationer's shop; he went into a coffee-house, called for a cup of coffee and the ink, and wrote a descriptive paper on that scene; when it was done he took it to the office of a great daily paper, and asked to see one of the subeditors. His paper was read and accepted; he was told that he might bring more; he did bring more; he became one of the staff; he was presently sent abroad on the business of that paper. I do not know whether he thought fit to tell the editor anything about his own record. Well, the man ought to have become one of the submerged; but, you see, he was a scholar and a man of imagination; he had been engaged, it is true, in frauds, and was morally hopeless and corrupt through and through, but he had not lost his power of will; he had had no experience of the disappointments and the step-by-step descent which rob the submerged of his energy and his resource. The example only proves that journalism opens its doors in vain for the ordinary submerged who has lost his grasp of realities.

For those who are strong enough to walk about the streets at an even pace for a great many hours a day the sandwich offers a tolerably safe means of living. Remember, however, that your truly submerged very often, by reason of age and infirmities,—some physical weakness generally appears after a time to aggravate the misery,—cannot undergo the fatigue of carrying the boards all day. If, however, the strength is there the work can generally be found at a shilling or one shilling and twopence a day. It is work which entirely suits any man who has left off trying. At the same time, it is a help to the young man who for the moment may be down on his luck. For the former it means simply the fatigue of walking about for so many hours on end. It is interesting to walk slowly along the pavement while the single file of sandwich men pass along, one after the other. They never talk, there is no exchange of jokes, they never chaff the workmen or the girls or the lads or the drivers who threaten to run over them; on the other hand, no one chaffs them; they are by common consent held sacred, as men in the world but not of the world. Some of them carry a pipe between their lips, but merely as a habit; it is an empty pipe; there is no speculation in their faces; they manifest no interest in anything; there may be a police row and a fight, there may be a horse down, the sandwich man pays no attention; he looks neither to the right nor to the left; the show that he advertises is not for himself; the wares exposed in the shop-windows are not for him to buy; the moving panorama, the procession of active and eager life along which he marches is nothing to him; he takes no longer any interest in anything; he is like the hermit, the anchorite, the recluse—he is dead to the world; he is without friends, without money, without work, without hope; his mind has nothing to occupy it; he thinks of vacant space; he walks in his sleep; he is comatose; if he lifts his eyes and looks upon the world it must be in wonder that his own figure is not in its proper place, its old place—it ought to be there. Why is it not? How did he get into the gutter, one of a line in single file, with a board in front of him and a board behind him? Newsboys shout their latest; the shops light up till every street is a fairyland of brightness; the carriages go up and down. To all the sights around him, to the meaning of the show and to the dance of life, which is so often the dance of death, the sandwich man remains indifferent. He has nothing left of all the joys and toys and dreams and vanities of the world; the past is a blurred memory on which he will

Sandwich-men.

not dwell if he can help it; there is no future for him, only the day's tramp, the shilling at the end of it; fivepence will give him warmth, light, a bed, and a modicum of food; eightpence, or, if he is lucky, tenpence, must find him food, drink, and tobacco for the following day, with some means of keeping the mud and water out of his boots.

A small contingent of the submerged is formed by the men who, not being habitual and hardened criminals, have been in prison and have not only found employment difficult and even impossible in consequence of a misfortune which many worse than themselves escape, but have returned to the world broken down by the terrible discipline of an English prison. The prison receives a man; it turns out a machine, an obedient machine, as obedient as the dog which follows at heel: it obeys cowering; the machine has no self-respect left, and no power of initiative; the prison bird can only henceforth live in a cage where he is not called upon to earn his livelihood or to carry on a trade. I know little about prisons in other countries, but I doubt whether any system has ever been invented more effective in destroying the manhood of the poor wretches who are subjected to its laws than the prison system of Great Britain. There is no sadder sight imaginable than the reception of a released prisoner by the Salvation Army Refuge for these unfortunate men. Every day their officer attends at the prison doors at the hour of discharge, and invites the men, as they come out, to the refuge. They come in dazed and pale; the light, the air, the freedom, the absence of the man of authority with the keys—all together make them giddy; they are received with a welcome and a handshake which make them suspicious; they are invited to sit down and take food; they obey with a shrinking readiness which brings a flush of shame to the spectator's face. See; after a little they push the plate away; it is solid food—they cannot take it; they have been so long accustomed to gruel that a plate of meat is too much for them; they can neither eat nor talk; they cannot respond even to kindliness; they cannot understand it; the man—the lost manhood—has to be built up again. The Salvation Army's Helping Hand rescues some; it fails with some; even where it fails, some good effect must be left in their minds by the show of friendliness and kindness.

The best place to find the submerged is at one of the shelters of the Salvation Army. Here they give for fourpence a large pot of coffee, tea, or cocoa, with a hunch of bread; it is probably the best meal that the men have had that day; the fourpence also entitles them to a warm and well-lighted room with benches and tables, the means of getting a good wash and a bed. For a smaller sum the accommodation is not so good. Every evening the shelters are quite full; every evening there is held that kind of service, with addresses, prayers, and the singing of hymns, which is called a Salvation Meeting. Well, the men feel, at last, that they are with friends; the lasses with the banjos and the tambourines, the men in the jerseys who speak to them—these are not making any money out of them, they are working for them, they are taking an immense amount of pains entirely on their behalf; I cannot but believe—indeed, I know—that among this poor wreckage of society their efforts meet with the kind of response that is most desired.

Or, if you can get so far out, there is Medland Hall by the riverside at Ratcliffe. It was formerly a Dissenting chapel; it is now a free lodging-house. No one pays anything; there are bunks ranged in lines over the floor—they are rather like coffins, it is true; these bunks are provided with mattresses, and for sheet and blanket with American cloth, which can be easily kept clean. I believe that bread is also provided. An effort is made to find out a way of helping the men to work; the likely young fellows are sent to the recruiting sergeants; some connection has been formed with the railway companies for men young and strong.

The casual ward is a place to which no one will go if he

can possibly avoid it. This refuge will only receive the actual destitute, those who have no money at all; their rations of food are light, to say the least. The allowance for young and old, strong and weak, is the same—for breakfast, half a pound of gruel and eight ounces of bread; the same for supper; for dinner, eight ounces of bread and an ounce and a half of cheese; for drink, cold water. The casual is put into a cell by himself and there locked up; in the morning, when he ought to be out and looking for work, he is detained to do stone-breaking or oakum-picking—half a ton of stone-breaking or four pounds of oakum, a task so heavy that it takes him the best part of the day, and he is lucky if he is not detained as a punishment for another night and day, with a corresponding increase in the task imposed upon him.

One would like to take some of the permanent officials of the Local Government Board and set them to the same work *on the same food.* What is the man's crime? Poverty. There may be other crimes which have reduced him to this condition of destitution, but no questions are asked. It is poverty, poverty, nothing but poverty, for which this treatment is the punishment. I once visited a casual ward; it was, I believe, Saturday afternoon. I was shown one cell occupied by a woe-begone young country lad; he was sitting alone; I think he had done his task; he was to be a prisoner till Monday morning—such was the infamy of his poverty. Lucky for him if he was not kept over Monday, to pick more oakum and to reduce his strength and impair his constitution by more starvation on gruel and bread weighed out by ounces. With refuges for the destitute where they are starved and made to work hard on insufficient food, with prisons for the criminal where manhood is crushed and strength is destroyed by feeding men on gruel, we support bravely the character of a country obedient to the laws of God and marching in the footsteps of Christ.

Such are the submerged—an army of brokendown gentlemen, ruined professional men, penniless clerks, bankrupt traders, working-men who are out of work through age or infirmity, victims of drink, ex-prisoners and convicts, but not habitual criminals. It is a helpless and a hopeless army; I have said already that this is the note of the submerged. We shall see presently what is done for this great body of misery. One thing must be remembered. There are lower levels than those reached by this army; physicians, clergymen, missionaries, journalists, whisper things far worse than can be alleged against the submerged. And we have not included among them the tramp, that class whose blood is charged with restlessness hereditary, who cannot remain long in any place, who cannot enter upon steady work, who are driven by their restlessness, as by a whip of scorpions, along the roads. Not the tramp, nor the sturdy rogue, nor the professional criminal, nor the vile wretches who live by the vilest trades, may be numbered among the submerged. They fall noiselessly from their place of honor, they live noiselessly in their place of dishonor; they might perhaps be brought back to work, but the cases of recovery must be very few in proportion, because the causes which dragged them down are those which prevent them from being dragged up. If any physician can give back to the submerged patience, resolution, will, courage, hope, he may reclaim them. If that cannot be done they must remain as they are.

My illustration of the submerged seems to have little to do with East London. As a fact, there is no respect paid to places. When a man has belonged to the West End his wandering feet, over which, as over his other actions, the patient has no control, carry him about the scenes of his former prosperity without his taking any steps to prevent it. Old acquaintances recognize him, and pass him by with a cold eye which denies the recognition and conceals the pity. He himself sees nobody and remembers nobody. In the same way a man who belongs by birth and habits to

East London will remain there after he has come to grief. Or, if the former gentleman, for some reason, gets into East London and finds out its ways, with the cheap lodgings, the shelters, the "ha'penny" cups of cocoa, and the many helping hands from which he may get some kind of relief he will stay in East London. We need not hesitate about awarding the palm of nourishing or starving more or fewer of the submerged to East or West London. It is enough to know that they exist in both quarters, and that, according to statistics, there are over ten thousand of them in East London alone. If any help can be found for this mass of wreckage let us find that help and give it with full hands and in measure overflowing, for indeed of all those who are poor and distressed and unhappy the company of the submerged are the most wretched. Even if, as is almost always the case, they have brought their punishment upon themselves by the folly of the prodigal, the weakness of those who take the Easy Way, and the wickedness of those who indulge the natural inclination to vice, let us not inquire too closely into the record; let us still stretch out our hand of help; if we can restore some of them—even a few, even one here and there—to the life of honesty among folk of good repute, we must still leave them the shameful memory of the past. That punishment we cannot avert; we cannot remove it from them. The world will forgive them, but how shall we find that Lethe whose waters will enable them to forgive themselves? "Arise"—it is easy for the world to say—"thy sins shall no longer be imputed to thee for a reproach and a hissing." Alas! When the better self returns, how shall that poor wretch cease to reproach himself?

X

THE MEMORIES OF THE PAST

X

THE MEMORIES OF THE PAST

I HAVE so often insisted that East London must be regarded as a city of many crafts—the working-man's city—that it may seem contradictory to call attention to another aspect. That part of East London with which we have been most concerned is the densely populated part lying north of the river and including all that part west of the river Lea as far north as Dalston, Clapton, and Hackney, and east of that river, including Bow, Stratford, Walthamstow, Wanstead, Forest Gate, Bromley West, and East Ham and Barking. It includes, in a word, very nearly all the ancient villages and hamlets whose names may be found upon the map. But there is a fringe, and there are extensions. When one emerges at last from streets which seem to have no end, when the nightmare of a world which is all streets, with never a field or an orchard or a hillside left, begins to break, when it is cleared away, as an ugly dream by the daylight, by the reappearance of trees and large gardens and wide roads, then we discover the fringe. Part of Stoke Newington, part of Stamford Hill, a small part of Tottenham, part of Snaresbrook, belong to the fringe. Here we get roads lined with trees, villas with trees in front gardens, modern churches built all after the same half-dozen patterns, in true proportions, correct and without inspiration; here we get windows filled with flowers, and here presently we get houses well apart and a wealth of creepers and of flowering shrubs;

which means that the breath of the crowded City is left behind.

But there are further extensions; the suburbs of East London are not confined within the limits of the map of London; they stretch out far afield, they include Chigwell and Chingford and Theydon Bois, and all the villages round Epping Forest. Dotted about everywhere in this extension are stately houses with large gardens and grounds, the residences of the manufacturers and the employers, not those of the small trades of East London, where the master is often but one degree better off than the employee, but those of the factories and the works; theirs is the capital invested; theirs is the enterprise; theirs the wit and courage which have made them succeed; theirs is the wealth. This extension is a delightful place in early summer; it is full of trees; there are old churches, and there is "the" forest—the people of East London always speak of "the" forest, for to them there is no other. It is, also, a part of London very little visited; it is, to begin with, somewhat inaccessible; one who would visit it from the West End has to get first into the City. In the next chapter we will discourse on what may be seen by the curious who would explore the forest and its surroundings. Let us return to my group of villages.

To the American, and to most of my own people, the names of Stoke Newington, Hackney, Stepney, Mile End, and the rest are names and nothing else; they awaken no more memories than a list of Australian or American townships. Let me try to endow these names with associations; I would make them, if possible, venerable by means of their association with those who have gone before. The suburban life of London belongs essentially to the eighteenth and the nineteenth centuries. In the former only the wealthy had their country, as well as their town, houses; in the latter there have been no town houses left in the City at all, and the whole of the people who every day carry on their business in the City have now their suburban residences.

The introduction and the development of the suburban life effected a revolution in the City. It destroyed the social side of the City by the simple process of driving out all the people. When the citizens lived over their offices and their shops they belonged to a highly sociable and gregarious City, its society having no kind of connection with the aristocratic side of the west, and its gregarious nature preserving due respect and distinction to City rank and position. Every man had his weekly club and his nightly tavern. Here, with his friends of the same street or the same ward, he discussed the affairs of the day. He was a politician of advanced and well-defined views; he confirmed, by many a commonplace uttered with solemnity, his own and his friends' prejudices; the use of conversation, when men read nothing more than was provided by an elementary press, was mainly the development and the maintenance of healthy prejudice. This was all the amusement that the good man desired—how great was the interval between two of John Gilpin's pleasure jaunts? "Twice ten tedious years!" Wonderful! To be sure, he had his City company, and its dinners were events to be remembered. The City madams had their card-parties; for the *élite* there was the City Assembly. For those who wanted pleasure there were the gardens—Vauxhall, Ranelagh, Marylebone, Bagnigge Wells, any number of gardens.

The daily work, the business done on 'change, the counting-house, the shop, all this formed part and parcel of the family life; it was not cut off and separated as at present; from his counting-house the merchant went to his "parlor" —it was under the same roof—when dinner was called. And all the year round he slept under the same roof over his place of business.

A hundred and fifty years ago the people began to leave the City; the wealthiest merchants went first; then the less wealthy; finally the shopkeepers and the clerks; the private houses were converted into offices and warehouses and chambers; the old City life absolutely vanished. Everything disappeared; the club, the tavern, the card-parties, the assembly, the evenings at Vauxhall—all were swept away. The life of the City man was cut in two, one half belonging to his office in the City, the other to his suburban villa, with the night and three or four of the waking hours. He took breakfast at eight; he went off after breakfast, catching an early omnibus; he returned at six or seven; he dined; he sat for an hour or two; he went to bed. No life could be duller; of social intercourse the suburban resident had little or none; visiting was limited; at rare intervals there were evenings with a "little music"; dances were few and far between; the old circles were broken up and no new ones formed; the occupation and social position of neighbors were not known to each other. For amusements the girls had their slender stock of accomplishments; the sons, whenever they could, ran up to town and got into mischief; and the *père de famille*, not knowing or suspecting the narrowness and the dullness of his life, solemnly sat after dinner with a book in his hand or took a hand at cribbage, and went to bed at ten. There were no theaters, no evening entertainments, no lectures even, no concerts, no talk of amusements. As the evangelical narrowness was widely spread over all the London suburbs, if a young man spoke of amusements he was asked if he could reconcile amusement with the working out of his own salvation. The church, or the chapel, was in itself the principal recreation of the ladies. They found in religious emotions the excitement and the interest which their narrow round of life failed to supply.

As for the theater, it was natural that, with such views as to amusement, it should be regarded with a shuddering horror. No young woman who respected herself would be seen at a theater. However, it was quite out of the question, simply because the theater was inaccessible.

Such has been the suburban life of London for a hundred

"A Quiet Dullness"

years, so dull, so monotonous, so destitute of amusement. So lived the residents of Hackney, Clapton, and Stoke Newington before their quiet dullness was invaded by the overflowing wave—irresistible, overwhelming—of the working swarms.

This side of London life deserves to be studied more attentively; it accounts for a great many recent events and for some of the governing ideas of Londoners. This, however, is not the place; let it suffice to pay it the tribute of recognition.

It is now fast passing away. New forces are at work; the old suburban life is changing; the rural suburb has become a large town, with its central boulevards, shops, and places of resort; there are theaters springing up in all the suburbs; there are concerts of good music; there are art schools; there are halls and public dances; there are late trains connecting the suburb with the West End and its amusements; there are volunteer corps, bicycle clubs, golf clubs, tennis clubs, croquet clubs, amateur dramatic clubs; above all, there is the new education for the new woman; whatever else she may do or dare, one thing she will no longer do: she will no longer endure to be shut up all day in a suburb left to the women and children, and every evening, as well as all day, to be kept in the house, with no gaiety, no interests, no pursuits, and no companions. In all these ways the dull suburban life has been swept away, and a new social life, not in the least like that of a hundred years ago, is being established and developed.

Let us pass on to the memories and associations of these hamlets. They are of two kinds—those which appeal to all who belong to this country by descent and inherit our literature and call our great men theirs as well, and those which appeal to ourselves more than they can be expected to do on the other side of the Atlantic. I propose to speak more especially of the former class. It will be seen that the memories of the past belong peculiarly to the history of Nonconformity, but I shall be able to connect East London with many persons distinguished in literature, art, science, and

The Street and Old Church Tower, Hackney.

politics. East London has also its eccentrics. And it has its villains.

Let us, however, consider one or two of these places separately, and note certain things worth visiting in those streets where no traveler's foot ever falls.

Hackney, to begin with, is a very ancient place; the manor belonged to the Knights Templars for about two hundred years; a house, now taken down, used to be shown as the Templars' Palace. It was an ancient house, but not of the thirteenth century: it probably belonged to the reign of Henry VIII. On the suppression of the Templars the manor was given to the Hospitallers, whose traditional house was also shown till about sixty years ago, when it was destroyed. This house was also the traditional residence of Jane Shore, one of those women who, like Agnes Sorel and Nell Gwynne strike the imagination of the people and win their affections. Even the grave and serious Sir Thomas More is carried away by the beauty and the charm of Jane Shore, while the memory of so much beauty and so many misfortunes demands a tear from good old Stow. The name of a street—Palace Road—preserves the memory of the house.

Standing alone in its vast churchyard crammed with monuments, mostly illegible, of dead citizens all forgotten long ago, stands a monument for which we ought to be deeply thankful. They pulled down the old church, but they preserved the tower. It is a tower of singular beauty, the one ancient thing that is left in Hackney. Beneath the feet of the visitor on the east side lie the bones of the buried Templars, proud knights and magnificent once, beyond the power of the bishop, rich and luxurious; with them the dust of their successors, the Knights Hospitallers, and now all forgotten together. In another part of the churchyard they erected a singularly ugly new church—a capacious barn. Outside the churchyard the tower looks down upon a crowded and busy thoroughfare, the full stream of life of this now great town of Hackney. Omnibuses and tram-cars run up and down the street all day long; there is an open market all the year round, with stalls and wheelbarrows ranged along the pavement; a railway arch spans the street, the frequent train thunders as it passes the Templars' tower; the people throng the place from six in the morning till midnight. In many towns I have watched this stream of life flowing beside the gray survivals of the past; nobody heeds the ancient gate, the tower, the crumbling wall; nobody knows what they mean; the historical associations enter not at all into the mind of the average man; even amid the ruins of Babylon the Great his thoughts would be wholly with the present; he has no knowledge or understanding of the past; his own life is all in all to him; being the heir of all the ages, he takes his inheritance without even knowing what it means, as if it grew spontaneously, as if his security of life, his power of working undisturbed, the peace of the City, his freedom of speech and thought and action were given to mankind like the sunshine to warm him and the rain to refresh him. Yet the presence of this venerable tower should have some influence upon him, if only to remind him that there has been a past.

One who walks about an English town of any antiquity —most of them are of very considerable antiquity—can hardly fail of coming from time to time upon a street, a place, a square, a court, which takes him back two hundred years at least, or even more, to the time of the first George, or even to that of Charles II. Sometimes it is a single house; sometimes it is a whole street. In this respect, one or two of the East London suburbs are richer than those of the west or the south because they are older. Hackney and Stoke Newington, Stepney and Tottenham, were villages inhabited by wealthy people or noble people when the suburbs of the south were mere rural villages, with farms and meadows among their hanging woods.

There are two such places which I have found in Hackney. The first is a wide and open place, not a thoroughfare for vehicles; it may be approached by a foot-path through Hackney churchyard. It consists of a row of early eighteenth century houses on the south side, and another row of houses, probably of late eighteenth century, on the north. There is nothing remarkable about the place except its peacefulness and its suggestion of authority and dignity. You may frequently find such places adjoining old churches. It is as if the calm of the church and the tranquillity of the church-

An East London Suburb, Overlooking Hackney Marshes.

yard overflowed into one at least of the streets beside it. The clergy who used to live in this claustral repose have left this memory of their residence; in such a place we look up and down expecting to see a portly divine in black silk cassock, full silk gown, white Geneva bands, and wig theological, step out into the street and magisterially bend his steps toward the church where he will catechize the children.

The second place is also on the east of Hackney church; it is a long and narrow winding street, called magnificently the High Street, Homerton. It contains three great houses and many small ones, mostly old; in spite of its name, which conveys the suggestion of a town, it is a secluded street, remote from the ways of man; it might be a street of some decayed old town, such as King's Lynn or Sandwich; there are no children playing in the road or on the door-steps. Half way down the street stands a church, the aspect of which proclaims it frankly and openly as belonging to the reign of the great George, first of the name. It was a place of worship simply, without special dedication or presentation to any religious body; it has been sometimes a chapel of ease to the parish church; sometimes it has been an independent chapel, having a service of its own. There it has stood since the year 1723, testifying to possibilities in the way of ugliness which would seem like some dream of architecture, fantastic and visionary, impossible of achievement. Yet it somehow fits in with the rest of the street; the ugliness of the chapel is not out of harmony with the street, for the early eighteenth century claims the houses as well as the church. All should be preserved together among the national monuments as a historical survival. This, it should be said, was how they built in the twenties of the eighteenth century.

If we leave Hackney and walk north we find ourselves in the village of Clapton, more suburban than Hackney, but not yet rural. Clapton lies along the western valley of the river Lea, which here winds its way at the bottom of a broad, shallow depression. There is one spot—before the place was built over there were many spots—where one may stand and, in the summer, when the sunshine lights up the stream, gaze upon the green meadows, the mills, the rustic bridges, the high causeways over the marshes, and the low Essex hills beyond. The Essex hills are always far away; there is always one before the traveler; if he stands on an eminence he sees them, like gentle waves of the heaving ocean, across other valleys, and I would not affirm that this is more lovely than any other; indeed, one knows many valleys which are deeper and more picturesque, planted with nobler woods, shadowed by loftier hills. Yet look again. You remember the lines—

> Sweet fields beyond the swelling flood,
> Stand dressed in living green:
> So to the Jews old Canaan stood,
> While Jordan rolled between.

Mark how exactly the view fits the lines, and how the lines fit the view. This is as it should be, for good old Isaac Watts stood often here and gazed upon that scene; the swelling flood was the winding river Lea; the sweet fields lay before him in living green. That is why I have brought you to this place. Dr. Watts might have stood here at another season, when a low, white mist hung over the sweet fields and obscured the swelling flood, and when the Christian knew not what lay between him and the everlasting hills beyond, where he fain would be at rest.

He lived not at Clapton, but at Stoke Newington, on the west of Clapton. If we could have seen this suburb seventy years ago! But the place is overgrown and overcrowded; workmen's houses cover its gardens like a tangle of ugly weeds. Still there is one place left which it will please you to visit; on the map of 1830 it is the only street in the village. It is called Church Street; you enter it from the high road running north; it promises at the outset to be common, mean, and without dignity or character. Patience! we pass through the mean part and we emerge upon a Street Beautiful. It consists of houses built of that warm red brick which,

Clapton.

as Ruskin has pointed out, grows richer in color with age; they are houses of the early eighteenth century with porches and covered with a wealth of creepers; the street has associations of which I will speak presently. Meantime, it is delight enough merely to stand and look upon it. The street ends with two churches. Happier than Hackney, Stoke Newington has been able to build a new church, and has not been obliged to pull down the old one. You see the new church; it is in the favorite style of our time, perhaps as favorable a specimen as can be found; in a word, a large, handsome, well-proportioned church. It was good that such a church should be built, if only to show that when Stoke Newington passed from a small rural village to a great town it did not outgrow its attachment to the Anglican faith. The old church could no longer accommodate the people; a new one therefore was built, a church urban, belonging to a great population beside the other. The old church is not dwarfed by the new; happily, the broad road lies between; it is a charming and delightful village church, standing among the trees and monuments of its churchyard. It has been patched, repaired, enlarged; it is, I dare say, a thing of patchwork—an incongruous church; yet one would not part with a single patch or the very least of its incongruities. There is Perpendicular work in it, and Decorated work; there is also nondescript work. They did well to keep it standing; it is a venerable monument; its spire is much humbler than that of its splendid successor, still it points to heaven; it has what the other will never have, the bones of the villagers for two thousand years; and still, to admonish the men of to-day as of yesterday and the day before, over the porch hangs the dial, with the motto, "Ab Alto"—"From on High," that is, "cometh Safety, cometh Wisdom, cometh Hope" in the language of the ancient piety.

I have spoken of the intimate connection of these villages with Nonconformity. The Nonconformist cause was very strong among the better class of London merchants during the hundred and fifty years from 1650 to 1800. Hackney and other places in this part of the London suburbs are occupied to a large extent by their country houses. When the Act of Uniformity was passed and the Nonconforming ministers were ejected, many of them were received by the merchants of London in their country houses, and when the Conventicle Act of 1663 forbade the Nonconformists to frequent any place of worship other than the parish church, it was in their private houses at Hackney and other suburbs that the merchants were able, unmolested, to worship after their own consciences.

Before this, however, there had been Puritan leaders in the place. Two of them were regicides. On the east of the tower in Hackney churchyard stood until recently a chapel or mortuary chamber built by one of the Rowe family and called the Rowe Chapel. There was a Sir Thomas Rowe (or Roe), who was Lord Mayor of London in 1568; he married the sister of Sir Thomas Gresham, who founded the Royal Exchange; his son was also lord mayor in his time; his grandson, Sir Henry Rowe, built this chapel. Among the descendants was one Owen Rowe, citizen and haberdasher, a fierce partizan—in those days every one was a partizan and every one was fierce. He was colonel of the Green Regiment for the Parliament, so that he could fight as well as argue. Owen Rowe, unfortunately for himself, was one of those who took a leading part in the trial and execution of the King, being a signatory to the warrant for that execution. After the Restoration he surrendered, and by an act of clemency, of which Charles was sometimes capable, he was not executed, but sentenced to imprisonment in the Tower of London for the rest of his days. He died in the December following, and was buried in this chapel.

The other regicide of Hackney was John Okey, one of the Root and Branch men. He was a very turbulent Parliamentarian; he was of humble origin, beginning, it is said, as a drayman; he had no education, but he developed military genius of a kind and became a colonel of cavalry under Cromwell. After the Restoration he fled to Germany, where he might have continued in security to the end of his days, but being tempted to venture into Holland was there arrested by the English minister, Sir George Downing, and brought over to England with two other regicides, Miles Corbet and John Barkstead. Pepys records the event. It is astonishing that Sir George Downing should have done this, since he owed everything he had in the world to the favor of Cromwell. However, it was done, and on March 16, 1662,

Pepys says that the pink *Blackmore* landed the three prisoners at the Tower. He adds that the Dutch were a long while before they consented to let them go, and that "all the world takes notice of Sir George Downing as a most ungrateful villain for his pains." A month later, on April 19th,

The Old Church, Stoke Newington.

Pepys goes to Aldgate and stands "at the corner shop, the draper's," to see the three drawn on their way to execution at Tyburn. "They all looked very cheerful and all died defending what they did to the King to be just." While at Hackney, Okey lived in a house called Barber's Barn, formerly the residence of Lady Margaret Douglas, Countess of Lennox, and mother of Lord Darnley, husband of Mary Queen of Scots, a curious little fact which connects Hackney with Queen Victoria, Darnley's descendant. The regicide's estate was confiscated, but his widow got permission to retain Barber's Barn, where she lived till her death. Okey himself was buried somewhere in Hackney churchyard.

Let us turn to more pleasing associations. In the village

of Hackney during the Commonwealth there lived a certain Captain Woodcock. Among his friends was the Protector's Latin secretary, John Milton, a person of very great consideration. John Milton in 1656 was a widower, but he was not a man who could live without the society of a wife. Captain Woodcock's daughter, Catharine, pleased the Latin secretary; they were married on November 12, 1656, and she died on October 17th in the following year.

But there are other Cromwellian associations with Hackney and Stoke Newington. The American visitor to London would do well to give a day to a quiet ramble in this quarter, once so sturdy in its Puritanism and independence.

Leading out of Church Street, Stoke Newington, there is a place called Fleetwood Street. This street covers the site of an Elizabethan house which was once the residence of Colonel Fleetwood, Cromwell's son-in-law. His second wife, Bridget Cromwell, however, did not live in this house, because Fleetwood got it, after her death, with his third wife, Lady Hartopp. He was left unmolested by the government at the Restoration, and died in this house in 1692. He lies buried in the Nonconformist cemetery of Bunhill Fields.

Another member of the Cromwell family, Major Cromwell, was a resident of this quarter. He was the son of Henry, and the grandson of the Protector. He married, in 1686, Hannah, eldest daughter of Benjamin Hewling, whose sons suffered for joining Monmouth. One of her children, at least, was born at Hackney. This was Richard, who became an attorney and solicitor in chancery. It is pleasant to record that when this Richard married the wedding was solemnized in the chapel of Whitehall, in memory of his great grandfather's occupation of the palace.

I have already mentioned Isaac Watts as a resident in this part of London. He was born at Southampton in 1674. At the age of sixteen he was placed under the care of the Rev. Thomas Rowe of London, and chose the calling of a

Nonconformist minister. For five years he was tutor in the family of Sir John Hartopp, Colonel Fleetwood's stepson, at Stoke Newington; he there became acquainted with Sir Thomas Abney, whilom Lord Mayor of London. He preached for ten years in London, under the Rev. Dr. Chauncey. Then an attack of fever prostrated him, and he was obliged to give up preaching altogether for the rest of his

A Street in Stoke Newington.

life. He was invited by Sir Thomas Abney to his house at Theobald's, where he stayed till Sir Thomas's death. He then removed with Lady Abney to her house at Stoke Newington, where he remained an honored guest, or rather one of the family, until his death in 1748. He was a painter as well as a poet, and until the house was pulled down certain paintings on the walls were shown as his.

A more sturdy and combative Nonconformist was Daniel Defoe, also a resident of Stoke Newington. The site of his house survives in a small street named after him. He was born at Cripplegate, just outside the walls of London. He was sent to school at Newington Green, so that he was more or less connected with this quarter all his life. The school was kept by one Murton, and among his school-fellows was Samuel Wesley, father of John and Charles. Defoe came to live in Stoke Newington early in the eighteenth century. It was here that he wrote "Robinson Crusoe" and his novels. His house has long been pulled down, but a large part of his garden-wall still stands.

Matthew Henry, the commentator, lived at Hackney for some time. Among Nonconformists we must not forget Mrs. Barbauld. Her husband, Rougemont Barbauld, of French descent, was Unitarian minister at Newington Green. Unfortunately, his mental powers declined, and in a fit of insanity he threw himself, or fell, into the New River. Mrs. Barbauld's brother, Dr. Aikin, lived also at this time at Stoke Newington. Mrs. Barbauld removed to his house and died there. She is buried in the churchyard of the old church. There are many better poets than Mrs. Barbauld, but her memory should survive for one little scrap in which for once she is inspired, and speaks, as a poet should, out of the fullness of heart common to all humanity.

> " Life! we have been long together
> Through pleasant and through cloudy weather;
> 'T is hard to part when friends are dear,—
> Perhaps 't will cost a sigh, a tear;
> Then steal away, give little warning,
> Choose thine own time;
> Say not ' Good night,' but in some brighter clime
> Bid me ' Good morning.' "

Also in Church Street, Stoke Newington, lived Isaac Disraeli, author of the "Curiosities of Literature" and the "Quarrels and Calamities of Authors." This estimable and amiable writer died in 1848. His son, Lord Beaconsfield, born here in 1805, was educated in a private school in the neighborhood until he was articled to a lawyer. He belonged, therefore, essentially to a middle-class family; he was not wealthy by birth, but he was not poor; he had the advantage, or the reverse, of being a Jew by descent and a Christian by conviction. To the former fact he owed much of his intellectual powers, to the latter the possibility of rising to the highest distinction and responsibility that the state has to offer, because at the outset of his career even the beginning would have been impossible to one of the ancient Hebrew faith.

The philanthropist John Howard was also a native of Hackney. He belonged, like so many others of the place, to the Nonconformists. His father was an upholsterer in the City, and he himself was at first made apprentice to a wholesale grocer. He was, however, unfitted for that kind of work, and as soon as he could he bought himself out. This is not the place to enlarge upon the work accomplished by this extraordinary man. After being a prisoner of war in France he became wholly possessed with one resolution—to reform the management of prisons. How he traveled through Great Britain first and the continent afterward, how he published reports which revealed the plague spots called prisons all over Europe, is matter of common fame and history.

I think that my claim for these suburbs, that they were a stronghold of Nonconformity, has been proved by these associations. There are, however, more. Everybody has read "Sandford and Merton," both that of Mr. Thomas Day and the other, equally instructive, of Mr. Burnand. Thomas Day belonged by residence to Stoke Newington. His house is still pointed out. In Clapton, on the other side of the high road, lived and died an amiable and accomplished novelist, Grace Aguilar. Here was born a philanthropist, also among the Nonconformist ranks, the late Samuel Morley. Here was born another Nonconformist, the late Sir William Smith, editor of so many classical and antiquarian dictionaries and other aids to learning.

Enough of Nonconformists. Let us turn to other associations. Stoke Newington is connected with the name of Edgar Allan Poe. It was here that he was at school, where he was brought over by the Allans as a child. The house still stands; it is at the corner of Edward's Lane, which runs

House in Stoke Newington in which Edgar Allan Poe Lived.

out of Church Street. Let us hope that the eccentricities of this wayward poet were not due to the influences of Nonconformist Newington.

In the churchyard of Hackney may be seen the tombs and monuments of certain members of the André family. The unfortunate Major André was born at Hackney. His history is well known; our American visitors have been taught to think that Washington's act, severe indeed, was just and warranted by the facts of the case. That will not stifle the regret that a soldier of so much promise should have met with such a death. The time has gone by, or should have gone by, when the name of André called forth bitterness and recrimination.

One more note to connect suburban East London with America. In the year 1709 a great number of refugees—Palatines, Swabians, and others—came over to England, being driven out of their own country by the desolation of war. There were between six and seven thousand of them, all, or nearly all, being quite destitute. The Queen ordered a daily allowance of food to be bestowed upon these unfortunates, and tents were put up for them in various parts round London. The parish of Stoke Newington possessed at that time a small piece of ground, which was lying unoccupied. The parishioners undertook to build four houses on this field, and to receive twenty persons from the refugees. Other parishes offered to do the same. Finally, however, the government disposed of them. The Roman Catholics were sent back to their own country; the Protestants were settled, some in Ireland and the rest in the American colonies. A few went to Carolina; the rest, twenty-seven hundred in number, were shipped to New York, where they arrived in June, 1710. They were allotted ten acres of land to each family. Most of them, however, for reasons of some dissatisfaction, removed to Pennsylvania, where they settled, and where their descendants, it is said, still preserve the history of their misfortunes and their emigration.

The history of these suburbs is unlike that of any other part of London. From the middle of the seventeenth century until far in the nineteenth they were rural retreats; a few houses were clustered about a church; a meeting-house stood here and there; upon the whole place, on the faces of the residents, was the stamp of grave and serious religious thought and conviction; grave and serious Nonconformist divines or grave and serious merchants of the City professing Nonconformity walked about its lanes and among its gardens. As recently as the thirties they retained this character. The map of 1834 shows fields and pasture and garden where there is now a waste of brick and mortar; the little stream known as Hackney Brook meandered pleasantly through these fields; Stoke Newington, though it could boast so many distinguished natives and residents, consisted of one long street, mostly with houses on one side only, and a church. The place is now entirely built upon; a few of the old houses remain, but not many, and the old atmosphere only survives in places which I have indicated, such as Sutton Place, High Street, Homerton, and Church Street, Stoke Newington. And I fear that to the visitor, to whom these associations are not familiar, there is no dignity about these streets other than is conferred by the few surviving mansions.

We have seen that the suburb of Hackney is connected with Queen Victoria by the early residence there of Darnley, husband of Mary Queen of Scots. There is, strangely, another house connecting this suburb with the Queen by another ancestress. Darnley was the father of James I; the Princess Elizabeth, known afterward as the Queen of Bohemia, was the daughter of James. Elizabeth had twelve children; the youngest, Sophia, was the mother of George I. Elizabeth lived for a time at Hackney, in a house called the Black and White House near the church—it is now destroyed; the house had formerly been the residence of Sir Thomas Vyner, Lord Mayor of London.

There are still more associations. Hackney is, in fact, richer in memories of this kind than any other suburb of London. Sir Walter Raleigh and Sir Thomas More belong to American as well as English history, both of them because they precede the colonial time and the former because he foresaw the boundless possibilities of America and attempted to found a colony there. Tradition—a vague tradition only—assigns to Sir Walter a residence in Hackney. History points with certainty to Sir Thomas More's connection with the place. His daughter Cecilia married one George Heron, son of Mr. Thomas Heron, Master of the jewel house to Henry VIII. The family house was a mansion, long since pulled down, on Shacklewell Green, and hither Sir Thomas must have come to visit his daughter.

All Americans who visit London go to see the Charter House. It is one of the really ancient and beautiful things still left standing. One can make out the disposition of the buildings, the cloisters, refectory, chapel, and cells of the Carthusian monks. One can also study the more recent buildings which converted the monastery into an almshouse and a school. The transformation was effected by Thomas Sutton.

This excellent person, the son of a country gentleman, filled many offices during a long life of over eighty years. He was Master of the Ordnance to Queen Elizabeth; he became, at the advanced age of fifty, a citizen of London, joining the Girdlers' Company, and married the widow of one John Dudley, lord of the manor of Stoke Newington. On her death he removed to Hackney, living in a great house which you may still see standing at the present day, one of the very few old houses remaining. It is a house with a center and two wings; formerly there was a large garden behind it. Sutton died in 1614, only a few weeks after signing deeds by which he endowed the Charter House with his estates for the maintenance of eighty almsmen and a school of boys. The foundation still exists; they have foolishly removed the school; the almsmen remain, though reduced in numbers. Colonel Newcome, as of course you remember, became one of them.

Enough of great men. Let us speak of smaller folk who have distinguished themselves each in his own way.

It is given to few to achieve distinction by ways petty and mean and miserable, or bold and villainous. These suburbs can point to one or two such examples, adduced here on account of their rarity. Perhaps the most illustrious of the former was a certain hermit. His name was Lucas; he belonged to a West Indian family; he became a man of Hackney only when he was buried in the churchyard. His house was about thirty miles north of London; on the death of his mother he became suddenly morose; he shut himself up alone in the house; he refused all society; he barricaded his room with timber and lived by himself in the kitchen, where he kept a fire burning night and day, wrapped himself in a blanket, slept upon a bed of cinders, and neither washed nor cut his hair nor shaved, but remained in this neglected condition, which he seems to have enjoyed greatly, after the manner of hermits, for twenty-five years, when he died. He lived on bread, milk, and eggs, which were brought to him fresh every day. He was an object of great curiosity; people came from all parts to gaze upon the hermit; he was very proud of a notoriety which he would probably have failed to acquire by any legitimate efforts; and he conversed courteously with everyone. He was found in a fit one morning, after this long seclusion, and was removed to a farmhouse, where he died the next day.

We may revive the memory of John Ward, formerly of Hackney, as a specimen of the villainous resident.

His career was chequered with coloring of dark, very dark, and black shade. He began life in some small manufactory; he wriggled up, and became a member of Parliament; he was prosecuted for forgery, he was pilloried, he was imprisoned, and he was expelled the House of Commons. He was also prosecuted by the South Sea Company for feloniously concealing the sum of £50,000. He suffered imprisonment for this crime. He is held up to execration by Pope:

> "there was no grace of Heaven
> Given to the fool, the mad, the vain, the evil;
> To Ward, to Waters, Charters and the Devil."

He added to his villainies a kind of pinchbeck piety, that perverted piety which manifests itself in beseeching the Lord to be on his side in his money-getting. The following is, I imagine, almost unique as a prayer.

"O Lord, thou knowest that I have nine estates in the City of London and likewise that I have lately purchased an estate in fee simple in the county of Essex: I beseech thee to preserve the two counties of Middlesex and Essex from fire and earthquakes: and as I have a mortgage in Hertfordshire, I beg of Thee likewise to have an eye of compassion on that county and for the rest of the counties Thou mayest deal with them as Thou art pleased. O Lord, enable the bank to answer all their bills, and make all my debtors good men.

"Give prosperous voyage to the *Mermaid* sloop, because I have insured it: and as Thou hast said that the days of the wicked are but short, I trust in Thee that Thou wilt not forget Thy promise, as I have purchased an estate in reversion, which will be mine on the death of that profligate young man Sir J. L."

Such a prayer would seem to argue some mental twist; but strange are the vagaries of the pinchbeck pious.

Two more villains, and we make an end. The first of them was the bold Dick Turpin. Have the achievements of Dick Turpin crossed the ocean? Surely they have, if only in the pages of the "Pickwick Papers," where Sam Weller sings part of a song written in praise of the highwayman. The verses are generally believed to be by Charles Dickens himself, but that is not so. They are by James or Horace Smith, or both, the authors of the "Rejected Addresses," and are the two opening stanzas of a long poem. Dick Turpin lived for a time at a house in Hackney Marsh, near a tavern and a cockpit, and passed for a sporting gentleman free with his money. Few highwaymen were so successful as the gallant rider of Black Bess, and very, very few arrived, as he did, at the age of thirty-four before undertaking that drive to Tyburn Tree, which was the concluding act in his profession. Indeed, the grand climacteric for a highwayman seems to have been twenty-four.

The other villain for whom Hackney blushes was a native of Homerton. This was none other than the famous "Jack the Painter," who formed the bold design of setting fire to all the dockyards in the country. The story of his attempt in Portsmouth Dockyard, and of his failure and trial, forms one of the most singular chapters in the criminal history of the last century. He was executed in 1776, and his body hung in chains on the shore near Portsmouth for a great many years. I have myself conversed with persons who could remember the gibbet of Jack the Painter, and his blackened, tarred remains dangling in chains. But they were old men, and they were seafaring men. And when the mariner grows old his memory lengthens and strengthens and spreads.

XI

ON SPORTS AND PASTIMES

XI

ON SPORTS AND PASTIMES

WE have dwelt so long on the melancholy pictures of the houseless and the starving that there is danger of falling hastily into the conclusion that East London is the favorite residence of Poverty, Misery, and Necessity—those Furies three. We must not think this. East London is, as I have said before, above all things the city of the working-man—the greatest city of the respectable working-man in the whole world. Fortunately he is, for the most part, in good and steady work. Those are not his daughters who march arm in arm down Brook Street, lifting the hymn, which has no words, of irrepressible youth; nor are those his sons who hang about the corners of the streets near the public house; nor has he any connection with the shuffling, ragged outcasts whom we call the submerged.

The great mass of the population consists of the steady craftsmen, with the foremen, and the managers of departments, and the clerks employed in the factories and the works. I am about to point out some of the ways in which these people brighten and enliven their days.

A certain joyousness has always been the keynote of London life. A volume might be written on the cheerfulness of London; it is not gaiety—Paris or Vienna is a city of gaiety; it is a more valuable possession; the citizen of London is not light-hearted; he is always, in fact, possessed with a wholesome sense of individual responsibility; but he is cheerful, and he loves those amusements which belong to the cheerful temperament. It must also be acknowledged that he loves sport, and everything connected with sport. Now this cheerfulness of London a hundred years ago seemed well-nigh destroyed. The old social life of the City was broken up by the abandonment of the City; the suburban life, without centers of attraction, such as the little City parish, or the ward, or the City company was wont to offer, was dull and monotonous; the working-men, long left to themselves without schools, or leaders, or masters, or discipline of any kind, were sunk deep in a drunken slough, and the industrial side of London had hardly yet sprung into existence. In another place I have considered the suburban life; here let me speak only of the people who make up the crowds of East London. Without apparent centers round which they could group themselves, the people, by instinct, when they found themselves thus massed together, revived the old cheerfulness of their ancestors. East London, for its sports and pastimes, when we look into them, reminds us of London of the twelfth century as described by Fitzstephen—a city always in good spirits, joyous, and given to every kind of sport. Not quite in the same way; the houses are no longer decked with flowers—it would be too ridiculous to decorate a street leading out of the Commercial Road with flowers; nor do we see any longer the old procession where the minstrels went before,—if it was only the tabor and the pipe,—while the lads and lasses followed after. Yet in its own way this new city is full of cheerfulness; it contains so many Hooligans and casuals and outcasts that it ought to go about with a face of dismal lines; but there were outcasts and casuals even in the twelfth century; quite another note will be struck by one who investigates; there is no city more cheerful and more addicted to enjoyment than East London.

Like all industrial cities—you may note the fact especially in Brussels—the young seem out of all proportion to the old;

ON SPORTS AND PASTIMES

this is of course partly because the young people come out more; they crowd the leading streets and the boulevards; they seem to have nothing to do, and to want nothing but to amuse themselves every evening.

I have already twice called attention to the very remarkable change that has gradually transformed the life of the modern craftsman. We have given him his evenings—all his evenings; we have postponed his going to work by an hour at least, and in many cases by two hours; this means a corresponding extension of the evening, because when a man had to present himself at the workshop at 5:30 or 6 A. M. he had to get up an hour before that time, therefore he had to be in bed by an early hour in the evening. This point is of vital importance; it is affecting the national character for good or evil; it is full of possibilities and it is full of dangers.

Our young people, who are those most to be considered, for obvious reasons, are now in possession of the whole evening. From seven o'clock till bedtime, which may be eleven or twelve, they are free to do what they please; the paternal authority is no longer exercised; they are, in every sense, their own masters. In addition, we give them the Saturday afternoon and the whole of Sunday free from the former obligations of church. We also give them the bank-holidays, with Christmas Day and Good Friday. In other words, we give them, if you will take the trouble to calculate, more than a quarter of the solid year, reckoned by days of twenty-four hours. If we reckon by days of sixteen hours we give them more than one third of the whole year, and we say to them, "Go; do what you please with one third of your lives." This is a very serious gift; it should be accompanied by admonition as to responsibilities and possibilities. Anything may be done for good or for ill, with a whole third part of the working year to work at it. The gift, so far, and with certain exceptions, as of the ambitious lad who means to rise, and will rise, though it means hours of labor when others are at play, has been, so far, generally interpreted to mean, "Go and do nothing, except look for present enjoyment."

The winter, by universal consent, comes to an end on Easter Sunday, which may fall as early as the fourth week in March or as late as the fourth week in April. The breath of the English spring is chill, but the snow and the cold rains and the fogs have gone; if the east wind is keen it dries the roads; the bicycles can come out; there is not yet much promise of leaf and flower, but the catkins hang upon the trees and the hedges are turning green, and the days are long and the evenings are light. I think that Easter Monday is the greatest holiday of the year to East London.

It has replaced the old May-day. Formerly, when by the old style May-day fell on what is now the 14th, it came very happily at the real commencement of the English spring. We are liable to east winds and to cold and frost till about the middle of May, after which it is seldom that the east wind returns. On that day the whole City turned out to welcome summer. Think what they had gone through; the streets unpaved, mere morasses of mud and melting snow; the houses with their unglazed windows boarded up with shutters; the long evenings spent crouching round the fire or in bed; no fresh meat, no vegetables, only salted meat and birds, and, to finish with, the forty days of fasting on dried fish, mostly so stale that it would not now be allowed to be offered for sale. And here was summer coming again! Out of the City gates poured the young men and the maidens to gather the branches and blossoms of the white-thorn, to come back laden with the greenery and to dance and sing around the May-pole.

May-day has long ceased to be a popular festival. The Puritans killed it. Yet there still linger some of the old signs of rejoicing. To this day the carmen deck their horses with ribbons and artificial flowers on May-day. Until quite recently there were one or two May-day processions still to be seen in the streets. The chimney-sweeps kept up the custom longest. They came out in force, dressed up with fantastic hats and colored ribbons. In the midst was a moving arbor of green branches and flowers, called Jack in the Green. Beside him ran and danced a girl in gay colors, who was Maid Marian. Before him went a fife and drum or a fiddler, and they stopped at certain points to dance round Jack in the Green. Another procession, discontinued before that of the chimney-sweeps, was that of the milkmaids. The dairy women, dressed in bright colors and having flowers in their hair or in their hats, led along a milch cow covered with garlands. After the cow came a man inside a frame which bore a kind of trophy consisting of silver dishes and silver goblets, lent for the occasion and set in flowers. Of course they had a fiddler, always represented in the pictures as one-legged, but perhaps the absence of a leg was not an essential.

May-day is gone. Its place is taken, and more than taken, by Easter Monday. It is the fourth and last day of the longest holiday in the whole year. From Good Friday to Monday, both inclusive, no work is done, no workshops are opened. The first day, the Day of Tenebræ, the day of fasting and humiliation, is observed by East London as a day of great joy; it is a day on which the men seek their amusements without the women; on this day there are sports, with wrestling and boxing, with foot-ball and athletics; the women, I think, mostly stay at home. On the Saturday little is done but to rest, yet there are railway excursions; many places of amusement, such as the Crystal Palace and the Aquarium (they offer a long round of shows lasting all through the day), are open. Easter Sunday is exactly like any other Sunday. But Monday—Monday is the holiday for all alike, men, women, and children. Poor and miserable must that man be who cannot find something for Easter Monday.

There used to be the Epping Hunt. This absurd burlesque of a hunt was the last survival of the right claimed by the citizens of London to hunt in the forests of Middlesex. On Easter Monday the "hunt" assembled; it consisted of many hundreds of gallant huntsmen mounted on animals of every description, including the common donkey; there were also hundreds of vehicles of every kind bringing people out to see the hunting of the stag. It was a real stag and a real hunt. That is to say, the stag was brought in a cart and turned out, the horsemen forming an avenue for him to run, while the hounds waited for him. There was a plunge, a shout; the stag broke through the horsemen and ran off into the cover of the forest, followed by the whole mob at full gallop; the hounds seem to have been for the most part behind the horses, which was certainly safer for them. The stag was not killed, but was captured and taken away in the cart that brought him. The Epping Hunt is no longer celebrated, nor is Epping Forest any longer one of the haunts of Easter Monday.

Five miles from St. Paul's cathedral lies a broad heath on the plateau of a hill. This is Hampstead Heath. Two hundred years ago, on the edge of the heath was a Spa, with a fashionable assembly-room and a tavern. The Spa decayed, and the place became the residence of a few wealthy merchants, each with his stately garden. Some of these houses and these gardens survive to this day; most of them are built over, and Hampstead is now a suburb of eighty thousand people, standing on the slope and top of a long hill rising to the height of nearly five hundred feet. The heath, however, has never been built upon. It is a strangely beautiful place; not a park, not a garden, not anything artificial, simply a wild heath covered with old and twisted gorse bushes, with fern and bramble, and in spring lovely with the white-thorn and the blackthorn and the blossoms of the wild crab-apple, Britain's only native fruit. The heath is cut up into miniature slopes and tiny valleys; a

Hampstead Heath, Looking "Hendon Way."

ON SPORTS AND PASTIMES

high causeway runs right across it; the place is so high that there is a noble view of the country beyond, while at rare intervals, when the air is clear, the whole valley of the Thames lies at the spectator's feet, and London, with her thousand spires and towers is clearly visible, with St. Paul's towering over the whole.

The heath is the favorite resort of the holiday makers of Easter Monday; a kind of fair is permitted on one side, with booths and the customary bawling. There are never any shows on Hampstead Heath—I know not why. The booths are for rifle galleries, for tea and coffee and ices, for cakes and ginger-beer, for crafty varieties in the game of dropping rings or pretty trifles for bowls and skittles, and for "shying" sticks at cocoanuts. No stalls are allowed for the sale of strong drink. Here the people assemble in the morning, beginning about ten, and continue to arrive all day long, dispersing only when the sun goes down and the evening becomes too cold for strolling about. They may be numbered by the hundred thousand. Here are the factory girls, going about in little companies, adorned with crimson and blue feathers; they run about laughing and shrieking in the simple joy of life and the exhilarating presence of the crowd; they do not associate with the lads, who dress up their hats with paper ribbon and hurl jokes, lacking in originality as in delicacy, at the girls as they run past. There are a great many children; the policemen in the evening bring the lost ones, disconsolate, to the station. Some of them have come with their parents; some of them, provided with a penny each, have come alone; it is wonderful to see what little mites run about the heath, hand in hand, without any parents or guardians. There are young married couples carrying the baby. All the people alike crowd into the booths and take their chance at what is going on; they "shy" at the cocoanuts as if it were a new game invented for that day, they dance in the grass to the inspiring strains of a concertina, they swing uproariously in the high wooden carriages, they are whirled breathlessly round and round on the steam-conducted wooden cavalry, and all the time with shouting and with laughing incessant. For, you see, the supreme joy, the true foundation of all this happiness, is the fact that they are all out again in the open, that the winter is over and gone, and that they can once more come out all together, as they love, in a vast multitude. To be out in the open, whether on the seashore or on Hampstead Heath, in a great crowd, is itself happiness enough. There is more than the joy of being in a crowd; there is also the joy of being once more on the green turf. Deep down, again, in the hearts of these townbred cockneys there lies, ineradicable, the love of the green fields and the country air. So some of them leave the crowd and wander on the less frequented part of the heath. They look for flowers, and pick what they can find; the season is not generally so far advanced as to tempt them with branches of hawthorn, nor are the fields yet covered with buttercups; the buds are swelling, the grass puts on a brighter green, but the spring as yet is all in promise. There are other country places of resort, but Hampstead is the favorite.

For those who do not go out of London on Easter Monday there are more quiet recreations. On that day Canon Barnett opens his annual exhibition of loan pictures at his schools beside his church at Whitechapel; to the people of his quarter he offers every year an exhibition of pictures which is really one of the best of the yearly shows, though the West End knows nothing about it, and there is no private view attended by the fashionable folk, who go to see each other. There is a catalogue; it is designed as a guide and an aid to the reader; it is therefore descriptive; in the evening ladies go round with small parties and give little talks upon the pictures, explaining what the artist meant and how his design has been carried out. Such a party I once watched before Burne-Jones's picture of "The Briar Rose." The people gazed; they saw the brilliant coloring, the briar-rose everywhere, the sleeping knights, the courtyard—all. Then the guide began, and their faces lit up with pleasure and understanding, and all went home that evening richer for the contemplation and the comprehension of one great work of art.

At the People's Palace there are concerts morning and evening; perhaps also there is some exhibition or attraction of another kind; there are other loan exhibitions possible besides those of art.

Some of the people, but not many, go off westward and wander about the halls of the British Museum. I do not know why they go there, because ancient Egypt is to them no more than modern Mexico, and the Etruscan vases are no more interesting than the "Souvenir of Margate," which costs a penny. But they do go; they roam from room to room with listless indifference, seeing nothing. In the same spirit of curiosity, baffled yet satisfied, they go to the South Kensington Museum and gaze upon its treasures of art; or they go to the National Portrait Gallery, finding in Queen Anne Boleyn a striking likeness to their own Maria, but otherwise not profiting in any discoverable manner by the contents of the gallery. And some of them go to the National Gallery, where there are pictures which tell stories. Or some get as far as Kew Gardens, tempted by the reputation of the houses which provide tea and shrimps and water-cresses outside the gardens, as much as by the Palm House and the Orchid Houses within.

The streets on Easter Monday present a curious Sunday-like appearance, with shops shut and no vehicles except the omnibus, but in the evening the theater and the music-hall are open, and they are crammed with people.

Therefore, though Easter Monday is the greatest of the people's holidays, it is so chiefly because it is the first, and because, like the May-day of old, it stands for the end of the long, dark winter and the first promise of the spring.

Even in the streets, the streets of dreary monotony, the East Londoners feel their blood stir and their pulses quicken when the April day draws out and once more there comes an evening light enough and long enough to take them out by tram beyond the bricks.

The holiday of early summer is Whit-Monday, which is also a movable feast, and falls seven weeks after Easter, so that it is due on some day between May 12th and June 12th. I have already observed that the cold east wind, which retards our spring, generally ceases before the middle of May, though in our climate nothing is certain—not even hot weather in July and August. When it falls reasonably late, say in the first week of June, there is some probability that the day will be warm, even though there may be showers; that the woods will be resonant with warblers, the fields golden with buttercups, the hedges bright with spring flowers, the bushes white and pink with May blossom, and the orchards glorious with the pink of the apple and the creamy white of the cherry and the pear. On this day the East Londoner goes farther afield; he is not content with Hampstead Heath, and he will not remain under cover at the Crystal Palace. Trains convey him out of London. He goes down to Southend, at the mouth of the Thames; there, at low tide, he can gaze upon a vast expanse of mud or he can walk down a pier a mile and a half long, or, if it is high tide, he may delight in the dancing waters with innumerable boats and yachts. Above all, at Southend he will find all the delights that endear the seaside to him; there is the tea with shrimps—countless shrimps, quarts and gallons of shrimps; he is among his own kind; there is no one to scoff when, to the music of the concertina, he takes out his companion to dance in the road; he sings his music-hall ditties unchecked; he bawls the cry of the day, and it is counted unto him for infinite humor. Southend on Whit-Monday is a place for the comic man and the comic artist; it is also the place for the humorist.

The Shooting-Gallery.

One must not be hard upon the Whit-Monday holiday-maker. He is at least good-humored; there is less drunkenness than one would expect; there is very little fighting, but there is noise—yes, there is a good deal of noise. These children of nature, if they feel happy, instinctively laugh and shout to proclaim their happiness. They would like the bystanders to share it with them; they cannot understand the calm, cold and unsympathetic faces which gaze upon them as they go bawling on their way. They would like a friendly chorus, a fraternal hand upon the shoulder, an invitation to a drink. Let us put ourselves in their place and have patience with them.

I have already mentioned Epping Forest in connection with the cockney hunt of Easter Monday. But to be seen in the true splendor of its beauty Epping Forest must be visited in early June. It is the East Londoner's forest; fifty years ago he had two; on the east of Epping Forest lay another and a larger, called Hainault Forest. It was disforested and cleared and laid out in farms in the year 1850. Epping, however, remains. It is about sixteen miles north of the river; encroachments have eaten into its borders, and almost into its very heart. For a long time no one paid any attention. Suddenly, however, it was discovered that the forest, which had once covered twelve thousand acres, now covered only three thousand. Three fourths had been simply stolen. Then the City of London woke up, appointed a verderer and rangers, drew a map of what was left, and sternly forbade any more encroachments. What is left is a very beautiful wild forest; deer roam about its glades; for the greater part of the year it is quite a lonely place, only receiving visitors on Saturday afternoons and Sundays. It is a narrow, cigar-shaped wood about a mile broad and eight miles long. There are outlying bits on the north and on the south. The ancient continuity of the forest is gone, but there are tangles of real wood and coppice here and there;

T

the central point of the forest, that which attracts most people, is a small bit of wild wood lying on a hill. Here the ground is rough and broken; everywhere are oaks, elms, beeches, and hornbeams, with a veritable jungle of wild roses, sloes, thorns, and brambles. The woods are filled with singing birds; the ground is covered with wild flowers. Imagine the joy of the East Londoner on Whit-Monday when he plunges up to his knees in the buttercups, the wild anemones, and the flowering grasses, while the lark sings overhead, and thrush and blackbird call from the woods around him, and the sun warms him and the sweet air refreshes him. Such an one I followed once and watched. He was a young fellow of twenty-one or so, with his wife, a girl of nineteen, behind him. He had taken the pipe out of his mouth; instinctively he felt that the pipe was out of place; he threw himself down upon the grass and clasped his hands under his head. "Gawspel truth, old gal!" he cried, out of the fullness of his heart. "It's fine! It's fine!"

It was fine, and it was Whit-Monday, and a hundred thousand others like unto this young fellow and his bride were wandering about the forest that day.

There are not many students of archæology in East London, which is a pity, since there are many points of interest within their reach. All round the forest, for instance, and within the forest there are treasures. To begin with, there are two ancient British camps still in good preservation; there is a most picturesque deserted church, called old Chingford church; there is the ancient Saxon church, whose walls are oaken trunks, put up to commemorate the halt of those who carried St. Cuthbert's bones; there is Waltham Abbey, where King Harold lies buried; and if you take a little walk to the east you will find yourself at Chigwell, and you may dine at the inn where, in the Gordon troubles, as presented in "Barnaby Rudge," the landlord found a trifle of glass broken. But the joy in things ancient has not yet been found out by the London workman. Now and again he is a lover of birds or a student of flowers; for such an one Epping is a haunt of which he can never tire, for it is the only place near London where he can watch heron, hawk, kingfisher, and the wild water-fowl.

Or the people go farther afield by cheap excursion trains. Their coming is not welcomed by the inhabitants of the towns which are their destination. They go to Brighton or to Hastings; they sit in long rows, side by side, upon the shingle idly watching the waves; they go to Portsmouth and sit on Southsea beach watching the ships. They even get across to the Isle of Wight. Last year I was at a little town in that island called Yarmouth. I there made the acquaintance of an ancient mariner who was employed by Lloyd's to take the names of all the ships which passed into the Solent, here a narrow strait. He told me in conversation that I ought to see their church, which is old and beautiful. I replied that I had attempted to do so, but found the door shut. Upon which he gave me the following remarkable reason for this apparent want of hospitality. I quote his words to show the local opinion of the tripper. "You see," he said, "it's all along of they London trippers. One Whit-Monday they came here and they found the church doors open and in they went, nosebags and cigarettes and all. Then the parson he came along, and he looked in. 'Well,' says the parson, 'Dash my wig!' he says. 'Get up off of them seats,' he says, 'and take your 'ats off your 'eads,' he says, 'and take they stinkin' bits o' paper out of your mouths,' he says, 'and get out of the bloomin' church,' he says. And he puts the key in his own pocket, and that's why you can't get into the church." The remarkable language attributed to the parson on this occasion illustrates the depth of local feeling about East London out on a holiday.

The August bank-holiday is a repetition of Whit-Monday, without the freshness of that early summer day. By the end of July the foliage of the trees has become dark and heavy; the best of the flowers are over in field as well as garden; the sadness of autumn is beginning. All through the summer, especially on Saturdays and Sundays, the excursion trains are running in all directions, but especially to the seaside; the excursion steamers run to Southend, Walton, Margate, and Ramsgate. For those who stay at home there are the East-End parks, Victoria Park, West Ham Park, Finsbury Park, Clissold Park, Wanstead Park. They are thronged with people strolling or sitting quietly along the walks. All these parks are alike in their main features; they are laid out in walks and avenues planted with trees; they contain broad tracts of green turf; there is an inclosure for cricket; sometimes there is a gymnasium, and there is an ornamental water, generally very pretty, with rustic bridges, swans, and boats let out for hire. Where there is no park, as at Wapping and Poplar by the riverside, there are recreation grounds. In all of them a band of music plays on stated evenings.

This restoration of the garden to the people is a great feature of modern attempts at civilization; it seems terrible that there should be no place anywhere for children to play except the streets, or for the old people to sit except in the public house. London is now dotted with parks, chiefly small and covered with gardens. Nearly all the churchyards have been converted into gardens; the headstones are ranged along the walls; they might just as well be taken away; one or two "altar tombs" are left. The rest of the ground is planted with flowering shrubs—lilac, laburnum, ribes, the Pyrus Japonica, and the like; the walks are asphalted, and seats are provided. Nearly all the year round one may see the old people walking about the paths or sitting in the sun; part of the ground is given to the children. It is difficult, indeed, to exaggerate the boon conferred upon a crowded city by these breathing-places, where one can be

On Margate Sands.

quiet. The summer amusements of the people, you will observe, are not all made up of noisy crowds and musical trippers; add the summer evening walk in the park and, all the year round, the rest in the garden that is a disused burial-ground.

For the children there is the day in the country. Every summer day long caravans of wagons filled with children, singing and shouting as they go, drive along the roads to the nearest country place, or excursion trains crammed with children are carried off to the nearest seaside places. They run about on the seashore, they bathe, they sit down to a tea of cake and buns, and they are taken home at night tired out but singing and shouting to the end. This summer "day out" is the one great holiday for the children; they scheme to get put on the lists of more than one excursion; they look forward to it; they count upon it. Every year vigorous appeals are made in the papers for help to send the children away upon their annual holiday; these appeals are of course pitched extravagantly high; they talk a conventional jargon about the little ones who grow up without ever gazing upon a green leaf or a tree. Rubbish! There is not a street anywhere in London where a garden, if it is only a disused burial-ground, is not accessible if the children choose to go there. Mostly the very little ones prefer the dirt pies in the gutter, but even for them the wagonette comes now and then to carry them off for the whole day to the grass of Victoria Park. Still, it is a very great thing that they should, once at least in the year, be carried away into real country and have a glimpse of meadows, woods, and cows and sheep.

When they grow older they are still better off. It is quite common now for young men who carry on the Settlements and the boys' clubs to get the lads under their care to save up week by week until they have amassed the sum of five shillings. On this capital, with management, they are enabled to get a week's holiday by the seaside. It is a glorious time for them. A convenient place is found; it must be on the seashore; it should be quite free from any town or village; there must be no temptations of any kind; the lads are there to breathe fresh air and life, quite cut off from any suggestion of town life. They sleep, every boy in his own rug, on dry, clean straw in a barn, which is also their refectory, their lecture-hall, their concert and their singing-room. On the seashore there are boats for them; they row and sail and they go deep-sea fishing; they bathe every day, and they have swimming matches; on the sands they run races; in the evening they sing, they box, they look at dissolving views, and they lie down on the straw to rest. Their food is plain; it consists principally of boiled beef and potatoes, with cocoa and coffee and bread and butter. Of course this magnificent holiday demands a head and leader and obedience. But there is hardly ever any hitch or breakdown or row among the lads.

The hopping, considered as an amusement, should be placed next, but we have already shown the place it takes in the year of the factory girl. It is indeed amusement to all concerned, especially if the weather be fine; it is amusement with profit; the hoppers come home with a pocket full of money; they have left their pasty cheeks in the country, and they bring back rosy cheeks and freckled noses and sun-burned hands, with the highest spirits possible. The hopping, I confess, is not always idyllic. Last autumn it was reported that Maidstone Gaol was filled with hoppers charged with being disorderly; their camps might be conducted with more care for cleanliness; London roughs should not be allowed to come down on Sunday and mar this Arcadia. But the complainant, a well-known clergyman of the district, spoke with moderated condemnation. A more careful classification of the families in each encampment, he thinks; some check on the Sunday drink, which now flows at the sweet will of the people; some hindrance to the incursion of the Sunday rough; a more careful system of inspection—these things would go far to remove all reproach from the hopping. Meantime, as a proof of the substantial results of the work the roadway outside the principal station for their return was this year observed to be strewn with the old boots discarded by the hoppers when they bought new ones on their way home.

The river Lea, which, according to some, is the natural boundary of East London,—but it has leaped across that boundary,—is part of the summer amusements. The stream at its mouth, where it is a tributary to the Thames, is a black and murky river indeed. Higher up above the works it is a pleasant little river, winding along at leisure through a broad, marshy valley. The ground is soft and easy to be worked, the incline is so gradual that it might easily and at small expense be made an ornamental stream, moderately broad and able to carry racing boats, flowing beside gardens and under summer-houses and between orchards from its source to its mouth. Instead of this, it has been mercilessly divided into "cuts," channels, and mill-streams running off at wide angles, joining again lower down, separating again into other cuts and channels, again to unite. On its way it receives the refuse of mills, the refuse of towns; it passes Ware and Ryehouse, Tottenham, Clapton, and Hackney; its course unfortunately lies for the most part through a broad level of soft earth—marshy and low—which permits these cuttings and humiliations. It is accused of being a sewer; young men row upon it; boys bathe in it, but with remonstrance and complaint. The stream is, it must be confessed, in its lower reaches, offensive. Sore throats are caught beside its banks; sometimes people write indignantly about it to the papers. There is a little fuss, summer passes, in the winter no one goes near the river Lea, things are forgotten, and all goes on as before.

It is not possible for a river to flow for thirty miles without having lovely stretches and picturesque corners. The

Lea, with all its drawbacks, does possess these inevitable lapses into beauty. But in these pages we cannot stop to point them out. Where the Lea is beautiful it is outside the widest limits assignable to East London. Where the Lea is ugly, dirty, and disreputable, it used to form the eastern boundary to East London.

In the brief sketch of the summer amusements I have said nothing of the bicycle. Now, all the roads outside London are on Saturday and Sunday dotted with the frequent bicycle. It goes out in companies of twenty and thirty; it goes out by twos and threes; it goes out singly. On one Sunday twenty-five thousand bicycles were counted crossing one bridge over the Thames and making for the country beyond. And it seems that there are none so poor as not to afford a bicycle. The secret is, I believe, that a second-hand bicycle, or a bicycle of the last fashion but one, or a damaged bicycle, may be purchased of its owner for a mere trifle, and these lads learn very quickly how to repair the machine themselves.

But the summer all too quickly draws to an end. By the middle of September twilight falls before seven. There are no more evening spins ten miles out and back again; by the end of October twilight falls at five; then there are no more Saturday afternoons on the road. The weather breaks, the roads are heavy, the bicycle is laid aside for the next four months, perhaps for more, because the cold east wind of early spring does not make the roads pleasant except for the hardiest and the strongest. The winter amusements begin. For the factory girls and the dockers we have seen what they are: the street first and foremost; always the street, imperfectly lit, the pavement crowded; always the street, in which the girls march up and down three or four abreast. Their laugh is loud, but it is not forced; their jokes and their badinage with the lads are commonplace and coarse, but they pass for wit; they enjoy the quick pulse when all the world is young; they are as happy as any girls in any other class; they need not our pity; youth, if it has enough to eat and its evening of amusement, is always happy.

They have, then, the boulevard without the café, the street with the public house and the invitation from youth, prodigal of its pence, to step in and have a drink. In addition, they have the music-hall and the theater. For some there is the club; but only a few, comparatively, can be persuaded to go into the club for an hour or two every evening. Most of them have no desire for a quiet place; they are obliged to be quiet in the factory; at night they like to make up for the day's long silence.

So with their companions, the casual hands, the factory lads, the Hooligans, the children of the kerb, they rejoice in the days of their youth.

Let us mount the social scale; we come to the craftsman in steady work, to the small clerk, to the small shopkeeper. Not that these are of equal rank. The working-man consorts with other working-men; the small clerk calls himself a gentleman; the small shopkeeper is a master. What have they for amusements? The small shopkeeper seems to get along altogether without any amusement. He keeps his "place" open till late in the evening; he shuts it, takes his supper, and goes to bed. His social ambitions are limited by the distinctions to be acquired in his chapel; he reads a halfpenny journal for all his literature.

As for what is offered to those who will accept these gifts, there are lectures first and foremost; there are the lectures offered every winter at Toynbee Hall. These lectures are not, if you please, given by the "man in the street"; the lecturers are the most distinguished men in their own lines to be found; there is no talking "down" to the Whitechapel audience; those serious faces show that they are here to be taught, if the lecturer has anything to tell them, or to receive suggestions and advice; they are all of the working-class; they are far more appreciative than the audiences of the

West End; they read and think; they have been trained and encouraged to read and think by Canon Barnett for many years; they are very much in earnest, and they do not come with vacuous minds; as Emerson said of the traveler so we may say of a man who listens to a lecture—he takes away what he brought with him. About the Settlements and the

Toynbee Hall and St. Jude's Church.

gifts which they offer, with full hands, to the people, I speak in the next chapter.

What Barnett and Toynbee Hall have done for the intellectual side the People's Palace has done for the musical side. Its cheap concerts have led the people, naturally inclined to music, insensibly into ways of good taste; the palace was fortunate, at first, in getting a musical director who knew how to lead the people on; one of the most gratifying successes of this institution has been its music. They have now their own orchestra, vocal and instrumental. At the same place are held exhibitions, from time to time, of East London industries, of pictures, of arts and crafts of all kinds.

Here is the finest gymnasium in London, and here are many clubs—for foot-ball, cricket, and games of all kinds.

One omission in the amusements of London must be noted. There are no public dancing-halls. I see no reason at all why a public dancing-hall should not be carried on with as much attention to good behavior as a private dance, or a theater, or any other place where people assemble together. It requires only the coöperation of the people themselves, without the aid of the police. Meantime, there is no form of exercise, to my mind, so delightful to the young and so healthful as dancing; nothing that more satisfies the restlessness of youth than the rapid and rhythmic movement of the limbs in the dance. Nature makes the young long to jump about; education should take in hand their jumping and make it part of the orderly recreation which we are substituting for the old brutal sports. Dancing was tried at the People's Palace; it was a great success; the balls given in the Queen's Hall were crowded, and the people were as orderly as could be desired. But, indeed, the whole feeling of the assembly was in favor of order.

The theater and the music-hall claim, and claim successfully, their supporters; concerning the former one has only to recognize that it may be a school of good manners, as well as of good sentiments, and that it is also an institution capable of ruining a whole generation. The pieces given at the theaters of East London are, so far as I have observed, chiefly melodramas. The music-halls are places frankly of amusement, and for the most part, I believe, vulgar enough, but not otherwise mischievous.

And there is the public billiard-room, with all that it means —the betting man, the professional player, the proximity to the bar, the beer and the tobacco, and the talk. It attracts the young clerk more readily than the young craftsman. It is his first step downward. If it does not plunge him beneath the waves after the fashion that we have witnessed, it will keep him where he is and what he is—a writing machine, a machine on hire at a wage not so very much better than a typewriting instrument, all his life. Let us rather contemplate the thousands of lads who attend the classes at the palace, the polytechnics, and the Settlements; let us rather think of those who crowd into the concerts, sit as students at the lectures and listen and look on while the guide leads them round the exhibitions.

In this long list of amusements I must have omitted some, perhaps many. For instance, I have not spoken of reading or of literature. The craftsman of East London has not yet begun to read books; at present he only reads the paper; his children read the penny dreadfuls, and are beginning to read books.

Considering that Sunday afternoon is especially the time of rest, we must not forget one form of recreation peculiar to that time. It takes the form of an address given in some chapel. There is generally a short service, with prayer and the singing of a hymn; the people who attend and crowd the chapel seem to like this addition to the address which follows. It is intended to be of a kind likely to interest and to instruct; the first duty of the lecturer is to choose a subject which does both; I have myself on more than one occasion attempted to address working-men on the Sunday afternoon; I have found them easy to interest and quick to take up points. As at Toynbee Hall, one must not talk "down" to them. Indeed, the men who come to such lectures are the most intelligent and the best educated of the whole population. It is pleasant and restful for them; the chapel is warm; the singing is not disagreeable, even though in their own homes psalmody is not commonly practised; to be called away on a dark and gloomy November afternoon and led gently into another world, with new scenery and other conditions, is that complete change which is the best rest of all. The lecturer need not be afraid of tiring his audience; he may go

ON SPORTS AND PASTIMES

on as long as he pleases; when he leaves off they will crowd round him and beg him to come again.

Many other omissions I have made purposely. There are the drinking and the gambling clubs, the betting clubs, haunts, and dens, if one choose to consult the police and to hunt them up, which would enable one to finish this chapter with a lurid picture. Where there are so many men and women there will always be found a percentage of the bad, the worse, and the worst. It is the hopeful point about East London that wherever the better things are offered they are accepted by the better sort; not by a few here and a few there, but by thousands who are worthy of the better things.

: XII

THE HELPING HAND

XII

THE HELPING HAND

THE work that lies before us in every city waiting for the Helping Hand—the human wreckage, bankruptcy, age, sickness, poverty, which must always be forming anew however we may meet it and find alleviation—will certainly not decrease as the years roll on. The point for us to consider here is not the volume and variety of the forces which cause this wreckage, but the attempts which are now being made to find this alleviation and, if possible, a remedy.

The Helping Hand has a history, and it is very simple:

1. First of all it threw a penny to the beggar because he was a beggar.

2. Secondly, it offered free meals and free quarters in every monastic house to every beggar because he was a beggar.

3. It continued to give the penny and the free meals and the lodging to the beggar because he was a beggar, but it ordered the beggar to go back to work.

4. It arrested, imprisoned, branded, and flogged the beggar because he was a beggar. It continued also to give him a penny for the same reason.

5. It founded almshouses for some of the aged poor; those who could not get in continued to receive their penny and their flogging because they were beggars.

6. It founded workhouses, Bridewell, and houses of cor-

rection for the beggar. And it continued to give that penny to the beggar because he was a beggar.

7. It built houses for the reception of the poor who could no longer work, infirmaries for the sick, orphanages and homes for poor children, casual wards for the homeless. It made begging an offense in the eyes of the law. Yet it continued to give the beggar a penny because he was a beggar.

8. It discovered that a multitude of rogues and people who will not work trade upon the charity and the pity of people, sending around letters asking for help. It therefore established an association, with branches everywhere, to expose the fraudulent. Yet it continued to give the beggar a penny because he was a beggar.

In other words, the Helping Hand has never been able to refrain from giving that penny which encourages the "masterless" man, and the man who will not work, and the fraudulent, and the writer of the begging letter. Could the Helping Hand be persuaded to refuse that penny for a single fortnight, to turn a deaf ear resolutely to the starving family on the road, to the starving children on the pavement, to the starving woman who stands silent, mournful, appealing with mute looks of misery, only for a single fortnight, the existence of the beggar would come to a sudden end. This the Helping Hand can never be persuaded to do. Therefore we have with us not only the real misery caused by fate, by fortune, by the natural consequences of folly and weakness and crime, but also the pretended misery of those who live upon the pity of the world and trade on that strange self-indulgence which gives the dole to remove an unpleasant object out of sight and to awaken the glow which follows with the sense of charity.

I leave aside in this place the casual dole—the penny to the beggar because he is a beggar; it is illustrated for all time by the partition of the cloak between St. Martin and the beggar. The saint, then a gallant cavalryman, did not stop—or stoop—to inquire into the merits of the case; here was a beggar. Was he really starving? could he work? were his sufferings pretended? was he really cold? did he deserve any help at all? Was he, on the contrary, well fed and nourished, money in purse, food in wallet, a sufficiency of clothes on his back, a fire and a pot over it at home, with a well-fed family and a wife on the same "lay" at the other gate of the city? Let us leave the Bishop of Ligugé as a type for all the centuries of the unthinking charity which gives the penny to the beggar because he is a beggar.

Let us turn to other and later developments. The Helping Hand has founded and endowed and now maintains by voluntary contributions hospitals of every kind for the sick; by rates and taxes, workhouses for the poor, schools for the children. Yet there has passed—there is now passing—over the work of charity a great and most remarkable revolution; it is a revolution characteristic of a time in which every theory of social life, social conditions, and social responsibilities has been completely changed. The old duties remain still; schools and hospitals have been multiplied; if almshouses have not increased, the workhouse system has become better organized. But we have become aware of other duties, of new responsibilities. It is now understood that it is not enough to put the children to school from one to fourteen; they must be looked after when they leave school; it is not enough to provide for the diseases of the body; we must make provision for the diseases, and the cause of the diseases, of the mind. The Helping Hand is at work in these days for the arrest of degeneracy; for the opening up of art, literature, music, science, culture of all kinds, to the better sort among the working-classes; for the wider extension of the area and the depth of culture; for the creation of that kind of public opinion which, more than anything else, makes for public order and the maintenance of law; for the care and safeguarding of young people at the perilous time of emancipation from school; for the rescue of those who can be rescued; for the cleansing of the slums; for the restoration to the world of those who, as we have seen, have dropped out; and for the prevention of pauperizing by ill-considered schemes of ill-informed benevolence.

These are general terms. In order to carry out its work in detail, the Helping Hand looks after the children in their homes, while the Board-school looks after their teaching; it provides cases for the hospital, and aids the parish authorities during sickness in the home; it introduces the social side into the lives of the better sort; it devises attractions for the young people who stand at the parting of the ways, where temptation is strong and the primrose path is bright with flowers; it teaches the lads a trade, and the girls a love for the quiet life; it wages war with the public house and the street; it endeavors to bring back the lowest strata to a sense of religion which they have come to think the peculiar and rather unaccountable property of "class"; it brings friendliness among folk who have only known the order of the policeman.

The New Whitechapel Art Gallery.
(The building to the right is a free library.)

These are some of the functions which to-day are exercised by the Helping Hand. In East London we can see the hand at work with greater energy, wiser supervision, and in directions more varied than in any other city of Great Britain. I do not venture, for the obvious reason of ignorance, upon comparison with American cities, but I should think that we have in East London, with its vast population of working-people of all kinds, ranging from the highly-paid foreman to the casual hand, the lad of the street, the wastrel, and the wreck, a mass of humanity which is not paralleled anywhere, and a corresponding amount of philanthropic endeavor which it would be impossible to equal elsewhere.

In this immense multitude there are many slums of the worst kind; but they are now much fewer, and they are much less offensive, than they were; the most terrible of the plague spots seem to have been improved away; to find the real old slum, the foul, indescribable human pigsty, one must no longer look for it in East London. That is to say, there are, I dare say, a few of the old slums left, but the places—there were then many of them—into which one peered, shuddering, twenty years ago, have now vanished. The police, the clergy, the ladies who go about the parish, can still take the visitor into strange courts and noisome tenements, but he who remembers the former state of things feels that light and air and a certain amount of public opinion, with some measure of cleanliness, have been brought to the old-fashioned slum by the modern Helping Hand.

If the American visitor to London desires to see a real old-fashioned slum—one where all the surroundings, physical and moral, are, to use the mild word of the day, absolutely "insanitary"—I would recommend him not to try East London, where he would have to search long for what he wants, but to pay a visit to Guy's Hospital on the south side of the Thames and to seek the guidance of one of the students through the courts of crime and grime which still lie pretty thickly round that fortress of the army of health.

If you read novels of the day describing things brutal beyond belief, it will be well to suspect that the situations are a little mixed. Art must exaggerate; art must select; art must group. In this way it is quite possible that a picture tendered as of to-day may really belong to twenty years ago. There is still plenty of misery left in East London—we need, in fact, no exaggeration; I could fill these pages with lamentable histories; the people are still very much "down below"; some of them are a long way down; they are not only suffering for the sins of their fathers, they are busily piling up by their own sins sufferings for their children. Terrible has been their own inheritance; more terrible still will be the inheritance of the children.

Among these people, being such as they are, a whole army is at work continually. Let me now, in such short space as is at my command, consider in detail some of the more important methods by which this army is at work. It is not yet an army completely drilled and subdivided and commanded; some of their work overlaps, or hinders, other work. Perhaps it is not to be desired that this army should be completely drilled and organized. We do not ask for the crystallized methods of French education, or the iron drill of the Prussian sergeant. Let us leave some room for individual choice. Given certain principles of action, the element of personal freedom in carrying out these principles becomes of vital importance.

I have spoken of the revolution in opinion as to the responsibilities of the better educated and the wealthier toward those below them. Perhaps the situation may be illustrated by considering the change that has passed over us in our conception of what civilization should mean. The view of the eighteenth century was that civilization, culture, the pursuit of art, reading, learning of all kinds, science, the power, as well as the right, of government belonged essentially to the upper classes. When the good people of Spalding, for instance, in the year 1701, founded a literary society they called it the "Spalding Gentlemen's Society"—only gentlemen, you see, could be expected to take any interest in things that belong to civilization. It was further considered that it was impossible to expect civilizing influences to bear upon the working-classes. They were kept in order by discipline, by the prison, and by the lash. To open the doors of education, to give them access to the tree of knowledge, would be a most dangerous, a most fatal, mistake. Even at the present day one hears, at times, the belated cry that the working-classes need no more than the barest elements of learning.

In certain circles the distinction between the cultured class and those outside was marked by artificial notes of manner and of speech. The limits were intolerably narrow; outside these circles there was no leadership, no statesmanship, possible.

But apart from the pretensions of the eighteenth-century aristocracy it was considered by the middle class and the professional class alike dangerous to interfere with Providence; the working-class were born to do service: let them learn to do it. Religion, of course, they could have if they wanted it; the church was there, the doors were open every Sunday, anybody might go in; the clergyman would visit the sick, if he were invited; the children were baptized in the church; some of the people were married in the church; all the people were buried in the churchyard, with the service of the church by law established. That was all; there were very few schools; education, even if the parents wished it, was not to be had, and the folk were left altogether to their own devices. They had been forced out of the City to make room for warehouses and offices; they lived in their own quarters, especially along the riverside and in Whitechapel, and they were left quite alone to their own devices.

There were no police; the hand of the law among these crowded streets was weak; they did what they pleased. There is a story belonging to the year 1790, or thereabouts, of a man living in Wapping, just outside the Tower of London, which was always garrisoned with troops. This man gave offense to his neighbors by complying with some obnoxious law. He heard that they were going to attack him, meaning that they were going to murder him. The man had the bulldog courage of his time; he sent away his wife and children; he got a friend as brave as himself to join him; he closed his lower shutters and barricaded his door; he laid in ammunition, and he brought in and loaded two guns, one for himself and one for his friend.

At nightfall the attacking party arrived; they were armed with guns and stones. They began with a volley of the latter; the besieged paid no attention; they then fired at the windows; the besieged received their fire, and while they were loading again let fly among them, and killed or wounded two or three. They retired in confusion, but returned in larger numbers and with greater fury. All night long the unequal combat raged. When their ammunition was spent the two men dropped out of a back window into a timber yard, where they hid in a saw-pit. Observe that this battle lasted all the night, close to the Tower, and that no soldiers were sent out to stop it till the morning, when the mischief was done and the house was sacked. And no one was arrested, no one was punished, save the men who were shot. Can any story more clearly indicate the abandonment of the people to their own devices?

Reading these things, remembering how brutal, how ignorant, how degraded were whole masses of our people at that time, I am amazed that we came out of that long struggle of 1792-1815 without some awful outburst, some Jacquerie, like that of the Parisian mob, which might have drenched our land, as it did that of France, with blood and murder. And I think that when the social history of the nineteenth century, which we who have lived in it cannot grasp, save in parts, comes to be really and impartially considered, the chief feature, the redeeming point, will be that it began to recognize in practice the elementary truths that we are all responsible for each other, that each is his brother's keeper, that no class can separate itself from the rest, and that no civilization is durable or safe unless it includes the whole people.

What, then, have we done? What have we attempted? What are our present aims? It is not my purpose either to defend or to attack. I have only to state what is being done. Nothing can be attempted in this direction that is not open to abuses of one kind or another. The relief of distress encourages the idle; help of every kind is seized upon by the fraud and the impostor; if we feed and clothe the children their parents have more money for drink; the most we can do is to choose the line that seems open to the fewest objections and to exercise the most unremitting vigilance, care, and caution. The worst feature in the whole chapter of modern charity is that love and forbearance the most unwearied, devotion the most unselfish, seem too often only to pauperize the people, to induce more impudent frauds. But not always; we must take the line of the greatest, not the least, resistance,—that which is hardest for the worker, and certainly most unpopular with the subjects,—and we must judge of results from what follows. All modern philanthropic effort must, in order to be successful, be based upon the people understanding quite clearly that such effort cannot, by any ingenuity or any lies and legends, be turned to the encouragement of those who will not work.

I begin with the parish. There is at the present moment no more active clergy in the world than our own; there is no organization more complete than that of a well-worked London parish. The young men who now take Holy Orders know, at the outset, that they must lead lives of perpetual activity. There are the services of the parish church, with outlying mission churches; there are Sunday-schools, there are clubs, there are mothers' meetings, there are amusements for the people—concerts and entertainments for the winter; there is the supervision of the visiting ladies who go about the parish and learn the history of all the tenants in all the courts. There is the choir to be looked after, there are the sick to be cared for, there are always people in distress and in need of help—people for whom the vestry officers and workhouse officers can do nothing; the despairing young clergyman very soon finds out that the more you give to people who want help, the more people there are who clamor for help; he has to learn, you see, the great lesson that in certain social levels, where not to work should mean not to eat, no one will do a stroke of work if he can avoid it. Some of the clergy never do learn this lesson; they go on, all their lives, giving, doling, distributing, and pauperizing.

The organization of a London parish on the modern line is amazing in the extent of the aims and the variety of the work done. I have before me the annual report of a parish. From this document, which is like most of the other parochial annuals, it would seem the resolved endeavor of the clergy to make every kind of helpful and civilized work spring from the church and rest upon the church. In this report there are notices of seventy-five associations of various kinds; among them are gilds and fraternities, schools and classes; there are institutions purely religious and purely secular; with the Bible classes and the gilds we find the penny bank, the sharing club, the sale of clothes, the library, the maternity society, the mothers' meetings, the cookery class, and the blanket society. All these associations are conducted by the vicar and his four curates, assisted by a voluntary staff of about twenty ladies. It is evident that without unpaid and voluntary assistance the work could not be even attempted. The remarkable point—the "note" of the time—is that this voluntary assistance is like the widow's cruse—it never fails.

If, on the other hand, it is asked how far the people respond to the assumption that everything is done by the church, it is necessary to reply that the church, as a rule, remains comparatively empty. We have seen elsewhere that the percentage of attendance at the Sunday services of the

The East London Mission.

parish or the district church was, fourteen years ago, a little over three. Occasionally, however, when the vicar is a man of exceptional character, one who succeeds in winning the respect and the affection of the people so that they will follow him even into his church, the services are well attended, and in the evening crowded. There is, for example, a church in a district—a very poor and humble district near Shoreditch: the church was built through the exertions of the present vicar, who has succeeded in making the people attend. The history of the man partly explains the phenomenon. Fifteen years ago, when he went there, the place, consisting of a dozen miserable streets, was one of the vilest kind. Violence, robbery, drunkenness, murder, life in the most uncleanly forms imaginable prevailed in this slice of a large, crowded parish, which this man cut off to make a parish by itself. He sat down in the midst of them all, and he began. Observe that the first lesson he had to teach them was that he was not afraid of them; he was neither afraid of their threats nor of their proffered violence nor of their tongues; he went about among the women—the owners of those tongues—and opened up conversation with them; he spoke them friendly; they gave him the retort unfriendly; he replied readily and boldly, carrying the laugh against his adversaries; the common bludgeon of Billingsgate he met with the gentle rapier of "chaff," insomuch that the women were first infuriated, then silenced, and then reduced to friendliness, and, in this more desirable frame of mind, so remain. He put up a temporary church; beside the church he started schools; he opened a club for lads and the younger men; he provided his club with things that attracted them—rough games and gymnastics; more than this, he gave them boxing-gloves and taught them how to fight according to the strict rules of the prize-ring. You think that this is not the ideal amusement for a clergyman—wait a bit. The rules of the prize-ring are rigid rules; they demand a good deal of study; they make boxing a duello conducted according to rules of honor and courtesy. Now, when a lad has learned to handle the gloves according to the rules he becomes a stickler for them. Like Mrs. Battle over a game of whist, he exacts the rigor of the game. As for the old methods—the stones in the knotted handkerchief, the club, the short iron rod, and the cowardly boot—he will have no more of them. Moreover, fifteen minutes with a stout adversary, two or three returns to earth, and a shake-hand at the end, knock the devil out of a lad—the devil of restlessness and of pugnacity—give him a standard of honor, and make the rough-and-tumble in the street no longer worthy of consideration.

Then the vicar built a "doss-house," a place where men could sleep in peace and cleanliness. And he lived among his people, spending every evening of his life in club and doss-house and all day in the parish, so that the people trusted him more and more; and not only did his club overflow, but his church also began to fill—by this time it is no longer a temporary thing of iron, but a lovely church, with painted windows and carved work. In his services there is plenty of singing; he has processions, which the people like, with banners and crosses, the choir singing as they go. He also has incense, which I have never understood to be other than a barbaric survival. Nor can I understand how any one can endure the smell. Still, I suppose the people like it or he would not have it, and, after all, for those who do like the smell it is apparently harmless.

How many others have tried the same methods, but have failed! Why? Because the one thing necessary for success in such work as this—nine parts philanthropic and one part religious—is the magnetic power which we call, in practical work, sympathy, and, in art or literature, genius.

The clergy, with or without this magnetic power, work day and night. Never before has the Church of England possessed a clergy more devoted to practical work. Never before, alas! has the Church possessed so few scholars or so few preachers. Learning, save for a scholar here and there, has deserted the Church of England. Eloquence has passed from her pulpits to those of the Nonconformists. But the clergy work. Unfortunately, the parishes are large; even a district church has often ten thousand people or more, and those mostly poor, so that the struggle would be, if it were not supplemented, almost hopeless.

It is supplemented in many ways. To begin with, in its

civilizing work, by the Board-school. The action of the London School Board is always subjected to the fiercest light of hostile criticism, especially that of the ratepayers, who have seen with disgust the rate mounting year by year. There is, however, a consensus of agreement that the influence of the schools has been to humanize the people in a manner actually visible to all. The results are before us. The children of to-day are, it is confessed even by opponents to the policy of the School Board, in every respect better than those of twenty years ago, and this although, despite laws and inspectors, there are still many children who escape the meshes of the school net. The mothers understand that the teachers demand certain things of them; that the children must present themselves with hands and faces washed and with some attempt at neatness in their dress; this gives rise to a certain shame at letting the children go unwashed; perhaps, also, the thought of the school tyranny makes the father remember on Saturday afternoon the responsibility of the children, even to knocking off a pint or so.

As for the children themselves, they love the school and the teachers and the lessons; this part of the day is their happiness. Whether in the after life they will remember much of the scraps they learned—crumbs of knowledge: the historical crumb, the geographical crumb—I know not, but the important lessons of order and obedience are not readily forgotten; they will remain; when these children grow up some of them will perhaps join the company of disorder; but they will be rebels, not untaught savages who know no law.

I have already spoken of the clubs for boys and girls. These clubs are simply invaluable. They take the young people at a time when habits are most easily formed, at a time of life when it is most desirable to give them occupation and pursuits which will take them away from the dangers of the streets.

For the better class of boys, those who should be taught

the better trades, especially those which require a knowledge of drawing, designing, or machinery, there are the continuation schools, which are carried on in the evening, and the Polytechnics. A Polytechnic is to the young working lad what a public school or a college is to the upper class. It not only teaches him a trade, that by which he is to live, but it gives him discipline, obedience, responsibility, and the sense of duty. It makes a man of him; it gives him honor and self-respect. There are now lads in the London Polytechnics by thousands; many of them will go out to the colonies; whether they emigrate or whether they stay at home, they will become the very cream and flower of the working-people; they will stand up wherever fate leads them as lifelong champions for soberness and for industry. Not for them will be the wild dreams of anarchy; not for them the follies of an impossible socialism; not for them the derision of religion; not for them the hatred of the rich or the jealousy of class. Not the least among the benefits and advantages of the Polytechnic is the *esprit de corps* promoted among them; they are as proud of their "Poly" as any lad of Eton or any man of Balliol. And the latest arrival from the place, wherever he goes, is sure to find friends and advisers and helpers among the old boys of his "Poly."

The Helping Hand in education is of such great importance that one may dwell a little upon the machinery by which a clever and persevering lad may rise from the very lowest levels to any honor or distinction which the country has to offer. It is chiefly the Technical Education Board, a body which has been in existence for some ten years, which supplies the ladders. This Board is empowered by the London County Council to assist in supplying technical instruction to schools and institutions which are not conducted for private profit. The Board spends the sum of £170,000 a year in maintaining and developing classes for technical education. The most important of these institutions are the

Polytechnics above mentioned. There are twelve of these in and about London, of which two are in our quarter of East London. The number of students in Polytechnics —all of them, it is needless to say, of the working-class —amounts to 45,000. The cost of maintaining them is £120,000, of which the Board of Technical Education contributes £30,000; a large sum is given by the City Charities Commission, and the rest is given by half a dozen rich City companies. It is evident we have here a very serious attempt at providing technical education for lads who are to become the skilled workmen of the future. Formerly they were apprenticed to various trades; the system of apprenticeship has fallen into disuse; but it is found highly necessary, if this country is to hold her own against foreign competition, to train the lads in workshops and laboratories where they may learn every branch of their own trade. There are excellent and fully equipped laboratories at the People's Palace and one or two other Polytechnics. As for the trades taught, they are far too numerous to set down. All those trades which are connected with engineering, with metal work, with gold- and silver-smiths' work, with enameling, wood engraving, bookbinding, decorating and painting, carpentry, furniture- and cabinet-making, and a hundred other trades are taught in these colleges of industry. There are art schools also for the teaching of design, decoration, and all the art requirements of the trades.

For the encouragement of the lads who have left school and are willing to carry on their work the continuation classes were formed. The Technical Board has established a system of scholarships by which a ladder is placed in readiness for any boy or girl who can climb it. There are six hundred small scholarships given every year by examination to boys and girls who have passed the sixth standard in the elementary schools; they are in value £8 for the first year, and £12 for the second year. After two years the second ladder is reached. The student who has shown, so far, that he is able to climb the ladder and would now give further proof of ability, must be under sixteen, and his parents must not be in the receipt of more than £400 a year. He may then gain by open competition a scholarship giving him free education at some recognized college of higher education, together with about £30 a year in money. After three years, if he is able to climb still higher,—the number of competitors now narrows,—he has a grand chance before him; he may win a scholarship giving him free education at any university he may choose, with £60 a year, tenable for three years. There are at present many such scholars in residence at Oxford, Cambridge, and other universities.

In addition to these, the Board gives scholarships for art, for science and technology, for horticulture, for sanitary science, and for domestic economy. Besides this industrial help, the Board provides lectures, especially for clerks, on commercial subjects.

It will be understood that by means of these scholarships a boy may work his way, at little or no cost to his friends, from the position of craftsman to that of a graduate in honors of Oxford and Cambridge. Think what this means! The boy is lifted straight from the life of manual labor, very likely monotonous labor, which is the lot of most, in which he can never attain to fortune, honor, or distinction, to the life of intellectual work; his companions will be those who stand in the very forefront of science, literature, and art. A fellowship at his college will enable him to be called to the bar; he may then aspire, with reasonable hopes of success, to the honors of Queen's counsel, Judge, Solicitor-General, Chief Justice, or even Lord Chancellor. He may go into the Church, and look forward, if with learning he has acquired administrative power and preaching power, and, let us add, manners, to becoming a bishop; he man remain at the university, a lecturer and teacher of his own subject;

he may become a professor of science, or he may become an expounder of history. He may become a physician or a surgeon. He may become a journalist, a dramatist, a novelist, a poet. Whatever line he enters upon, he has climbed, by means of these three ladders, up into the higher ranks, with all that the word means. He has become, if he chooses, —and he cannot help choosing,—a gentleman. The poor lad who climbs up does not always, it is true, become a gen-

The New Model Dwellings.

tleman. Sometimes there remain still clinging to him certain rusticities; sometimes ancestral traits, such as a thirst for strong drink, seize him. As a rule, however, the lad who has climbed remains, he and his children after him, in the rank, so dear to the British soul, of undoubted gentility. If the sins of the father are visited upon the children, then, surely the achievements and the virtues of the father shall bring their rewards to the children—yea, even unto the third and fourth generation.

After the parish work and the work of education I had placed that of housing, but this has already been sufficiently considered.

The care of the sick comes next upon my list. There is a continual cry ascending to the regions of the rich concerning the insufficiency of hospital endowments. There is certainly no city better provided with hospitals than London, nor any city where more money is annually subscribed for their maintenance, nor any where the medical staff are paid so little and do so much. In East London there is the magnificent foundation of the London Hospital, which receives 11,500 in-patients every year, has an endowment of £20,000 a year, and an additional income, from voluntary subscriptions, of £40,000 a year. The story of the Children's Hospital and its beginnings in the hamlet of Ratcliffe has been already told. And there are, in addition, "homes" of all kinds, crèches for infants, nursing societies, and dispensaries. One mentions these in passing, but a catalogue of endowments is not necessary.

Among the organizations for help must not be forgotten the fraternities for mutual assistance, such as the Odd Fellows, the Foresters, and the Hearts of Oak. These associations do not belong exclusively to East London, but they have extensive branches here, and are, I believe, well managed and on sound principles. They offer assistance in times of misfortune, medical aid in sickness, and care of the widows and fatherless. In this place they can only be mentioned.

For the women, a very large society is that called the M. A. B. Y. S.—*i. e.*, the "Metropolitan Association for Befriending Young Servants." It began by befriending young servants from the workhouse—girls generally friendless and very forlorn—and has now extended its work to include all young servants. Every lady in the society undertakes the care of one or more servants, whom she visits or invites to her own house on the Sunday "out." These friendships are often lifelong, and produce the best possible results.

The position of the workhouse girl is sometimes very pitiful. One such girl recently came to my knowledge. In this case the girl had been picked up as a baby in the streets; she had no family, no name, no friends, no birthday even. When she found a friend in the M. A. B. Y. S. she asked permission to take her friend's birthday for her own, and to call her friend's cook her aunt, so that she might feel that she too could enjoy, if only in imagination, what all the rest of the world possesses—a birthday and a family.

There are six or seven free libraries in East London. Who was the benefactor to humanity who first invented or discovered the free library? Who was the philanthropist who first advocated the free library? I do not know. But when one realizes what the free library means one is carried away by admiration and gratitude. By means of the free library we actually give to every person, however poor,—we *give* him, as a free gift,—the whole of the literature of the world. If he were a millionaire he could not acquire a greater gift that the poorest lad enjoys who lives near a good free library. He can take books home with him; he can study any subject he likes, if he is a student; or he may read for his own pleasure only, and for amusement. More than this, since none but good and worthy literature should be admitted to the free library the readers cannot use its treasures without forming, purifying, and elevating their taste. Now, taste in literature leads naturally, it is believed by some, to corresponding preferences as regards the major and the minor virtues and their opposites. For my own part, I regard the librarian of a free library as a guardian of morals, a censor, a teacher; those who receive books of him receive the continual admonitions of the wisest and the best of men. A course of Shakspere is in itself an education; a course of Scott may be said to teach history; and a course of the best fiction in our language teaches what is meant by the grand old name of gentleman. I look for the time when the demand for books by the mass of the public will be in itself a selection of the best and finest; when it will be impossible to reproach the people, as is done to-day, with buying the ephemeral trash that is offered at a penny, and neglecting the scholars and the poets and the wise ones of ancient days. The free library is doing for the working-people what the circulating library cannot do for its readers who go in broadcloth and in silk. In the time to come, in the immediate future, it will perhaps be the latter who read the rubbish and the former who will create the demand for the nobler and the higher work.

Mention has already been made of the Sunday afternoon lecture. Other attempts have been made to brighten the Sunday afternoon, always in winter a difficult time to get through. There are organ recitals at the People's Palace, social meetings, with talk and sometimes lantern views, and short addresses.

Perhaps the work that is done in East London for the waifs and strays is the most remarkable, as it is certainly the most interesting.

Those who have read Defoe's "Colonel Jack" will remember the wonderful picture which he presents of the London street boy. That boy has never ceased to live in and about the streets. Sometimes he sleeps in the single room rented by his father, but the livelong day he spends in the streets; he picks up, literally, his food; he picks it up from the coster's barrow, from the baker's counter, from the fishmonger's stall, when nobody is looking. For such boys as these there are Barnardo's Homes, where waifs and strays to any number are admitted, brought up, trained to a trade, and then sent out to the colonies. Five thousand children are in these homes. The history is very simple. Dr. Barnardo, a young Irish medical student, came to London with the intention of giving up his own profession and becoming a preacher. He began by preaching in the streets; he picked up a child, wandering, homeless and destitute, and took it home to his lodgings; he found another and another, and took them home too. So it began; the children became too many for his own resources; they still kept dropping in; he took a house for them, and let it be known that he wanted support. The

Dr. Barnardo's Home, Stepney Causeway.

rest was easy. He has always received as much support as he wanted, and he has already trained and sent out to the colonies nearly ten thousand children. There are also many less important homes and associations for indigent children, homes for homeless boys, homes, refuges, and societies for girls; industrial homes, female protection societies, orphanages, in long array. Most of these societies are, however, limited as to income; a great part of their funds goes in management expenses. If they would be persuaded to unite, a great deal more might be done, while each society, with its honorary officers, could be carried on in accordance with the intentions and ideas of its founders and supporters.

Homes and schools for the boys and girls, hospitals for the adult, there remain the aged. Dotted about all over London there are about a hundred and fifty almshouses; of these about half are situated in and about East London. Not that the people of East London have been more philanthropic in their endowments than those of the west, but, before there was any city of East London, almshouses were planted here on account of the salubrity and freshness of the air and the cheapness of the ground. Some of these have been moved farther afield, their original sites being built over. The People's Palace, for instance, is built upon the site of the Bancroft almshouses, founded in 1728 for the maintenance and education of one hundred poor. Their original house has gone, but the charity is still maintained.

I have always been astonished to think that this most excellent form of charity, one least of all liable to be abused, has gone out of fashion. If I were rich I should rejoice in creating and founding an almshouse for the admission and maintenance of as many old men and old women as I could afford, or as the college which I should build would admit. There are still some delightful almshouses left in London, although so many have been removed; those that remain stand beside the crowded thoroughfares, each one a lesson in charity and pity; there is the stately Trinity Almshouse in the Whitechapel road, with its two courts and its chapel and its statue of the founder and the good old men, the master mariners, who live there; and close beside, unless it has been lately removed, an almshouse of the humbler kind, but quite homely and venerable. My almshouse, if I were privileged to build and endow one, should have its refectory, as well as its chapel; my old people should have their dinner together, and their common hall for society in the winter evenings; they should have, as well, their gardens and their quadrangle and the sense of belonging to a foundation beautiful in its buildings, as well as charitable in its objects.

The existing almshouses by themselves go very little way toward keeping the aged out of the workhouse; but there are other aids which carry us on a little farther, societies which give annuities and pensions to various persons. On the list more than a hundred different trades are represented. Among them is one for flower girls and water-cress venders. This, however, despite its unpretending title, has grown into a very large and important society. Under this title are conducted industrial and servants' training homes, a cottage hospital, a home for waif girls, an orphanage, a shelter and clubroom for street flower-sellers, and a seaside holiday home for blind and helpless and crippled girls, ineligible for ordinary homes—the whole with an income of over £7000, and giving assistance to 12,000 girls a year. This, like the association for befriending young servants, has grown gradually out of small beginnings, and in a space of thirty years has attained to its present dimensions.

So numerous are the societies and the charities of every kind that one thinks there ought not to be any distress, any destitution, any vice in this City of London. Alas! It is a city of five millions, and out of this multitude there are many who will not work, many who deliberately desire the life of vice and crime, and still more who, if the Helping Hand offers relief without question or condition, will swell the numbers of those who are wilfully helpless and deliberately destitute. The power of working is easily lost, and with difficulty regained. The administration of charitable funds is a most difficult task.

Fourteen years ago, in a time of exceptional distress, the Lord Mayor, in the kindness of his unreflecting heart, opened a subscription for the relief of the unemployed. A very large sum was collected in a few days. Of course this became known not only over all London, but over the whole country. Then there began a mighty migration; wave after wave of hungry applicants arrived by every train; the glorious prospect of obtaining a gift of money without doing anything for it attracted thousands; they gave up work in order to be eligible; they magnified the amount of the gift, in anticipation; when the day of distribution arrived they fought for admission, they threatened to brain the distributors, they took tickets which entitled them to food and sold them at the public house; in the end that act of charity developed and strengthened the pauper spirit in hundreds of thousands; those who had been working for the better exercise of charity were in despair; to this day the memory of that day of free gifts, without question and without conditions, lies in the mind of the working-man who will not work, and nerves him for another spell of idleness and starvation.

In this attempt to stay the hand that grants the unthinking dole the Charity Organization Society stands in the forefront. It has offices and branches everywhere; it intervenes between the rich man and the poor; it says to the former, "Never give him money, you will only keep him poor; make him understand that money means conditions of work and effort; do not turn the unemployed into a pauper." To the workhouses the Charity Organization Society says, "Do not give outdoor relief; do not accustom the sturdy poor to look for doles of bread and orders on the butcher. Make them go into the house if they want help." It is better to be cruel when kindness means weakness, and doles mean pauperizing. The temptation to give is like the temptation to take opiates. To give relieves the discomfort of knowing how others are suffering. To give brings food to the children, fire to the hearth; it also enables the breadwinner to spend in drink what he should take home to his wife, and it makes the wives and children accustomed to receive alms, and to look to alms for the supplies which are only deficient through their own improvidence and vice. The Charity Organization Society is known and detested by every thriftless loafer, every beggar, every impostor, every begging-letter writer in the country; it is also known and detested by that large class of sentimentalists who give money wherever there is none, who bribe the women by doles to come to church, and who interpret certain words of our Lord, as they were interpreted by the monastic houses, into an injunction to give without question and to relieve without condition.

I come next to a form of philanthopic endeavor concerning which it is difficult to speak unless in terms of extravagant admiration.

I mean the Settlement, which is spreading and taking root in all great cities both in America and in Great Britain.

The Settlement very properly began in East London, as the place which stood most in need of it. There are now some thirteen or fourteen Settlements in London, of which six, I believe, belong to East London. There are Settlements in Glasgow, Bristol, Manchester, and Edinburgh. There are, I believe, speaking under correction, more than twenty in the greater cities of the United States.

It is now fifteen years since the first creation of the Settlement. What is it? What was at first proposed? What has it done? We may answer these questions by the help of Canon Barnett, its real founder. (See "University and Social Settlements," chapter ii.)

The Settlement sprang out of a profound distrust of the machinery by which the Helping Hand could reach the people. It seemed to many that this machinery hindered rather than helped. The Charity Organization Society was proving with pitiless statistics and cruel logic that the widespread system of doles was crushing the spirit of independence in the poor; the experience of the present, as well as that of the past taught them that laws cannot touch the restless and the improvident; they saw that refuges might receive the unhappy, but could not touch or remove the cause of unhappiness; they discovered that societies for relieving the poor were too often machines which blindly acted by a hard-and-fast rule, maintained many officials, and made no attempt at prevention or improvement. Also they saw that with all the machinery of the parish and despite the self-denying work of the clergy there had been little less than a complete failure in inspiring among the people the faith and hope of religion and its self-restraining powers.

There was also, thanks to certain influences which it would take us long to discuss, a growing recognition of certain evils, such as the separation of the rich from the poor, the withholding from the poor of so many things enjoyed by the rich, the condescension of rich to poor, an exclusive spirit on the one side and a natural resentment on the other, and a conviction that something should be done to resist these evils. In other words, the feeling was gradually growing, especially among certain groups of young men of Oxford and Cambridge, that civilization should belong not to one class but to all classes; that the things which we believe to be the most important—knowledge, art, manners, beauty, purity, unselfishness—should be made possible for the working-man, if he will accept them, as well as for the rich. The root idea, therefore, of a Settlement is the example, the teaching and the maintenance of what we call the life of culture among the working-classes.

By example—for the members of the Settlement live among them, go about with them, live in the sight of all The working-man dines with them, spends the evening with them, talks with them. He finds that their mode of life is simple; that the luxury he has been taught to believe as the common rule among the easy class does not exist among these members of that class; that cleanliness, using the word to cover everything—the home, the meals, the person, the daily habit—is the first thing necessary; that knowledge may be pursued for its own sake, and not because it has a commercial value and is saleable; and that these men and women have come to live in his quarter without the least intention of giving him any money or of taking off his shoulders any one of his own responsibilities.

Next, by teaching. The Settlement has its library, its class-rooms, its lecture-room, and its fifteen hundred students—yet it is not a college. The residents do not all teach. The visitor thinks perhaps that if they are not come to teach, their object is to preach temperance and to get a hold over the criminal classes. Nothing of the kind; the Settlement is not a mission. Nor, again, is it a Polytechnic, despite the manifold studies that are carried on. The lads of the Polytechnic learn a trade by which to live; the students at the Settlement make a study of some science. Nor is it in the narrow sense a charitable institution. In a Settlement every resident carries on his own life in his own way; he does not stoop to the ways of the people around; he is not their benefactor; he is not a superior person; he is just one man among the men all round him into whose interests he enters and whose ideas he endeavors to understand.

In all countries governed by our institutions or by those which have our institutions as their basis the duty of the individual citizen to his town and to his state is assumed as essential for the government of the people by the people. A man who deliberately abstains from exercising the right to vote, who leaves to any who please to snatch it the government of his own city, is little less than a traitor to the cause of freedom; he enjoys rights which have been won for him by his fathers, but refuses to watch over and to defend those rights. It is the work of the Settlement to teach this duty and to set the example. The constitution of a municipality assumes that citizens will give, freely and without pay, such time as is wanted for the conduct of the municipal affairs. In local government the Settlement carries on a quiet work which is perhaps more effective than its classes and its lectures. The members become guardians and vestrymen; they

Mile End Almshouses.

sit on school boards, they are school visitors, they inspire every branch of local government with the sense of duty and of principle. For the members themselves the Settlement teaches and requires, as Canon Barnett points out, "the surrender of self-will and of will worship."

For those who come under the influence of the Settlement it destroys class suspicion, it removes prejudices; the workingmen discover that those whom they call, in a lump, the rich are not what their radical orators of Whitechapel Waste believe and teach; they make friends where they thought to find only enemies; they learn the things in which the rich are happier than themselves—the cleanly life, the power of acquiring knowledge, the possession of, or the access to, art of all kinds, more gentle manners, greater self-restraint, and in the cases before their eyes unselfishness and the power of working without pay, without praise, without apparent reward of any kind. Above all, there is no hidden motive; Canon Barnett's church stands beside the Settlement of Toynbee Hall, but there is no invitation, no condition, no pressure put upon the people to step out of the Settlement into the church. There is no teaching of politics; there is no attempt to introduce shibboleths; there are no bribes, unless it is the pressure of the friendly hand and the pulse of the sympathetic heart; the evenings spent with gentlewomen and gentlemen, the patient teaching, the lecture by a man whose name is known over the whole world—unless these things be considered bribes, then the Settlement offers none.

In education, then, the Settlement has classes which learn all kinds of sciences, but not for trade purposes; it has lectures by great, or at least by distinguished, men; it offers exhibitions of pictures the same as those presented to West End people; it encourages the formation of clubs and associations of all kinds; it opens the library to everyone; it leads the way in local government; it offers recreation that shall be really *recreative;* it enrolls the boys in athletic clubs, and gives them something to aim at and to think about; it gathers in the girls and keeps them from the dangers of long evenings with nothing to do; it is a center for the study of the labor problems and difficulties of all kinds. In one word, the Settlements of East London, where I know most of their workings, are set up as lamps in a dark place; they are not like an ordinary lamp which at a distance becomes a mere glimmer; the lamp of the Settlement, the more widely its light penetrates, the farther the darkness recedes; the deeper is the gloom, the more brightly shines the light of this lamp so set and so illuminated and so maintained.

Should the workhouse be considered as any part of the work of the Helping Hand? It should be, but it cannot be. Whatever the state touches in the way of charity or philanthropy it corrupts and destroys, whether it is the workhouse or the prison or the casual ward. As for the London workhouse, it is simply a terrible place. It is a huge barrack; it contains over a thousand inmates; they are all alike herded and huddled together, the respectable and the disreputable; there is no distinction between misfortune and the natural consequence of a wasted life. The system is a barbarous survival of a time when the system was not so barbarous because the respectable poor were much rougher, coarser, ruder, and nearer to the disreputable poor. It must be reformed altogether. There ought not, to begin with, to be this kind of barrack life for the respectable poor; there should be municipal almshouses. Meantime the poor folk themselves hate the workhouse; they loathe the thought of it; they are wretched in the shelter of it; you may see the old men and the old women sitting in gloomy silence, brooding over their own wreck; they have nothing else to do; they are prisoners; they cannot go in and out as they please; they are under strict rule, a rule as rigid as that of any prison; they have no individuality; they all try to cheat the officers by smuggling in forbidden food; they are at the mercy of Bumble, who may be a very dreadful person, not comic in the least. The most unhappy are those who should be the objects of the greatest pity, the brokendown, able-bodied man, too often bent with rheumatism—the English agony—or some other incurable disease. Such an one enters into this place, where all hope must be abandoned; we use the phrase so often that we hardly understand what it means. No hope at forty but to lead the rest of life without work, without change, without comforts; to be deprived of tobacco, beer, meat, society, mental occupation; to live on among the other wrecks of humanity, with so much bread every day, so much suet pudding, so much cocoa, so much pea soup, so much tea. Can the workhouse be truly called part and parcel of the work of the Helping Hand?

Let us end, as we began, with the lower levels. Very far, indeed, below the working-men who attend the lectures and the drawing-room of Toynbee Hall are the submerged and the casuals, the dockers, the wanderers, and the criminals at large. What is done for them? They are, of course, looked after with the utmost zeal and attention by the police, by the officers of the vestry, and by the magistrates. But these agencies are not exactly reformatory in their character.

I have spoken of the Settlement as one of two forces now acting upon the mass of the people which seem to promise the most powerful influence upon the future. The second of these two forces I believe to be the social work of the Salvation Army. I am not speaking of their religious efforts; they do not appeal, as a rule, to the educated; on the other hand, I would not speak a word in disrespect of efforts which I know to be genuine and which I know to have been attended with signal success in the reclaiming of thousands from evil ways.

The first step in the social work of the Salvation Army is the opening of a lodging-house of the cheapest kind. So far, against great opposition, they have, I believe, succeeded in keeping it free from the ordinary law as regards common lodging-houses—viz., the visit of the policeman whenever he chooses either to see that there is no disorder or because he "wants" somebody, and so in the middle of the night tramps round the dormitories, turning his bull's eye upon the faces of the sleepers. It is most important that the poor creatures in the place should feel that in that shelter at least they will not be hunted down. The men have to pay for their lodging—the price of a bed varies from twopence to fourpence; the beds are laid in bunks; they are covered with American cloth; they are provided each with a thick blanket; foot-baths and complete baths are ready for them; a cup of cocoa and a large piece of bread cost a trifle; they are received in a light, warm, and spacious hall; they are invited every evening to join in a short service, with singing and an address. In the morning those of them who choose lay their cares before the superintendent, who sends them on to the Labor Bureau, where in most cases, if the man is willing to work, something is found for him.

They have, next, workshops where all kinds of work are undertaken and turned out; homeless and friendless lads are received in these workshops and taught trades. Whatever may be the previous record of a case, the man received is treated as a friend; his past is regarded as already finished and done with, perhaps already atoned. He is made to understand that if he would return to the world he must work for every step; by work alone he is to get food, shelter, and clothes; beside him at every step stands the officer in whose charge he has been placed. He is constantly watched, without being allowed to entertain any suspicion that his conduct is under careful supervision.

If you visit one of these workshops you will be astonished at the show of cheerful industry. Everyone seems doing his very best. Some of this apparent zeal is genuine; some of it is inspired by passing emotion and evanescent passion or repentance; out of the whole number so many per cent. give up the work and go back to the old life. But some persevere.

I have already spoken of the English prison. The cry of the wretched prisoner goes up continually, but in vain. The long agony and torture, especially to the young, of the solitary cell, the enforced silence, the harsh punishments, the insufficient food, the general orders which will allow of no relaxation in any case, the system which turns the most humane of warders into a machine for depriving his prisoner of everything that makes a man—these things crush the unhappy victim. After a long sentence—say of two years—this poor wretch comes out broken; he has no longer any will, any resource, any courage; he is like a cur whipped and kicked into a thing that follows when it is bidden.

Let me again recall the appearance of these unhappy creatures on the morning of their deliverance. They sit spiritless, obedient, not speaking to each other or to their new friends, waiting for some fresh order. It is pitiful to look at the semblance of manhood and to think that this—this is the method adopted by the nation in its wisdom in order to punish the crime and to reform the criminal. When the sentence is over they escort him to the gates of the prison; they throw the doors open wide and say, "Go, and sin no more." What is the wretched man to do, but to go and sin again? No one will employ him. He has lost his skill and sleight of hand. He has lost his old pride in his work; he cares for nothing now. It is a hard world for many; it is a black, hopeless, despairing world for the man who once enters or comes out of an English prison. There is a poem, written the other day, by one who endured this awful sentence—a scholar and a man of culture:

> "With midnight always in one's heart,
>   And twilight in one's cell,
> We turn the crank, we tear the rope,
>   Each in his separate hell.
> And the silence is more awful far,
>   Than the sound of a brazen bell."

> "And never a human voice comes near,
>   To speak a gentle word.
> And the eye that watches through the door
>   Is pitiless and hard;
> And by all forgot, we rot and rot,
>   With soul and body marred."

The officers of the Salvation Army's Home welcome their guests with warm hand grasps and friendly words. What, however, is to be done to find them work to go on with? Not far from the home there is a disused chapel; in this place some thirty or forty of the discharged prisoners are engaged in sorting waste paper. Others go out and collect it; there is paper of all sorts—fine note-paper, coarse paper, packing paper, newspaper, everything. The men sort this in crates, and so earn a few pence a day. It is a rude beginning for the new life; many of them lose heart; the uphill fight, the long strain of patience until work of a better kind is found is too much for them; they relapse, they disappear in the streets, they are seen no more for a time, until one day they are met again at the prison gates and are led back to the home they deserted, where they meet with the same welcome and where they are encouraged to make another attempt.

Some five and thirty miles from London on the east, where the coast of Essex rises in a low hill facing the Thames estuary and overlooking an island which has been reclaimed from the mud, there lies a large farm, which is unlike any other farm in the country. It is, in fact, the colony of the Salvation Army. Here they bring men whom they have dragged out of the mire and the depths. They bring here the clerk who has ruined himself by a loose life, the working-man who has fallen by reason of drink, the weak creature who has habitually taken the Easy Way, the criminal from the prison, the sturdy rogue, the slouching thief—they are all brought here and they are turned on to the farm. There are between two and three hundred of them. When they come here they are for the most part unable to do a day's work; they are unable to lift a spade or to wield a hoe. They are set to light work until they recover a little strength and muscle—there is work of all kinds on a farm. On this farm they grow fruit and vegetables; they have dairies, and make butter and cheese; they have cattle and sheep and pigs and poultry. And they have a very large brick-making industry. The men live in small detached barracks; there are not many rules of conduct; they are paid by the piece, and they buy their own food, which is sold at prices as low as will pay for the cost; they may smoke in the evening if they please; they may read; they may go to bed when they please; they are not perpetually exhorted to religion, but they are made to feel that the house rests on a religious foundation.

How does the farm get on as a commercial venture? Does it pay its way? To begin with, it belongs to the Salvation Army; there is consequently no rent to pay; against this advantage must be set the fact that the men, when they are first sent down, are practically useless, and that it takes three or four months before their strength returns to them. The farm, however, pays its way, or very nearly. If it did not, it would still, with certain limits, be an economical concern. For, if we consider, every one of these men, if left to himself and his own promptings, would cost the country, including his maintenance, without counting the loss of his labor and including the expenses of prisons and police to take care of him, at least £100 a year. We have, therefore, a very simple sum. How much can the colony afford to lose every year, and yet remain an economical gain to the country? On a roll of 250 there is the gain to the community of £25,000 a year. If, therefore, the colony shows a deficit of £3000 a year the country is still a gainer of £22,000. Any one may carry on this little calculation. Suppose, for instance, that even fifty per cent. of the cases prove failures; the remaining fifty save the country £12,500 a year. And, what is much more, they, being honest themselves, bring up their children to ways of honesty—their children and their grandchildren for generation after generation, and who can calculate the gain in a single century?

"The Bridge of Hope," a Well-known East End Night Refuge.

I do not speak here of other branches of the Salvation Army's social work. To receive the discharged prisoner, to find him work, to train lads to steady work, to give back to the soil the wastrels who were devouring and spoiling honest men's goods in the cities, to restore to a man his pride and his self-respect, to give him back his manhood, to fill him with new hopes and a new purpose—this is surely a great and a noble work.

On more than one occasion I have publicly testified to my own belief in the efficacy of the social work of the Salvation Army. There is one point on which it contrasts with every other effort either of philanthropy or of religion. The work is carried on by a vast multitude of eleven thousand officers, men and women, young men and maidens. They are bound by no vows; but they might, if they chose, wear the rope with the triple knots of the Franciscans. For they follow, without vows, the three Franciscan virtues of obedience, poverty, and chastity. Add to these, if it is a virtue, total abstinence from strong drink. They go where they are sent, they do what they are ordered to do, they carry out the military duties of obedience, they draw pay barely enough for the most modest standard of living, and their lives are blameless on the score of purity. So long as these virtues remain with them, so long will they prevail. If, as happened with the Franciscans, the praise of the world, which certainly is coming to the Army as well, turns their heads and corrupts their zeal, if they take money and make money by their work, then the social side of the Salvation Army will, like so many human systems, fall to the ground and be trampled in the dust. At present they are all poor together; poor and not dissatisfied; not a man or woman among the whole eleven thousand has a bank account of his own; they all live from hand to mouth, and when the word comes from headquarters that there is to be a week of self-denial they live for that week as they can, without any pay. And if we are fain to confess that their work is good for the unfortunates, whom they chiefly befriend, what are we to say or to think of the good which their work confers upon themselves? Surely, the Helping Hand raises its owner as well as those whom it lifts. The twopenny doss-house, the refuge, the home, the rescue, the colony—do they not also raise and rescue and strengthen the people who administer and direct them?

Matthew Arnold once visited East London in verse:

"I met a preacher whom I knew and said:
'Ill and o'erworked, how fare you in this scene?'
'Bravely!' said he; 'for I of late have been
Much cheered with thoughts of Christ, the living bread.'
O human soul! as long as thou canst so
Set up a mark of everlasting light,
Above the howling senses' ebb and flow,
To cheer thee and to right thee if thou roam—
Not with lost toil thou laborest through the night!
Thou mak'st the heaven thou hop'st indeed thy home."

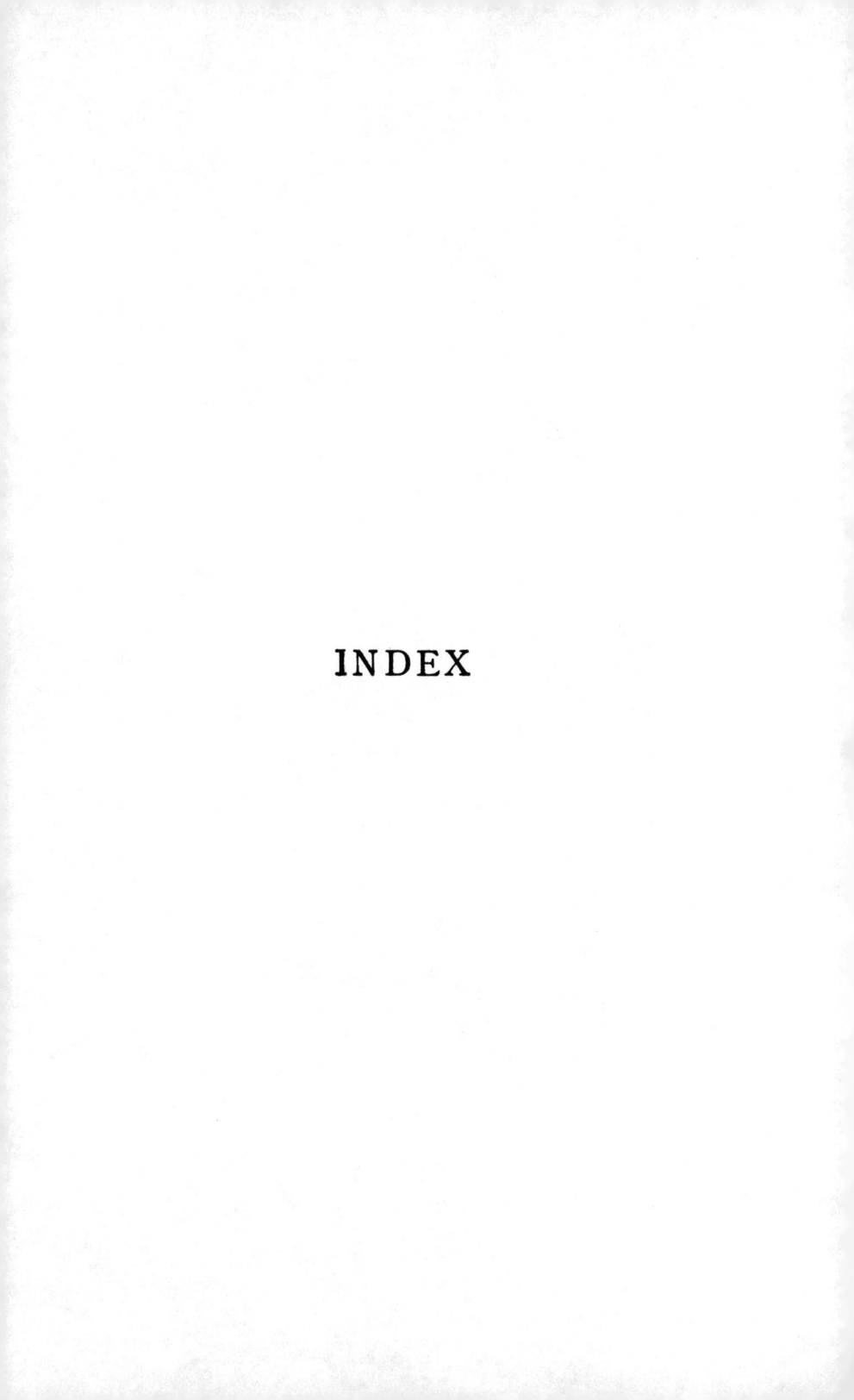

INDEX

INDEX

ABNEY, Lady, 274
— Sir Thomas, 274
Aguilar, Grace, 276
Aikin, Dr., 275
Aliens in London, 187
Anarchists, 206
Appeals for Day in Country, 307
August Holiday, 303

BAD BUILDING, Bribery of Inspectors, 220
Bancroft Almshouses, 341
Barbauld, Mrs., 275
Barking, 104, 111
Barnardo's Homes, 339
Barrack Life, 223, 224
— and Salvation Army, 224
Beating the Bounds, 60
Beds hired out, 212
Bethnal Green Crowded District, 221
Billingsgate, 52, 54, 55
Bishop's Manor, 4
— Palace, 7
Bicycle round London, 310
Blackwall Basin, 95
Booth, General, 225
Boundaries of East London, 4
Bow Creek, 99
Bradwell, 109
Breathing Places, 302
Bridge, First London, 53

CASUAL WARD, Stupidity of, 249
Census, Religious, 37
Centenarian, The, 201
Chapels on the Wall, 110

Chapels on Bridges and Walls, 110
Charity Organisation Society, 343
Charter House, 280
Chaucer, 47, 55
Children's Day in Country, 307
Chinese in London, 204
Church of England, 331
City, 257
Clapton, 267
Club of Factory Girls, 142
— of the baser sort, 315
Colet, Dean, 7
Continuation Schools, 333
Coopers' Company, 82
Cromwell, Major, 273
— Oliver, 271
Crowded Part of Bethnal Green, 221
Custom House, 55

DAGENHAM, 111
— Whitebait Dinner, 111
Dancing, none in East London, 313
Day in Country for Children, 307
Defoe, 47, 274
Discharged Prisoners, 241
Disraeli, Benjamin, 275
— Isaac, 275
Docks, St. Katharine, 62
— London, 68
— West India, 95
— Blackwall, 95
— Millwall, 95
— Attractions for boys, 96
Dogs, Isle of, 91
Drury Lane, Barracks in, 222
Dutch in Spitalfields, 192
— Church, 192

EAST END Parks, 304
East Ham, 7, 213
East London, History mostly a blank, 3
—— Boundaries of, 4
—— Nature of ground, 4
—— Collection of villages, 8
—— No centre, 8
—— Not a city, 8
—— No newspapers, 8
—— No people of fashion, 8
—— Filled with working class, 8
—— Population of, 8
—— No hotels, 9
—— New Zealander in, 9
—— No restaurants, 9
—— Rapid rise, 10
—— A manufacturing city, 10
—— Not a trading city, 10
—— Resembles Old London, 10
—— No book shops, 13
—— No literary power, 14
—— No garrison, 14
—— No recruiting, 14
—— Monotony, 15
—— Meanness, 15
—— Streets all alike, 15
—— No old buildings, 16
—— An unlovely city, 16
—— Fine roads, 17
—— Life not monotonous, 16, 17
—— City of many crafts, 21
—— Distribution of trades, 22
—— Factories in, 23
—— Proportion of professions to crafts, 24
—— The curse of labour, 27
—— Division of labour, 28
—— Demand for skilled labour, 29
—— Wages in, 30
—— Sweating, 30
—— Co-operative labour, 33
—— An experiment, 33
—— Not a slum, 38
—— A hive of workers, 116
—— Huxley on, 127
—— Ministering ladies, 128
—— Fringe of, 255
—— Matthew Arnold on, 358
Easter Monday, 290, 291, 295
Eighteenth century, 325

Emigrés, 189
Epping Forest, 256
Epping Hunt, 291, 301
Excursion trains, 303
Execution Dock, 78
—— Escape of a man, 78

FACTORY GIRL, Chapter V.
Fairy Lights, 239
Fight near Tower, 326
Fleetwood, Cromwell's son-in-law, 271
Flower Girls' Society, 342
Foreshore, Rescue of, 110
Fraternities, 337
French in Spitalfields, 188
French Revolution, 188
Fringe of East London, 255
Future—the man who looks forward, 56

GAMBLING, Chinese, 205
Gardens in London, 304
George's, St., in the East, 72, 73
German clerks, 191
— Jews, 190, 192
Ground, Lie of, 4

HACKNEY, Churchyard, 263
— Old Town, 263
— 18th-century Houses, 264
— Barber's Barn, 272
— Darnley, 272
— Captain Woodcock, 273
— Major Cromwell, 273
— Hartopp, Sir John, 274
— John Howard, 276
— André, 277
— Princess Elizabeth, 279
— Sir Walter Raleigh, 279
— Sir Thomas More, 279
— Thomas Sutton, 280
— John Ward, 281
— Lucas, 281
Ham, West, 7
Hampstead Heath, 292
—— on Easter Monday, 295
Hangman's Acre, 79

INDEX 363

Heckford, Dr., 85, 86
Helping Hand, The, Chapter XII.
— — History of, 319
— — and the beggar, 320
— — and St. Martin, 321
— — new developments, 321
Henry, Matthew, 275
Hewling, Benjamin, 273
Holidays, 289
Homerton, High Street, 267
Hopping, 308
Hospitals, 337
Housing of the People, 212
— and London County Council, 225
Huguenots in London, 188, 192
Hunting Rights, 7
Huxley on East London, 127

IDLERS on London Bridge, 42
Immigration, 190
Increase of Population, 213
Industrial Villages, 225
Irish Colony, 36
Isle of Dogs, 91
— — Origin of name, 92
Italians, 191, 203

JACK the Painter, 283
Jay, Osborne, The Rev., 329
Jewish quarter, 193
Jews, Alleged Superiority, 194
— Trained intellect, 194
— Unpopularity of, 195
— Sunday morning with, 196
— Salesmen, 196
— Physical degeneration, 199
— Oriental note, 200
— The, old man, 201
— The Synagogue, 202
Journalism and the Gaol Bird, 242
Judenhetze, 195

KEY of the street, 155
Key, Price of the, 211

LABORATORIES at People's Palace, 334
Labour Aristocracy, 119

Ladies in East London, 128
Lads in the Country, 307
Lawlessness in 18th Century, 325
Lea River, 7
Libraries, Free, 338
Liz, The baby, 119
— London Street, 119, 120
— Home, 120
— Furniture of home, 120
— Hardening the baby, 122
— Parents of, 122
— Food of, 121, 122, 123
— Beer, 123
— The school, 124
— Washing of, 124
— Leaves school, 127
— Forgets her teaching, 127
— Appearance of, 128
— Character of, 129
— Ignorance of, 129, 130
— Conversation and ideas, 130
— Interests of place, 133
— goes to work, 134
— Sailor cousin, 133
— in a jam factory, 135
— goes a-hopping, 136
— A day at factory, 137
— Christmas Feast, 133
— Breakfast, 137
— Dinner, 137, 138
— on strike, 141
— Independence of, 143
— Ladies' Club, 143
— Bank Holiday, 144
— at seventeen, 147
— on Sunday, 147
— Her sweetheart, 148
— Marriage of, 150
— A wife and a mother, 151
London, the old families, 34
— — devours her children, 34
— Vanishing of old families of, 35
— Influx of new blood, 36
— The Port of, 41, 42
— Docks, 68
— Street, 119, 120
— A City of Refuge, 187
— and the Alien, 187
— — County Council, 225
— — School Board, 332

Long Hours of Idleness, 289
Lord Mayor's Fund, 343
Lowe, Bob, 141
Lucas, 281

MAN, Two varieties of, 56
Manor of Bishop of London, 4
Match Tax, 141
May Day, 290
Medland Hall, 248
M.A.B.Y.S., 337
Memories of the Past, Chapter X.
Millwall Dock, 95
More, Sir Thomas, 7, 279, 280
Morley, Samuel, 276
Music Halls, 322

NANTES, Edict of, 188
New Docker, The, 52

OKEY, JOHN, 271
Opium Den, 205
Organised Robbery, 48
Osborne Jay, The Rev., 329
—— Work of, 330
—— The Boxing Class, 330
—— The Doss-house, 331
Overcrowding, 213, 214
— A million affected, 218
— Case of A.B., 218
— Vitiation of Air, 217

PALACE of Bishop, 7
Palatines, The, 188, 278
Parish Work, 327
— Unpaid Assistants, 328
Past, The Man who loves the, 54
People, Housing of, 221
People's Palace, 297, 312, 313, 334
Pepys, 91
Persian Scholar in East London, 204
Peter, St., ad Vincula, 60
Polish Jews, 192
Polytechnics, 333
Poor, Generosity of, 121
Port of Billingsgate, Ancient, 52

Port of London, Increase of Trade, 48
—— Riverside People, 48
—— A.D. 1700, 48
—— A.D. 1400, 46
—— Lightermen formerly organised plunderers, 51
Poplar Recreation Ground, 304
Population of East London, 8
—— Proportion of those born, 36
—— Rapid increase, 213
Prisoners, wreck of manhood, 351
— Welcomed in the Salvation Army, 247, 353
Prisons, 352, 353, 357

RAINES CHARITY, 68, 71
Ratcliffe, 81
— Highway, 71
— Stairs, 81
— Cross, 82
— Shipwrights' Company, 82
— Willoughby, 82, 85
— The Italian Ghost, 87
Refuge, the City of, 187
Religion, Indifference not hatred, 37
Rent, Increase of, 211
Rescue of Foreshore, 110
Revolution, French, 181
River Lea, 309
Riverside, 48
Riverwall, 103, 104, 105, 107, 109, 112
Rowe, Owen, 271

ST. AUSTIN'S Church, 192
St. Katharine's by the Tower, 65
—— Dock, 62
—— Liberty of, 65
—— Destruction of, 66
—— Regent's Park, 66
Salvation Army Barracks, 224
—— Shelters of the, 248
—— The Farm, 353
—— Social Work, 350
—— Lodging Houses, 350
—— Work shops, 350
—— Prisoners, 247, 353
—— Does it Pay? 354
—— The Modern Friars, 357

INDEX

Salvation Army, A Company of Self-denying workers, 357
Sandwich Man, The, 240
Scholarships, 334
— Possibilities of, 335
School Children, 332
— — Humanising influence of, 332
Settlement, the, and Lads, 307
— Origin of the, 344
— Working of, 345
— What it is, 346, 348
Shacklewell Green, 286
— — and Sir Thomas More, 286
Shadwell, 79
Shakespeare, 47
Shipwrights' Company, 82
Shopkeepers, no amusement for, 311
Sick, care of, 337
Slums, 323
— Exaggeration of Novelists, 324
Smith, Dr. William, 274
South London, Barracks in, 222
Spitalfields and French, 188
Sports and Pastimes, Chapter XI.
— in the Street, 310
Stepney, 7
Stoke Newington, Dr. Aikin, 275
— — Mrs. Barbauld, 275
— — Church Street, 269
— — Thomas Day, 276
— — Defoe, 274
— — Isaac Disraeli, 275
— — Fleetwood House, 273
— — Nonconformity in, 270
— — Puritan Leaders in, 271
— — John Okey, 271
— — Palatines, 278
— — E. Allan Poe, 277
— — Owen Rowe, 271
Stow, 59, 67
Stratford Langthorn, 111
Strype, 67
Submerged, of all classes, 229
— Where found, 230
— of the eighteenth century, 232
— Inoffensive, 233
— Causes of wreck, 233
— in Police Court, 234
— the case of A.A., 237
— in the Sixpenny Hotel, 238

Submerged, in Oxford Street, 239
— of various trades, 240
— The odd job, 241
— Pennyworths, 241
— The Sandwich Man, 244
— Ten thousand of them, 251
— A lower depth still, 250
Suburban Life changing, 261
— — Destruction of City Social Life, 257
— — Dulness of, 258
— — Clubs and Amusements, 261
— — Awakening of Society, 261
— — Theatres in, 261
Suburbs, growth of, 67
Sunday lectures, 339
Sutton, Thomas, 280
Swedish Church, 73

Technical Education Board, 333
The lad of the street, 156
— — at school, 159
— — leaves school, 160
— — Prospects, 160
— — What he knows, 161
— — His temptations, 162
— — The barges left in the mud, 165
— — His pair of hands, 165
— — City boys, 166
— — Railway for, 166
— — Factories for, 167
— — Van and horse, 167
— — Beer boy, 167
— — Meals, 168
— — Porter's work, 168
— — Degeneration of, 171
— — Long evenings, 171
— — Boys' Clubs, 172
— — Classes, 172
— — Music Halls, 173, 181
— — Mimicry of, 174
— — Casual hand, 177
— — Street amusements, 177
— — at Epsom, 177
— — Hooligans, 177
— — Street fights, 177
— — The Reformatory, 178
— — Gamblers, 178

The lad, Reading, 181
— — keeps company, 181
— — Ordeal of street, 182
— — Loafers, 183
Theatre regarded with horror, 258
Thousands driven out homeless, 222
Tower Hill, 55, 56
— Terrace on, 55, 56, 59, 61
— of London, 59
— Bridge, 61, 62
— Liberties, 66
Toynbee Hall, Lectures at, 311
Tramps and Rogues, 250
Trinity Almshouses, 341
Turpin Dick, 282

WALL by River, 103
Wapping, School and churchyard, 73, 74

Wapping Old Stairs, 77
— Recreation Ground, 304
Ward, John, 281
Wat Tyler, 7
Watts, Dr. Isaac, 268, 273
West Ham, 7, 214
West India Dock Road, 203
West India Docks, 95
Whitechapel Picture Exhibition, 296
Whit Monday, 298
Whittington, 47
Winter amusements, 310
Woodcock, Captain, 272
Workhouse, The, 349
Working class, Better Sort, 119

YARMOUTH Church, why closed, 303

The List of Titles in the Garland Series

1. Walter Besant. **East London.** London, 1901.
2. W.H. Beveridge. **Unemployment. A Problem of Industry.** London, 1912.
3. Charles Booth. **The Aged Poor in England and Wales.** London, 1894.
4. Clementina Black, Ed. **Married Women's Work. Being the Report of an Enquiry Undertaken by the Women's Industrial Council.** London, 1915.
5. Helen Bosanquet. **The Strength of the People. A Study in Social Economics.** London, 1903 (2nd ed.).
6. A.L. Bowley and A.R. Burnett-Hurst. **Livelihood and Poverty. A Study in the Economic Conditions of Working-Class Households in Northampton, Warrington, Stanley, and Reading.** London, 1915.
7. Reginald A. Bray. **Boy Labour and Apprenticeship.** London, 1911.
8. C.V. Butler. **Domestic Service.** London, 1916.
9. Edward Cadbury, M. Cécile Matheson and George Shann. **Women's Work and Wages.** London, 1906.
10. Arnold Freeman. **Boy Life and Labour. The Manufacture of Inefficiency.** London, 1914.

11. Edward G. Howarth and Mona Wilson. **West Ham. A Study in Social and Industrial Problems.** London, 1907.
12. B.L. Hutchins. **Women in Modern Industry.** London, 1915.
13. M. Loane. **From Their Point of View.** London, 1908.
14. J. Ramsay Macdonald. **Women in the Printing Trades. A Sociological Study.** London, 1904.
15. C.F.G. Masterman. **From the Abyss. Of Its Inhabitants by One of Them.** London, 1902.
16. L.C. Chiozza Money. **Riches and Poverty.** London, 1906.
17. Richard Mudie-Smith, Ed. **Handbook of the "Daily News" Sweated Industries' Exhibition.** London, 1906.
18. Edward Abbott Parry. **The Law and the Poor.** London, 1914.
19. Alexander Paterson. **Across the Bridges. Or Life by the South London River-side.** London, 1911.
20. M.S. Pember-Reeves. **Round About a Pound a Week.** London, 1913.
21. B. Seebohm Rowntree. **Poverty. A Study of Town Life.** London, 1910 (2nd ed.).
22. B. Seebohm Rowntree and Bruno Lasker. **Unemployment. A Social Study.** London, 1911.
23. B. Seebohm Rowntree and A.C. Pigou. **Lectures on Housing.** Manchester, 1914.
24. C.E.B. Russell. **Social Problems of the North.** London and Oxford, 1913.
25. Henry Solly. **Working Men's Social Clubs and Educational Institutes.** London, 1904.
26. E.J. Urwick, Ed. **Studies of Boy Life in Our Cities.** London, 1904.

27. Alfred Williams. **Life in a Railway Factory.** London, 1915.

28. [Women's Co-operative Guild]. **Maternity. Letters from Working-Women, Collected by the Women's Co-operative Guild with a preface by the Right Hon. Herbert Samuel, M.P.** London, 1915.

29. Women's Co-operative Guild. **Working Women and Divorce. An Account of Evidence Given on Behalf of the Women's Co-operative Guild before the Royal Commission on Divorce.** London, 1911.

   bound with Anna Martin. **The Married Working Woman. A Study.** London, 1911.

Augsburg College
George Sverdrup Library
Minneapolis, Minnesota 55454